T-6

A Pictorial Record of The Harvard, Texan and Wirraway

Books by Peter C. Smith

DESTROYER LEADER
TASK FORCE 57
(Foreword by Admiral of the Fleet, Lord Fraser of North Cape)
PEDESTAL
(Foreword by Admiral of the Fleet, The Lord Lewin)
STUKA AT WAR
(Foreword by Oberst Hans-Ulrich Rudel)
HARD LYING
BRITISH BATTLE CRUISERS
WAR IN THE AEGEAN
THE STORY OF THE TORPEDO BOMBER
HERITAGE OF THE SEA
ROYAL NAVY SHIPS' BADGES
R.A.F. SQUADRON BADGES
BATTLES OF THE MALTA STRIKING FORCES
PER MARE, PER TERRAM
(Foreword by The Earl Mountbatten of Burma)
FIGHTING FLOTILLA
(Foreword by Mrs R.M.J. Hutton)
ARCTIC VICTORY
DESTROYER ACTION
(Foreword by Admiral Sir Gresham Nicholson)
BATTLE OF MIDWAY
THE GREAT SHIPS PASS
HIT FIRST, HIT HARD
(Foreword by Vice-Admiral B.C.B. Brooke)
IMPACT!
ACTION IMMINENT
CRUISERS IN ACTION
DIVE BOMBER!
HOLD THE NARROW SEA
H.M.S. *WILD SWAN*
(Foreword by Bob Burns)
INTO THE ASSAULT
VENGEANCE!
JUNGLE DIVE BOMBERS AT WAR
VICTORIA'S VICTORIES
(Foreword by David Chandler) ·
THE ROYAL MARINES – A PICTORIAL HISTORY
(Foreword by Lieutenant-General Sir Steuart Pringle)
MASSACRE AT TOBRUK
DIVE BOMBERS IN ACTION
BATTLESHIP *ROYAL SOVEREIGN*
EAGLE'S WAR
STUKA SQUADRON

For Arthur and Audrey Pearcy

Good friends indeed in hour's need!

T-6

A PICTORIAL RECORD OF THE HARVARD, TEXAN AND WIRRAWAY

PETER C. SMITH

Airlife

Copyright © 1995 by Peter C. Smith

First published in the UK in 1995
by Airlife Publishing Ltd

British Library Cataloguing in Publication Data
A catalogue record for this book is available from the British Library

ISBN 1 85310 115 X

Typeset by Litho Link Ltd, Welshpool, Powys
Printed in Singapore by Kyodo Printing Co (S'pore) Pte Ltd

Airlife Publishing Ltd
101 Longden Road, Shrewsbury SY3 9EB, England

Contents

Preface

The T-6 and its many variants have had a lifespan of more than fifty years so far. During that time it has served with almost every air force in the world in a wide variety of roles. Since its demise as a front-line military training aircraft its versatility has ensured equal global coverage in hands of the display team and the enthusiast as well as the aeronautical museum.

This book has attempted to cover pictorially the many facets of this hugely versatile and uniquely ubiquitous aircrafts' repertoire as is possible within a limited number of pages. While it is obvious that not every aspect of the T-6's career could be encompassed, effort has been made to include a broad range of subjects.

In my search for photographs I have contacted air forces, museums, flying teams, individual owners, enthusiasts and first-rate aerial photographers the world over. Not all my searches were successful. Many air forces, including, sadly, the Royal Air Force, could not see their way to helping. Many others ignored all requests and the same situation was found from other individuals and organisations who had splendid material but were not willing to make it available. This is a sad reflection of modern attitudes but, happily, this type of reaction was far outweighed and indeed was swamped by the generous and willing support and the enthusiastic backing of others from all parts of the world, eager to share their best and their love of the T-6 with a wider audience.

I do not claim to have uncovered a startling amount of fresh information, although this volume does contain much that has not been included between hard covers before. A few myths have been laid; for example – gallant and dramatic as the use of the Mosquitoes was during the Korean War, it is NOT the case, as is frequently claimed, that this represented the *first* military use of such machines in this role. The work of the LT-6Gs was as brave and stirring an episode of the T-6's life as any, but it was *preceded* by identical work conducted by the Australian Wirraways between 1943 and 1945, and by equally effective action by Harvards of the Royal Indian Air Force during the 1947 Kashmir conflict. Nor have I found the slightest documentary evidence to support the oft-trumpeted claim that a German submarine was sunk by a Mexican T-6 during the World War II. However, as a historian of long standing, I stand prepared to eat my words at any time!

As for my own errors, I am sure to have made some in a book of this nature. I apologise for these in advance and will hope to make corrections (and perhaps additions) in future editions of the book. I have tried to update material as far as possible to include interesting stories up to the end of 1989, as well as a balanced historic perspective. Inevitably of course, not everyone's favourite T-6 topic, aircraft or story will be included here, but I trust that my selection is as comprehensive as it could possibly be made.

In view of the valuable combat work done by ground-to-air rocket attacks post-war in Korea by American T-6s, it was natural that similar experimentation should take place elsewhere with standard rockets mounted on rails beneath the wings, and that the Harvard should be so adapted that training in this form of attack could be part-and-parcel of its itinerary.

The North American in fact proved a good steady platform for the delivery of such ordnance against land targets and its low speed made for accurate targeting. Here Harvard 2930 of the Royal Canadian Air Force carries out such shooting with three rockets fired and a fourth yet to leave the rack. Notice also the four small practice bombs in place outboard of the rocket mountings on each of the aircraft's wings. The chequered tail markings are typical of RAF and RCAF squadrons during the 1950s period when this photograph was taken, although the exact date is not known. (*Courtesy of Canadian Forces Photographic Unit, Ontario*)

Acknowledgements

From the vast amount of really superb photographic material made available it has been a very difficult task to trawl down to the section presented here. The parameters which decided the final selection were guided by the following factors, each of which had to be balanced carefully. There was the need for as complete an historical coverage as possible and as universal a coverage as possible. These requirements did not always sit happily for the over-riding concern of both author and publisher alike for *quality* of photograph. Finding fifty-year-old photographs to illustrate rare and special windows on the T-6's long career while attempting to couple that with the very high standards demanded by the printing and photographic requirements of the 1990s caused the author many a headache. As always in such cases, compromise has to be made. So, if a particular use or incident is not pictured in these pages it is more likely that the quality of the original negative brought about its omission rather than lack of such a photograph in the first place. We hope the reader will understand the dilemma and accept that the aim of presenting as high a quality of reproduction as possible was done with their interests in mind.

So many otherwise deserving or unique photographs I had to leave out. But I would like to thank the following individuals and organisations, presented here in strictly alphabetical order, for their highly-appreciated contributions and help, whether used or not, all of which helped make this book as careful and appreciative a tribute to the T-6 family as possible. For those who gave permission for their outstanding pictorial work to be reproduced in this book, a very special thank you.

William J. Armstrong, Department of the Navy, Washington, DC; Colonel Sabri Aydogan, Ministry of Defence, Ankara; D.S. Baker, Hawker de Havilland Victoria Ltd, Melbourne; Dr Fred Beck, Office of Air Force History, Bolling AFB; Major-General Ahmed I. Behery, Commander Royal Saudi Air Force, Riyad; Mrs Anne Bell, Fleet Air Arm Museum, Yeovilton; M. Benoits, SIRPA, Paris: David V.S. Berrington, Ohai; Warrant Officer P.L. Boulton, Air Staff Defence HQ, Wellington; Chaz Bowyer, Mulbarton; Commander B.J. Bromfield, Royal Australian Navy, RAN Air Station Nowara; Jack Bryant, TAGS, Langley; Meg Campbell, Palmerston North; Herr Cimander, Armando da Silva Coelho, Forca Aerea Portuguesa, Lisbon; Der Bundesminister der Verteidigung, Bonn; Group Captain B. Cole, Ghanian Air Force HQ, Accra; Dr Ira Chart, Northrop Corporation, Hawthorne, CA; M.B. Chenel, Musée de l'Air et de l'Espace, Le Bourget; John A. Collver, Lomita, CA; Terry Dowman, RNZAF Museum, Christchurch; Group Captain Theo J. MacLean de Lange, Rotorua; Chas. Dellow, Mermaid Beach; Steven D. Eisner, Van Nuys, CA; Major K.W. Farrell, Canadian Forces Photographic Unit, Ottawa; Colonel Francesco Fino, Stato Maggiore dell Aeronautuca, Rome; James L.R. Flynn, Ringwood, Vic; Warrant Officer D.W. Gardner, RAAF Museum, Point Cook; Group Captain John E. Gerber, RAAF, Turner, ACT; Wing Commander Arthur Murland Gill, Llanwarne; Colonel H.R. Haberli, Bern; Brian Hall, Myrtle Bank, SA; Anthony E. Hutton, The Squadron, North Weald; Dr J.A.M.M. Janssen, Royal Netherland Air Force, Soesterberg; Coronel Eduardo Jimenez-Carles, Madrid; Lieutenant-Colonel Sidney F. Johnston, Jr, Albuquerque; Lieutenant-Colonel Zeev Lachish, IDF, Tel Aviv; J. Laneiro, Loures; Reine Maily, Canadian Government

9

Expositions and A.V. Centre, Ottawa; Doug McPhail, Dundas, Ontario; Cyril J.B. MacPherson, East Ringwood, Vic; Ten QFO Solandge Teixeria de Menezes, Ministerio de Aeronautica, Brasilia-DF; Paul L. Muir, Condell Park, NSW; Brigadier-General Hanna Najjar, Royal Jordanian Air Force, Amman; William C. Northrop, Jr, RCMB Inc. Newport Beach; Arthur Pearcy, Sharnbrook; Bob Piper, Royal Australian Air Force Historical Officer, Canberra ACT; Flight Lieutenant P.B. Ratnayake, Sri Lanka AF HQ, Colombo; Air Commodore S. Sahay, Air HQ IAF, New Delhi; Sadao Seno, Kanagawa-ken; Hanfried Schliephake, Konigsbrunn; F.D. Sheppard, RAF Museum, Hendon; Ray C. Sturtivant, St. Albans; Group Captain Bhisit Sukhum, RTAF, Bangkok; Anna C. Urband; Dept of the Navy, Washington DC; Bill C. Walmsley, Rockwell International, Los Angeles; Nick Williams, American Aviation Historical Society, Waverly, IA; Helen Vaughan-Dawkes, National Archives, Wellington; Nick Veronico, *In Flight*, Woodside, CA; Louis J. Vosloo, Fish Hoek, SA; Dr G.A. 'Doc' Swayze; David Wilson, Department of Defence, Canberra ACT.

Peter C. Smith, Riseley, Bedford.

1 Origins and Ancestors

The most widespread and versatile training aircraft ever built; an aeroplane used by more air forces world-wide than any other; a brilliant concept developed and modified through a decade and resulting in more than 17,000 flying machines, more than 600 of which are still flying fifty years later; the best-loved and most-remembered single-engined training aircraft of all time; an adaptable and rugged aircraft that performed in the unexpected roles of fighter aircraft, dive-bomber, COIN airplane, ground-attack machine, observation aircraft, and on extensive anti-guerrilla suppression roles. An aircraft that has served at various times and various dates as airliner, mailplane and pylon racer. The aircraft still most commonly seen at air displays and air races; beloved by stunt aces and formation teams alike but best-remembered as the aircraft that spawned several generations of young pilots in countries as diverse as Brazil and the Soviet Union. All these aircraft are one aircraft, the North American 'T-6'.

The aircraft had almost as many official designations and names as it has uses and users! NA-26, BC-1, NA-44, AT-6, SNJ, 'Texan', J-Bird, Harvard, Wirraway, Ceres and a host more variants, marks and modifications to the same standard design proliferated down the years as engines and concepts changed and were altered around the same basic airframe. And then there were the nicknames bestowed by the flyers themselves down the years 'Pilot Maker', 'Mosquito' and more.

This work is not claimed as *the* definitive history of the T-6, so much as a loving pictorial tribute. The author is continuing exhaustive research for a future major study of the T-6 which is well underway and which will ultimately tell the full and complete story of this, the most universally-utilised and most significant military training aircraft in aviation history. However, for now and in this volume, we must confine ourselves to the salient details and trust our selection of photographs tells the story in its own special way.

The names of North American Aviation and the brilliant designer James H. 'Dutch' Kindelberger, are synonymous. The two first came together when Kindelberger and John Leland 'Lee' L. Atwood, respectively the former vice-president in charge of engineering and chief structural engineer of the Douglas Aircraft Company (both of them active in the development of the equally famed Douglas DC-1 transport aircraft) re-organised the General Aviation Manufacturing Corporation during 1934. The manufacturing operations of this Delaware company, which had originally been founded on 6 December 1928, were taken under the North American name on 1 January 1935. The new base for the re-generated company was the former Curtiss-Caproni factory at Dundalk in Maryland. Meanwhile work commenced on the construction of new plant incorporating the latest assembly techniques and equipment, at the massive Mines Field at Inglewood, California.

Among a host of antecedent operating airline companies and airplane manufacturers that formed the original base of the engineering and manufacturing organization of North American Aviation, were names like Sperry, the Fokker Corporation of America, incorporated in 1923 and acquired by General Aviation in 1930, and the Berliner-Joyce Aircraft Corporation, acquired by North American in the same year and merged in 1933 with General Aviation. By 1938 the new organisation had shed its airline holdings like TWA and concentrated solely on production.

With the outstanding kudos of what was to be the world-famous Dakota design behind them, Kindelberger, Atwood and the team they brought with them, confidently began to enter their advanced concepts for United States Army Air Corps design contracts. The new team scored an instant initial success with their GA-15 observation aircraft, a three-man, mid-wing design, built in less than nine weeks. It won the Air Corps competition at Wright Field, Ohio and became the XO-47 and finally the NA-25, the O-47. Another General Aviation concept, was the GA-16. This was a smaller two-seat in tandem, open-cockpit, low-wing, monoplane training aircraft. Like its contemporaries it was a fabric-covered aircraft, powered by a 400 hp Wright R-975-7 nine-cylinder, air-cooled Whirlwind engine. The GA-16 had been flight-tested under civilian licence number X-2080 at Logan Field, Baltimore and the Air Corps expressed interest. The re-organisation completed, this design was modified and re-introduced for the first time under the North American banner. This was the 'Basic Trainer', which, as the NA-16, Kindelberger entered for the 1934 competition.

As was to be expected, the North American team came up with an aircraft design that incorporated a whole host of radical and innovative features. In effect Kindelberger looked at the Basic Trainer concept laterally and functionally, with one eye on the looming war clouds gathering in Europe and the feel that massive expansion of the world's air forces was imminent and that fighter designs were changing completely with the introduction of monoplane interceptors like the German Me 109, the British Hawker Hurricane and Supermarine Spitfire and the America P-40 on the drawing-boards. Clearly the days of the old 'wings-wires-and-struts' type of biplane trainer were also numbered as a new generation of aircraft would require their pilots to be more highly-skilled in high-speed, low-drag monoplane flying. But it had to be simple enough for novices to fly with some confidence, rugged enough to withstand the treatment handed out by student pilots and versatile enough to be repairable economically. With these widely-differing requirements all firmly in mind the NA-16 was unlike any of its competitors.

First flown by test pilot Eddie Allen on the unauspicious date of 1 April 1935 from Dundalk, the NA-16 had taken six weeks to prepare and by the end of the month was ready to be put through its paces.

The features which won the 1935 Air Corps competition for North American and with it a contract to build forty-two of these training aircraft under the Air Corps designation BT-9, were the same features that ensured this initial order was but the forerunner for seventeen-thousand plus descendants world-wide. They were summarised by the company thus:-

> *(1) Accessibility of internal mechanisms.* By the removal of quickly detachable fuselage side panels and engine cowlings, it was possible to obtain convenient and complete access to the internal structure and mechanisms of the aircraft for inspection, replacements and repairs. This feature was possessed by the BT-9 to a greater extent than by any other aircraft then in existence. It was an extremely important feature to the Air Corps and other purchasers of the aeroplane, concerned then as now with keeping the maximum number of available training aircraft in flying condition.
>
> *(2) Interchangeability of parts and components.* Through design of the airplane in logical components which were quickly detachable and attachable, and through assembly of those components in precision steel jigs, North American achieved a new high in interchangeability. For example, the tips of the wings were designed as quickly detachable assemblies so they could be replaced without a long inactivation period when the wing-tips scraped the runway in a ground loop, as frequently happened when student pilots were at the controls. As another illustration, the entire power-plant installation was designed as a unit, which could be detached and replaced in a matter of eight man hours. Or, an entire wing outer panel could be removed with amazing

speed because it was held to the centre section simply by bolts through flange angles.

(3) Duplication of handling characteristics of combat aircraft. To a remarkable degree, the BT-9 and its descendants duplicated the performance characteristics of single-engined combat aircraft. The transition from a trainer airplane to a pursuit or attack airplane was thus made easier for the student pilot, and the Air Corps training programme was greatly facilitated.

The BT-9 itself was modified by Air Corps requirements to feature an enclosed aerodynamic canopy over the whole of the considerably-widened tandem cockpit and the instruments changed to suit the laid-down Army-style layout. Otherwise the airplane was much the same, other than for an enlarged air intake for the Whirlwind engine forward of the cockpit. Perhaps the most retrograde feature in an otherwise very forward-looking design was the fixed-undercarriage with each fully-faired oleo leg mounted on the forward edge of the central wing section. The wheels themselves were spatted outboard only. The initial use of fixed-landing gear on the NA-16 may have been for strength.

The fuselage was a fabric-covering over a steel frame, and the three-piece wings were all-metal, stressed-skin and flush riveted, all features common to the DC-2, with the two outer panels bolting to a constant-chord centre-section. The wings were forty-two feet in length with a full-span flap on the wing centre section balanced by split flaps on both outer wing panels. These outer panels, leading and trailing edges, as well as the wing dihedral angle, also matched that of the DC-2. As related above, the fuselage was constructed in sub-assemblies for easy replacement, with the separate sections of the engine cavity, cockpit area, upper and lower rear fuselages all being bolted together and fitted with fabric-covered easy-access panels to allow engineers to reach any section of the fuselage simply and quickly.

The basic Army paint scheme of the period was for a blue fuselage with yellow wings and the resultant prototype machines received the company designation of the NA-18. Further modifications, for which provision was made at that time, was for the replacement of the Whirlwind with a 600 hp Pratt & Whitney R-1340 Wasp power-plant and the mounting of machine-guns for armament training. It was proposed that two fixed forward-firing .30 calibre weapons be fitted to the cowling with a single gun of the same calibre on a flexible mounting in the rear cockpit. But the Army rejected both concepts. But of course North American had other fish to fry when it made these provisions, for the Air Corps were far from their only potential customers as we have seen. Nor was it being marketed abroad solely as a trainer.

The first production BT-9 flew on 15 April 1936. In the event, the second Air Corps production order was for forty more aircraft. BT-9As (NA-19s) were equipped with modified outer wing panels to overcome an initial stall problem, which featured a two degree 'wash-out' built into them. Stability was also improved by lengthening the fuselage by five inches overall and the aircraft had built-in provision for both machine-guns and cameras. The fitting of leading edge slats to the outer wing sections necessitated the relocation of the Pitot tube inboard, which gave a long-range clue between the two models. A solitary fixed forward-firing .30 gun was provided on the starboard side of the cowling with a single flexible-mounted weapon of the same calibre in the aft cockpit. The height of the canopy had been increased slightly for crew comfort.

These minor alterations completed, the BT-9 proved a great success in service, so much so that, in 1937 the Air Corps came back with repeat orders for no less than 117 aircraft. The following year the Army dropped the machine-gun requirement once again and as the BT-9C sixty-seven further machines were ordered for use by the USAAC Organized Reserve. Only one BT-9D was ever built. This was an experimental aircraft which appeared in 1938 and was a BT-9B with the tail surfaces and wing panels re-designed for trials.

It was to meet the requirements of the other major Stateside customer, the United States

Navy, that the soundness of the alternative engine design thought out earlier came to the fore. The US Navy did not rate the Wright engine very highly and had always favoured the Pratt & Whitney instead. To meet that preference, and so open up the BT-9 to Navy orders, North American took the first standard BT-9C and replaced the Wright engine with a 600 hp Pratt & Whitney R-1340-41 Wasp radial. Because of dire shortage of funds the Navy was unable to finance this experiment, so this aircraft, the NA-28, became the Army Y1BT-10. This was later redesignated as the BT-10. Evaluation testing followed.

Meanwhile the US Navy had approved the Pratt & Whitney-engined BT-10 and when they had sufficient funds, under the 1937 naval estimates, they immediately ordered forty of these aircraft under the designation NJ-1. Under Navy nomenclure N stood for training aircraft, J for the North American company and 1 indicted the first machine from this firm. All these NJ-1s featured the relocation of the engine airscoop from the top of the cowling to below it. None of the naval trainers were equipped with any armaments. Nor were they equipped for carrier deck landings and none had tail hooks or strengthening.

Deliveries commenced as early as July 1937. The US Navy colour scheme at that time was bright aluminum fuselage and wings with the upper-wing surfaces a vivid orange. Those aircraft utilised for instrument training were distinguished by broad red bands around both fuselage and wings.

All these machines were to be fitted with the Wasp engine except for the final production model of the series. This machine was fitted with yet another alternate power-plant, the 550 hp Ranger XV-770-4 inline engine. This gave a whole new profile to the BT-9 (or the NJ-2 as this aircraft was for a while designated), but the experiment was not a happy one and, after reversion to the normal power-plant, this aircraft was finally delivered to the Navy as a standard NJ-1.

The fitting of the Pratt & Whitney engine with its greater power to the Navy variants, gave a strong performance to the basic model and led to the next home-orientated development. By fitting the 450 hp Pratt & Whitney R-985-25 Wasp Junior engine to the new BT-9D (NA-58) another great stride forward was made.

The NA-58 saw the composite fabric-covered fuselage dropped in favour of the more revolutionary all-metal, aluminium semi-monocoque type of construction, which was both sturdier and lighter. The fuselage was lengthened by fourteen inches. By contrast the wing span was reduced to forty-one feet, by having a broad-chord, but squared-off, wing-tip following further stability tests. The forward edge of the vertical tail surface was much further raked and the formerly distinctly rounded rudder was cut in a sharply angular style that was to become one of the aircraft's most highly distinctive recognition points. Other physical feature changes were brought about by the need for a larger cowling for the new engine, with the exhaust-pipe positioned astern of it on the starboard side. Taking on a decisively modern appearance, the YBT-14's undercarriage still stubbornly remained of the fixed, half-spatted type as before.

Evaluation by the Army Air Corps proved the advantage of these improvements and with re-armament at last gaining some momentum in the States as a result of the international situation, an unprecedented order for no less than 251 BT-14s was placed. The latter end of this batch, some twenty-seven aircraft, were modified while still under construction in 1941, to carry the 400 hp Pratt & Whitney R-985-11A engine.

In the interim, and with firm US orders safely under their belt as an affirmation to the rest of the world of the soundness of the BT-9 design, production was now well under-way at the new Inglewood plant.

> 'Many export sales were found for the trainer series, each requiring design revisions to the specific requirements of the export customer.'

The first of these customers was France. By the end of 1938 it was clear to the French Government that war with Hitler's Germany was almost inevitable. A purchasing mission, under M. Jean Monnet, was sent to the States to explain their dire needs and see if the

Americans would be willing to help. As Monnet himself stated to Captain John H. Towers of the United States Bureau of Aeronautics, 'The French and British Governments had been compelled to accept the terms of the Munich Agreement solely because of the preponderant strength of the German Air Force . . . both the French and British Governments realized further demands could be expected from Germany.' Due to the lamentable state of their own aircraft industry, France's only hope of building up its air strength quickly lay in the bulk purchase of the latest American types. The stumbling block was the American Neutrality Act. A sympathetic President Franklin D. Roosevelt was trying to have this nullified but had to tread carefully. Delicate negotiations continued apace and finally, on 16 January 1939 M. Monnet's mission sent a cable to Paris recommending that the French Government order 555 aircraft of all types, including fighters, bombers and dive-bombers. But by far the largest part of this intended deal was for 200 North American basic training aircraft. Authorisation was received from Paris to go ahead without further delay.

Supply by the American builders presented no problems, delivery of the aircraft was something else. On 9 November 1939 it was reported that fifty-four North American trainers were crated and ready for shipment to France with five more expected to be ready by the end of that month. The problem for the French was shortage of suitable shipping to transport these machines across the Atlantic in convoy, only three such ships being available for December with a capacity of fifty to sixty aircraft each. German submarine activity also brought about further delay when the ports of destination in mainland France were altered to disembarkation at Casablanca in Morocco. Even when the first aircraft arrived there on Christmas Day 1939, few facilities had been prepared for the disembarkation and assembly of the aircraft.

At the time of the French surrender on 15 June 1940 of the forty North American trainer aircraft received at Casablanca, thirty-eight had been successfully transferred to the French Air Force and the other two were still being assembled.

As the North American NA-57, the French ordered 230 BT-9Bs customised to their own special requirements. These aircraft were therefore fitted with reversed throttles and were powered with the 420 hp Wright R-975-E3 engine. All were delivered (despite the American neutrality laws and other restrictions introduced on the outbreak of war in Europe in September 1939), apart from the final batch of sixteen machines. The French surrender in June 1940 left these aircraft still in the States.

It was thanks to the foresight of M. Jean Monnet himself, who worked hard from 3 September 1939 onwards, that the joint Anglo-French Economic Co-ordinating Commission had been formed to ensure both nations got the best from the United States aircraft industries output during their hour of need.

The British also became beneficiaries of all outstanding French orders for American planes. Thanks to the courage of the French representative on the Anglo-French Purchasing Commission in the United States, all French contracts for American planes and arms were signed over to the British on the night of 17 June 1940.

Thus, as with so many other outstanding aircraft orders for occupied countries, the British Government quickly stepped in and purchased them to prevent them falling into German hands. The sixteen NA-57s were diverted to Canada and taken on the inventory of the Royal Canadian Air Force. Being American training aircraft they were allocated names to fit into the British scheme of things and being training aircraft were named after the famous American college of Yale, these sixteen aircraft becoming the Yale Mark I.

But French orders had not been confined to the NA-57, they had also placed contracts for a further 230 NA-64 trainers, which were Pratt & Whitney-equipped BT-14 aircraft, the R-985-25 type being utilised. Along with all the usual French modifications this later order commenced delivery after the outbreak of the war and was therefore only half complete at the time of the surrender. There were 119 outstanding NA-64s on hand and these were also taken into the RCAF and RAF training schools in Canada, and, confusingly, these were also christened Yale Mk.Is. The reverse throttles and other French fixtures remained unchanged in RCAF service. In a similar manner the many NA-57s and NA-64s that fell into German hands were put to good use by their new owners, the Vichy French Government, who also allowed their use by the Luftwaffe training units in both occupied France and Germany with their *Flugzeugführer Schules* and continued in this use for several years.

Following the US Army requirement for a two-seater trainer issued in 1934, the initial response had come from General Aviation, Dundalk, Maryland. It featured the Wright R-975 400 hp radial engine. When North American took them over this machine received the new designation of NA-16 (X-2080) and first flew in April 1935.

With the introduction of closed cockpits and fairings, streamlining the fixed landing-gear, the NA-16's engine was changed to the Pratt & Whitney R-1340 Wasp. This became the NA-18 for Argentina, but the next batch of forty-two machines ordered by the US Army Air Corps as the NA-19 were given the classification of BT-9. They featured a landing gear that had been moved forward and outer wing slats operated by a manually-operated hydraulic system. The Wasp engine was re-introduced. These were Basic Trainers, but there was a need for an even more tame variant for novice pilots, the Primary Trainer.

The aircraft shown here was in fact the ninth BT-9 ordered from North American by the US Army but was experimentally evaluated in this role as the NA-22 with primary trainer features. This included open cockpits, a Townsend ring cowling and much simplified handling equipment. (*Courtesy of Rockwell International Archives*)

The BT-9 itself was modified by Air Corps requirements to feature an enclosed aerodynamic canopy over the whole of the considerably-widened tandem cockpit and the instruments changed to suit the laid-down Army-style layout. There was also an enlarged air intake for the Whirlwind engine forward of the cockpit. The BT-9 proved a great success in service, so much so that, in 1937, the Air Corps came back with repeat orders for no less than 117 aircraft. (*Courtesy of Rockwell International Archives*)

It came about in 1937 that even before the first BT-14 had taken to the sky plans were in hand to convert a standard NA-16 to take the folding landing-gear and this became the North American NA-36. As well as having the aircraft wheels retracting fully into wells in each of the extended wing's main sections, this aircraft was given the acclaimed Pratt & Whitney R-1340-S3H1 air-cooled engine which was rated at 600 hp and drove a twin-bladed variable-pitch propeller.

Although the fuselage at this stage remained fabric-covered, some further re-design work was incorporated which included another canopy modification and the re-introduction of armament fittings. Provision was made for the re-introduction of the single, fixed, forward-firing .30 calibre machine-gun on the starboard cowling and the .30 gun on the flexible mounting aft. The reasons for this were related to Kindelberger's ideas on export potential, but also to demonstrate a new concept he was putting across to enable the Air Force to overcome the limitation of funding on all but pure combat-type aircraft at this period.

The North American concept was that the NA-36 represented not just an advanced trainer but something completely new, as a Basic Combat type of aeroplane. Thus, as the BT-9D (and then as the BC-1) the new trainer was advanced as a kind of cheap, second-level pursuit and attack machine. Such a category was obviously more than just a trainer and thus qualified for more generous funding. When Kindelberger proposed this concept to General Henry H. 'Hap' Arnold, who was to become Commanding General of the Army Air Forces, it won instant approval and a new Army specification was written around the NA-36 for just such a type. Not completely surprisingly in the ensuing competition for such an aircraft, the BC-1 fitted the bill exactly! Thus appeared the NA-26 shown here, or the North American BC-1. (*Courtesy of Rockwell International Archives*)

The NA-44 charge number was allocated on 9 December 1937 to the prototype machine for the Canadian Government (NX-18981). (Factory Serial Number 44-747.) This experimental model was the forerunner of thousands of Harvards supplied by the parent company but also built under licence by the Noorduyn Aviation Ltd., of Montreal, Quebec after the Canadian Government had secured a licence for the manufacture of the type in Canada. The Royal Canadian Air Force received thirty Harvard Mk Is in July, 1939.

The Harvard Mk II entered service on 19 June 1940 and by 1945 a total of 1,876 had been accepted. The first assembly line successor began to appear in April 1941. The Canadian output of this machine reached a total of 2,775 Mk IIs with a peak production rate of 113 per month. Many of the Canadian-built Harvards were delivered to the Royal Air Force, but, even so, the Harvard was the second most numerous aircraft type to serve in the RCAF. The Harvard was 'officially' phased out of the RCAF on 14 December 1960. (*Courtesy of Rockwell International Archives*)

The T-6 was one of the most successful aircraft designs of all times. Its arrival filled an urgently-felt need in the air forces of not just the major powers like the United States, Great Britain, France, Canada and Australia, but a whole host of lesser nations that wished to modernise their air fleets under the impetus of World War II. The Texan was the right aircraft at the right time in more ways than one! But before we examine in detail the enormous diversity of customers for the T-6 and the variety of uses that they put this little aircraft to, let us take a look at the final conventional developments of the type by North American in the closing stages of the war, along with a few of experimental and 'oddball' customisations of the basic airframes that took place during this same period.

Many other nations took the earlier NA types in the pre-Lend-Lease era among them Argentina, Brazil, Chile, China, Honduras, Peru, Sweden and Venezuela all took delivery of such aircraft.

On 30 November 1939, Siam ordered ten of the two-seat NA-69 Attack Bomber variants, equipped with the 785 hp Wright R-1820-F52 Cyclone engine, a three-bladed propeller and five .30 calibre wing-fuselage and swivel-mounted machine-guns and bomb fixtures under the fuselage and wings. They never reached the country of their destination but were appropriated by the USAAC (as the A-27) and expended in defence of the Philippines in 1941-42. Brazil purchased thirty of a similar type (NA-72) and Chile twelve (NA-74). China took delivery of fifteen NA-16-3Cs (NA-48) on 23 February 1938. They were similar to the BC-1 except for the engine.

Concentrating solely on the T-6 variants, Latin-American nations naturally constituted a good market for North American early on. Venezuela ordered three NA-71s (NA-16-3) on 18 January 1940. These aircraft resembled the NA-59 except that they carried two fixed, forward-firing machine-guns. Like the RAF the Venezuelans also omitted the flagpole of a radio mast smack in front of the pilot's vision! Under the designation NA-72 (NA-44, BC-1A) Brazil placed a large order on 13 January 1940 for thirty machines for use as Attack Bombers. They were basically NA-59/AT-6s equipped with two wing-mounted machine-guns and direction-finding (D/F) gear. Finally Chile followed suit on 8 August in the same year with an order for a round dozen NA-74s (NA-44) which were identical to the NA-72, except for the extra provision of under-wing racks for light bombs.

This photo shows one of the first of the export types, one of three NA-45s, the Venezuelan government ordered in 1938. (*Courtesy of Rockwell International Archives*)

(*above*)

The NA-56 was a batch of fifty BT-9Bs which North American constructed for the Government of China from 18 April 1939 onwards. They took the serial numbers 56-1453 to 56-1502. Already fully engaged in a long-running war with Japan, the Chinese were desperate for modern aircraft of all types. It was from export orders like these that the fledgling North American Company kept itself afloat and was able to bring forward its improved designs that were to result in the famous AT-6 later. Already the parenthood is obvious.

At this time, with Hitler gulping down the remnants of Czechoslovakia in Europe as well as the Sino-Japanese situation, the need for training aircraft was beginning to boom all around the world and North American were well placed to benefit from it, even if its own Government were still luke-warm. (*Courtesy of Rockwell International Archives*)

(*below*)

The NA-45 was the North American charge number allocated on 14 December 1937 to three trainers built especially for the Venezuelan Air Force under the designation of NA-16-IGV. The factory serial numbers were 45-693, 45-694 and 45-695. These aircraft had been ordered by Venezuela on 18 January 1940 and resembled the NA-59 (AT-6) except that they carried two fixed, forward-firing machine-guns. Like those built for the Royal Air Force, the Venezuelan aircraft omitted the siting of the massive radio mast right in front of the pilot's vision.

All markings were in Spanish. The national markings were on the rounded rudder (like the BT-9) but the rest of the fuselage was painted jungle green. (*Courtesy of Rockwell International Archives*)

Following the successful completion of the Navy tests an initial batch of sixteen NA-52s was placed, and these joined the fleet in May 1939, under the designation SNJ-1. They were delivered to NAS Anacostia on the 29th of that month in an all-over aluminium finish. It was basically this aircraft that was to interest the British and become the initial Harvard, as we shall see later.

The final transitions now began to take place. A solitary BC-1B was built to test a new centre wing section, increased capacity fuel tanks and an improved version of the retractable landing-gear. All these features would be incorporated on future models.

After the Army had looked hard at its own BC-1s and B-14s and the Navy's SNJ-1s they came up with a new specificiation incorporating the best from each model. Three BC-2s were constructed with the all-metal semi-monocoque, lengthened fuselage and retractable landing gear. The hitherto rounded wing-tips of the BC-1/SNJ-1 duo were squared off in a similar manner to the angular rudder modifications which were also adopted. The air intake became a large and obvious scoop positioned under the forward fuselage behind the cowling. These aircraft also featured an experimental three-bladed propeller fitted to the Pratt & Whitney 600 hp radial R-1340-45 engine which necessitated a second air intake positioned on the port side of the fuselage abaft the cowling. The new propeller was fitted with the hope that this would further improve the aircraft's performance. The experiment took place at Wright Field, Ohio, but was a failure and was not proceeded with. This is the NA-52, or North American SNJ-1 in 1939. (*Courtesy of Rockwell International Archives*)

The North American NA-55, proved itself a winner and the Army placed contracts for fifty-four of these aircraft to equip the Air Reserve training force, with an additional twenty-nine to equip the Air National Guard as the BC-1A. By now the war in Europe was in full-swing, Congress had released enormous funds to increase America's armed forces while they still had the time and the new factories were going flat-out to meet the demand of both home and continued British orders. The need for the Basic Combat designation was seen as no longer applicable, there were ample true Attack types under development as it was. So the category was changed once more to Advance Trainer (AT) and the North American NA-59, as it became, went to war under the designation it was to become most famous, the AT-6. Thus, of the original order for 180 BC-1s the Army had ninety-two modified as BC-1As in which capacity they served mainly as flexible gunnery trainers rather than 'pilot makers'. Nine others stayed in the plant and became the first of the 'AT-6 period' as they were later dubbed by American instructors and trainees alike. Late in 1940 the Army Air Corps placed orders for ninety-four of these AT-6s and the dynasty had commenced.

The North American BC-1A (BC Standing for Basic Combat) became the AT-6 (AT for Advanced Trainer) and combined with all-metal fuselage of the BT-14, slightly lengthened, with the retractable landing-gear and wings which featured the 'squared-off' tips. The rudder became angular in shape and the air intake was made into a shallow scoop positioned slightly abaft the engine cowling. This is a 1941 view which shows some of these features to good advantage. (*National Archives, Washington DC*)

The early war years were studded with problems of supply and delivery for North American due to the political ramifications of neutrality that were not cleared-up until the Lend-Lease Act came into force. 'When a new contract for Harvard trainers was placed with North American late in 1939, the British decided to concentrate training activities in Canada, and to have the Harvards flown directly to training centres in the Dominion. Until revision of the Neutrality Act took effect in September 1940, it was necessary to have these planes pulled across the international boundary by Canadian nationals, where they were turned over to Canadian pilots.

The first plane hauled across the international line by manpower was delivered in the summer of 1940 from Pembina, North Dakota, a small town near the Canadian border. Altogether about twenty-five Harvards were delivered in this fashion before direct delivery was legalized. Subsequently the Harvards were flown direct from the factory near Los Angeles to the training bases where they would be used in Canada. This tremendous delivery job was performed by a staff of skilled American pilots who delivered the trim monoplanes in Canada and returned by scheduled airlines for the next delivery flight. By the end of 1940 North American had delivered more than 800 Harvard advanced trainers to various parts of the British Empire. In January 1941 Kindelberger received a personal cablegram from Lord Beaverbrook, British Minister of Aircraft Production, congratulating the company on its achievement in bettering the production schedule set for 1940 on the Harvard II type.' (*Courtesy of Rockwell International Archives*)

The classic profile of the Harvard II on the concrete at Inglewood in 1940. Between July 1941 and May 1942, 305 Harvard IIs were directly flown across the US/Canada border to equip training units of both the EATS and the BCATP, as well as SFTS squadrons where they joined RCAF Harvards. At the same time shipments to Southern Rhodesia via South African ports continued from August 1941 onwards, some 103 Mk IIs being thus despatched, while forty-seven others ultimately ended up in the Middle East. Four Mk IIs reached India but were soon expended in accidents and, finally, direct shipment of thirty-eight Mk. IIs equipped the training squadrons of the Royal New Zealand Air Force.

The Harvard Mk IIA was the equivalent of the American AT-6C. No Mark IIAs were shipped to the United Kingdom but were instead allocated to EATS units both in the Middle East (one hundred Mark IIAs) and South Africa (a total of 436 Mk. IIAs) from October 1942, and these despatches were followed by fifty-three machines to New Zealand (commencing in December 1942) and 149 to Southern Rhodesia (starting in January 1943). Later in the war the Royal Navy's Fleet Air Arm units, No. 789 Squadron at Wingfield, South Africa and No. 757 Squadron at Pattalam, Ceylon (Sri Lanka), took some. (*Courtesy of Rockwell International Archives*)

Wings for the world. The supplying of the T-6/SNJ/Harvard variants from the expanding North Amerian aircraft plant mushroomed as the war in Europe accelerated and the threat to the United States became ever greater. This 1940 photograph shows the wing racking with both USAAF and RAF markings painted up.

When the company had originally moved its operations to Inglewood, California from Dundalk, Maryland, on the basis of the Air Corps order for the original eighty-two BT-9s in November 1935, they had initially taken seventy-five key employees with them to form the nucleus of the new organisation. By January 1936, double this number of men moved into the new 158,678 square-foot factory which had the transplanted tooling and machinery installed. By 1938 this workforce had risen to 2,730 people and by 1 September 1937 to 3,400 and the factory area had expanded to almost 800,000 square-feet by November of that year.

Impressive though this expansion was with the President's call for 50,000 aircraft per annum, the two-year period between the outbreak of war in Europe and Pearl Harbor saw these totals pale into insignifance. North American increased its monthly aircraft output from seventy to 325 units, its personnel from 3,400 to 23,000 and its factory floor area to 2½ million square-feet. Even this was not to be enough. Despite further expansion at Inglewood it was clear that the plant just could not meet the flood of orders for the advanced combat trainers and other aircraft. (*Courtesy of Rockwell International Archives*)

2 The SNJ/AT-6 Development

What was to prove the final preliminary step in the progression to the AT-6 took place in 1937 and was the result of another piece of 'Dutch' Kindelberger's opportunism. The fixed landing-gear of the earlier North American trainers was looking progressively retrograde as the months went by and a main factor in limiting the aircrafts' best speed to 190 mph. The fact that both Army and Navy were now firmly wedded to North American for their standard training aircraft led the company to feel that it was time to take the next step forward.

It was a logical advance therefore to create a test model with a much improved performance, to enable the aircraft to act as an advanced trainer certainly, but also to provide the flexibility that North American required to extend the range of its potential export capabilities into general purpose and even limited fighter roles. To achieve all this a 'clean-up' design was needed which necessitated the adoption of a fully-retractable landing gear. At the same time, although the composite fuselage structure was acceptable, both the American services made it clear that all-metal construction was what they most favoured and most welcomed in future aircraft of this type. Combining both internal and external needs North American came up with the NA-26, which at its most simplistic form was a NJ-1 with retractable undercarriage.

The final step was to be the ironing out of most of the frustrating differences between the Army and Navy specifications for what was, after all, a standard Advanced Trainer aircraft for both. They could never be completely harmonious of course, as with the chartboard, the need for life-jacket stowage and, later, tailhooks and strengthening for carrier deck landings, the two services could never be absolutely compatible. But with war fast approaching they could clearly be much more amenable to each other's viewpoints and training aircraft requirements than they could ever hope to be with combat aircraft needs. Both had been for so long traditional rivals in competition for meagre Government defence funds that it took no little persuasion for the two services to harmonise their needs for the benefit of both North American, the US Government inspectors of the Bureau of Ordnance and the Allied war effort alike, but eventually it was done. And *when* it was the T-6 had finally, and absolutely, arrived!

The catalyst of this ultimate joining was of course the vast expansion programmes following the German victories in Europe and *prior* to America's entry into the war after the Japanese Navy attack at Pearl Harbor on 7 December 1941. One result of all this was a colossal expansion of the American aircraft industry and the need for brand-new factories to be built to meet the insatiable demand.

As the company history records;

> 'The large and vital trainer programme for the Army Air Corps and US Navy got underway in earnest shortly after the President's National Defense message to Congress in May of 1940. On the strength of verbal indications from Air Corps officers that a quantity of AT-6 combat trainers would be required when and if appropriations became available, the management issued a general order for the manufacture of the first group of these planes

on 28 June 1940, and work proceeded immediately. The board of directors of the corporation formally supported this action by the management in a resolution adopted at its meeting on 12 July 1940. The supporting contract was executed by the Government on 13 August 1940, calling for 637 planes of the AT-6A type (later changed to 517 AT-6A type for the Air Corps and 120 SNJ-3 type for the US Navy). Thanks to the head-start gained by the company by going ahead with production work on its own risk, the first airplane under this contract was delivered to the Air Corps on 27 September 1940, with production accelerating rapidly thereafter. The entire order for 637 planes had been completed in August 1941, just one year after the date of the contract. The first unit delivered under this contract late in September, 1940, just forty-five days after the contract was signed, was the first aeroplane delivered to the Government under a National Defense programme contract.

Shortly after this initial National Defense delivery, the company received a contract for the manufacture of 1,480 AT-6A and SNJ-3 trainers. This was the first contract undertaken by the new Dallas plant. In August of 1941, approximately four months after the first deliveries were made from the new Dallas plant, the last advanced combat trainer to be produced by the Inglewood plant under domestic contracts was delivered to the Army Air Corps. Thereafter all Army and Navy trainer deliveries were made from the Dallas plant, which then became a self-sufficient production unit capable of conducting the entire manufacturing operations on trainers.'

There were labour shortages in the Los Angeles area at that time and so North American cast about for a site for a brand-new complex, somewhere with ample space and plenty of people available to work there. Not surprisingly, their choice fell on Texas.

The company found the site it considered the most desirable next to Hensley Field, the Army Reserve airfield close to Dallas, Texas. This was also the major population centre of the American South-west. However, it was discovered that the Consolidated Aircraft Corporation was also after this site for a new plant to build their B-24 Liberator bombers. As the company history later recorded;

Although Consolidated had previously indicated to the Air Corps its desire to use this location, North American Aviation was given preference by the Air Corps. The determining factor was the pressing need for production of North American's advanced trainer; this programme was ready to go immediately, whereas Consolidated's programme was still far in the future. The Dallas plant was to be built with Defense Plant Corporation funds.

The first public announcement of selection of this location for North American's new trainer manufacturing plant was made on 17 August 1940. Ground-breaking ceremonies were held on 28 September on the bare expanse of Texas plain adjoining the Army field. The general contract for construction of the plant was not awarded until 13 November, due to delays occasioned by the D.P.C. arrangement, but events moved at top speed after the contract was awarded.

Work on the 1,022,400-square-foot plant commenced on 2 December and North American personnel began to move into the still uncompleted plant on 20 January 1941. Less than three months later, on 8 March, the first manufacturing operations commenced at the factory and on 7 April the first three AT-6A advanced trainers were turned over to the Air Corps on the occasion of the plant dedication ceremony. This was just 120 days after construction had begun.

Nor was the training programme for the new employees any less spectacular. The first class of thirty-five men was enrolled in the Dallas training school on 4 November 1940. Under the Dallas training plan, 100 new applicants were to start each fortnight on a two-week training course calculated to serve also as an entrance examination. At the end of the two-week period those who had successfully completed the course were placed on the payroll and assigned to departments for which they were best fitted, after which they began actual production work under adequate supervision as the final phase of their training.

To each plant was sent a small nucleus of supervisory personnel from among the experienced employees of the Inglewood plant. The organizational structure set up in each plant was basically similar to the Inglewood organizational structure. The work of all plants was co-ordinated by administrative staff groups in Inglewood, later to be formalized as the corporation's general office staff. As an illustration of the tremendous training job faced in these new plants, only about seventy-five men were transferred from Inglewood to the Dallas plant as its supervisory and training nucleus prior to the plant dedication in March, 1941. At the end of 1941 it was estimated that at least ninety-five per cent of the total payroll in the Dallas plant comprised native Texans who had no previous aircraft experience before being employed by North American Aviation.

Involvement in the war and rapid expansion was fine, but of course it also brought about production problems. Although the USA, as the 'Arsenal of Democracy', was completely immune from bombing attacks or indeed almost every other form of enemy intervention, the actual supply of raw materials *could* (in theory) be disrupted by the German U-boat fleet which, in 1941/42 enjoyed enormous success off American coastal areas.

This brought about the first serious alteration to the Texan's design because imported aluminium was deemed to be at a possible premium. Desirable as both Army and Navy deemed it to have all-metal fuselages for their trainers, the US War Department decided, wisely, that the needs of combat aircraft in this respect must take priority.

As a result of this decision North American brought in a series of wooden composite fuselage parts abaft of the fire-wall to compensate and lessen demand for this vital metal. Later the whole of the rear section of the fuselage was built of three-ply mahogany plywood sheeting as were the cockpit floorboards. Other internal fixtures were built of native spruce wood. This achieved a saving of 200 lbs of aluminium per aircraft. Thus composite Texans began to appear in large numbers, and, in the end, 1,243 AT-6Cs and 1,040 SNJ-4s were built to this specification. The predicted shortage of aluminium never, in fact, materialised and later production of the all-metal fuselage type was resumed as the norm.

This set the standard for further designations and that of all subsequent 'navalised' trainers. Both versions could be adapted as target tugs by the provision of cabling gear fitted on the underside of the fuselage abaft the rear cockpit.

The North American NA-88 (Army AT-6C, Navy SNJ-4) represented the ultimate amalgamation of ideas and varied little from their forebears save for certain internal alterations. Also the SNJ-4 incorporated the third machine-gun and the bomb racks carried by the Army variants which made them even more identical.

(*above*)
The US Navy, which did not rate the Wright engine very highly and had always favoured the Pratt & Whitney instead, had approved the Pratt & Whitney engined BT-10 and when they had sufficient funds, under the 1937/38 naval estimates, they immediately ordered forty of these aircraft under the designation NJ-1. Under Navy nomenclature N stood for training aircraft, J for the North American company and 1 indicted the first machine from this firm. All these NJ-1s featured the relocation of the engine airscoop from the top of the cowling to below it. None of the naval trainers were equipped with any armaments. Nor were they equipped for carrier deck landings and none had tail-hooks or strengthening.

Deliveries commenced as early as July 1937. The US Navy colour scheme at that time was bright aluminum fuselage and wings with the upper-wing surfaces a vivid orange. Those aircraft utilised for instrument training were distinguished by broad red bands around both fuselage and wings.

This photo is the NA-52 (SNJ-1), the first of a batch of sixteen such trainers given that designation on 28 September 1938. (*Courtesy of Rockwell International Archives*)

(*right*)
With a brand-new North American aircraft plant firmly established at Dallas, Texas, work got underway in earnest to try and meet the needs of North American's many customers for its outstanding product, the 120 SNJ-3s (North American NA-77, Navy Bureau of Aeronautics Requisition 1255), which had its first flight in March 1941, and the 517 AT-6As (North American NA-78, Army contract AC-15977). As we have seen, with Government prodding, these two variants were largely standardised versions of the same aircraft and the majority of the aircraft's sections, including the wings, airframe and tailplane (with the Army's triangular configuration becoming the norm), and associated nuts, bolts, seats, instrumentation, radio and other basic fittings were totally interchangeable, while visually they were were almost identical.

The wingspan of both these types was 42 feet ¼ inch, a reduction overall of 6¾ inches. In both also the fuel tanks were made removable from the centre section of the wing. Both carried the same armament of .30 Browning M2s, one a single, fixed, forward-firing weapon mounted atop the fuselage just in front of the pilot's windscreen on the starboard side, and the other a single, swivel-mounted rear-firing .30 machine-gun, with ammo box and link collector box and a stowage slot atop the aft fuselage. This latter weapon had a full, 360 degree swivelling seat for gunnery practice. Both versions featured a forward-folding rear canopy to give the rear-seat man a temporary windscreen.

Only when it came to the engines and armaments did minor differences begin, and then they were largely cosmetic for both variants used 600 hp Pratt & Whitney R-1340 power plants, the Navy version being the AN-1 (AN = Army/Navy) and the Army the 49. When later the Army in its turn also adopted the AN-1 as the AT-6B (North American NA-84), even this modest distinction vanished. (*National Archives, Washington, DC*)

In December 1941, 203 of the new advanced trainers were accepted from the Dallas plant. Thus came about the earliest nickname for the AT-6, which was appropriately enough christened the 'Texan'. Actually those aircraft built at the new Dallas plant had the suffix NT to distinguish those built at Inglewood which carried NA. (*National Archives, Washington, DC*)

The versatile T-6/SNJ was not only used for pilot training by the USAAF and the USN during the war years. They were readily adaptable for training of air gunners also. But, in addition, the same cockpit layout and reliability of the aircraft itself also lent itself to other training roles. The Royal Australian Air Force was the first to use its variant of the universal North American as a combat spotter/recce aircraft in the south-west Pacific. Post-war many other Allied nations were to adapt their T-6/ Harvard allocations for the same purpose and in Korea the AT-6 was widely used thus. But during World War II the US forces only used the rear-seat camera facilities for training of operators in this increasingly vital and essential role as this 1944 photo shows. (*National Archives, Washington, DC*)

The US Navy's SNJ-3s proved very versatile in service. For the B series an additional .30 Browning M2 machine-gun was mounted in the starboard wing and provision was made for underwing racks capable of carrying four 100-lb practice bombs. These machines did not carry the swivel seat as they were principally used for gun training which was naturally conducted with the gun trained on the after-firing arcs.

This splendid photo shows such a configuration at a Florida base with the trainee air gunner ready for another training sortie. (*National Archives, Washington, DC*)

Another wartime development of the standard T-6 in the United States, this affected the last series of Harvard marks for British service also. Starting in the summer of 1943 a fresh variant appeared.

There were no external differences but there was for the first time a duplication of the most important instruments in both cockpits fore and aft. This was a most welcomed addition as far as the instructor was concerned, as he now had control over the power of the landing-gear and flaps in an emergency. Another change was to the standard electrical equipment, which, hitherto for the T-6 had been of the 12-volt system but now a change-over was made to the 24-volt system. Other internal changes were the installation of a VHF four-button communications radio and an Automatic Direction-Finding (ADF) receiver. Intitially also, a larger propeller spinner was installed on the Ds but this proved so troublesome in service that it was soon withdrawn again. These alterations were reflected by the resulting change of designation to NA-88, of which the Army and Navy designations became the AT-6D/SNJ-5. In all other respects these aircraft were repeats of the standard AT-6C/SNJ-4. In fact being intermixed on the Dallas production line 440 BT-6D and 276 SNJ-5 appeared with the composite wooden fuselage structure although the majority were of all-metal stressed-skin construction. Total output of this variant was 3,958 AT-6D and 2,198 SNJ-5. Those strengthened for carrier deck landings with tailhooks again had the suffix C added.

In the RAF these became the Harvard III and 537 were delivered. These included 143 for the Royal Navy, with twenty-five others transferred later. Thus this Mark became by far the most widely used Fleet Air Arm Harvard. The allocations of the Mark III were seventy to the EATS in Southern Rhodesia between December 1943 and July 1944, 197 to South Africa during the same period, eight-one sent to the Middle East and forty-one shipped directly to New Zealand between November 1943 and November 1944.

By 1945 few Harvard Is remained in service with the RAF, the main variant in the post-war Flying Training Command being the Harvard IIB. The Harvard II was one of the mainstays of the wartime training programme in Canada, and the Mks. IIA, IIB and III saw service mainly in Southern Rhodesia.

This Harvard III is 7111 of the South African Air Force, taken in April 1987 near Cape Town, and features the then standard trainer markings of red tail and rear fuselage, engine cowling and leading edge and wing-tip with the standard yellow blocked out number. She was one of the Central Flying School's formation team at that time, hence the red strips adorning the leading edges of the wings. (*Courtesy Arthur Pearcy, Sharnbrook*)

Among the earliest of the 'Warbird' restorations of the SNJ workhorse post-war was this splendid example photographed by Jim Larsen in 1976. Its proud owner was Ben Harrison of Seattle, Washington, USA. The aircraft itself was painted in the colours of the Pensacola Training School during the period 1940-41. Not only was the colour scheme authentic but much painstaking work went into the rest of the restoration.

The entire airframe and the engine itself were also carefully overhauled and refurbished with the same devotion to detail. Many remanufactured or new parts had, perforce, to be incorporated although the bulk of the original airframe was maintained complete. The cockpit instrumentation was restored to its original positioning and brought up to factory-freshness. However, some compromise had to made to fit modern flying conditions and some new lightweight electronic gear was substituted for the old navigation equipment to fit 1970's laws.

The feature of the swivelling rear seat for rear gunnery training was one point in case for the US Navy's SNJ-3s were often used for this role. None of the original flexible mounted machine-guns could be fitted but of course the unusual rear canopy mechanism and seat functions were retained in Ben's Warbird.

Fully airworthy again N2864D was one of the pioneer efforts which showed just what could be done and set the trend towards T-6 restoration and revival after decades in which the more glamorous (and expensive) fighter types had predominated the civil scene. (*Courtesy Jim Larsen collection*)

The Hamilton Standard two-bladed propeller was fitted to the standard production T-6s no matter which powerplant the Army and Navy initially decided upon. Standardisation was not to be achieved until well after the war had got underway.

Thus the first BC-1 prototype took to the air on 11 February 1938, only a day after the first flight of the BT-14. Engined by the 550 hp Pratt & Whitney R-1340-47 Wasp radial, trials and evaluations resulted in minor alterations to the rudder, it being made larger with the bottom edge being squared-off to aid directional control. The streamlining effect of the new undercarriage, plus the new engine, combined to give the BC-1 a top speed of 209 mph.

Impressed, the Army placed an initial contract for 180 BC-1 trainers. Of these, three dozen were actually completed as instrument training aircraft and given the designation BC-1I (I for Instrument). In these aircraft hoods were fitted to the rear cockpit for blind-flying instruction. They could also be identified by the manually controlled radio loop-antenna which was carried abaft

the landing-gear on the underside of the wing.

Progress was also made on the other home-front at this time, for the US Navy also trialed and evaluated the BC-1 throughout the summer of 1938. The Navy was also switching over to monoplane aircraft, with fighters like the Grumman Wildcat, dive-bombers like the Vought Vindicator and torpedo planes like the Douglas Devastator, and with improved models of all three types on the drawing boards (Hellcat, Dauntless and Avenger). They were thus very interested in the new advance trainer concept.

It was Navy needs that saw the final stage of the metamorphosis completed, for they stipulated in their September specification to the company that the all-metal fuselage, as in the BT-14, was an essential feature. This was wedded to the retractable landing gear and armament of the BC-1 and the adoption of the 500 hp Pratt & Whitney R-1340-6 engine in place of the existing powerplant. North American quickly complied with all these wishes and the resulting aircraft, the NA-52, was delivered towards the end of the year for trials. (*Courtesy of Rockwell International Archives*)

Here a large formation of Navy SNJ-3s head out on a mass flight under lowering clouds and thunderheads in 1943. All-weather training over water and long-distance navigation were of course a must for US Navy carrier aircrew due to join carrier Task Forces for the closing actions of the Pacific War against Japan. The all-metal construction of the Dash-3 was regarded as one of its strengths early on. However, strangely, in the early months of American involvement in the shooting war there were doubts about the wisdom of this. (*National Archives, Washington, DC*)

(below)
The US Navy made extensive use of its SNJ trainers throughout World War II. With the bulk of the available manpower serving at the front and overseas, the US Navy like most combatants, relied increasingly on female recruits to keep the aircraft flying.

Here a bunch of Navy WAVES, (left to right) Inez Waits, S1/C AMM; Lucille H. Henderson, S1/C AMM and Mary Anne Gasser, S1/C AMM, Helen Adams, 3/C and Leona Curry, S1/C AMM, all Aviation Metal Smiths, are seen checking out an SNJ engine in the assembly and repair department of the Naval Air Station at Jacksonville, Florida, prior to its take-off. The ladies are posed for the camera around the 500 hp Pratt & Whitney R-1340-6 engine which drove the two-bladed controllable-pitch propeller. The first SNJ had been delivered in May 1939 and thousands rolled off the production lines in the years that followed, gradually becoming standardised with the Army's T-6. (*National Archives, Washington DC*)

(left)
When the Navy came to adapt fifty-five of the original SNJs for carrier deck landings at NAS Pensacola by the installation of a tailhook, the suffix C (for Carrier) was added to their designations and that of all subsequent 'navalised' trainers. Both versions could be further adapted as target tugs by the provision of cabling gear fitted on the underside of the fuselage abaft the rear cockpit.

The North American NA-88 (Army AT-6C, Navy SNJ-4) represented the ultimate amalgamation of ideas and varied little from their forebears save for certain internal alterations. Also the SNJ-4 incorporated the third machine-gun and the bomb racks carried by the Army variants which made them even more identical. (*National Archives, Washington, DC*)

'Texan Away!' A flight-deck scene from the late war period.

In America the US Navy's SNJ-5Cs modified for carrier landing training with navigation tables and tailhooks had continued in service working from the training carriers (TCVs) USS *Sable* (IX. 81, formerly the mercantile *Greater Buffalo*) and USS *Wolverine* (IX. 64, formerly the mercantile *Seeandbee*). These were Great Lakes paddle-tankers modified like escort carriers by the fitting of 500 foot-long wooden flight-decks. They had been converted in 1942 for this role and worked out of Chicago on Lake Michigan steadily until they were finally scrapped in 1947 and 1948. The SNJs were not based on these vessels of course but flew out to them from the Glenview Naval Air Station in Illinois for each

day's training. A proper seagoing escort carrier, the former British *Charger* (CVE. 30, formerly the mercantile *Rio de la Plata*) had operated in a similar capacity off the Pensacola navy base, on the Florida coast during the same period. The post-war replacement of these training carriers were the two former light carriers USS *Saipan* (CVL 48) and USS *Wright* (CVL. 49), completed in 1946 and 1947 respectively and they continued in service in the training role until the advent of jet trainers made them redundant in the late 1950s. They were capable of thirty-three knots as against the earlier ships' best of eighteen knots which made for more realistic deck operations for the SNJs. (*US National Archives, Washington DC*)

(below)
An undignified re-entry to the world. Carrier-based operation was a hazardous enough operation out at sea during wartime conditions, but for many rookie pilots getting their SNJ off the giant runways of the Navy flying schools sometimes proved just as awesome until one got the hang of things. This is one such SNJ that went 'into the drink' and had to be recovered by the salvage men – it was more-or-less in one piece. (*Courtesy of the late Herb Cook, INTERCOM, Fort Worth*)

(left)
A US Navy SNJ 'Winds up' in preparation for take-off from the flight deck of the USS *Long Island* (ACV 1) used for training purposes in the war. Pilot qualification period included deck take-offs and landings and this photograph was taken on 28 January 1943. (*US National Archives, Washington DC*)

A beautiful study of a restored US Marine Corps SNJ-2 (N5208V) in the original colour scheme belonging to VM-308 at Pensacola, Florida, training base, owned and flown by Frank Compton.

Early in 1940 the US Navy was once more active and had contracted for an additional sixty-one SNJ-2s (North American NA-65). These were really SNJ-1s with a few minor changes. The SNJ-2 had its maiden flight on 20 March 1940 and was powered by the 600 hp Pratt & Whitney R-1340-36 radial again with a two-bladed prop. This combination gave the aircraft a best speed of 214 mph with a ceiling of over 24,000 feet. Modifications involved the removal of the carburettor air scoop to the port side of the fuselage abaft the engine cowl, which itself had a larger ring fitting. An additional vent scoop was located below the cowl due to the repositioning of the oil cooler to the port side of the engine.

The SNJ-2s could be distinguished by their retention of the rounded rudder form and from the clumsy and awkward positioning of the large radio antenna mast which was plonked slap in the pilot's line of vision on top of the fuselage abaft the engine cowling. Close-up the Navy's standards of fitments evidenced themselves in leather headrests and the need for a chart board for the pilot for over-water navigation. The initial order for three dozen aircraft was for the Naval Reserve units and was followed by a repeat order to twenty-nine more as Congressional funding became available for Roosevelt's 'Two-Ocean Navy' following the fall of France. (*Courtesy Dr Ira Chart*)

A unique aerial photograph of a unique aircraft. The one and only T-6 with an in-line engine!

The in-line engine had been heavily promoted by Fairchilds before the war and they presented several advantages of this type over the radial. Such engines gave a low profile forward and thus the pilot had a much improved view out of his forward wind-screen, essential for high-speed fighter tactics as epitomised by the British Supermarine Spitfire and German Messerschmitt Me. 109 in the Battle of Britain, the aerial combat which became every air force's bench-mark after 1940. Such in-line engines had the natural advantages of smoother running and less vibration with their balanced crankshaft-connection rod arrangements, which equated with less wear-and-tear on both machine and pilot. Also, because the in-line engine's prop shaft would always be the physically highest point of the engine, a larger diameter propeller could be mounted for more efficiency, or, alternately, with the same-size propeller a shorter undercarriage could be utilised, and this equated with less weight and better landing visibility.

Weighing all these factors in the balance the go-ahead was given by the Army for the experiment to be conducted. The result was the XAT-6E. FEC's Haggerstown, Maryland, airfield was the test-bed site for the work and here a 575 hp Ranger air-cooled inverted 12-cylinder SGV-770-D4 in line engine, which drove a two-bladed propeller fitted with a spinner and which was supercharged for high-altitude flights, was installed in an AT-6D (No 42-84241). This engine gave 520 hp for take-off, 80 hp less than the Pratt & Whitney R-1340. The two-feet longer nose required by the Ranger meant the complete rebuilding of the airframe forward of the fire-wall and strict rebalancing to compensate. Overall length was thirty-one feet.

Work was complete at Haggerstown during 1944 and the XAT-6E was then transported to Elgin Army Air Force Base in Florida and air tested against a conventional 600-hp radial-engined AT-6D.

Comparison of test figures showed the following results. At sea-level the XAT-6E had a bare 3 mph speed advantage over the AT-6D, 196 mph against 193 mph. The higher the altitude the greater this advantage became, being 19 mph at 10,000 feet (220 mph against 201 mph) and 59 mph at 20,000 feet where the in-line continued to increased to 231 mph while the radial fell off dramatically to 172 mph. At 22,000 feet no figures were given for the conventional Texan but the supercharged XAT-6E was clocking 236 mph. Final testing pushed the service ceiling up to 30,000 feet and registered a top speed of 244 mph.

The Ranger-engined XAT-6E was therefore proven to be both the fastest and the highest-flying of all the Texans, but only the one prototype was ever built and no production orders followed. (*National Archives, Washington, DC*)

The USS *Wolverine* (IX. 64, formerly the mercantile *Seeandbee*) was a sister ship of the *Sable*. They were both Great Lakes paddle-tankers modified like escort carriers by the fitting of 500 foot-long wooden flight-decks. They had been converted in 1942 for this role and worked out of Chicago on Lake Michigan steadily until they were finally scrapped in 1947 and 1948. The SNJs were not based on this vessel of course but flew out of them from the Glenview Naval Air Station in Illinois for each day's training.

Taken off Chicago, Illinois in December 1942, this photo shows crewmen working on a deckload of SNJs whose engines have been warmly muffled to keep out the bitter cold of the Great Lakes in winter. (*US National Archives, Washington, DC*)

(below)
The control panel in the after (instructor's) cockpit of SN-2J G-6. The original caption for this photograph read as follows:- 'From this control panel in the rear cockpit, instructors can temporarily 'upset' instruments in the cadet's front cockpit to simulate emergencies during flight training in the new XSN2J-1 trainer developed by North American Aviation, Inc., for the US Navy. The Navy has ordered the plane for evaluation in connection with its modernized pilot training programme.' (*Courtesy of Rockwell International Archives*)

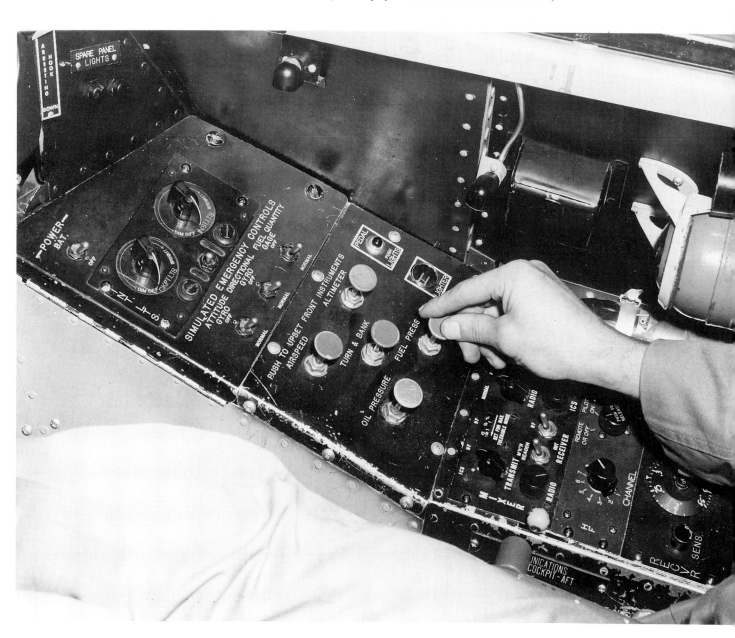

(left)
The USS *Wolverine* (IX. 64, formerly the mercantile *Seeandbee*) was a sister ship of the *Sable*. Here the decks have been swept of snow as the carrier operates just north of the city of Chicago, Illinois, in December 1942. As an SNJ (6972) runs up its engine, deck crew stand-by with fire extinguishers, 'just in case'. (*US National Archives, Washington, DC*)

Many famous pilots have cut their teeth on the Harvard or the T-6 down the years. This photograph shows one of the most famous of them all. His Royal Highness, The Duke of Edinburgh is pictured here 'Going Solo' for the first time on his advanced pilots' course in a Harvard. The photo was taken by Charles E. Brown in another Harvard piloted by Flight Lieutenant C.R. Gordon, the Duke's flying instructor, over Windsor Castle. Air traffic conditions from Heathrow were not then what they have become today obviously! (*Charles E. Brown photo courtesy of R.C. Sturtivant Archives*)

3 The Versatile Harvard

Before moving on to cover the final wartime developments of the American versions of the Texan and the several variants adapted for other roles than training, we must retrace our steps a while to examine the equally large British and Commonwealth involvement with the type.

Resident British representatives arrived at the Inglewood plant during July, and the first Harvard produced was test flown from the adjoining airfield on 28 September 1938. After the completion of test flight and the formal acceptance by the British of this machine in the middle of October, the aircraft was shipped from Los Angeles aboard the SS *Lochatrine* of the Furness Line, sailing on 24 October by way of the Panama Canal to Liverpool. A company pilot from North American had been sent to England to conduct the initial flights and he was joined by a staff of mechanics whose duty it was to assist the British in uncrating, assembling and testing the Harvards as they arrived from overseas.

The enthusiasm for the Harvard by some British instructors was rather muted as it was a complex aircraft to understand after the simple trainers hitherto in use, like the gentle de Havilland Tiger Moth and such. It also had vicious spin tendencies which could fatally catch out novice pilot and veteran teacher alike. Nonetheless it was instantly recognised as a distinct advance on what had gone before. One anonymous RAF Chief Flying Instructor was quoted in the New York *Sun* newspaper as being wildly over the top about his new charge.

> 'What I think so good is their marvellous cockpit layout. It's like a car. In some aeroplanes the controls seem to be put anywhere there is space. The result is knobs, buttons and levers everywhere; under the seat, behind your back, over your head, under your arms. The Harvard trainer gives the impression that the designer sat down and made a plan of his controls before he began to build his machine. It was decided that one place was just right for every instrument and gadget and there it went. We call it the Yankee layout.'

The desperate war situation and the loss of western Europe finally awoke most Americans to their own isolation in an ever-hostile world. This enabled President Roosevelt to push through the historic Lend-Lease deal under the terms of which US Military funding purchased huge numbers of both American and foreign-built aircraft. Under these contracts the US Army or Navy then Lend-Leased these self-same aircraft, under American designations and serial numbers but with foreign markings and serial numbers actually factory painted on them, to 'deserving' nations. Officially the aircraft would then be returned by the countries in question to the United States at the end of hostilities. The majority of the British and Commonwealth Harvards were, although many others had been crashed, wrecked, scrapped and also transferred to other countries in the interim, even some going back to the USAAF. Keeping track of all these 'paper exchanges' is a nightmare best left to the super-fanatical enthusiast – suffice it that this very generous ploy worked well for Britain when she needed it most. Under the terms of the new Lend-Lease Bill the RAF contracted for 747 AT-6Cs as Harvard IIAs. Another 1,500 Harvard IIs built in Canada were funded by the US Army. British contracts had reached 1,100 before Lend-

Lease and total deliveries to British Commonwealth Air Forces exceeded 5,000. This included 400 Mk. I, 1,173 Mk. II, 726 Mk. IIA, 2,485 Mk. IIB and 351 Mk. III.

Meantime, on 3 December 1938 the first aircraft of the initial order had arrived from Liverpool docks for trials and tests at the Aeroplane and Armament Experimental Establishment at Martlesham Heath. From these tests the British Pilots Notes were prepared. Number 7000 was the first of the many Harvards that were to serve in British and Commonwealth air forces. The Harvard Is were serialled N 7000-N 7199 and P 5783-5982. Later versions ranged between AH 185 and KG 309, delivered in 1944.

The Harvard was to remain standard equipment for the RAF's Flying Training Schools for more than sixteen years. Unfortunately N 7000 was almost immediately written-off when, on 16 February 1939, a spin caused it to crash at Eyke, close to Woodbridge in Suffolk, killing both crew members. Its replacement N 7001 had already arrived at Martlesham the month before and N 7002 arrived at the Central Flying School the same month for instructors to gauge the new aircraft. The Flying Training Schools also began to receive their due allocations soon after, the first being twelve to FTS at Spitalgate, Grantham in January.

Outwardly, if not internally, the British modifications were modest. Following the precedent set by Yale the new trainer took the name Harvard quite naturally. The radio equipment was the main alteration in service, along with some instrumentation and the seats were altered so that seat-pack parachutes could be carried. This meant the radio mast in front of the cockpit was deleted while a large heating muffler was fitted to the exhaust on the starboard side to heat the cockpit in Britain's bleak skies.

Pre-war shipments had progressed steadily from Inglewood.

> 'Export records were shattered from time to time on the British and French contracts. For example, on 31 March 1939, twenty crated Harvard airplanes were shipped from Los Angeles harbor aboard a single vessel bound for Liverpool. This shipment then constituted the largest quantity of airplanes of a single type ever to leave the United States on one vessel. The last airplane of the initial RAF contract for 200 airplanes was shipped from Los Angeles harbor on 20 May 1939, less than eleven months after the company had received the contract from the British Air Ministry. Meanwhile the plant was busy producing 200 additional Harvard airplanes, which had been added to the contract.'

It is relative to include here a look at the French Government order for what was basically the same aircraft, because ultimately many of them were later to enter service with the RAF and not the French Air Force. The initial contract from the French government for the manufacture of 230 NA-57 basic trainer type aeroplanes (similar to the BT-14) was approved on 14 February 1939. The contract also provided for twenty-seven equivalent airframes as spare parts at a total cost in excess of seven million US dollars. The first production article was accepted at the factory by representatives of the French government in April. Just as the British orders, the airframes were crated at the Inglewood factory, trucked to Los Angeles harbour and shipped to France on vessels of a French steamship company.

> 'The first NA-57 trainer was flown at Châteaudun, France, on 29 June 1939, by a company test pilot despatched from England for that purpose. Soon thereafter a staff of factory mechanics was established at Châteaudun to assist the Armée de l'Air in uncrating and assembling the aircraft. Export shipping records established in the shipment of Harvards to Great Britain were shattered on 31 July 1939, when a total of forty crated NA-57 trainers were shipped out of New Orleans, which had been substituted as the port of embarkation in order to rush deliveries, destined for Le Havre aboard the French Line SS Louisiane.

The typical two-seat Harvard with the all-metal stressed-skin construction had a wingspan of 42ft ¼ inches, a length of 28 feet 11⅞ inches, and a height of 11 feet 8½ inches and a total wing area of 253 square feet. Weight empty was 4,158 lb, loaded 5,250 lb, maximum speed was 205 mph at 5,000 feet, cruising speed 170 mph. Initial climb was 1,350 feet per minute and it had a range of 750 miles, an endurance of 3.9 hours and a service ceiling of 21,500 feet.

The equivalent to the American AT-6A, the Harvard IIB was licence-built in Canada by Noorduyn Aviation Company of Cartierville, near Montreal, Quebec, who produced 2,798 of them. At its peak Canadian production rate reached 113 per month. 1,500 of these were subsequently turned over to the US Army Air Corps which, because of their different instruments, were designated as the AT-16. The Canadian-built Mark IIBs formed the greater bulk of all British-flown Harvards and these began to arrive at EATS, BCATP and Canadian SFTS units from May 1942 onward. In all, 639 Mark IIBs were delivered up to the end of 1943. Seventy-two of the Canadian allocated Mark IIBs were subsequently shipped to the UK in March 1944 where they joined hordes of the same type which had been shipped over from April 1943 onward via Speke, near Liverpool for initial assembly and ultimately to the various Maintenance Units (MUs) across the country where they were stored pending allocation to squadrons. In fact there was an over-supply by this period of the war and some never saw anything other than storage and scrapping. Others were re-allocated to the USAAF and other Allied nations during and after the war's end.

Foreign deliveries of the Mark IIB included 507 to the RAF in India from February 1943 onward, (seventeen more were lost at sea) and forty-two modified for target towing sent to the Middle East in January 1945. In the British Fleet Air Arm the Harvard III was the variant that featured most strongly, along with a few Mk. IIBs.

Here a North American Harvard IIB (FE992 – G-BDAM) is seen revving up on the ground at RNAS Yeovilton on 19 December 1985. (*Fleet Air Arm Museum, Yeovilton*)

The British aspect of the North American trainer programme involved those aircraft built for the Royal Air Force (and other air forces of the Empire) which were constructed in the American plants, and also numerous others which were licence-built both in Canada and Australia.

In April 1938, the newly-formed British Purchasing Commission arrived in Washington DC empowered to spend 25 million dollars with which to purchase vitally needed American aircraft types to equip the expanding Royal Air Force. The first aircraft they selected for purchase was the North American NA-49 and, on 22 June 1938, they placed an order on behalf of the British Air Ministry for 200 Harvard I type aeroplanes (plus twenty-five equivalent airframes in spare parts) under Contract Number 791588/38 from the Inglewood plant. The total cost of this order was six-and-a-half million US dollars. The Harvard I (commencing with serial number N 7000) was the British version of the US Army Air Corps' BC-1 of 1937, and the initial contract for two hundred was completed in June 1939. The RAF acquired 200 as Harvard Is and the RCAF received thirty. These became the Harvard Mk.I and were to be fitted with some British instrumentation on their arrival in the United Kingdom.

With home orders at that time thin on the ground, the North American concern went out of its way to please this important new client. As it later recorded, 'When the first order for 200 of North American's BC-1 type combat training airplanes was placed by the British Purchasing Commission in the summer of 1938, the company's engineering department shattered all design records in revising the basic airplane to meet British requirements and accommodate British equipment. Although 990 of the original 2,200 design drawings required changes for this rush export project, the engineers performed their work so rapidly that the first completed airplane was test-flown in England only 120 days after design work had started, and so well that the British almost immediately ordered additional quantities of the sturdy Harvard trainer, as it was called'.

This early photo was taken in the summer of 1940 and shows instructor and trainee boarding their mount at a Canadian airfield under the Empire Air Training Scheme while one of the ground crew makes some last minute adjustments for the benefit of the cameraman! (*Courtesy of the Canadian Forces Photographic Unit, Ottawa*)

In the late 1940s eight RCAF Harvards were sold to Turkey, seventeen to France, one to Italy and one to the RCN. Similarly of the 494 Mark IIBs Sweden bought 142, the Royal Netherlands Air Force forty-nine, the Royal Danish Air Force four, the Royal Norwegian Air Force seven, the Swiss Air Force two and the Israeli Defence Force one.

That still left many hundreds in service with the RCAF itself and they continued to serve for many years as trainers until replaced by the new jet generation. Other uses were found for them by the services of course.

Between 1962 and 1964 the most famous unit was the RCAF's 'Goldilocks' aerobatic team which put on impressive displays all across Canada. The Harvard remained on the RCAF's inventory until 1965. On 19 May of that year, at No. 4 FTS, Penhold, Alberta, Flight Lieutenant J.A. Cratchley and his student, Officer Cadet J.W. Lussier, flew Harvard 20384 into history on the last training mission on this aircraft type with the RCAF.

Here the distinctive gold Harvard IV, with its red flash and bird-of-prey fuselage scheme, stands out boldly in this unique aerial view. (*Courtesy Jim Larsen, Kirklands, Washington*)

The first fateful steps! A young Canadian pilot walks out with his instructor to take his first flight at an RCAF training base in 1964. The versatility of the T-6/Harvard concept enabled this reliable machine to carry on in its basic training mode long after the advent of jet trainers for advanced duties and ensured that it was one of the most long-serving military aircraft of any era. (*Courtesy CFPU, Ottawa, Canada*)

Early wartime colour photography is extremely rare but Harold Bennett took this photograph of a wartime training flight over Canada which is notable for its clarity considering the age of the negative. The Harvard Mark II in the foreground, AJ-930, (Construction number 76.3900) was originally built as part of the French Government's order for 450 machines but was taken-over by the RAF on completion in 1940. She spent some time with 39, 34 and 13 Service Flying Training Schools in Canada before being transferred to the Royal Canadian Air Force. (*Courtesy R.C. Sturtivant*)

The faithful old Harvards were finally phased out of the Flying Training Schools with the introduction of Vampire T.II jet trainers in 1954/55.

It was not until 23 March 1955, however, that the very last RAF pilots were to gain their 'wings' by qualifying on the North American Harvard trainer. This event took place at No. 3 FTS Feltwell. This was not, however, the end of Harvard quasi-military service in Britain, as for long after this they continued to fly in Home Command's University Air Squadrons. A few lingered on as communications aircraft, while others saw combat operations against the Mau Mau uprising in Kenya and the communist insurgents in the Malayan jungle.

Among the Harvards to fly on in the United Kingdom was this veteran AT-6C Mark IIA, the former 88-10108, 41-33365, EX392, here carrying its old South African Air Force marking of 7185 in the yellow panel, as well as the civilian registration of G-BGOU. This aircraft was registered to A.P. Snell in January 1983 when she received these markings after formerly belonging to Europworld International at Biggin Hill. She is seen here taxying up the runway at West Malling airfield on 26 August 1985 on one of her last flights. On 7 September of the same year this machine crashed at Bourn killing her owner-pilot. (*RAF Museum, Hendon, London*)

Shown here in a somewhat world-weary condition is an ex-Royal Canadian Air Force Harvard IV, CF-URH (20367). She was rescued from oblivion and is pictured here at Long Beach, California, in July 1968, prior to her re-building.

The Canadian Harvard Aircraft Association is another outstanding organisation with a large, and very knowledgeable, membership. In 1989 they had five machines, a mix of North American, Noorduyn and Canadian Car and Foundry-built types. There is also the Canadian Warplanes Heritage Group, Ontario, which currently have four flyable Harvards in their team and they also boast the only T-6G in Canada. The CHAA have a very wise and enthusiastic chronicler in Doug MacPhail of Dundas.

Just across the US border, a trio of ex-Spanish T-6s work together over the Lake Michigan area, piloted by Dick Hansen, Russ Cook and Ron Kuhny. (*Courtesy Nick Williams Collection*)

A refined version of the NA-55 (BC-1A) was ordered by Great Britain as the war got under way in earnest. On 17 November 1939 some six hundred were ordered and designated Harvard IIs. A further British order followed specifically for the Royal Canadian Air Force, then a separate order for the RCAF, while undelivered orders to France were also taken-over under the same designation. This gave a grand total of 1,275 Harvard IIs. They carried a wing-mounted gun, and the engine exhaust was muffled to aid in cockpit heating in northern climes.

Shown here is one of the Harvard IIs given a NA-75 charge number on 3 June 1940. This was one of the direct-purchase order from the British Government for the Royal Canadian Air Force for 100 machines (Serials 75-3048 to 3057 and 75-3418 to 3507). (*Courtesy of Rockwell International Archives*)

Line-up of Harvards at a snow-bound Canadian flying school in the Toronto area in the winter of 1941. While the majority have adopted the standard RAF Yellow overall paint scheme, at least one (2557) has the early two-tone scheme.

The large orders received from both Britain and France in 1938/39 enabled the company to proceed with its expansion plans with a great degree of confidence. By the outbreak of war in Europe, North American had almost completed the first two British contracts, totalling 400 trainers, and were well on the way with the French order for 230 of the same type.

This initial order was soon increased. On 11 November 1939 an order was placed for 600 Harvard IIs (BC-1A/NA-55). A second direct-purchase British order followed for the Royal Canadian Air Force, a total of 100 Harvard IIs (NA-75s) being procured. As with the Yale, on the fall of France, Britain was able to step in and secure some 450 NA-76s ordered by that nation. British equipment replaced the French but the radio mast remained *in situ* in these machines after delivery. They were rated as Harvard IIs.

Yet a further batch of Harvard IIs (NA-81s) was ordered on 11 July 1940, this being a combined RAF/RCAF order for 125 aircraft. However, not all saw service with these air forces for some of these were appropriated by the USAAC before delivery with only insignificant alterations to them. (*Courtesy of Canadian Forces Photographic Unit, Ontario*)

What was to prove the last aeroplane under the second French contract for 230 basic trainers was not completed until August 1940. 'Since German troops had entered Paris on 14 June and France had sued for peace on 17 June, the undelivered portion of this contract was taken-over by the British government, and the aeroplanes were delivered to Canada.'

For the RAF personnel from the very first flight with No. 3 SFTS, at Grantham, what one Canadian history described as 'the Harvard's characteristic rasping note' was to become a familiar sound over airfields across the whole world and more than fifty years on it is just as distinctive. This highly individual grating was caused by the direct-drive prop with its high tip speeds and earned the T-6 yet another of its many epithets, that of the 'Noisy North American'. However much it jarred on the ears it is a sound that is still well remembered by a hundred thousand novice pilots and worried instructors, from Brazil to Minsk, from Medicine Hat to Queensland and from Montrose to Alipore. It is never forgotten by all who flew it.

Here a flight of three Harvards (2928, 2631 and 2917) are seen over Canada in 1941. Note the variations in their identity markings. (*Courtesy of Canadian Forces Photographic Unit, Ontario*)

North American Harvard IIs of 20 Service Flying Training School lined up at Cranbourne, near Salisbury (Harare) Southern Rhodesia (Zimbabwe) during the war. The unit was equipped with Mark IIs from the autumn of 1941 until the end of the war, about 114 reaching them and fellow schools in that country during this period, of which forty were lost through crashes during the Empire Air Training Scheme programmes.

At the end of the war a further thirty-one Mark IIs were scrapped in situ in November 1945. Of the thirty odd survivors a dozen were sold to the Southern Rhodesian Air Force in February 1949 and carried on with their duties in the training role for many years before being sold on again. (*RAF Museum, Hendon, London*)

Crash! Where novice pilots were concerned not all flights in the Harvard had happy endings. Some errors were paid for dearly.

The wrecked remains of a Harvard II (AJ715 E) of 20 Service Flying Training School after an horrific crash at a farm near Salisbury, Southern Rhodesia, (now Zimbabwe) on 4 April 1942. Normally based at Cranbourne, this particular flight was made from the Pendennis Relief Landing Ground. (*RAF Museum, Hendon, London*)

Ready for the off!

A posed for the camera view of two RAF flying personnel seated aboard a North American Harvard II (DC) of 11 Service Flying Training School, Royal Canadian Air Force, taken at Yorkton airfield, in December 1941.

By March 1941, Inglewood had passed the 1,000 quantity mark on the Harvard for the British and Empire Air Forces, which at that time, was an all-time record for a single model of airplane. Although identified as a single model, these were not 1,000 identical planes, however. Actually there were 2,500 drawing changes made after the first Harvard was produced, and among the 1,000 combat trainers there were actually more than twenty-five different models, each varying from the others in some major or minor detail of construction.

Between July 1941 and May 1942, 305 Harvard IIs were directly flown across the US/Canada border to equip training units of both the EATS and the BCATP, as well as SFTS squadrons where they joined RCAF Harvards. At the same time shipments to Southern Rhodesia via South African ports continued from August 1941 onward, some 103 Mk IIs being thus despatched, while forty-seven others ultimately ended up in the Middle East. Four Mk IIs reached India but were soon expended in accidents and, finally, direct shipment of thirty-eight Mk.IIs equipped the training squadrons of the Royal New Zealand Air Force.

Three Harvards of the Royal Canadian Air Force over a snowy backdrop in 1941.

When the fighter operational training units were redesignated as OTUs in March 1940 their establishment strength already included numerous Harvard Is. Finally, with the setting-up in the same month of the British Commonwealth Air Training Plan (BCATP) in Canada and the Empire Air Training Scheme (EATS) in Southern Rhodesia (now known as Zimbabwe), direct shipping to 20 and 20 Service Flying Training Schools (SFTS) from the States was undertaken. This was accelerated when the whole of the British training effort was shifted there in July of the same year, some 216 British-based Harvards being packed for transhipment at Cardiff and Odiham for the southern African destination, with a further eight going to the Middle East. Very few Harvards remained flying over the UK although units like 15 SFTS at Lossiemouth continued to feature Harvard Is until April of the following year. The Harvard, in all its guises, was the second most numerous aircraft type to be used in the BCATP.

Meanwhile Harvard IIs were arriving in both Canada, where twenty equipped the BCATP units and eight more in the UK, being followed by a further six (with another six going down with their ship after a U-boat attack in the North Atlantic *en route*). Two of these were subsequently allocated to the USAAF and the rest joined the Mk.Is.

No obvious place to put down! Both pilot and instructor had more than the scenery on their minds during this mid-50s training flight.

Set against the magnificent backdrop of the Rocky Mountains this duo of Royal Canadian Air Force Harvards (20248 and 20293) come from the Canadian Car and Foundry-built batch of 555 Mark IVs which were built from 1951 onward and were the Canadian-built version of the T-6G. They could be readily identified by the small type ADF mounting carried astern of the cockpit. They also had an exhaust shroud on the right-hand side not visible in this photo. (*Courtesy of the Canadian Government, Ottawa*)

In Canada the Harvard equalled the longevity of the American T-6. The first three had been received in Vancouver in July 1939 and had been accepted at Camp Borden in August. They were used as advanced trainers at Nos 1, 2, 6, 8, 9 and 13 RCAF Service Flying Training Schools at Camp Borden, Ottawa, Dunnville, Moncton, Summerside and St. Hubert. In addition they were used by Nos 31, 32 and 39 RAF SFTSs at Kingston, Moose Jaw and Swift Current. They were still working as standard equipment in the summer of 1963 with No.2 Flying Training School at Moose Jaw and No. 3 FTS at Penhold. A total of 2,063 Harvards were eventually used by the RCAF. Trainee pilots were initially given instruction at schools like St. Kitts, Ontario, receiving sixty-five hours of basic training on the Fleet Finch and the de Havilland Tiger Moth, before moving on to the Harvard. In Canada, Harvards were also used by Nos 14, 111, 115, 123, 126, 127, 129, 130, 132, 133, 135, 163, 166 and 167 RCAF Squadrons for training and communications work. In all some 11,000 Canadian and 8,000 Allied pilots were trained in Canada on Harvards under CATS.

All the 224 Mark II former RAF Harvards that remained behind when the CATS had been pulled out of Canada in 1944 became RCAF property. When Canada became part of NATO in August 1949, a further 6,000 pilots learned to fly in Canadian Harvards. Allocations were also made to NATO allies. The Canadians also adopted the T-6G conversions and this machine of the Royal Canadian Navy in its distinctive markings was one of the last of the type to see active service there. (*Canadian Forces Photographic Unit, Ottawa*)

Zimbabwe (Southern Rhodesia before Independence) had twelve Harvard Mark IIs as its initial aerial strength on the formation of its air force in February 1949. They purchased nine more from South Africa in April of the same year and a further eleven from the UK in August 1951. These were later exchanged for Mark IIAs.

In RAF service a pair of Harvard Is flew in Southern Rhodesia until November 1945, while the very last two saw service in the Middle East in January 1947. Three Harvard Mark IIs survived in the Rhodesian Air Training Group until December 1949, before being 'Struck Off Charge'. With the Mark IIA, a solitary survivor served at Deversoir until November 1950, others lingered on until sold abroad as above. The last Harvards to be used of the Mark III type were those flying with the Royal Navy Reserve Squadrons, which used them until 1956. The final Harvard IIBs survived in University Squadrons and at Hong Kong until 1957, while the last one serving with an FTS was working from Feltwell prior to April 1955. Two of this Mark (FT 375 and KF 183) still survive and serve the RAF at Boscombe Down in flyable condition.

One of these aircraft (7185 G-BGOU) is shown here with its original markings, taxying at West Malling airfield on 26 August 1985. (*RAF Museum, Hendon*)

This Harvard was one of the latest flying originals and was unique. It is the Royal New Zealand Air Force Harvard (NZ934) which was presented to the Royal Australian Air Force Museum.

This former RNZAF Harvard had been grounded since 1962 and was stored at Shepparton Museum of Aviation. It was restored in 1988 and flew again in March of that year in Australia. Give the name *City of Canberra* the restoration work cost some 80,000 Australian dollars. Unfortunately this aircraft was involved in a bad crash at Canberra airport on 9 July 1989, blocking the intersection of two of the main runways there. Apparently the landing gear collapsed during a circuit flight touch-down and the Harvard finished up on its belly. The pilot and passenger were both unharmed but extensive damage was done to the wings, undercarriage and propeller of the Harvard itself.

At the time of writing it is hoped that the machine can be salvaged but whether it will ever again be airworthy is questionable.

RAAF Point Cook Air Museum also received an ex-RNZAF Harvard as a static display item. (*Courtesy of RAAF Museum, Canberra ACT*)

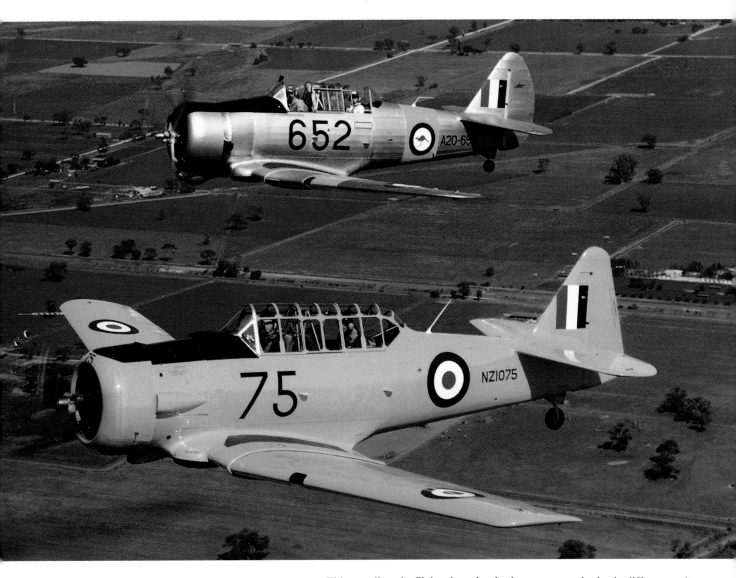

This excellent in-flight view clearly demonstrates the basic differences in appearance of the North American Harvard and the Commonwealth Wirraway.

The occasion was the Antique Aeroplane Association of Australia's annual 'Fly-In', which was held at Easter 1989.

The Harvard in the foreground (NZ1075) is owned by John Barnes of Melbourne and was flown on this occasion by Steve Chapman. The Wirraway in the background (A20-652) is owned and was flown by Stephen D. Eath, of Albury, New South Wales. (*Copyright, 1989, N.M. Parnell*)

Flyable Wirraways are something of a rarity nowadays. This is A20-653 (BF-F) in the original wartime operational colours of the SE Asia combat zone of World War II coming in to land at the 'Fly-In' held at Air World, Wingratta, Victoria. The date was 29 March 1986 and the pilot on that occasion was Alan Searle. (*Courtesy N.M. Parnell*)

4 The Wirraway Story

The Wirraway CA1 General Purpose aircraft, was named from the Aboriginal word for Challenge, which was appropriate enough for it was the first aircraft to be built by the newly formed Commonwealth Aircraft Corporation Proprietary Limited of Port Melbourne, Victoria.

The origins of both the company and the concept can be traced back to an evaluation of the future role of the Royal Australian Air Force (RAAF) made by Marshal of the Royal Air Force Sir John Salmond as early as 1928, the Salmond Report. Lack of funding, public apathy and no obvious threat delayed any implementation of even the preliminary scheme for five squadrons for almost a decade. But with the Japanese invasion of China, Hitler's rise to power in Germany, Mussolini's bully-boy tactics in Ethiopia and other grave events, by the mid-1930s a different mood was beginning to appear in Australia as in the other democracies. Influencial Australian businessmen like Essington Lewis returned from Europe deeply concerned at Australia's vulnerability in this field.

It was a statement issued by the then Prime Minister of Australia, Archdale Parker, on 18 June 1936, when it was first becoming clear that the threat of war in Europe might leave Australia unable to rely on the traditional British guarantee for protection against Japanese expansion, that proved the final catalyst. Parker expressed the view, now common among his countrymen, that there existed a need for the Commonwealth to manufacture its own aircraft and aero-engines and be self-reliant in both respects. 'The development of such manufacture by Australian interests within the Commonwealth is regarded by the Government not only as essential to the defence of the Commonwealth, but in addition, a decided benefit to Australian industry.'

It was as a direct result of this statement that a mission was sent to Britain, Europe and the United States to examine and evaluate foreign designs that would be suitable for the initial production runs of the proposed new industry. The three men of this mission were Wing Commander Wackett and Squadron Leaders Harrison and Murphy, RAAF, and their brief was to select a relatively simple, modern and reliable aircraft with General Purpose (GP) abilities. The aircraft were to have all the most up-to-date features, variable-pitch propellers, low-wing form, stressed-skin, all-metal fuselage, and were to become the first forty such Australian-built aircraft. It was not high performance that they were seeking so much as a good, modern and easy-to-build type on which to establish the new industry.

Hitherto it had been a matter of routine, indeed patriotic faith, that British types were automatically selected and used by the RAAF. It is a measure of the Australians' growing independent spirit and hard-headed business sense that no such inhibitions influenced the mission on this occasion, for their final recommendations were for the adoption under licence of the North American NA-26 trainer. There were protests from some of the traditionalists in the Government at the acceptance of an American rather than British aircraft but these were very sensibly overruled.

Commonwealth Aircraft Company records provide a detailed description of how the Wirraway was constructed.

The mainplanes were of aluminium alloy construction employing a single spar with channel section spar caps and sheet metal webs. Both upper and lower spar caps were divided into sections, being spliced at each joint with a short length of similar section. The spar web was made of four sheets of aluminium alloy of varying thicknesses, which were joggled and lap jointed. Reinforcements and rib attach angles were riveted to the faces of the spar. Flanged type ribs extended from the spar to the trailing edge and forward of the spar to the leading edge. The former ribs were known as trailing edge ribs. The entire assembly was covered with aluminium alloy sheet reinforced with stringers.

Flanged intercostals supported ailerons and flaps along the trailing edge. The ribs were attached to spar and intercostals by means of formed angles. Access doors were provided on the lower surface to facilitate servicing. These could be used, if convenient, for access to the interior, for repairs. All ribs were pressed aluminium alloy sheet, with channel type flanges and pressed lightening holes. The trailing edge consisted of a formed section of aluminium alloy riveted to the upper skin covering and extended inboard from the aileron cut-out in each wing. Wing-tips of aluminium alloy consisted of two ribs, two intercostals, and top and bottom covering. Bolt angles, made from aluminium alloy extruded section, formed the medium by which the outer wing panels were bolted to the centre section.

The centre section of aluminium alloy construction throughout, incorporated riveted channel section spars and pressed channel-type ribs. Reinforcement and rib attach angles were riveted vertically across the faces of the spars. Machined aluminium alloy blocks were bolted inside the top spar caps to form the attach for the centre section to the fuselage. The covering was aluminium alloy sheet varying in thickness at different stations; the upper skin between the spars being reinforced by a corrugated section. The centre ribs were cut to give accommodation for the fuel tanks. Trailing edge ribs extended from the rear face of the rear spar.

The wheel housing assembly was riveted to the front face of the front spar. The lower surface of the centre section between the spars was made up of a removeable portion, known as the fuel tank cover, which was attached to each spar by means of anchor nuts located along the inside of the lower spar caps. When this cover was bolted into position it formed an integral part of the centre section construction. The major sub-assemblies of the complete wing assembly could be removed from the fuselage as one unit, or removed individually. Removal of the complete wing assembly or centre section could be accomplished with landing gear installed on centre section and locked in the extended position.

The landing flaps were of aluminium alloy construction throughout incorporating a 'hat' section spar and pressed channel ribs. A 'Z' section formed the leading edge, the trailing edge was a standard formed section. Flaps were secured to the wings by a continuous-type hinge. Actuating rods were attached to the flap spar by eyebolts which rotated in phosphor-bronze bearings. Dive bombing flaps, interconnected with the landing flaps and operated by the same hydraulic jack, were fitted to Mk. III aircraft, (Nos. A20-623 onward). These flaps opened upwards as the flaps moved downwards.

The ailerons' construction was similar to that of the flaps and incorporated a pressed channel type spar, flanged nose and trailing ribs and channel section trailing edge suitably reinforced by gussets. Cat aluminium alloy hinge brackets were provided. Covering forward of the spar was sheet metal, whilst fabric formed the covering for the trailing edge and also extended over the nose skin. Ailerons were fitted with three hinges. Each aileron incorporated a booster tab.

The fuselage frame consisted of the engine mount, the forward and aft sections of welded chrome-molybdenum steel tubing and steel fitting construction and the bottom section, aft of station number six, which was of aluminium alloy semi-monocoque construction. An auxiliary tail skid and jack pad were riveted to the aft end of this monocoque. An overturn structure was incorporated in the forward section of the fuselage frame, behind the front cockpit, for protection of the crew in event of a nose-over. The fire-wall was a single sheet of aluminium alloy, provided with reinforcing angles about its circumference.

Fuselage side panels were fabric-covered aluminium alloy frames readily detachable, being secured to the fuselage by screws. The two tandem cockpits were under one enclosure incorporating individual manually-operated sliding sections at each cockpit, for entry and exit. Both sections could be locked closed or in several intermediate positions. Seats were mounted on steel tubes and were adjustable to selective vertical positions. The rear seat was reversible, being pivoted on a bearing incorporated in the fuselage frame. Provisions were made for an instrument flying hood in the front cockpit of the Mk. I and II aircraft.

The landing gear was of a single leg, half-fork, fully cantilever design. Each unit consisted of a cylinder and piston, by means of which shock absorption through air and oil was provided. The piston and cylinder were interconnected by forged chrome-moly steel torsion links. A heat-treated steel fork was bolted to the lower end of the piston and carried the axle. This fork was heat treated to 160,000-180,000 psi. The gear was fully retractable inboard and forward of the wing centre section front spar. Hydraulic power was supplied normally by an engine-driven hydraulic pump and in the event of failure of that pump or its connections, by means of a hand operated pump. The landing gear was operated by double-acting rams, with mechanically operated spring-load latches and lockpins at the retracted and extended positions respectively. The gear could be lowered from either cockpit but as a safety catch was incorporated in the front cockpit quadrant, it could not be raised by rear cockpit controls.

Mechanical indicators and an electric warning horn were located in the front cockpit. Hydraulic wheel brakes were fitted. The tail-wheel assembly consisted of an aluminium (later magnesium) alloy wheel support casting attached to two fittings bolted to the rear end of the monocoque, a swivel post assembly and fork, mounted on roller bearings in the support casting and a pneudraulic shock strut. An eleven inch diameter wheel and tyre was mounted on the axle which was an integral part of the fork. The wheel was steerable and controlled by the rudder pedals and cables incorporated in the rudder control system. A tail-wheel locking device was also fitted. The tyre pressure was 60 psi. The hydraulically operated landing flaps were controlled in a manner similar to the retracting landing gear. A calibrated indicator, adjacent to the landing gear position indicator in the front cockpit, showed the position of the flaps from the UP position (0 degrees) to the DOWN position (60 degrees). The hand pump was used for emergency operation of the landing gear and flaps.

Of the Wirraway's tail unit, the rudder frame was of aluminium-alloy construction consisting essentially of a torque tube, pressed flanged ribs, channel trailing edge and metal covered leading edge were fabric covered. The elevators consisted of two interchangeable sections. The construction of the elevators followed the pattern of the rudder, including the fabric covering. The tailplane also comprised two interchangeable sections each of aluminium alloy construction and consisting of a front and rear spar, pressed flanged ribs, stiffening intercostals and metal covering. The fin was of aluminium alloy construction throughout, the assembly consisting of a front and rear spar, pressed flanged ribs, stiffening intercostals and metal covering. Trim tabs were fitted to the rudder and elevators.

With regard to the electrical system on the Wirraway, an engine-driven generator of voltage controlled type and control panel were fitted. A 12-volt battery was mounted on a shelf at the right hand side of the fire-wall, below the oil tank. All wiring, with the exception of H.T. wires, was of glazed cotton-braided type with metal terminal lugs pressed and soldered into place. Each wire was numbered or coded with a colour designation like the wiring diagram. Two 240-Watt landing lights were fitted to the aircraft and built in the leading edge of each wing. Navigation lights were built into wing-tips and fin; indentification lights being fitted in the rear fuselage. A heated Pitot static head was located on the starboard wing.

All the instrument panels were mounted on shock absorbers to prevent damage to the instruments due to engine vibration. A sub-panel was also fitted in the front cockpit below the main instrument panel and a small panel installed aft of the rear cockpit on the port side at the prone bombing position. The main panels were directly illuminated by lamps located behind a hinged reflector covering each panel. The following instruments were installed on the instrument panel in the front cockpit: air speed indicator; turn and bank indicator; rate of climb indicator; directional gyro; gyro horizon; altimeter; compass; clock; exhaust gas analyser; tachometer; manifold pressure gauge; engine gauge unit; and engine cylinder head temperature indicator. On the sub-panel were located, air temperature indicator; suction gauge; connections for camera; engine starter switch; bomb jettison switch. The rear cockpit panel had altimeter; air speed indicator; turn and bank indicator; clock; compass; tachometer. The bomb-aimer's panel contained an air speed indicator and altimeter, which were not fitted on later Mk.III Wirraways.

The fuel and oil tanks and hydraulic fluid reservoirs were manufactured from aluminium-alloy and were repairable by welding. The fuel tanks were covered with a rubber and canvas fire proofing medium but after aircraft No. A20-768, this protection was discontinued.

The Wirraway's armament comprised two forward-firing .303 inch Vickers machine-guns with synchronising gear plus a freely rotating Vickers G.O. No 1 which was carried on a hydraulically controlled hoist in the rear cockpit in the Mk I and II aircraft. The gun could move on a track in the form of a circular arc. Eight magazines, each holding sixty rounds were carried. A camera-gun could be mounted on the gun hoist, replacing the gun. Pyrotechnics included a Very pistol for signal flares, located on the right hand side of the front cockpit, stowage for eight cartridges being provided opposite.

On Mk I and II aircraft two forced-landing flares could be dropped through launching tubes in the rear fuselage; reconnaissance flares (when used) were carried on centre section mechanical bomb carriers and released by the bomb release mechanism and controls. Eighteen bomb slips were built into the aircraft; there were two universal carriers on each outer wing. Total normal bomb load was 500 lb, but for the overload case 1,000 lb could be carried. Light series carriers were located in the trailing edge portion of the centre section, just forward of the flaps. These carried practice bombs. A course-setting bomb-sight, Mk VII or IX, was fitted below the rear cockpit floor. Later aircraft, Mk IIIs from A20-623 onwards, had all-gun armament (including the camera gun) deleted and the aft end of the cockpit enclosed by a streamline steel-framed Perspex canopy. The radio transmitter and receiver were fitted in the rear cockpit, together with a trailing aerial and winch. The aerial had to extend 200 feet to be effective. Other equipment carried in this cockpit included a hand-operated carbon-tetrachloride fire-extinguisher, readily accessible from the ground as well as from the cockpit, by opening a hinged door. An F24 camera could be installed when it was not desired to use the prone bombing position.

The Wirraway's flying controls consisted of those operating the rudder, elevators, ailerons and trim tabs. Non-corrodible flexible steel cables were used. Smooth and effective control was assured by use of sealed type ball bearings at all pulleys, bellcranks and control-surface hinge points. These were packed with lubricant on assembly and required no further lubrication. A complete set of flying controls was installed in each cockpit, all controls being readily adjustable. A surface control lock was provided in the front cockpit. Engine controls comprised throttle, mixture and propeller control handles all assembled in a single quadrant located on the left side of each cockpit and interconnected by rods. Hot air from the exhaust manifold shroud could be taken into the carburettor through a valve in the air mixture chamber: this was controlled by a handle with notches providing vernier adjustment. The hand fuel pump handle was located on the left side of each cockpit, while fuel selector valve controls were adjacent. The engine starter push-button was located on the instrument sub-panel in the front cockpit. The engine switch was placed ahead of the rear cockpit on the left side. It was operated by mechanical linkage via a lever in the front left-hand corner of each cockpit, ahead of the throttle controls.

The Pratt & Whitney Wasp engine powered this aircraft, driving a *three-bladed*, controllable-speed, metal propeller. The engine was a nine-cylinder, single row R-1340 S1H1G radial, the first of many to be built under licence from Pratt & Whitney by the CAC

Engine Division. This engine was rated normally 550 hp at 5,000 feet at 2,200 rpm, take-off as 600 hp at 2,250 rpm. Thus maximum horsepower was 600 and the weight was 1,750 lb. Rate of climb was 1,950 feet per minute and endurance at operating speed was 3.07 hours. The range at operational speed at 450 hp was 640 miles, and at best economical speed was 850 miles. The engine could be turned with a hand starting crank which was stowed inside the fuselage side access door.

Maximum speed at crusing altitude (8,600 feet) was 220 mph; with 177 mph at sea-level, 199 mph at 9,000 feet and 209 mph at the critical altitude of 13,000 feet. The service ceiling was 23,000 feet. Landing speed at normal weight with flaps down was 65 mph, with flaps up, 70 mph.

Gross weight for the Wirraway was 5,575 lb normal, 6,450 lb maximum. Fuel capacity was ninety-two gallons total and reserve was sixteen gallons. Oil capacity was 8¾ gallons. The Wirraway's wing area was 256 square feet, span forty-three feet. Overall length came out at 27 feet 10 inches. Normal wing loading was 21.98 lb per square foot and power loading normal at 9.3 lb/hp.

The Wirraway at war. An Australian Commonwealth Wirraway conducts a very low-level sweep over the beaches at Port Douglas, North Queensland, on 17 March 1944. The occasion was the 6th Division's landing exercises conducted there during Exercise 'Douglas'.

Both Wirraways and Boomerangs of No. 5 Squadron, RAAF, were used to simulate Japanese opposing air strikes against the landing craft and invasion fleet during this operation, conducting mock strafing and bombing runs over the beach-heads. (*Courtesy of Australian War Memorial, Canberra. A.C.T.*)

Following the acceptance of Australian Mission's report a consortium of six of the leading Australian industrial companies formed the CAC with working capital of one million Australian pounds, on 17 October 1936. A factory was established the following April at Fishermen's Bend, Melbourne and work commenced. The Company's first aircraft were the two North American types which were used as received from North American Aviation, Inc. in mid-1937 and evaluated by the RAAF. They were assigned the RAAF numbers A20-1 and 2 respectively. Two versions were offered for selection. The first was the NA-32 (NA-16-1A), later the Yale, which featured a fixed undercarriage and a two-bladed propeller (Serial number 32-387). The second was the NA-33 (NA-16-2K) with the retractable gear and a three-bladed propeller (Serial number 32-388). Following their transfer to the RAAF on 2 February 1938, it was the latter that was finally chosen.

In June 1938 the Australian Government announced the awarding of a contract to CAC for the first forty Wirraways, (the construction of which had already been mooted the year before) with the firm intention to order another sixty or seventy later. This was despite a disparaging report by Marshal of the Air Force Sir Edward Ellington, who expressed reservations about the Wirraway's fitness for GP or light bombing duties, indeed for anything other

than air training. The Air Board stoutly defended their choice (and were to be proved right by events) while the Government assured the public that the price paid for the licence was 'satisfactory'.

In fact Kindelberger had struck a hard bargain for the licencing agreement. North American was paid an initial licence fee of one hundred thousand US dollars, royalties of thirty thousand US dollars for the specifications and manufacturing data plus a royalty of one thousand US dollars for each of the first batch of twenty-five aircraft produced. Furthermore, additional royalties of six hundred US dollars per aircraft were to be made on the next seventy-five machines before all payments ceased.

Various modifications, including fitment of twin, synchronized, forward-firing machine-guns in the upper forward fuselage firing through blast troughs, bomb gear and associated rear assembly strengthening for dive-bombing, camera and radio, were suggested and incorporated, and the name Wirraway assigned. The first of the series made its maiden flight, piloted by Flight Lieutenant H. Boss-Walker, RAAF, on 8 March 1939, as the Wirraway Mark I. In July 1939 the first three production Wirraways were accepted into service by the RAAF. (*Courtesy of Rockwell International Archives*)

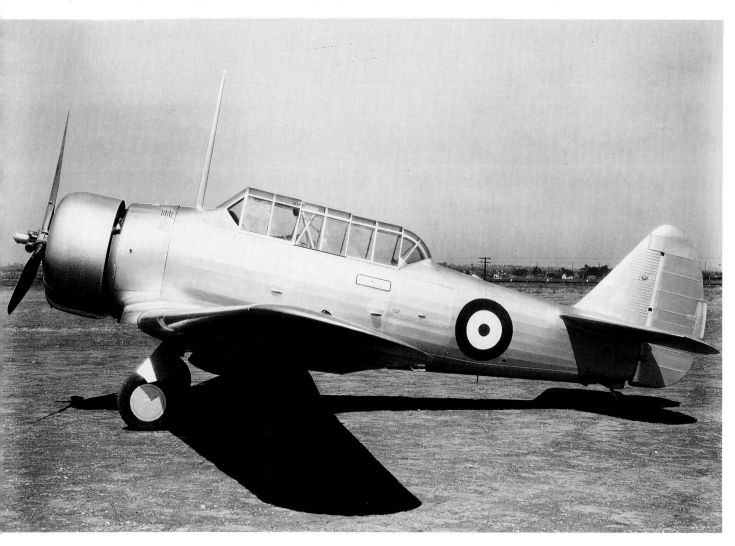

Work underway on Wirraway aircraft. Total production was 755 machines built between March 1939 and June 1946. (*Courtesy Hawker de Havilland Archives, Melbourne*)

The success of the first experimental Wirraways resulted in further orders on the outbreak of war in September of that year and production was increased to forty-five aircraft a month in 1941. The Wirraway was never intended to be in any way a combat aircraft but circumstances dictated otherwise. However, from the start the Wirraway was built with an armament of two machine-guns and could carry underwing bombs. Thus when No. 21 squadron RAAF was sent to Malaya just prior to the Japanese invasion they were soon thrown into the turmoil of total war. Other Wirraway-equipped squadrons went to New Guinea where they fought gallantly against heavy odds. Others served in the south Pacific island campaigns in New Guinea and onward as target spotters, dive- bombers, supply and transport aircraft and observation machines. The Australian Wirraways were by far and away the most combat-used version of the T-6 during World War II and we will return to some of their outstanding actions in a later chapter.

In addition to their impressive battle record, the chief role of the Australian Wirraway remained, as with their American, Canadian and British bretheren, that intended for them, advanced training aircraft. Wirraways were the mainstay of the Empire Air Training Scheme (EATS) in Australia and it was largely due to the enterprise of CAC that this scheme was carried out so completely and that it was able to accomplish the training of many thousands of young Australian pilots and aircrew who later served the world over. Here a stepped echelon formation of Wirraways with yellow engine cowlings is seen on a training flight during 1943.

The original Wirraway programme was for 620 machines and this was completed by June 1942, but a further programme for additional aircraft of this type increased the grand total constructed to 755. As with the Texan and Harvard, however, the story of the Wirraway was far from finished with the arrival of VJ day! (*Department of Public Records, Canberra ACT*)

(above)
One of the very early Commonwealth Wirraways (A20-21) is seen to good advantage in this air-to-air photograph. The aircraft's armament is clearly displayed with the two forward-firing .303-inch Vickers machine-guns with synchronising gear plus a freely rotating Vickers G.O. No 1 which was carried on a hydraulically controlled hoist in the rear cockpit in the Mk I and II aircraft. The gun could move on a track in the form of a circular arc. Eight magazines each holding sixty rounds were carried. Alternately a camera gun could be mounted on the gun hoist, replacing the gun. Pyrotechnics included a Very pistol for signal flares, located on the right-hand side of the front cockpit, stowage for eight cartridges being provided opposite.

On Mk I and II aircraft two forced-landing flares could be dropped through launching tubes in the rear fuselage; reconnaissance flares (when used) were carried on centre section mechanical bomb carriers and released by the bomb release mechanism and controls. Eighteen bomb slips were built into the aircraft; there were two universal carriers on each outer wing. Total normal bomb load was 500 lb, but for the overload case 1,000 lb could be carried. Light series carriers were located in the trailing edge portion of the centre section, just forward of the flaps. These carried practice bombs. A course setting bomb-sight, Mk VII or IX, was fitted below the rear cockpit floor. Later aircraft, Mk IIIs from A20-623 onward, had all-gun armament, (including the camera gun) deleted and the aft end of the cockpit enclosed by a streamlined steel-framed Perspex canopy. The radio transmitter and receiver were fitted in the rear cockpit, together with a trailing aerial and winch. The aerial had to extend 200 feet to be effective. (*Courtesy Department of Public Records, Canberra ACT*)

A fine aerial study of Commonwealth Wirraway 142 of the Royal
Australian Air Force on a training mission.

There were several variants to the standard Wirraway design, both
completed and proposed. The Mark I was a GP design which had the
CAC contract number CA1. They were allocated the serial numbers 1 to
40 and took RAAF numbers A20-3-42 (Mk I). Further batches of GP
Wirraways followed, the Mark II, (contract CA3) taking serial numbers
41-100 and RAAF numbers A-20-43-102 (Mk.II); CA5, serials 103-134
and RAAF numbers A-20-103-134 (Mk.II); CA7, serial numbers
135-234 and RAAF serials 135-234 (Mk.II). A combined GP/Trainer variant
followed under contract CA8, with serial numbers 436 to 635, and RAAF
numbers A-20-235-434 (Mk.II) and this was followed by a dive-bomber
variant under contract CA9 with serial numbers 636-823, RAAF numbers
A-20-435 to 622 (Mk.II). A further GP batch under contracts CA10 and
CA10A were later cancelled, but another dive-bomber group went ahead
under contract CA16, with serial numbers 1075 to 1224 and RAAF
numbers A-20-623-722 (Mk.III). Finally under contract CA20 another
dive-bomber batch was proposed for conversion for RAN use but
subsequently cancelled. Total production was therefore 755 between
March 1939 and June 1946.

They were all two-seat, low-wing monoplanes. The Wirraway had a
welded steel tube fuselage and wings of stressed-skin construction. The
tail unit was metal with fabric covered control surfaces. (*Courtesy
Department of Public Records, Canberra ACT*)

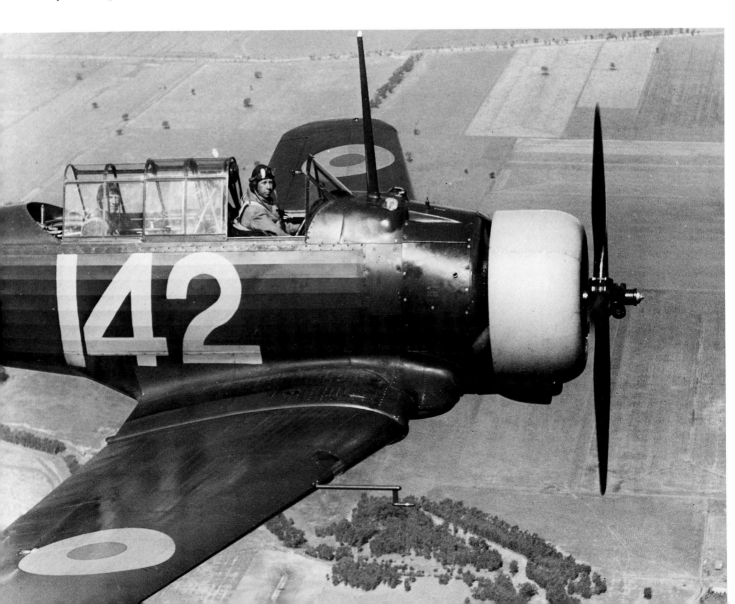

Another variant from the T-6 stable was the Australian Commonwealth Boomerang single-seater fighter. This was developed from the NA-16 from the NA-33 Wirraway built under licence. The Royal Australian Air Force designated it as the A-46 and, as such, it was the only Australian home-produced fighter-bomber built during World War II. Born as a direct result of the crisis situation of 1941-42 and the need for fighter aircraft CAC utilised the Pratt & Whitney 14-cylinder Twin Wasp engine. To speed production the Boomerang line utilised an adaptation of the Wirraway cockpit with a fairing, as well as the now reinforced centre section, undercarriage, tail assembly and other components, all built directly from Wirraway drawings. Although it looked similar to the American P-64 fighter, North American had absolutely no design input into the Boomerang itself.

   This is A46-128 in flight and showing to good advantage the 'spined' engine exhaust, gunsight and one of the two 20-mm cannon, which, along with four Browning machine-guns, formed the Boomerang's armament. (*Copyright Trethewey, Oppem, Belgium*)

The Wirraway at war. Mareeba, North Queensland, Australia, 8 May 1944. Boxes containing field operations rations are being fitted underneath the mainplanes of a Wirraway of No. 5 Squadron, Royal Australian Air Force. These boxes of rations were dropped to the troops of the 17th Infantry Brigade during a combined supply dropping exercise.

The RAAF's Wirraways were frequently used in this role during the campaigns in New Guinea and Burma and proved invaluable in keeping the forward troops supplied in thick jungle territories.

In the background is the fighter derivative of the Wirraway, the Commonwealth Boomerang (A46-192) with the white tail and rear fuselage markings common to the S.E. Asia Theatre of Operations. (*Courtesy of Australian War Memorial, Canberra. A.C.T.*)

(*right*)
The most celebrated combat of the war involving a Commonwealth Wirraway was probably that which took place on 26 December 1942, over Gona, New Guinea. Pilot Officer Jack Archer was on routine reconnaissance patrol over the famous wreck in the harbour there in Wirraway A20-103 ('Chuff-Chuff') in company with another Wirraway. Fortunately this aircraft, as well as being used for dive-bombing operations at the time with universal bomb carriers under the wings, was also fitted with two forward-firing machine-guns.

Another aircraft was spotted by Archer's observer, Sergeant J.L. Coulston, some 1,000 feet below them. At first it was taken for a friendly but then Coulston yelled a warning over the intercom. 'Hell, it's a . . . Zero'. And so it was, a Japanese Navy Mitsubishi A6M Reisen 'Zeke' or 'Zero' fighter, considerably faster, more powerfully armed and more manoeuvrable than the Wirraway, or indeed most contemporary Allied fighter planes!

It was a time for quick action and Archer did the only thing possible to prevent the destruction of two Australian machines, he attacked!

As he dived towards the enemy, which fortunately had still not spotted them, Archer pressed the firing button at 200 yards range and kept his finger firmly on the trigger until within fifty feet of the Japanese machine. To his intense relief as he pulled his Wirraway in a tight turn, Archer saw the Zero fall flaming into the sea.

Coulston, later said that Archer had done the only possible thing when he attacked. Had he missed things would have turned out very differently for them all. Asked how it felt to attack a Zero in a Wirraway, Archer replied he couldn't say, 'I didn't have time to think about it. I was lucky to get in the first burst. It was certainly good to see him crash into the sea.' He was duly rewarded with a crate of beer on his return to base!

Post-war after many adventures, Archer's mount was eventually salvaged and restored and is now on display at the Australian War Memorial. (*Courtesy Australian War Memorial, Canberra ACT*).

Another unique event. The last-ever Commonwealth Wirraway to fly on active service with the Royal Australian Air Force is pictured here making her farewell flight over Sydney Harbour Bridge. Very few survive today but in recent years some worthwhile efforts have been made to preserve some, even if few of them are flyable.

The story of Archers' A20-103 Wirraway is the most well-known of these few survivors. After being passed on to another pilot in his unit for a time, this machine was returned to Australia for a refit and refurbishment. Archers' personal 'Chuff Chuff' emblem, a wheeled Chinese Dragon, his red and white 'Rising Sun' kill marking and three yellow bombing mission registers, were painted over and replaced by the Squadron Crest. All the aircraft's armament was removed at the same time and the Wirraway was operated by No. 3 Communications Unit for a while. Then it went to No. 7 Aircraft Depot for storage. It survived many years of neglect and today has been fully restored and is a static display at the Australian War Memorial in Canberra, A.C.T. (*Courtesy Hawker de Havilland, Melbourne*)

5 Exports and Offspins

The T-6 was one of the most successful aircraft designs of all times. Its arrival filled an urgently-felt need in the air forces of not just the major powers like the United States, Great Britain, France, Canada and Australia, but a whole host of lesser nations that wished to modernise their air fleets under the impetus of World War II. The Texan was the right aircraft at the right time in more ways than one! But before we examine in detail the enormous diversity of customers for the T-6 and the variety of uses that they put this little aircraft to, let us take a look at the final conventional developments of the type by North American in the closing stages of the war, along with a few experimental and 'oddball' customisations of the basic airframes that took place during this same period.

The story of the Ranger-engined Texan is a complex one. The Fairchild Caminez Engine Corporation was set up as a subsidiary of the Fairchild Aviation Corporation in 1925, becoming just the plain Fairchild Engine Corporation four years later. When, during the same period, the noted engine designer Walter F. Davis came up with an in-line, air-cooled inverted cylinder aero-engine at Wright Aeronautical it found no favour there. Seeking a more successful engine to market than his own failed four-cylinder, four-stroke, Caminez cam-drive disaster, the head of the Long Island company, Sherman Fairchild, took Davis and his engine onboard immediately.

The original six-cylinder Ranger 6-390 in-line engine was progressively developed through to the Model 770, a 290 hp, 12-cylinder inverted engine which had rows of cylinders in a 60-degree 'V' form. Uprated steadily through to a 575 hp model, the Ranger in-lines found some limited use with Fairchild training aircraft but no large contracts, and even after the outbreak of war in Europe its projected use in the Navy's Curtiss SO3C-1 never materialised and the reputation of the engine itself suffered unfairly accordingly. A similar fate befell the projected Bell Aircraft Corporation's XP-77, a wood-construction, high-speed fighter, which was also cancelled.

It was then that Fairchilds proposed the marriage of the upgraded 770 in-line engine with North American's outstandingly successful trainer in order to provide both a market for their engines and also the Army Air Force with a training aircraft that more reflected the type of aircraft their new young fighter pilots would be flying in combat.

The T-6 is famous for its radial engine, both because of its distinctive sound and for its readily identifiable shape. The United States Navy had always favoured radial-engine aircraft from the 1930's onward, but the USAAF was less enamoured, and, other than for fighters like the Republic P-47 Thunderbolt, it was the inline-engined fighters like the Curtiss P-39 and P-40 Kittyhawks and Warhawks and North American P-51 Mustang that predominated. This fact was coupled with the fear that huge demand for the Pratt & Whitney Wasp engine might result in shortages and bottlenecks in production, and helped turned the USAAF's attentions to Fairchild's suggestions on the possibilities of developing an inline-engined version of the T-6 for their future air training needs.

It was not a success and only one prototype was ever built. Fairchilds, the engine manufacturers, had lost their last gamble and went to the wall. The reasons for the rejection, despite the very impressive figures achieved, are these. First-and-foremost, like the anticipated aluminium shortage earlier, the feared shortage of Pratt & Whitney engines never materialised. Reliability and continuity of production far outweighed the height and speed advantages of the XAT-6E which after all was a *trainer* and not competing as a fighter with the AT-6D. It did not need either of the former's desirable assets to continue to churn out thousands of young pilots year-after-year!

Secondly was the unreliability and temperament of the Ranger engine itself. Noisy it might be, rough-and-ready also, maybe, but the good 'ole P & W kept flying steadily on and required but minimum care and maintenance to keep it that way. The in-line was smaller, had to work harder for the same effect and thus suffered from gross over-heating. Although Fairchilds' engineers desperately tried to overcome these problems by the fitting of sheet metal baffles between each cylinder, and also invented a chemical bond heat-dissipating fin to each cylinder barrel, the *Al-Fin* process, they could not save the day. Thirdly, by the time the trials were over the end of the war was clearly in sight. There were thousands of surplus Texans all over the free-world, jet fighters were already in the skies and money was getting tight again as Governments started to cut back on funding. The XAT-6E was doomed before it even flew; but it was a nice try.

One final word on this aircraft is required. It is a fact that North American official records show only a single XAT-6E conversion. It is also a documented and photographically-proven fact that *two* such machines competed against each other in post-war civil air races. How can these two facts be squared?

The original North American/Fairchild conversion was bought privately and registered as NX7410. Piloted by Margaret McGrath it became the top qualifier for the 1947 female competition, the Halle Trophy Race, held at the National Air Races at Cleveland, Ohio, logging 223.325 mph and was said to have exceeded 240 mph. However, the old engine unreliability let it down again and she later had to withdraw.

The other 'XAT' was a conventional T-6 bought and converted privately by Dori Marland. It carried civilian registration N61268. It carried at various periods of its brief life the names 'Wingwax' and 'Spray Wax', large numerals '49' on its main fuselage and the 'Sohio' sponsorship logo on the streamlined fairing abaft the cockpit. This particular machine crashed during the self-same 1947 Halle Trophy Race.

The AT-6F/SNJ-6 was the final war production model of the Texan. These were AT-6Ds taken from the existing NA-121 contract and modified. The most obvious external change was the fitting of an integral, one-piece moulded Plexiglas (Perspex) rear canopy section in place of the previous ribbed movable section. This was made possible due to the complete dropping of the all machine-gun and bomb-carrying potential from the model. Complementary to this the rear seat was no longer required to swivel and was made a forward-facing fixture. The wing and nose machine-guns were also deleted, as were the underwing racks for light bombs. In place of the latter came an under the centreline fuselage fixture for mounting a twenty-gallon drop tank for extra fuel bunkerage. It was positioned just abaft the wheel wells.

Another identifying feature of this Mark of Texan was the fitting of a large propeller-spinner to complete the aerodynamic clean-up of the aircraft. Not obvious was the fact that the outer wing panels were strengthened on this model. The original US Army Air Force order was for 1,375 of these aircraft, but these included the Navy orders which, in common with earlier dashes, were procured on Army Air Force contracts. From this total 417 were cancelled at the end of the war and the Navy took delivery of 931. Of the twenty-five that were completed as AT-6Fs these were mainly assigned to Army Air Force Reserve units. None of these aircraft were transferred to the RAF or related air forces, so consequently there was no Harvard equivalent of the AT-6F.

So much for the conventional development of the Texan. Apart from the metric-metered T-6s sold to France before her defeat in 1940, the American and Canadian-built Harvards and the Australian-built Wirraways, T-6s (or their derivatives) equipped numerous other air forces' inventories by 1945. And not just those of Allied nations!

Apart from the 111 aircraft actually supplied from the 230 French *Armée de l'Air* batch of

NA-57s of 5 September 1939, which fell intact into German hands in June 1940, and which were given Swastikas and *Balkenkreuz* and then pressed into *Luftwaffe* service, North American scored a more obvious 'own-goal' by supplying two of their early trainers (and consequently the wherewithall to construct good imitations of them), to the Japanese enemy.

These aircraft were not Texans but of the fixed-fuselage Yale types, a NA-16-4R with a 450 hp Pratt & Whitney R-985-8CG engine and a three-bladed propeller, the first arrived in Japan in September 1937. Later a NA-47 (NA-16-RW) was delivered in December of the same year and again was a one-off built for Japan that was identical to the BT-9 except for the fact that it was fitted with a larger engine, the Wright R-975-E3 and a two-bladed propeller. This machine (47-699), along with full manufacturing rights, was sold outright to Mitsubishi Heavy Industries and shipped disassembled to them at Yokohama on 16 December 1937. These aircraft were evaluated by the Japanese Navy as the KXA1 and KXA2 respectively as Navy Experimental Type A Trainers. The Japanese Navy found them good enough to imitate and the licence and manufacturing rights were purchased through an intermediary trading company. As the NA-16-4R and many modifications, chief of which was the fitting of a Nakajima 600 hp Kotobuki 2 Kai air-cooled radial engine, this Japanese version was built by K.K. Watanabe Tekkosho, who had the prototype flying by 1941. The Japanese aircraft also featured enlarged vertical tail surfaces. A batch of twenty-five more Navy Type 2 Intermediate Trainers followed up to November 1942, as the K1OW1.

Further Japanese production runs were carried out by the Nippon Hikoki KK, and, as the K5Y1, they built 150 of them between February 1943 and March 1944. Armament was a single, forward-firing 7.7 mm Type 97 machine-gun and maximum speed was 152 knots. In the Pacific War this American-styled trainer was allocated the usual Allied code names, which for trainers were trees. So, to the Texan, the Harvard, the T-Bird, the Wirraway and the many other names by which the T-6 flew, another can be added, the Oak.

Two special one-offs were built at Inglewood for overseas customers pre-war. The first was produced for Canada as the BC-1 (NA-36, 26-202) and was similar to the BT-9 except that it featured fully retractable landing-gear and had an armament of two. 30 machine-guns. Power plant was the larger Pratt & Whitney R-B40 engine. The order was dated 20 October 1936 and the purpose of the machine was for use as a demonstration aircraft for the basic trainer.

In Europe another such 'customer' was found in the form of the Dutch aircraft manufacturer Fokker Aircraft, who purchased a one-off NA-27 as its demonstration machine of a basic trainer for the European market. They ordered from the Inglewood plant on 1 December 1936 and took delivery of this machine (NA-16-2H, 27-312) which was similar to the NA-26, on 15 April 1937.

Also, in Scandinavia, the Royal Swedish Air Force, the *Flygvapnet*, on 2 August 1937 took delivery of one NA-16-4M, (31-386) which was similar to the BT-9 but with a different engine, the Wright R-975-E3 driving a two-bladed propeller. This machine was fitted with the broad Goodyear Airwheels to take into account soggy conditions on Lapland strips. The *Flygvapnet* also bought the airplane and manufacturing rights. The Swedes received a second machine of the same type (identical to the NA-31) on 28 September of the same year (38-540) which was shipped unassembled as part of the manufacturing agreement.

Once evaluated an initial order for thirty-five machines resulted in July 1938, the Swedish designation being SK 14. These had started to enter service by the following May. SAAB received two contracts, for eighteen and for twenty-three of these machines which were delivered during the war. Subsequent orders for Texans were to result from their experience with the Yale, and Sweden later purchased direct a total of 263 later models, which comprised 145 AT-16s (Swedish designation being SK16A), 112 T-6s (the SK16B) and six SNJ-2s (the SK16C).

On 10 January 1944, the US Army procured eighty-one AT-6Ds (NA-119) under Lend-

Lease for the Brazilian Air Force. Of this total, sixty-one were shipped south as completely-assembled airframe kits for final assembly on-site; ten as complete airframe sub-assemblies and the final ten as complete airframe partially sub-assembled in Texas. No US Army serials were allocated to these aircraft.

Reverting again to strictly Lend-Lease procurements, on 2 December 1941 the Bolivian Air Force, the *Cuerpo de Aviadores Boliviano*, was the recipient of three North American AT-6A-NTs and these were the sole representatives of this dash to reach South America under the agreement. One of these machines was actually for use by the US Army Air Corps mission in that country, although it was nominally charged against Bolivia's account.

During 1942 there was a vast increase in deliveries, and for Brazil, the *Aviacao Exercito do Brasil* (fourteen AT-6B-NTs in April), Chile, the *Fuerza Aerea Nacional de Chile* (fifteen AT-6B-NTs in April), Columbia, the *Fuerza Aerea Colombiana* (four AT-6B-NTs in April), Ecuador, the *Fuerza Aerea Ecuatoriana* (four AT-6B-NTs in April), Mexico, the *Fuerza Aerea Mexicana* (six AT-6B-NTs in June), Peru, the *Cuerpo de Aeronautica del Peru*, (nine AT-6B-NTs in April) Uruguay, the *Aeronautica Militar Uruguaya* (four AT-6B-NTs in February) and Venezuela, the *Servicio Aereo Militar Venezolana* (four AT-6B-NTs in March) received between them a total of sixty AT-6Bs.

Dan Hagedorn described their reception thus:

> 'These aircraft were intended as morale boosters and a statement of intention to honour obligations, and they achieved these purposes marvelously. Besides propaganda value, the AT-6B variant offered at least limited defensive and offensive capabilities as well, and proved ideally suited to Latin American conditions at practically every turn. It is not surprising that, of all types sent to the theater, Texans were the most numerous (483) . . . T-6s supplied under Lend-Lease and other US air programmes to follow (not to mention quantities purchased surplus) soon became the most common aircraft in military colours in South America.'

In 1943 this trickle became a flood which eventually totalled 545 Texans making them easily the most numerous US aircraft sent to South American air forces. Bolivia received nine AT-6C-10-NTs and fifteen AT-6D-NTs; Brazil twenty AT-6C-NTs, five AT-6C-5-NTs, ten AT-6C-10-NTs, thirty-five AT-6C-15-NTs, twenty-five AT-6D-NTs and twenty AT-6D-1-NTs, five AT-6C-15-NTs, ten AT-6C-15-NTs, and thirty-two AT-6D-NTs (one of which was lost in transit); Columbia, two AT-6C-NTs, two AT-6C-10-NTs, four AT-6C-15-NTs, thirty-eight AT-6D-NTs and six AT-6D-1-NTs; Ecuador three AT-6C-NTs, three AT-6C-15-NTs and six AT-6D-1-NTs; Guatamala, the *Cuerpo de Aeronautica Militar Guatemalteca*, three AT-6C-15-NTs; Haiti, the *Corps D'Aviation D'Haiti*, two AT-6C-15-NTs; Mexico thirty-one AT-6C-NTs, six AT-6C-5-NTs, twelve AT-6C-10-NTs, ten AT-6D-NTs, and twenty AT-6D-1-NTs; Nicaragua, the *Fuerza Aerea de la Guardia Nacional de Nicaragua*, three AT-6C-15-NTs; Paraguay, the *Fuerza Aerea Nacional del Paraguay*, three AT-6C-NTs; Peru twenty-five AT-6D-NTs; Salvador, the *Aviacion Militar Salvadorena*, three AT-6C-NTs and three AT-6D-1-NTs; Uruguay six AT-6D-1-NTs; and Venezuela five AT-6C-5-NTs, three AT-6C-15-NTs and five AT-6D-NTs.

In all, 192 T-6Cs and 219 T-6Ds were sent while ten AT-6F-NTs were supplied to Cuba, the *Cuerpo Aerea Ejercito de Cuba*, in addition to six AT-6C-NTs and three AT-6C-10-NTs.

Other Allied governments were in ready receipt of the Texan also, including the China and the Netherlands government in exile, and the Soviet Union which had eighty-four AT-6Cs assigned to them, of which eighty-two were delivered. Thirty of these trainers were shipped by way of the Arctic convoys to Archangel, the other fifty-four were handed over in Alaska in 1945, for transit through Siberia (the Alsib ferry route). But they returned none of them!

Finally, among the many variations on the basic T-6 theme were some single-seater fighter adaptations that deserve mention. The first of these was the NA-50A. This aircraft was a direct development from the NA-16 and seven were contracted by the Peruvian Air Force on 9 February 1939 as the NA-50 (50-948 to 50-954). North American chopped five feet from the overall wingspan of the AT-6 and one foot from the fuselage length. The reduced canopy was faired over to the rear with the radio stack shifted aft. An Aldis gunsight tube was fitted forward of the pilot's cockpit. The old-style BC-1 type rudder and fin shape was retained with a fixed tailwheel but the main undercarriage was fully retractable.

To give the new aircraft fighter credibility an 870 hp Wright R-1820-77 engine was fitted which drove a three-bladed propeller. This combination gave it a trial speed of 295 mph and a service ceiling of 32,000 feet. The Peruvian batch were fitted out as fighter-bombers and thus were armed with both guns and bombs. These guns were four Colt-Browning. 30 calibre weapons, carried one in each wing and two more, fully synchronised, mounted in the actual engine cowling itself. Light racks under each wing gave it a bomb-carrying capacity of 550lb. Range unladen was 645 miles.

The NA-50A had its first flight on 1 September 1940 and all seven fighters were delivered to Peru by early 1941.

Following their own inspection and air testing of the first NA-50A in September 1939, the Siamese government (now Thailand), to whose original specification it had been designed, ordered six of these fighter aircraft on the following 30 November. They asked for some modifications, mainly to the armament which was upgraded to match European War standards where the need for a heavier punch was manifest. As well as the two 8-mm machine-guns in the wings and two more in the engine cowling, the Siamese fighter had two single 20-mm cannon slung in underwing fairings under each wing outboard the machine gun station. Being delivered later they incorporated the distinctive T-6 angular tailplane and rudder configuration, and had no Aldis sighting tube emplaced. Except for an improved landing gear equipment they were in all other respects identical to their Peruvian cousins and were completed and shipped out of Los Angeles harbour as the NA-68 (NA-50A, 68-3058 to 68-3063) in 1940.

These aircraft were destined never to reach Siam. While still at Hawaii, Vichy-France and Siam fought a brief and vicious little war that is now all but forgotten. Under the strict terms of the Neutrality Act the United States was loath to assist either side (one an ally of Nazi Germany the other flirting with Japan) and so the state Department acted swiftly and revoked their export licences.

The six fighters were returned to the States and taken into the USAAC inventory at Luke AAFB as 'fighter-trainers'. They were assigned the standard designation of P-64 and used by Training Command throughout the war. Five were scrapped but one survived to be sold privately and later became one of the exhibits of the Experimental Aircraft Association at Oshkosh in Wisconsin, a very unique relic indeed!

Yet a third single-seater fighter was developed from the basic NA design, this time in Australia where the CAC came up with the Boomerang concept. Early in 1942 the Japanese were sweeping all before them in their drive to conquer their 'Co-prosperity Sphere'. Hong Kong, the Philippines, Borneo, Malaya, Singapore, the Dutch East Indies, New Britain, Burma and New Guinea, all fell like a house of cards before them. The position of Australia looked very precarious indeed and the Japanese Zero fighters had met no serious aerial opposition while cutting their swathe of victories through the Pacific. Certainly these fast and agile fighters completely outclassed anything Australia could pit against them at this time and there was little prospect of either the British or the Americans being able to supply many in the foreseeable future.

A locally-constructed, highly manoeuvrable and hard-hitting interceptor was desperately needed. The people to quickly produce such a home-produced fighter seemed obvious and the manager of the Commonwealth Aircraft Corporation, Wing Commander Lawrence

Wackett, put his design team to work at once. The Australian Government gave design approval as early as 21 December 1941, and, on 2 February 1942, the initial contract for 105 machines was placed before a single machine had been built!

The idea that they evolved was for a small fighter using the most powerful engine then readily available to them (the 1,200 hp Pratt & Whitney R-1830-S34C-G 14-cylinder Twin Wasp radial then in local production for the twin-engined Beaufort torpedo-bomber) and around it to construct the machine. To save on man-hours as the need was urgent, the use of existing tooling and as many CAC Wirraway components as was possible was made integral to the design. Thus the Boomerang had centre section, undercarriage and tail unit almost identical to the Wirraway.

The fuselage structure was of steel tube with a wooden monocoque fairing extending from the cockpit to the rudder. A seventy gallon bullet-proof fuel tank was fitted in the fuselage, behind the pilot and two forty-five gallon tanks of moulded wood construction were located in the centre section. Increased range was afforded by a seventy gallon drop-tank. This gave a range of 1,600 miles. After the 106th aircraft, the pilot's seat and wing-tips were also constructed of moulded wood. The cockpit was amply protected with armour plating behind the pilot and a bullet proof windscreen was fitted. The armament consisted of two 20mm Hispano cannon and four .303 Browning machine-guns mounted in the wing. There were also underwing bomb racks. The wings, fin and tail were all-metal stressed skin construction, the control surfaces being fabric covered. The Boomerang was fitted with a three-bladed de Havilland propeller.

The first CA.12 Boomerang, made its debut flight from Fisherman's Bend on 29 May 1942, flown by test pilot Ken Fruin, just fourteen weeks after the rough drafts had been approved. The only major modifications required after tests were to the oil cooling system. A spinner was added to the propeller as well. 105 ordered off the drawing board and by September a steady flow was joining the RAAF. The wingspan was 36 feet, total wing area being 225 square feet. The length was 25 ft 6 inches and height was 11 feet 6 inches. All-up weight of this little fighter was 8,032 lb and its maximum speed was 305 mph at 15,000 feet. It had an outstanding climb rate claimed to be 2,940 ft./min which was better than the Spitfire I, Focke-Wulf 190 F-3 and the Curtiss P-40N Warhawk, and a service ceiling of 36,000 feet.

Since the Twin Wasp was a medium supercharged engine giving its greatest power with the high-speed blower at about 15,000 feet, this gave a limitation to the aircraft's performance. To overcome this a Boomerang was converted to take an improved supercharger. This aircraft became CA.14 and its performance was considerably higher than that of the CA.12. Further improvements were made including the fitment of sliding gills and an engine cooling fan. The intercooler air scoop on the port side of the CA.14 was deleted, the air being directed from the engine bay. A square fin and rudder replaced the conventional Boomerang type and this greatly modified aeroplane became the CA.14A.

However, at about this time, American high-altitude fighters were being landed and assembled in Australia, so that further work on the CA.14A was dropped. In total, 250 Boomerangs, including the CA.14A, were built. The various batches of CAC Boomerang fighters can be summarised thus: Contract CA12, Fighter Interceptor, Serial numbers 824 to 928, RAAF numbers A46-1-105; Contract CA13, Fighter Interceptor, Serial numbers 929 to 1023, RAAF numbers A46-106-200; Contract CA14, Fighter (with supercharger), 1073, RAAF Serial number 1001; CA14A, Fighter with supercharger, square fin and rudder, 1073, 1001; CA19, Fighter, Serial numbers 1024 to 1072; RAAF Serial numbers A46-201-249.

In America the US Navy's SNJ-5Cs modified for carrier landing training with navigation tables and tailhooks had continued in service working from the training carriers (TCVs) one of which was the USS *Sable* (IX. 81, formerly the mercantile *Greater Buffalo*).

These two photographs were taken in May 1945 aboard the *Sable*. The second view shows the Texan of Captain Schoech, USN, touching down on the flight-deck a little later. In the background a Grumman Wildcat fighter awaits its turn to follow suit. (*US National Archives, Washington, DC*)

Here a SNJ can be seen taking-off from the flight-deck (note the raised arrester-hook just in front of the rear wheel) while in the background another circles the carrier awaiting the chance to land back on again (notice the extended arrester-hook of the distant machine). (*US National Archives, Washington DC*)

Post-war, the T-6 continued to give good service in training aircrew for the building-up of brand-new air forces from those of former enemies and Allies who now found themselves in the new Alliance, that of the Anti-Communist Free World. Having spent six years destroying the air arms of Germany and Japan, both the United States and Great Britain now had to allocate resources to re-equipping these nations and the North American trainer played a great part in this.

Here is shown the very first North American T-6G trainer (2861-29) to be painted with the Rising Sun emblem of the Japanese Air-Self Defense Force which was turned over from a United States Air Force unit at Camp Matsushima, in the Miyagi Prefecture in 1954. Note the tail markings incorrectly show this as a 'JS Air Force' machine. (*Courtesy of Tadashi Nozawa*)

West Germany received large batches of T-6s and Harvards. On 1 July 1955 the *Bundeswehr* ordered 135 Harvard Mark IVs under the MDAP programme in order to set up the Temporary Flying Training Command. The 7.351 Flying Training Wing established at Landsberg first flew these aircraft and was followed, on 24 September 1956, by further imports of T-6J-CCFs from North America. With the *Flugdienststaffel* (FFS) these machines served faithfully and well, undergoing several minor modifications, until the early 1960s. A few served with WaSLw 30 (the Operational Training School for the F-84F fighters). Yet another T-6 nickname could be added to the seemingly endless list for the chrome-yellow coloured unarmed FFS training machines were dubbed 'Zitronen-bombers' (Lemon bombers) by the instructors and novice pilots.

In addition to training some Harvards served as target tugs for radar-controlled flight-controller training with F1Kdo TSLw 1 at Kaufbeuren from 1964 onward. The FFS 'A's aerobatic team flew their Harvard IVs from Landsberg for many years. The final West German Harvard flight took to the air on 30 January 1962 with the machines flown by *Oberleutnant* Garske, *Leutnant* Kruger, *Leutnant* Stehli and SU Rohl. A final farewell ceremony was held at Kaufbeuren in the summer of 1964 when a check-nosed Harvard IV, suitably bedecked with black mourning crêpe ribbon from both wingtips, was officially 'discharged' from the service. (*German Federal Government Photograph Archive, Bonn*)

Three Dutch Harvards outside the Fokker factory for refurbishing after their hand-over from the Royal Air Force. Nearest the camera is FS737, which, on being handed over in September 1946, had seen no previous service with her original owners at all. FT148, beyond her, was handed over in August 1947, and similarly had not been flown before entering Dutch service.

A further forty ex-RCAF Harvards were delivered to the Netherlands East Indies in August 1948, two of which were damaged in transit. They were flown as trainers at the flying schools at Kalidjati. Those that survived were handed over to the Indonesian Republic in 1950 on independence. (*Courtesy Arthur Pearcy Archives*)

The Turkish Air Force received a grand total of 196 T-6/Harvard aircraft. The first batch of one hundred machines, AT-6Cs, arrived in the country on 2 August 1948 and were given Turkish Serials 7251 to 7350. These were later supplemented by eighteen ex-RAF Harvard Mark IIBs from the Royal Norwegian Air Force, six arriving on 4 October 1955 and twelve more on 6 November 1955. They received the Turkish Serials 7351 to 7368. These were followed, on 18 July 1956, by a further eight Mark II Harvards that arrived from RCAF sources and were numbered 7369 to 7376.

Under the NATO Mutual Air Programme Turkey received yet further batches of North American COIN and trainer aircraft. The first of these new assignments were sixteen former LT-6Gs. These arrived on 7 September 1957 and were assigned Serial Numbers 7277 to 7392. They were followed by three more of the same type on 7 October 1957 (7393 to 7395) along with eleven T-6Gs (7396 to 7399 and 7501 to 7505).

Two more consignments were shipped to Turkey in 1958. On 13 January of that year twenty-one machines arrived and were numbered 7508 to 7528), while on 5 May 1958 a final batch of nineteen were received (7529 to 7547).

All these aircraft served on the Turkish Air Force Inventory for over twenty-five years, the final T-6 being phased out in 1976. (*Author's collection, courtesy of Turkish Air Force, Ankara*)

The use of Harvards/T-6s for Military COIN (Counter-Insurgency) and close-support aircraft was widespread post-war. One of the foremost users of such machines in this role was the Portuguese Air Force. Many were used thus in the Angola conflict, a few falling victim to the shoulder-launched Soviet SAM-7 missiles supplied to the Communist guerrilla forces.

The final combat usage of the Harvard however, was closer to home, when, on 11 March 1975, two of them (1737 being one of these) were used to bomb an Army barracks close to Lisbon during an abortive coup against the new Government which had overthrown the old right-wing ruling party the year before. Three years later the type was finally withdrawn from official combat usage and many were sold overseas.

Fortunately, thanks to the dedicated work of Colonel Fernandes Nico, commandant of *Base Aerea 6* at Montijo, who recovered and maintained T-6J 1774, the *Museu do Ar* at Alverca was persuaded to save two of these machines in airworthy condition. The FAP staff at another airfield, *Base Aerea 7* at San Jacinto, hid a second machine (1769) away from the scrappers and ground-ran the engine at frequent intervals to keep it serviceable.

Eventually Colonel Nico was allowed to add this to the first machine together with a large stock of T-6 spares. Both are airworthy and hopefully can be kept flying for another decade yet. Here 1769 is seen over the Portuguese coast in 1989, the underwing machine-gun pods and rocket launchers can be clearly seen under the nearside wing in this photograph. (*Courtesy J. Laneiro, Lisbon*)

Right up to the present day the T-6 has proved itself a popular choice for the entertainment industry also. From early wartime black and white motion picture epics, like *I Want Wings*, which starred Brian Donlevy and Veronica Lake, through to wide-screen film presentations like *Tora, Tora, Tora* and *The Battle of Midway*, and on through the TV series *Black Sheep Squadron* (as suitably willing victims of 'Pappy' Boyington's Marine Corps Chance-Vought Corsairs), the T-6 has been filmed.

At first in its original authentic form, but more recently, they were modified with new cowling, rudders, canopies, wing-tips and paint-jobs to double-up, almost endlessly, as Japanese Mitsubishi Zero fighters, Nakajima Kate torpedo-bombers and a whole host more, at Hollywood's behest. They have become mock Republican Thunderbolts in *A Bridge Too Far*, (featuring similar checkerboard cowling markings to N2861G which is shown here, in a photograph taken at Van Nuys airfield, California in July 1968, although without the tail gun!) and metamorph-ised into Soviet Yaks. T-6s have been altered and disected for all manner of aerial imitation and promotion. (*Courtesy Nick Williams Collection*)

The *Marine Luchtvaartdienst* (Royal Netherlands Navy) obtained six Harvard Mark IIBs from the Royal Netherlands Air Force on loan in 1946. After three years they were returned. A further four were similarly loaned from 1958 onward and a final quartet were transferred at de Kooy in 1965 and 1966. Although the lion's share of the Dutch Harvards job was, of course, advanced training for air force pilots, a small number were used for communications and courier services, *Basisvlucht* duties. Six camouflaged Harvards, stationed at Deelan airbase, formed a photographic flight and had a reconnaissance task. In addition to military training further Harvards were also used as a training aircraft for civil pilots.

Here maintenance work is taking place on one such Harvard. The overall paint scheme has now reverted to the traditional NATO yellow with black markings. (*Author's collection, courtesy Royal Netherlands Air Force*)

An underside look at a trio of French Harvards. The French air force had first received replacement for all the T-6s lost in 1940, when three ex-RAF Harvards joined a training establishment in Syria in 1943. In January 1944, a fighter transition school was established at Meknes, Morocco and its establishment included some T-6s. Towards the end of 1944 the RAF gave two more Harvards to the French air training school at Blida, Tunisia. These few relics remained the sum total strength in French service until the formation of NATO in 1949, then things changed dramatically.

A brand-new training base was established at Marrakech on 1 January 1949 ready for the T-6s. A second ATS flew Harvard IIs at Salon de Provence, southern France between 1949 and 1952. France received thirty Harvard Mark IIBs in April and May 1949 from the RAF. Under MAP the USAF was delivered a further 119 T-6Ds which joined training establishments in Morocco. In the same year, and under the same scheme, France also received fifty-one Harvard IIIs (forty-five via the USAF and six from the RCAF), also in Morocco. In 1952 the Aéronavale, also under MAP and also in Morocco took delivery of fifty-six SNJs and a further seventeen Mk IIs arrived from Canada. A fresh batch of forty-nine AT-6Ds arrived here between October 1951 and April 1952, some of which survived until 1958 when the unit moved to Tours. Odd machines also served at the Rochefort and Saintes Mechanics' schools as static airframe workshops in the 1950s and flew from the Cazaux Test Centre on liaison duties in the same decade.

With Moroccan independence the French school was moved to Cognac in September 1961 and the Texans continued to train 200 French pilots a year until phased out of service in 1965 when they were replaced by Fouga Magister 170 jet trainers. (*Courtesy SIRPA/ECP Armées, Fort D'Ivry, Paris*)

Final notes on the Dutch use of the North American trainer was when a further forty ex-RCAF Harvards were delivered to the Netherlands East Indies in August 1948, two of which were damaged in transit. They were flown as trainers at the flying schools at Kalidjati. Those that survived were handed over to the Indonesian Republic in 1950 on independence.

Here an echeloned stack of Royal Netherlands Air Force Harvards is caught over the south of the country in immaculate formation. (*Author's collection, courtesy Royal Netherlands Air Force*)

The *Fliegerabwehrtruppen* (Swiss Air Force) purchased forty Noorduyn-built Harvard IIBs from the RCAF in 1947 and these were given the Swiss Serials U-301 to U-340. On their arrival in Europe they were given a complete overhaul by the Dutch firms of Aviolanda and Fokker of Amsterdam and Schipol. From 1949 to 1968 they served with great success as blind-flying instruction machines, for, in this period, practically all military trainee pilots obtained the blind-flying qualification. They were employed strictly as training and liaison aircraft and no armament was *ever* carried. (*Author's collection, courtesy of Swiss Air Force*)

The ultimate stretching and modification of the T-6 having already been achieved, North American continued to widen its range of alternatives building on its acknowledged solid base for training aircraft. The ultimate wartime result of all their experience was this machine, the X-SN2J-1 experimental Scout/Trainer aircraft developed by North American in 1945 for the US Navy.

It featured a whole host of innovations which wartime training programmes had shown to be desirable. The adoption of the double-bubble canopy improved all-round vision for both pupil and instructor, while a whole range of automatic devices were built-in to the rear cockpit to enable the teacher to simulate all manner of 'emergencies' to be practised for in advanced training modes. As at this stage of the war the desirability of combining functions to effect cost savings was obviously desirable, the defeat of the enemy being clearly only a matter of time and the wartime budgets would obviously be severely cut-back, the same observation qualities were directly applicable to aircraft with a scouting role. However, this type had already been combined with the dive-bomber in the US Navy and there was no longer a requirement for a separate type. (*Courtesy of Rockwell International Archives*)

6 Re-Birth and Re-Generation

In the United States the advance training programme had followed broadly similar lines to those conducted by the British in Canada and Rhodesia and the Australians at home except it was on a larger scale and more lavish. The qualified pilot requirement rose from 30,000 in October 1941 to 50,000 a year later. American Cadets went through four stages, Primary, Basic, Advanced and Transitional. The AT-6 Texans performed the Advanced role at the beginning of the 1940s with the Stearman PT-17 (a biplane and the American equivalent to the British Tiger Moth), along with the Fairchild PT-19 and Ryan PT-22 (both monoplanes) performing the Primary roles, and the Vultee BT-13A carrying out the Basic training function. The British Commonwealth Air Training Plan training system left out the Basic stage completely and moved the '65-hour Student' straight on to the Harvard from Tiger Moths or Fleet Finch Primary trainers. The Americans later adopted this approach. From 1943 onwards the influx of powerful modern fighter aircraft like the Chance Vought Corsair and Republic Thunderbolt hitched requirements and expectations up a notch and the students moved straight on to the AT-6, which took over the Basic training role for a more realistic scenario.

British and Canadian pupils were trained in the Harvard, but the only real difference in the machines were that the modern American style pistol-grip control moulded to the hand and fingers, was replaced by the old-style RAF style circular stick-grip, which again reflected the different fighter controls of the respective nations. The Harvard also had a circular compass of imposing size and weight let into the cockpit floor instead of the neater console-mounted AT-6 version. By 1943-44 the influx of hopeful pilots far exceeded the requirement or needs of the Allies, who had an abundance of trained and skilled pilots to spare, but were desperately short of foot soldiers on the ground. Subsequently there were wholesale cutbacks in entries in both nations and many cadets had their flying careers abruptly terminated before they ever began. This policy was naturally paralleled in the requirement and needs of the training aircraft themselves, and many AT-6/SNJ/Harvard orders were cancelled. Many others in the USAAF, RAF, RCAF and others air arms were assigned to combat squadrons as 'Hacks' and spent their whole lives a personal taxi and stores shifters for senior personnel. Canadian-built Harvards and Australian-built Wirraways alike saw service in the USAAF and a hopeless mix of types, marks and serials resulted. At the time it seemed unimportant, only in retrospect does the tracking down of individual aircraft histories seem essential to the enthusiast.

The ending of World War II saw the disposal of hundreds of AT-6s, Harvards and the like at knock-down prices. As in most such cases disarmament was rapidly carried out by war-weary governments, too hastily carried out as events were to prove only too quickly. There were bargains aplenty with such a short-sighted policy, often perfectly airworthy aircraft being sold for under five hundred dollars. Both foreign governments and civilian aviators benefitted from this, but within a few years the realities of the Cold War saw a reversal of thought and the T-6 (as it was re-designated by the USAF in 1947) was to undergo a startling change of fortune.

The disposal programmes and immediate post-war career of the Texans is similar for most of the larger nations therefore. Let us examine them alphabetically merely for convenience sake.

Very few Wirraways survived for preservation, those that have are featured in these pages. The fate of the Boomerang was to be similar. Production ceased with A46-105 in June 1943. Boomerangs had served with No.2 OTU at Port Pirie, SA and Mildura, Victoria from 10 October 1942 onwards, but their careers were relatively brief. No. 84 Squadron had ceased to use the Boomerang as early as 15 October 1943, No. 8 Communications Unit flew its last Boomerang sortie on 5 August 1944 and next to give up the machine was No. 85 Squadron until 27 January 1945. The remaining operational units were not far behind, with Nos 4, 5 and No. 83 Squadrons all ceasing to fly Boomerangs from 15 August 1945.

One Boomerang survived, the Mark I A46-30. This aircraft was the thirtieth production aircraft built and was completed in February 1943. It had its initial forty-five-minute flight from Fisherman's Bend on 2 February and then was flown to No 1 Aircraft Depot at Laverton where it was handed over to the RAAF three days later. After the usual checks the Boomerang was sent to No 2 OTU at Mildura and then to No. 83 Squadron at Strathpine, Queensland on 20 April. During the mythical 'Japanese Task Force' scare A46-30 was one of the many aircraft hastily flown to reinforce No. 85 Squadron at Guildforth, Perth, on 6 May.

Routine patrol, convoy escort and fighter training missions followed and after a rough landing had resulted in a wing replacement the aircraft underwent repairs and maintenance before rejoining No 85 Squadron on Christmas Eve 1943. Another accident occurred on 5 July 1944 involving replacement of the port wing. Further brief service with No. 85 Squadron was followed by storage at No 4 Aircraft Depot, Kalgoolie, WA from 11 December 1944 until 21 March 1945. A46-30 then joined No. 83 Squadron at Menagle, Sydney, NSW for home defence duties.

An interesting interlude followed when it was disguised as a Lockheed Altair aircraft for a film about Charles Kingsford-Smith which was being shot. Its regular pilot Warrant Officer Brian Thompson flew it for several sequences. Thus it survived when all of No 83 squadron's other Boomerangs went to the scrapyards at Tocumwal on 24 September 1945. A46-30 on the other hand went to Richmond for ten months before being handed over by the Australian Government to the Australian Air League at the Cabramatta Company's base near Sydney on 29 August 1946.

For the next two decades it rotted away at Blacktown NSW and was vandalised. Not until 1964 did Richard Hourigan persuade Wing Commander Keith Isaacs at Williamstown to obtain the aircraft back from the Air League to save it from a final demise. This was done and restoration was commenced at Williamstown where it was placed on display two years later. In April 1977, forty-three years after it had left Fisherman's Bend A46-30 returned there and CAC under project officer Ian Royle, who faithfully restored it and it also is a static display at the Australian War Memorial.

The crop-spraying derivative, the Ceres, met similar indifference, although just as unique an aircraft. The full list of Ceres aircraft and their original owners is given here for historical records as follows:

CA28-1*	VH-CEA (VH-CEX)	Proctor's Rural Services
-2	-CEB	Airfarm Associates
-3	-CEC	Airfarm Associates
-4	-CED (ZK-BPU)	Aerial Farming, NZ
-5	-CEF (VH-SSZ)	Coondair Tintinara SA
-6	-CEG	Airfarm Associates
-7	-CEH (ZK-BXW)	Aerial Farming NZ
-8**	-CEI (ZK-BXY)	Aerial Farming NZ
-9	-CEL (ZK-BZO)	Cooksons Airspread NZ
-10	-CEK (VH-SSY)	Airfarm Associates
-11	-CEM (ZK-BVS)	Wanganui Aerowork
-12	-CEN (ZK-BVS)	Aerial Farming NZ
-13	-CEO (VH-SSF)	Marshall Spreading Service
-14	-CEP (VH-DAT)	Doggett Aviation WA
-15	-CEQ (VH-WAX)	Airland Improvements

-16	-CER	Marshall Spreading Service
-17	-CET (VH-WHY)	Airland Improvements
-18	-CEX (VH-SSV)	Airfarm Associates
-19	-CEU (VH-WOT)	Airland Improvements
-20	-CEV	New England Aerial Top Dressing
-21	-CEW	Airfarm Associates

* This aircraft rebuilt and became CA28-18
** This aircraft was written off in a crash.

Back in the military field with the T-6G, the revitalisation of the Texan through the NATO policy of the late 1940s brought a new generation of pilots into contact with this aircraft.

Although not directly a part of this revitalised NATO policy North American themselves took advantage of the situation to upgrade the Texan themselves. They saw the need for a cheap and reliable aircraft, moderately armed for ground support and anti-guerrilla warfare operations which could be a cheap form of air support for poorer nations in the troubled post-war world of nationalistic and communist-inspired rebellion.

Accordingly, a solitary FT-6G was built as a Counter-Insurgency (COIN) prototype to test the market. Underwing pods carrying .30 calibre machine-guns were fitted, along with ground-strafing potential with racks for up to 400lb of bombs, rockets and napalm containers being fitted. This idea never took-off, but the concept was basically a sound one and similar adaptations were later made by a variety of air forces around the world, as we shall examine later.

The T-28-C showing the three-bladed propeller, the tricycle under-carriage, bubble canopy and marked dihedral of the wings, strengthened and extended tail fairing which showed the way for the final generation of post-war prop trainers and the final transition between prop and jet training requirements of the late 1940s and early 1950s. Although a very different machine to the old T-6 the ancestry can clearly still be traced. (*Courtesy of Rockwell International Archives*)

The reconstructed Royal Netherlands Air Force received 150 Harvard Mark IIBs from former RAF stocks plus fifty more from the RCAF between August 1946 and November 1948. In this photo a batch of these can be seen undergoing stringent overhauls at the factory of Aviolanda/Fokker before entering Dutch service. In addition another twenty former RAF Harvards were purchased from training school surplus stock in South Africa and shipped via the UK in February 1947 for use as spares. They were used as advanced trainers and later some were utilised for communications aircraft. The final Harvards were withdrawn from service in 1968. (*Courtesy Arthur Pearcy Archives*)

A beautiful in-flight view of a United States Air Force T-6G (TA-143 – 93143).

The wholesale post-war disposal and scrapping programme embarked upon with such enthusiasm in 1945 came to a halt with the establishment of NATO in the face of the Soviet take-over of Eastern Europe and its massive threat to the rest of that continent. A crash programme was therefore started to refurbish and modernise 2,068 of the T-6Cs and T-6Ds that remained on the new United States Air Force's inventory.

This programme resulted in the T-6G variant. The type was given a North American NA designation as the NA-168, although, in reality these were not new production models at all. For the Air Force all the airframes finally taken in hand for modernisation under this scheme, were re-built by the parent company. Full-scale modernidation took place at four plants, each factory having its own identifying code letter added to the serials, North American's Downey (NI) and Fresno (NF), the Douglas plant at Long Beach (NA), all in California, and the former Curtiss plant at Columbus, Ohio (NH), although for a short time these were designated as T-6Hs.

The outward and visible changes were relatively slight. Mid-bracing was removed from the cockpit canopies and replaced by larger clear-panels for much improved visibility. All provision for machine-gun armament was removed. The 550 hp Pratt & Whitney engine still remained as the -G's power plant and the modest streamlining did not push up the speed above 205 mph. (*Courtesy of Rockwell International Archives*)

Under the same programme the US funded the successor of Noorduyn, the Canadian Car and Foundry Company, to refurbish some 285 Harvard Mk.IVs to a similar standard under the Mutual Defense Assistance Program (MDAP). Once completed most, although not all, of these T-6Js, were assigned to help rebuild the NATO air forces of Belgium, France, Italy and West Germany. From 1951 onward also, the Canadians also engaged on a fresh construction programme on their own account, utilizing available material, engines and parts on hand. Some forty of these machines, designated as the Harvard IV, were completed at the Fort William, Quebec, plant of CCF. The modifications followed almost exactly the -G programme across the border. They were followed by a further 515 of the same specification, built from scratch. Again, under MDAP American funds purchased no less than 285 of these and supplied them to European air forces as the T-6J.

This beautiful air-to-air photograph of Royal Canadian Air Force trainers from Goderich was taken in 1955 over Lake Huron. Note the leader's bands on the nearest aircraft's tailfin and rudder. (*Canadian Forces Photographic Unit, Ottawa*)

Between 1948 and 1953 the Royal Australian Navy (RAN) also acquired and used sixteen Wirraways (for which the designation CA-20 is said to have originated) for both pilot and ground crew training at HMS *Albatross*, the Naval shore base located at Nowara, New South Wales. Of these A20-28 served with No. 723 Squadron; A20-133 and -139 with Nos. 723 and 816 Squadrons; A20-141 with No. 805 Squadron, A20-145 with No 723 Squadron and was written-off after an accident on 18 June 1953, A20-168 with Nos. 723 and 724 Squadrons, A20-176 with No. 723 Squadron, A20-209, -211, -214, -225, -237, -250 and -469 with Nos. 723 and 724 Squadrons, and A20-490 and -752 with Nos. 723 and 724 Squadrons.

None of the RAN Wirraways were ever utilised for deck landing training, although tail codes were allocated, NW for Nowara, K the aircraft-carrier HMAS *Sydney* and Y, then M, the aircraft-carrier HMAS *Melbourne*. All the RAN Fleet Air Arm Wirraways were finally sold off at disposal to Lund Aviation Inc., of New York, USA during 1957. None has ever re-appeared on the US Civil Register so it is assumed that these aircraft were purchased merely for the engine and propellers and were scrapped *in situ*.

This is A20-168 (972) of the Royal Australian Navy parked outside 'J' hangar (near the stop butts) at RAN Air Station Nowara in 1950. (*Official Royal Australian Navy Photograph*)

A final commercial spin-off from the Wirraway led to a continuation of the type in civilian hands despite the Government restrictions. This was the CA-28 Ceres Agricultural aircraft. It should be emphasised right from the start that the Ceres was *in no way* a modified Wirraway. Some Wirraway components fully inspected and in perfect condition were modified and incorporated into the Ceres but in all other respects it was a new design, built specially for agricultural work. Nonetheless the linage with North American's original product is there, however distant and tenuous.

Two prototypes were built and tested before production was commenced. The performance of the prototype Ceres A gave a maximum speed of 140 knots, a cruise speed of ninety knots and a landing speed of forty-seven knots. There was little change in performance of the production Ceres although the gross weight was increased to 7,410 lb. The standard Ceres Model B was fitted with the Wasp-geared engine and a DH Hamilton propeller, while Model C had the same engine type but with a 'high solidity' propeller. On aircraft number six and subsequent aircraft, the cockpit enclosure was extended aft to enclose a rear passenger compartment. The extended enclosure had clear acrylic panels each side and faired at the aft end with a hinged aluminium alloy door which swung sideways for access. The Ceres gained DCA approval for pilot and two passengers.

For the new post-war generation of US Navy pilots training continued from Pensascola, with the big carrier *Wasp II* (CV.18) acting as training deck for a period and giving a broader expanse of deck for the cadets to practise alighting upon than the old *Charger*, with her stubby, confined flight-deck, had offered their fathers. Even the big brand-new 'Midway' class carriers were hosts to SNJs from time-to-time, and their decks were broad enough for aircraft to land side-by-side.

The date is 14 September 1953 and a double-landing involving an F4U and a SNJ takes place aboard the United States Navy aircraft-carrier *Franklin D Roosevelt* (CVA 42). The SNJ (878) has taken the arrester wire succesfully on the right-hand side of the flight deck as the Chance Vought Corsair (308) with arrester hook extended, thumps down on the teak a few seconds later to the left.

The final flight of the SNJ-7 took place from Barrin Field, Alabama, on 14 March 1958. Apart from Air National Guard units, one official user in the States continued to fly Texans for a few more years yet and that was 35 Air Rescue Squadron, part of the US Civil Air Patrol. This unit was Uncle Sam's last contact with North American's finest product. (*US Navy photo, Courtesy National Archives, Washington, DC*)

The wholesale disposal and scrapping programme embarked upon with such enthusiasm in 1945 came to a halt with the establishment of NATO in the face of the Soviet take-over of Eastern Europe and its massive threat to the rest of that continent. All of a sudden it was not a safe world after all and one demise of one awful dictator had resulted merely in his being supplanted by an even more dreadful one. Early in 1950 stock was taken of the run-down arsenals of the west and among the many deficits were adequate training aircraft to fuel the new aerial expansion of the USA and her NATO allies. A crash programme was therefore started to refurbish and modernise 2,068 of the T-6C and T-6Ds that remained on the new United States Air Force's inventory, along with fifty Navy SNJs, to fill the gap until new types could take the strain. (Incidentally, due to shortages of available stock, it also meant in some cases the re-purchase of recently disposed-of airframes at vastly inflated prices, such has always been the military way!)

The outward and visible changes brought about by the refurbished American T-6Hs were relatively slight. Mid-bracing was removed from the cockpit canopies and replaced by larger clear-panels for much improved visibility. All provision for machine-gun armament was removed. The 550 hp Pratt & Whitney engine still remained as the -G's powerplant and the modest streamlining did not push up the speed above 205 mph.

In Canada the story was somewhat different. The Canadian Car and Foundry company built no less than 555 Harvard IVs brand-new from 1951 onwards. Apart from the elongated exhausts on the right-hand side and cockpit canopy strutting and appearance, the only difference between them and the American T-6H modifications was the much less prominent ADF antenna abaft the instructor.

Here an immaculate formation of the new Harvard IVs belonging to the Royal Canadian Air Force are seen on one of the last 'official' training flights by these machines. (*Canadian Forces Photographic Unit, Ottawa*)

(above)

A CA-28 Ceres Agricultural aircraft comes in to land. The Australian farmers and graziers were among the earliest to promote crop spraying from the air. In terms of ease of use and cost they were soon convinced this was the way to go. It must be remembered that the adverse environmental aspects were not to the forefront of people's thoughts in the late 1940s and 1950s as they are today. By 1959, well over two million acres were being treated with super-phosphate, seed, insecticides, herbicides and other materials from the air.

With such a startling growth in the industry the need for an Australian designed aircraft became obvious. The CAC investigated all aspects of this problem placing the emphasis on first cost, safety and economical operation. The result was the Ceres concept. By good design and the utilization of some components of the Wirraway Trainer, the Ceres could be produced for a selling price of 14,000 Australian pounds.

The wing area was 312 square feet, the fixed slats on the outer half of the wings and large slotted flaps resulted in excellent flying characteristics right down to the stall (at fifty knots) which was entirely without vice. The wing loading in the normally fully loaded condition of 6,900 lb was 22.1 lb per square foot. The Pratt & Whitney engine was fitted with a three-bladed Hamilton propeller. The Ceres was sold in both Australia and New Zealand, and twenty-one machines were registered. (Only twenty were actually built, the extra machine being a re-build after a crash.)

Span was 46ft 11 inches, overall length 30 feet 8½ inches, height 12 feet 5 inches and ground angle 12 degrees 54 minutes. It had a wheel track of 12 feet 6¾ inches and fuel capacity of eighty Imperial gallons. The Ceres had a two hour endurance and a landing ground run of 175 yards. Cruising speed was 110 knots, with a rate of climb of 1,520 feet per minute and a range of 500 nautical miles.

Although only a handful of the Ceres type were built before production ceased, their usage was to have useful repercussions. (*Courtesy Hawker de Havilland, Melbourne*)

And so into the 1990s and the T-6 had undergone yet a third re-birth, this time as one of the most popular flying veteran aircraft of all time with civilian owners and Warbird Associations. This renewed popularity should see the Texan, in all its many guises, gracing our skies (and deadening our eardrums) well into the 21st Century, a fact that 'Dutch' Kindelberger and his small team could hardly have predicted back in 1937!

We have seen how tight were the restrictions placed on the former military Wirraways in Australia and how limited was their subsequent civilian role post-war as a result. By way of strict contrast, in the United States one of the most common outlets for former AT-6 and SNJs was the commercial, rather than the sport

and pleasure, fields. That is not to say that the latter did not predominate, but they tended to be individualistic efforts.

Apart from National Guard duties (which by 1947 had become the Air National Guard or ANG), the popularity of the T-6 in the civilian field extends back to the immediate post-war era. Although the commercial aspect of its use has naturally declined with increasing running costs (with the Pratt & Whitney guzzling up half a gallon of fuel each minute) and shortage of spares, the private use for pleasure and sport has grown steadily ever since.

An excellent aerial study of N5500V, an SNJ belonging to the famous Confederate Air Force collection. (*National Archives, Washington DC, courtesy of Dr Ira Chart*)

The CAC Ceres was an all-metal, low-wing monoplane powered by a 600 hp Pratt & Whitney Wasp R-1340 S3H1-G, nine-cylinder radial air-cooled engine. Agricultural loads of up to 2,327 lb of dust or 250 gallons of spray were carried in a stainless-steel hopper having a capacity of forty cubic feet and which was located over the centre of gravity, which gave negligible change in the aircraft's fore-and-aft trimming. An emergency dump gate jettisoned the entire load in a few seconds. The change to liquid load was made by replacing the dust gate with an assembly carrying the air-driven pump, valve and filter. This unit had a capacity of up to 120 gallons per minute. Discharge was through a spray boom forming the trailing edge of the flap, which gave an effective swathe width of ninety feet.

CAC gave careful consideration to the cockpit and pilot comfort in this little machine. Footsteps and handgrips on either side enabled easy entry and exit, and the all-round vision was particularly good. The flight controls were conventional for the period, trim controls for elevator and rudder were fitted. The flaps were operated by a cranked handle operating a screw jack, but the flaps could be left in an intermediate position during operations, being lowered for landing. In some Ceres aircraft extra seating accommodation was provided for a crew member in a ferry flight, behind the pilot and facing aft.

This particular Ceres (VH-SSF) was owned by Blaney Air-farmers of Bathurst, New South Wales and is pictured landing at the company air strip in March 1979. Note the increased wingspan, raised cockpit, fixed undercarriage and the hopper location. (*Copyright, 1979, N.M. Parnell*)

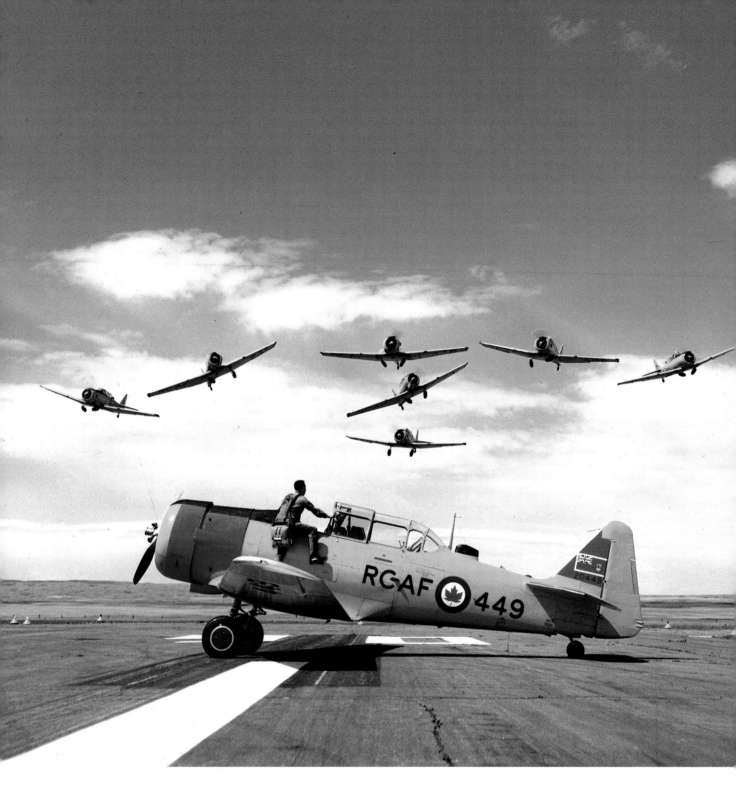

Although not completely docile, the Harvard lent itself to formation team work and was so exploited throughout its long career. The list of Harvard Display Teams in service use is a long one, and nowadays there are several formation teams which employ the good old 'Texan' or its derivatives to put on stunning spectacles all over the world at Meets and Fly-Ins.

This Canadian formation team shows their skills during a practice 'aerial dance' routine in the mid-1960s and shows what could be done with the Harvard in experienced hands. (*Courtesy Canadian Government Official Archives, Ottawa, Canada*)

The equipping of all the NATO air fleets post-war was conducted as part of the Allied policy of combined strength and included in this latter day post-war equivalent of 'Lend-Lease' initiated under the Marshall Plan were of course both refurbished T-6s and Canadian-built Harvard IVs.

A late model Texan, known as the T-6H, (MM54111 – AA-51) of the Italian *Aeronautica Militare* running up her engine at a training base in 1972. (*Author's collection via Official Italian Air Force Archives*)

Seen over the Rockies in 1961, these two Royal Canadian Air Force Harvards show very well the cockpit canopy differences between the Harvard IIIs and IVs although otherwise the machines have been re-furbished to the same standards.

Internally the changes on both these and their American T6-H cousins were more far-reaching and important. On the latter the fuel capacity was increased from 110 gallons to 140 gallons by the fitting of two 15-gallon bladder-type fuel tanks, one being located in each outer wing panel. The rear seat was raised by six inches. The communications equipment was up-graded with the fitting of multi-channel VHF and UHF equipment and an oval rugby-football shaped ADF receiver was fitted abaft the re-located aerial, now fitted behind the cockpit in the Harvard style and out of the pilot's line-of-sight at last. Even when slightly offset to the left this had been a retrograde fitting and it is to be wondered that it lasted as long as it did in the US-built Texans. After-all novice pilots had enough problems without such an unnecessary hindrance

to vision. Landing the AT-6 over that great hump of a cowl was hard enough anyway and involved a kind of crab-wise progression down the runway until fully confident.

The power button system was also brought up to date with its replacement by direct actuation of both landing-gear and the wing flaps. Merely putting the gear handle to 'down' carried out the full landing-gear functions without any further intervention on behalf of the pilot. This meant the elimination of the hydraulic pressure gauge from the instrumentation layout. The later -F type tail-wheel locking/steerable system became standard on the -G. Under this system the tail-wheel was made free-swivelling by the pilot neutralizing the rudder pedals and pushing the control stick forward. This made for a much simpler operation and helped cut down on the Texan's passion for ground-looping. Final confirmation of their 'status' was the adoption of British Harvard-style all-over yellow paint scheme. (*Canadian Forces Photographic Unit, Ottawa*)

A CC & F-built Harvard IV shares the runway (and the limelight) with other veterans at Downsview airfield, Ontario, sometime in 1958.

There never was a Harvard IV in RAF service. The British Government had disarmed more completely, more quickly and more disastrously than had the Americans after 1945 and found themselves in the same mess a few years later. In fact they were in worse trouble, more directly threatened by Soviet expansion but with no cash in the coffers to rectify the situation as was done in Canada and the USA.

Great Britain had already liberally supplied Commonwealth and Allied air forces with batches of its own Harvards of various marks, both during and immediately after the war. The RNZAF took delivery of thirty-eight Mark Is, fifty-three Mark IIs, and forty-one Mark IIIs, while the South Africans were allocated 436 Mark IIs, and 197 Mark IIIs during the war. Immediately after the war fresh consignments were made of almost brand-new, straight from the stores, models to various friendly governments in Western Europe and also to help the newly-emerging independent air forces of the former empire as the latter disintegrated at an accelerating pace between 1947 and 1967. (*Canadian Forces Photographic Unit, Ottawa*)

In South Africa civilian Harvards have been rare until fairly recently, despite the preponderance of military machines still flying. There were some civil registrations many years ago but these civil markings were merely test registrations for Syrian Air Force examples, which were overhauled and refurbished by the Field company at Rand Airport.

In 1989 twelve former Mozambique Air Force Harvards (originally Frelimo, French and Luftwaffe aircraft) were at Syferfontein airfield awaiting sale 'as seen' on the civilian market. (*Courtesy L.S. Vosloo*)

Another South African Harvard, this machine (7569) belonged to the Central Flying School and was based at Dunnottar, some 1,000 miles from the Cape in the Transvaal. It is pictured here at Ysterplaat Air Force Base, Cape Town, in May 1989. It features an all-metal fuselage. and ailerons etc with yellow outer wings. This machine was repainted in 1987 in the World War II Joint Air Training Scheme colours and today is frequently seen, as a regular CFS aircraft, taking part in air displays around South Africa.

Already having the largest Harvard fleet in the world, the SAAF will probably be still flying them in 2000 AD.

The first civilian Harvards for many years were seen in South Africa in 1989, there were civil machines many years ago but these were merely civilian test registrations for some Syrian Air force examples being overhauled and renovated by the airwork firm of Fields at Rand Airport. Others were the twelve ex-Mozambique Air Force Harvard Mk IVMs (originally FAP and Luftwaffe machines) which ended up at Syferfontein airfield awaiting rebuilding for the civilian market.

Among the preserved machines is 7729, a Mark III Harvard, which was for a long while at Fort Klapperkop Military Museum, but which has more recently been transferred to the South African Airways Apprentice School. (*Courtesy L.J. Vosloo, Fish Hoek*)

To just what lengths a real enthusiast will go to build and fly their own T-6 is illustrated by the 1972 Grand Champion Warbird, an immaculate aluminium T-6 (N3682F), *How Sweet It Is* illustrated here on her maiden flight, which was built from scratch using new surplus parts from all over the USA by Dr Gerald A. Swayze of Mesquite, Texas. He later told the story of how it all came about.

'I looked at quite a few T-6s, but most left a lot to be desired. It was impossible to find one that didn't have zinc chromate peeling off on all the interior surfaces. Very few of them are clean and dent-free enough to look good with a polished aluminium exterior. Besides, I had always wanted a new T-6 and for that I had been born too late.

In 1968 at a C.A.F. Airshow, I saw a beautiful Bearcat, N-9G, the magnificent bird of Gunther Balz. This airplane gave me the inspiration I needed to begin the project that had been teasing my brain. Why not build a new T-6 with new surplus parts? So the decision was made and N3628F with a run out engine was bought. In order to put together a new T-6, I would have to first tear an old one apart to see how to do it. Besides, some parts might be available and old ones, especially non-moving castings, could be made new.

Parts were secured from all over the country. The main suppliers were Don Wise and Southwest Aero Sales. A new left wing was unavailable so a used one was completely remanufactured at a cost of over 3,000 US dollars. I bought a new rear fuselage section, but decided to put a new skin on it because of numerous scratches from years of storage. I found five brand-new right wings in Dallas still in factory crates. Three of these wings were coated with cosoline and in mint condition. I still have two right-hand wings and don't know what to do with them.

(Courtesy Dr G.A. 'Doc' Swayze)

The South African Air Force has for a long time now retained the largest numbers of Harvards on its books of any air force in a variety of roles and seems likely to continue to operate this hardy veteran for some time yet! Parts and spares are not too difficult to come by and machines of various marks continue to be airborne on into the 1990s, a remarkable testimony to both the soundness of the original design and the versatility and resiliance of the type.

This photograph shows 7082 and 7406 on the ground at Swellendam airfields, in southern Cape Province, east of Cape Town, in September 1976. Both machines at that time belonged to No. 7 Squadron SAAF. (*Courtesy L.J. Vosloo, Fish Hoek*)

The burnished prop and yellow cowling of 'Doc' Swayze's first baby. He continues the story of how he assembled the necessary equipment after a nationwide hunt.

'A new wing center section was found and new gas tanks were installed. All of the parts in the center section are new including the landing-gear, wheels and brakes.

New engines were not to be found and I wanted a custom-built one anyway. How I ever got lucky enough to find Mr Faxel and Mr Cleveland of Fort Worth Engine Overhaul, I don't know. They did a magnificent job with the R-1340 An-1. It is the smoothest, most economical 1340 with respect to both fuel and oil consumption, that I have ever sat behind.

Initially, I thought it would take about three years to complete the project if I worked on it almost every day and that's hard to do when you are married and are a practising family doctor. It would have taken six years had I not had the constant help of Mr Redell Gross, who was also my pit man and crew chief from T-6 racing days.'

(*Courtesy Dr G.A. 'Doc' Swayze*)

122

The cockpit controls of 'How Sweet It Is'. If building the airframe and assembling the T-6 was difficult enough, getting it all wired up and passed fit to take to the air was a nightmare. Many would have given up at that stage, but 'Doc' stuck to it as he recalled later.

'The real monster in this project was the electrical system. I was determined to do it myself. To do so required that I learn soldering and the reading of electrical diagrams. It took four months and when later assembled all the goodies worked with the proper switch – that was a surprise. I really thought it would burn.

On May 14, 1972, I climbed into the cockpit for the test flight after Mr Bob Card made a thorough inspection of everything. I'll have to admit that after rigging the aileron boost tabs, it flies as pretty as it looks.'

Since then 'Doc' has gone from strength to strength and has re-built a further six AT-6s, three of which were remanufactured from primarily new surplus parts.

'I did not build these aircraft by myself, nor could have done so without the help of my loyal volunteer crew. They include Mr Redell Gross, Mr Tom Ryan, Mr Frank Goodloe, Mr Jim Walters and more recently Mr Dave Groark, who, by the way, flew 107 missions over North Vietnam. His SNJ-5 was the last aircraft we built, it is a sister ship to my latest one which is 5486V. It has the same paint scheme, which is Pre-World War II Navy from the Carrier *Saratoga*. Previously we had won 'Grand Champion Warbird Award' twice in 1972 and 1973.

(*Courtesy Dr G.A. 'Doc' Swayze*)

The home-built North American of 'Doc' Swayze shows her classic lines. To get her in this pristine flying condition took a great deal of hard work, improvisation and scheming as he relates.

'Much of the work was done at home. The garage was scattered with parts. The study, upstairs, served as a storage area for completed parts and sub-assemblies. The cabinet in the den was full of completed small parts. Most of the time there were T-6 parts on the bar in the breakfast area.

My wife was then a school teacher of first and second graders, and she was used to seeing toys peppered all over and in general she was quite tolerant of it all. Once, however, while doing the electrical system (wires were all over the kitchen amidst dripping little balls of solder), I saw her standing, hands on hips, tight-lipped with her right foot tapping the floor. She got over it after I retreated with my wires. I was finished anyway!'

(*Courtesy Dr G.A. 'Doc' Swayze*)

7 At War

And so the revitalised T-6G/SNJ-7 soldiered on into the 1950s and beyond in fresh guises as a training aircraft. The -Gs gave excellent value for money before they were finally phased out of the USAF and USN inventories. In the 1950s the Texans assumed the fresh duty for those who were part of the Training Command and became Primary Trainers (PTs). In this configuration rather than being the daunting third step on the road to being a pilot, as during the 1940s, the Texan was now thought docile enough to be the very first aircraft the novice took into the sky! After twenty hours (as against the WW II period of twelve to eighteen) of dual-control, aspiring aces went solo on the T-6. From there they graduated to the Lockheed T-33 jet trainer which began entering service in 1947. It was not until 1956 that the Air Force finally got rid of the sturdy Texan, which was 'officially' retired from duty at Bartow Air Force Base, Florida on 17 September of that year.

For the US Navy the story was much the same. The training continued from Pensacola, with the big carrier *Wasp II* (CV.18) acting as training deck for a period and offering a broader expanse of teak for the cadets to thump down on than the old *Charger*, with her stubby, confined flight-deck, had offered their fathers. The final flight of the SNJ-7 took place from Barrin Field, Alabama, on 14 March 1958. Apart from National Guard units one official user in the States continued to fly Texans for a few more years yet and that was 35 Air Rescue Squadron, part of the US Civil Air Patrol. This unit was Uncle Sam's last contact with North American's finest product. With the RAF also, in addition to such diverse duties as photo-reconnaissance, target-tugs, glider-tugs, instrument training, flying weather monitors, map-makers and the like, Harvards continued to be used as station hacks.

But before it finally departed from the USA and British military air scenes the incredible T-6 trainer was destined to carve further significant niches in combat history. In fact, the Texan and Harvards world-wide combat operations in the post-World War II period, if anything, *exceeded* their combat usage during that conflict. Also, following the lead set by the FT-6G, several nations produced their own versions of the Texan in a COIN role. Others made more primitive conversions to suit the immediate needs of the moment.

During the Korean War, when at first North Korea and then Communist Chinese Army divisions invaded South Korea and were resisted by United Nations' troops, the only modern aircraft that the victim nation had to defend itself with were two T-6Ds. The ROK Navy later modified a crashed T-6F by fitting the repaired wreck with floats from a former Japanese Nakajima A6M2-N ('Rufe') fighter seaplane and wingtip tanks from a F-80 Shooting Star jet. It entered service in 1951 as the one and only KN-1.

The ROK T-6s were utilised in strictly a training role and had no armaments. They continued to serve in this capacity and although the ROK Air Force was to be built up in the ensuring years it was in fact the USAF, USN and US Marine Corps, with help from the British Flect Air Arm Sea Fury fighter-bombers, who provided the bulk of the close-range air support for the troops on the ground with aircraft like the Mustang and Corsair. All the old lessons of such direct support, which had been so painfully learnt by trial-and-error during World War II, had to be virtually re-learnt from scratch and a fierce debate ensued over the accuracy and reliability of such air support. This was especially so when the new jet-powered F-80C Shooting Stars and F-84 fighter-bombers began to be extensively employed. Because of their speed, and also the lack of suitable training of the pilots, it was claimed by ground forces that they were at best inefficient, at worst downright dangerous to their own side.

The ground control and direction methods of World War II were re-introduced in the US 5th Air Force at this time but, following the example set by the Australian Wirraways in the last three years of the Pacific War, slower propeller-driven aircraft were employed as aerial Tactical Air Controllers or Target Spotters.

A special unit was set up, 6132 Tactical Air Control Group. General Earl Partridge is credited with adopting the old Australian ploy once more and it was put into effect on 10 July 1956 with three Stinson L-5G aircraft and seven officers based at Taejon air strip, which was described as, 'a loose gravel runway about the width of a country road and not much else'. It recognised early on, that the conventional observation and spotter/liaison aircraft, like the L-5 and the L-9, lacked both speed, ruggedness and efficiency in such a role. For this mission the reliable old Texan entered the conflict in new guise, as the LT-6G.

The first Texan to enter the fray was a re-built T-6C, a former hack of 35 Fighter Interceptor Group based in Japan. It had not flown for more than a year but was quickly given priority for refurbishment. The T-6 was kitted out with an AN/ARC-3 radio set capable of communication with both the ground controllers in the front line and the incoming fighter-bombers. This pioneer TAC reached Taejon on 10 July 1956 and was in action immediately, crewed by First Lieutenant James A. Bryant and First Lieutenant Frank Mitchell. Reserve was First Lieutenant Harold A. Morris. They quickly proved their value by locating a North Korean armoured column containing forty-two heavy tanks at Chochiown. Bryant signalled this news and the precise location to a formation of F-80Cs who arrived soon after to deliver a devastating rocket and strafing attack which knocked out seventeen of the enemy tanks. It was a stunning debut and the scouring of back-area bases for redundant T-6s began in earnest.

The T-6 pilots' duty was to patrol along the front-line and to report on enemy troop dispositions, movements and activity. A heavy responsibility lay with these flyers. The Air Force, Navy and Marine jets were only able to remain over the target for a matter of seconds due to the long ranges at which they operated and their short endurance. Moreover the heavy concentrations of light flak guns that the Communists assembled over vital objectives like bridges and artillery concentrations, made any lingering overhead a very risky and dangerous occupation. There was also the ever-present possibility of being 'jumped' by Yak-9 prop-driven fighters and later MiG-15 jets and it was not always possible to have a friendly North American Sabre on hand for protection. One 'Mosquito' pilot, Lieutenant Dick Meade, when he was 'jumped' by a Yak, fired his rockets at it in desperation, missing by yards but scaring the enemy fighter away.

Despite these hazards the lone Mosquito pilot had to accurately observe and mark the target for the fighter-bombers to strafe and bomb. They did this by precisely marking the enemy positions with 2½-inch smoke rockets and flares. These units gradually developed their skills and flew an enormous number of combat missions. On 15 July 5 Air Force HQ assigned a call sign to the FAC patrols that were stinging the enemy so badly, 'MOSQUITO'. The raucous noise of the T-6's Pratt & Whitney had only been slightly subdued by the fitting of a square-tipped propeller and was still a distinctive sound. The noise and the call-sign together made it inevitable that the FACs soon adopted the name by which they became famous, being dubbed the 'Mosquitoes'.

Although established and working, the 6132 had no 'official' status as a flying unit and found itself everybody's friend but nobody's baby. They received ample and heartfelt praise and congratulations but few supplies, little equipment, food, storage, fuel or support and had to scrounge aircraft and weapons as and how they could. They had grown to twenty-five personnel with twelve aircraft in varying states of readiness. Never has had the description 'ad hoc' formation been more suitably employed to describe a fighting unit operating in the fog of war!

The initial Communist onrush almost succeeded and the South Korean and UN forces were hemmed into the Pusan pocket, from where the 'Mosquitoes' operated as best they could from Taegu airstrip. Some three weeks after their first operational sortie the unit finally became a genuine USAF outfit when it was re-established as the 6147 Tactical Control Squadron (Airborne) on 29 July 1950. The commander of the new unit was Major Merrill H. Carlton. (He was to be relieved on 28 March 1951 by Colonel Timothy F. O'Keefe.) By the time they had become 'official' they had already flown 269 sorties in a three-week period.

For the next two months they continued to operate from Taegu. On some missions which required extremely close support the Mosquitoes used 1:50,000 maps to pinpoint targets within one hundred yards of friendly forces. In one such mission, against enemy troops holding the walled-city of Kasan, seven miles north of Taegu, and two adjacent ridges, a Mosquito directed a flight of B-26s over the target in a night mission in which the LT-6G pilot used his landing lights to expose the enemy target.

The position became fluid again for, with the breakout from Pusan by 5 Army, their bases became mobile once more. As the UN forces drove the North Koreans back behind their own borders and beyond in November, the Mosquitoes shifted base firstly to Seoul City airfield, South Korea, and then to Pyongyang East in North Korea, which they reached on 27 October in bitterly cold weather. In the period from 9 July to 25 November intensive operations were conducted and 4,902 combat missions were flown. By the end of August out of fifty-five pilots on the TAC(A) roster, seventeen had already completed a normal fifty mission tour of duty. The 6147 TCS(A) was credited with helping in the destruction of 436 enemy tanks, 598 artillery pieces and field guns, 2,332 soft-skinned motor transports, eight railway engines, twenty-seven ammunition dumps, ninety-eight fuel dumps and 228 supply dumps.

In one incident there had been a particularly heavy UN artillery barrage directed by the Mosquitoes onto a target near the Hwachon reservoir. The LT-6G overflew the target afterwards in the normal manner to assess results in preparation to directing the fighter-bombers onto any survivors. But by this time even the Chinese soldiers had got the message of what followed a Mosquito run! Enemy troops were observed clambering out of their trenches and foxholes and waving white sheets and clasping their hands on their heads in mute appeals of surrender. The Mosquito pilot quickly appraised the situation and, rather than waste good napalm on an already defeated enemy, directed the F-80 strike at fresh targets while the Chinese tramped over no-man's land to surrender in scores to the British troops opposite.

The intervention of massive Communist Chinese Army formations overwhelmed the extended UN forces by sheer weight of numbers and drove them back towards the 38th Parallel once more. The American President sacked General Douglas MacArthur when he requested Chinese targets be bombed to stem the flood and the retreat became a rout. The Mosquitoes once more had to pull back, again to Seoul and then south again to Chunchon airfield. Here they established themselves a main base for the first time in the war and were further expanded.

The Mosquito unit now became the 6147 Tactical Control Group which contained two Airborne squadrons, 6148 TCS (Western Sector) under Colonel Watson, and 6149 TCS (Eastern Sector) equipped with the modified T-6s, and one administrative, mechanical support and forward air control teams, as a general Ground squadron, 6150 TCS. The hastily-adapted AT-6Ds and AT-6Fs were gradually replaced with more sophisticated versions, especially modified for the work in hand. These were the LT-6Gs of which ninety-seven were eventually built. Their main difference over the basic T-6G was the additional radio communications equipment packed into the cockpit. They carried three basic sets, AN/ARC-3, AN/ARN-6 and SCR-522A. For target marking they were fitted with no less than six underwing racks capable of carrying three rocket launchers for either six 5-inch or eighteen 2½-inch white phosphorous smoke rockets each, while pods were slung under each wing fitted with two .30 calibre machine-guns for strafing opportunities. (These were later dropped to give a few knots extra speed over heavy flak concentrations.) Red identification stripes were marked diagonally across their wings for identification by friendly aircraft.

Against the now static front line, which settled down to a fair resemblance of the Western Front during World War I, the Mosquito units perfected their low-level reconnaissance patrol, identification and support techniques. Many pilots now commenced, and completed, a second tour of duty. The LT-6Gs sat in sandbagged revetments with engines running permanently on call. On one memorable day, 14 December 1950, no less than twenty-five machines were airborne on station at one time waiting for the fighter-bombers. The three-man ground teams (Tactical Air Control Parties) were equipped with jeeps and radio communications equipment. Each team comprised an officer, the Mosquito pilots rotated on this duty to gain experience, a radio man and a driver/mechanic. These teams spread out across the peninsular and kept in immediate contact with the Army's infantry and artillery HQs. They worked with the British, South Korean and other Allied troops as well as US land forces.

They were able to liaise directly with both ground troops and patrolling fighter-bombers and call in strikes independently themselves if the need arose. More often than not they called in the airborne Mosquitoes, one of which was kept over each half of the front line all the time, for aerial target identification and marking prior to the strikes, and aerial confirmation on the effectiveness of the attacks after the bombing and rocketing. The LT-6Gs duties also included artillery spotting, casualty evacuation, aerial photography, deep penetration, night direction of B-26s, directing naval bombardments, supply missions, long-range reconnaissance to study enemy build-ups behind the lines and limited interceptor roles against enemy observation aircraft, like the Soviet-supplied PO-2 night harassment biplanes. During lulls in operations some were fitted with DDT tanks and spray nozzles and used for fighting their namesakes which were a menace to local farmers and supplies during the summer months. Their work was honoured at the highest level on 4 February 1951 when the unit was presented with the Distinguished Unit Citation at Taegu West Airfield. A radio broadcast by the famous journalist Edward R. Murrow over the CBS network on 6 February, brought to the people back home news of what the LT-6Gs were doing in the almost forgotten war.

By the time the war petered out with the July 1953 cease-fire (it has never officially ended to this day) the Mosquitoes had lost forty-two of their aircraft to accident and ground fire, and thirty-three of their crew had been killed in action. The enemy concentrated their anti-aircraft fire power over the front, with the 20mm and 40mm pieces barraging at 3,000 feet and over while small-arms fire coned up to 1,200 feet. The Mosquitoes tried to operate in the narrow band in between those two parameters, but in reality there was nowhere to hide and it was rare for a mission to be completed without some ground-fire damage.

But the LT-6Gs conducted no less than 40,354 combat sorties and had helped with the destruction of enough tanks to equip five Communist armoured divisions as well as 563 guns and more than 5,000 soft-skinned untracked supply vehicles. It was an enviable record of dedication and service and one that crowned an already illustrious career.

The T-6 consistently broke aviation records in the States. With regard to its reliability, students at Craig Field, Alabama, a USAAF training unit, flew T-6s for 23 million miles without one single accident attributable to mechanical failure. At the other end of the scale another Craig Field T-6 showed what these aircraft had to endure in the course of routine training operations. This machine flew 2,000 hours during which time it was involved in eleven accidents, required seven new wings, five new landing-gear struts and six new propellers. During one intensive period the aircraft was in the air twenty-two hours a day. At Napier Field in the same state in October 1944, a Texan established the record for continuous service by completing 5,000 hours of flying time. This aircraft averaged three hours forty-five minutes flying time per day, or around 111½ hours per month and flew approximately 750,000 miles, (approximately thirty circumnavigations of the globe). Seven engine replacements were required in achieving this feat.

For adaptability the T-6 had few equals as we have seen. One duty it undertook was as a flying storm spotter with the US All-Weather Flying Center, known as 'The Hurricane Hunters'. A few Texans were reported fitted with skis for service in the Arctic and assisted in the rescue of crashed aircraft in Alaska, Greenland and Iceland. There was the instance of the floatplane version at Kwangji, Korea already mentioned. The machine successfully flew in August 1951 but was written off in a crash in November of the same year.

The SNJ trained some 40,000 Navy pilots during the war and the most decorated US Navy flyer of World War II, Lieutenant E. C. Dickinson, called the SNJ 'the best scout trainer in the world'. That sentiment was echoed and re-echoed by military pilots around the globe.

With the -G refurbishment programme begun on 5 October 1949, the USAF took 641 of the Downey remanufactured and modified T-6s (as the NA-168), and 59 LT-6Gs. The National Guard units took a further fifty. In the repeat order of 8 February 1951, 824 NA-182s were given the same treatment at Columbus. Long Beach-modified aircraft (NA-188s) were ordered on 11 April 1951 and totalled 107, and Fresno rebuilds (NA-195) from 19 March 1952 totalled eleven, with a further 110 T-6Ds brought up to -G standard (NA-197) for the National Guard at Fresno from 16 June 1952 onwards. The 240 SNJ-8s (NA-198) had their contracts terminated on 3 July 1952, as related, after some SNJ-6s had been updated to SNJ-7 by the US Navy Overhaul and Repair Facility at Naval Air Station Pensacola, Florida, in 1952.

In March 1956, 150 T-6GS were ordered by the French Air Force and they began to arrive at Bordeaux docks, ferried across the Atlantic on the decks of US aircraft carriers, in October of the same year. A second order of 150 was placed in November and others followed. Under the T-6G scheme no less than 693 of these re-manufactured trainers arrived in France.

Once landed, the French drastically modified these trainers to fit their new role. Armour plate was added to protect the crews from ground fire. The single nose-mounted .30 machine-gun was replaced by a heavier punch. There were two versions, one type equipped the T-6G with two 7.5mm guns, mounted in pairs on underwing pods, with four racks fitted under the wings for four SNEB 68mm rockets and six T-10 rockets and 110-lb bombs. The alternative payload comprised four 7.5mm machine-guns in underwing pods, two racks for 110lb bombs and four SNEB 68mm rockets and six T-10 rockets. Extra radio-equipment was fitted. Their aircrews underwent special ERALA conversion and training courses at Blida, Reghala and Caen. At their peak no less than thirty Texan-equipped ERALA squadrons were operational.

Once again that distinctive noise was heard in battle, this time over the desert wastes. And once more their unique howl brought about another nickname for the T-6 and they became known as 'Tomcats'. The Tomcats became the mainstay of close-support operations all through this bitter conflict up to 1961 and elsewhere. During that period they suffered the loss of 255 aircrew. They flew intensive missions and, by March 1957, had notched up 10,000 sorties. This total had increased to 106,512 during the first ten months of 1958, where they flew from seventy-two different airstrips and clocked up 115,000 flying hours.

With the end of the war the Tomcats' work was done and they were laid up for sale and scrap. Some went to private buyers and Air France bought a dozen for airline pilot training (sans weapons!). Others were returned to the USA. Many French Tomcats were sold to foreign air forces who had a need for such ground-attack aircraft, Morocco, Tunisia, Portugal, Spain and India. Unofficially, some found their way back into African war conditions in the hands of mercenary pilots during the Congolese and Biafran wars of 1964.

Sixteen Harvard Mk IIIs were transferred from the Royal Navy to the *Forca Aerea Portuguesa* (FAP – Portuguese Air Force) in March 1956. South Africa contributed fifty-nine more Mark IIA Harvards in 1969, while the Belgian Air Force transferred seven further Mark IIAs and three Mark IIBs. This batch was followed by another ten from the same source in 1962. Later additions include twenty surplus USAAF AT-6A and AT-6Bs, and twenty-five T-6Gs supplied under the Mutual Defense Assistance Program. In addition, the *Aviacao Naval* (Portugese Navy) acquired six SNJ-4s (Serials I-1 to I-6) from the USA and fifteen former Royal Navy Harvard IIIs which were handed over in 1956. Others (Serials 1701 to 1799) came in from sources as varying as Belgium, France and West Germany over the years. They were all used in their intended training role to start with.

Like most European powers with colonies Portugal had to fight several nationalist uprisings and wars in Africa and elsewhere post-war. They used armed T-6s in their colonial wars in Angola, where they proved very handy, but the introduction of Soviet-supplied SAM-7 shoulder-launched surface-to-air missiles soon showed up the vulnerability and several were lost. The COIN adaptations were also used in similar operations in Mozambique and Guinea up to August 1974.

The final (and most dramatic) combat action for the T-6 in Portuguese use was during the March 1975 uprising against the revolutionary government. Two machines bombed and strafed a loyalist Army barracks on 11 March, causing a large amount of damage. Those still employed as training machines were not finally withdrawn from combat operations until 1978.

Photographs showing Harvards actually dropping bombs are extremely rare indeed, hence the need to include this unique air-to-air shot in my collection for posterity. This is AJ596, a Mark II machine which initially served with 31 Service Flying Training School between May 1942 and May 1944, before being handed over to the Royal Canadian Air Force. She is pictured here in 1959. (*Courtesy R.C. Sturtivant*)

In actual war conditions the T-6 fought as hard with the French as with anyone. With the eruption of the Algerian uprising the *L'Armée de L'Air* began using converted AT-6Ds from the Marrakech school and then imported the huge numbers of T-6Gs to employ in the Ground-Support Light Aviation Command (ERALA) in the COIN role. The early conversions proved superior in this role to French types. They could operate from 800- metre long airstrips, had an endurance of almost five hours giving them a range of over 800 miles, and a relatively high cruising speed which, as the Mosquitoes had shown in Korea, were all commendable attributes, giving loiter time and ruggedness of operation in primitive conditions. (*SIRPA/ECPA France*)

During the war the Dutch pilots in exile were trained on RAF Harvards at Langham airfield in Norfolk. With the re-establishment of the *Koninklijke Luchtmacht* (Royal Netherlands Air Force) on its own liberated soil a flying training school was established at Gilze-Rijen airfield in 1946.

The Royal Netherlands Air Force took delivery of 200 Mark IIBs Harvard trainers from both the RAF and the RCAF in the immediate post-war years. This Dutch machine, (66) is shown with camouflage paint scheme overall, including the engine cowling as well as the standard national markings of the period. (*Author's collection, courtesy Royal Netherlands Air Force*)

Spanish T-6s disembarking from the US aircraft carrier *Corregidor* (CVE 58) at Santander in 1958.

Spain acquired her first batch of sixty AT-6D Texans when they arrived at Santander airfield between August and October 1954. They received the Spanish serials E.16-1 to E.16-60 and were basic aluminium coloured aircraft. They were destined for the training establishments at Matacan and Villanubla. The first unit to receive delivery was No. 74 *Agrupacion Aerea* while others modified for ground-attack work, went to the No. 3 *Cazabombardeo Tactico*.

During 1958 a second consignment of sixty aircraft was purchased, this time it was T-6Gs that were received. They were given the Spanish serials E.16-61 to E.16-120 and were used to replace the older models at both training centres and also those of the No. 3 Tactical Squadron.

During 1957 the situation in Spanish Morocco escalated and the *Ejercito del Aire* decided to utilised the older AT-6Ds as close-support aircraft to give assistance to the front-line F-86 Sabre jets. Between 1959 and 1963 these aircraft were refitted privately by the American firm Charlotte Aircraft Engineering to become almost brand-new machines. Seventy other machines were obtained, SNJ-4, -5 and -6 models, all of which were based at Matacan and other air bases. These new additions were given the Spanish serials E.16-21 to E.16-190.

In the COIN configuration modified AT-6Ds were equipped with wing-mounted Breda 7.7mm machine-guns and also had underwing racks capable of mounting a dozen Oerlikon ATG rockets or ten 221-lb bombs. This transformation was carried out at the AISA factory at Carabanchel and they were re-designated as C.6 Attack aircraft. (*Author's collection courtesy of Royal Spanish Air Force, Madrid*)

The T-6 saw considerable combat in the Korean War. The ground control and direction methods of World War II were re-introduced in the US 5th Air Force at this time but, following the example set by the Australian Wirraways in the last three years of the Pacific War, slower propeller-driven aircraft were employed as aerial Tactical Air Controllers or Target Spotters.

A special unit was set up; 6132 Tactical Air Control Group. General Earl Partridge is credited with adopting the old Australian ploy once more and it was put into effect on 10 July 1956 with three Stinson L-5G aircraft and seven officers based at Taejon airstrip, which was described as, 'a loose gravel runway about the width of a country road and not much else'. It recognised, early on, that the conventional observation and spotter/liaison aircraft, like the L-5 and the L-9, lacked both speed, ruggedness and efficiency in such a role. For this mission the reliable old Texan entered the conflict in new guise, as the LT-6G.

From their radio call-signs they became known as the MOSQUITO units. They proved brilliantly successful. As well as the target-marking Mosquito missions in Korea this versatile machine flew photo-reconnaissance missions over the front line. Here Major Angus J. Walker. DIR Photo Division of General Headquarters, Far East Command, poses ready to take-off on a T-6 Photo-recon mission near Taegh on 19 August 1950. (*US Army Photo, Courtesy National Archives, Washington DC*)

In the Korean War the Mosquito unit became the 6147 Tactical Control Group which contained two Airborne squadrons, 6148 TCS (Western Sector) under Colonel Watson, and 6149 TCS (Eastern Sector) equipped with the modified T-6s, and one administrative, mechanical support and forward air control teams, as a general Ground squadron, 6150 TCS. The hastily-adapted AT-6Ds and AT-6Fs were gradually replaced with more sophisticated versions, especially modified for the work in hand. These were the LT-6Gs of which ninety-seven were eventually built. Their main difference over the basic T-6G was the additional radio communications equipment packed into the cockpit. They carried three basic sets, AN/ARC-3, AN/ARN-6 and SCR-522A. For target marking they were fitted with no less than six underwing racks capable of carrying three rocket launchers for either six 5-inch or eighteen 2½-inch white phosphorous smoke rockets

each, while pods were slung under each wing fitted with two .30 calibre machine-guns for strafing opportunites. (There were later dropped to give a few knots extra speed over heavy flak concentrations). Red identification stripes were marked diagonally across their wings for identification by friendly aircraft.

LT-6Gs conducted no less than 40,354 combat sorties and had helped with the destruction of enough tanks to equip five Communist armoured divisions as well as 563 guns and more than 5,000 soft-skinned untracked supply vehicles. It was an enviable record of dedication and service and one that crowned an already illustrious career for the sturdy and surprising T-6.

North American T-6G, 42-86074A, K-16 at Seoul airport, South Korea on 23 May 1954. The unit markings are in yellow and black. (*Courtesy of Arthur Pearcy Archives*)

81573A.C. USAF Mosquito T-6 landing at a forward airstrip after making rocket strikes on Communist positions. (*Smithsonian Institute, Washington, DC*)

166862A.C. (AF3923.1) USAF armourer fitting smoke rockets beneath wing of Mosquito aircraft. (*Smithsonian Institute, Washington, DC*)

83699A.C. (SP2/30-272) Mosquito units at the revetments on a forward airstrip in Korea. (*Smithsonian Institute, Washington, DC*)

Two Tomcats patrolling the Sahara Desert. (*SIRPA/ECPA France*)

(*above*)

The cockpit layout of the preserved ex-Portuguese Air Force Harvard 1769 (ex 52-8565) at Montijo. This machine had in excess of 4,000 flying hours on the clock in 1989 and is still in flying condition after undergoing a detailed inspection in that year.

As well as the two fully airworthy examples preserved by the *Museu do Ar* 1769 (ex-52-8596) and 1774, there is another stored at Alverca in rather dilapidated condition, 1737. This machine is minus engine and the wings are dismantled, there is no propeller and the cockpit is incomplete. There are some hopes of restoration as a static display in the future. (*Courtesy J. Laneiro, Lisbon*)

(*below*)

A dozen or so former Mozambique Air Force Harvards used by the Frelimo, but also previously seeing service in the French and German air forces were located at Syferfontein after being declared surplus to requirements. They were all in a sorry state as these two photographs show.

They were all rescued in 1988 by a South African enthusiast, Brian Zeederberg, who purchased a job-lot and shipped them to South Africa. In 1989 three of these machines Nos. 1727, 1731 and 1751 were sold to South African Airways apprentice school, No. 1762 was sold in Durban, No. 1748 in Johannesburg and No. 1754 in Cape Town, all to civilian buyers, for approximately £15,000 each. (*Courtesy L.S. Vosloo*)

His instructor makes last-minute checks on his pupil before the take-off. A scene repeated a hundred thousand times in the T-6's long training career. Here the aircrew are Italian flyers of the *Aeronautica Militare* some time in the mid-1960s.

The first Italian Harvard was an ex-RCAG Mark II taken over from No. 15 MU, at Wroughton on 2 July 1947. The Italian air force subsequently received thirteen Harvard Mark IIs on 10 May 1949 (registered as T-6Ds on Italian records) via US allocation of acquired ex-RAF South African stock post-war. These joined the training school at Lecce.

Five further T-6s were delivered on 12 January 1951, four on 16 February, one of 14 March direct from the States. This gave a total of forty-three machines of which twenty-seven were operational. With the expansion of the Italian air force new schools were set up at Cagliari, Sardinia using Alhgero and Elmas airfields each with

six aircraft. Further expansion took place in 1952 under NATO auspices and the first of a consignment of thirty T-6Gs began to arrive from America (some re-furbished AT-6Fs were included under the designation of T-6H). These were followed in 1953/54 by a further batch of sixty-nine Canadian Harvard IVs (also confusingly designated T-6H). A central flying school was also established at Foggia with eight T-6s, five of them operational. These machines continued to serve as basic trainers well into the 1960s.

The final 'official' Italian flight in a T-6 was made by Colonel Sergio Ponzio of 53 *Stormo* at 166.12 on 13 February 1979 from Cameri airfield. In actual fact a later (and highly unofficial) flight was made in an Italian Air Force Texan five days later by an anonymous Colonel from No. 330 *Gruppo*! (*Courtesy Aeronautica Militare, Roma*)

The T-6's commercial roles included civil airline pilot and general public
aero training. The T-6 was widely used for crop-spraying in the States. A
rather extreme example of re-building of two former SNJ-5s for this role
which was carried-out by Bob Stroop. He ripped off the canopies and
inserted a large chemical tank in the rear cockpit. Routine stuff, but to
give the machine a slow, almost-hovering ability, he bolted a whole upper
wing to struts on the lower wing and upper fuselage to produce two
biplane variants, probably the only ones ever constructed anywhere. His
customer was a crop-duster from Monroeville, Alabama, J.F. Carter who
used them, precariously, for a number of years. They probably proved
more successful than the specially-built CAC Ceres machines in Australia.
These proved themselves rather expensive to run in practice and they
needed a longer take-off and landing distance than usually available to
crop dusters. In the event only twenty were ever built.

A more conventional SNJ-5 preservation is seen here sporting her
'Two-Star Admiral' markings over the modern aircraft carriers and
guided-missile frigates of the US Fleet. (*Jim Larsen Photographs,
Kirkland, Washington*)

8 At Work and at Play

Apart from the major nations' air forces, the T-6 has seen post-war service in a huge variety of roles in the inventories of military air arms all over the world since 1947. What is presented here is a brief summary of the most important of them.

On 18 March 1961, a squadron of eighteen Spanish C.6s was transferred *en mass* from Villanubia to Jerez to form No. 7 *Buchones del Ala*. These machines were used against guerrillas in Spanish Sahara desert colonies during the 1970s. The final ten Spanish Texan acquisitions came from the French *l'Armée de l'Air* surplus stocks of T-6Gs, which arrived in 1965 and received the Spanish Serials E.16-191 to E.16-201.

In 1974 the AT-6Ds were pulled out of the Sahara colony being replaced by Mirage F-1Cs for close-support. The -Ds continued to be used for reconnaissance and observation duties. By 1976 the greater part of the remaining -Ds were assigned to No. 90 *Escuadrillas Grupo* at Getafe and as various air base hacks. During their final service days at San Javier the survivors were re-designated as the CE.6.

The T-6Gs that remained as training aircraft were used by 741 and 742 *Escuadrones* at Matacan until 1972 when the unit was transferred to San Javier and formed the 793 *Escuadron*. They were ultimately replaced in the training role by the CASA C-101 type.

Subsequently the Air Force Aerobatic team performed with these T-6s for a considerable period. The last official flight by Spanish Air Force T-6s took place from 31 June 1982.

The Belgian Air Force took delivery of fifty-six Mark IIA and Mark III Harvards between February and May 1947 which came to them from South Africa via the UK. Most of these aircraft were flown from UK to Brustem airport which had hardly re-emerged from its wartime devastation. Ten Mark IIB Harvards were received in August to October 1949, along with one from the Royal Netherlands Air Force, with another ten arriving from Britain between September and October of the following year. Between October 1952 and March 1953 ten more were received from the Dutch.

Two dozen more Mark IIA Harvards were added to the Belgian fleet in November 1953, being surplus to British requirements with the closure of the RATG. An advanced flying school was set up at Kamina in the Belgian Congo to take advantage of all-round climate conditions in a similar manner to the British experience in Rhodesia earlier. Thus, these machines were available for hasty conversion and, from July 1960 onwards, they served in the COIN role during the war of Independence in the Belgian Congo.

After independence had been granted the bulk of the training aircraft were written-off and scrapped when the Belgian Air Force pulled out but six of the Harvards subsequently served with the Air Force of Ruanda-Urundi. From 1960 to 1962 they fought again during their own Congolese Civil War.

The Royal Danish Air Force obtained twenty-seven Mark IIB Harvards from the RAF from December 1946 to September 1947, plus four more from Canada. From South Africa via the UK a further seven were received for spares.

The Royal Norwegian Air Force received twenty-three Harvard Mark IIBs from the former Norwegian Training Base at Winkleigh on its closure in November 1945. Seven further ex-Canadian Harvards joined them later.

The Royal Swedish Air Force as related equipped itself with 144 ex-Canadian Mark IIBs (as the SK-16). They also bought former SNJ-2, -3 and -4s from surplus stocks post-war. A total of 257 aircraft were purchased in this manner. These all served with the F5 Primary Training School at Ljungbyhed through to 1968. One of these trainers survived, Fv16109 (formerly FE 632) and is now preserved at the Swedish Air Force Museum at Linkoping.

The *Fliegerabwehrtruppen* (Swiss Air Force) purchased forty Noorduyn-built Harvard IIBs from the RCAF in 1947 and these were given the Swiss Serials U-301 to U-340. On their arrival in Europe they were given a complete overhaul by the Dutch firms of Aviolanda and Fokker of Amsterdam and Schipol. From 1949 to 1968 they served with great success as blind-flying instruction machines, for, in this period, practically all military trainee pilots obtained the blind-flying qualification. They were employed strictly as training and liaison aircraft and no armament was *ever* carried.

When the new Pilatus P3-03/05 training aircraft arrived, blind-flying instruction was commenced in the flying schools, so that the AT-6 was less and less required. Furthermore, by 1968, they were well overdue for a major overhaul of airframe parts suffering from fatigue. The whole AT-6 fleet was therefore withdrawn from service and scrapped, except two aircraft and four engines which were retained as exhibits.

Aircraft number U-322 was bought by an English instition. It received the civil registration G-AXCR and was flown from Dubendorf to London via Kloten and Cologne on 10 April 1969. With the exception of those retained for exhibits, all engines, plus propellers and engine mounting units, were purchased by an American aircraft maintenance company and delivered to Dallas, Texas for use in twin-engined ground-spraying aircraft.

The Royal Hellenic Air Force obtained thirty-five Harvard Mk IIAs from South Africa via Britain between March and August 1947 and thirty Mark IIBs direct from the UK from July 1947 onwards.

The Turkish Air Force received a grand total of 196 T-6/Harvard aircraft. The first batch of one hundred machines, AT-6Cs, arrived in the country on 2 August 1948 and were given Turkish Serials 7251 to 7350. These were later supplemented by eighteen ex-RAF Harvard Mark IIBs from the Royal Norwegian Air Force, six arriving on 4 October 1955 and twelve more on 6 November 1955. They received the Turkish Serials 7351 to 7368. These were followed, on 18 July 1956, by a further eight Mark II Harvards that arrived from RCAF sources and were numbered 7369 to 7376.

Under the NATO Mutual Air Programme Turkey received yet further batches of North American COIN and trainer aircraft. The first of these new assignments were sixteen former LT-6Gs. These arrived on 7 September 1957 and were assigned Serial Numbers 7377 to 7392. They were followed by three more of the same type on 7 October 1957 (7393 to 7395) along with eleven T-6Gs (7396 to 7399 and 7501 to 7505).

Two more consignments were shipped to Turkey in 1958. On 13 January of that year twenty-one machines arrived and were numbered 7508 to 7528), while on 5 May 1958 a final batch of nineteen were received (7529 to 7547).

All these aircraft served on the Turkish Air Force Inventory for over twenty-five years, the final T-6 being phased out in 1976.

The Yugoslavian Air Force obtained ten Harvard Mark IIBs, direct from the UK to use at the local Flying Training School, which was then operating as part of the Allied Mediterranean Air Force, in March and April 1945. Post-war, the Communist Government emulated their Russian mentors and held on to their 'loaned' aircraft after the war had terminated.

In the Middle-East the former Royal Iranian Air Force had armed T-6Gs on its strength prior to the overthrow of the Shah, which it used against Kurdish insurgents.

Harvards served with the Israeli Defence Force and Air Force during the 1948 War of Independence where they fought armed as dive-bombers with two .50 calibre machine-guns in the wings and a .30 gun on a flexible mounting aft. They were also adapted to carry eight 110-lb bombs on underwing racks or alternatively 400lb of bombs.

Again in 1956 rocket-firing and bombing Israeli T-6s fought against Egyptian armoured forces. However, they suffered severe damage from the sophisticated Egyptian anti-aircraft defences and were not combat employed again. They were pensioned off from training duties in 1965.

There were twenty Syrian Air Force armed Harvards T-6s. Ten of these were ex-RAF Mark IIBs from South African stocks in 1956.

Three Harvard Mark IIBs from the RAF's 1340 Flight in Kenya were re-supplied to the Royal Jordanian Air Force in January and February 1956.

The Lebanese Air Force obtained sixteen Harvards which it obtained from various British sources between 1952 and 1954.

In Africa the Mozambique Government inherited some former Portuguese Air Force Harvards after Independence. These were soon withdrawn from flying duties and were parked in open storage at Maputo Airport, where they remained exposed to the elements and steadily deteriorated.

Biafran insurgent forces, using mercenary pilots, flew twelve ex-French T-6s against Nigerian forces during their struggle for independence between 1967-1970 and are credited with destroying one Nigerian Air Force MiG-17 'Fresco' jet fighter on the ground in that conflict.

South Africa has long been the major user of the Harvard. Indeed it owns the largest Harvard air fleet in the world. Several score remain of the hundreds she inherited from the war and remain on her training school inventory today. She was also a major user of the type in the ground-attack role particularly against SWAPO guerrilla forces in South-West Africa (Namibia) and against Mozambique incursions across her frontiers.

Although the RAF continued to fly Harvard aircraft from Negombo (now Katunayake) airfield right up to 1952, none were taken into service when Ceylon became independent Sri Lanka.

The Indian Air Force Harvards initially saw much hard *combat* duty during the Kashmir Operation, which commenced on 28 October 1947. Pakistan and India fought over this disputed territory and ground-strafing became a priority. Two days later two IAF Harvards, which had been hastily adapted to the close support role at Ambala, were rushed forward to work from Srinagar airfield. On 31 October these Harvards gave air support to the infantry and two further machines were sent to join them. Aviation fuel had to be flown into the advance airfield by Dakotas, transferred to buckets and poured in the Harvards' fuel tanks to keep the missions going. On 4 November 1947 the Harvards again sortied over the battlefield in the Badgam-Baramulla Sector to good effect.

Reconnaissance missions were flown over Kotli by the Harvards on 3 November and they also attacked Pakistan fortified positions. Another valuable contribution the IAF Harvards from Srinagar gave the Army was rendered on 5 November when four machines were sent out to first locate, and then guide an Indian armoured column from the Banihal Pass to Srinagar, which it did in the following two days. This enabled the major Indian ground attack to be put in on the 7th.

When the Indian advance was held up near Rampur on 12 November, two Harvards joined in the close-support missions and attacked Domel, Kotli, Mirpur and Uri, and the latter town fell next day. On 16 November close-support was given to Indian troops at Uri and enemy positions around a road block at Milepost 67 were bombed, strafed and destroyed by them.

Back in the more tranquil training role the Harvards continued to give their usual sterling service. Late in 1963 the Indian Air Force Harvards were concentrated soley at the AFFC. Ten years later the Harvard was still being used, alongside the new Indian-designed and built HJT-16 Kiran jet trainer, with the AFA. Not until 1975 was the last Harvard phased out of service on the sub-continent, after more than thirty years faithful flying.

In September 1946, the Royal New Zealand Air Force formerly absorbed the survivors of all her wartime deliveries, plus acquiring one Mark IIB in 1948. They served until 24 June 1977. One still survives, NZ1015 (formerly the RAF EX193) and is part of the RNZAF Historic Flight.

The Japanese Self Defense Force took delivery of both T-6Fs and SNJ-6s early in October 1957 and used them until 1976. Japan became the fourth nation to build the type under licence (after Sweden, Australia and Canada).

The Laotian Air Force T-6s flew missions against the Communist Pathet Lao guerrillas and along the Ho Chi Minh Trail during the Vietnam War.

The Royal Thai Air Force obtained T-6s direct from the States between 1948 and 1957. They operated with 1, 2, 3, 4, 5, 6 and 7 Wings and they formed three Attack Groups with them. The T-6s served as well as the RTAF Flying Training School at Don Muang, Bangkok, until 1974.

The Chinese Nationalist Air Force in Formosa also acquired a number of T-6s. Likewise the Philippine Air Force was the recipient of many T-6Gs.

In South America, Brazil used armed T-6s, fitted with underwing racks for rockets and light bombs in the COIN role. T-6GS also served with the Liaison and Observation Squadrons of the Brazilian Air Force in this configuration and were equipped with a life-raft carried in an under-the-fuselage container. The premier Brazilian formation team to use the Harvard was the *Esquadrilla de Fumaca* (Smoke-trailing Squadron). They gave numerous displays in their T-6s, which were strikingly painted with red wing-tips, black underbellies and a horizontal red lightning flash down the white fuselage. They served in this duty from 1956 until 7 February 1963 when the T-6s were replaced by FAB T-24 jet trainers.

The Chilean, Mexican, Uruguayan and Venezuelan Air Forces were among many Latin American air fleets equipped with AT-6Ds post-war. Some South American nations still fly the odd T-6 in the COIN role today.

In the last two decades, however, it is as a civilian pleasure machine that the Texan has spent its most productive years. A whole variety of roles have presented themselves to the North American, and I have tried to include as many representatives as possible in these pages to cover these, from stunt machine to racer to rebuilt show machine.

In the latter configuration, in 1989, the Oshkosh Grand Champion was a Harvard Mark IV (20247). This aircraft contained almost all its original authentic parts rather than being built from new ones. This model was a Canadian Car and Foundry produced aircraft, the final one of the series, built in 1955. It was based at Penhold, Alberta with 4 Fighter Trainer Squadron, RCAF, and logged 4,191 hours of flying time. After an accident in 1958 it was repaired and overhauled with new right elevator, wing flaps, centre section, vertical stabilizer, starboard wing and hydraulic assemblies. It then soldiered on at Penhold until 1964, totalling 6,512 flying hours and six engine changes. On retirement its wings were removed, engine and propeller moth-balled and the aircraft placed in storage. It was finally struck from charge on 28 February 1966.

The Harvard was ferried to Chino, California and remained stored until 1988 when Bill Melamed of Los Angeles bought her to restore her. The work was done by John Muszala of Pacific Fighters using as many of the original parts as possible. The engine was overhauled and inspection showed the original fabric of the control surfaces in perfect condition. The original radio was made to work, but the addition of modern equipment was deemed necessary for safety, but it is mounted on a removable panel. By the time the aircraft was complete it was more than ninety-seven per cent original. Painted yellow, with day-glo pink cowling and rudder, Bill's Harvard was the deserving winner after all this careful work.

Long may the 'Noisy North American' continue to grace the skies of the world.

(*previous page*)
The T-6 and its many variants are now the most popular of the propeller driven vintage civilian aircraft still flying today. Their popularity has undergone troughs and peaks since that time, because keeping them flying costs a lot of money and time. In 1952 just over three hundred remained on the register, but, in reverse ratio to the machines' age, this figure began to rise once more, helped by the retirement of numerous machines from the military services, to over four hundred two decades later.

Here Jim Larsen's immaculate camera work catches an equally immaculate 'JAX' over the Sierras in the late 1970s. (*Jim Larsen Photographs, Kirkland, Washington*)

Whole societies have grown up, again especially in the States, built around the Texan. The more recent 'Warbird' scene is one of the more interesting innovations. Here T-6s and Harvards have again featured strongly (if not always very accurately) in the re-creation of wartime aircraft in flyable form down to passing imitations flown for fun and spectacle, with no pretence at 'exactness' of colour scheme or markings. NA-16s and their successors are classified as officially 'Classic' aircraft by the Experimental Aircraft Association in its Antiques and Classics Division. The Sport Aviation Association section of this organisation has offices at Franklin, Wisconsin and a European branch at Welwyn Garden City, just north of London.

Here a Mark IV Harvard, (AJ832 BH-S) is seen with wheels down coming in for a landing and carrying an RAF dazzle paint scheme complete with duck-egg blue band around fuselage, yellow wing-tips, propeller extremeties and edging to the old-type roundels. (*Jim Larsen Photographs, Kirkland, Washington*)

'GOTCHA!' Making a stunning contrast between the sparkling Pacific ocean and the gleaming scarlet of her paintwork this T-6G is one of many restored to their former glory and fully flightworthy after dedicated work by T-6 enthusiasts in the States.

The North American Trainer Association is another really flourishing organisation and, under the Presidentship of Stoney Stonich, has almost four-hundred pilot members in the States. The T-6 Owners Association flourishes and in conjunction with the Warbirds of America encourage the maintenance, promotion and safety aspects of T-6 restoration, flying and exhibition. There is also an equally active and wide-ranging 'Mosquito' Association for LT-6G veterans of the Korean conflict. (*Jim Larsen Photographs, Kirkland, Washington*)

A splendid airborne view of *How Sweet It Is* from the Swayze team of Mesquite, Texas, who regularly sweep the board at Oshkosh with their immaculate paintwork and meticulously assembled flying T-6s. This glittering all-metal finish beauty was his first effort and well worth every loving hour of care spent on her. (*Courtesy 'Doc' Swayze, Mesquite, Texas*)

Another 'Doc' Swayze re-build, one of six T-6s he and his team have lovingly built and flown down the years. This is the latest, an SNJ-5 (N5486V) which carries the pre-World War II paint scheme of the US aircraft carrier *Saratoga* with red tail and cowling and yellow wings.

Totally built from new surplus parts and completed in June 1987, 5486V won for the Swayze team their third National Award for the Best AT-6 at Oshkosh in 1987. (*Courtesy 'Doc' Swayze, Mesquite, Texas*)

Air Racing has been another aspect of aviation interest to strongly feature the T-6 in all its many aspects. Pylon and Long-Distance meetings always feature several of the type at any assembly. When the National Air Races at Cleveland resumed, the prestigious female event, the Halle Trophy Race, was dominated by T-6s with cockpits removed and engines supercharged for those vital extra knots. It was won that year by Ruth Johnson flying a highly 'souped-up' AT-6, in which she achieved a speed of over 223 mph, after the X-Birds had both dropped out as related earlier. Second place was taken by Grace Harris. In 1948 this event became the Kendall Trophy race and Grace Harris won it in that year, and the next, by which time supercharged engines and three-bladed propellers had been banned from the competition.

Again, there was a two-decade lull in the sport but, in 1967, the T-6 re-appeared at the National Air Races now held at Reno, Nevada. This set the ball in motion once more and the following year there were seventeen entries for the Bardahl Trophy race for standard T-6s, and so it has continued to this day.

Here an early T-Bird flyer (N7067C) is shown at Monterey, California, airstrip in July 1968. (*Courtesy Nick Williams Collection*)

(*above*)
Gary Numan inverted! Since joining the Harvard Formation Team the pop star and showman has enthusiastically embraced the Harvard flying technique and lent his own brand of uniqueness to their flying displays and aerobatics! The team travel all over the world giving their displays and between May and October of most years are fully committed in the United Kingdom as well. Although the former RAF fighter base located close to Harlow New Town has had a slice of its runway cut off by the M11 motorway, it is still more than adequate to house the team and the Annual 'Warbirds Fighter Meet' takes place there as well.

The Harvard Team is sponsored by Tarmac Construction of Milton Keynes and each year at the famous Cranfield Air Races and Air Show, held annually at the Bedfordshire airfield, there is a special 'Harvard Trophy' to be competed for on an individual basis. (*Courtesy of The Squadron, Harvard Formation Team, North Weald*)

(*below*)
Two T-6s drop down on the dusty airstrip at Mojave, California, in October 1974, while in the distance, another brace circle in readiness to follow them down. 'Air Meets' of this kind have increased the popularity of the T-6 family with civilian owners the world over.

Flyable aircraft are always more exciting than static display models of course, although, usually, the latter are much more likely to be both authentic machines and well documented. However, there are exceptions! In South Korea, for example, the Korean War Museum in Seoul has a static ROKAF T-6 on display. In 1989 Captain Russ Turner, USAF, reported on this aircraft. 'Although weathered, it's complete. It has two machine-gun pods and four bomb racks. The display states that the initial invasion from the north was met by South Korean T-6s pelting the communists with grenades!' Just what the Mosquito veterans think of that claim is uncertain!

In Australia and New Zealand both Harvard and Wirraway have been enjoying similar popularity and only a shortage of suitable aircraft has prevented a similar expansion to that found in the UK and the USA. (*Courtesy Nick Williams Collection*)

(above)

This SNJ is seen landing at the Hawthorne Air Fair in 1987. Painted brilliant red it has the markings 'China Lake' on its tail. China Lake, California, is a Naval Weapons Test Station but this is probably just a restoration by enthusiasts there, although very well done.

The fiftieth anniversary of the North American Texan type was marked in 1988 by a number of special celebrations around the world. In the States the North American Trainer Association marked the event at Kenosha, Wisconsin, between 23 and 27 July when almost 150 T-6s and derivatives flew in what was the largest gathering of the type in one place since the US military discontinued the type in service.

As things look today the planning for the 60th, and even the 70th anniversary of this remarkable aircraft can be started with confidence. The resilience of the T-6 marks it out as one of the most outstanding aircraft of all time. Long may she continue to grace our skies! (*Courtesy Dr Ira Chart*)

(*overleaf*)

It was the relative simplicity of the T-6 that enamoured it of civilian owners, especially in the USA. In November 1945 only small modifications were needed to bring the AT-6/SNJs into line to meet Government guidelines. This allowed them to gain the required Commercial Civil Aircraft licence 'ticket' for revenue operating, (although it was only the Category 2-575 certificate). It did not prove possible for the former military Texans to gain the full Approved Type certificate (ATC) in the States. It was Autair, a London company, that later received the more limiting AR-11 'Restricted' ticket for the AT-16s. In this way more than eight-hundred former T-6 variants were on the civilian register by 1947, working in a wide variety of roles.

This appeal is world-wide and this privately-owned and exotically painted T-6H was proudly on display at a 'Fly-In' in West Germany in 1988. (*Courtesy Hanfried Schliephake Archive*)

Appendix 1: T-6 Namecheck:

Throughout its long career the North American trainer has received a whole variety of names quite apart from the many company and official designations. Depending on how pendantic the reader is (or how much of a 'nit-picker') the blood pressure of enthusiasts rises in proportion to the number of times the 'wrong' word is used. In this volume, as a very general rule of thumb, the name 'T-6' has been used as the overall covering name for *all* the variants. Beneath this blanket, in order to prevent too much repetition, the name 'AT-6' has been used for older models and 'T-6' for all post T-6Gs. Appendix 2 covers the company and official designations.

   For the rest, the following list gives a quick summary check on the various official and unofficial titles received by the aircraft described in this book, with a brief word on the probably origins.

BACON SUPER: an American one-off civilian conversion of a standard T-6 into a counter-insurgency/ground-attack aircraft.

BOOMERANG: the CAC-designed and built WW II Australian fighter aircraft built utilising some Wirraway parts and fixtures.

C.6: the Spanish post-war ground-attack conversions.

CERES: not a conversion but a CAC Australian-built and designed post-war crop-spraying aircraft.

HARVARD: the British and Commonwealth name given to American and Canadian-built variants of the T-6. Four different Marks.

HURRICANE HUNTER: not strictly the name of the aircraft themselves but their unit, the American All-Weather patrols, but sometimes applied to the aircraft themselves.

J-BIRD: the popular US Navy term for the SNJ variants.

LEMON BOMBER: derisive West German Luftwaffe term for post-war T-6 trainers derived from their colouring.

MOSQUITO: the radio call-sign of the American LT-6G close-support aircraft in the Korean War which was adopted for both the aircraft and the unit itself.

NOISY NORTH AMERICAN: a wry British term used mainly by ground staff and aircrew in the UK, for obvious reasons.

OAK: the Allied WW II codename allocated to the Japanese training derivative, the Kyushu K10W.

RANGER: general term for the Ranger-engined XAT and its post-war copy.

SK-16: the Royal Swedish Air Force licence-built variant of the T-6.

TEXAN: the 'Official' name given to Dallas-built AT-6s said to have originated from both the plant and the numerous Texas-based flying schools. Later applied to all AT-6 and T-6s, but *not* generally adopted by the American aircrews themselves during the war.

TOMCAT: the French Air Forces' name for their ground-attack conversions during the Algerian war.

WIRRAWAY: the WW II CAC Australian licence-built trainer/dive-bomber variant of the AT-6.

YALE: British and Commonwealth name allocated to the American-built fixed-under-carriage predecessor of the AT-6.

Appendix 2:
NAA Variant Listing:

On 27 May 1956, North American Aviation issued Report 'O' from which a breakdown of the company Charge Numbers and designations, along with quantities and serial numbers of all the trainers of the series could be listed. This enabled the company Charge Number (NA-) to be checked against the Model designation (AT-). An original (more detailed) compilation was done by historian Dustin W. Carter many years ago, to whose dedication and application I am accordingly deeply indebted.

This listing serves two functions. Firstly, it enables the direct lineal descent of the T-6 to be followed in a chronological sequence. Secondly, it assists further research. As both the original company drawings and many major sub-assemblies are solely identified by the NA-numbers, this cross-over reference is important for archive checking. It is also important for the reader to understand that *only* machines actually constructed or modified by NAA are included in this list. For private conversions, Canadian, Australian and other licence-built variants, along with USAAF, USAF and USN modifications are *not* included here.

CHARGE No.	DATE	DESIGNATION	CUSTOMER	QUANTITY	FACTORY S/N
NA-16	–	NA-16	–	1	NA-16-1
NA-18	13-5-35	NA-18	Argentina	–	NA-18-1
NA-19	10-3-35	BT-9	USAAC	42	NA-19-1 NA-19-3 NA-19-5/11 NA-19-20/34 NA-19-50/67
NA-19A	–	BT-9A	USAAC Reserve	40	NA-19-4 NA-19-12/19 NA-19-35/49 NA-19-68/83
NA-20	–	NA-16-2H	Honduras	1	NA-16-2
NA-22	–	NA-22	USAAC	–	NA-16-1
NA-23	1-12-36	BT-9B	USAAC	117	NA-23-85/201
NA-26	20-10-36	BC-1	Canada	1	26-202
NA-27	1-12-36	NA-16-2H	Fokker	1	27-312
NA-28	14-12-36	NJ-1	USAAC for USN	40	28-313/352
NA-29	22-12-36	BT-9C	USAAC Reserve	32	29-353/384
		YIBT-10	USAAC	1	29-385
		BT-9C	USAAC	34	29-505/538
NA-30	–	YIBT-10	–	–	–
NA-31	2-8-37	NA 16-4M	Sweden	1	31-386

NA-32	10-3-37	NA-16-1-A	Australia for CAC	1	32-387
NA-33	10-3-37	NA-16-2K	Australia for CAC	1	33-388
NA-34	19-3-37	NA-16-4P	Argentina	30	34-389/418
NA-36	16-6-37	BC-1	USAAC	85 92	36-420/504 36-596/687
NA-37	2-9-37	NA-16-4R	Japan	1	37-539
NA-38	28-9-37	NA-16-4M	Sweden	1	38-540
NA-41	23-2-38	NA-16-4	China	35	41-697/731
NA-42	9-12-37	NA-16-2A	Honduras	2	42-691/692
NA-43	9-12-37	NA-16-1Q	Brazil	–	Cancelled
NA-44	9-12-37	NA-44	Canada	1	44-747
NA-45	14-12-37	NA-16-IGV	Venezuela	3	45-693/695
NA-46	2-12-38	NA-16-4	Brazil	12	46-972/977 46-1991/1996
NA-47	16-12-37	NA-16-4RW	Japan	1	47-699
NA-48	23-2-38	NA-16-3C	China	15	48-732/746
NA-49	7-2-38	NA-16-IE Harvard I	UK	200 200	49-748/947 49-1053/1252
NA-50	9-2-39	NA-50	Peru	7	50-948/954
NA-52	28-9-38	SNJ-1	USN	16	52-956/971
NA-54	3-10-38	BC-2	USAAC	3	54-688/690
NA-55	–	BC-1A	USAAC	83	55-1548/1630
NA-56	18-4-39	NA-16-4	China	50	56-1453/1502
NA-57	21-2-39	NA-57 (BT-9B)	France	230	57-1253/1452 57-1518/1547
NA-58	28-4-39	BT-14	USAAC	251	58-1655/1905
NA-59	–	AT-6	USAAC	94	59-1631/1639 59-1906/1990
NA-61	25-5-39	NA-16-IE	Canada	30	61-1503/1517 61-1640/1654
NA-64	5-9-39	NA-64	France	230	64-2033/2232 64-3018/3047
NA-65	25-9-39	SNJ-2	USN	36	65-1997/2032
NA-66	17-11-39	Harvard II	UK	600	66-2234/2833

NA-68	30-11-39	NA-50A (P-64)	Siam	6	68-3058/3063
NA-69	30-11-39	NA-44	Siam	10	60-3064-3073
NA70	9-1-40	Cancelled	–	–	–
NA-71	18-1-40	NA-16-3	Venezuela	3	71-3074/3076
NA-72	13-1-40	NA-44 (BC-1A)	Brazil	30	72-3077/3096 72-4757/4766
NA-74	7-8-40	NA-44	Chile	12	74-4745/4756
NA-75	3-6-40	Harvard II	Canada	100	75-3048/3057 75-3418/3507
NA-76	5-6-40	Harvard II	UK	450	76-3508/3957
NA-77	28-6-40	AT-6A SNJ-3	USAAC	517 120	–
NA-78	1-10-40	AT-6A SNJ-3	USAAC USN	1330 150	–
NA-79	–	SNJ-2	USN	25	78-3983/4007
NA-81	11-7-40	Harvard II	UK	125	81-4008/4132
NA-84	6-12-40	AT-6B	USAAC	400	78-7412/7811
NA-85	–	SNJ-3	–	–	To NA-78
NA-88	10-4-41 –	AT-6C AT-6D SNJ-4 SNJ-5	USAAF USAAF USN USN	2970 2604 2400 1357	
NA-119	10-1-44	AT-6D	USAAF (for Brazil)	81	119-40086/40166
NA-121	11-2-44	AT-6D AT-6F	USAAF	800 956	121-41567/42366 121-42367/43322
NA-128	1-6-44	Cancelled	–	–	–
NA-168	5-10-49	T-6G	USAF	641	168-1/371 168-387/440 168-450/500 168-511/560 168-571/620 168-631/680 168-681/691
		LT-6G T-6G	USAF ANG	59 50	168-692/750 168-372/381 168-441/450 168-501/510 168-561/570 168-621/630
NA-182	8-2-51	T-6G	USAF	824	182-1/824

NA-186	22-6-51	T-6J	USAF	–	Design data
NA-188	11-4-51	T-6G	USAF	100 7	188-1/100 188-101/107
NA-195	19-3-52	T-6G	USAF	11	191-1/11
NA-197 FO.8002	16-6-52	T-6G	USAF (T-6D to T-6G for ANG)	50 60	197-1/50 8002-1/60
NA-198	Terminated 3-7-52		USN	240	–

For acrobatic display and formation flying, few aircraft can beat the North American trainer. The combined racket of six or more P&Ws snarling overhead is usually worth the admission money alone! Instant reaction had long been a hall-mark of the North American trainer and superb wing-tip to wing-tip displays are grist to its mill. During the war inverted flight time was limited to ten seconds due to the dry-sump oil condition but the machine is light on the controls.

In Great Britain the premier team is 'The Harvard Formation Team' based at the former Battle of Britain airfield of North Weald, near Harlow, Essex. Here 087 of that team bids a fond farewell to Oshkosh! (*Courtesy of The Squadron, Harvard Formation Team, North Weald*)

Sky-writing and publicity banner-hauling has also naturally featured on the working T-6's itinerary down the years. In the mid-1960s a new slant on that old advertising ploy is used by the American firm of Skytypers East, based at Flushing, New York. Six former SNJ-2s are used in a technique known as 'Skytyping'. Linked together electronically, a 'master' lead plane acts as guide and controller with a main computer and transmitter aboard. On the word from this machine all six aircraft, known as the Miller Squadron after the Brewery firm which sponsors them, simultaneously 'type' out a letter by emitting smoke balls at about 1,000ft altitude. Seen from the ground this merges into readily readable writing at the rate of nine characters per minute. This is a ten-fold improvement on the old-style skywriting and has proved a big hit. Each 'letter' extends over about five miles of airspace and is highly effective.

The line-up of the Skytyping T-6s (with N66082 in the foreground) is seen here at Long Beach, California, in July 1968, where a West Coast team was set up. (*Courtesy N.M. Williams Collection*)

Classic Gardens

Translated from the French *Jardins à la française*
by Harriet Mason

Designed by François Chevret
Plans by André Leroux

This edition first published in the United Kingdom in 2000
by Thames & Hudson Ltd, 181A High Holborn, London WCIV 7QX

© 2000 Thames & Hudson Ltd, London and The Vendome Press, New York

Original edition © 1999 Imprimerie nationale Editions, Paris

British Library Cataloguing-in-Publication Data
A catalogue record for this book is available from the British Library

ISBN 0-500-51030-X

Printed and bound in France

Classic Gardens
The French Style

Jean-Pierre Babelon and Mic Chamblas-Ploton

Photographs by Jean-Baptiste Leroux

Pathways of the Sun

Jean-Pierre Babelon

Courances, looking out over the garden.

THE DREAM OF VAUX

WHEN ACANTHE *fell asleep one spring evening, he dreamed that Sleep would allow him to see the palace of Vaux and its gardens.*

JEAN DE LA FONTAINE

When Nicolas Fouquet urged him to write in praise of the splendours created at Vaux, La Fontaine turned to the literary device of the dream, and later explained: 'As the gardens at Vaux were newly planted, I could not describe them as they were then without giving a rather unattractive idea of the place, which would anyway be quite different twenty years later. So I had to anticipate, which could only be done in three ways: by magic, conjecture or dream.'

The use of dream allowed him to visualize Fouquet's estate as it would become, and gave his imagination free rein to lead his reader on a fanciful walk through the gardens. He continued, 'My precedents were the *Roman de la Rose*, the *Hypnerotomachia Poliphili* (the *Dream of Poliphilus*) and the *Dream of Scipio*.' Since antiquity, dreams had been used by poets to depict an ideal world, both philosophical and sensual, and a garden is surely the most beautiful possible setting for our dreams, a part of his world in which man contends with the power of the elements. In the stories of old, it is only after he has successfully undertaken the various symbolic trials that he encounters in the forest, and followed the paths of love, that man can reach the supreme good of wisdom, and go on his way with understanding.

In the Garden of Eden, Adam experienced happiness, and then the agony of temptation, finally giving in to the devil, before humankind was saved by a second Adam in the Garden of Gethsemane. In the thirteenth century, the authors of the *Roman de la Rose*, Guillaume de

Lorris and Jean de Meung, and at the end of the fifteenth, the author of the *Hypnerotomachia Poliphili*, Francesco Colonna, also chose a carefully structured natural setting for their heroes' quests, intended as a metaphorical initiation for their readers. In the former, the narrator enters the walled orchard of Love, and finds the pool where long ago Narcissus tried in vain to capture the beauty of his own reflection; in the latter, Poliphilus searches for his beloved Polia through a series of imaginary landscapes, filled with temples, allegorical sculptures and classical ruins.

Like all educated people at the time, La Fontaine knew these books. Jean Martin's French version of the Colonna story, published in 1546, was widely read. Both the text and the illustrations made it a key book for garden designers, who found in it the vocabulary they needed. It was crucial to the birth and development of the formal garden.

La Fontaine was not the only one to give detailed descriptions of gardens. There were many other guides written to help enthusiasts in the 'Grand Siècle' to plan their walks, such as those of André Félibien, Madeleine de Scudéry and Piganiol de La Force. They were reprinted several times to satisfy a constant demand, and to spread the word about the latest wonderful sights. The 'Précieux' were uncompromising in their attempts to establish a refined lifestyle, and, among other things, encouraged the new passion for gardens, which was rooted in the powerful allure of nature illustrated in many influential literary and artistic works.

Agriculture was in fashion in France, thanks to the impetus given by King Henri IV (1553–1610) at the end of the civil war. In 1600, a manual of farming methods and domestic economy, *Le Théâtre d'agriculture et mesnage des champs* by Olivier de Serres, promoted by the King and Sully, his Chief Minister, was published to support the efforts of farmers. It also covers horticulture and arboriculture, advising the planting of flower gardens with roses and carnations.

The appearance of the French countryside had been changed by the construction of new châteaux or the rebuilding of old ones, deprived of their fortifications on the orders of

Richelieu, Chief Minister of Louis XIII, and all now with gardens. Financiers had taken enormous risks and made a fortune backing the monarchy, the *nouveaux riches* had accumulated substantial revenues from their agricultural estates – they climbed the social ladder, obtaining posts in the royal household and gaining other important public positions, and invested their money in luxurious dwellings, both town houses and châteaux, and in their gardens. The public was allowed to share in the festivities to some extent through reading the guides and journals, and accepted this conspicuous display of wealth without too much complaint.

Throughout his work, La Fontaine shows a devotee's enlightened appreciation of the art of making gardens: 'Gardens are mostly silent places, speaking only through my book' (*L'Ours et l'amateur des jardins*). In his descriptions of the enchanted places prepared by Cupid for the beautiful Psyche, he introduces with ease references to the best-known gardens of his own time, listing them in the style of a recipe:

> *Mix together, without ever going there,*
> *Vaux, Liancourt and their fair naiad daughters,*
> *Adding to them also, should you care,*
> *Rueil with its clear cascading waters.*
> *Then scatter far and wide throughout this space,*
> *Artfully set in each enchanted place,*
> *Myriad fountains pointing to the skies,*
> *Canals that stretch away beyond men's eyes.*
> *Rim them with orange, myrtle, jasmine, whose sweet scents delight,*
> *Grown to gigantic stature, while our own are dwarfed in height;*
> *Pile them with nurseries on every side;*
> *Plant them with whole dense forests, vast and wide....*
> *That in this district with such charm replete*

Pomona should with Flora here compete
To make a show of all their plenteousness.

Here is the first description, in 1669, of a *jardin à la française* – a garden in the French style. It is significant that the examples have not been taken from Louis XIV's properties, but from some of the renowned, innovative private gardens. The French 'mode' or style of garden design was gradually developed during the sixteenth century by the aristocracy, who retained strong links with their country estates. They were freer than the king to choose how and when to spend their money, and the great landowners experimented with new ideas and new layouts, which were only later adopted in the royal gardens. This liberating independence gathered pace during the French Wars of Religion (1562–98) and then in the reign of Louis XIII (1610–43), reaching its peak with Nicolas Fouquet at Vaux, seeming to justify the daring motto of his heraldic squirrel, 'Quo non ascendet' – 'To what heights will he not climb?'

LOUIS XIV CAME TO THE THRONE in 1643 and when he was old enough he took charge of the royal inheritance and made it his own. He intended to create the most magnificent surroundings possible for himself, but also wanted a suitable setting for the sumptuous rituals of the centralized and personalized State which ruled the daily lives of the courtiers. Metaphorically, they were bound to the King by the magnificent garlands of flowers painted on the ceilings of the Grands Appartements; and the gardens played an even more important part than the château in defining the royal domain, providing an even wider setting for every aspect of the monarch's public image, from his appearance, to his promenades, parties and fêtes. The perfection that had been the aim of Louis XIV and André Le Nôtre, the garden designer, made Versailles into a universal model, an inspiration for future projects of any size by members of the French or European nobility.

Detail of the Jardin d'Amour at Villandry, covered with snow...

...and in the springtime.

The hornbeam hedges around the Bassin des Dames at Beloeil in Belgium.

View of the Baroque pavilion in the garden at Kromeriz, in the Czech Republic.

IN THE BEGINNING
THERE WAS THE CHATEAU

A DESCRIPTION that concentrates on the formality, straight lines and symmetry strictly imposed in a French seventeenth-century garden gives only a very limited idea of its distinctive appearance. Jacques Boyceau de La Barauderie wrote in his *Traité du Jardinage selon les raisons de la nature et de l'art* (1638) that 'the gardens with the most variety will be found to be the most beautiful'. An appreciation of the character of such a garden can best be achieved by strolling around it.

It is clear straight away that the garden's visual links with the château are paramount; the French style is defined by its carefully arranged hierarchy of spaces, very different from Italian gardens. For example, at the Villa Lante at Bagnaia the house consists of no more than two square pavilions built in the corners of the *parterre*. In France, the opposite is the case. The garden radiates from the château; everything both leads away from it and returns to it.

In feudal times, the castle, seat of the overlord and symbol of his power, was surrounded with fortifications as a defence against the outside world; in keeping with its name, *castrum*, it was cut off and separated from its surroundings. The lord and his family lived in a protected environment in which there was only space for a small and utilitarian garden. But later French knights returned from the Crusades greatly impressed by the gardens they had seen in the eastern Mediterranean, and a new era of garden design developed in the fourteenth century, inspired by the concept of the secret garden and representations of paradise found in both sacred and profane literature. Gardens were now placed outside the castle's enclosing wall, even if they had to be defended with more walls, as they were at the Louvre in Paris in the time of King Charles V (1337–80); the garden or *hortus conclusus* was by definition an enclosed space.

At the same time, a new kind of stately home was beginning to develop: the *manoir de plaisance*, dear to King René of Anjou. Here there were lodges, courtyards, galleries, arbours and pergolas, encouraging aristocratic society to enjoy the flowers and fruits of nature; a way of life widely depicted in miniatures and tapestries. As a result of French wars with Italy, there was a second important influence on garden design; Kings Charles VIII, Louis XII and François I discovered sunny gardens there, filled with unfamiliar scents, gardens that surrounded the house and provided both food and pleasure for the titled families who left their town palaces for a while to be refreshed by the country air and streams.

The 'Humanist' gardens such as those of the Medici in Tuscany (Poggio a Caiano, Castello), the vineyards of the Roman cardinals and the first Papal gardens at the Vatican, in Rome, and particularly the magnificent ensemble of terraces and *parterres* built above the Bay of Naples for King Alfonso II at Poggio Reale, were built on a system unknown at that time in France: landscape and buildings were built together to an architect's overall design. The first architect known to have advocated this idea was the great theoretician of beauty in design, Leon Battista Alberti. Nature was made into works of art, rivalling some of ancient Rome's finest achievements such as Hadrian's Villa at Tivoli.

French travellers also discovered the idea of a single axis linking the rear façade of the house and the layout of the geometrically planned gardens. This new approach was soon applied to the landscape of their own estates, although an axial and symmetrical composition was only possible with new constructions, freed from the constraints of the older fortress setting. The pioneers were the Maréchal de Gié, Pierre de Rohan, who laid out regularly shaped gardens at his Château du Verger in Anjou, on either side of the defensive ditches, and Cardinal Georges d'Amboise who had a large rectangular garden designed for the open area behind his château at Gaillon in Normandy; a decisive step was taken by Florimond Robertet, who built a château and garden to a strict geometric plan at Bury, a few kilometres from Blois, in 1511; the plan of the château and garden together formed a double square, the two linked by a monumental perron and double flight of steps leading down to the square *parterres*. Only traces of it remain today. Thanks to the imagination of Robertet, who served both Louis XII and François I as a minister, a garden layout designed for Italian hillsides was transposed to the flat Loire landscape, and the idea of the physical and ideological linking of the château and the garden that characterizes the French style was born.

The kings had less scope than their inferiors, as they were restricted to using their inherited properties on the Loire, fortresses built on high promontories above the river. The gardener Pacello da Mercogliano was brought from Italy to improve unpromising sites with regularly laid-out gardens at Amboise, within the castle walls, and at Blois, on level ground outside the walls.

Bury was for a long time an isolated example. There is no record of François I having grand plans for the gardens at Chambord, although he had been responsible for building the château, and at Fontainebleau, where the irregular plan precluded a dominant axis, he laid out gardens at a tangent to the buildings. Diane de Poitiers, Henri II's mistress, did the same in 1552 with the garden at Chenonceau, within a sort of bastion on the banks of the river Cher.

It was not until the second half of the sixteenth century that the great innovative architects returned to the axial principle. Sebastiano Serlio used it at Ancy-le-Franc, built for Antoine de Clermont, who had really wanted a château in the Italian style, and Philibert de L'Orme created axial plans at Anet for Diane de Poitiers and at the Tuileries, in Paris, for Catherine de Médicis. From then on, the single axis running through both château and garden was rigidly imposed on the site in its entirety – the entrance, the courtyard, and even the outer courtyard and the outbuildings – so that a visitor would immediately be aware that the whole composition was governed by a harmonious unifying plan.

The French principle was adopted for garden design, and dictated the plans of the great château gardens of the end of the sixteenth century – Verneuil, Charleval, Montceaux – as described by Jacques Androuet du Cerceau in his *Les Plus excellents bastiments de France*.

During the first half of the seventeenth century, this gradually led to changes in the design of the château itself. The quadrilateral plan was abandoned in favour of the horseshoe and then the horizontal block, which in turn meant a radical change in the relationship between the building and the garden.

One man, François Mansart, had the vision to anticipate all the possibilities of these developments, allowing a new treatment of space, opening it up towards the horizon, and taking complete control of the landscape. His contribution was a key one, first through his own work and then as the teacher and example for André Le Nôtre. At the beginning of the 1630s, Mansart built a château and grounds at Balleroy in Normandy, with an axial road that took the pyramidal building as its focal point. The estate stands prominently on the side of the valley, with its decorative *parterres*. At Blois, he persuaded Gaston d'Orléans to build a colossal bridge across a ravine in order to extend a great geometrical garden behind the recently completed main building. His masterpiece was Maisons, built on a raised plinth and standing at the end of a vast perspective, stretching from the Fôret de Saint-Germain to the Seine, with paths at right angles to it creating unexpected views. He was in direct competition with Louis Le Vau, who used the same technique at Vaux. There, the contrasting architecture of the outbuildings emphasizes the impact of the château standing on its podium, surrounded by defensive ditches and enclosed on three sides by the *parterres*.

At Versailles, the same formula was applied on a scale that has never been equalled: the design included a new town on the orders of Louis XIV, following the example set by the cardinal and minister Richelieu on his own estate. The great axis begins in the town, with three avenues forming a huge *patte d'oie* and crossroads. The axis of the central Avenue de Paris continues across the Place d'Armes, through the *avant cour* flanked by the Ministry wings, then the Cour Royale, into the inner sanctum of the Cour de Marbre, heart of the original château, and finally through the gardens and the Grand Parc. An interrelation of spaces on such a scale had never been attempted before. The garden itself is not visible from the town, although before the north and south wings were completed in 1689, some of the *parterres* and foliage could be seen to the right and left of the horseshoe-shaped palace. Since Versailles became the seat of sovereign power, entailing the construction of the wings, it has formed a huge continuous barrier 670 metres (2200 ft) long, which blocks the view of the grounds and separates two distinct worlds, the constructed world and the world of vegetation.

The residences of other European monarchies employ the same hierarchy of courtyard, château and gardens, for example at Schönbrunn in Austria, Caserta in Italy, or Peterhof in Russia. The need for access through the architectural mass of the palace, from the courtyards to the gardens, was resolved most spectacularly by the architect Gabriel-Germain Boffrand for Duke Léopold de Lorraine in his château at Lunéville. There, three tall arcades let light into the central pavilion and give a clear view of the gardens with the sun penetrating from all sides.

By the Grand Canal at Versailles.

The *avant cour* at Versailles.

Two views in opposite directions at La Roche-Courbon.

The east–west perspective from the perron of the château.
In the foreground, the *parterre* dotted with topiary and beyond,
the canal and the *allée d'eau*.

The château seen from the top of the double flight of steps
framing the *allée d'eau*, showing the same view from the
opposite end of the perspective.

Above: aerial view of the Château de Chenonceau, showing in the foreground the Jardin de Diane de Poitiers, and beyond, from left to right, the gallery over the river Cher, the Bohiers' château, and the Jardin de Catherine de Médicis, with the Tour des Marques and inner and outer courtyards lying in front of it.

Below: Vista along the transverse arm of the Grand Canal at Versailles, from the Trianon. Louis XIV's Ménagerie was at the far end of the canal.

Above: the Gloriette in the gardens of Schönbrunn, Vienna.

Below: A play on lines and changes of level in the garden at Cormatin, in Burgundy.

The gardens at Vaux-le-Vicomte seen from the terrace of the château.

THE WELL-KEPT
AND THE WILD

In urban Paris, the formal garden arrived just as soon as houses were built with enough space behind them. However, the *parterres* that were created for these *hôtels* ('an almost infinite number', as Henri Sauval wrote in the middle of the seventeenth century), even when they were designed by the greatest masters, were merely a miniature version of those built on the huge scale that the French style demanded, and it was sometimes necessary to resort to false perspective to create an illusion of greater space.

Two palaces originally built just outside the capital avoided the constraints imposed by a small plot; these were Catherine de Médicis' Palais des Tuileries and Marie de Médicis' Palais de Luxembourg. The two Florentine queens brought the Medici taste for gardens to France, along with a familiarity with the execution of large-scale designs. At the Palais de Luxembourg, the Florentine precedent of the Palazzo Pitti and the Boboli Gardens led to a close relationship between the building and the garden, enclosed within terraces culminating in a semi-circular apse; similar designs were created at Anet, Charleval, Maulnes en Tonnerrois and the Tuileries. Originally, the Luxembourg axis was terminated by a grotto, and it was only much later that a long avenue was cut through, bringing the Palais de l'Observatoire into view at the end of the main sight line. At the Tuileries, André Le Nôtre re-created Catherine de Médicis' level, enclosed garden, making the two matching lateral terraces and extending the central *allée* beyond the walls into an avenue lined with a double row of elms, now the Champs Elysées, towards the raised ground of Chaillot.

However, these are the exceptions, as the scale of gardens *à la française* at their grandest demanded a rural setting. Large areas of good arable land with adequate irrigation were

necessary to feed a prince or a king's entourage. Hunting was a favourite pastime in a society eager for physical exercise, and that regarded riding and jousting as a peaceful alternative to the joys of real combat, and so it became an important factor in the choice of locations and the orientation of the châteaux.

In those days the forests were denser and much more extensive, the trees crowding close to the great houses; the guests expected to be able to enjoy a range of hunting nearby in the forest and brushwood, rabbit warrens, heaths or ponds. The kings favoured their estates with a variety of wild natural habitats, so that they had the daily choice of either furred or feathered game, deer, wolves and boar. The first building at Versailles was a lodge for Louis XIII, used when the hunt drew him out of the Forêt de Saint-Germain to look for game in the Val de Gally; the Hapsburgs' Schönbrunn, near Vienna, then known as the Katterburg, was originally used for hunting parties, and was bought by Emperor Maximilian II (1527–76) to pursue his passion for hunting. The obsession was widely shared among the aristocracy, and explains the particular arrangement of the châteaux built and rebuilt in the middle of France's biggest forests, such as Chambord, Saint-Germain in the Fôret de Laye and Madrid in the Bois de Boulogne, which provided extensive accommodation for guests, and terraces to watch the departure and return of the horsemen and their hounds. The abiding popularity of Fontainebleau with the French monarchy, from the Capetian kings to Napoleon III, rests on the huge extent of the forest. At Versailles Louis XIV, Louis XV and Louis XVI continued to enlarge the great hunting park, at the expense of surrounding villages, marshes and arable land; at the end of Louis XIV's reign it already covered 6614 hectares (15,000 including the Forêt de Marly) while the Petit Parc was 1765 hectares and the gardens 93. Fouquet's estate at Vaux amounted to 500 hectares; today Saint-Cloud is 400 and Sceaux 200 hectares.

Gardens were carved out within these cultivated or wild areas of vegetation, like shorn patches on a fleece. Nature was always an indispensable part of the whole; the visual contrast between the 'natural' areas and the garden added to the impact of the man-made environment.

Part of the *vertugadin* on the north–south axis at Villarceaux,
which links the Château du Haut and the lake.

As the proud owner of an estate at Ferney, Voltaire remarked in 1772: 'I have everything in my gardens – *parterres*, small ornamental ponds, formal walks, very informal woodland, little valleys, fields, vineyards, vegetable gardens with espaliered fruit trees covering their walls; both the well-kept and the wild...'

The development of the French style was dictated by the relatively level terrain of the Val de Loire, and later that of the Ile-de-France. The natural lie of the chosen landscape lent itself to a series of terraces, allowing an emphatic single direction for the site. By contrast, gardens in the Italian hills of Tuscany and Lazio were designed using dramatic cantilevered effects, but rarely included long perspective vistas. In some areas of France, however, a wide river such as the Seine – ideal terrain though it was for winding pathways with panoramic views – prevented the imposition of the usual strict grid for the château and garden; in such cases, a more Italian approach was used. Axes at right angles to the river were created, at a distance from the house itself, and the changes in level were used for magnificent water features. This was done at Saint-Cloud, and also at Saint-Germain, where a charming compromise was reached by treating the two parts of the site differently. The Château Vieux had a huge horizontal terrace designed by Le Nôtre, stretching between the forest and the valley of the Seine; meanwhile, the Château Neuf, a small, low building that was gradually extended, stands tall above the series of ramps, terraces and grottoes descending to the level of the river, reminiscent of the Villa d'Este at Tivoli.

Was there a particular reason why Louis XIV gave Saint-Cloud to his brother, and Saint-Germain to the deposed King of England, James II? Perhaps it shows that he did not want to live in a restricted landscape, however prestigious it might be. A large-scale project with a system of interrelated axes required a fairly level site, which could be moulded and had open views, even if, as Louis de Rouvroy, Duc de Saint-Simon noted with some exaggeration, 'it is the most mournful and unpromising of places, lifeless, with no woods, no water and no earth because it is all soft sand and marshland.' For Louis XIV, the waters of the Seine or the Eure

were a means of filling the fountains and the canal at Versailles, and he diverted them at great expense; he was not concerned with natural rivers as features of the royal landscape.

It had always been the case that the untamed countryside which provided the privileged with the pleasures of hunting was also a dangerous place, inhabited by armed bands and brigands, and both towns and châteaux surrounded themselves with defensive walls. The internal warring of the 'Ligue' and popular unrest and disturbances during the 'Fronde' era were reminders right up to the accession of Louis XIV that such times were not yet passed. New châteaux continued to be built with defensive walls, barbicans, ditches and drawbridges, but this was largely because such features conferred an exalted status on the landowner, a particularly attractive prospect to new members of the second tier of royalty.

The inclusion of these features, although cleverly integrated into the overall character of the plan and the design by the architects, had an impact on the landscape and the relationship of the building with the garden. The four-sided keep surrounded by ditches was still built, with the château standing on a protective plinth. Isolating the château, as happened at Vaux and Maisons, did offer protection against petty attack, but resistance to siege would have been impossible; it did, however, reinforce the 'imposing air of dignity' and 'majesty' of the place, qualities much commented on in writings of the time.

THE ORIGINAL VERSAILLES had been fortified, and it was only in 1668 that the defensive ditches were filled, when Le Vau doubled the size of Louis XIII's main building. Now there was direct access to the *parterres* and the great terrace overlooking the whole site, from both the open bays of the ground-floor central gallery and from the great rooms on either side. A revolution had taken place, and the walls had definitively come down.

Two years later Louis XIV ordered the ramparts of Paris to be razed, believing that the future security of the capital was assured by the strongholds on the kingdom's frontiers. On the same principle, the entire park at Versailles was ringed with a wall 43 kilometres (27 miles) long, with twenty-five gates. The wall was not, however, allowed to block the perspective views along the axial and radiating avenues. Because of invisible ditches and ha-has of varying widths, the horizon was clearly visible and the crops growing on the Plaine de Gally could be seen from the Trianon, bringing a view of the surrounding landscape into the very heart of the royal park.

The purpose of a terrace constructed in front of a château is to give a panoramic view of the whole layout of the grounds, with its main perspective, the axes at right angles to it and the many other sight lines, and to make clear the balance between the open areas and the thickly wooded ones. A raised terrace is an integral part of such a design, and the recent restoration of the Tuileries gardens has included the rebuilding of the terrace in its position in front of the 'phantom' palace.

The château at Versailles stands on the highest ground of the site, an isolation required for security considerations, but also for health reasons – the sun and wind dispel the miasmas caused by the still waters below. This places the château at the peak of a pyramid, an appropriate geometric figure to describe the hierarchical social structure under the Ancien Régime. Authority is expressed in the series of descending levels, the terraces linked by stairs and slopes, both straight and curved, which form the framework of the theatre where the drama of power is acted out. Their masters were on display, and the public were part of the show as well as being spectators. The great gardens had always been freely accessible, permitting the mingling of the social classes. Like the rich in ancient Rome, kings and princes offered the people access to their own pleasure gardens, an amenity nowadays provided by public parks.

The great spaces around the palace of Versailles are bathed in sunlight. Phoebus, or Apollo, rules unchallenged here, producing flashes of brilliant light from the gravel on the paths, the marble of the copings of the *bassins* and the statues, and the drops of water from the gushing fountains. The power of the sun myth is felt by every visitor even if the mythology itself is unfamiliar, or the royal symbols unknown. At Versailles the identification of the king

with the sun is at its most insistent, though poetic licence has been allowed. The sun god's chariot does not travel in the natural direction of the sun as it illuminates and warms the earth; instead, Apollo makes use of the orientation of the site, facing into the sun for the most dramatic effect, as it rises over the town and sets at the far end of the Grand Canal. Here, the sun god rises from the waters of the fountain in the west, and rests from the heat of the day in the cool of Thetis' grotto to the east near the château (where the Chapelle Royale now stands), after passing the scene from his childhood represented at the Fontaine de Latone. The paths of the king and the sun god cross here, as La Fontaine described with a touch of humour:

> *Behold, in golden chariots, the Prince and all his court*
> *Ride out to taste the freshness as the daylight hours run short:*
> *Sun and Sun King, each unique in legend and in story,*
> *Flaunt to all who look on them their power and their glory.*
> *The King of France and Phoebus vie to dazzle mortal eyes;*
> *We often cannot rightly judge to whom to give the prize:*
> *Both are so filled with brilliancy and radiant with fame.*
> *If only, when I called for aid, Memory's daughters came!*
> *Then, when I compared the two, what shafts of wit would follow!*
> *Versailles would readily become the Palace of Apollo;*
> *The beauties of the Court would be mistaken for the Seasons.*

The blazing sun did not please everyone. Courtiers who accompanied the King, wearing wigs and formal clothes, dissatisfied with 'always being in the countryside' since the King ordered it in 1682, had to face that 'huge torrid zone, in which there is nothing to do but go up and down' (Saint-Simon). Even though the water cooled the atmosphere when the fountains were playing, the shady trees were a long way off. At the end of his life, the King accepted the difficulty – at Marly, where the gardens were more compact than at Versailles, he increased the number of outdoor 'rooms'. Philippe de Courcillon, the Marquis de Dangeau wrote in May 1695 that 'on his most recent visit the King created a very pleasant area that could be called the Appartements Verts, where it will be possible to remain in the shade at all hours of the day.' On walking by a few weeks later, 'he saw the ladies sitting there, working at their embroidery'.

View of the Etang de la Vinette from the terrace at Villarceaux.

The gardens at the Manoir d'Eyrignac blend into the 'Périgord noir' landscape.

The tall hornbeam hedges at Cordés contrast with the countryside
of the massif du Mont-Dore, in Auvergne.

43

Cormatin, in Burgundy. The moated *parterre* in front of the north façade symbolizes the Garden of Eden.
To the left, the outbuildings screen the kitchen garden.

Schönbrunn in Vienna was named after a spring, the Schöner Brunnen.

The 'green bastion' of Canadian thuyas at the
Château de Hautefort, in Périgord.

GARDENS FOR THE INTELLECT, GARDENS FOR THE SENSES

IN THE SEVENTEENTH CENTURY it was the fashion to enjoy a promenade, especially when combined with reflections on man's destiny. It was the role of poets such as Colonna and La Fontaine, the heirs of the great classical poets Virgil and Tibullus, to initiate visitors by elucidating the philosophical principles behind the design of the garden: they held the key to the sanctuary. In La Fontaine's poem, four spirits are brought together by Oronte (Fouquet) to compete for the prize of excellence at Vaux: Palatiane (Architecture), Apellanire (Painting), Hortésie (Gardening) and Calliopée (Poetry), and Calliopée has the last word as she is the only one to have the use of language, which is universal and eternal:

> *The gifts of Hortésie in leafy shade*
> *Have more charm in my verse than those she made.*

Lucien Corpechot made the same definition of gardens *à la française* in 1912 in his book *Les Jardins de l'intelligence* (Gardens of the Intellect). But La Fontaine was not to be limited by a single interpretation. As well as mysteries, there were sensual pleasures, and he was a man who appreciated these too. Against a background of symbols and evocations of antiquity and humanism, Le Nôtre or Jean-Baptiste de La Quintinye designed gardens for the senses, concerned with the pleasures of seeing, smelling, hearing, touching and eating.

> *He loved gardens, and was a priest of Flora;*
> *But was even more devoted to Pomona.*

Fifty years earlier, the last of the Valois, Queen Marguerite, wrote to her husband Henri IV that she was going to Fontainebleau 'to see that earthly paradise, that beautiful garden of exquisite pleasures'.

Our ancestors tasted the apple in Paradise and when they were expelled, they were condemned to cultivate the earth. One of the oldest traditions of gardening, particularly in ancient Greece, was the association of the utilitarian with the pleasurable. The flower garden, vegetable garden and orchard were planted together, satisfying all the senses, and giving the proprietor the pleasure of extolling the virtues of his own private universe; these were the kind of gardens praised by François Rabelais, gardens providing not simply food but also remedies, with their collections of 'simples', herbs with known beneficial properties.

Ever since the Carolingian period, monks had been highly skilled at managing the large areas they used to cultivate nature's produce, under the watchful eye of the Creator. The plots were meticulously irrigated, divided into squares separated by paths, and sometimes contained arbours to rest in at the intersections; this regular plan was copied early on in immaculate pleasure gardens such as the one at Blois, where the little rest house used by Anne de Bretagne can still be seen.

The gardens at Villandry, restored with an admirable enthusiasm by Joachim Carvallo in the early twentieth century, give an idea of those huge monastery vegetable gardens, where an appreciation of the beauty of colour combinations, of the variety of shapes and the juxtaposition of flowers, vegetables and fruit trees, was the result of the highest scientific and practical expertise. The tradition continued into the Grand Siècle. Sauval wrote that the Capucin monks in Paris 'cultivated some cabbages, root vegetables and herbs. They grow them in beds in their *parterres*, and these make a more pleasing sight than the creations of our most admired flower gardeners.'

La Quintinye was responsible for planting the Potager du Roi, the king's vegetable garden at Versailles; it was a centre for production and experiment, and he took great pride in the sunken areas he devised for the maintenance of micro-climates suitable for the propagation of exotic plants. Many other kitchen gardens *à la française* have been either salvaged or re-created in modern times, in France (at Saint-Jean-de-Beauregard) and in America, by enthusiastic garden lovers. This was the gardeners' heyday, toiling from dawn to dusk in their straw hats and busily maintaining the *parterres* for our pleasure. In the writings of Pliny or Cicero, the Latin word for gardener is *topiarius*: a person who has learned to tame nature, to restrain, cut and bend growing things, to impose a shape on them, give them a purpose and make them part of a unified design. The art of topiary as we understand it today is an ancient one and was mentioned by one of the first garden theorists, contemporaneous with the *Roman de la Rose*, the Italian Pietro di Crescenzi in his *Le Livre des prouffitz champestres et ruraulx*; and arcades of trained shrubs feature in a painting by Andrea Mantegna and the engravings that illustrate the *Hypnerotomachia Poliphili* show laurels and box bushes clipped into the most unlikely shapes, in imitation of sculpted figures or fragments of architecture. Paradoxically, living matter is trained to emulate the inanimate.

In the Middle Ages, such visual games involving references and jokes in a pleasure garden setting were very popular and the seventeenth-century 'Classicists' used them as their starting-point when they restructured their landscapes. It is impossible to think of a French formal garden without the manipulation of vegetation which creates all the shapes, shadows and perspective views. The hand of the artist is revealed: he achieves his effects with shears, using them to make pictures; as Pliny had said long before, *picturas operis topiarii*.

These effects were used to make the carpets of vegetation spread out in front of the house – the *parterres* and their intricate designs have for a long time represented the pinnacle of the gardener's ingenuity. This was a two-dimensional composition, on a par with drawings, prints, book covers and embroidered cloth, and the terms *brodeur* and *broderie* were soon used to describe it. The first *parterres de broderie* were made in the sixteenth century, during the reign of Catherine de Médicis, when the art of embroidery on cloth was experiencing a 'golden age'.

Those *parterres* included the ones at Anet, designed, according to the king's gardener Claude Mollet, by the architect Etienne Dupérac on his return from Italy in 1582. Only dwarf box trees from Italy were suitable for the degree of precise trimming required, and Mollet established tree nurseries to acclimatize and propagate them under French conditions. This also allowed him to provide sufficient trees for Henri IV and his gardens at Saint-Germain, Montceaux and Fontainebleau.

The first geometrical *parterre* designs were the *parquets* at Amboise by Pacello da Mercogliano, and consisted simply of medium-sized squares arranged in chessboard fashion and separated by a grid of paths. Later designs were more extensive, varied and complex; they introduced rectangles and circles, and later abandoned simple geometric forms in favour of cut-off corners, indentations, concave and convex curves and scrolls.

Box is the raw material of the garden *brodeur*. Like a calligrapher's brush, which can flatten or make a point, it can be made to draw downstrokes and upstrokes, straight lines, curves and full stops, a whole playful range of leaf designs, palmettes and interlacing, with intermingled cryptic signs, initials, coats of arms and mottoes. Claude Mollet made a design at the Tuileries which included the initials and emblems of Henri IV in one of the central compartments. At Villandry, Dr Carvallo laid out the symbolic designs of his 'gardens of love' three hundred years later.

The *parterre* was the masterpiece of the profession, to which the gardener devoted all his skill or inspiration, and highlighted the pre-eminence of those who worked for the king. Like Mollet, Jean Le Nôtre was awarded the title 'Plant and Garden Designer to the King', and André Le Nôtre made his name with his design for the *parterre* in the Queen's garden at Fontainebleau. The full effect of a *parterre de broderie* could only be experienced from an elevated position, having been, as Mollet wrote, 'designed to be easily seen and contemplated from the windows'. Le Nôtre agreed and, according to Saint-Simon, declared that 'they were only appreciated by the nursemaids who, unable to leave the children in their care, walked there in their imagination and admired them from the second floor.' Sometimes a few steps (of 'pink marble', according to the poet) were constructed around the *parterre* so that it could be viewed outside from above, rather in the same way that the sloping lawns and grass amphitheatres make a hollow, relieving the monotony of long, horizontal esplanades.

The entwined shapes of the box hedges called for some contrasting background colours to make the patterns decipherable: black earth, pale sand, cinders, crushed brick. Alternatively, they could edge patches of grass in *parterres à l'anglaise*, or could be used even more effectively as borders for beds of flowers.

The 'mille-fleurs' tapestries of the Middle Ages are a reminder of the prevalent taste for country flowers, the wild varieties native to the area, such as autumn crocus, violets, primroses, crocus and columbine. King René of Anjou was a great horticulturalist and introduced the Italian *rosa gallica* into Provence, and then Anjou. In the seventeenth century, displays of flowers became even more popular. To underline the merits of planting *parterres* near the house, La Quintinye wrote, 'There is nothing more attractive than to see a rich variety of flowers there in successive seasons, with new blooms taking the place of the ones before. They are like set changes in a theatre, while the stage remains the same; they are a perpetual source of pleasure, both for their appearance and their perfume' (*Instruction pour les jardins fruitiers et potagers*, 1690).

The quest for rare and exotic plants widened, urged on by the passion of the Dutch for tulips; they had gone as far as Constantinople to procure them, and collected them with increasing dedication. The science of botany gained authority and appealed to the curiosity of garden lovers such as Gaston d'Orléans and Louis de Bourbon, the Grand Condé, who planted the most beautiful species in their flower gardens just as they collected objects to display in their cabinets of curiosities. Painters could not resist them, houses were adorned with them, and they were represented in watercolour in the pages of sumptuous herbals.

In his book *Théâtre des plans et jardinages* (1652) Mollet invites his readers to distinguish between three types of flowers for planting in their *jardins de plaisir* – tall flowers, those grown from bulbs and those that grow close to the ground. He says they should be carefully chosen bearing in mind the best arrangement of the beds, considering the height and width of the edging plants and the desirability of a continual year-round flowering. The first group are hardy or biennial, such as hollyhocks, sunflowers, French marigolds, stocks, white and yellow lilies, larkspur, poppies and columbine; the bulbs include irises, tulips of all colours, crown imperials and narcissi, and favoured low-growing plants are wild thyme, violets, carnations, and especially oxalis, 'a small, very squat plant bearing a very pretty small white flower'.

THESE CARPETS SPREAD OUT ON THE GROUND needed contrasting vertical elements; yew trees provided a soft, dark texture, suitable for making shadow effects. They were trimmed into shapes such as balls or cones, chess pawns, urns, animals or human figures, and were derived from the visual games popular in the Middle Ages, competing with the statues to create a dream world made with consummate skill.

Further away, dense masses of trees were enclosed within a rigid wall of hornbeam hedges, which formed the framework of the garden. Mollet and his gardener contemporaries had understood the particular usefulness of hornbeam to make *palissades* or fences, *berceaux* or arbours and *bosquets*, since it 'grows densely right to the ground', and is strengthened by being clipped at the top. Fir, beech and maple were also sometimes used. The hornbeam hedge, standing as straight as a wall and sometimes embellished with niches and arcades, is the most consistent feature of the *jardin à la française*.

Above the hedges, the trees themselves were shaped to fit in with the overall picture. Only the outer face was cut, or the junction of two rows of trees, above the pathways; they were cut *en drapeau*, *en marquise* or *en berceau*. The equipment and techniques used in the seventeenth century, such as wheeled scaffolding, templates and cutting *au croissant*, were crucial to the practical task of controlling the blocks of greenery in the landscape. The elms, oaks, beeches and horse chestnuts managed in this way, and particularly the limes which are so easily trained, make frames for the *allées* and determine both their real and apparent dimensions.

Mollet laid down some rules: 'The widest *allées* that you plant will be the noblest; but the width must be in proportion to the length you can give them; for instance if they are 150 *toises* [300m] long, then they must be five *toises* [10m] wide to allow for the diminishing effect of perspective. The hedges on either side will also thicken, so that if your *allées* are planted five *toises* wide, with time they will be only four and a half *toises*.'

This advice on the geometrical use of space was part of the knowledge passed on to André Le Nôtre by previous generations of royal gardeners, but his inspired approach meant that he was eventually able to leave behind their doctrines to pursue the exceptional breadth of his own vision.

View over the massive hornbeam hedges
at the Château de Cordés, in Auvergne.

A bright flower-bed along the wall between the royal palace
at Drottningholm, Sweden, and its garden.

An *allée* in the *jardin à la française* at Bouges.

The design of the kitchen garden at Villandry is based on ancient monastic precedents; its nine squares are laid out with variations on the cross motif. The colourful effect is maintained with two plantings a year.

The Potager du Roi at Versailles was created by La Quintinye to supply Louis XIV's table, and his methods are still being practised; old varieties of fruit trees are trained into thirty different shapes, such as tridents, diamonds, palmettes, candelabras, double Us, urns and goblets. In the distance, the Cathédrale Saint-Louis de Versailles.

The beds of flowers for cutting at Saint-Jean-de-Beauregard make a colourful division between the kitchen garden and the orchard.

At Bouges the old kitchen garden has been made into a garden of flowers for cutting, to decorate the rooms in the château.

Potager du Roi, Versailles.

From his vantage point on the terrace named after him, the royal gardener La Quintinye surveys
his achievement; the garden was created between 1678 and 1683, and is managed today by
the Ecole Nationale Supérieure du Paysage, or National School of Horticulture.

On the esplanade leading up to the Château de Hautefort, a *parterre* of both common and variegated box and yews follows the layout of the old ramparts.

The lively style of the Malta Garden at Queluz in Portugal.

WATER
AND THE GODS

ARTH ALONE, however expensively remodelled with new levels and slopes, cannot be transformed into a beautiful garden without the essential element of water to give it life and movement. Without it, there can be no garden. 'The bigger the area of water, the more beautiful we find it, and its vibrancy and movement is essential to the life of gardens' (Boyceau de La Barauderie). Water is the magical element in the gardens of the Islamic world, and in those of the Alhambra in Spain; it surprised and enchanted French visitors to Italy, and they found the greatest pleasure in its reviving coolness under the hot Mediterranean sun.

In northern France the use of water was restricted for some time to ornamental fountains and fish ponds, and the art of water gardens was hardly known, which explains Michel Eyquem de Montaigne's amazement when he discovered the fountains at Pratolino and the Villa d'Este in Italy, with their ingenious mechanisms for activating spectacular effects that he described as 'an infinity of jets of water controlled and ejected by a single spring, triggered from some distance away'.

Before reaching the display of fountains, the visitor would enjoy the great horizontal sheets of water called *les eaux plates*, with their reflections of the sky and the movement of the clouds. The great French gardens of the end of the sixteenth century had an abundant network of canals, on an even larger scale than the Italian *canali*; including those at Anet, Vallery, Joinville, Charleval, Fleury-en-Bière, Fontainebleau and particularly Courances: 'Its clear, flowing waters gave Courances its name' (Dezallier d'Argenville). Health considerations became as important as the creation of a beautiful view: it was often necessary to drain marshy land and to revive stagnant pond water by diverting a nearby stream through it.

At the beginning of the following century, wider canals were built which took pride of place along the central axis of the composition. This was largely due to the influence of an Italophile

Preceding pages: In the Allée des Charmes at Eyrignac the consoles of hornbeam and columns of yew are regularly spaced as far as the Chinese pavilion. The Allée is framed on either side by a quincunx of apple trees trained into rounded shapes, with clusters of santolina at their feet.

Frenchman, Etienne Dupérac, and two Italian engineers sent by the Medicis, the brothers Tommaso and Alessandro Francini, who had a central role in garden architecture in the reign of Henri IV. The grand canal at Fontainebleau was dug in 1609, and is 1200 metres (3936 ft) long and 40 metres (131 ft) wide; it is the outstanding creation of its time, an artificial river spread out below the château windows, in the middle of the great *parterre*.

At Vaux there were two distinct phases in the construction of the gardens and the displays of water. The first canal was built at right angles to the central axis, of modest size and split into two halves, then a second beyond, with the same relation to the central axis, but uninterrupted and much larger (1 km or ⅝ mile in length). Seen from the great square *miroir*, it is a sudden and striking sight, an exceptionally impressive expanse of water dominating the area below it, between the cascades and the grotto. It is incontrovertibly the work of Le Nôtre, dating from after his arrival at the site, and was constructed on additional land that Fouquet had bought to enlarge his gardens. At Sceaux the linked systems of the canal and great Octogone *pièce d'eau* are to be found at the side of the château.

At Versailles a quite different scheme was adopted, with the intention of displaying a grand sequence of features in one exceptional perspective, 8 km (5 miles) long. It begins with the Parterre d'Eau (whose present arrangement dates from 1683), followed by the Bassin de Latone between the curved ramps; then, beyond the vast Allée Royale with the Tapis Vert running down the middle, lie the Bassin d'Apollon and the Grand Canal, 1650 metres (5412 ft) long and 62 metres (203 ft) wide, leading the eye to the vanishing point of the perspective, a clear horizon framed by tall poplars. The two lateral arms of the canal, one leading to the Ménagerie and one to the Trianon, form the last of a series of axes perpendicular to the château, a series which begins between the Orangerie and the Bassin de Neptune. At Chantilly, Le Nôtre produced a superb and unusual design, capitalizing on a natural site so overflowing with water from its rivers and lakes that the château had been built on an island, like Azay-le-Rideau and Chenonceau.

Great axial canals were used to create the grandeur of gardens in Lorraine or Alsace such as Lunéville, Commercy and Saverne, as well as at Hampton Court in England and Nymphenburg and Schleissheim in Bavaria. At Queluz in Portugal the canal flows between banks lined with coloured tiles, and at Caserta, Italy, the axis formed by the canal runs the entire length of the site.

Some gardens are situated on steeply sloping land, allowing the water to fall from the still pools above, like a mountain torrent or a river interrupted by rapids. In Italy such cascades were made into 'stairways' of water, 'water chains' or *rivières*, such as those at the Villa Lante at Bagnaia, Caprarola, the Villa d'Este at Tivoli, and the Villa Aldobrandini at Frascati. These were an innovation, and so much admired that similar effects were constructed at Saint-Germain, Rueil, Liancourt, Marly (now destroyed), Saint-Cloud, Sceaux and La Granja; at all of these the perpetual movement and sound of the water almost seems to bring to life the statues of gods and heroes that line the banks.

Displays of running water were created on a colossal scale in Russia by Peter the Great (1672–1725), as part of his monument to his victorious Northern war. At Peterhof, the huge stepped waterfall, framed by a mass of fountains and golden statues, flows straight into the ship canal which joins the Gulf of Finland, and the waves and sea spray become part of the drama. Neptune reigns, applauding the Tsar's heroic deeds, which are symbolized by the sculpture of Samson wrenching open the jaws of the lion, standing high on a rock and spurting a jet of water 20 metres (66 feet) high.

The wonderful effects created with water in Italian gardens demanded the mastery of new technical skills, and became a source of fascination for the European aristocracy. Already in the Middle Ages, the mechanics of water pressure had been used to animate automata, a pastime much enjoyed by Comte Robert II d'Artois in his 'galeries des engiens d'esbattement'; a display of mechanical 'toys' at his château, Hesdin.

However, it was the Francini brothers who introduced the new techniques to France, and the engineer Salomon de Caus later published a treatise on the subject, *Les Raisons des forces mouvantes* (1615). Spurred on by Louis XIV's insistent demands to tackle the unpromising

terrain at Versailles, the theorists were obliged to deal with practicalities. Now indispensable, water became a significant expense, requiring an extensive infrastructure including reservoirs, water towers, feeder pipes, pumps to raise water or cut it off, and stone drainage channels. At Vaux, Fouquet had the benefit of a plentiful supply of water from the river Anqueil, but at Versailles the King struggled throughout his reign for an adequate solution, finding himself obliged to bring water from the distant Eure (via the aqueduct of Maintenon), from the Seine (using the engine at Marly) and, more prosaically with the aid of gravity, from the lakes at Saint-Quentin which the learned Abbé Picard had been able to prove were on a higher level than the gardens at Versailles. The gardeners of the classic period also inherited an architectural style for garden buildings from the sixteenth century which was specific to the cult of water. Grottoes and nymphea were in fashion until around 1670, before reappearing in a new 'natural' style in the picturesque early Romantic gardens.

Fontainebleau, Meudon, the Tuileries, with its rustic vases by Bernard Palissy, Gerbéviller, Noisy, Rueil, Effiat, Wideville, the Château Neuf at Saint-Germain, Maisons and of course Versailles (the Thetis grotto) all have buildings which were designed as a 'natural' setting for the divinities of the waters. Unsuspecting visitors could find themselves soaked by trick fountains, although by the end of the century, such devices came to be regarded as childish:

> *A thousand rain-like jets come by surprise*
> *To soak the imprudent and to soak the wise.*
> LA FONTAINE

Other styles of garden architecture, among them those in *Hypnerotomachia Poliphili*, had already provided plenty of inspiration, reinterpreting an urban classical style suitable for the gods and heroes commemorated there: triumphal arches, arcades, colonnades and peristyles, created from marble masonry or trellis fences, while the water gushed and poured into the *bassins*, fountains, *buffets* and *cabinets d'eau*.

The *miroir* at the Château de Courances.

STATUARY is as much part of the framework of the French-style garden as water is, giving it life and meaning. In Roman antiquity, statues were erected in gardens as a focus for the worship of the household gods and the gods of nature, and to deflect the misfortunes that threatened the harvests; they were known as the *satyrica signa*. Like the domestic gods, or lares, the satyrs watched over the gardens, as did the Fauns, Priapus and Venus, goddess of April and protectress of vine growers and gardeners. Elaborate schemes were devised to fill the gardens of the Emperor and the aristocracy with tableaux representing dramatic legends, particularly those that featured hunts, such as Niobe and her children or Meleager, as well as the Farnese Bull or Orpheus.

In the Renaissance, gardens reflected the taste of princes and cardinals for the antique, and were in effect outdoor museums. This fashion crossed the Alps, and became widespread in France in the seventeenth century. Following the examples of François I and Richelieu, Louis XIV commissioned copies of antique statues from students of the Académie de France in Rome to erect in the gardens at Versailles. A collection of busts was displayed at the Trianon, and at Marly the Bosquet des Bains d'Agrippine was created.

However, it was the link between the garden and the powers of nature, identified and made into divinities by the Greeks and Romans, that provided the principal theme for the sculptors' commissions. It seems that the Sun King learned the stories from a pack of cards invented by Desmarets de Saint-Sorlin; the 'Fable', as ancient mythology was called then, was assiduously taught by the Jesuits to their pupils, who gained a thorough knowledge of the classical authors and especially of Ovid, the author of *Metamorphoses*, the prime reference book for artists.

An easily deciphered anthropomorphism resulted in the language of poetic convention, and when La Fontaine wrote:

> *In your deep, echoing grottoes, fill the air with cries,*
> *Weep, O you nymphs of Vaux, and make your waters rise,*
> *And may the swollen stream wreak havoc on the treasure*

Strewn by Flora on its banks with her bounty beyond measure....
The Fates are satisfied: Orontes is unhappy.

his readers did not need notes to understand the references to the plight of Fouquet, and to join with the protestations of the gods, whose statues were familiar from the gardens at Vaux.

In the Grand Siècle, fine sculptors turned to mythological themes and their work contributed to the lasting fame of the *jardin à la française*. The greatest artists were commissioned to make urns and statues for the *parterres*, *bosquets* and fountains at Versailles, Marly, Sceaux and Saint-Cloud, among them François Girardon, Antoine Coysevox, Thomas Regnaudin, Jean-Baptiste Tuby, Gaspard and Balthazar Marsy and Pierre Puget; in the following century, the fine urns at La Granja were sculpted by René Frémin to the designs of Gilles-Marie Oppenordt.

Yet again, Fouquet took the lead at Vaux. It was no longer enough to make single figures the focus of a *parterre* or the highlight of an axis; now an iconographic programme had to be devised to bring the whole garden to life and provide it with a theme. The most respected painters were brought in to make the maquettes and supervise the whole commission; Nicolas Poussin designed some terms for Fouquet, and Charles Le Brun took over responsibility for all the King's garden design.

Throughout the long process of its creation, sculpture was used at Versailles to represent the philosophical theme, intending to hold up a mirror to the world in marble and bronze. The visitor leaves the Parterre d'Eau and the recumbent figures of the rivers of France – no longer the Nile and the Tiber – glorifying the natural riches of the kingdom, and is challenged by the rhetorical gestures of the children astride sphinxes at the entrance to the Parterre du Midi, representing a philosophical debate between impulse and reflection. The Grande Commande statues approved by Jean-Baptiste Colbert in 1674 were installed in front of the hornbeam hedges on the west front and along the two sides of the Parterre du Nord; they all represent phenomena numbered in fours: the seasons, the elements, the corners of the world, the ages and temperaments of man, the poetic styles.

To the north, water determines the theme of the prescribed route. After being confronted by Neptune and the other sea gods, and after slaying the Dragon, the hero Apollo completes his ritual, slowly walking up the Allée d'Eau, charmed by the little smiling figures holding their marble fountain basins, and stops before the Bains des Nymphes, a variation on the grotto theme; finally, on the Parterre du Nord stand the Fontaine de la Pyramide and the Bassins des Couronnes, symbolizing recognition of all his efforts and successes.

However, these figures intended to provoke reflection did not replace the great set pieces with multiple statues, which give an atmosphere of permanent drama. At Versailles, the Bassin de Latone represents one of the archetypal scenes from classical mythology. On the top of a marble pyramid, surrounded by water, is Latona, mother of Apollo and Diana, with her little children clinging to her knees, and she implores the gods to rescue her from the ridicule of the Lycian peasants. Her wish is immediately granted, and her wretched tormentors are by degrees turned into frogs, faithfully re-creating Ovid's tale. Further down along the great perspective, Apollo's chariot takes off from the water of the fountain, pulled by the horses of the Sun, and hailed by the Tritons with their conches. Elsewhere, fighting animals are reminders of the importance of the hunt.

In all of Europe's great residences we find themes linked by a common culture. Just as at Drottningholm in Sweden there is a water terrace as an echo of the calm waters of Lake Mälar, at the Spanish castle of La Granja there is a Latona fountain, and a fountain dedicated to Fame. Enormous petrified tableaux were ideal vehicles for the Baroque aesthetic of movement and emotion. A magnificent operatic scene of the death of Actaeon crowns the great perspective at Caserta, the seat of the Bourbon kingdom of the Two Sicilies; it stands in a contrived 'natural' setting of rocks and splashing waters. At Schönbrunn, Thetis pleads with Neptune for Achilles. At Veitshöchheim, seat of the Prince-Bishop of Würzburg, all the residents of Mount Parnassus are assembled on a rock, with Pegasus rearing up on the summit. In 1778 Hubert Robert made a significant return to the past at Versailles when he created a new 'rustic' setting for the groups of sculptures originally made for the grotto of Thetis.

Alongside the Grand Canal at Versailles.

A double row of limes beside the *parterres* at Drottningholm,
in Sweden.

The cascade at Sceaux and its dazzling sheets of water.

One of the 'open-air rooms' along the east–west perspective leading
to Frederick II's New Palace at Sans-Souci in Germany.

Above: A pool at the meeting place of several paths, on one of the subsidiary axes of the *parterres* at Schönbrunn, Vienna. The palace can be seen in the distance framed by the trees.

Below: On the *parterre* at Cormatin, the pool in the shape of a square superimposed on a quatrefoil stands for the union of Heaven and Earth at the moment of Creation. A Tree of Life stands in the middle, with tortoises representing the Rivers.

Above: The palace of La Granja, near Madrid, seen from the
fountain of the Three Graces sculpted by René Frémin.

Below: The Bain de Ninon, the lake, the *vertugadin*
and the Château du Haut at Villarceaux.

The Bosquet de l'Encélade at Versailles.

The statues at Schönbrunn, carved from Sterzing marble, were made from 1773 onwards by Beyer and his twelve assistants. They are drawn from mythological and historical subjects.

Pluto's rape of Proserpine, by Girardon,
in the Bosquet de la Colonnade at Versailles.

The great central *parterre* at the foot of the steps of the palace of Sans-Souci in Germany displays sculptures of the gods of Olympus, and allegories of the Four Elements by the Adam and Pigalle brothers, artists from Lorraine and France.

Statue of Hercules at the foot of the steps leading to the orangery at Sans-Souci, Germany.

THE
DRAMA OF SHADOWS

A N ARCHITECTURE OF TREES provides the framework of the sun's domain; although they depend on the sun's life-giving warmth, gardens also need shade and coolness. They were therefore planned with areas of *couvert* or shade composed of *allées* through widely spaced trees, suitable for walks sheltered from the sun, but still with clear views of the rest of the garden.

By contrast, the *bosquets* or groves were carved out of dense areas of trees, and created a hidden, secret world, an Arcadia entered with hushed curiosity, soon turning to surprise at the unexpected. Winding paths leading off the main axes led into a mysterious world of outdoor rooms, arbours, drawing rooms and theatres hidden in the clear spaces or *bosquets* within the little woods. A precedent had been set at Hadrian's Villa at Tivoli, where several well-known classical buildings had been re-created for the pleasure of the 'collector' Emperor, juxtaposed like pages from a travel book. Later, *Hypnerotomachia Poliphili* was used by designers as a source of ideas, and Jules Hardouin-Mansart probably referred to it before planning the Bosquet de la Colonnade at Versailles.

These secluded areas of the garden were ideal settings for sculptural representations of the struggle between the forces of darkness and the cosmic order imposed by the Olympians. The fashion started in Italy, with the *Bocca d'Inferno* and the intimidating figures in the Sacro Bosco at Bomarzo. The subject of Giulio Romano's powerful fresco of the Defeat of the Giants at the Palazzo del Té in Mantua was the inspiration for the Bosquet de l'Encélade at Versailles, where the rebellious giant, a colossus of gilded lead, lies crushed beneath the rocks he has been hurling at Jupiter; a powerful jet of water thrown high into the air represents his cry of despair.

There is clearly a political message here, just as in the Bassin de Latone: rebellion against the divinely appointed King never goes unpunished.

One of the heroes often represented was Hercules; he belonged to the forces of good because he had conquered monsters, but he is nevertheless awe-inspiring because of his super-human physique. He was given no place at Versailles, perhaps because Fouquet had chosen the Farnese Hercules to dominate the entire length of the rising perspective at Vaux. However, Henri II had installed Michelangelo's Hercules at Fontainebleau in the Cour de la Fontaine, later moved by Henri IV to the Jardin de l'Etang. The landgrave Charles von Hesse-Cassel returned to the theme in 1717, with the obelisk supporting a colossus at the top of the great cascade at Wilhelmshöhe.

Other *bosquets* featured amphitheatres of rockery, or had water effects with parallel rows of water jets, such as the Grille d'Eau at Vaux; or there were the *cent tuyaux* (a hundred pipes) in the Bosquet de l'Obélisque at Versailles and the pyramid at Peterhof (505 pipes), or jets of water placed among the leaves of the trees, as in the Bosquet du Marais created by Mme de Montespan at Versailles; no doubt that was the inspiration for similar effects in the pines and one of the oak trees at Peterhof, which also boasted an artificial sun turned by water power.

The fashion for labyrinths came from the idea of offering visitors a kind of treasure hunt in the footsteps of Theseus, who overcame the monstrous Minotaur in the tragic legend by negotiating the labyrinth. Similar diversions, then known as *dedalus*, were introduced in the gardens of Charles V and René of Anjou, as well as later at the Tuileries. At Versailles the route through the gardens was given a simultaneously playful and instructive character with scenes from Aesop's Fables at intervals along the route. This idea was a familiar one in garden design from the Renaissance onwards, when pleasure gardens were used for games, sports, displays and celebrations. An *allée* for playing *pail mail* was laid out at Chenonceau and at Montceaux, integrating an area to be used for a particular purpose into the overall design. In his old age Louis XIV was keen to provide games for his grandchildren, and at Marly a series of grounds were prepared for playing *mail*, for swings, and for a *roulette*, a kind of roller-coaster. Later the Duc de Bourbon had his Jeu de l'Oie at Chantilly, and Marie-Antoinette her Jeu de Bague at the Petit Trianon at Versailles.

Prolonged stays in one place called for a selection of places to walk to, and subsidiary buildings were erected where a few hours could be spent, a meal enjoyed, and perhaps even a stay of a few nights planned. Accordingly, summer houses were built around the edges of the park, designed to distract the courtiers by providing variety. They were not as yet designed as the 'rustic arbours' of Anglo-Chinese gardens, but were a range of elegant secondary dwellings at some distance from the principal château, miniature palaces or hermitages.

In the sixteenth century François I built the Pavillon de Pomona near the grotto at Fontainebleau, and the Cardinal de Bourbon built a pleasure house, the Maison Blanche, in the middle of a delightful water garden at the far end of the park at Gaillon, on the site of the Lidieu. The Pavillon de l'Aurore was the pride of Sceaux, and Trianon and Marly are the grandest examples of this desire to create satellites around the palace. All the great parks of Europe have sumptuous subsidiary buildings, foremost among which are Frederick the Great's Sans-Souci and Peter the Great's Peterhof, whose pavilions have names such as the Hermitage, Marly and Monplaisir.

The aviaries and menageries of exotic beasts, which had been very popular in the Middle Ages, and later the orangeries and huge greenhouses, were all part of an all-embracing vision of the garden as the entire world in miniature.

The Ile d'Amour in the park at Chantilly, with its gloriette and statue of Eros.

The labyrinth *parterre* in the garden at La Gaude, Aix-en-Provence.

The tall hornbeam hedges at Cordés, in Auvergne.

The play of light and shadow on the Tapis Vert at Versailles,
between the Bassin d'Apollon and the Parterre de Latone.

Decorative trellis work on the terrace of the Sans-Souci Palace.

THE SATISFACTION
OF TAMING NATURE

HAVING THOROUGHLY EXPLORED THE GARDENS shared by the gods and man, we now take a trip on the canals seeking, if not the temple of Venus at Cythera, then at least a quiet spot away from the crowds, and so find ourselves back on the central axis. Le Nôtre preferred a clear view of the horizon to the finality of a building; Nicodemus Tessin tried to persuade Louis XIV that one of the axes at Versailles should end with an architectural feature, but the King was not in favour of it. However, at Het Loo in the Netherlands, the view is enclosed within two colonnaded arcs; at Schönbrunn it ends at the Gloriette.

Looking back, we now face the palace, which imposes its powerful presence on the whole landscape. Everything is clearly organized according to a single overriding idea. Yet again, La Fontaine provides us with the best choice of words: 'the intellect which is the soul of these wonders'. He is thinking here of Le Nôtre, but it is important to understand that the creation of a *jardin à la française* was the work of two minds, two imaginations and two approaches which have coincided, that of the master and that of the manager of the project. It could even be said that the garden demands more personal, detailed and even obsessive involvement than the house does on the part of its financial backer, prince, lord or bourgeois owner. It is a commitment that easily becomes a passion, stimulating the instincts of ownership as well as the pursuit of pleasure in daily life, the quest for beauty and the enjoyment of the new, and can lead to glorious achievements.

In the scale of aristocratic values in the seventeenth and eighteenth centuries, military glory came first, followed by the glories displayed in a fine garden, often more prized even than imposing buildings. It has been observed that in ancient Rome the ever increasing domination of imperial power had effectively neutralized the aristocrats, who lost interest in public life and

concentrated on their gardens, and that Roman Hellenism dated from this period of political apathy on the part of the upper classes. It seems likely that the same situation arose in France when Louis XIV assumed absolute personal power, and the idleness of the nobility led to the extraordinary scale of garden construction on their estates. This was certainly true of the royal princes; distanced from any political responsibilities and from military campaigns in which they might risk undermining the prestige of the king, they were left with their gardens and estates. Monsieur had Saint-Cloud (where he received his brother, Louis XIV, with a note-worthy enthusiasm in October 1678), the Grand Dauphin had Meudon and the Grand Condé had Chantilly. Some architectural projects were under way too, such as the vast works under-taken at Blois by Gaston d'Orléans; these were secretly welcomed by Mazarin, chief minister to Louis XIV, thinking that the new château would provide a distraction from his frustrated ambitions.

Was gardening regarded as a noble art? Henri IV had encouraged his landed gentry to return to their estates as part of an attempt to revive his kingdom, exhausted by wars; he hoped to break the cycle of raids and pillage that had followed a period of general unrest, and dispel the warlike frame of mind and political ambitions of landowners seeking independence of action and autonomy for the provinces. It became necessary to encourage them to sustain an income from their land, and at the same time to dissuade them from raising funds by selling their mature timber, or 'jouer des hauts bois'.

The King himself had set an example of 'practical gardening' by cultivating mulberry trees on his estates and embellishing his gardens at Fontainebleau and Saint-Germain with them. Olivier de Serres, who spread the new doctrine, was a gentleman landowner from the Vivarais. Four other gentlemen had been given the title of chief steward, administrator, or steward of the royal gardens in the reigns of Henri IV and Louis XIII: they were Louis de Bordeaux, André Bérard de Maisoncelles, Jacques Boyceau de La Barauderie and Jacques de Menours. Boyceau de La Barauderie had spent most of his life on 'projects of the utmost importance' in the service of Henri IV, before concentrating on the art of garden design in the service of Louis

XIII. They and the two Mollets, father and son, defined the new skills, and popularized them through their treatises.

Le Nôtre added a new dimension to the art of gardening:

With Le Nôtre every path is a fine broad walk....
Hitherto such enchantments were quite unknown.
All parks were once orchards in days long ago;
Now all orchards are parks: the past masters know
How to make small gardens fit for royal pleasure,
And then these in their turn fit for godly leisure.

LA FONTAINE

He and Louis XIV had a unique relationship, a closeness which the King never shared with any other artist, architect, painter or sculptor in his service. This meant that for many years Le Nôtre was able to reign supreme over nature, which he controlled and perfected but at the same time treated with great respect. His brilliance is apparent in every one of his creations, at Vaux, Versailles, Trianon, Marly, Saint-Germain, Meudon, Saint-Cloud, Sceaux, Chantilly, Maintenon and Dampierre, as well as in the gardens he designed abroad for kings and princes.

Like François Mansart, Le Nôtre was able to see his ideas perpetuated by his nephews, Michel Le Bouteux and Claude Desgots, who created the gardens at Champs-sur-Marne; an even more influential follower was Dezallier d'Argenville, whose treatise *La Théorie et la pratique du jardinage* was first published in 1709 and reprinted many times. It reiterated Le Nôtre's ideas while guiding the reader towards a less ornate, sophisticated and rigid interpretation of his principles; from now on it became acceptable to 'make art give way to nature'.

The impact of this development was noticeable towards the end of the reign of Louis XIV, as a reaction to mannerism and the Baroque, and was acknowledged by Jacques-François Blondel in his *Cours d'Architecture*. A taste for 'the lovely simplicity of nature' and not only 'the

exertions of the human spirit' began to predominate. From then on the phrase *jardin français* was used to describe a type of layout different from its successor the *jardin naturel*. Louis XV followed this style when he planted the *parterres*, lime arbours and small-scale groves on his private estate La Nouvelle Ménagerie (1750), which was called the Jardin Français in 1774 to distinguish it from the Jardin Anglais laid out behind the Petit Trianon.

It was this specifically French taste in garden design which was recognized and re-created in gardens in other countries. The Swedish architect Nicodemus Tessin, a disciple of Le Nôtre, perpetuated the style with his designs for the King at Drottningholm, while exploiting the potential of its extraordinary site. Following the example of d'Argenville, he wrote a treatise *Remarques touchant les jardins de propreté et premièrement de leur situation* for the King's son Carl Gustav, which elevated the theories of the French master to a universally accepted art form. The formal garden was further developed in the Age of Enlightenment by the Prince de Ligne in his gardens at Beloeil in Belgium, renowned for the huge scale of its hornbeam hedges.

The eighteenth century saw a definite change of taste, led by the preference of the English aristocrats for a 'natural' landscape, combining a Chinese influence with a new philosophical mood, in reaction against the constraints of classical art and the artifice of its mythology. But neither these developments nor the sarcastic comments of Voltaire, Rousseau, the Chevalier de Jaucourt and the Marquis de Girardin succeeded in entirely discrediting the 'French formal style', as it was known. When Louis XVI ordered large-scale felling at Versailles in 1774 to allow a natural cycle of renewal, he did not replant in the English style.

The fame of the gardens of the Grand Siècle persisted in the nineteenth century, although they were gradually damaged by neglect, unchecked growth of plants and trees, structural changes and lack of sympathy with their principle. At the turn of the twentieth century a new generation of landscape architects set to work to rediscover the values of the French formal style, first Henri and Achille Duchêne (father and son), then others such as Ferdinand Duprat. Their first task was to reconstruct the vanished masterpieces, Vaux, Champs and Breteuil, and they used the knowledge gained to create new gardens in a similar style at the Château de

Marais and the Château de Voisins. Later, new gardens were made on the Côte d'Azur, and in California; in England the French *parterres* have been reconstructed at Blenheim, in the style of Le Nôtre which has also inspired revivals at Greenwich, Windsor and Hampton Court. The trend has continued, keeping pace with the demand demonstrated by newly created gardens at La Roche-Courbon, Effiat, Hautefort, Cordés, Sassy, La Gaude, Eyrignac and Cormatin.

The meticulous restoration of the great historic gardens, led by work at Versailles, underpins the theoretical basis of this art of the intellect and the senses, and it continues to inspire the great contemporary landscape designers. It shows them the organization of vistas, shapes and colours in a unified space, open to the horizon and welcoming to its visitors, and thereby gives them the powerful sensation described by Saint-Simon as 'the supreme satisfaction of taming nature'.

Above: The start of the Grand Canal at Versailles, seen from the Bassin d'Apollon.

Opposite: The other end of the Grand Canal. The transverse arm of the Canal can be seen between the screens of trees, and along the line of the perspective are the Bassin d'Apollon, the Tapis Vert, the Bassin de Latone and the Château.

The Trianon de Marbre at Versailles.

A game of hide and seek; the clipped yews
on the *parterre* of the Château de Sceaux.

The Cent Marches, or Hundred Steps,
leading to the Orangerie at Versailles.

The following descriptions of individual gardens are divided according
to seven themes which form the first part of this book: 'The dream of Vaux',
'In the beginning there was the château', 'The well-kept and the wild',
'Gardens for the intellect, gardens for the senses', 'Water and the gods',
'The drama of shadows' and 'The satisfaction of taming nature'.
An approach that highlights the experience of the senses seemed more appropriate than
a prosaic alphabetical list, bringing out the particular qualities of each garden in all their richness,
and showing how the inexhaustible creativity of the designers of the *jardins à la française* was used
to impose a geometrical system on nature and, paradoxically, enhanced it. They were the
poets of clipped yew, geometrical reflecting pools, straight allées and *parterres de broderie*,
the moving spirits behind the marriage of the earth and the sky; their achievements,
continually evolving, still give undiminished pleasure.

Some Special Gardens

Mic Chamblas-Ploton

Vaux-le-Vicomte

THE INSUFFERABLE
HUBRIS OF THE MINISTER

At the end of the *parterres*, the Grand Canal crosses the main axis at right angles, spreading out in front of the grottoes. Two ramps edged with shady clipped bushes lead up to the Bassin de la Gerbe and the Farnese Hercules at the end of the perspective.

WHAT WAS NICOLAS FOUQUET, the powerful Superintendent of Finances, thinking about on that hot summer evening of 17 August 1661, as he stood in his room with its painted ceiling by Charles Le Brun, showing the sun god Apollo illuminating the world? The lights of the magnificent entertainment he had given for Louis XIV were extinguished, the King had set out on his return journey to Fontainebleau, and the thousand guests had disappeared. Everything had been perfect: the refreshments served on the arrival of the royal party, the tour of the garden filled with playing fountains, the music in the arbours, Molière's comédie-ballet *Les Fâcheux*, written for the occasion and performed in front of the Grille d'Eau; then the dinner served on gold plates, the firework display created by the 'Grand Sorcier' Torelli, the gilded gondolas floating on the *miroir*, and the tombola with its sumptuous gifts. As his friend La Fontaine was to say later: 'Everything vied to give pleasure to the King: the music, the water displays, the lights and the stars.'

Unfortunately for him, the man, whose motto was 'To what heights will he not climb?' and whose emblem was a squirrel, had no idea that at that very moment, in the royal carriage, his fall from grace was already being arranged. Fouquet had been imprudent enough to make a display of magnificence that surpassed even that of the King, at a time when the royal finances were at their lowest ebb, and he himself was suspected by Jean-Baptiste Colbert of making huge profits from the fraudulent use of public funds. This lavish display only hastened his ruin. Three weeks later, Louis XIV had him arrested at Nantes by d'Artagnan, captain of the Musketeers.

Louis XIV had known for a long time that the grounds of Vaux were the scene of a project that was out of the ordinary. For the last five years the Superintendent's property, situated between the two royal residences of Vincennes and Fontainebleau, had undergone earth-moving operations on a massive scale, requiring the labour of eighteen thousand men. Although Fouquet was reckless by nature, he had built the perimeter wall as quickly as possible so that work could proceed unobserved. Alerted by discreet hints from Mazarin and Colbert, Louis XIV made it known that he wanted to see the grounds for himself, which was the reason for the lavish invitation from the imprudent owner. An intellectual, and greatly interested in the arts, Fouquet had ambitious plans for his new property; as he said later, 'it was a place which I regarded as my principal residence, and I wanted to leave there a permanent reminder of my achievements.' He had therefore engaged the architect Le Vau, the painter and interior decorator Le Brun and the garden designer Le Nôtre. Le Vau and Le Nôtre, who had met while working for Simon Vouet, were to complement each other perfectly, and create here the archetypal estate *à la française*, which would be the reference point for all subsequent developments, including Versailles.

After Fouquet's arrest, Vaux was confiscated, and many of the Superintendent's statues and orange trees found their way to Versailles. Madeleine Fouquet and her son eventually recovered their property, which was sold in 1705 to the Maréchal de Villars, and then in 1764 to the Duc de Choiseul-Praslin. Vaux was spared damage in the Revolution, but was in a very neglected state when the industrialist Alfred

Sommier bought it at auction in 1875, and he and his son launched a fifty-year programme to restore it to its seventeenth-century glory. Contemporary engravings and plans were used as references by the landscape artists Laîné, and later Duchêne, for the restoration of the gardens.

The château lies on a north–south axis; it is built in Creil stone and stands on a plinth of Fontainebleau sandstone surrounded by a moat, dominating the composition. A gateway flanked by terms marks the entrance. Handsome brick outbuildings stand to the right and left. A grass-covered *avant cour* followed by a gently sloping paved inner court lead to the perron where Fouquet received his guests, more than three hundred years ago. The axis runs through the middle of the château, where the vestibule and huge oval Grand Salon by Le Vau occupy the full height of the building, and reaches the perron overlooking the gardens. After descending several flights of steps, it crosses the *parterres de broderie*, the Rond d'Eau, and runs between the two canals which mark the transverse axis: one leads eastwards to the Grille d'Eau which was the setting for Molière's play, and the other westwards to the gate of La Quintinye's former kitchen garden, flanked by two pavilions. A few steps further on, the main axis meets the former Allée d'Eau, now grassed over and ornamented with flower-filled urns standing on pedestals, and then continues between the two huge Bassins des Tritons, to the square Grand Miroir.

Beyond that, the axis leaps over the Grandes Cascades below, crosses the Grand Canal, vaults the grottoes and the Grande Gerbe, then climbs the sloping Tapis Vert towards the statue of Hercules. In the course of following the great axis, it becomes clear that although the garden appears to be flat from the terrace, it actually plays constantly on the differences of level, creating a series of surprises for the visitor walking through it. From the château, the Grandes Cascades and the canal are completely invisible, and the *parterres de broderie* are edged with raised paths, so that they can be seen from a slightly higher viewpoint. To the right and left, the former Parterre des Fleurs and Parterre de la Couronne are either revealed or hidden according to the viewer's position. On days when the water is flowing, the sound hints at the otherwise completely unsuspected, ravishing spectacle presented by the Cascades.

Inevitably, thoughts turn to the poem *Songe de Vaux* by La Fontaine, written in defence of his friend and patron, forever incarcerated in the Pignerol prison, deprived of walks, books and even paper and ink, so that he was driven to write in soot on his white shirts:

'In your deep, echoing grottoes, fill the air with cries, / Weep, O you nymphs of Vaux, and make your waters rise; .... You for whom he made such a beautiful home, / Nymphs whose very charms to him are owed, / If Louis should tread where your streams flow, / Try to weaken his resolve, soften his heart.'

Even though Louis never returned to Vaux and did not change his mind about Fouquet, who died after nineteen years of imprisonment, the Nymphs remain constant and still murmur the sad story of the man who was deprived of his masterpiece, which afterwards became the touchstone of the Grand Siècle.

'There is not a single corner where he has failed to add something beautiful',
said Madeleine de Scudéry of the proprietor of Vaux.

Fontainebleau

OF GARDENS
AND FASHION

TODAY, THE FONTAINE BELLE EAU, after which the château was named, continues to play in the Jardin Anglais, oblivious of passing fashions. There have been many changes to the spring's original forest setting, the various proprietors of the estate having created ambiences that were alternately monastic, Renaissance, classical and a sophisticated version of a 'natural' style. Of the three areas of garden at the château, two are in a so-called English style. This might seem like a paradox at a property which France's greatest kings had been seeking to embellish since the twelfth century. But the 'king's pleasure' can have contrasting facets, and both the architecture and the gardens at Fontainebleau show perhaps more clearly than anywhere else the extent of the monarch's will in indulging his fancies. The Jardin Anglais is squeezed between the wing built by Jacques-Ange Gabriel for Louis XV (which replaced the Galerie d'Ulysse decorated by Francesco Primaticcio, one of the great lost

masterpieces of Fontainebleau) and the famous Etang des Carpes, a vast irregularly shaped stretch of water, which, like the spring, has existed there since the earliest times. This part of the garden was originally enclosed for the use of the monks of La Sainte-Trinité, who had been housed by Saint Louis near the medieval château which was the first building on the site. François I brought the elegant atmosphere of the Italian Renaissance to the garden, with an area of pines chequered with flower beds, covered walks and private corners aimed at providing seclusion for people walking there. A shadowy grotto supported by sandstone giants and with fresco decorations (now the Grotte des Pins) was then at the end of the Galerie d'Ulysse. Henri IV and his *jardiniers*, Claude and Jacques Mollet, gave it a new face with a series of gardens linked by paths edged with high *palissades*. Louis XIV called on the 'magicians' Le Nôtre and Le Vau, who had so impressed him with their work at Vaux-le-Vicomte, to redesign the Fontainebleau garden in the classical style. It was treated separately from the *parterre* which was the focal point, and was made into a series of *bosquets* reached by diagonal pathways. In 1810 Napoleon found the palace stripped of its furniture and the gardens completely neglected. He brought in Hurtault to turn an area that had been used as a special military academy after the Revolution into an idealized landscape, through which a winding river flowed among lawns and rare trees. It is this garden, further modified by Napoleon III, which survives today. The Jardin de Diane, the palace's other *jardin à l'anglaise* has had a similar history. It also retains a mythological character; its central decorative feature, the Fontaine de Diane, was made by Francini for Henri IV, and has recently been restored to its original condition. Nestling between the Galerie des Cerfs, the Galerie de Diane, the royal apartments, the Chapelle de la Trinité and the Jeu de Paume, the garden has

The Grand Parterre, and the Tiber statue in the Rond d'Eau on the north–south axis. Spread out along the *parterre* from west to east (from left to right in the picture) is the group of buildings that form the château: the Belle Cheminée Wing, the Pavillon de la Porte Dorée, the Salle de Bal, the Chapelle Saint-Saturnin, the Porte Dauphine and the Kitchens.

At the far end of the *parterre*, a change of level conceals the Cascades by the Francini brothers,
lying in front of the Grand Canal.

had several different names and has undergone reorganization under each successive master. Le Nôtre designed four regularly planned *parterres de broderies* and a decorative basin for the fountain. Napoleon later used the expertise of Hurtault to transform it into a *jardin à l'anglaise*, and this design remained unchanged, in spite of subsequent programmes of renovation under Louis-Philippe and Napoleon III. This part of the garden, with its carefully labelled trees and shrubs, now opens towards the town, inviting passers-by to come in and share centuries of secrets.

The centrepiece of the gardens is, however, thoroughly French. An immensely long esplanade is lined to the north by a series of buildings which make up the palace: the Porte Dorée, the Salle de Bal, the apse of the Chapelle Saint-Saturnin, a wing of the Cour Henri IV, and to the west by the Allée de la Chaussée, which borders the Etang des Carpes, and finally to the south by the forest. Henri IV had determined the huge scale of the gardens in 1606, when he undertook the digging of a canal 1200 metres (3940 ft) long designed by André Mollet, running below the esplanade eastwards into the Grand Parc. Mollet had already created a garden for the King in front of the château, consisting of extensive *compartiments de broderie* and areas for games, surrounded by a complex arrangement of canals.

Le Nôtre had the smaller canals filled in, retaining only the canal in the Grand Parc in his new project based on two axes at right angles to each other. The first crossed the *parterre* in front of the buildings and ran towards the forest. The starting-point of the second was a pretty octagonal summerhouse built on an island in the Etang des Carpes (it still survives, rebuilt under Napoleon); from there, the axis ran through the middle of the *parterre* and continued uninterrupted along the path of the canal. Then, as now, the *parterre* was divided into four big squares, with a square central *bassin* and fountain, Le Pot-qui-bout. The cleverly designed scrolls of box, cut into the initials of Louis XIV and Marie-Thérèse, could be admired from the slightly raised terraces edged with tree-lined *allées* on all sides. The *parterre* was extended to the north, to include a round *bassin* with a statue representing the River Tiber, and canals and banks edged with *allées* forming a half octagon. In the other direction, above the canal, a terrace looks down on the huge cascade built in 1664 by Tommaso and Alessandro Francini. Water spurts from its four hundred pipes, sometimes with a murmur, sometimes rushing and crashing down in a tumult of thunderous sounds. Two ramps with balustrades lead into the Petit Parc with its *bosquets*, lying on both sides of the canal.

The majestic composition that the visitor sees today is relatively unchanged. Even though the *parterre* has lost its sophisticated *broderies*, the beautifully harmonious arrangement of colours in the flower beds delights the eye as it takes in the grandeur of the whole layout. One of the miracles of Fontainebleau is the perfect balance of pleasure in discovering its many secret corners, and at the same time enjoying its magnificent Grand Siècle spaciousness; qualities which together make up a 'special garden', capable of responding subtly to the visitor's every mood.

Chenonceau

A   RENAISSANCE   ISLAND

The Jardin de Diane de Poitiers, seen from the gallery over the Cher built by Catherine de Médicis.

AT CHENONCEAU the château and its gardens seem to be floating on the water, waiting to drift away with the visitor to an enchanted, fantastical and unreal world. But before embarking, the visitor walks down an *allée* of tall plane trees, passes two sphinxes, and arrives at the lawn of the *avant cour*. There, a choice must be made between three directions, three journeys, which complement, challenge and echo each other. Straight ahead is the château, an elegant island of white and grey standing in the waters of the river Cher, and accessible via a drawbridge. To left and right are two green and pink peninsulas: upstream lies the Jardin de Diane de Poitiers on a vast artificial platform, and downstream, on a smaller scale, the Jardin de Catherine de Médicis. Another island, the bare *cour d'honneur*, links the *avant cour* and the château; it marks the place where the first château, owned by the Marques family, stood in medieval times. It was demolished in 1513 by Thomas Bohier when he built his own fine residence. Only the former donjon or Tour des Marques and a well remain of the earlier building. The powerful financier had a poetic inspiration when he decided to build his château out over the water, using the piles of the former estate mill. In 1535 the property came into the hands of François I, in payment of Bohier's debts to the crown, and from 1547 it belonged to Henri II, who gave it to his beloved mistress, Diane de Poitiers. Her first concern was to make the ground fruitful, later indulging herself with luxurious additions. In 1552 she began the expensive process of constructing the east *parterre* (today the Jardin de Diane de Poitiers) by raising the level of the ground and reinforcing the banks. The layout was symmetrical, with two diagonal *allées* crossing each other and forming four triangles, each then subdivided in two; the most ordinary fruits and vegetables grew alongside the most rare, while the simplest flowers of the local woods and fields were planted next to the most recent botanical discoveries, worthy of the *parterres* of a royal residence. Diane cut *allées* through the surrounding forest, and made outdoor 'rooms', a labyrinth and spaces for games there. The beautiful Duchesse de Valentinois was keen to offer lavish entertainment at the château, and commissioned Philibert de L'Orme to build a bridge across to the left bank of the river so that her guests could hunt there. A covered gallery was to be added, but almost as soon as the bridge was completed, Diane lost her royal lover in a tournament, and had to give up Chenonceau to his wife, Catherine de Médicis, in exchange for Chaumont.

Catherine was now able to savour her long-awaited revenge, holding memorable entertainments on the very spot where her rival had shone. She completed work begun by Diane, and dreamed of other projects which were never realized. Another *parterre* planted with exotic vegetables was created on the banks of the Cher; it included a fountain, a menagerie, an aviary, and although it covered a smaller area than

Diane's pastoral garden, it greatly surpassed it in extravagance. In 1564 a 'garden of delights' designed by Bernard Palissy enhanced the left bank of the Cher, and huge caryatids representing the gods of Olympus were added to the façade of the château.

Today, the Jardin de Diane de Poitiers consists of eight grass-covered triangles decorated with volutes of santolina, and edged with flower beds punctuated with hibiscus and clipped yew, re-creating the refinement and elegance of the Renaissance innovations. The circular *bassin* in the Jardin de Catherine is a diminished reminder of the extravagant fountain that used to play there. Without the perseverance of Chenonceau's great restorers, Marguerite Pelouze from 1864, then the Menier family in the 1950s, the château of the two rivals and its gardens would have drifted off forever with the gently flowing river. Echoing the old Labyrinthe de Diane, which has long since disappeared, a new one has recently wound its way round a circular clearing, surrounded by a hornbeam hedge; standing in front of it are the figures of Hercules, Pallas, Apollo and Cybele: the caryatids mounted on the façade of the château by Catherine, but removed by Marguerite Pelouze when their authenticity was doubted.

Chenonceau in all its splendour. The diagonal *allée* across the Jardin de Diane de Poitiers leads the eye towards the château built over the river.

La Ferté-Vidame

THE MARQUIS
DE LABORDE'S PALIMPSEST

Beyond the weather-stained balustrades, the ruins of the Marquis de Laborde's château give
a romantic charm to the great classical park, which at one time belonged to Saint-Simon.

TODAY, ONLY SIXTY HECTARES REMAIN of some thousands originally enclosed within a wall 14 kilometres (8 ½ miles) in length: this was once the huge estate of the Marquis de Laborde, an extremely rich banker to the Court, who died on the scaffold in 1764. Formerly the property of the Duc de Saint-Simon, Laborde bought it in 1764, and its network of radiating *allées* remained intact until 1937. It was cut in two when the new owner, the shipping magnate Vieljeux, sold most of the land to André-Gustave Citroën. Since then, the great east–west perspective behind the château has been ruthlessly severed by an impenetrable wall of trees, completely screening from view the Octogone which used to be the centrepiece of a sophisticated pattern of *parterres*. There is certainly no possibility of appreciating it from the first floor, as was the custom; the château that had been built for the banker by Mathieu Le Carpentier was confiscated during the Revolution, then sold to a property speculator and shamelessly dismantled. The two fine Pièces d'Eau du Miroir and du Bourg on either side of the great axis are still there, but are nowadays known prosaically as ponds. Nevertheless, the lawns, canals edged with balustrades and long avenues lined with trees are a reminder of the estate's former grandeur. The great perspective still runs unhindered for 1600 metres (5248 ft) from the façade of the house to the Saut du Loup (which replaced the *grille d'honneur* in 1880) and on to the Rond Victoire along the Route de Réveillon, between two rows of recently replanted limes beside the trapezoidal Etangs de Mousseuse: this used to be the ceremonial approach to the château.

A secondary north–south axis crosses the great perspective on the central *parterre*. For a short time it became the main axis of the composition when Louis-Philippe converted Saint-Simon's outbuildings in 1845. Unable to undertake the restoration of the château, he enlarged the buildings dating from the Regency, making a triangular courtyard and a formal garden with *parterres* and *bassins* following the north–south axis.

Today the original axis has been reinstated, and it still retains its unique character, peopled with its well-loved and famous ghosts; to them should be added that of the Duc de Penthièvre, who became so obsessed with the place that he forced Laborde to sell it to him in 1784. This whim led to the creation of a new garden by Laborde at Méréville, though this time it was an informal one.

Les Tuileries

BETWEEN

THE CITY AND THE SKY

Aerial view of the Grand Carré.

IN EARLY AUTUMN THE TUILERIES GARDENS are the temporary resting place of some long-distance travellers: they would have been unfamiliar to Le Nôtre when he redesigned the original garden of Catherine de Médicis, with additions by Henri IV, in 1666. Clouds of black-headed gulls arrive from the coast, following the Seine, giving this most Parisian of gardens a feeling of the beaches of Normandy. These graceful birds are quite at home in the royal garden – they bathe in the *bassins* on the *parterres*, dry themselves facing into the wind on the green lawns, and readily make fun of the hieratic pose of the *Centaure Nessus enlevant Déjanire*, or of Millet's *Cassandre* by alighting on their heads. The garden's other visitors (some six million a year) are used to sharing it, and hardly notice them; they are preoccupied with finding a chair in the sun, enjoying the view or admiring the subtle combinations of colours in the borders full of flowers. Such is life in this garden, which has been washed by the tide of historical events ever since it was created. A new terrace has been built by I. M. Pei on the site of the palace that was burned down by the Communards in 1871; twelve steps lead down to the gate into the Tuileries Gardens, where the visitor's journey through the garden begins. Almost as soon as he has passed the huge garlanded urns from Versailles, standing on high pedestals, his gaze is drawn beyond the *parterres* towards the trees and the even more distant Obélisque, the Arc de Triomphe, and the Grande Arche. The pleasure of leaving the city behind for a while is mingled with the excitement of being able to wander freely in a place imbued with four centuries of history. Today's alert explorer is open to any clues offered by the garden. First, he crosses the open Grand Carré with the *parterres* of flower-edged lawns which have replaced Le Nôtre's *broderies*. The original three *bassins* are still there, two small ones and one larger, arranged in a triangle so that they would appear to be linked when viewed from the terrace or the upper floors of the

now vanished château. In 1831 Louis-Philippe, followed by Napoleon III in 1858, made part of the Grand Carré into the Jardins Réservés, separating it from the public gardens with a ditch; they planted rare trees there, and adorned the area with statuary. There are still many statues around the gardens, notably by the Grand Bassin, including spectacular works such as the *Serment de Spartacus* (Oath of Spartacus) by Louis-Ernest Barrias, *Thésée combattant le Minotaure* (Theseus and the Minotaur) by Etienne Ramey, or *Prométhée* by James Pradier, and on either side of the central axis, the majestic *Hercule Farnèse* by Comino and *Jules César* by Parisi, two seventeenth-century works. It is interesting that in Le Nôtre's time there were very few statues in the gardens, and they began to grace the Tuileries in greater numbers from the reign of Louis XV onwards. On the right flank of the gardens lie the Esplanade des Feuillants and the raised Terrasse des Feuillants, linked to the Rue de Rivoli by a gate dating from the reign of Napoleon. Before this road was cut through by Napoleon in 1801 the royal stables and the convent des Feuillants stood here. On the left the other raised terrace, the Terrasse du Bord-de-l'Eau, lies alongside the river Seine; under Napoleon I and then Napoleon III, it was used exclusively by their young sons, the Roi de Rome and the Prince Impérial, as a playground.

Continuing on the axial route, the visitor reaches the second part of the garden, the Grand Couvert, a tree-covered area. When Le Nôtre was the royal gardener, the trees were made into a range of *bosquets*. There were 'open air rooms and *bassins de gazon*', 'little wooded areas', as well as an open-air theatre *à l'antique* called the Salle de la Comédie. Each space was surrounded by *allées* of chestnuts and dense yew hedges. The modern restorers of the garden, Pascal Cribier, Louis Benech and François Roubaud, won a competition organized by the Ministère de la Culture to plan a programme of renewal in the gardens, running from 1990 to 1998; they worked

Between the eastern *parterre* of the Fer à Cheval and the great octagonal *bassin* stands the statue of the Nile carved for Louis XIV by Lorenzo Ottoni.

'layer by layer', in order to retain as many features as possible from each historical period. They wanted to give the visitor a feeling of restfulness and freedom of movement, and avoided creating enclosed spaces, while at the same time they preserved some secluded areas for quiet contemplation. For example, the former exedrae, or 'outdoor rooms' for meeting and conversing, created under the Convention Nationale at the end of the eighteenth century, have now been turned into water gardens filled with lotus flowers and water-lilies. Casts of some of the statues from Marly, *Vénus Callipyge, Faune au chevreau* (Faun with a Goat), *Apollon*

poursuivant Daphné, Hippomène and *Atalante* make an impressive sight. These slightly mysterious, romantic parts of the gardens are reminiscent of the *giardini segreti* of Italian villas, places for dreaming, for secret conversations, for periods of reflection and meditation. Other spaces within the quincunx of chestnuts have been made into a grid of neat grass *parterres* with sloping banks similar to Le Nôtre's *bassins de gazon*. Here and there, a statue adds an enigmatic highlight.

The visitor emerges into full daylight again in the Parterre du Fer à Cheval, the third distinct part of the garden, where Le Nôtre's setting is still unchanged. At ground level is a great octagonal *bassin* ringed with statues – the *Fleuves* or Rivers by Guillaume Coustou, Van Clève, Ottoni and Bourdy, as well as the *Vestale* by Legros, *L'Eté* by Coustou, *L'Hiver* by Raon, *Pomone* by Barois, among other seventeenth-century works – and two *parterres* with intricate cut-box hedges and exuberant floral planting. A horseshoe ramp on the right leads up to the Jeu de Paume, and on the left up to the Orangerie, to meet the Terrasse du Bord de l'Eau and the Terrasse des Feuillants. Beyond the gate to the gardens on the Place de la Concorde, between the superb flourishes of the statues of *Mercure* and *La Renommée* (Fame) by Antoine Coysevox, the visitor takes in the continuation of the immensely long perspective laid out three hundred years ago by Le Nôtre: he intended it to run the full length of the Champs-Elysées (then still open country) until it reached the terrace of the château de Saint-Germain. If the visitor now turns round he can try to imagine the dome that used to crown the palace in the centre of the perspective, and can see in the distance the Carousel triumphal arch, built by Napoleon to commemorate the victory of the Grande Armée at Austerlitz. It has recently become the entrance to a new garden created by the designers Jacques and Peter Wirtz as a living counterbalance to the powerful sculptural impact of the Louvre and the Cour Napoléon. Belvederes, lawns and yew hedges are now the precisely laid-out setting for statues by Aristide Maillol, and lead the eye back towards the Tuileries.

Since 1998, works by Rodin, Dubuffet, Etienne Martin, Germaine Richier, Giacometti, Max Ernst, Henry Moore and many others complement each other from all corners of the gardens. This homage to twentieth-century sculpture was initiated by the installation of the Maillol pieces by André Malraux, and the tradition continues today under the direction of the sculptor Alain Kirili.

Two statues by Antoine Coysevox that originally stood on the Terrasse de l'Abreuvoir at Marly stand above the entrance from the Place de la Concorde; this one represents Mercury riding Pegasus, and opposite him is Fame.

Sceaux

A CUBIST SLANT ON

CLASSICISM

The Grand Canal from the Terrasse des Pintades.

IN 1903, A CERTAIN HENRI-ALBAN FOURNIER, the future writer Alain-Fournier, while still a pupil at the Lycée Lakanal, used to walk up and down the *allées* in the Parc de Sceaux, gathering priceless memories, which together with those of the misty atmosphere of the Sologne, would resurface when he began to write his novel, *Le Grand Meaulnes*. The 'long green room, the colour of leaves' in the young Meaulnes' dream, into which streamed 'such a soft light that one could almost taste it', could have been prompted by recollections of the Parc de Sceaux, where the straight, curtain-like rows of clipped trees seemed like the walls of beautifully decorated rooms. The present perfect condition of the estate gives no clue to the many trials history has inflicted on it. First, it was confiscated during the Revolution from the Duchesse d'Orléans, daughter of the Duc de Penthièvre, and sold to Hippolyte Lecomte, who pulled down the château and turned the park over to the cultivation of crops. The park was restored and a new château built in 1856 by the Duc de Trévise, Lecomte's son-in-law; but during the wars of 1870 and 1914 the whole estate was taken over by the army, and seriously damaged. It was not until the 1920s when the mayor of Sceaux, Jean-Baptiste Bergeret de Frouville, committed himself to its restoration, that the estate began to regain its former glory.

At Sceaux, as elsewhere, it has been necessary to choose between an exact historical restoration and a more contemporary interpretation, reflecting the new role of the park since it became publicly owned. The main outlines of the original layout of the park still exist, as do the *pièces d'eau*, Mansart's Orangerie and the delightful Pavillon de l'Aurore built by Charles Perrault for Colbert, and decorated by Le Brun. The park was created by Le Nôtre for Colbert between 1675 and 1685, and was subsequently embellished and enlarged to four times its original size by the son of Louis XIV's Minister Colbert, the Marquis de Seignelay. The twentieth-century architect Léon Azéma drew up a simplified version of this design, retaining the two principal axes, at right angles to each other, which meet in front of the château. One continues the line of the fine entrance avenue, crosses the *avant cour* and the *cour d'honneur*, passes through the middle of the château (now the Musée de L'Ile-de-France), then falls away sharply in the direction of the hills of Châtenay through the grass-covered *parterres* and the great lawn of the Quatre Statues. The seventeenth-century *parterres de broderie* were replaced by extensive lawns; the ones nearest to the château are edged with massive cone-shaped yews, which make a constant play of shadows according to the time of day and season. The other axis starts from the Allée de Diane to the north, passes the façade of the château, joins the Allée de la Duchesse, pausing for a moment before revealing one of the park's masterpieces, the Grandes Cascades; the rush of water collects in a vast *pièce d'eau*, the Octogone, which has a powerful central jet of water. Azéma entirely rebuilt the cascade in the 1930s, after its ruthless destruction by Lecomte in 1798. The pared-down geometrical design is a reminder that he was also the architect of the Trocadéro gardens in Paris. The water gushes now from two 'grotesque' masks by Rodin, made for the Paris World Fair of 1900; in the seventeenth century it flowed from the urns held by the statues of river gods in rock niches at the top of the *escalier d'eau*. Successive sheets of water slide down towards the Octogone, making sparkling curtains between each step. The new

The Orangerie; a new enclosed garden with trellis fencing has recently been created nearby.

version of the Grandes Cascades is an illustration of how well the Art Deco style, with its debt to Cubism and reliance on the use of geometric forms, fits into a great formal garden which relies above all on an elaborate play of straight lines. A second north–south axis, parallel to the one followed by the cascade, was added by Colbert's son. In 1687 he cut the Grand Canal, which runs for a kilometre along this axis, almost its entire length. Added slightly later, the Petit Canal links it to the Octogone, forming a new east–west axis at right angles to the Grand Canal, leading to the Plaine de Châtenay, and beyond it to the Pavillon de Hanovre. This elegant eighteenth-century building was dismantled and brought here in 1930 from its original site on the Boulevard des Italiens in Paris. On either side of the Plaine de Châtenay, *bosquets* planted with cherry and wild cherry trees are a delight to visitors in the spring, with their frothy pink and white flowers; they make a charming allusion to the Salle de la Cerisaie which was planted before 1785 near the Orangerie of the Marquis de Seignelay. This building still stands, and a new garden was created beside it in 1990; the trellis fences surrounding the central *bassin* support a display of climbing roses and jasmine. There were several such gardens at Sceaux in the seventeenth century, which were designed by Le Nôtre himself.

It is tempting to mourn the disappearance of the *bosquets*, the labyrinths, the covered *allées*, the *parterres de broderie*, the outdoor rooms with their ornamental *bassins* and marble statues, and the marvellous entertainments. But what matters is that this fine 160 hectare park, thanks to a protracted programme of restoration, is now able to satisfy a variety of different needs, those of walkers, sports enthusiasts, fishermen, ramblers, and visitors who enjoy history and concerts, without losing its original identity: a highly impressive achievement.

The *parterres* with their rows of cone-shaped yews.

La Roche-Courbon

PIERRE LOTI'S
'SLEEPING BEAUTY'

'THOSE PLACES IN WHICH WE HAVE NEITHER LOVED NOR SUFFERED leave no traces in our memory. On the other hand, those where our senses have experienced unparalleled enchantment are never forgotten. So it is that the dell where I first learned about love, with its ferns, its mosses, its mysterious grottoes, and even its delicate, shimmering dragonflies, has ever since held a strong nostalgic attraction for me.' After his life-changing experiences there in the arms of a beautiful gypsy, the writer Pierre Loti always cherished the vivid memory of the forest of ilexes which surround the Château de La Roche-Courbon, at Saint-Porchaire in Charente-Maritime. In 1908, the great trees of his beloved forest were reduced to cinders by property developers to make charcoal, and the lovely feudal manor was threatened with demolition; the author of *Aziyadé* wrote an

eloquent appeal, published on the front page of *Le Figaro*, for a 'prince' who could rouse the domain from a hundred years of sleep: 'At the end of the avenue, the green half-light suddenly gets darker; here the great ilexes are centuries old, with moss and ferns growing from their strong branches. Finally the Sleeping Beauty's castle begins to come into view. Still in semi-darkness, we can make out first of all the old wrought-iron gate and mossy perron of a huge, regal terrace with a balustrade, and then beyond, still far off, in a gap between the branches, a façade and turrets gilded by the autumn sun. Two Louis XIII wings, shut up for a hundred years, stand at the sides of this deserted terrace, which looms thirty or forty feet above the sunken river, another world of shivering poplars and ilex trees, a confusion of greenery, rushes, water ferns and lilies, the inextricably tangled jungle below.' However, it was not until 1922 that Loti met Paul Chenereau, a *polytechnicien* from Saintonge, who committed himself to taking charge of the château, the gardens and the forest.

In this story unlike any other, it seems that the good fairies were struggling against the malevolent ones, just as in Perrault's tale, and got the better of them in the end, with just a bit of ingenuity. It so happened that a picture was found in one of the rooms of the château, painted around 1660 by the Dutchman Jan Hackaert, which showed the gardens in all their glory and in great detail. This picture formed the basis of the restoration which then began under the direction of the landscape architect Ferdinand Duprat. A seventeenth-century painter came to the rescue of a famous twentieth-century writer to save the whole estate from oblivion: an apt image for La Roche-Courbon. From 1928 to 1936, the owner and his landscape architect devoted themselves to re-creating the classical garden. The façades of the plain feudal

View of the canal, *parterres* and château from the top of the double flight
of steps framing the *allée d'eau*.

manor had, over the centuries, been enriched with additional windows, a balustraded terrace and an 'Italian loggia', and now a *parterre* was established on the east–west axis, in front of the house, punctuated with topiaries, urns and statues. The axis continued with a *pièce d'eau*, a double staircase framing an *allée d'eau*, until it reached one of four columns in the forest marking the points of the compass. A plain straight avenue of handsome trees was planted, leading up to the château's *cour d'honneur*. Unfortunately, a few years later, the bad fairy managed to make trouble, and the enchanted surroundings of the château were threatened; the gardens stood on reclaimed marshland, and started to sink inexorably into the water. Paul Chenereau's heir and son-in-law, Jacques Badois, a civil engineer, perfected a system of piles which rest on a solid base several metres deep (following Venetian practice), and support oak planks placed under the *parterres*, with their *allées* and decorative features. This is the magical garden that we are lucky enough to be able to visit today. 'Such Gardens of Eden should be jealously guarded, as in future neither the will to do it, nor unlimited money will ever be able to re-create them', wrote Pierre Loti, as early as 1908.

Above: The *parterres* in front of the château.

Below: The Allée d'Eau and the steps leading up into the forest.

Craon

INVITATION TO A JOURNEY ✦

An unusual perspective: in 1770 the Baron de Craon chose to line up the principal axis
of his garden with the public road.

THE MARQUIS PIERRE-AMBROISE DE LA FORÊT
D'ARMAILLÉ, the last Baron de Craon, had a
commanding view from his hill-top estate, and
took a pragmatic, megalomaniac or perhaps
poetic decision when choosing the orientation
of his grounds. When he built the château of
his dreams, he used a ready-made principal axis,
that of the straight Pouancé-Laval road that
descended the hill directly opposite his property.
Accordingly, a lovely house built of white Vallée
de Loire stone, with two symmetrical wings,
was built in 1770 among the fields, and awaited
an appropriately grand garden setting. However,
the Revolution unfortunately put an end to any
prospect of creating it. The estate was bought
in 1830 by M. de Champagné, who rejected the
vistas, *parterres* and *bosquets à la française* planned
by the previous owner, and set an English-style
parkland around the château, watered by the
river Oudon.

It was not until a hundred years later that
another man of vision, the Marquis d'Andigné,
understood the possibilities of the site. With the
help of the landscape designer Redont, he gave it
back its true identity, and realized the unfulfilled
dreams of the Baron de Craon.

Today, the long vista leads from the south-
west façade of the château through the *jardin à
la française*, crossing the grass *parterres* edged
with double rows of limes, passes the gate with
its two lodges, dropping down the hill to the
public road which then takes up the perspective.
The forty-two hectares of *parc à l'anglaise*, which
includes a huge kitchen garden, an ice house and
an old wash-house, is now the outer framework
of the formal garden.

Blenheim

FRENCH AND ENGLISH
STYLES SIDE BY SIDE

LOUIS XIV PLAYED AN UNENVIABLE ROLE
in the first garden at Blenheim: a giant bust
of him, captured after the battle of Tournai,
was triumphantly placed by the Duke of
Marlborough above the south front portico,
where it looked down onto a 'bastion'-shaped
terrace with a *parterre* of box hedges,
representing a fortification of the type
constructed by Sébastien Le Prestre de Vauban
(Louis XIV's military engineer), and heroically
breached by the valiant John Churchill, first
Duke of Marlborough. Today, a portrait of the
French King by Pierre Mignard takes pride of
place in the second saloon of the palace, close to
a tapestry illustrating the battle of Bouchain, in
which Marlborough again distinguished himself
against the Sun King's troops; and now *parterres
à la française*, re-created in the 1920s, occupy the
terraces to the east and west of the palace.

The Duke of Marlborough became a national
hero after his victory in 1704 at Blenheim on the
north bank of the Danube, and in recognition of
his triumph Queen Anne gave him the royal estate
of Woodstock in Oxfordshire. The former hunting
lodge of King Henry II was in a ruinous condition,
but the Queen promised to build a palace there –
Blenheim – that would do justice to his fame.
Her promise was only half fulfilled, however;
following a quarrel, Marlborough and his forceful
wife Sarah found themselves obliged to pay part
of the cost of the building. Regardless of this,
the palace built by John Vanbrugh was conceived
both as a homage to the sovereign and as the
private residence of a prominent member of the
court, and was therefore built on a grand and
luxurious scale in the English Baroque style.
Vanbrugh's garden designs were conceived in
collaboration with the Queen's gardener Henry
Wise, who had already established himself with
his work at Hampton Court. As well as the south
terrace already mentioned, they were responsible
for a flower garden *à la française* to the east for
Sarah, a huge walled kitchen garden 800 metres
(2625 ft) from the palace, and a landscaped park,
with two great avenues planted with fully grown
elms, so that the Duke did not have to wait
to enjoy the full effect. Vanbrugh also built a
monumental bridge to link the two sides of the
valley of the river Glyme and its tributaries, and
improve its marshy appearance: the bridge was
intended to include little rooms for use in the
summer, looking out over an ornamental lake.
After Marlborough's death, his widow erected the
40 metre (130 ft) high Column of Victory, on the
north–south axis, topped by a statue of the first
Duke, as well as a triumphal arch, which is now
the main entrance to the palace. Infuriated by
what she considered Vanbrugh's extravagance,
Sarah entrusted a former soldier with the task
of constructing canals to carry the waters of
the Glyme.

In 1758 George Spencer, fourth Duke of
Marlborough, inherited the estate. By this time
the fashion for the informal had taken over, and

'Capability' Brown, who personified the 'English garden' just as Le Nôtre did the 'French garden', was engaged to completely reappraise the grounds at Blenheim. He brought the lawns into the Great Court of the palace, removed the formal beds on the south terrace, and dammed the river to form an asymmetrical lake on either side of Vanbrugh's great bridge, partly submerging it. The Blenheim landscape garden we know today was born, with its waterfalls, its sparkling lake, its clumps of great trees evoking a painting by Turner, and its hundreds of peacefully grazing sheep.

Much later, Charles, the ninth Duke of Marlborough, became dissatisfied with this idealized view of nature, and wanted to restore some of the original, more formal character to the surroundings of the palace. In the 1920s he brought in Achille Duchêne to re-create the Blenheim *parterres*. The two men shared a willingness to see things on a big scale, but unfortunately not always from the same point of view. Duchêne leaned heavily towards a 'Le Nôtre' approach, while the Duke favoured a 'Bernini' style. Duchêne loved ostentatious water fountain displays, while the Duke preferred still waters that would not contrast with the peaceful lake. They managed to agree on an 'Italian' garden to the east, consisting of a *parterre de broderie* that was in fact more French than Italian, arranged around a fountain with statues of mermaids; to the west they made a *jardin à la française* overlooking the lake, with two monumental *parterres*. The Duke wrote to Duchêne: 'It is an absolute stroke of genius on your part to have raised the water to the level of the first terrace. I never would have thought of it myself, and doubt if any English architect would have done either.' This represented a partial retribution for the aggression of the English lions, carved on either side of the clock in the Great Court, which have been sinking their claws into dying French cockerels for two centuries:

the raised *parterre d'eau* was directly inspired by those at Versailles. It consists of a series of linked *bassins*, each surrounded with box-bush *broderies*. The outer *bassins* are slightly raised, allowing thin sheets of water to glide down into the central one. The lower of the two terraces has two rectangular *bassins*, one of which contains the maquette of Bernini's River Gods fountain in the Piazza Navona, Rome. The enthusiasm of the Duke and Duchêne for large projects included the re-paving of the Great Court, grassed over by 'Capability' Brown, and the replanting of the Great Avenue of elms running north–south to the Column of Victory. Blenheim had regained the subtle balance of the formal and the picturesque, of art and nature, which makes such a harmonious whole.

The elms have now been replaced by limes as a result of Dutch elm disease, and the eastern avenue was replanted with alternate limes and plane trees. One summer's day in 1908, Winston Churchill (born at Blenheim in 1874) and Clementine Hozier did not choose either of these avenues for their walk, taking instead a path that leads from the lower terrace to the arboretum, the rose garden and the cascade, and stopped at the Temple of Diana by William Chambers, built on a rise in the time of 'Capability' Brown: it was on this romantic spot that Winston asked Clementine to marry him.

Blenheim Palace is today the seat of the eleventh Duke of Marlborough, and is a Unesco World Heritage site. At the same time as meticulously preserving his family's traditions, the Duke has provided little train and boat trips for visitors, and an amusement park within the brick walls of the old kitchen garden. The most spectacular feature is the Marlborough labyrinth, whose hedges are cut into a symbolic representation of the battle of Blenheim, the event which led to the building of the palace – perhaps a present-day version of the original south terrace 'bastion'.

On the second terrace, to the right, is the maquette of Bernini's outstanding River God fountain.
from the Piazza Navona, Rome.

The entrance court side of the Palace.

Saint-Cloud

MONSIEUR'S
'HOUSE OF DELIGHTS'

THE PREOCCUPIED MOTORIST driving along the majestic avenues of the huge park of Saint-Cloud is probably unaware that his road is part of one of Le Nôtre's most ambitious schemes, created for Louis XIV's only brother, the Duc d'Orléans, known as 'Monsieur'. A painting by Etienne Allegrain in the museum at Versailles shows the estate in around 1680, when 'a thousand *calèches*' were available for visitors to explore Monsieur's park; would the modern motorist exchange his car for one of them? The painting gives a bird's-eye view of Philippe d'Orléans' 'house of delights' after the completion of works by the *jardinier du roi* dating from 1665. Perched on a hill above the Seine, the great size of the U-shaped château dominates the composition. A series of

geometrically placed terraces, ramps and *allées* delineate the many areas of *parterres de broderie*, *bosquets* and ornamental lakes – a great variety of shapes and designs. Monsieur's imposing country retreat corresponds exactly with the magical domain described by Saint-Simon: 'The pleasure of many kinds of games, the very individual beauty of the place made accessible even to the most lazy by the provision of a thousand *calèches*, the musical performances, the excellent refreshments, made it a house of delights on a grand scale.' Today, the château for which this legendary setting was created has disappeared. Prussian soldiers took refuge there during the siege of Paris in 1870, and the luxurious dwelling was destroyed when they were fired on with shells by the French forces. Tall cones of yew mark the outline of where it used to stand, on the vast terrace looking down on the Seine and Paris. The plan of the park as it is today remains largely that of Le Nôtre. Here, the inspired designer not only had to deal with problems particular to a steeply sloping site, but he also had to take previous designs into account. Before Louis XIV gave Saint-Cloud to Monsieur, a house was built there by Jérôme de Gondi, Catherine de Médicis' equerry, completed in 1577. It was famous for its magnificent 'Italian' terraced gardens with their fountains, grottoes and statues, and had itself replaced the Hôtel d'Aulnay. After the Gondi family came Barthélemy d'Hervart, Mazarin's Controller of Finances, who considerably enlarged both the château and the gardens, and received the young Louis XIV there: he in turn was so attracted by the site and its proximity to Paris and Versailles that he decided to buy it in 1658. When Philippe d'Orléans took over the property, he began to expand the grounds, so that their area grew from fourteen to four hundred hectares between 1658

From the terrace of the former château, the Allée de la Balustrade, one of the three main axes which
run through Le Nôtre's vast park, can be seen beyond the Bassin du Fer à Cheval.

and 1701. Le Nôtre had to keep up with Monsieur's acquisitions, and laid out three principal axes in the gardens. These carefully preserved routes are the ones that the modern visitor is able to enjoy today. The first, lying north–south, parallel to the Seine, follows the lines of the Gondi gardens. Starting from the terrace of the original château – enlarged for Monsieur by Antoine Le Pautre and then Jules Hardouin-Mansart – it slopes down past the Bassin du Fer à Cheval, climbs the Allée de la Balustrade, with its grass amphitheatre added by Contant d'Ivry in the reign of Louis Philippe, and reaches the Rond de la Balustrade, where the same architect built a belvedere with a spectacular view over the Seine and Paris. The second axis leads to the west, also from the terrace of the former château. It crosses the Terrasse des Orangers (the site of Monsieur's orangery which was an extension of the north wing of the château), climbs the Allée des Statues, joins the *bassin* and canals of the Vingt-Quatre Jets, follows the Tapis Vert, and reaches the Bassin de la Grande Gerbe before disappearing into the distance among the clipped foliage of the Allée de Marnes. The third axis is an oblique and sloping avenue to the north-east, leading to the château after running alongside extensive outbuildings. Below the Bassin du Fer à Cheval, stairs lead down to a canal, and then to the upper part of the famous cascade designed by Le Pautre for Monsieur. To see the complete effect, the visitor must descend some more steps

The Grande Cascade by Le Pautre, and the Grandes Nappes, or sheets of water, by Jules Hardouin-Mansart in front of it.

which lead gradually down a wooded slope to the square Bassin du Grand Jet, enclosed in a *bosquet* embellished with statues. To the left, the Allée du Tillet separates the two parts of the Grande Cascade, the *buffet d'eau* built into the steepest part of the hillside, and then the Grandes Nappes, sheets of water created later at the foot of the Cascade by Hardouin-Mansart. This leads to the Jardins du Bas, now unfortunately missing its former fine decorative features, and without its previous access to the river.

An exploration of the park could continue for hours, with countless further surprises. Some date from the Grand Siècle, like the Allée d'Eau des Goulottes which follows the east–west axis towards the Bassin des Chiens and the Bassin des Trois-Bouillons; there are bonuses from the nineteenth century such as the Trocadéro *jardin à l'anglaise*, created by Hurtault for Louis XVIII and reached by a narrow flight of steps from the terrace of the former château. It is also possible to simply wander around, following one of the straight *allées* with their evocative names: the Allée de l'Etang Vieux, the Allée des Cerfs, the Allée de Monsieur, which cross each other at right angles or converge at cross-roads. Since the estate was listed in 1994, a huge programme of restoration of the *allées*, *parterres*, *bosquets* and hydraulic systems has been undertaken, creating a vast island of skilfully planned ornamental parkland on the site of the old royal estate, on the doorstep of the capital.

Sans-Souci

THE GOLDEN
RETREAT OF FREDERICK II

Beneath the hornbeam arbours in the Sicilian Garden.

AT THE PALACE OF SANS-SOUCI, built as a summer residence by Frederick the Great (1712–86), King of Prussia, one of the five guest rooms in the west wing is still called 'The Voltaire Room'. It is delightfully decorated, with walls of yellow silk patterned with colourful garlands of flowers and birds. The French poet spent nearly three years between 1750 and 1753 as the guest of the King he called 'the Solomon of the North'. The dinners held there in the Marble Saloon, looking out over the gardens and terraces, were famous throughout Europe; the conversation was in French, and the participants were some of the most brilliant minds of the time. Voltaire remarked in his *Mémoires*: 'Nowhere else in the world was it possible to discuss man's superstitions so freely, or with such humour and cynicism. God was treated with respect, but those who had cheated people in his name were not spared. No women or priests were allowed to enter the palace. In short, Frederick lived there with no court, no council and no confessional.' The name Sans-Souci (without cares) is written in capital letters on the cornice of the central dome of the palace, representing an absence of protocol where life was devoted to the arts – Frederick was a flautist and composer – and the delights of conversation. The royal family, the Hohenzollerns, had been enchanted by the landscape around Potsdam, with its delightful lakes and forests, since the middle of the seventeenth century. At Potsdam Frederick I had maintained a court that claimed to be the equal of the court of the Sun King. When Voltaire arrived, the royal country retreat of Frederick

the Great had been in existence for six years. The palace itself, built in a dazzling Rococo style, with spectacular terraced vineyards laid out before it, had been finished three years before. Frederick and his architect Georg Wenzeslaus von Knobelsdorff had laid out several axes starting from the centre of the palace. One led from the courtyard side towards the Mount of Ruins, a classical composition concealing a reservoir that supplied water to the fountains. On the garden side, the eye was led to the lush banks of the River Havel. Along this axis, a huge staircase bisected the terraces and finished at a *parterre à la française* with a central *bassin*, encircled with marble statues of the gods of Olympus and allegories of the Four Elements. Further on, two sphinxes marked the entrance to the formal garden; crossing it at right angles was a secondary axis which later became the central *allée* of the park. This led at its eastern end to the Obelisk Gateway and the exit from the park; statues of Flora and Pomona stood at the ends of a balustrade terminated with Corinthian columns. Nearby, Frederick planned a Neptune grotto and, on either side of the palace, a greenhouse above a terraced kitchen garden and an orangery above a sloping cherry orchard. It was important to him to mingle beauty and practicality in his garden, to enjoy both extravagance and the everyday. But he was a man of his time, and could not resist the temptation of adding the delicious *chinoiserie* features which create the illusion of a different time and place. Johann Gottfried Büring built the green and gold Chinese Pavilion – one of the most beautiful examples of *chinoiserie* in one of the more informal southern parts of the park.

Frederick may have felt a lack of space in his golden palace, since it only had ten rooms, but loved it so much that he spent every summer there until his death. He commissioned Büring

Frederick II's palace, with before it the stepped terraces of vines. In the foreground, the *parterre* with the statues of the gods of Olympus and the allegories of the Four Elements.

to replace the greenhouse where he grew bananas with a gallery to display his collection of paintings; he was a great admirer of Jean-Antoine Watteau. Sixteen years later a matching building replaced the orangery, providing rooms for his guests. By the time he became one of Europe's most powerful monarchs after the Seven Years' War (1756–63), he had already completed his second or New Palace, this time on a grandiloquent scale complete with extensive outbuildings. It terminates the east–west axis running 2½ kilometres (1½ miles) across the garden from the Obelisk gateway. The palace is in the Rococo style, like the first; on the ground floor an extraordinary grotto was created to mirror the Neptune grotto to the east, with five great French windows leading out onto a semi-circular *parterre à la française*. The New Palace was built to accommodate the royal family, but Frederick largely ignored it in favour of his beloved Sans-Souci and the attraction of its more intimate scale. On the other side of the tall hornbeam hedges, which form a stylish border to the *parterre* in front of the New Palace, the King built two temples, one on each side of the central axis. One is known as the Temple of the Antique, and housed his collection of antiquities; the other, the Temple of Friendship, was dedicated to his sister Wilhelmina, who was also a friend of Voltaire. Frederick's last project in his remarkable park was the building of the Dragon Pavilion in an area to the north-east planted with more vines; it is based on the Pagoda at Kew in London, and was the eccentric home of the gardener who tended the vineyard. A little further on, a tower-like belvedere was constructed on the Klausberg hill, to provide an overall panorama of his wonderful domain.

In 1825 the future Frederick William IV (then still the Crown Prince) launched a second phase of embellishments at Sans-Souci when he inherited some land to the south of the park.

He was a great Italophile, and built the neoclassical Charlottenhof Palace in an idealized landscape laid out by Peter Josef Lenné; it was surrounded by flower gardens, and a Roman bath was built in the grounds as part of a historical reconstruction of life in classical times. When he became king in 1840, he envisioned a massive orangery on the hill overlooking the whole garden to the north, a Florentine palace with a terraced garden, directly rivalling the terraced vines of his ancestor. One of the great rooms of this palatial building houses fifty copies of paintings by Raphael.

A walk along the main axis of the park gives a good idea of the alternating areas of 'the well-kept and the wild', that were so dear to Voltaire, and which complement each other so well at Sans-Souci. Whether the paths that cross it are at right angles, diagonal or winding, they are always a clue to some new exciting discovery. To the east, the Dutch garden lies in front of the Picture Gallery; the name comes from the busts of members of the House of Orange, relatives of the Hohenzollerns, that used to stand there. It is a slightly sloping formal garden, impeccably designed, defined by hedges, pergolas and avenues of limes, all closely clipped. A marble balustrade with groups of mischievous cupids offsets the changes in level. On the far side of the Dutch garden stands the Church of Peace, built by the side of a lake by Frederick William IV in the style of the earliest Christian churches. It is the focal point of a group of buildings and gardens conceived in a Romantic style by Lenné and the architect Ludwig Persius, who also created the delightful rustic garden named Marly on the site of the former kitchen garden made for Frederick II's father, Frederick William I.

Leaving behind Sans-Souci and its terraces, we can see the Chinese Pavilion glittering in its idyllic setting; the central avenue, lined with tall hornbeam hedges, comes to a meeting of paths

The New Palace is more formal; it was built by Frederick II as his family's residence and as a symbol of the Empire.

marked by a pool and statues. Another path leads to the New Apartments, and on the way we pass through the Sicilian Garden with its Mediterranean plants in pots, followed by the Nordic Garden planted with conifers; both were created by Lenné. Further on to the right, a diagonal path gives a view of Frederick William IV's immense orangery, with a sequence of terraces laid out before it. As it crosses the deer park, unchanged since the eighteenth century, the path breaks free from its constricting hedges and spreads out across the soft, glowing landscape.

Two statues mounted on columns indicate the return to the more formal setting of the *parterre* in front of the New Palace. Sans-Souci, the parks and other buildings make up the 'cultural landscape' that Frederick William IV entrusted to the landscape designer Lenné. The entire estate is today listed as a Unesco World Heritage Site.

155

Effiat

SEAT OF THE MARÉCHAL DE FRANCE

156

The *parterres* of the Château d'Effiat, seen from the terrace of Volvic stone, shaded by oak trees almost four hundred years old. The great park was created by the Maréchal d'Effiat, third most powerful person in the kingdom after the King and the Cardinal, and father of the Marquis de Cinq Mars.

IN 1625, ANTOINE COËFFIER, Marquis d'Effiat Ruzé and Louis XIII's Chief of Artillery, ordered the demolition of the village of Effiat to create a 132 hectare park at his ancestral home, to add to the *parterres* designed by André Mollet. This was just what Louis XIV had done when he wiped the village of Trianon off the map in order to enlarge the Grand Parc at Versailles. Nothing was impossible for the Marquis d'Effiat, Maréchal de France, who enjoyed the approval of Cardinal Richelieu. The great park with its lake and network of *allées* has now disappeared, given over to agriculture. The fine terrace of Volvic stone, 135 metres (443 ft) long, was embellished with carved niches and planted with majestic oaks in 1627 – it separated the château grounds from the park, and now marks the division between the grass and box bush *parterres* and the yellow waves of vast fields of corn. The château stands exactly in the centre of a huge rectangle, with a moat on two sides. A paved path lined with two-hundred-year-old limes leads up to the *cour d'honneur* and a porch of Volvic stone, with the Maréchal's coat of arms on the pediment. On the garden side of the house, four *parterres* of lawn with narrow edging paths and dotted with cone-shaped box bushes surround an octagonal *bassin*, reflecting the austere form of the house among the trees and the clouds. The *parterres* are lined on two sides by *allées* of limes, the Allée du Maréchal and the Allée Cinq Mars, with each tree standing on a square of grass. The Marquis de Cinq Mars, born at Effiat, was the son of the Maréchal. From the middle axis, a bridge crosses over the moat to a grotto with a pebble-covered vault, nestling under the raised terrace. At the back of the grotto water flows from a carved mask into a lava-stone bowl, and from there in *chaînettes de diamant* into a *bassin*.

On either side of the grotto flights of steps ornamented with military trophies lead up to the terrace and the shade of the oak trees planted two years before Richelieu's visit to Effiat. From there is a fine overall view of the proud Louis XIII building; inside, much of the original décor has been preserved, including some Italian Renaissance-style panelling with monochrome painted decoration, an innovation known as *camaïeu* in the eighteenth century.

A terraced garden facing onto the open countryside. In the distance
is the summit of the Montagne Sainte-Victoire.

La Gaude

A PROVENÇAL GARDEN WITH AN ITALIAN FLAVOUR

THE EVOLUTION OF THE GARDEN at La Gaude is somewhat mysterious, like the famous summit of the Montagne Sainte-Victoire in the chilly morning light, the garden's majestic backdrop to the east. At first sight the general layout of the garden is typical of a large Provençal 'bastide' on a wine-growing estate, in the heart of the lush Vallée des Pinchinats near Aix-en-Provence. Such gardens are the ornamental part of Provençal agricultural estates, and traditionally follow the pattern of a *jardin à la française*. The house, plain and imposing, stands at the centre of an axis along which *parterres* and *bassins* are laid out, flanked by symmetrically arranged clipped hedges in the Mediterranean style; beyond the garden, lies an extensive view of the countryside and the cultivated land of the estate. Urns and statues demonstrate the owner's taste for the arts

and emphasize his social standing. Beyond an imposing gateway with stone pillars, an avenue of trees bordered with clipped hedges leads up to the house.

The meticulously planned garden at La Gaude certainly conforms to this typical French plan, but because the site is sloping, the opportunity has been taken to construct a terraced garden and add subtle variations to the outline plan, inspired by Italian Renaissance garden design. For example, on the second terrace there is a moated island with a stylized labyrinth *parterre* of clipped box – the labyrinth was a favourite motif in Italian gardens from the fifteenth century onwards, and was used in a great variety of forms in gardens all over Europe. Two statues of dogs and a wrought-iron gate guard its entrance. On either side are thickly planted areas of trees containing a *tèse* or area of clipped hedges designed to catch small birds, attracted by the berries, in nets arranged among the branches. The island and the *bosquets*, although slightly lacking in scale and theatricality, are an inevitable reminder of the *isolotto* in the Boboli Gardens in Florence, a magical island symbolizing the end of a prescribed route, which a wanderer can only reach after passing various metaphorical 'tests' in the shadowy *bosquets*. The *tèse* is a variation on the *toiles d'araignée* or spider's webs, the intricate networks of paths and drinking places designed to catch birds, which commonly surround gardens in the south-east of France. The style and symbolism of the Italian Renaissance garden seem to have been absorbed into this corner of a French hillside as part of the dream of a rich aesthete in the eighteenth century. According to Jean Boyer, chief curator of Musées de France, the La Gaude estate was

sold in 1778 by Jean-Joseph de Silvy, lawyer
to the Parlement, to Charles-François-Joseph
Pisani de la Gaude, vicar-general and future
bishop of Vence, who considerably enlarged
it. He added to the house and decorated the
gardens with sculptures by the two Chastels,
father and son. Pisani fell into serious debt,
and was obliged to sell his estate in 1786. After
a series of changes of ownership, the estate was
acquired in 1938 by the Baron de Vitrolles, who
restored the château and the garden and revived
the vineyards. It was his wife that designed
the garden's third terrace, a lawn dotted with
clipped yews surrounding a circular *bassin*,
which makes an effective transition between
the garden and the open countryside.

Shaded 'outdoor rooms' can be explored on either side
of the central axis.

Marly

'MARLY, YOUR MAJESTY!'

COMING FROM VERSAILLES, Louis XIV used to enter the estate of his Marly 'retreat' by the Grille Royale on the east side of the park. His coach travelled down the impressive paved avenue from Louveciennes, cutting through the hill between plain high walls. On reaching a crossroads the carriage passed through another gate, flanked by the Guards' lodge and the Chapel. The King alighted at the steps of his 'Palladian' villa, then entered the Salon Octogonal, the focus of life at Marly. The magnificent perspective spread out to the north, descending by degrees with terraced *pièces d'eau* and inclines to the Abreuvoir or Watering Place. From the south, he could hear the tumultuous sound of La Rivière, the most beautiful cascade a King could wish to have. To the west, he could observe the whirlwind of preparations in the servants' quarters caused by his arrival. The thirty to fifty courtiers who had 'requested Marly', and had the honour of being chosen, would make their way to the lodges where they were allocated apartments according to their rank and degree of favour. The twelve lodges were arranged symmetrically on either side of the central axis, with its double row of intricate hornbeam hedges, like planets revolving around the sun: the women were accommodated on one side, the men on the other. You could hear the rustle of velvets, silks and lace, and the fluttering of fans, and see rich satins and taffetas catching the light, while swarms of valets opened travelling cases and arranged the rooms. The lodges on the east side stood in front of the Bosquets de Louveciennes, those to the west backed onto the Bosquets de Marly, named after the two villages on either side of the valley; the site had been chosen by the King and moulded in shape by Hardouin-Mansart.

Today, the visitor is free of the restrictions of etiquette, and can enjoy the most exclusive of royal parks, in all weathers; the Abbé de Polignac declared to Louis XIV 'the rain is not wet at Marly'. If the visitor chooses to enter by the more discreet side gate on the Côte du Coeur-Volant, he can take the tree-lined path sloping gently down to the Abreuvoir, and admire the famous 'Marly Horses' by Coustou, the same ones which stand in Paris at the start of the Champs Elysées. In fact, the originals were brought to Paris in 1794 and are now in the Louvre; the horses and their grooms have been replaced by replicas both in their position above the royal watering place at Marly and at the entrance to the most beautiful avenue in the world. Their dramatic impact is still considerable, and even though they are copies, it is still satisfying to see the statues standing in their intended place.

Alternatively the visitor can take the same starting-point, the Coeur-Volant gate, and climb southwards back towards the château. In that case he will follow an informal path which wanders where the Bosquets de Louveciennes used to be; they and the lodges have completely disappeared. As he looks back into the Grand Siècle through the screens of trees now left unclipped by the gardeners, the modern visitor will see the evocative rows of yew cones, standing like trained courtiers to mark where the lodges used to be. Their plain geometric outlines overlook the grass-edged *pièces d'eau*, home to mallard and seagulls. Further up a platform surrounded with lime trees shows where the King's residence used to be, while a long *tapis vert* runs down the hill to the south where the royal Rivière originally flowed in cascades, arabesques and sheets of water down the sixty-two red and green marble steps. Two white marble groups by Coustou stand on the spot where steps used to lead down to the Rivière; they each show a hunter, one battling with a boar, the other with a stag, and give an idea of the splendour of the original sculptural display.

The restoration project undertaken in 1997 for the preservation of Marly does not claim to be able to revive its glorious ghosts, and even less the gold and polychrome of its buildings. It does, however, aim to complete the work of restructuring, replanting and marking out of *allées* begun by Duchêne and Granger-Veyron in the 1930s, and to renew the impact of the north–south axis, whose monumental style remains impressive, as well as to reconstruct some of the displays of statuary and *pièces d'eau* that were such an essential part of this favourite among Louis XIV's enchanted domains.

The famous 'Marly Horses' by Coustou still look down on the Abreuvoir below, beyond the balustrade.

164   The plain grass edges of the *miroir* mark a departure from the classical norm; a row of cone-shaped yews shows the position of the missing lodges.

Chantilly

THE 'TRÈS RICHES HEURES' OF THE GRAND CONDÉ

THE PRICELESS LIBRARY AT CHANTILLY, accumulated during the life time of the Duc d'Aumale, is one of the most remarkable in the world; one of its outstanding possessions is the illuminated manuscript *Les Très Riches Heures du duc de Berry*, which was discovered by chance in a religious boarding school near Genoa. The famous miniatures in this book show several fairy-tale châteaux, with graceful turrets and soaring roofs picked out in gold, against precisely drawn landscapes. The Château de Chantilly, reflected in the waters of the moat, could easily be one of them, a fine example of the elegance and inventiveness of Renaissance architecture. The grounds at Chantilly were Le Nôtre's favourite among his projects, and in a letter to the Duke of Portland he declared that they were

his most representative work. This is unexpected, since the composition places the château to one side of the main axis, implying a secondary role. But perhaps Chantilly is the exception which proves the rule, and in its own authoritative way shows how all gardens *à la française* take the château as their starting-point, and reinforce its commanding role with a symmetric arrangement of *parterres*, *pièces d'eau* and *bosquets*.

There had been a château at Chantilly in the Middle Ages; it stood on a rocky outcrop looking out over marshland, and controlled the road from Paris to Senlis. The Connétable Anne de Montmorency, a comrade-in-arms of François I, inherited the estate in 1522, enlarged it by buying surrounding land, and rebuilt the Grand Château with his architect Pierre Chambiges. Jean Bullant built the Petit Château, which still stands on the esplanade facing the *cour d'honneur*. Henri I de Montmorency, son of the Connétable, built the Maison de Sylvie, which some years later became the refuge of the poet Théophile de Viau, hounded by the Parlement because of the decadent tone of his writings. As a mark of his gratitude, de Viau dedicated a poem to Marie-Félice des Ursins, wife of Henri II de Montmorency, naming her Sylvie in the poem. The house with its trellis-work garden, rebuilt and enlarged over the years, still stands at the western end of the park. The vast *pièce d'eau* in front of it is linked to the west with the moat, and is known as l'Etang de Sylvie.

In 1643 the estate passed to the Condé family after the marriage of Marguerite de Montmorency and Henri II de Condé. Their son, Louis II de Bourbon, the Grand Condé, inherited it in 1650. The victor of the battle of Rocroi was fascinated by Vaux and Versailles, and wanted to create the same enchantment at Chantilly; so, in 1662, he summoned Le Nôtre, his nephew Claude Desgots, and the famous fountain engineers of Versailles. They found

The *miroirs* on the north *parterre* and the Allées des Philosophes seen from the Canal des Brochetons. In the distance is the Grand Canal and the *vertugadin* with its statue of Hercules

The park was created as a setting for luxurious celebrations, and has many delightful surprises for the curious visitor.

some of their favourite 'raw materials': a terrain with a promising variety of levels, vast forests, numerous springs and a river, the Nonette. The position of the château and the complexity of its architecture meant that it could not take centre stage in the composition, so Le Nôtre focused his perspective on an equestrian statue of the Connétable, facing the main entrance. The central axis still begins where several avenues meet, and continues to the ceremonial gateway and its two lodges; from there it extends right up

to the statue of the Connétable Anne de Montmorency, and pursues a straight line down the Grand Degré, crosses the Bassin de la Gerbe and runs the length of the Manche – a branch of the Grand Canal lying in the middle of the *parterre d'eau*. After crossing the Grand Canal it reaches the grassy incline and the statue *Hercule enlevant Déjanire*, finally disappearing into the distance along a vast tree-lined avenue. An east–west axis follows the dip of the valley, crosses the central axis and takes the route of the Grand Canal for a mile. At its eastern end it begins at the Grand Rond, which collects the water channelled from the River Nonette; this splashes noisily down the three levels of the cascade into the Hexagone, the large pool at that end of the Grand Canal. The axis runs the entire length of the canal to the west, delimiting the boundary of the park.

Le Nôtre remodelled the Connétable's gardens to the west in line with contemporary taste, and replaced the kitchen garden with an orangery and *parterres*, which have since disappeared. He also created a network of *bosquets* linked by radiating paths, enlivened by magnificent fountain displays, including the Grande Cascade and the Fontaine de la Tenaille. All were lost when that part of the park was destroyed during the Revolution. The Ile d'Amour and the *buffet d'eau* called the Fontaines de Beauvais (similar to the cascade at the Villa d'Este at Tivoli) have fortunately survived in the *parc à l'anglaise* designed by the architect Victor Dubois in 1817, after the Condé family regained possession of their estate.

At the end of the seventeenth century, Henri-Jules, son of the Grand Condé, continued some projects begun by his father, including the reconstruction of the Grand Château by Hardouin-Mansart, and the design of the Petit Parc, on the far side of the Pont du Roi, which lines up with the main entrance to the Grand Château. Several 'outdoor rooms' were fitted out with appropriate entertainments for guests at Chantilly, among them a labyrinth, a riding paddock, and games such as *jeu de l'oie*, *jeu de mail*, *longue paume*, and shooting with harquebus and crossbows. Walking today in this wooded area, criss-crossed with paths leading to many hidden corners, the visitor can still find inscrutable statues, oblivious to the changing seasons which transform the colours of their backdrop of dense walls of foliage.

In 1774, Louis-Joseph de Condé, great grandson of Henri-Jules, created a *hameau*, or hamlet, in a marshy field between the Grand Canal and the parallel Canal des Morfondus to the east. Pre-dating Marie-Antoinette's similar project, it is still almost intact, with its five little half-timbered houses, the Salon, the Grange (barn), the Cabaret (inn), the Etable (stable) and the Moulin (mill), linked together by curving paths edged with winding streams.

During the Revolution the Grand Château was emptied of all its valuables and demolished. Between 1875 and 1885 it was rebuilt on the foundations of the medieval fortress by Honoré Daumet for the Duc d'Aumale, son of Louis Philippe and heir to the Condés, who transferred his considerable collections of paintings, books and manuscripts there.

A walk in any direction here is exhilarating. The formal approaches, the château itself and its immediate surroundings, the *parterre d'eau* and

The network of *allées* and 'outdoor rooms' containing busts or statues add continual interest to a walk in the grounds.

the canals are all in the grand style; the *bosquets* of the Petit Parc are more enigmatic, while a walk in the *hameau* is charming, and the Jardin Anglais has a rustic, romantic quality. Water, with its reflections and mirrored clouds, covers 25 of the 115 hectares of the park, and leads the visitor on a walk back through time, and offers a comprehensive view of the art of garden design. We owe this privilege to the generosity of the Duc d'Aumale, who gave his estate to the Institut de France in 1884.

Le Tertre

A PARK

BLESSED BY THE MUSES

The classical *bassin* is placed between the *parterres* and the park,
and was designed by Roger Martin du Gard.

WHEN HE BOUGHT THE CHATEAU DU TERTRE
from his wife's family in 1924, the writer Roger Martin du Gard had been 'possessed' by the place for a long time: for him it was an ideal setting for the creation of something out of the ordinary. A gentle walk from a formal area to a more secluded one is appealing to any writer seeking both order for their thoughts and a more relaxed atmosphere in which to explore the more troubled areas of the imagination. Views over the open country and woodland are a reminder of the continuing presence of the outside world.

In front of Le Tertre, a Louis XIII-style château built at the beginning of the seventeenth century by Bry de La Clergerie, is a simple grass *parterre*, dotted with ball-shaped yew hedges, and edged with two *allées* of limes cut *en marquise*. A central *allée* leads to a few steps, below which lies a grassed terrace, surrounded by groups of tall beech trees; in the middle of this space is a large quatrefoil *bassin*. From the belvedere, the Musoi, there is a view to the right towards the forest and the church of Saint-Martin-du-Vieux-Bellême. It is balanced on the left by a fountain with a statue of Flora, which marks the beginning of the landscaped park.

The writer wanted to make Le Tertre into a work of art; he designed the terrace and belvedere, and organized the building of the *bassin* and the installation of a hydraulic ram to provide the necessary water. The nine-hectare park which adjoins this classical part of the estate to the south-east was designed in 1802 by the Comte Josef Abrial, who also added two wings to the château. The park has a Masonic theme, with several garden buildings, such as a Temple of Reason built above a grotto, a Temple of Philosophy, and a turret hidden among the trees. Just as he had built a terrace in front of the château to give views over the Perche countryside and from which to enjoy the sunsets, Roger Martin du Gard also constructed an arbour where he could write in the Allée du Bréviaire, a particularly romantic area of the park. The author of *Les Thibault* was also responsible for an imposing avenue of thuya pines, which form a kind of living Gothic nave that can only be approached with reverence, so vivid is the elusive presence of the Muses.

Cormatin

A WORLD OF SYMBOLS

The *parterre* seen from the château. To the left, the entrance to the labyrinth.

The north façade and *parterre* from the Bosquet d'Albion.

An urn in the Salle des Tulipiers.

IN THE SUMMER APARTMENTS in the north wing of the Château de Cormatin is an unusual *cabinet* or study; it was decorated in the Louis XIII style in 1626 for the Marquis d'Uxelles, a brilliant soldier, gentleman of Marie de Médicis' court and governor of Chalon. It depicts St Cecilia, symbol of harmony, with Juno, Minerva and Venus, representing the three lives of man, active, meditative and sensual – the Renaissance ideal was to achieve an exact balance between them. The modern visitor will particularly enjoy this special place if he keeps in mind that it reflects principles, shared by an intellectual elite, that were current at the beginning of the seventeenth century. As he moves from one space to another, from surprise to surprise, he will enjoy the pleasures of the intellect and the pleasures of the senses in equal measure. The owners of Cormatin did not set out to re-create the original garden when they began their restoration project in 1981 – all records were lost – but they were keen to make a perfect partnership between the château and its grounds, hoping to echo the richness of the symbolism of the decoration inside with the garden. It was important to them to create a living place, transposing ideas into their modern equivalent, rather than slavishly following rules laid down at the beginning of the seventeenth century. For example, all the pathways at Cormatin are grassed over, because for citizens of the twentieth century, it is a welcome change to see and walk on grass rather than gravel, whereas in the seventeenth century a carefully raked path was the height of luxury. The designs of the various parts of the garden have been inspired by contemporary examples which may have been known to the original owners: the work of Dezallier d'Argenville, André and Claude Mollet or Boyceau at La Barauderie, the kitchen garden at the Abbey of Saint-Gall or the Garden of the Planets at Twickenham. All that was best in garden design up to the beginning of the seventeenth century is reinterpreted using the distance and experience of the twentieth century.

The garden consists of a number of linked compartments: *parterre*, labyrinth, *bosquet*, *miroir*, *tapis vert*, kitchen garden, arboretum and the Jardin des Planètes currently under construction. All can be seen from different levels, and the whole composition is united by the square outline imposed by the moat. To the north, the *parterre* in front of the summer apartments of the Marquis and Marquise d'Uxelles has a very specific intellectual schema, involving the château in a form of dialogue. It represents the Garden of Eden, and includes an apple tree and statues of Adam and Eve; as tradition dictates, it contains sixteen triangles of lawn, edged with yellow, blue and white flowers: the colours of God. In the centre is a quatrefoil *bassin*, symbolizing the union of sky and earth at the moment of Creation; from this Fountain of Life spring four tortoises, which represent the rivers of the world and spout water in the direction of the points of the compass. A little bridge leads from the *parterre* across a moat to the labyrinth, which represents man's tribulations after being expelled from paradise. On either side of the bridge stand a statue of a dancing Faun (Folly) and a statue of Aesculapius (Wisdom), intended to represent the routes between which man must choose before starting to negotiate the labyrinth, or his life's journey. The aviary in the centre symbolizes the kingdom of Heaven, the goal of a disciplined life.

After the trials of the labyrinth, the visitor can allow himself the pleasure of wandering in the *bosquet* planted with alders, oaks, maples, silver birch, planes and chestnuts, and along the way can admire the tulip trees from Virginia, planted as a reminder of those brought from America at the end of the eighteenth century by Pierre Desoteux, then the proprietor of the estate. Beyond that is the Allée Lamartine, which runs for 500 metres (1640 ft) alongside the waters of the River Grosne, channelled in 1627 by the creators of the first garden. Lamartine was a frequent visitor, and in 1812 had a liaison with Pierre Desoteux's capricious daughter, Nina. Through the branches of the ancient limes that edge the poet's *allée*, the visitor can see the *miroir*, a dominant feature of the gardens, and then the open-air theatre within a quincunx of liquidambar. This lies at the southern end of the garden, where another canal runs at right angles to the first. A *tapis vert* lies at the back of the château, and beyond that is the kitchen garden, embellished with English roses, rosemary and lavender, and also the planned Jardin des Planètes. This garden, intended for completion in 2000, will use several varieties of plants to represent the five circles of Ptolemy's planetary system, which placed the earth at the centre of the universe. The design dates from 1610, based on ideas contemporary with the building of the château. A little further on, a two and a half hectare arboretum is planted with rare trees, continuing a tradition followed by successive owners of Cormatin. This 'alliance with the past' is of great importance to the present owners, and forms the basis of their whole project.

The kitchen garden strikes a relaxed note between the Jardin des Planètes and the farmyard.

Villandry

THE QUINTESSENTIALLY
FRENCH GARDEN

The gardens from the air. To the right are the ornamental gardens, in the centre the nine squares of the kitchen garden and to the left is the garden of medicinal plants. At the top, on the right, is the château.

BETWEEN 1907 AND 1920 the last Renaissance château to be built in the Val de Loire was restored to its former splendour by a Spanish doctor, Joachim Carvallo, and his American wife, Ann Coleman. Their finished creation was deemed 'quintessentially French' by Hugh Johnson of the Royal Horticultural Society. They undertook a meticulous and imaginative reconstruction of the château and gardens, after considerable research; they visited all the manor houses and châteaux in the region, studied the most authoritative books on the art of garden design, and above all studied the plans in Jacques Androuet du Cerceau's book *Les Plus excellents bastiments de France*, and a text by the Benedictine monks of the community of Saint-Maur, *Monasticum gallicanum*. The château had been built in 1536 by Jean Le Breton, a minister of François I; the misconceived eighteenth-century additions made by the Marquis de Castellane were unacceptable to the discerning eye of Carvallo, conflicting with his almost mystical need for order and harmony. After removing the frivolous ornaments from the château, he turned to the gardens that had been superseded by a *parc à l'anglaise*, and revived the fertile dialogue between man and nature which was the hallmark of the Renaissance. On the slopes of the valley, 1500 metres (4920 ft) from the meeting of the two rivers, the Loire and the Cher, vast terraces covering seven hectares were re-created, balancing perfectly with the nearby forest, fields, and the village with its beautiful twelfth-century church. Carvallo explained in 1923: 'There are three superimposed cloister-like

terraces, each a continuation of one of the floors of the château, and each containing a different kind of garden. The first enclosure is the kitchen garden; the second, the ornamental garden, and the third, the water garden.... The kitchen garden is on the lowest level, continuous with the basement floor of the château and level with the stables; the ornamental garden is level with the ground floor and is an extension of the salon, in fact an open air salon. Lastly, the water garden is on the third level, and the surrounding terraces are an extension of the third floor of the château.'

Three generations later, Villandry is as impressive as ever, and undergoes regular fine-tuning by the descendants of its creator and a dedicated team of gardeners with the same exacting standards. The kitchen garden is the showpiece of the estate; it is based on monastic layouts, with nine square divisions, overlooked by a pergola of vines. Each square has a different cross motif outlined in little box hedges, with the spaces filled by all kinds of vegetables, chosen for their harmonious shapes and colours; they are bordered with flowers and dotted with standard roses and pear trees. The paths between the squares are edged with trellised fences of oak which support espaliered apple and pear trees. The intersections have a central fountain and four arbours 'à la Philibert de L'Orme', covered with roses and honeysuckle. The extraordinarily exuberant planting, which contrasts with the extreme rigidity of the composition, is renewed

The ornamental gardens, a masterpiece of the art of topiary, were designed by the Andalusian painter Lozano for Joachim Carvallo. In the distance is the village and church of Villandry.

completely twice a year, in the middle of March and around 20 June. Beyond the elegant carved white stone balustrades, which border the terraces and the moat on the second level, lies the Jardin d'Ornement; it was designed by the Andalusian painter Lozano in the Spanish *mudejar* style, the legacy of Arab craftsmen who stayed in Spain after its return to Christian rule; one of the rooms in the château has a ceiling in the same style. This part of the garden is made up of squares or rectangles of taller box hedging; within them are symbolic geometrical shapes, filled with flowers in delicate or vibrant colours. 'Mute servants' of clipped yew – a type of topiary characteristic of Villandry – are placed at regular intervals around the edges; their originality and perfectly trimmed forms are essential to the composition, as too is the balance that a vertical element provides. The Jardin d'Amour is below the reception rooms of the château, and its motifs in the shape of hearts, masks, fans, daggers or lances evoke in turn the various stages of passionate love, from the tender harmony represented by pink flowers, to the drama of betrayal illustrated with yellow ones. A little further on, the *parterres* of the Jardin de Musique are planted with imaginative and colourful designs based on musical instruments. Gently sloping ramps lead to the *allée* of lime trees cut *en marquise* which marks the change to the third level and the Jardin d'Eau. Here is a classic large *miroir*; Carvallo called it 'the eye of the estate, filled with light from the sky'. It has a grass border and four grass 'carpets' with little circular fountains in the middle of each. The water from the *miroir* flows into a canal edged with balustrades, before mingling with water in the moat and the reflection of the château.

The kitchen garden at its colourful best, and the château with its twelfth-century tower: a perfect match.

The twelfth-century tower, part of the Renaissance building by Jean Le Breton, is topped with a terrace that overlooks the whole garden. At the end of the *allée* of lime trees, the hornbeam labyrinth can be seen; it is based on the one created by the Italian garden designer Pacello da Mercogliano at Gaillon. Then on the far side of the kitchen garden to the west is a garden of aromatic, culinary and medicinal plants. On the edge of the wooded park beyond the Jardin d'Eau a new garden of 'mixed borders' has been planted as a tribute to Hatfield House, Hertfordshire, whose famous garden is twinned with Villandry. This may be a place full of history, but it is nonetheless still evolving.

Saint-Jean-de-Beauregard

THE GRAND
SIÈCLE WAY OF LIFE

Between the kitchen garden and the orchard is a dividing wall, sheltering a border of medicinal plants.
On the right is the garden of flowers for cutting.

THE SAINT-JEAN-DE-BEAUREGARD ESTATE dates from the seventeenth century and has retained its original design; a harmonious layout of perspective, *parterre à la française*, courtyard, *avant cour*, country-style outbuildings, dovecote and kitchen garden around the Louis XIII and Louis XIV period château. Three important festivals are the highlights of the year, and illustrate its individual character.

In the spring the festival of hardy perennials reflects the interest of the proprietor in these freely growing plants as a decorative feature of the kitchen garden. In September the craftsmen's fair is held in the picturesque courtyard of the stable buildings and the old hay barns, where thirty or so craftsmen re-create an atmosphere of the past; a blacksmith, a potter, glass-blower, weaver, woodturner, bronze caster, stained-glass window maker and sculptor demonstrate their skills and their application to the restoration and maintenance of historic monuments. At the fruit and vegetable fair in November, old or rare varieties of kitchen garden produce are displayed, all grown according to traditional methods. One of the main attractions of this occasion is the collection of squashes and gourds, with their wide range of colours and unusual shapes. There are also specialist nurserymen who come to show, sell and identify forgotten varieties of fruit tree.

During these three open days, visitors are invited to explore the kitchen garden, centrepiece of the estate, and its unusual combination of plants. It consists of a large, walled rectangle, covering two hectares, of which about two thirds is given over to vegetables; dividing walls separate this area from the orchard. The kitchen garden is divided by earth or grass paths into squares, which are edged with free-standing espaliered pear and apple trees or beds of annual flowers in shades of yellow, pink or blue. A round *bassin* stands in the middle, and gaps in the wall give a view across the ditch to the formal perspective of the château and the park. The walls of the kitchen garden and orchard are edged, according to their orientation, with shade- or sun-loving plants, soft fruits, climbers and shrubs. The dividing walls are bordered on one side by culinary, aromatic and medicinal plants, and on the other by a collection of old roses. Part of the orchard is planted with flowers for cutting, in borders edged with dwarf box hedges; beyond this are two vine houses and some informal flower borders. Stores for the grapes, fruit and vegetables complete this balanced picture, an unusual surviving reminder of the Grand Siècle way of life.

Hautefort

THE STRATEGIC USE
OF TOPIARY

IN THE TWELFTH CENTURY the troubadour
Bertran de Born was the lord of the medieval
fortress that used to stand on this site; it was
destroyed in the seventeenth century by François
de Hautefort when he built the château we see
there today. Bertran was both a poet and warrior,
and gave the place a lasting subtle duality, a
combination of charm and austerity. The present
proprietors of the château and their gardeners
continue to maintain a complex and creative
dialogue between the robust architecture of
the château and the sophisticated gardens that
surround it. The Château de Hautefort stands in
the middle of a hill-top esplanade, surrounded by
the levelled ramparts of the old medieval fortress;
it is quadrilateral in shape, consisting of a main
block with two end pavilions on the north side,

and an east and west wing at right angles to it,
each ending with a large round tower topped
with a dome and small lantern. To the south
a terrace edged with a balustrade gives a wide
view of a lush protected landscape: Hautefort
is a listed site.

The gardens gradually created from the 1930s
onwards by the Baron and Baroness de Bastard
cover the irregularly shaped terraces between the
château and the ancient ramparts. The *parterres*
visible from the windows of the austere building
have retained a seventeenth-century character,
and have been ingeniously designed to fit into
an awkward site. The château is reached along
a sloping path bordered with topiary shapes that
include a pyramid, column, swan, mushroom
and eagle, showing the owners' and their
gardeners' taste for a light-hearted and flexible
approach to the taming of nature. With the
entrance of the château now in view, a small
bridge crosses the deep dry moat, and on either
side geometrically shaped hedges in several
shades of green follow the outlines of the old
ramparts, the first indication of the links between
the living garden and the strong architectural
lines of the château. A long pergola of Canadian
thuyas lines the north side of the open space
before the fortified entrance to the château and
its drawbridge; the trees have been moulded into
the shape of a roofed military bastion with arrow
slits, a shady and scented pathway to the north
terrace. Here there is a row of silent sentinels:
cylinders of yew, each topped with a ball, framed
on two sides by crenellated hedges. At the foot
of the walls box hedges in Greek key patterns,
crosses and squares are interspersed with brightly
coloured patches of flowers. Below the ramparts,
a quincunx of lime trees planted with military
precision reflect the underlying defensive
metaphor. To the east, a large asymmetrical
parterre is also covered in geometric motifs using
dwarf box and flowers, with a fountain playing

'Carpets' of clipped box decorate the dry moat on either
side of the drawbridge across to the château.

On the east terrace, yews cut into hemispheres echo the domes of the château, built in the seventeenth century by François de Hautefort.

in the middle. Enormous yews clipped into two superimposed half spheres mirror the domes of the château and of the hospice chapel below, built for the village by Jacques-François de Hautefort, grandson of the château's builder. The beds of the southern *parterres* are edged with box, cut at intervals into balls and cones, and a hedge of magnolia grandiflora is espaliered on the walls of the terrace. In the summer the vast park on the far side of the little bridge can be visited by horse-drawn carriage; it is planted with beeches and oaks, as well as many rare tree species.

Kromeriz

THE FANTASIA
OF THE PRINCE-BISHOPS

The octagonal Baroque pavilion stands in the centre of the garden
like a sentinel, and dominates the composition.

ONCE THERE WAS A FRENCH FORMAL GARDEN at the Bishop's Palace at Kromeriz in Moravia, commissioned in the middle of the seventeenth century by Charles von Lichtenstein from the architect Giovanni Pietro Tencalla. Today there is little trace of it, as it was made into a picturesque park at the end of the nineteenth century, and has been frequently altered since. However, at about the same time, another garden was created by Filiberto Luchese and Tencalla for the Prince-Bishop of Olomouc, a learned patron of the arts. This was the Pleasure Garden (today the Flower Garden) that lies beyond the ramparts of the old town of Kromeriz. In spite of a few later alterations, it retains the original 1665 plan. This walled pleasure garden replaced an orchard that had been created on marshland, and is closely modelled on the garden of the residence of Duke William at Munich. The northern part is a huge square subdivided into four smaller squares by a cross, and then again by symmetrical secondary paths, either at right angles or diagonally. The axes are bordered with clipped hedges or tall *palissades*, and form the outer edges of compartments planted with *parterres de broderie* of box, which in the summer are filled by beds of colourful flowers. In the middle is an octagonal Baroque summerhouse, topped with a cupola and lantern – the starting-point for the radiating principal axes. It was originally decorated with frescoes of mythological scenes, and included grottoes and water displays; since 1908 it has housed a Foucault pendulum, installed by a Kromeriz astrophysicist. Some of the intersections of the garden's secondary axes are marked by water features, such as the fountains with lions and tritons. The Colonnade, a covered walk 243 metres (800 feet) long, runs the width of the garden on its northern side, and is embellished with busts and statues of mythological figures; the entrance to the garden is in the middle of the Colonnade. Two of the compartments contain mazes, one of them with paths at right angles and the other with concentric circular paths.

The garden extends to the south with a rectangular area of the same width as the northern side, about 300 metres (984 ft). It is divided into two parts by the central axis. Each contains a pool and fountain with a mythological theme, and there are the remains of a little mound on which a small garden building originally stood. The southern part is today planted with limes, but used to include an aviary and a pheasantry, as well as a Dutch garden and an orangery. The total length of the north and south gardens is nearly 500 metres (1640 ft). When it was first made the garden was renowned for the harmony of all its different elements: it had a balance between art and nature, a precisely calculated use of water, and a balance between flora and fauna that made it a vision of paradise. Since 1964 it has been undergoing a programme of restoration aimed at re-creating its original appearance after the many changes that time and misfortune have inflicted over the years.

The gardens at Cordés

AN EAGLE'S NEST
A LA FRANCAISE

WHEN YVES DE TOURZEL, Marquis d'Alègre and Maréchal de France, had the garden made that Le Nôtre had designed for him in 1695, he first had to demolish the outer walls of his château, bought by his father from the Châlus family who had owned it since the thirteenth century. In their place he created monumental green ramparts to both conceal and set off the old feudal building, and made new windows in its thick walls. As a result, in spite of being perched on a steep site 274 metres (900 feet) high, only the stone tiled roofs can be seen above the immense walls of beech and hornbeam, which in some places are 8 metres (26 feet) high.

This eagle's nest is reached through a gate opening onto a straight *allée*, which leads up to the courtyard of the château with its pillared gateway and two lookouts. The *allée* is edged with a double row of dense *palissades* which enclose terraces with formal *parterres*. The semi-circular *cour d'honneur* also has a double border of hornbeam hedges, and follows the line of the old ramparts. *Bassins* and yew topiary underline the classicism of the design; a double staircase on either side of the gateway to the courtyard leads into the *parterres*. These rectangular open-air salons have a central *bassin*, and paths edged with flowers and topiary radiate out from the middle. Openings in the double row of *palissades* lead from one 'room' to another, and to the grass-covered oblong salon to the right of the château, which was used for musical recitals. On two of its sides the garden has new *palissades*, whose long intersecting walks are laid out like a labyrinth. It is a pleasure to lose oneself among these extraordinary *allées*, and to be struck by the daring of the Grand Siècle garden designers; how wonderful it would be to go back three hundred years and witness some of the festivities that took place in these magnificent surroundings.

The medieval château, protected by its breathtaking green ramparts.

Eyrignac

AN AESTHETE'S WAKING DREAM

Circular 'green room', with windows onto the countryside, and a central paved area showing the points of the compass. Beyond is the Allée des Vases.

The *parterre à la française*, a very individual interpretation by Gilles Sermadiras de Pouzols de Lile.

EVEN WHEN HE WAS A CHILD, Gilles Sermadiras de Pouzols de Lile was dreaming up magical new features for the Manoir d'Eyrignac. His family home dates from the seventeenth century; although out of keeping with the architecture, the grounds had been redesigned in the nineteenth century in a picturesque style, which gradually fell into neglect. He had a designer's eye, trained by years of contemplation of the Sarlat countryside, and when he grew up he put his childhood dreams down on paper, and eventually realized them on the ground by completely redesigning the garden. He returned to the basic plan and the decorative elements introduced by an Italian architect in the eighteenth century, and created a space which made a feature of using every possible shade of green, and an infinite variety of shapes using cut yew, box and hornbeam. There are console-shaped blocks of hornbeam clasping cylinders of yew, pyramids of yew with tops cut into diamonds, balls, *broderies* and spirals, and yews cut into flat discs, scattered here and there on either side of the grassy *allées*, decorating a *parterre*, framing urns and standing at regular intervals along the length of a hedge. Openings in the many tall hedges invite the visitor to go from one 'room' to another, to sit down in the seclusion of a Chinese 'salon', and enjoy framed views of the Périgord countryside through windows in the walls of an open-air theatre. The names given to the *allées*, statues and secluded corners of the garden are clues to this enchanted world. Although primarily descriptive, the names Allée des Charmes and the Allée des Vases conjure up a magical atmosphere as surely as the Terrasse Enchantée and the statue of the Dieu du Temps qui Passe. It is a very individual garden, created with an aesthete's fertile imagination to realize a long-cherished dream. Every year Eyrignac receives thousands of visitors, showing that the search for balance and harmony evokes a universal response.

The *parterre* in front of the manor house.

Courances

A   SUPREME   HARMONY

A side view of the *miroir*.

THE 'LIVING PILLARS' OF THE PARK AT
COURANCES, its plane trees, have been reflected
in the calm waters of the wide canals for more
than two hundred years. Sometimes the sound
of the wind in the leaves sweeps up the main
avenue, one of the most beautiful in the Ile-de-
France, beyond the gates of the château, to the
ruffled waters of the *pièce d'eau* in the gardens
by the Fer à Cheval, the refuge of the statue of
Arethusa. Many statues were abandoned with
the destruction of the Sun King's 'hermitage' at
Marly, and were taken to other gardens – this
is how Arethusa found her way to an empty
plinth at Courances.

Courances, with its seventeen natural
springs, was chosen as a seigneurial estate in
the thirteenth century. In the sixteenth century,
Cosme Clausse, Secretary of Finance to King
Henri II, became the first of many important
public figures to own it. Claude Gallard,
councillor and secretary to the king, bought
Courances in 1622, and transformed the original
medieval château into an elegant Louis XIII
residence with slate roofs; it is thought that his
son called on Le Nôtre to design the grounds.
After passing through five generations of the
Gallard family, the estate came into the hands
of the Nicolays in 1708, who managed to keep
it, in spite of the upheavals of the Revolution,
until 1830. After a serious family rift, the last
heir of Courances went to live in Switzerland,
and the park was abandoned for forty years.
Both park and château were almost forgotten,

but still attracted artists such as Auguste Renoir
and Alfred Sisley, who used to take walks there.
In 1870 the Baron von Haber, the great-great-
grandfather of the present owner, acquired the
estate. He added the unusual staircase on the
entrance façade based on one at Fontainebleau,
and replanted part of the park in the English
style. His granddaughter Berthe, wife of Jean
de Ganay, commissioned Achille Duchêne to
restore the garden to its original appearance by
clearing the *allées* and restoring the *bassins* and
parterres. From 1948 onwards Hubert de Ganay,
his son Jean-Louis and his wife Philippine have
restored the park after the damage it suffered
during the Occupation.

The exact layout of the original garden is
no longer known, nor whether Le Nôtre was
really responsible for its design. The clear water
pouring from the mouths of fine stone dolphins
washes away Courances' secrets, with no thought
for the past. The well-designed *jardin à la
française* visible today is a flexible interpretation
of the genre with a character of its own. There is
the usual central axis on which the general plan
of the garden is focused. It starts from the centre
of the building's façade, passing between two
symmetrical *parterres de broderie*, crosses a perfect
miroir in the middle of a great lawn edged with
benches and statues, and arrives at a Baroque
bassin with a cupid astride a dolphin. After
cutting across a subsidiary axis, it reaches the
bassin and statue which close the perspective;

no terraces or slopes interrupt its progress.
On a walk down any of the right-angled paths,
on either side of the *miroir*, the visitor can feel
the magic of the grounds, casting a powerful
spell with its careful balance of formality and
grace. The wide grass *allées* muffle the sound of
footfalls; edged with meticulously clipped box
hedges, the tall beeches, hornbeams and ash rise
above with their branches unrestricted. To the
right, the Allée de la Table ends at the octagonal
Bassin de la Gerbe, close to the beginning of the
Grand Canal, a favourite place of the swans.
A little further on a transverse *allée* leads to the
Cascatelles, an enchanting rectangular *bassin*
with glistening sheets of water falling in curtains
from step to step with a clear crystalline sound.
A little classical temple can be seen at the end
of the *allée* through the delicate foliage, and the
atmosphere of this part of the park makes such
a strong impression that it is no surprise to find
two marble wolves and two lions as its guardians.
Another secret place is the Anglo-Japanese
garden, created near the canal on the site of an
old fulling mill; it was made in 1925 by Berthe
de Béhague with an English friend, Kitty Lloyd
Jones, who was a professional garden designer.
It is laid out around a *pièce d'eau* with a central
island, and stands out from the rest of the
park because of the variety of its species, both
indigenous and Japanese, its spring flowers
and its autumn colours.

The Cascatelles in the snow: a magical scene
in the middle of the park.

Queluz

THE SUMMER
PALACE OF THE INFANTES

The Neptune Bassin in the middle of the Raised Garden,
in front of the Ceremonies Façade.

IMAGINE A RECEPTION AT THE INFANTES' SUMMER PALACE AT QUELUZ, on an August evening in 1781. The guests are arriving at the Robillion pavilion along the straight paths of the garden and the embankments of the Azulejos canal, illuminated by multi-coloured lanterns for the occasion. At the top of the monumental Lion Steps, deliberately designed like a stage set, stands the *castrato* Francisco Farinelli, and the almost supernatural sound of his singing fills the night air. Members of the court listening below the Raised Garden, near the labyrinth, are enraptured. The Infantes' birds in their crystal and gold cages stop singing; musicians, dancers, pyrotechnists, set designers, fountain engineers and valets walk on tiptoe as they prepare the next part of the entertainment.

Today, concerts and ballets still take place on the monumental marble Robillion Steps, built in 1760 by the French architect Jean-Baptiste Robillion. He is almost certainly unknown to audiences at these entertainments; the brilliant apprentice of the silversmith Thomas Germain, he came to live in Lisbon in 1743 and offered his services to the future King Pedro III and his architect Mateus Vicente de Oliveira. A large part of the palace's Rococo decoration was designed by him, including the Throne Room, the Music Room and the Ambassadors' Room, and the wing named after him with its six rooms decorated in a particularly sophisticated style.

The gardens at Queluz, today covering fifteen hectares, are divided into two sections: the upper gardens, designed to be an extension of the palace's salons, and the park, divided up by a series of criss-crossing pathways. The upper gardens – the Malta Garden and the Raised Garden – were also designed by Robillion. They are separated by a balustrade, and both are planted with box hedges trained into geometric patterns *à la française*, and decorated with fountains and statues. The Malta Garden retains the shape of a previous *bassin*, and is level with the white and gold Throne Room in the east wing. The princes of the Infantes' family, heirs to the Queluz estate, were Grand Masters of the Order of St John of Malta, hence the name of this part of the garden. The Raised Garden lies in front of the Ceremonies Façade in the north wing, and is built over the reservoir supplying the fountains. This façade used to be the principal entrance to the palace; it is the starting-point for the axis which crosses the garden from north to south, passes through the Cavaliers' Gate with its marble statues of Fame astride Pegasus, and runs between the hornbeam hedges as far as the grandiose Great Cascade. On the western side of the building is the Robillion Pavillion and the Lion Steps, the architect's spectacular link between the higher and lower parts of the garden.

The labyrinth, the botanical garden where Pedro III grew pineapples, the kitchen garden where the Infantes learned about horticulture and the Chinese summerhouse have all now disappeared, but it is still possible to wander beside the majestic Azulejos canal, flowing with

Above: Mischievous putti stand at intervals along the balustrade of the Malta Garden.

Below: The Azulejos canal.

the waters of the River Jamor, which crosses the garden in an arc from east to south. As they passed along it by boat, the royal family enjoyed looking at the blue and white tiles, depicting river and maritime ports, that decorate its banks. The canal leads to the most secluded part of the estate, where a long avenue passes through an area of secret enclosures to the Medals Bassin by Robillion. The French architect was not the first to make his mark at Queluz. Two centuries before the estate became the favourite summer residence of the princes, the Quinta de Queluz was a simple hunting lodge, which had been the property of the Marquis de Castelo Rodrigo since the sixteenth century. Then in 1640, when Portugal regained its independence from Spain, the property of nobles who had taken the Spanish side was appropriated by the Infantes' branch of the royal family. In 1747 Mateus Vicente de Oliveira was asked by the Infante Dom Pedro to transform the hunting lodge into a palace. At first this was a relatively modest undertaking, but when the Infante married his niece, Doña Maria, thereby assuming the crown of Portugal, the princely palace took on a different role; it became a royal residence, and the architects and their team of Portuguese, French and Italian craftsmen were expected to give it an even greater degree of splendour.

Pool hidden among trees, on the axis linking the
Raised Garden and the Great Cascade.

Villarceaux

NINON'S SECRET POOL

Louis de Mornay, lover of Ninon de Lenclos, lived in this *manoir* surrounded by
water, nestling in its little valley.

IN 1654 VILLARCEAUX WAS THE SCENE of the famous love affair between Ninon de Lenclos and Louis de Mornay, proprietor of the estate, lieutenant in the Dauphin's Household Cavalry, and master of the royal foxhounds. The attractive hilly landscape of the Vexin Français quickly puts the proximity of the capital out of mind and prepares the visitor for a glimpse of history. A long avenue of hornbeam hedges, a still *pièce d'eau*, a gateway, and it seems as if the little valley was made especially for this group of buildings, untouched by the passing of time. The place has a seductive charm, with its balance of pale stone, huge expanses of water and welcoming green spaces. The first thing the visitor sees is what remains of the old thirteenth-century fortified manor; this is the Tour Saint-Nicolas, a three-storey building containing a prison, chapel and pigeon loft, and in its cellar springs the clear water of the little River Chaussy. A wide *allée* leads up to the manor house, now known as the Manoir de Ninon. The main dwelling and its turret, dating from the fifteenth and sixteenth centuries, although alterations were made in the seventeenth, lie on the eastern side of a large paved courtyard lined with extensive outbuildings. A wooden staircase leads up to the rooms where the besotted Louis de Mornay installed the famous courtisan Ninon; here they conducted a passionate affair in complete seclusion. The ever-present water of the geometrically shaped canals, pond, *bassins* and *cascatelles* echoes the murmur of lovers' voices. Ninon de Lenclos was no ordinary woman, and it was considered a privilege to be offered her

friendship, or perhaps even more. Saint-Simon recognized that she owed her unusual destiny to her beauty, but even more striking was her intelligence, breeding and culture. He wrote: 'Ninon had all kinds of illustrious friends, and she was clever enough to keep them all, and to prevent them from falling out among themselves, or at least not openly. Relationships with her were conducted with a respect and outward decency that even the greatest of princesses would have difficulty in matching. As a result she had friends among the most popular and exalted members of the court; so much so that it became the fashion to be received by her, simply because of the people to be met there.' Among Ninon's many friends were Françoise d'Aubigné, wife of the poet Scarron and the future Madame de Maintenon. The morganatic wife of Louis XIV was by no means prudish, and appears, very scantily clad, in a painting hanging at the manor, by the persuasive Louis de Mornay himself.

Ninon was born in Paris, and was by nature a city dweller; she maintained a brilliant salon, frequented by all the capital's freethinkers, but also found herself revelling in the country charms of the estate and the details of the design of its gardens. A clever network of Italian-style terraces, linked by flights of steps or edged with avenues of sweet-smelling limes or chestnut trees, is arranged so that a walk around them can be completed entirely in the shade, without ever losing sight of the water. The Fontaine de Jeunesse and the Bain de Ninon are reminders to the visitor of the renowned beauty's private rituals when she was living here.

Today, Villarceaux offers another, more unexpected pleasure, with a vista Ninon could never have seen. Near the Bain de Ninon, the eye is drawn to a magnificent *vertugadin* on the far side of the pond; a series of ramps link areas of sloping grass banks, bisecting the hillside on the north–south axis with a classical formality. At the top stands the Château du Haut, built between 1755 and 1759 by the architect Jean-Baptiste Courtonne for the nephew of the Marquise de Villarceaux, Charles-Jean-Baptiste de Tillet,

Master of the King's Appeals. He chose a quite different ensemble, favouring a high viewpoint over the *pièce d'eau* on the garden side of the house, and on the northern, courtyard side, a drive lined with trees, whose forceful axis continues beyond the entrance gate and its lodges into the open fields. On either side of the *cour d'honneur* radiating straight paths cut through the wooded areas, making archways of trees that frame silhouettes of graceful statues against the sky. Here and there the walls open

The pool reflects the Château du Haut, standing at the top of the *vertugadin*.

onto the ha-ha, allowing the impression of infinitely extended perspectives, and conversely bringing the countryside into the garden.

In 1989 the estate was put into the hands of the Ile-de-France regional authority, whose Department for Open Spaces is now renovating the whole Villarceaux estate. In the meantime it is open to the public between April and October; every year there are young musicians' festivals led by eminent artists, as well as the opening ceremony of the Ile-de-France festival.

Villette

A GRAND SIÈCLE WATERFALL

Neptune wields his trident at the top of the *escalier d'eau*, whose design is based on the Rivière at Marly.

The water of the Villette *rivière* moves in many ways: there are flat sheets, curtains, sheafs, arcs, gushing jets, tall 'candles' and 'girandoles'.

THE CHÂTEAU DE VILLETTE, near Meulan in the Val-d'Oise region, stands on the path of a perspective running from one hill to another, between an obelisk towering above an *escalier d'eau* to the north-west, and some steps that appear to lead up to the sky to the south-east, giving an apparently unlimited dimension to the whole estate. It was designed by Mansart, near the end of his life, for Jean Dyel II, royal councillor and ambassador to Venice. A transverse axis crosses this major one on the garden side of the château, allowing glimpses on both sides of peaceful countryside. All the elements – earth, air, water and fire (in the form of the sun) – seem to have been brought together in one place as part of a celebration, composing a vista, both real and symbolic, that takes in all the points of the compass.

At Villette, the water displays have a classical theme of varying complexity. Yet the *escalier d'eau* waterfall, the most elaborate of these, has always been called simply the Rivière, suggesting that its creators had an artificial concept of 'nature', like those who planned the similar waterfall at Marly. The entrance hall of the château opens directly into the dining room, and the eye is immediately drawn to the Rivière, framed by the French window leading out to the gardens. But the rest of the surroundings are no less enchanting. The terrace rests on the surviving fragments of the old manor houses built here before the château, and overlooks the entire composition. A curved double flight of steps leads down to the grass *parterres* and the huge rectangular *miroirs* on either side of them, outlined with rows of trees and narrow channels of water.

At one end, the little stone bridges are guarded by statues of sphinxes brought from Marly.

A semi-circular lawn with statues lies at the foot of the Rivière. There are steps on either side of the cascade, so that the detailed decoration can be appreciated during the ascent to the grottoes at the top, with the central figure of Neptune wielding his trident. The water wells up from the rocks at the feet of the sea god and rushes down, first collecting in *bassins*, and then slides in glistening sheets down wide steps, between a hamadryad and a flute player, sculptures by Coysevox. The water grows still for a moment as it reaches a wide, indented *bassin*, before pouring steeply down with a thrilling sound, and filling the horseshoe-shaped *bassin* which completes the design. The Rivière was restored at the same time as the rest of the garden in the 1930s by Robert Gérard, then owner of Villette, and the architect François Duprat, according to the original seventeenth-century design.

The other side of the château continues the Grand Siècle theme, with a paved *cour d'honneur* and a grass *parterre* for the *avant cour*, lined with lime trees and fine outbuildings. To the right is a little garden with a monastic flavour, in front of a chapel. The central axis leaves the château behind and climbs the gentle slope to the entrance gate flanked by two lodges, and the eye carries on beyond the road, up the hill to the steps which take the perspective right to the horizon. Who was it that claimed *jardins à la française* lacked imagination? Perhaps it was Jacques-François de Grouchy, who bought the château in 1785, transformed the gardens *à la mode anglaise*, and received there the cream of the intellectuals of the time, such as the Marquis de Condorcet, Sébastien-Roch Nicolas Chamfort, Pierre-Jean-Georges Cabanis or La Fayette.

Drottningholm

HOMAGE
TO VAUX AND CHANTILLY

WITH THE HELP OF AN ENGRAVING OF 1692 and one of two years later by the same artist, it is possible to reconstruct the original Baroque design of the gardens at Drottningholm in Sweden. It consisted of a huge rectangle extending to the west from the façade of the palace to the open country. Straight tree-lined avenues surrounded this space on three sides. The garden was divided into three main parts, with the wide central avenue running from one end to the other as far as the thickly wooded areas of 'sculpted' trees. Below the terraces of the château lay the *parterre de broderie*, with its detailed designs of scrolls of box highlighted against the coloured gravel, reminiscent of similar patterns by Le Nôtre at Vaux-le-Vicomte. Each *parterre* was edged with an arrangement of shrubs, sometimes clipped, sometimes not,

contained within two box hedges. This motif was used in the first part of the central avenue, separating it into three. The Hercules fountain marked the division between the *parterres de broderie* and, a few steps further on, the *parterre d'eau*, based on the one at Chantilly. On either side of the central avenue were two lawns with cut-out geometrical shapes, and a border of bushes, which hold differently shaped *bassins* with tall fountains of water. Each *parterre* was edged by a straight wall of cascades, their muted splashing sound mingling with the sprays in the *bassins*. At either end of the cascades high hedges defined the area of the *bosquets*, whose succession of 'outdoor rooms' ran to the end of the garden and a star-shaped labyrinth.

Today, the general layout of the garden remains the same, but the distinctions between the different areas have inevitably had to be simplified. The sophisticated patterns of the *parterres de broderie* have been replaced with plain lawns, though still with their edging of double rows of box highlighted with yew topiary. Hercules is still in his place in front of the *parterre d'eau*, but the cascade at the other end of the *parterre* has been simplified. Four of the original formal *bosquets* remain, one with an open-air theatre, and beyond them are areas of more informal planting where the maze used to be. The formal parts of the garden are surrounded by the straight double rows of tall limes which continue to preserve something of the original feel of the gardens.

Over the years, more 'natural' areas have been created on either side of the Baroque garden; however, one major feature of Drottningholm is that the formal garden has never been encroached on, as so often happens in the history of a garden. The *jardin à la française* was designed for Queen Hedvige Eleonora, wife of King Carl X Gustaf, by the architect of the palace, Tessin the Elder, but was actually

The Hercules Fountain by the Dutch sculptor Adriaen de Vries
stands in the middle of the *parterre*.

A refreshing pause on the central axis, where the paths
to the *bosquets* and the open-air theatre meet.

constructed by his son, Tessin the Younger, from 1681 onwards. In 1750 the architects and sovereigns together began to produce ideas for the design of the areas outside the enclosed Baroque garden. The first new development was the Chinese pavilion, a special birthday present from King Adolf-Frederik to his wife Louise-Ulrike, and built in the utmost secrecy by the architect C. F. Adelcrantz. This exotic building was surrounded by delightful *bosquets* planted with scented flowering shrubs, which provided a sheltered spot for aviaries. The finishing touch to the picture was added thirty years later with the creation of a landscaped garden to the north of the site, commissioned by King Gustaf III and designed by Adelcrantz, and later by the architect Frederik Magnus Piper. Lakes, islands, winding rivers, clumps of trees in grassy dells, garden buildings and statues were all typical of the genre, with only one exception, the Monument Island – a little mound surrounded by water, with straight closely planted rows of limes climbing to its summit. To the east of the palace lies Lake Mälar, on which an idealized landscape of little islands linked by bridges was created. Since the 1950s different areas of the garden have undergone various phases of restoration, which continue today. Now the official royal residence, the palace and its theatre, gardens, park and Chinese pavilion have been listed as a Unesco world heritage site since 1991.

Above: The palace, seen from the lake.

Below: The cascades, between the *parterre d'eau* and the *bosquets*.

Caserta

VANVITELLI'S
MAJESTIC ALLEGORY

IMMEDIATELY AFTER ENTERING THE CHATEAU
from the former parade ground, the main axis of
the entire estate leads the visitor through to the
imposing rectangular building, designed by the
architect Luigi Vanvitelli for the King of Naples
in 1750. Charles de Bourbon, King of the Two
Sicilies, son of Philip V of Spain and Elisabetta
Farnese, wanted to build a new capital at Caserta
as Naples was geographically vulnerable and the
countryside at the foot of the Tifatini hills was
delightful, and rich with game. The central hall
gives access to the four symmetrical courtyards
formed by the cross shape of the palace and then
leads out into the park. From then on, the axis
takes a rising course two miles long, passing on
the way *tapis verts*, ramps, *bassins* and fountains,
settings for a host of mythological scenes and
statues, and culminating in a magnificent rock-
strewn cascade, rushing with a deafening sound
down the side of Monte Briano.

Open grass lawns spread out in front of the
palace, framed at the far end by a vast semi-circle
of trees, with marble terms placed at intervals
around it. To the right and left, paths lead into
thickly growing wooded areas, just asking to be
explored, but the attraction of the perspective,
with its fountains and distant cascade, is so
irresistible that such detours are inevitably put
aside. Luigi Vanvitelli had included *parterres de
broderie* in his original design, but the scale of
the building work on the palace and various
political changes of direction frustrated his plans,
so that it was his son Carlo who eventually
carried out the plans for the park, beginning in
1773. Although he was broadly faithful to his
father's design, he did have to submit to various
economic constraints.

The first fountain along the route, ringed
with grass and embellished with terms, is the
relatively modest Margarita fountain, with its
thin jet of water. To the right and left ramps
lead up to the Dolphin Bassin, first of the
masterpieces in this stunning aquatic metaphor.
Gaetano Salomone carved most of the park's
sculptures, including the dolphins exuberantly
spouting water from their mouths, in their
semi-circular grotto. A *tapis vert* lies between the
Dolphin fountain and the next, the fountain of
Aeolus and the Grotto of the Winds, an arcaded
crescent surmounted by a balustrade, its central
bay screened with a wide curtain of water falling
into an elaborately indented *bassin*. The statues
standing on the rocks in the water represent
winds and zephyrs on the point of being
unleashed, as they await the arrival of Juno and
Aeolus on their chariot drawn by peacocks; the
silvery curtain of the cascade conceals a passage
leading to the realm of the god of the winds. The
ramps leading up from the grotto to the *bassins*
on the next level are adorned with remarkable

The Ceres Bassin, halfway along the central axis as it climbs to the top of Monte Briano.
The goddess displays the Trinacria, symbol of the Kingdom of Sicily, to the Naiads.

Sculptures with mythological subjects, particularly from Ovid's *Metamorphoses*, line the ascent to the cascade at the top.

statues of slaves, supporting enormous shell-shaped urns on their shoulders. These may be modelled on the Muslim slaves who worked on the building of the palace.

In the long Bassin de Ceres, a sequence of small cascades spreads out from the fountain, which is a sculptural group showing the goddess Ceres displaying a medallion of the Trinacria, symbol of the Kingdom of Sicily, to the assembled Tritons and Naiads. Allegorical figures of the Sicilian rivers the Oreto and the Simeto and other statues join in paying homage, adding further jets of water to those of the dolphins. A long *tapis vert* leads to a spectacular *bassin*, the water breaking noisily all the way along it in twelve smaller rippling cascades – the cascatelles. Perhaps this long contemplative walk beside the water was intended as a preparation for the drama of the fountain of Venus and Adonis at the far end. Venus is surrounded by nymphs and cupids, pleading with the unwitting Adonis not to go hunting: the boar that is about to kill him is only feet away, ready to attack. The tension is palpable, but the tragic outcome is as yet only implied. The same cannot be said of the next set piece, the fountain of Diana and Actaeon, which a little further on forms the majestic finale of the whole sequence of mythological displays. This *bassin* receives the full force of the waterfall as it reaches the bottom of the steep hillside; to the right are Diana and her nymphs in a state of great agitation, and to the left is Actaeon, caught

The fountain of Diana and Actaeon is the focal point at the top of the steeply rising 'avenue of water'. Amid the water's tremendous noise, the visitor witnesses the drama of the unfortunate Actaeon, transformed into a stag and attacked by his own hounds, as a punishment for having watched Diana bathing.

as he watches the goddess bathing. His head has already turned into that of a stag, and his own pack of hounds is about to set upon him; the dramatic effect is heightened by the force and sound of the water. The powerfully realistic scene was sculpted by Paolo Persico, Angelo Brunelli and Pietro Solari.

On either side of the *bassin*, winding paths lead up beside the cascade and through the trees to the top of the hill, where the whole breathtaking perspective can be seen in its

At the fountain of Venus, the goddess pleads with Adonis not to go hunting, knowing that he will be killed.

entirety. To the right of the Diana fountain is the Giardino Inglese made for Marie-Caroline of Austria, wife of Ferdinand I, son of Charles de Bourbon. Venus is in her element there, surrounded by an ideal landscape created in 1782 by Andrew Graefer.

On returning to the Margarita fountain after retracing the long perspective, there are two other important features of the French section of the design to be seen, away from the main axis: the Peschiera Grande and the Castelluccio. Beyond the symmetrical *allées* of the old wood, to the west of the *parterres* directly in front of the palace, is the huge classical *pièce d'eau* called the Peschiera, with a central wooded island; it was intended as a place of entertainment for guests, with tournaments and balls, and was used, like most of the other *bassins* in the park, to supply the court with fish. In practice the royal family found that they preferred to use this secluded and peaceful spot as a place for private relaxation and boating. The thick vegetation on the island is now a favourite retreat for birds. A little further on stands the Castelluccio, a miniature fortified castle surrounded by a winding river, with little gardens of exotic plants reached by a small bridge; it was built for the young princes as a place where they could learn to shoot. It was restored in 1819, and is still a lovely place, adding a final touch to this huge, hundred-hectare park, which never fails to astonish.

The fountain of Aeolus and the Grotto of the Winds: the curtain of water screens a passageway leading to the realm of the god.

The ramp around the sides of the Grotto of the Winds, with its statues of slaves carrying shell basins on their shoulders.

Turmoil among Diana and her nymphs as
they watch the transformation of Actaeon.

Peterhof

THE ENCHANTED
PALACE OF PETER THE GREAT

The Golden Mountain cascade in the western part of the park,
near the Marly Palace.

Detail of the monumental *buffet d'eau* below Peter the Great's Palace,
facing the Baltic Sea.

INQUISITIVE, DARING, PROVOCATIVE AND NONCONFORMIST, Peter the Great (1672–1725), Tsar of Russia, had a gift for surprises. Nearly three hundred years after his death his summer palace at Peterhof, much of which he designed himself, draws astonishment from enthusiastic visitors from all over the world. At first there was nothing but a little wooden pavilion perched beside the Gulf of Finland. The story goes that it was Catherine, the Livonian serf whom the Tsar secretly married in 1707, who had the idea of building there; the pavilion was duly completed as a stopping place on the way to the island of Kronstadt where Peter was building a fortress to guard the approaches to his new capital, St Petersburg. When the Tsar began work on the Great Palace and its park in 1714, the modest wooden rest house became an elegant single-storey country retreat flanked by two colonnades with lodges, which he called Monplaisir. It became the stylish private home of this highly cultivated man, intent on living a relatively simple and secluded life, with a view of the sea (he was the founder of the Russian Navy), and familiar objects, books and paintings around him. As well as its dramatic seafront location, the Peterhof site presented Peter I with a remarkable opportunity in other ways. In 1717 he had visited Versailles and Marly; seeing himself as a reformer, keen to bring his country closer to its European neighbours, he wanted a residence to equal those of the continent's great monarchs. On the high ground at Peterhof were plentiful springs and lakes that could be used to create the park's fountains. With his architects Alexandre-Jean-Baptiste Leblond, Johann-Friedrich Braunstein and Niccolo Michetti, Peter the Great worked out plans for a palace looking down onto the sea from a hilltop, with grottoes, cascades and every possible kind of water display making a perennial wonderland. The scheme was never entirely completed in the Tsar's lifetime, but most of the projects subsequently undertaken were based on his original plans. He always arrived at Peterhof by sea, and it was his idea to link the great cascade below the Palace with the Baltic Sea by means of a canal, so that he would be able to sail right up to the palace steps.

Today, the ship canal, running from north to south, still divides the garden in two. At the landing stage, it is easy to imagine arriving, like the Tsar, by sea – in a small boat crossing the park between rows of water jets and gold grotesque masks, standing out against a backdrop of blue-green conifers. From here the massive *buffet d'eau* built into the side of the hill can be seen at its most dramatic, below the palace perched 16 metres (52½ ft) above; it is a double *escalier d'eau* decorated with bas-reliefs, urns and statues of gilded bronze, with a central cascade, and above it is the Balcony fountain, surmounted by two storeys of grottoes topped with marble balustraded terraces. The water bursts forth in 138 jets, and crashes down into several *bassins*, flowing down in smooth sheets and veils to the huge lower *bassin* which is linked to the ship canal. In the middle of the pool stands the muscular gilded statue of Samson, forcing open the jaws of a lion, and releasing a jet of water 20 metres (66 ft) high. This group did not exist at the time of Peter the Great; it commemorates the Russian victory over Sweden at Poltava on St Samson's day in 1709, hence the lion, which features on the Swedish coat of arms. The richness and complexity of this cascade, one of the grandest in the world, has necessitated numerous restoration programmes since the death of the Tsar in 1725, most recently in 1988 and 1995. The Great Palace was enlarged with two wings and corner blocks by Peter's daughter, the Empress Elizabeth. It was also during her reign that the architect Bartolomeo Rastrelli rearranged the gardens on the far side of the palace, towards the town, known as the upper park. It is made up of *parterres*, modest fountains, some *pièces d'eau* which were used to breed fish, and the hornbeam arbours and gazebos which date from the time of the Tsar. An imposing gateway of stone pillars, painted in white and ochre like the palace itself, separates the garden from the town. In the middle of the upper park's central axis stands a fountain with a statue of Neptune, forming a symbolic link with the Neptune who stands contemplating the sea near the Monplaisir palace, Peter the Great's favourite retreat.

The Tsar had other attractive hideaways at Peterhof, facing the sea like Monplaisir. The Hermitage is a small single-storey palace with a moat and drawbridge, and the superb palace of Marly, designed after his visit to France, stands where three paths meet in a *patte d'oie*. A large *pièce d'eau*, fountains and the Golden Mountain cascade contribute to the appeal of this peaceful and impressive place, the most isolated area of the park, and protected by a sea wall planted with a graceful row of limes cut into rounded shapes. On the other side of the ship canal, in the eastern part of the gardens, is the Chessboard Mountain cascade, a rather extravagant counterpart of the Golden Mountain; it consists of artificial grottoes, guarded by multi-coloured dragons perched on a black-and-white checked *escalier d'eau*. At its base is a *parterre* with exuberant Roman fountains, based on those in St Peter's Square, Rome; the polychrome marble glistens with the water from the fountain and the stiller water below it.

Other paths lead to magnificent sights such as the Pyramid fountain with its marble balustrade reminiscent of Versailles, the great single jet in the middle of the *parterre à la française* at Monplaisir, and the two fountains representing Adam and Eve symmetrically placed on either side of the canal, all of which are as Peter the Great intended, and have never been altered. There are some rare surviving examples of trick fountains, a genre that had been popular since the Renaissance. These include the Sun fountain, a disc with rays made with jets of water, and the Oak Tree and Umbrella fountains, which are a welcome diversion from the almost excessive splendour. The unwary visitor can be caught out by occasional pretend seats, such as the Little Divans in the garden at Monplaisir, one near the pavilion built for Elizabeth as an extension of her father's rural retreat, and the other in front of the Tsar's bathing pavilion; yet another example draws the visitor who attempts to evade the criss-crossing jets spouting from the Oak fountain. The 150 fountains spread over the 102 hectares of the park at Peterhof, whether as tricks, cascades, pyramids or still pools, give the Court of Tsar Peter its nickname of 'The Town of Fountains'.

On the terrace of the Monplaisir pavilion, Neptune surveys his domain. Peter the Great originally had a simple wooden house built here, before the construction of the Palace.

Het Loo

A MIRACLE
FROM THE ARCHIVES

WHEN QUEEN MARY II ASKED WALTER HARRIS, the
Court doctor, to give her a minute description
of her much missed garden at Het Loo, she
could not have known that what he wrote would
provide the basis for one of the most spectacular
reconstructions in the history of gardens, three
centuries later. In 1688 William III of Orange-
Nassau, Stadholder of Holland, became King
of England, and he and his wife Mary left for
England before their Dutch summer residence
had been completed. After their coronation Het
Loo had become a royal residence; extensions
and embellishments naturally followed and the
Queen wanted to be kept informed about them
from across the water.

The thoroughness with which Harris carried
out his task would later prove extremely useful.
Firstly, to his patroness, who could imagine
herself walking in the *allées* at Het Loo again
with the help of his description, and secondly,
to the restorers, who from 1977 onwards began
to re-create the appearance of the gardens at their
finest, at the end of the seventeenth century.

When he was still the Stadholder of
Guelderland, William III, an experienced
huntsman, had inherited some rich game
territory in Veluwe, and nearby was a medieval
moated castle, known today as Het Oude Loo.
He added the estate to his land, and in 1685
began the construction of a more modern palace,
choosing a site suitable for the creation of a series
of fountains in its gardens. A square plan was
divided between the entrance court, palace and
gardens; the main axis began to the south with
the avenue leading up to the house, and ran
through the square northwards in the direction
of Het Oude Loo. In the middle of the square
a wrought-iron gate led into the gardens. The
original layout of the garden was by the French
designer Daniel Marot, a Huguenot exiled in
the Netherlands, who also worked on the interior
decoration of the palace. In France, one of his
most important projects was the design of
Cardinal Richelieu's gardens.

From 1688 onwards, the gardens at Het Loo
were extended to the north. The semi-circular
colonnades linking the main building with
the wings were replaced by pavilions, and
reconstructed at the far end of the new or
Upper Garden, and the older part became
known as the Lower Garden. Beyond the walls
which enclosed these two sections lay the park
and the kitchen garden, fishponds and other
areas for domestic use, as well as the areas set
aside for entertainment, such as the labyrinth,
aviaries and the trick fountains. On the death
of William III, Stadholder of all the Dutch

The Fountain of Venus in the middle of the *parterre*.

provinces, William IV inherited Het Loo. It was not until his son William V inherited it that the garden underwent any major alterations, and he redesigned the Upper Garden in the English style. After a period of neglect, Louis Bonaparte, Napoleon's brother, who had become King of Holland in 1807, completed the work of his predecessor and had the entire estate landscaped, both park and gardens.

The garden as it is today, then, is a historical reconstruction of the original walled one, begun by Marot in 1686, and enlarged two years later after the coronation of William and Mary. The perspective starts from the gilded gate centred on the palace and crosses the *parterres*, passing cascades, *bassins* and fountains before slipping between the colonnades in the direction of Het Oude Loo. The Lower Garden is edged with raised terraces on three sides; its square *parterres*, four of *broderie* and four of grass, are all edged with flower-beds and a double row of clipped box. On the cross axis are the two remarkable fountains of the Celestial Sphere and the Terrestrial Globe, on either side of the central Venus Fountain, and the beautiful Arion Fountain *escalier d'eau*. A narrow channel of water edged with a double row of oak trees separates the two parts of the garden. Access to the Upper Garden is marked by a balustrade with statues of sphinxes. Here the space is divided up by *parterres*, fountains and colonnades, reflecting the harmony and elegance of the Grand Siècle. An old Virginia tulip tree and two copper beeches survive from the nineteenth-century plantings, having been retained during the restoration because of their great age.

Alongside the wings of the palace, two more private gardens, originally intended for the King and Queen, have also been restored. The King's consists largely of a smooth lawn, with some violet and orange flowers, the colours of the Orange-Nassau family also used in William III's bedroom. A grotto leads from the Queen's apartments to her garden, which contains decorative hornbeam arbours and flowers symbolic of the Virgin and femininity, as well as the Triton and Putti fountains: the charm of the place is all owed to Marot. The walls of both gardens are covered with espaliered fruit trees, using varieties known to have been in existence in the seventeenth century.

The painstaking twentieth-century restoration has been possible not only because of Harris's account, but also through old plans, engravings, State documents, diaries, records of visits to the gardens, contemporary accounts of seventeenth-century garden design as well as evidence on the ground. Matching bricks have been specially made to repair the garden walls, artificial stone has been used to reconstruct the colonnade, giant paper templates were made using slide projections to re-create the design of the *parterres*, and copies of missing or fragile pieces of decoration made from synthetic resin have been installed. In fact the whole range of modern technological aids was called upon by the directors of the Het Loo Museum, under the leadership of the architect Van Asbeck. Thus a seventeenth-century masterpiece, famous in its own time, has risen from the ground again and begun a new life, with spectacular results.

The reconstruction of the *parterres* was based on an early eighteenth-century plan by Cristiaan Pieter Van Staden. Shown here are the Upper Gardens.

La Granja

A DARING
CHOICE OF SITE

The Music Pavilion and the Fountain of the Three Graces.

The polychrome marble steps of the Great Cascade are centred
on the façade of the palace.

To the west, the Fountain of Fame, with its powerful jet of water that is said to be visible as far away as Segovia.

IT WAS NO DOUBT PRESUMPTUOUS to assume that a formal *jardin à la française*, with its strict axes, *bosquets*, fountains and statuary could be created on the steep foothills of the Sierra Guadarrama, a place of dark forests of pine and oak; nevertheless in 1720 that is what Philip V, first Bourbon King of Spain, decided to do. He was, after all, the grandson of Louis XIV, and it was his son, Charles de Bourbon, who thirty years later launched a similarly demanding project with the construction of the grandiose palace and gardens at Caserta, near Naples.

The name of the site means 'the farm', and gives no hint of the scale of the enterprise. This rugged and lonely landscape had been a royal game reserve since the fifteenth century, but was destined to undergo a series of metamorphoses to rival those described by Ovid; aptly, these became the subject of many of the statues for the garden's fountains. Two sites 5 kilometres (3 miles) apart were chosen by the Spanish Kings: San Ildefonso, where the present palace stands, and Balsaìn, where Henry III, King of Castile, built a hunting lodge, later rebuilt as a palace by Philip II (it was partly destroyed by fire in the reign of Charles III). It was Henry IV who took the first steps towards the building of the palace of La Granja. In 1450 he built a hermitage and chapel dedicated to St Ildefonso, whom he credited with having saved his life during a dangerous boar hunt. In the seventeenth century a community of monks of St Jerome decided to build their monastery and farm there, which was how it became known as La Granja. In spite of much later additional building, the monastery still forms the core of the royal palace.

In 1720 Philip V had decided to abdicate in favour of his son, and was looking for somewhere to live in his retirement. The site of La Granja made a strong impression on him, and he persuaded the monks to sell him their monastery, which he converted relatively modestly, concentrating on creating its magnificent gardens. However, on the unexpected death of his son in 1724 he resumed the throne, and made La Granja into a luxurious summer palace. Faced with such an intractable site, the French architect René Carlier, followed by Didier Marchand and the garden designer Etienne Boutelou, had to submit to the demands of nature rather than attempting to 'tame' it, in the famous phrase of Saint-Simon. All the same, 'picks, and quite often gunpowder, were needed to excavate the *bassins* and the *pièces d'eau*, to make holes to plant the trees, dig ditches for the *palissades* and the ground for larger areas of trees', as the writer described when he visited the gardens with the royal couple in 1722. However, 'sometimes the greatest obstacles can be turned to advantage', and the mountainous situation of La Granja was ideal for building a large number of fountains: 'there are *bassins*, canals, sheets of water, all manner of water effects; the water is most beautiful to look at, most delicious to drink, and flows in great abundance.'

The general plan of the garden has not changed very much, and still depends on water for its most dramatic effects. But large numbers of conifers were planted in 1870, and have to some extent undermined the design. Although they are not an indigenous species, they look as if they have come down from the mountain seeking revenge for the creation of these gardens, controlled with such care and designed with such sophistication, to try to return them to their natural state. To prevent this, a team of restorers,

including historians, forestry experts, biologists and landscape gardeners, are careful to maintain a balance of appearance and species.

In front of the palace and its terrace with sculpted sphinxes, the central axis follows the line of the polychrome marble Great Cascade and the eleven *bassins*, among them the Fountain of Amphitrite, the *cascatelles* and the Fountain of the Three Graces, and sets off to reach the top of the mountain, stopping first at a little hill topped by a Baroque music pavilion. Beyond that there are more *parterres* and *bosquets*, and a lake called the Sea, which was created to supply water to the fountains; Philip V used to listen to concerts while being rowed on the lake in a gondola. To the left of the palace another parallel axis links a string of fountains on a series of rising levels called the Horse Race; this dizzying display includes the Fan and the Snail pools, the magnificent *bassins* of Neptune and Apollo, and finishes with the Andromeda Fountain. The French sculptors René Frémin and Jean Thierry created nymphs, zephyrs, sea horses, cupids, tritons and naiads out of lead treated to look like bronze, and these carry the axis irresistibly upwards. The mythological scenes, with the added magic of the water effects, seem to be part of a ballet directed by a celestial choreographer. The cascade in front of the Andromeda Fountain divides to form a crescent, one arm feeding another parallel axis of water at the foot of a steep drop in the terrain. This canal is a favourite spot for the many water birds living in the garden, including whooper swans; it runs alongside the two other water axes, goes round the *bassin* of the Great Jet and its statues of Vertumnus and Pomona, and continues towards the village of San Ildefonso on the other side of

the high gateway. To the east of the last canal is
the recently restored labyrinth, based on a design
by Dezallier d'Argenville. To the right, on the
western side of the palace, a network of *allées*
crossing each other at right angles and diagonally
are the setting for even more fountains, of
which the most theatrical are the Fountain of
the Frogs, telling the story of Latona familiar
from Versailles – the inhabitants of Lycia being
changed into frogs for scorning the mother of
Apollo – and the Fountain of Diana, showing
the goddess just before she is caught bathing by
Actaeon; the tale that follows is told, as we have
seen, at the top of the great cascade at Caserta.

Below the horseshoe-shaped court on the
western side of the palace lies a sunken garden,
designed to be seen from a wrought-iron balcony.
With its geometrically shaped clipped box and
yews, its perfectly maintained lawns and grassy
slopes, it is one of the most successful *parterres*
at La Granja. Another fountain stands at the far
end of this *parterre*: the figure of Fame, with the
winged horse Pegasus, blows the most powerful
jet of water in the gardens from his trumpet,
reaching 47 metres (154 ft) up into the sky.
A monastic garden of medicinal plants has
recently been made alongside the *parterre* of
Fame, near to the Chapel of San Ildefonso
and the former monks' cells. Philip V had added
some outbuildings to house his guards, as well
as stables and carriage buildings. In 1759, Charles
VII built what amounted to a village on the
entrance court side of the palace, a charming
introduction to this extraordinary palace.

The Fountain of Diana, illustrating the same story as the
highest fountain at Caserta, but in a less dramatic way.

Beloeil

THE PRINCE DE LIGNE'S OPEN-AIR ROOMS

'I OWE THE GLORY OF MY BELOEIL TO MY FATHER. It is not too much to say that what he created is an epic poem. He is responsible for all that is great, just, noble and majestic there', wrote Prince Charles-Joseph de Ligne in his book *Coup d'oeil sur Beloeil*, printed on his private press at the château in 1781. An enthusiastic description of the garden follows: 'There are a great many *bassins*...and fine hornbeam hedges, which are neither tedious nor predictable as they are in other places, and which I have allowed to be simple enclosures for some secluded gardens; there are arbours *à l'italienne*, some magical, some very elegant, a charming cloister around a *pièce d'eau*, turfed drawing rooms; beds full of flowers, a little thicket of roses planted in a

quincunx; all the paths are green, and lead into the forest which surrounds my garden. This *terrain français* covers about two hundred acres. A twenty-acre *pièce d'eau* separates it into two equal parts, bound by canals, some of whose tributaries reappear as streams in my forest, encircling an area in which I breed wild animals to be released into my woods; these are five leagues in length and in some places two leagues wide. At the end of the great *pièce d'eau* is a swing bridge over the canal surrounding the garden, and on the other side is a great *patte d'oie*, which determines the layout of the forest; the middle pathway is twenty feet wide. I will only mention in passing the radiating paths, the large circuses where they meet, the most beautiful, grand designs; the extensive quincunx plantings of oaks and beeches stretching into the distance, where the stag and hounds run.... There are twenty acres of kitchen garden, surrounded by walls covered with the finest espaliers. There are four *bassins* with fountains, and in the middle a Temple of Pomona in which to eat the fruit. The hothouses, melon and fig gardens I hear are highly praised.'

Charles-Joseph de Ligne's lively description is almost the only guide necessary for a visit to the garden today. The *terrain français* does not seem to have suffered in the intervening time, and even if the network of straight paths in the surrounding forest has largely disappeared, the lovely enclosed spaces that give the garden its originality remain, laid out on either side of the six-hectare lake facing the château. Harmless rabbits have taken the place of the author-prince's wild animals in the forest, appearing from among the trees after visitors have passed. The great avenue is less wide than it was, but still impressive, and after crossing the *grand lac*, runs in a decisive straight line across fields for 5 kilometres (3 miles).

The Bassin des Dames to the west, between the Cloister and the Bassin des Glaces, has recently been restored. It was constructed with two depths of water for the benefit of swimmers.

Putti by the side of the great *pièce d'eau* in front of the château, a six hectare *miroir* watched over at the far end by Neptune, Aeolus and Apollo.

Les Miroirs, on the eastern side of the garden, between the Bassin Ovale and the Bosquet des Sources.
The height of the hedges is two thirds of the width of the *allée*, as recommended by Dezallier d'Argenville.

To right and left of the château, the secret gardens and outdoor *salons* are waiting to be explored, enclosed within imposing walls of hornbeam that stretch for some 10 kilometres (6 miles). Two majestic *allées*, the Allée du Doyen and the Allée du Mail, run for the whole length of the enclosed garden between the *palissades*. Whenever they cross another *allée*, at right angles or obliquely, there are idyllic glimpses of the *pièce d'eau* and the château, or the orangery and the Temple of Pomona. This vast rectangle of sixty hectares is defined to the north by the castle moat, and on all the other sides by canals, forming a magical island with areas that are open to the outside as well as some that are deliberately secluded.

The exploration of the *bosquets* traditionally starts on the western side, with the huge circular green carpet of the *boulingrin* or bowling green, which also served as an open-air theatre. Next comes the rose garden planted in a quincunx, as described by Charles-Joseph, where at one time the first Bengal roses imported to Europe in the seventeenth century grew. More hornbeam hedges divide up the grassy areas that used to be set aside for children's games. Charles-Joseph allowed himself to add one contrasting note to his father's classical garden: the Rieu d'Amour, a stream that winds its way in the same direction as the straight Allée du Doyen. Returning to the axis, the visitor finds himself in the Allée des Miroirs, where tall hornbeams enclose rectangular *bassins* designed to reflect the sky and the clouds, like a casket full of precious stones. A little further on is the secluded Bosquet des Sources, with three circular *bassins*, two of them enclosed within railings. Perhaps prompted by an unsettling picture in the château of a beautiful richly dressed young woman showing her hand to a fortune teller, the superstitious can throw a coin into the smallest of the three and make a

wish, hoping to see a few bubbles rise the top of the water – a sign that the wish has been granted.

All dark thoughts clear away on reaching the *allée* by the canal, bathed in light, and then the far end of the *pièce d'eau* with its triumphant sculpture by Henrion depicting Neptune, Aeolus and Apollo. The vista of the huge *pièce d'eau* and the château is superb, bringing to mind Charles-Joseph's descriptions of his idyllic boating sessions: 'I am beginning to have a sizeable fleet. One can sail on my great lake, which is linked to all the canals, *pièces d'eau* and rivers, which are equipped with drawbridges, swing bridges, sliding bridges and more; the ships are decorated with streamers and manned by little sailors dressed in my livery.' One of the swing bridges survives at the end of the axis of the château. From here can be seen the tops of the tall copper beeches planted in the 1950s by Prince Eugène, eleventh Prince de Ligne, making a startling contrast with the green of the hornbeams. Copper beeches became a feature at Beloeil after they were introduced from the Black Forest in the middle of seventeenth century by Claire-Marie, wife of Albert-Henri and then of Claude-Lamoral, the second and third Prince de Ligne. The secondary axis returns towards the château on the eastern side of the *pièce d'eau*, beginning with a sombre and mysterious 'cathedral nave' through the middle of a grove of trees, leading to the Cloister, a rectangular *bassin* surrounded by a *palissade* of arcaded hornbeam. The next *bosquet* is the Bassin des Dames, bordered with spectacular intersecting hornbeam arbours, where the ladies of the house used to swim in seclusion. It is followed by the Bassin des Glaces, which was used in winter to supply ice for the ice house. This was near the kitchen garden, which can still be seen on the other side of the canal, but unfortunately it is no longer maintained.

Instead of returning to the château, the visitor can take the winding path which follows the old moat, to find the Anglo-Chinese garden described in detail by Charles-Joseph in his book: 'I do not wish to have so near to the house anything that I would find in the fields, or in the immediate surroundings of my village. The pleasure of being "natural" applies to the poor and insignificant. Nor will I call these gardens "English", for they contain nothing alarming, no mountains or precipices; what I want is to have them decorated and furnished like a *salon*.' Remains of some of the former splendours described by the prince, such as the Temple de Morphée, originally surrounded with poppies, the Ruine and the trefoil-shaped Ile de Flore, which the ingenious prince used to reach by being winched down from the château library, offer clues to the setting he contrived to reflect the pursuit of pleasure and learning.

In 1610 the title of Prince de Ligne was conferred by the Emperor Rudolf II on Lamoral I and his descendants. Charles-Joseph was the seventh, and inherited the Beloeil estate from his father, Claude-Lamoral II. Although there was a garden from the beginning of the sixteenth century, it was Claude-Lamoral II who made it as it is today, with the French architect Jean-Michel Chevotet. The château has always remained in the hands of the de Ligne family; the great *miroir* proudly reflects its round towers with their slate roofs and the brick outbuildings, watched over by statues of putti and fantastic monsters, and by Neptune at the opposite end of the *miroir*. Eight centuries separate the original donjon, slowly transformed over the centuries into a country manor, and the elegant seventeenth-century style building that stands there now, reconstructed in 1900 after a fire.

The Château de Beloeil. It was damaged by fire in 1900, and has been meticulously reconstructed. The estate has belonged to the same family since the fifteenth century.

Bouges

ELEGANCE
A LA FRANCAISE

IT IS STILL UNKNOWN FOR CERTAIN whether the Italianate pavilion at Bouges, so close in style to the Petit Trianon at Versailles, is the work of Jacques-Ange Gabriel, or whether the formal gardens, integrated so successfully with the eighty-five hectare park, were redesigned by Achille Duchêne. The fact that the name of Louis XV's architect is inscribed on the building raises doubts, as it is said that he never signed his work. The assumption that the champion of the restoration of gardens *à la française* was involved rests on a bird's-eye view of the gardens that he drew between 1897 and 1910. Whatever the truth of these attributions, the modern

visitor will find the estate is a classic example of the balance of elements – the secret of the art of living in the French style. It was begun in 1765 for Charles-François Leblanc de Marnaval, 'the King's farmer', and subsequently belonged to Talleyrand, and later to Antoine-Achille Masson, who may be less famous, but is known to have had the park constructed in the middle of the nineteenth century. However, it was a twentieth-century businessman, Henry Viguier, chairman and managing director of the Paris department store Bazar de l'Hôtel de Ville, and his wife Renée, who in 1917 began to create the exceptionally elegant atmosphere that is characteristic of Bouges, and installed most of the rich furnishings for which the château is famous. They bequeathed their work to the National Fund for Historic Monuments and Sites, on condition that this stylish private home would be open to the public and maintained 'for the benefit of future generations'. The entrance avenue is edged with hundred-year-old chestnut and plane trees, and is nearly a mile long, with a riding track running alongside. There are screens of limes, *parterres de broderie*, *tapis verts*, *bassins*, lawns and topiary in balustraded enclosures; there is a flower garden in the former kitchen garden, greenhouses and extensive outbuildings: all the ingredients of the *style à la française* are there, orchestrated with consummate skill.

Play of light and shadow in one of the *allées* of the garden at Bouges.

Schönbrunn

THE HAPSBURGS' VERSAILLES

244

A view of the Palace of Schönbrunn, from the bottom of the *verugadin* in front of the Gloriette.
The building of the Palace to the west of Vienna began in 1695.

UNTIL RECENTLY, IN A LITTLE PAVILION IN THE PARK AT SCHÖNBRUNN, one could enjoy a glass of water from the spring discovered by the Emperor Matthias when he was on a hunting expedition at the beginning of the seventeenth century. The clear water from the Schöner Brunnen or 'fair spring' was still served at the table of the Austrian Archduke Josef I a century later, and gave its name to Schönbrunn. Since then both park and palace have provided a setting for the spring which pays tribute to nature on a grand scale, with majestic radiating *allées* lined with clipped trees outside, and exuberant Rococo décor inside the palace.

Before the spring was discovered, Schönbrunn was called Katterburg, and in what was then a rural area, there first stood only a farm and a windmill, and then later, a manor hidden away among gardens and vineyards. The surrounding forests were abundant with game, and eventually attracted some determined huntsmen: the Hapsburgs. Emperor Maximilian II bought the estate in 1569, enclosed it and converted the manor into a hunting lodge. This idyllic retreat was demolished by the Hungarians, and rebuilt by Maximilian's son, Emperor Matthias, who discovered the spring. The Turks destroyed the Italianate country palace which Eleanora di Mantua, wife of Ferdinand III, had built at Katterburg, and which was also much loved by Maria-Eleanora di Gonzaga, wife of Ferdinand II. The Hapsburgs', however, remained very attached to Schönbrunn, and King Leopold I conceived the idea of creating for his son, the future Josef I, a sumptuous summer palace that would rival Versailles, which had amazed the whole of Europe. So the architect Bernhard Fischer von Erlach, a pupil of Bernini, began to build the present Baroque palace, a symmetrical main building with one façade facing the great courtyard and the town, the other facing the gardens. These *jardins à la française* were designed by the Frenchman Jean Trehet, who was also responsible for the Augarten in Vienna. The perspective sails off towards the forest, *parterres de broderie* are laid out in front of the palace, straight *allées* lead to fountains and statues, and frame the outlines of the *bosquets*: the influence of Versailles is apparent everywhere at Schönbrunn. No significant changes were made either to the palace or the gardens until the Empress Maria Theresa, daughter of Charles VI, came to the throne in 1740. The mother of the future Queen Marie-Antoinette of France set about making Schönbrunn into a family home as well as an official residence for herself and her large family of sixteen children. She and her architect Nicolas Pacassi gave the façades of the palace their ochre colour, and created the reception rooms' Rococo decoration. She left the layout of the gardens untouched, but added most of the ornamental buildings and features, with the architect Johann Ferdinand Hetzendorf von Hohenberg, such as statues, artificial ruins, a cascade, grotto and Gloriette. Her husband, François de Lorraine, established a menagerie in the grounds, today the oldest zoo in the world; the royal couple could observe the exotic animals from the central pavilion in which they took their breakfast. A hundred years later, Franz Josef built the biggest hothouse in Europe in response to the Hapsburgs' keen interest in botany. Maria Theresa had employed the painter Johann Wenzel Bergl to decorate some of the ground-floor rooms facing the garden; he entirely covered the walls with colourful frescos of an 'Indian landscape', full of rich vegetation and tropical birds.

Maria Theresa's son, Josef II, opened the garden to the public in 1779. Today, thousands of visitors are free to walk among the many miles of *allées* edged with trees trained and cut into flat planes, sometimes as high as 12 metres (39 ft). Where the paths meet, and in the arbours, as well as in room after room of the palace, a multitude of ghostly figures from the past can be imagined by the visitor; among them, the seven-year-old Mozart giving his first recital in the Mirror Salon, and unceremoniously throwing his arms around Maria Theresa's neck; the tousle-haired Beethoven striding around the *allées* in search of inspiration for his opera *Fidelio*; the young Marie-Antoinette, performing and dancing in the delightful palace theatre, and L'Aiglon, the son of Napoleon and Marie-Louise, playing in the little wooden house built for him in the park: both of them spent their childhood at Schönbrunn. The visitor might also be reminded of Sissi, the famous wife of Franz Josef, who was bored at Schönbrunn, while Napoleon, when he lived there for a few months, enjoyed its combination of the domestic and the formal. But the image which stays in the imagination, even more enduringly than the Roman Ruins immortalized by Edmond Rostand in the fourth act of his play *L'Aiglon*, is the Gloriette which terminates the perspective running from the palace, across the *parterres* and over to the far side of the Neptune Fountain. Surrounded by a lawn, the triple triumphal arch was erected in 1775 by the Empress Maria Theresa to commemorate the Austrian victory over Prussia at Kolin. The visitor who reaches the terrace above the Gloriette can enjoy a view over the gardens, the city of Vienna and the woods, and for one glorious moment can imagine himself the proud owner of all that he can see.

The biggest palm house in Europe, the Palmenhaus, was opened by Franz Josef in 1882. It is a glimpse into the past, with Schönbrunn's historic collection of rare plants.

Versailles

LET THE CELEBRATIONS
BEGIN!

The great axis at Versailles, seen from the top of the steps leading down from the Parterre d'Eau.
In the foreground is the Bassin de Latone. To right and left are the Bassins des Lézards.
Further on are the Tapis Vert, the Bassin d'Apollon and the Grand Canal.

A VISIT TO VERSAILLES whets an appetite for discovery; it is as if the most mouth-watering delicacies are laid out in the secrecy of the *bosquets* as they were in the past, to tempt the hundreds of richly dressed guests. Newcomers try in vain to reconcile the lifeless commentary of their tour guide with the three-dimensional tableau spread out before their eyes; those who have visited before set off in a particular direction with proprietorial assurance. However, even they have not discovered all the secrets of the ninety-five hectares of the Petit Parc, which includes the *parterres* and the *bosquets*, or of the five hundred hectares of the wooded Grand Parc beyond. Louis XIV, who, with Le Nôtre, Le Brun, Le Vau, and later Mansart, designed this masterpiece, soon copied by other great European sovereigns, wrote a guide for its visitors called *Manière de montrer les jardins de Versailles*. He was not only fascinated with order and beauty, but also aware of the technical intricacies involved with the supply of water to his fountains, and the Sun King wanted to show his park to distinguished visitors at its best, dramatically enhancing the effect of tamed nature with his water displays. Almost exactly the same sequence prescribed by the King is followed by tourists from all over the world who are lucky enough to come on the days of the 'Grandes Eaux musicales' when the fountains are playing; for an hour and forty minutes of unrivalled pleasure they are transformed into guests at the time of the Grand Siècle.

The King decreed that 'on leaving the château...one goes out onto the terrace; one must stop on the steps to contemplate the arrangement of the *parterres*, *pièces d'eau*, and the fountains in the *cabinets*.' Almost as soon as the opening notes of a famous piece by Jean-Baptiste Lulli are heard, the waters of the *parterre* fountains shoot up into the sky and spray the white marble coping of the *bassins*, as well as drenching their bronze statues of the rivers of France. To the right and left of the central axis, in the two Cabinets des Animaux built of polychrome marble, statues of animals glisten in the criss-crossing arcs of water bursting from the mouths of lions, boars, tigers, wolves and dogs. Our royal guide carries on: 'Then one continues and stands above Latona, to contemplate her, the lizards, the ramps, the statues, the Allée Royale, Apollo and the Canal'. Looking straight down the perspective from the vantage point of the top of the great steps, the visitor is in the best place to admire the Bassin de Latone, showing the mother of Apollo and Diana getting her revenge on the peasants of Lycia, who after insulting her are transformed by Jupiter into terrifying giant frogs. At the far end of the Tapis Vert, Apollo and his four horses can be seen launching themselves through clouds of spray, on their eternally repeated journey. Further on again, the calm waters of the Grand Canal stretch out towards the west and the setting sun, whose fiery light sets the façade of the royal château ablaze, again underlining the metaphorical link between the King of France and the Sun God.

'On arriving at the sphinxes, a pause should be made to observe the Parterre du Midi.' The south *parterres de broderie* lie on the cross axis of the main one, and look down on Mansart's Orangerie below, beyond which is the Pièce d'Eau des Suisses. One of the majestic Cent Marches flights of steps, built over the two wings of the Orangerie, leads westwards to the lower part of the Petit Parc, where the King's itinerary begins with the exploration of the *bosquets*, the open-air 'drawing rooms' intended for entertainments, and nowadays usually closed to visitors. 'One proceeds to see the Salle de Bal.' Although Perrault's labyrinth decorated with scenes of animals from Aesop's Fables has long since disappeared, there is a delightful compensation for the visitor at the end of a narrow oblique *allée* – the *rocaille* amphitheatre called the Salle de Bal. The decoration includes a *buffet d'eau* encrusted with shells from Madagascar, with water flowing in smooth sparkling sheets, and urns and *torchères* of gilded lead, making an ideal setting for dancers and musicians. 'Next one enters the Colonnade.' The visitors follow the axis parallel to the main one, to the south, and pass two of the Bassins des Saisons, with Bacchus representing autumn and Saturn winter, their gilded lead gleaming in the spray from their water jets; then they come upon the dazzling Bosquet de la Colonnade built by Mansart, but considered inappropriate by Le Nôtre. It consists of a circular peristyle of slender columns of pink, ochre or blue-grey marble, with white marble fountains on pedestals between them; these each shoot up sprays of water which fall as a splashing shower, flowing down from the rim in smooth curtains; this was the sumptuous setting for the King's supper parties.

On the other side of the Tapis Vert the Bosquet des Dômes impresses with its aristocratic elegance. This is one of the most graceful parts of the park, with its balustrades of pink and white marble, set with bubbling jets of water. 'One moves on to the Lancellade.' Here, by contrast, a relentless drama is played out; the Bosquet de l'Encélade, recently restored, tells the story of Enceladus, the leader of the Giants, who

had revolted against the gods of Olympus and hurled rocks up at them in the sky. The fountain shows him punished by being trapped in a heap of gilded stones, and raging at his fate with a jet of water spurting from his mouth 23 metres (75 ft) up into the air. On the other secondary axis, parallel to the perspective on its north side, are the remaining two Bassins des Saisons, Flora as spring and Ceres as summer. Beyond is the Bosquet de l'Obélisque and its astonishing pyramidal fountain, with 230 closely packed jets of water shooting from a ring of metal 'reeds'. At the end of a winding *allée* nestles the romantic Bosquet des Bains d'Apollon, conceived in the reign of Louis XVI by the painter Hubert Robert. The sculptural group *Apollon servi par les Nymphes* was originally made for the Grotte de Téthys; its present informal setting dates from the demolition of the grotto to make way for the new north wing of the château. The King continues: 'One walks around the Dragon, and looks at the jets and the Pièce de Neptune.' The visitors return towards the château on the north side of the *bosquets*, as far as the Bassin de Neptune and the Bassin du Dragon. The charming Allée d'Eau or Allée des Marmousets contains fourteen bronze groups of laughing putti, each supporting a pink marble basin. The *allée* slopes gently up to the north *parterre*, and at the top reaches the Fontaine de la Pyramide, whose powerful flow of water pours down into four shallow superimposed bowls. It then joins the still water in the Bains des Nymphes just below, partly screening the naked nymphs on the superb bas-relief by François Girardon with a soft curtain of water. The jet of the Bassin du Dragon, at the bottom of the Allée d'Eau, is a more dramatic sight, rising to 27 metres

The Bassin d'Apollon.

Between the Parterre d'Eau and the Bassin de Latone.

The elegant Bosquet des Dômes, between the Bosquet de l'Encélade and the Fontaine de l'Obélisque.
It was laid out by Le Nôtre in 1675, and later altered by Jules Hardouin-Mansart, who added two
marble pavilions, which have since disappeared. The sculptures were added in 1704.

(88½ ft). The 'dragon' is the serpent Python, pursued by Apollo to avenge his mother. The *bassin* is the fanfare announcing the triumphant finale of the Bassin de Neptune; when all the other fountains in the park have ceased to play, it is at last Neptune's turn to unleash the full glory of the jets in his huge *bassin*.

'If one wants to see the Ménagerie and Trianon on the same day, after pausing beside Apollo, one must take a boat to the Ménagerie', according to the King. Unfortunately, the royal menagerie which used to be at the southern end of the lateral arm of the Grand Canal no longer exists. But the Trianon, at the northern end, has regained its original, striking appearance as part of a programme of restoration in the park expected to last twenty years; this was begun in 1990, following the great storm of that year and has included replanting trees, restoration of the *bosquets*, and reorganization of the floral decoration of the *parterres*.

Although the pyramids of fruit arranged in the park's *bosquets* for the pleasure of the courtiers were supplied by the Versailles cooks, Louis XIV does not reveal anything about his kitchen garden – the Potager du Roi – in his guide book, though he did invite private visitors such as ambassadors from Siam or the Doge of Venice to see it. In his alchemist's domain of nine hectares, his gardener La Quintinye started with the unpromising soil from the marshy land excavated to create the Pièce d'Eau des Suisses, and germinated seeds brought from all over the world, successfully growing exotic vegetables which thrived regardless of climate or seasons. La Quintinye contrived a system of sunken gardens and high protective walls, creating micro-climates which allowed production all the year round, and experimented with exotic breeds to surprise the diners at the royal table. The Potager du Roi was fortunately spared during the Revolution, since in 1798 it became a school of horticulture, a tradition it continues today.

During the Grandes Eaux musicales that take place every year from spring to autumn, Apollo's chariot rises up through a concerto of watery arcs, flourishes and jets.

The west-facing terrace in the Potager du Roi.

Garden plans and practical information

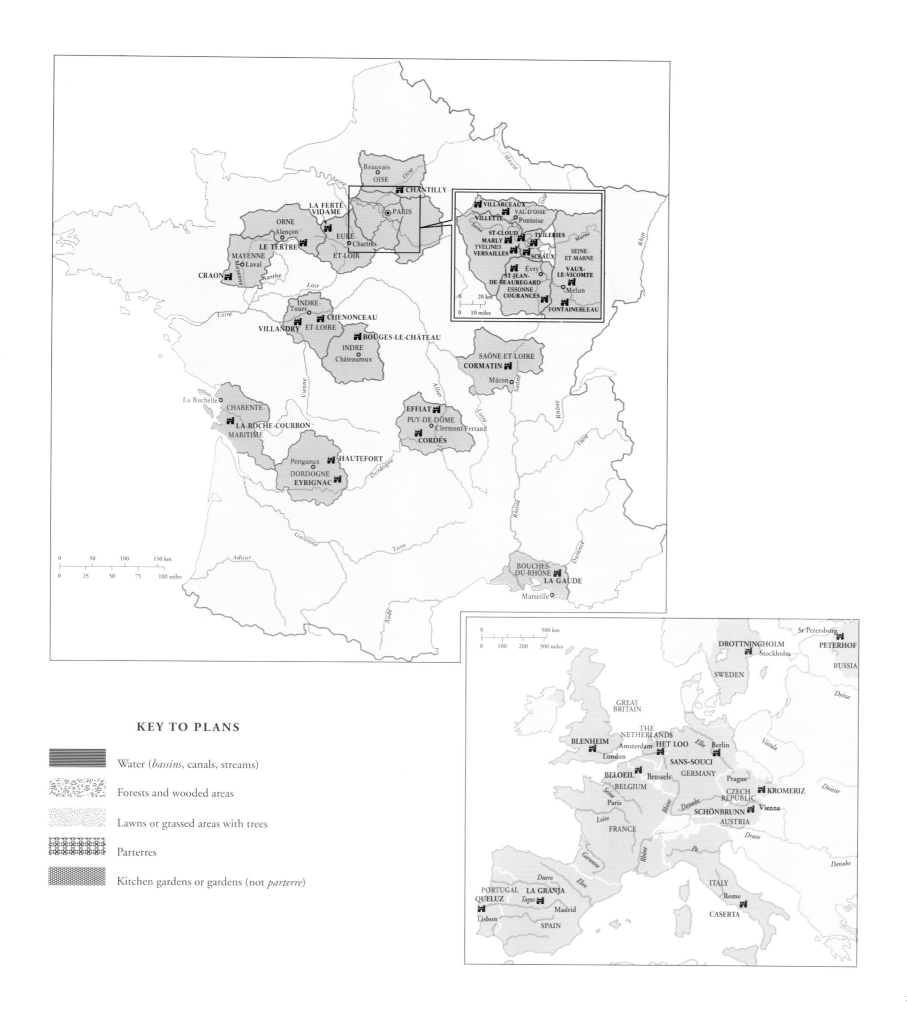

KEY TO PLANS

Water (*bassins*, canals, streams)

Forests and wooded areas

Lawns or grassed areas with trees

Parterres

Kitchen gardens or gardens (not *parterre*)

263

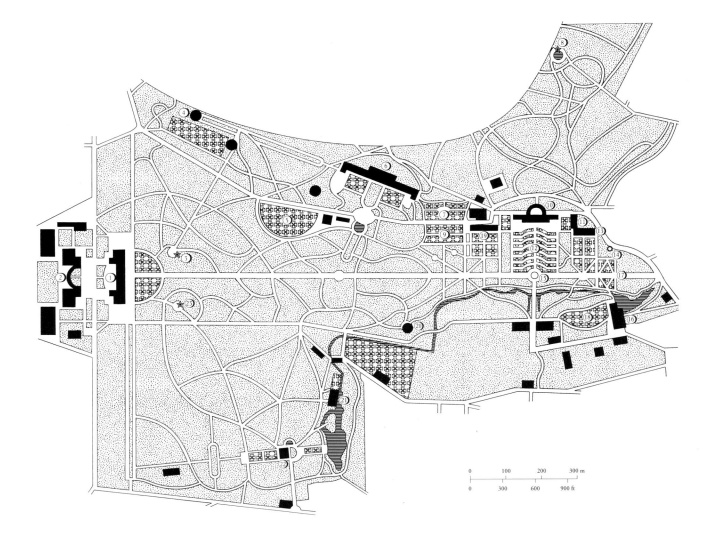

Sans-Souci

Germany (p. 150)

How to get there: the Park of Sans-Souci, Potsdam, Germany; 15½ miles (25 km) south-west of Berlin. Property of the State.

Palace: open from April to October, Tuesday to Sunday, 8.30am to 5pm; November to March, 9am to 12.30pm and 1pm to 4pm. Tel. 00 49 331 9694 190.

New Palace: open from April to October, Saturday to Thursday, 9am to 5pm; November to March, 9am to 12.30pm and 1pm to 4pm. Tel. 00 49 331 9694 255.

Picture Gallery: open from 15 May to 15 October, Tuesday to Sunday, 10am to 12.30pm and 1pm to 5pm.

The New Apartments: open from 1 April to 14 May, Saturday and Sunday, 10am to 5pm; from 15 May to 15 October, Tuesday to Sunday, 10am to 12.30pm and 1pm to 5pm.

Orangery: open from 15 May to 15 October, Tuesday to Sunday, 10am to 12.30pm and 1pm to 5pm.

Chinese Tea House: open from 15 May to 15 October, Tuesday to Sunday, 10am to 12.30pm and 1pm to 5pm.

Gardens: open every day from sunrise to sunset.

Further information: Potsdam Tourist Office, Tel. 00 49 331 275 580. Fax 00 49 331 275 5899.

1 Blenheim Palace
2 The Queen's Lake
3 The lake
4 The farm
5 Hensington Gate
6 The park and pleasure gardens
7 The Great Cascade
8 The *jardin à la française*

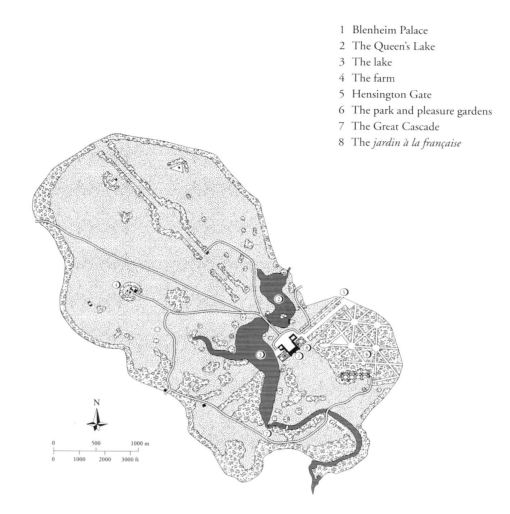

N

| 0 | 500 | 1000 m |
| 0 | 1000 | 2000 | 3000 ft |

Blenheim

England (p. 142)

How to get there: Blenheim Palace, Woodstock, Oxfordshire; 60 miles (100 km) from London. Privately owned by The Duke of Marlborough.

Palace, gardens, labyrinth, aromatic herb garden, butterfly house, motorboat trips, little train, boat hire, restaurants and shops: open from 15 March to 31 October, 10am to 5.30pm.

Further information: Tel. 00 44 1993 811325. Fax 00 44 1993 813527.

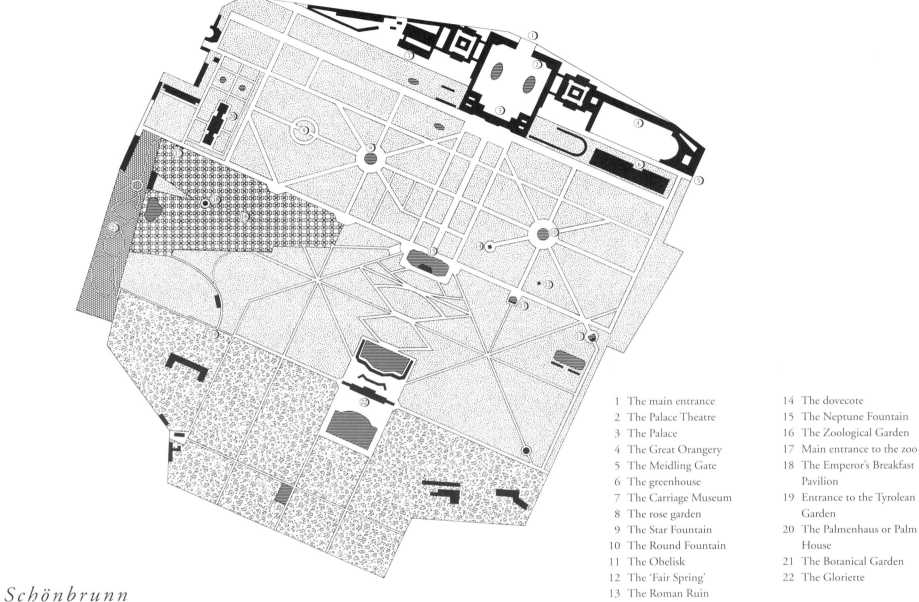

1	The main entrance	14	The dovecote
2	The Palace Theatre	15	The Neptune Fountain
3	The Palace	16	The Zoological Garden
4	The Great Orangery	17	Main entrance to the zoo
5	The Meidling Gate	18	The Emperor's Breakfast
6	The greenhouse		Pavilion
7	The Carriage Museum	19	Entrance to the Tyrolean
8	The rose garden		Garden
9	The Star Fountain	20	The Palmenhaus or Palm
10	The Round Fountain		House
11	The Obelisk	21	The Botanical Garden
12	The 'Fair Spring'	22	The Gloriette
13	The Roman Ruin		

Schönbrunn
Austria (p. 244)

How to get there: Palace of Schönbrunn, Vienna, Austria. Property of the State.

Palace: open from April to October, 8.30am to 5pm; from November to March, 8.30am to 4.30pm. Tel. 00 43 1 811 13 239. Fax 00 43 1 811 13 333.

Collection of historic vehicles/Wagenburg: open from November to March, 10am to 4pm (closed Mondays); from April to October, 9am to 6pm. Tel. 00 43 1 877 32 44.

Gardens: open all the year round from 6am to dusk. Tel. 00 43 1 887 50 87 0. **Gloriette:** open from May to October, 9am to 5pm. Tel. 00 43 1 879 13 11.

Palm House/Palmenhaus: open from May to September, 9.30am to 5.30pm; from October to April, 9.30am to 4.30pm. Tel. 00 43 1 887 50 87 406.

Butterfly House: open from May to September, 10am to 5pm; October to April, 10am to 3.30pm.

Zoological Garden: open February, 9am to 5pm; March and October, 9am to 5.30pm; April, 9am to 6pm; May to September, 9am to 6.30pm; November to January, 9am to 4.30pm. Tel. 00 43 1 887 92 94 0.

Concerts and ballets at the Orangery: Tel. 00 43 1 812 500 40, and in the **Palace Theatre:** Tel. 00 43 1 512 01 00.

Café: open from March to October, 8am to dusk; from November to February, 9am to dusk.

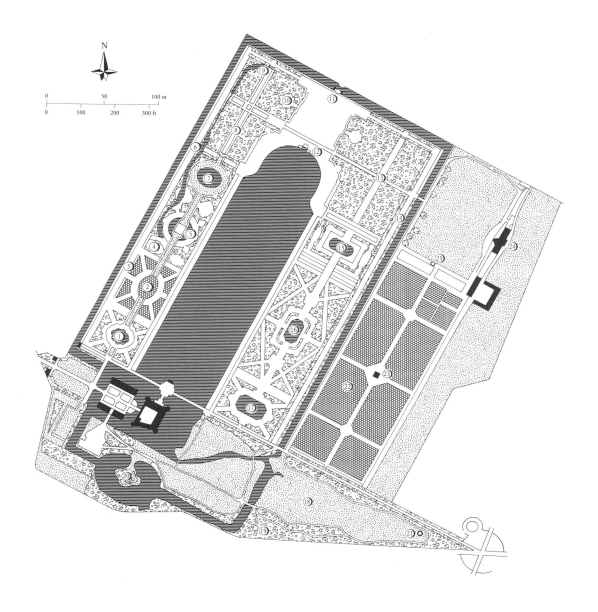

1 The 'bowling green', or *boulingrin*
2 The rose garden
3 The Allée du Doyen
4 The Jeux d'enfants
5 The Bassin des Poissons rouge
6 The Rieu d'Amour
7 The Bassin Ovale
8 The Allée des Miroirs
9 The Bosquet des Sources
10 The Salle du Grand Diable
11 A swing bridge
12 Neptune
13 The *quinconce*
14 The Allée du Mail
15 The Cloister
16 The Bassin des Dames
17 The Bassin des Glaces
18 The deer park
19 The Ruin
20 The Ile de Flore
21 The Temple du Morphée
22 The kitchen garden
23 The Temple of Pomona
24 The orangerie
25 The old copper beeches

Beloeil
Belgium (p. 236)

How to get there: 50 miles (80 km) south-west of Brussels. Privately owned by Prince de Ligne.

Gardens and château: open at weekends in May, 10am to 6pm; from June to September, every day from 10am to 6pm. Important music festival held in August.

Further information: the office of Fondation Ligne. Tel. 00 32 69 68 94 26. Fax 00 32 69 68 87 82.

1 The Palace
2 The Neptune Bassin
3 The Snail Pool
4 The Fan Pool
5 Apollo
6 The Sea
7 The Andromeda Bosquet
8 The Andromeda Fountain
9 The labyrinth
10 The 'Bouquet' Fountain
11 The Diana Pool
12 The Chapel of San Ildefonso
13 The Bosquet of Melancholy
14 The Queen's Gardens
15 The fishpond
16 The Corbeille

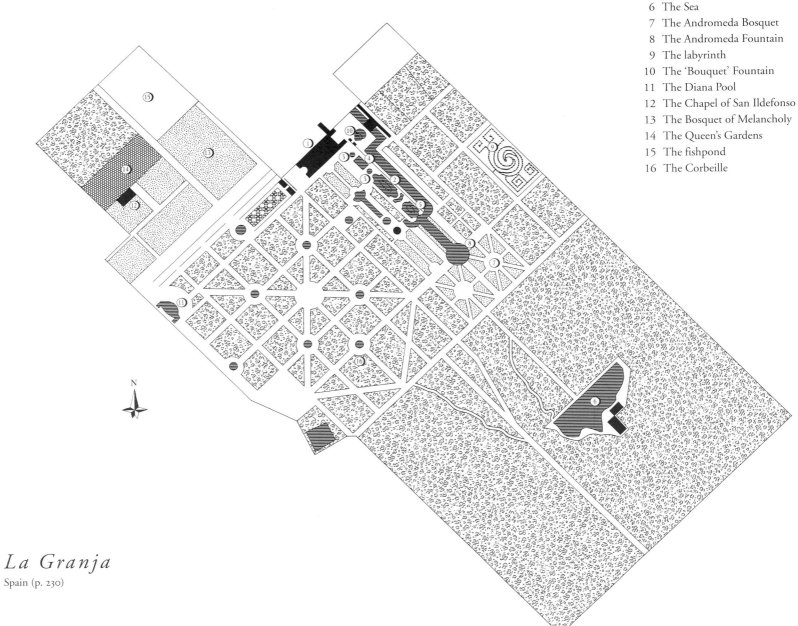

La Granja
Spain (p. 230)

How to get there: La Granja, San Ildefonso; 6½ miles (11 km) south-east of Segovia, 48 miles (80 km) north-west of Madrid. Property of the Crown.

Palace: open from October to March, Tuesday to Saturday, 10am to 1.30pm and 3pm to 5pm (Sundays and holidays, 10am to 2pm); in April and May, Monday to Friday, 10am to 1.30pm and 3pm to 5pm (Saturday and Sunday, 10am to 6pm); from June to September, every day except Monday, 10am to 6pm.

Gardens: open October and March, 10am to 6.30pm; from November to February, 10am to 6pm; April, 10am to 7pm; from May to September, 10am to 8pm.

Labyrinth: closes thirty minutes before the rest of the park.

Queen's Garden: open Friday, from 11.30am to 2.30pm and 4pm to 8pm.

San Ildefonso Hermitage: open Monday, from 3pm until thirty minutes before the closure of the gardens.

Fountain displays: from Holy Week until 25 August the fountains play in groups of four on Wednesdays, Saturdays and Sundays, at 5.30pm (for information, Tel. 00 34 921 470019). All the fountains play on 1 May, 30 May and 25 August at 5.30pm.

Further information: Tel. 00 34 921 470020. Fax 00 34 921 471895.

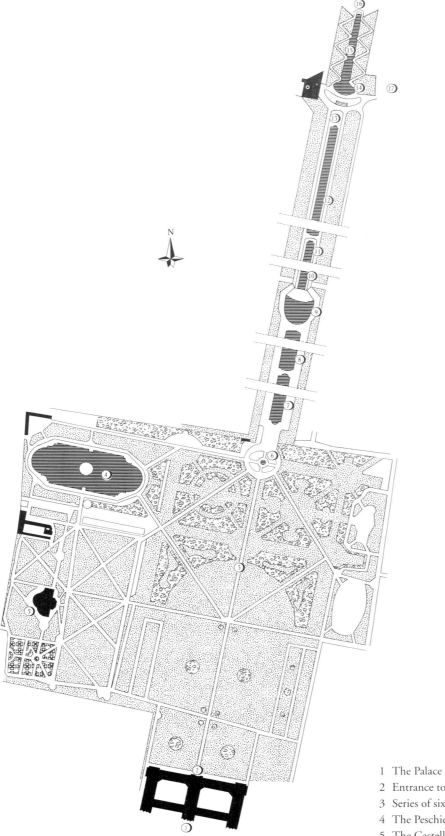

Caserta

Italy (p. 214)

How to get there: the Palace of Caserta, 12 miles (20 km) north of Naples. Property of the State.

Palace: open from 2 May to 31 October, Tuesday and Wednesday, 9am to 2pm; Thursday to Saturday, 9am to 2pm and 3pm to 7pm; Sunday, 9am to 8pm. From 1 June to 30 September, also open on Saturday from 9pm to 12 midnight. Closed on Monday.

Gardens: open from Monday to Sunday, 9am until one hour before sunset.

Giardino Inglese: guided tours every hour from 9am to 5pm.

Further information: Palace and Gardens, Tel. 00 39 0823 277111. Caserta Tourist Office, Tel. 00 39 0823 322233. Fax 00 39 0823 326300.

1 The Palace
2 Entrance to the garden
3 Series of sixteen statues
4 The Peschiera Grande
5 The Castelluccio
6 The Margarita Fountain
7 The Dolphin Bassin
8 The Dolphin Fountain
9 The Aeolus Fountain and Bassin
10 The Ceres Bassin
11 The Ceres Fountain
12 The Cascatelles
13 The Venus and Adonis Fountain
14 The Diana and Actaeon Fountain
15 The Cascade
16 The Grotto
17 Towards the Giardino Inglese

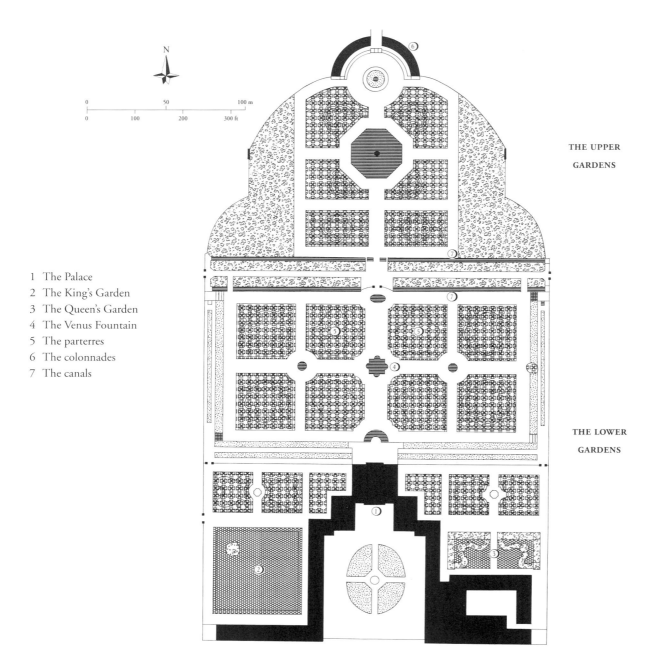

1 The Palace
2 The King's Garden
3 The Queen's Garden
4 The Venus Fountain
5 The parterres
6 The colonnades
7 The canals

THE UPPER
GARDENS

THE LOWER
GARDENS

N

0   50   100 m
0   100   200   300 ft

Het Loo

The Netherlands (p. 227)

How to get there: 1 mile (2 km) north-west of Apeldoorn. Property of the State.

Palace and gardens: open all the year round, Tuesday to Sunday, 10am to 5pm. Open on public holiday Mondays, closed at Christmas.

Further information: Tel. 00 31 55 577 24 00. Fax 00 31 55 522 18 35.

Queluz
Portugal (p. 200)

How to get there: 7 miles (12 km) west of Lisbon. Property of the State.

Palace and gardens: open from May to October, 10am to 6.30pm; from November to April, 10am to 5pm. Closed on Tuesday and public holidays.

Further information: Tel. 00 351 1 445 00 39. Fax 00 351 1 445 25 75

1 The Palace
2 The Robillion Steps, or the Lion Steps
3 The Azulejos Canal
4 The Medals Bassin
5 The Neptune Bassin
6 Queen Amelia's stables
7 The Ring of the Portuguese Riding School
8 The Jeu de Paume
9 The open-air New Riding Ring
10 The Great Cascade
11 The Shell Bassin
12 The Fame Gateway
13 The Raised Garden
14 The Malta Garden
15 The Ajuda Gateway
16 The Amphitrite Bassin
17 The Monkey Bassin
18 The Neptune Bassin

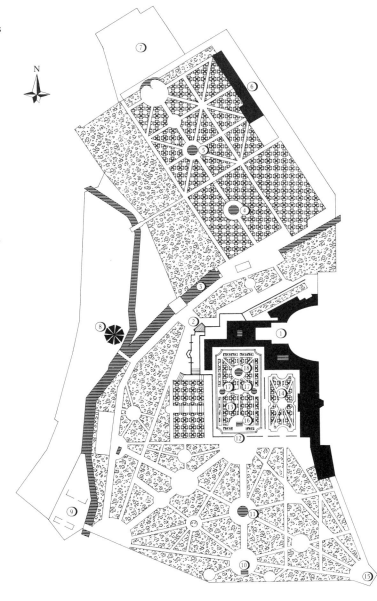

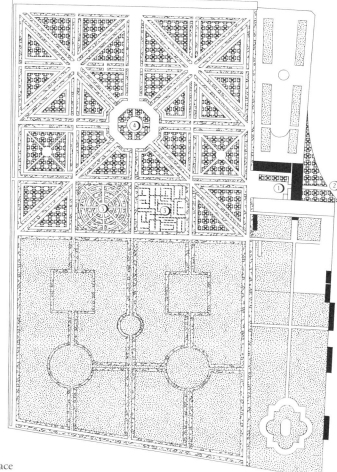

1 The Palace
2 The entrance
3 The mazes
4 The pavilion

Kromeriz
Czech Republic (p. 188)

How to get there: 168 miles (280 km) from Prague, 27 miles (45 km) from Olomouc. Property of the State.

Palace and gardens: open all the year round. In January and February, 9am to 5pm; in March and April, 7am to 6pm; in May, 7am to 7pm; from June to August, 7am to 8pm; in September, 7am to 6pm; in October, 7am to 5pm; in November and December, 7am to 4pm.

Further information: Palace, Tel. 00 420 634 21360 and 00 420 634 23311. Garden, Tel. 00 420 634 22218. Fax 00 420 634 21860.

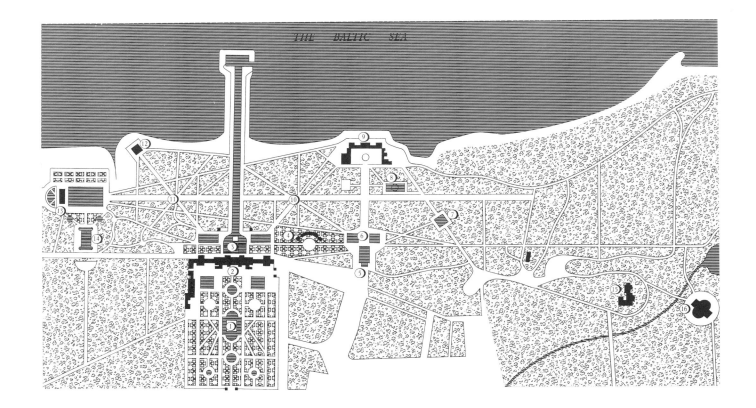

1 The Upper Garden	6 The Roman Fountains	13 The Marly Palace
2 The Great Palace	7 The Pyramid Fountain	14 The Golden Mountain Cascade
3 The Great Cascade	8 The Sun Fountain	15 The Farm Palace
4 The Orangery and the Triton Fountain	9 The Monplaisir Palace	16 The Cottage
5 The Chessboard Mountain Cascade	10 The Adam Fountain	
	11 The Eve Fountain	
	12 The Hermitage Pavilion	

Peterhof
Russia (p.222)

How to get there: 16 miles (27 km) from St Petersburg. Access by hovercraft from the Hermitage, St Petersburg, to the ship canal linking the garden and the sea. Property of the State.

Lower park: open every day, from 9am to 8pm, 9am to 9pm at weekends.

Upper park: free admission. Fountains play from 11am to 5pm, 11am to 6pm at weekends. The Great Palace, the Hermitage and Marly pavilions open every day, from 10.30am to 5pm, except Monday and the last Tuesday of each month.

Catherine's pavilion (formerly called Elizabeth's): closed on Thursday.

Further information: Great Palace, Tel. 00 7 812 420 0073. St Petersburg Tourist Information, Tel. 00 7 812 210 4527. Fax 00 7 812 210 4927.

1 The Palace of
   Drottningholm
2 The theatre
3 The stables
4 The *parterre d'eau*
5 The *parterre de broderie*
   and the Hercules
   Fountain
6 The theatre *bosquet*
7 The Chinese Pavilion
8 The Gateway
9 The Governor's
   Residence
10 Monument Island
11 The Carousel

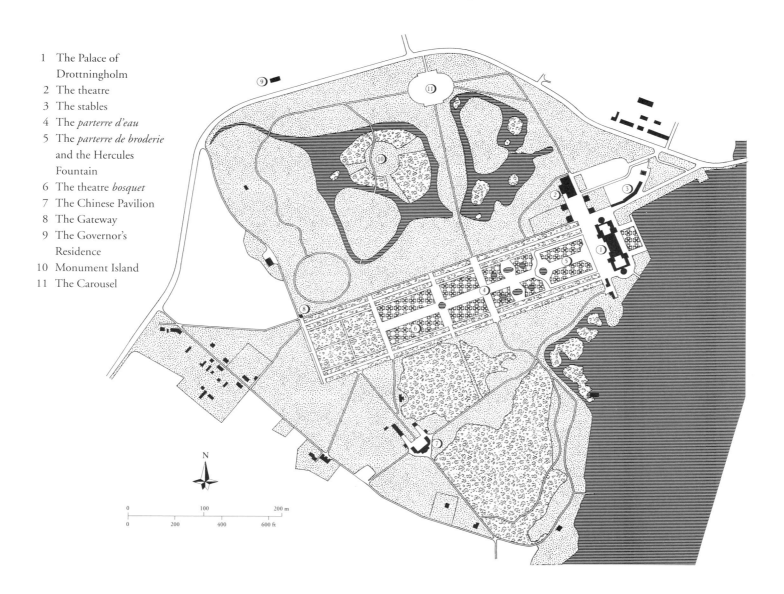

Drottningholm
Sweden (p. 210)

How to get there: on the island of Lovön, west of Stockholm. Access by boat or metro. Property of the Crown.

Palace: open every day from May to August, 10am to 4.30pm; in September, 12 noon to 3pm. Closed on 1 May and 19 June, and during official receptions.

Gardens: always open, day and night.

Further information: Tel. 00 46 8 402 62 80. Fax 00 46 8 402 62 81.

1　The Château
2　The cut-flower garden
3　The Tapis Vert
4　The *parterre à la française*
5　The lake

Bouges

Indre (p. 243)

How to get there: Château de Bouges, 36560, Bouges-le-Château; 24 miles (40 km) from Vierzon, 17 miles (28 km) from Châteauroux. Property of la Caisse nationale des Monuments historiques et des Sites (Department of Historic Monuments).

Château, park, garden, the old stables, saddle room and museum of horse-drawn vehicles: open weekends in March and November, from 10am to 12 noon and 2pm to 5pm; in April, May, September and October, every day except Tuesday, 10am to 12 noon and 2pm to 6pm; in June, every day, 10am to 12 noon and 2pm to 7pm; in July and August, 10am to 1pm and 2pm to 7pm, and evening openings. Closed from December to February.

Further information: Tel. 00 33 2 54 35 88 26. Fax 00 33 2 54 35 16 96.

1 The Great Stables
2 The Cascades de Beauvais
3 The Jeu de Paume
4 The Pont des Grands-Hommes
5 The Ile d'Amour
6 The Pelouse de Bucamp
7 The Petit Château

8 The Grille d'Honneur or main entrance
9 The *vertugadin*
10 The Bassin de la Gerbe
11 La Manche
12 The *miroirs*
13 The Château d'Enghien

14 L'Etang de Sylvie
15 The Allées des Philosophes
16 The Canal des Brochetons
17 The Patte-d'Oie
18 The Canal des Morfondus
19 The Maison de Sylvie
20 The Hameau buildings

21 The Prairie de Candie
22 The road to the Pont du Roi
23 The Hexagone
24 La Tête du Grand Rond, or the Cascade
25 The Grand Rond
26 The Musée Condé

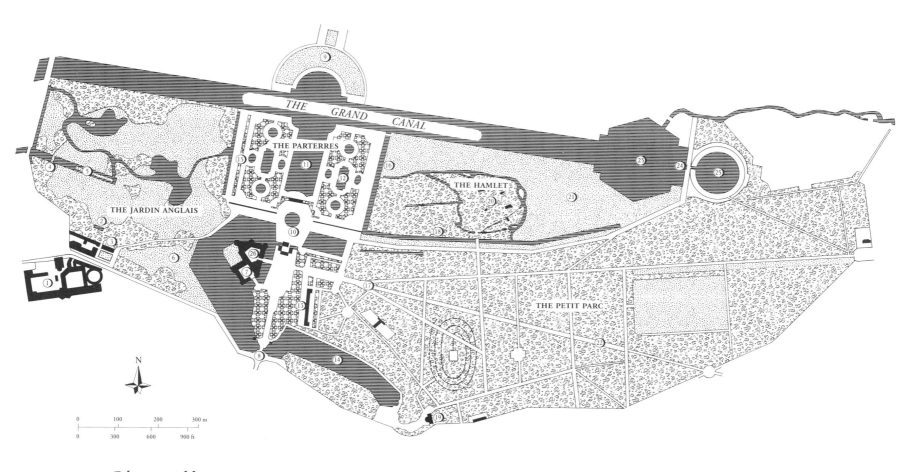

Chantilly
Oise (p. 166)

How to get there: Château de Chantilly and Musée Condé, Oise (60); 24½ miles (41 km) from Paris. Property of the Institut de France.

Park: open daily.

Château: open from 1 March to 31 October, 10am to 6pm; from 1 November to 28 February, 10.30am to 12.45pm and 2pm to 5pm; closed on Tuesday. The Duc d'Aumale Collections of paintings and rare books are among the richest in the world. Tel. 00 33 3 44 62 62 62. Fax 00 33 3 44 62 62 61. Book and gift shops.

'La Capitainerie' restaurant and tea-room in the château's old kitchens, Tel. 00 33 3 44 57 15 89. Teas available at the Hameau windmill in the park, from 20 March to 15 November, Tel. 00 33 3 44 57 46 21.

'Living Museum' of horses: in the Great Stables, open all the year round, 10.30am to 5.30pm, except Tuesday. Tel. 00 33 3 44 57 40 40.

'L'Aérophile' tethered balloon, from the beginning of March to mid-November, near the Hameau. Tel 00 33 3 44 57 35 35. Fax 00 33 3 44 57 29 62. Trips on the launch 'l'Hydrophile' on the Grand Canal. 'Nights of Fire' international firework display every two years in June.

Further information: Comité départemental du Tourisme de l'Oise, Tel. 00 33 3 44 45 82 12. Les Amis de Chantilly, Tel. 00 33 3 44 57 32 22.

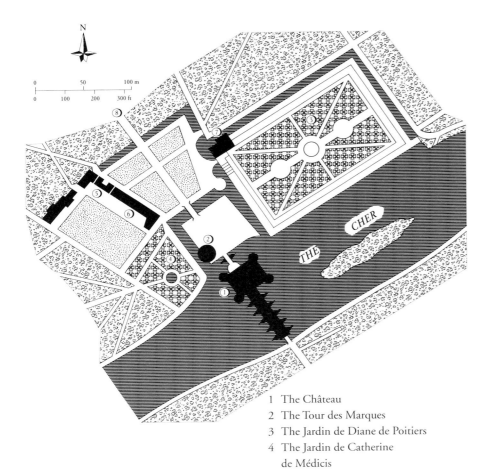

1 The Château
2 The Tour des Marques
3 The Jardin de Diane de Poitiers
4 The Jardin de Catherine
  de Médicis
5 The Waxwork Museum
6 The Dômes building
7 The Chancellerie
8 The entrance drive

Chenonceau

Indre-et-Loire (p. 122)

How to get there: Château de Chenonceau, Chenonceau (37); 128 miles (214 km) from Paris, 20 miles (34 km) from Tours. Privately owned by M. Menier.

Château and gardens: open every day, from 16 March to 15 September, 9am to 7pm; otherwise opens at 9am and closes between 4.30pm and 6.30pm, according to the season.

Waxwork museum in the old stables; exhibitions of modern painting in the Galerie Catherine de Médicis; son et Lumière; boat hire; and little train rides during July and August.

Souvenir shop in the Cour des Marques; flower shop in the former farm buildings (by the orangerie); visits to the cut-flower garden to watch the making of flower arrangements for the château.

The Dômes wine vault sells white, red and rosé Château de Chenonceau and Dômes de Chenonceau from the estate.

'L'Orangerie' restaurant, Tel. 00 33 2 47 23 91 97; and self-service restaurant in the Royal Stables.

Further information: Tel. 00 33 2 47 23 90 07. Fax 00 33 2 47 23 80 88.

Cordés

Puy-de-Dôme (p. 191)

How to get there: The Château de Cordés gardens, Orcival (63); 12 miles (20 km) from Clermont-Ferrand. Privately owned by M. and Mme Péchaud.

Gardens and château: open from Easter to All Saint's Day, every day from 10am to 12 noon and 2pm to 6pm. The rest of the year by appointment.

Further information: Tel. 00 33 4 73 65 81 34.

1 The Château
2 The terrace
3 The bassins
4 The parterres
5 The 'open-air salon'
6 The *cour d'honneur*
7 The hornbeam hedges

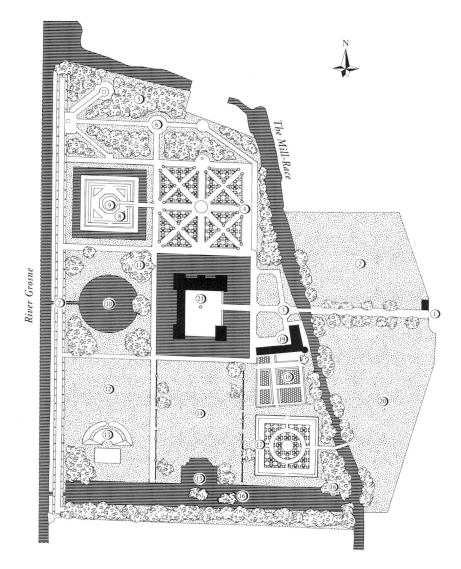

1 The entrance
2 The orchard
3 The farmyard
4 The parterre
5 The Bosquet d'Albion
6 The Salle des Tulipiers
7 The Allée Lamartine
8 The aviary
9 The labyrinth
10 The *miroir*
11 The great oak
12 The *quinconce*
13 The open-air theatre
14 The Tapis Vert
15 The canal
16 The seven 'cyprès chauves'
17 The Jardin des Planètes
18 The kitchen garden
19 The orangery and tea-room
20 The arboretum
21 The Château

Cormatin

Saône-et-Loire (p. 172)

How to get there: Château de Cormatin, Cormatin, Saône-et-Loire (71); 7 miles (12 km) north of Cluny. Privately owned by M. Marc Simonet-Lenglart, M. Pierre Almendros and Mme Anne-Marie Joly.

Château and gardens: open every day from Easter to 11 November; in April, October and November, 10am to 12 noon and 2pm to 5.30pm; in May, June and September, 10am to 12 noon and 2pm to 6.30pm; in July and August, 10am to 6.30pm (guided tours of the château, non-guided access to the gardens).

Further information: Tel. 00 33 3 85 50 16 55. Fax 00 33 3 85 50 72 06.

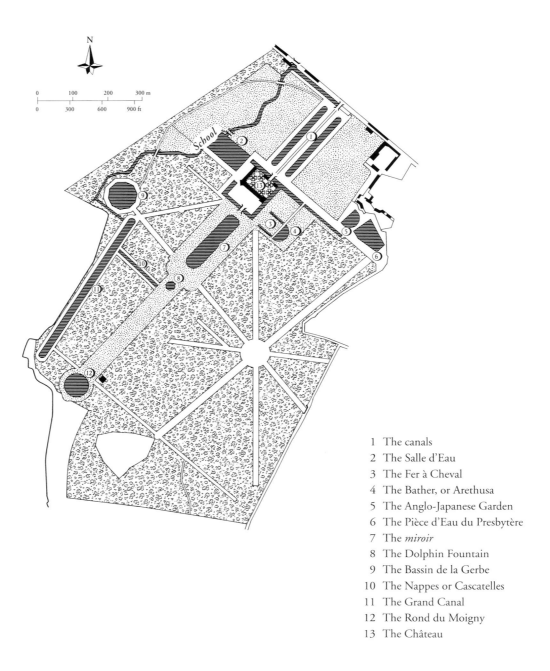

1 The canals
2 The Salle d'Eau
3 The Fer à Cheval
4 The Bather, or Arethusa
5 The Anglo-Japanese Garden
6 The Pièce d'Eau du Presbytère
7 The *miroir*
8 The Dolphin Fountain
9 The Bassin de la Gerbe
10 The Nappes or Cascatelles
11 The Grand Canal
12 The Rond du Moigny
13 The Château

Courances

Essonne (p. 196)

How to get there: 30 miles (50 km) south of Paris, 6½ miles (11 km) from Barbizon. Privately owned by M. and Mme de Ganay.

Château and gardens: open from 29 March to 1 November, Saturday, Sunday and public holidays, 2pm to 6.30pm (2pm to 5.30pm in October).

Further information: Tel. 00 33 1 40 62 07 62. Fax 00 33 1 47 05 04 89.

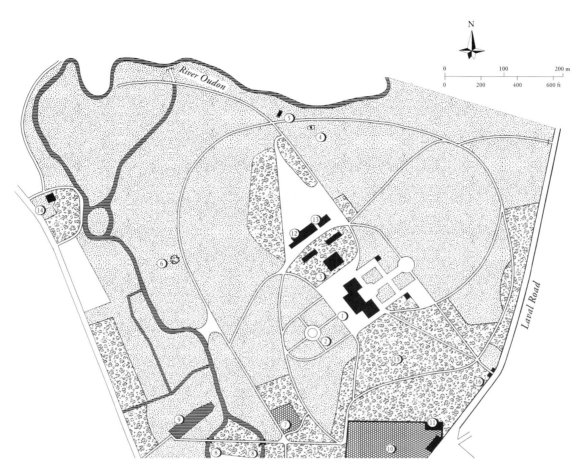

1 The Château
2 The *jardin à la française*
3 The bakery and the dovecote
4 The icehouse
5 The wash house or laundry
6 The oldest tree in the park
7 The Petit Jardin
8 The two bridges
9 The Bassin des Cygnes

10 The kitchen garden
11 The orangery
12 The outbuildings
13 The former orangery
14 The Chapel of Saint-Eutrope
15 Woodland
16 Entrance to the park

Craon

Mayenne (p. 140)

How to get there: Château de Craon gardens, Mayenne (53); 18 miles (30 km) from Laval. Privately owned by M. Louis de Guébriant.

Gardens: open from 1 April to 31 October, every day except Tuesday, 2pm to 6.30pm.

Château: open in July and August, every day except Tuesday, 2pm to 6.30pm. By appointment the rest of the year. Bed and breakfast available.

Further information: Tel. 00 33 2 43 06 11 02. Fax 00 33 2 43 06 05 18.

1   The Château
2   The canal and the grotto
3   The lime walks, called the
     Allées du Maréchal
4   The moat
5   The dry moat
6   The great gateway
7   The Church of Saint-Blaise
8   The former gardens of the
     military school
9   The annexe of the military
     school (bakery and linen room)

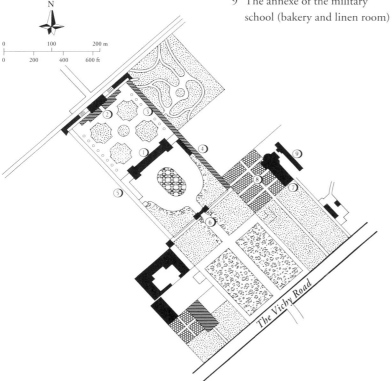

Effiat
Puy-de-Dôme (p. 156)

How to get there: Château d'Effiat gardens (63); 9 miles (15 km) from Vichy. Privately owned by M. de Moroges.

Gardens and château: open at weekends from 15 March; from 15 June to 30 June and from 1 to 15 September, 3pm to 7pm; in July and August, 9.30am to 12 noon and 2.30pm to 7pm (opens 30 minutes later on Sunday); candle-lit evening visits in July and August. Rest of the year by appointment. Open on public holidays.

Further information: Tel./Fax 00 33 4 73 63 64 01.

Eyrignac
Dordogne (p. 192)

How to get there: the Manoir d'Eyrignac gardens, Salignac (24); 8 miles (13 km) north-east of Sarlat, 15 miles (25 km) from Montignac-Lascaux and 24 miles (40 km) from Brive. Privately owned by M. Sermadiras de Pouzols de Lile.

Open: from 1 April to 31 May, 10.30am to 12.30pm and 2pm to 7pm; from June to September, every day, from 10am to 7pm; from 1 October to 31 March, 10am to 12.30pm and from 2pm to dusk. At other times by appointment.

Exhibition about the gardens, video presentation, sale of local produce, hall available for hire, restaurant and plant shows.

Further information: at Eyrignac, Tel. 00 33 5 53 28 99 71. Fax 00 33 5 53 30 39 89; Paris office: Tel. 00 33 1 47 66 51 21.

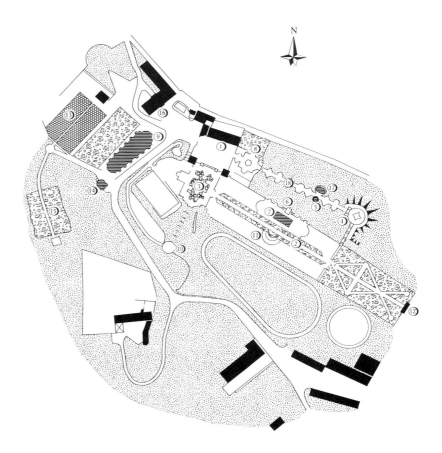

1   The manor house
2   The Allée des Charmes
3   The Jardin Français
4   The green rotunda
5   The Roman Fountain
6   The Portillon
7   The bassin
8   The Rond-Point de Repos
9   The fishpond

10   The Terrasse Enchantée
11   The Pavillon de Repos
12   The Chinese pagoda
13   The kitchen garden
14   The laundry
15   The tree nursery
16   The outbuildings
17   The Bassin Ovale
18   The Allée des Vases

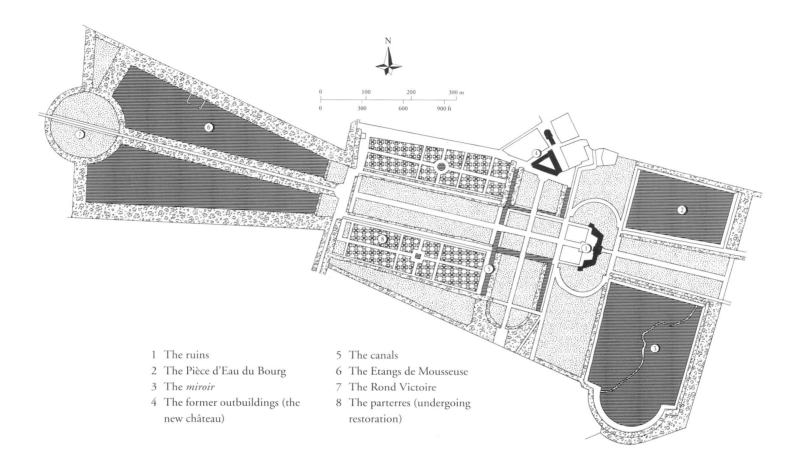

1 The ruins
2 The Pièce d'Eau du Bourg
3 The *miroir*
4 The former outbuildings (the new château)
5 The canals
6 The Etangs de Mousseuse
7 The Rond Victoire
8 The parterres (undergoing restoration)

La Ferté-Vidame

Eure-et-Loir (p. 126)

How to get there: La Ferté-Vidame, Eure-et-Loir (28); 75 miles (125 km) from Paris and 29 miles (48 km) from Chartres. Property of the département de Eure-et-Loir.

Château and gardens: open every day from April to October, 9am to 7pm; from November to the end of March, 9am to 5.30pm. Visits with talk every other Sunday, from 31 March to 31 October. Concerts in the summer months.

Exhibition about Saint-Simon and the history of the estate: Pavillon Saint-Dominique, at the entrance to the château. Information from les Amis de La Ferté-Vidame, Tel. 00 33 2 37 37 64 09.

Carriage rides in the park, Tel. 00 33 2 37 62 42 76.

Further information: from the Tourist Office, Tel. 00 33 2 37 37 68 59. From the Town Hall, Tel. 00 33 2 37 37 62 45.

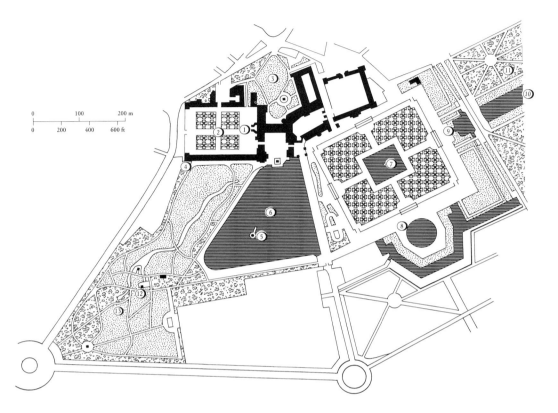

1 The Château	7 The Tiber statue
2 The Cour du Cheval-Blanc	8 The Romulus statue
3 The Jardin de Diane	9 The Cascades
4 The grotto in the Jardin des Pins	10 The canal
5 The Pavillon	11 The park
6 The Etang des Carpes	12 The Fontaine Bliaud
	13 The Jardin Anglais

Fontainebleau
Seine-et-Marne (p. 118)

How to get there: Château de Fontainebleau, Fontainebleau, Seine-et-Marne (77); 36 miles (60 km) from Paris. Property of the State.

Palace (the Renaissance rooms, the Grands Appartements, the Appartements de l'Empereur): open every day except Tuesday and 1 January, 1 May and 25 December. From November to April, 9.30am to 12.30pm and 2pm to 5pm; May, June, September and October, 9.30am to 5pm; July and August, 9.30am to 6pm. Evening festivities on 17 and 18 September. Occasional opening of the Empress Eugénie's drawing rooms and Chinese museum (enquire beforehand). Guided tour of the Petits Appartements and the Napoleon I Museum (rooms open in rotation, enquire beforehand).

Gardens: open from May to September, 9am to 7pm; April and October, 9am to 6pm; from November to March, 9am to 5pm.

Park: open from October to March, 7.30am to 7.30pm; from April to September, 7.30am to 9.30pm. Boat trips on the Etang des Carpes from 1 May to 31 October. Carriage rides and trips on the little train.

Further information: Tel. 00 33 1 60 71 50 70. Fax 00 33 1 60 71 50 71.

La Gaude

Bouches-du-Rhône (p. 159)

How to get there: La Gaude, Route des Pinchinats; 3 miles (5 km) north of Aix-en-Provence. Privately owned by Mme Beaufour.

Château: group visits on written application only. Tasting and sale of wine (Château de la Gaude red and rosé, AOC Coteaux d'Aix-en-Provence) from the estate.

Further information: Anne Beaufour and Michel Audibert, Tel. 00 33 4 42 21 64 19. Fax 00 33 4 42 21 56 84.

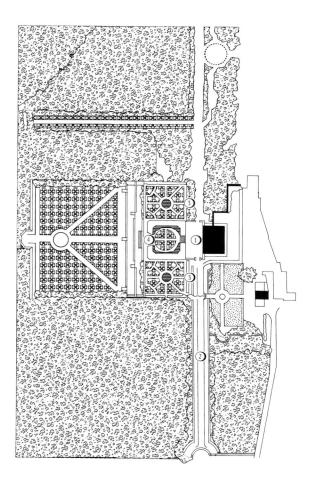

1 The Château
2 The entrance drive
3 The parterres
4 The labyrinth

1 The Château
2 The entrance drive
3 The park
4 The Pont Dormant
5 The esplanade
6 The dry moat

7 The drawbridge
8 The *cour d'honneur*
9 The terraced gardens
10 The thuya walk
11 The box parterre

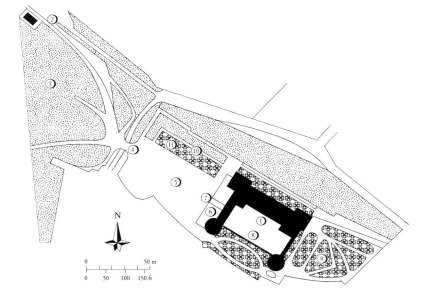

Hautefort

Dordogne (p. 184)

How to get there: Château de Hautefort gardens (24); 24 miles (40 km) from Périgueux. Privately owned by Fondation du Château de Hautefort.

Gardens and château: open every day from 5 April to 30 June and 1 September to 11 October, 10am to 12 noon and 2pm to 6pm; July and August, 9.30am to 7pm; from 12 October to 1 November, 2pm to 6pm. Out of season, open on Sunday afternoon, 2pm to 6pm. Annual closure from 14 December to 16 January.

Further information: Tel. 00 33 5 53 50 51 23. Fax 00 33 5 53 51 67 37.

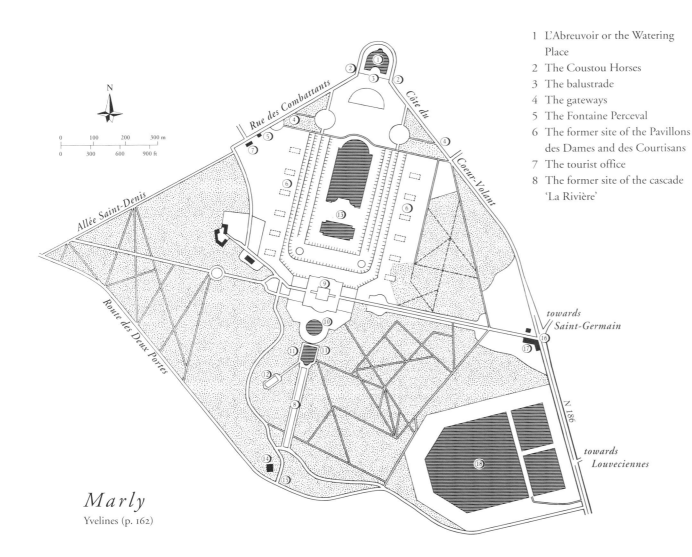

N

1 L'Abreuvoir or the Watering
   Place
2 The Coustou Horses
3 The balustrade
4 The gateways
5 The Fontaine Perceval
6 The former site of the Pavillons
   des Dames and des Courtisans
7 The tourist office
8 The former site of the cascade
   'La Rivière'

9 Site of the Château
10 The 'Grand Jet' Fountain
11 The Meleager statue
12 The open-air theatre
13 The Tapis Vert
14 The house in the woods
15 The site of the Ramasse
16 The Grille Royale
17 The musée-promenade
18 The reservoir

La Roche-Courbon

Charente-Maritime (p. 136)

How to get there: 21 miles (35 km) from
Rochefort. Privately owned by M. Badois.

Château and gardens: open every day from
15 June to 15 October, closed on Thursday out
of season, and on 1 January and 31 December.

Further information: Tel. 00 33 5 46 95 60 10.
Fax 00 33 5 46 95 65 22.

Marly

Yvelines (p. 162)

How to get there: Parc de Marly, Grille Royale, Louveciennes (78); 12 miles
(20 km) west of Paris, 3 miles (5 km) north of Versailles. Property of the State.

Park: open all the year round. From November to the end of April, 8am to
5.30pm; from May to October, 8am to 7.30pm. The 'Grand Jet' fountain plays
on one Sunday each month from May to October.

Visitors' centre: for the exploration of Marly-le-Roi/Louveciennes by the Grille
d'Honneur or Royale at the entrance to the estate. Permanent exhibition of the
history of the estate, also temporary exhibitions, workshops, themed tours, tours
and lectures, audio guides and use of library for researchers by appointment.
Open every day except Monday, Tuesday and public holidays, 2pm to 6pm.
Tel. 00 33 1 30 69 06 26. Fax 00 33 1 30 82 09 95.

Further information: Les Amis du Vieux Marly, Marly Town Hall,
Tel. 00 33 1 30 61 60 00.

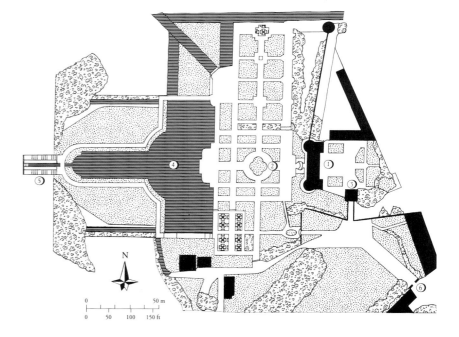

N

1 The Château
2 The *jardins à la française*
3 The donjon
4 The bassin
5 The escalier d'eau
6 The entrance to the estate

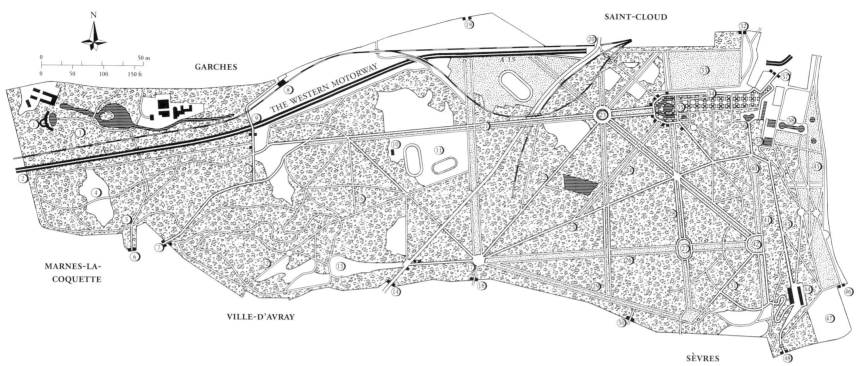

1 The La Fayette memorial
2 The Porte du Combat
3 The Parc de Villeneuve-l'Etang
4 The Plaine des Quatre Cèdres
5 The Porte de Marnes
6 The Place de Marnes
7 The Porte Blanche
8 The station at Garches
9 The Porte Verte
10 The pheasantry
11 The French stadium
12 The Brosse
13 The Lyre or Violin

14 The Grille de Ville-d'Avray
15 The Allée de la Porte Verte
16 The Allée de l'Etang Vieux
17 The Rond de Chasse
18 The Porte des Vignes
19 The Porte Jaune
20 The Grille d'Orléans
21 The Allée de Marnes
22 The Allée de la Grande Gerbe
23 The Grande Gerbe
24 The Allée des Glaises
25 The Allée de Versailles
26 The Allée de la Lanterne

27 The Rond des Gardes
28 The Allée de la Félicité
29 The Allée de la Broussaille
30 The Porte Brancas
31 The Allée Couverte
32 The Grille des Ecoles
33 The Jardin du Trocadéro
34 The Allée de la Carrière
35 Les Vingt-Quatre Jets
36 The Bassin du Fer à Cheval
37 The Grille d'Honneur or
    main gate
38 The Grande Cascade

39 The Grand Jet or great
    water jet
40 The Fer à Cheval
41 The Allée de la Balustrade
42 The Rond de la Balustrade
43 The Allée du Mail
44 The Pavillon de Breteuil
45 The Jardin Bas
46 The Grille de Sèvres
47 The national Sèvres factory
48 The Porte du Mail

Saint-Cloud

Hauts-de-Seine (p. 146)

How to get there: Domaine national de Saint-Cloud, Hauts-de-Seine (92); on the western outskirts of Paris. Property of the State.

Château and gardens: open every day from 7.30am; from 1 March to 30 April and 1 September to 31 October, gates close at 9pm; from 1 May to 31 August, at 10pm; from 1 November to 28 February, at 8pm. Carriage rides available around the Grand Parc.

The Musée du Domaine: open Wednesday, Saturday and Sunday, 2pm to 6pm. Fountain displays in the summer.

Restaurants and tea rooms: 'La Grande Gerbe', by the Bassin of the same name (open all the year round); the 'Café de Valois' and the 'En Vert du Décor', near the Vingt-Quatre Jets; the 'Oasis', near the Butte aux Chèvres; the 'Chalet du Fer à Cheval', by the Bassin of the same name; and the 'Chalet de Chamillard', in the Allée de Marnes.

Further information: Tel. 00 33 1 41 12 02 90. Fax 00 33 1 47 71 38 20.

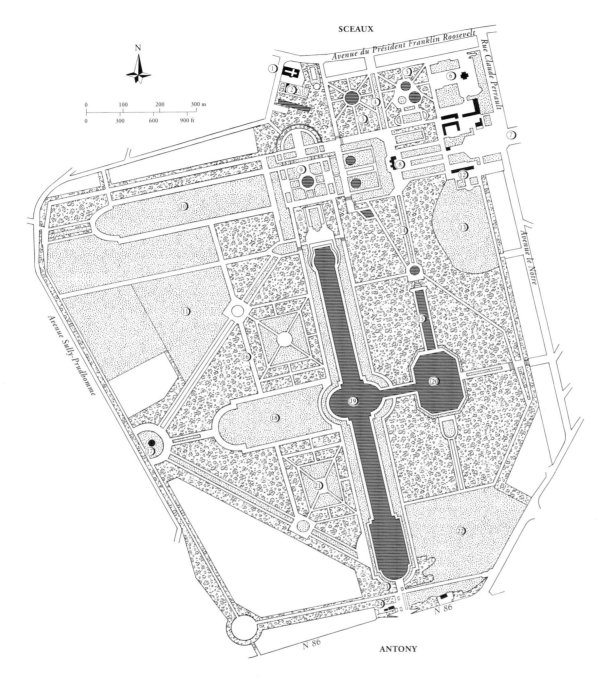

1   The church at Sceaux
2   The Petit Château
3   The Bosquet de Pomone
4   The Allée de Diane
5   The Plaine des Taureaux
6   The Pavillon de L'Aurore
7   The Allée d'Honneur
8   The Château and Musée de
    l'Ile-de-France
9   The Terrasse des Pintades
10 The Plaine des Quatre-Statues
11 The Plaine de la Pépinière
12 The Orangerie
13 The Plaine de l'Orangerie
14 The Allée de la Duchesse
15 The Cascades
16 The Allée des Cèdres
17 The Pavillon de Hanovre
18 The Plaine de Châtenay
19 The Grand Canal
20 The Octagone
21 The south *bosquet*
22 The Plaine de la Patte-d'Oie
23 The Grenouillère
24 The Maison du Parc

Sceaux

Hauts-de-Seine (p. 132)

How to get there: Domaine Départemental de Sceaux (92); 3 miles (5 km) from Paris. Property of the département des Hauts-de-Seine.

Park: open all the year round from sunrise to sunset, 7am or 8am to 5pm or 9pm. Fishing in the Grand Canal, nature trail, sports facilities.
Tel. 00 33 1 46 61 44 85.

Château: Musée de l'Île-de-France – history of the estate and other royal estates, ceramics and topography, paintings, sculpture, drawings and watercolours –
open every day except Tuesday, in spring and summer, 10am to 6pm; in autumn and winter, 10am to 5pm; Tel. 00 33 1 46 61 06 71.

Sceaux musical season: summer concerts in the Orangerie, Tel. 00 33 1 46 60 07 79.

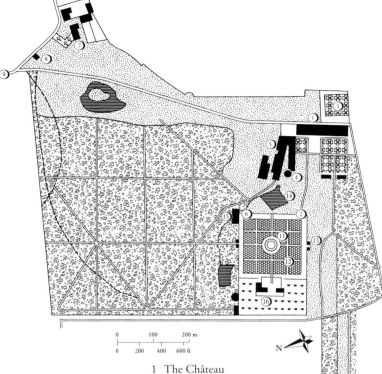

Le Tertre

Orne (p. 170)

How to get there: Château du Tertre, Orne (61); 48 miles (80 km) from Chartres. Privately owned by Mme Anne-Véronique de Coppet.

Château: Study and library of Roger Martin du Gard, open only by arrangement. Drama courses in speaking and interpretation; Franco-German music weeks; literary seminars.

Further information: Les Amis du Tertre, Tel. 00 33 2 33 73 18 30. Fax 00 33 2 33 73 11 46.

1 The Château
2 Entrance to the kitchen garden
3 Parterre with old roses
4 The dovecote
5 Outbuildings
6 Entrance to the kitchen garden
7 The chapel
8 Porter's lodge
9 Entrance to the estate
10 The perspective
11 The Rond d'Eau
12 The kitchen garden
13 The ha-has
14 The watering place
15 Fruit and grape store
16 Orchard and greenhouses

Saint-Jean-de-Beauregard

Essonne (p. 182)

How to get there: Domaine de Saint-Jean-de-Beauregard, Les Ulis (91); 17 miles (28 km) south of Paris. Privately owned by M. and Mme de Curel.

Château and gardens: open from 15 March to 15 November, Sundays and public holidays, 2pm to 6pm. Groups by arrangement, every day except Wednesday. Displays and sales, talks, demonstrations, tastings; hardy plants fair in April, craftsmen's fair in September, festival of fruit and vegetables of yesterday and today in November.

Further information: Tel. 00 33 1 60 12 00 01. Fax 00 33 1 60 12 56 31.

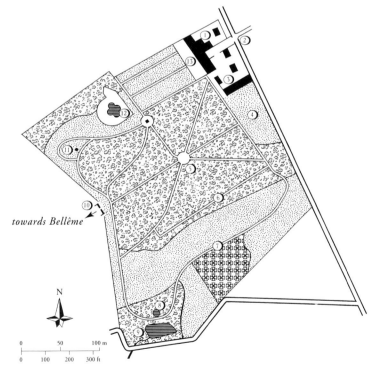

towards Bellême

1 The Château	8 The Fontaine des Peignés
2 Entrance to the estate	9 The lake
3 The outbuildings	10 The ha-ha
4 The kitchen garden	11 The Temple of Philosophe
5 The Rond de Diane	12 The Bassin
6 The Allée du Bréviaire	13 The terrace
7 The Allée des Thuyas	

287

1 The Galerie du Jeu-de-Paume
2 The Terrasse des Feuillants
3 The exedrae
4 The Bassin Rond
5 The Jardins Réservés
6 The small Bassins
7 Entrance to the garden:
   Terrasse Lemonnier (site of the
   former palace)
8 The Terrasse du Bord-de-l'Eau
9 The great octagonal Bassin
10 The orangerie
11 The Fer à Cheval

Les Tuileries

Paris (p. 128)

How to get there: Jardin des Tuileries, Paris Ist arrondissement. Property of the State.

Jardins du Carousel: always open.

Jardins des Tuileries: open 7.30am to 7.30pm, from the last Sunday in September to the Saturday before the last Sunday in March; 7am to 9pm from the last Sunday in March to the Saturday before the last Sunday in September. Tel. 00 33 1 40 20 90 43.

Free guided tours with a speaker from the Caisse nationale des Monuments historiques et des sites. Tel. 00 33 1 44 61 21 69/00 33 1 44 61 21 70. Meet at the Arc du Carousel at 3pm, Wednesdays, Fridays, Saturdays, Sundays and public holidays.

Lessons for children in the kitchen garden in the Grand Couvert, on the left looking towards the Place de la Concorde. Tel. 'l'Enfance de l'Art', atelier des Tuileries, 00 33 1 42 96 19 33.

Heritage bookshop in the gardens, below the Terrasse du Jeu de Paume, cafés and restaurants with outside seating.

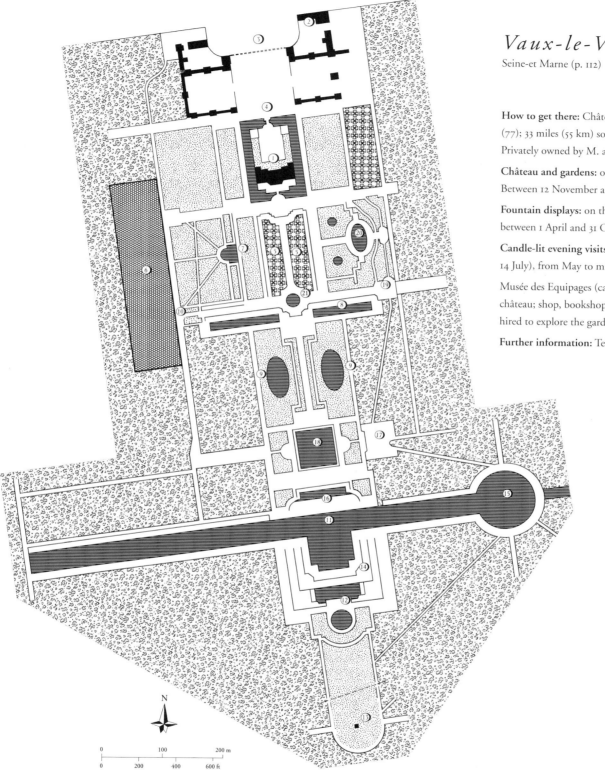

Vaux-le-Vicomte

Seine-et Marne (p. 112)

How to get there: Château de Vaux-le-Vicomte, Maincy, Seine-et-Marne (77); 33 miles (55 km) south-east of Paris, 3 miles (5 km) from Melun. Privately owned by M. and Mme Patrice de Vogüé.

Château and gardens: open from 1 March to 11 November, 10am to 6pm. Between 12 November and 28 February, groups by arrangement.

Fountain displays: on the second and last Saturday of each month, between 1 April and 31 October, 3pm to 6pm.

Candle-lit evening visits: on Saturdays and public holidays (except 14 July), from May to mid-October, 8pm to 12 midnight.

Musée des Equipages (carriages); audio guides available for tours of the château; shop, bookshop; 'L'Ecureuil' restaurant; electric buggies can be hired to explore the gardens.

Further information: Tel. 00 33 1 64 14 41 90. Fax 00 33 1 60 69 90 85.

1 The Château
2 The outbuildings
3 The Grille d'Honneur and its Terms
4 The moat
5 The *parterres de broderie*
6 The kitchen garden
7 The Bénitier, or font
8 The Petit Canal
9 The Bassins des Tritons
10 The gate to the kitchen garden
11 The Grand Canal
12 The Bassin de la Gerbe
13 The Farnese Hercules
14 The grottoes
15 The Poêle
16 The Bassin des Cascades
17 The Confessional
18 The *miroir*
19 The Grille d'Eau
20 The Bassin de la Couronne
21 The Rond d'Eau

Versailles

Yvelines (p. 248)

How to get there: 15 miles (25 km) west of Paris. Property of the State.

The Park

Park: open every day of the year from 7am (the Grille des Matelots and the Porte Saint-Antoine open at 9am) until sunset (between 5.30pm and 9.30pm, according to the season). Tours of the garden with commentary by lecturers from the Musées nationaux (National Museums service) or the Ecole nationale supérieure du paysage (National School of Landscape Gardening), Tuesday and Sunday at 2.30pm.

Further information: Tel. 00 33 1 30 84 76 18.

Grandes Eaux Musicales, or Fountain Displays with Music: every Sunday until 12 October (inclusive). The Grande Perspective, 11.15am to 11.35am; the Grande Perspective and the bosquets, 3.30pm to 5pm; finale at the Bassin de Neptune, 5.20pm to 5.30pm. No pre-booking required. Enter from the main entrance of the Château, then take the Passage des Princes on the left, or by the Deuxièmes-Cent-Marches, the Grille des Matelots, the Petite-Venise, the Neptune or Dragon gates. Additional performance 15 August.

Further information: Tourist Office, Tel. 00 33 1 39 50 55 12.

Evening entertainments: from June to September. Musical spectacles with fireworks and fountains, re-creating episodes from the history of the Château; at the Bassin de Neptune on Friday and Saturday at 10pm or 10.30pm, according to the month. Access from the Boulevard de la Reine. Reservations, Tel. 00 33 1 44 68 44 68, or Minitel 3615 Versailles, or the Versailles Tourist Office, Tel. 00 33 1 39 50 36 22.

The little train: leaves from the north parterre of the Château. The 35 minute grand tour includes the Bassin de Neptune, the Petit Trianon and the Hameau de la Reine, the Bassin des Trois-Jets (at the northern end of the transverse arm of the Grand Canal), the Petite-Venise (Grand Canal), the Trianon, Neptune, and back to the Château. Commentary in French and English, with seventeenth-century music; every day from March to November. Summer times are from 10am to 6.15pm. Ticket holders may leave and rejoin the train at any point throughout the day. Tel. 00 33 1 39 54 22 00.

Boat hire at the Petite-Venise: at the beginning of the Grand Canal, from 1 March to 1 November. Tel. 00 33 1 39 54 22 00.

Bicycle hire: from 1 February to the end of November, at the Petite-Venise or the Grille de la Reine (bring identification for security purposes). Tel. 00 33 1 39 66 97 66.

Carriage rides: begin at the Petite-Venise by the Grand Canal, weekends in May and June and every day in summer, from 10.30am to 7pm.

The Château

Open: from 2 May to 30 September, 9am to 6.30pm, and from 1 October to 30 April, 9am to 5.30pm. Information: from Action Culturelle, Tel. 00 33 1 30 84 76 18, or Minitel 3615 Versailles. Guided and private tours of up to ten people, Tel. 00 33 1 30 84 76 18.

Series of tours with a particular theme: Saturdays and Sundays at 2pm. Saturdays at 2.30pm, tour about the history of the Château, and of the Picture Collection; Tuesdays at 2.30pm, Life at Court. Information: Tel. 00 33 1 30 84 76 41.

Workshops for children, bookings, Tel. 00 33 1 30 84 76 20.

Introduction to the Organ in the Chapelle Royale: talk followed by a recital, one Saturday each month at 11am. Information: Tel. 00 33 1 30 84 76 41.

The Jeudis Musicaux: recital by the Pages de la Chapelle Royale, Thursdays at 5.30pm. Information: Tel. 00 33 1 30 84 76 18.

The Potager du Roi, or The King's Kitchen Garden

Open: from April to October on Saturday and Sunday, 10am to 6pm. Visits with lecturer 10.30am to 4.30pm. Sale of fruit and vegetables. Shop. Specialized tours with tastings on the first Sunday of each month, between April and October. Presentation and tasting on the subject of 'The flavours of the Potager du Roi' during the third week of October. Entrance at 6, rue Hardy. Information: Tel. 00 33 1 39 24 62 62.

Courses on gardening and garden design for non-professionals: Tel. 00 33 1 39 24 62 26.

1 The Château
2 The Cour d'Honneur
3 The Place d'Armes
4 The Potager du Roi
5 The Pièce d'Eau des Suisses
6 The Gardens
7 The Bosquets du Midi
8 The Bosquets du Nord
9 The Bassin de Neptune
10 The Bassin d'Apollon
11 The Grand Canal
12 The transverse arm of the
   Grand Canal (the Petit Canal)
13 The Petite-Venise
14 The Grand Trianon
15 The Petit Trianon
16 Marie-Antoinette's 'hameau', or
   hamlet
17 The ha-ha *étoile*

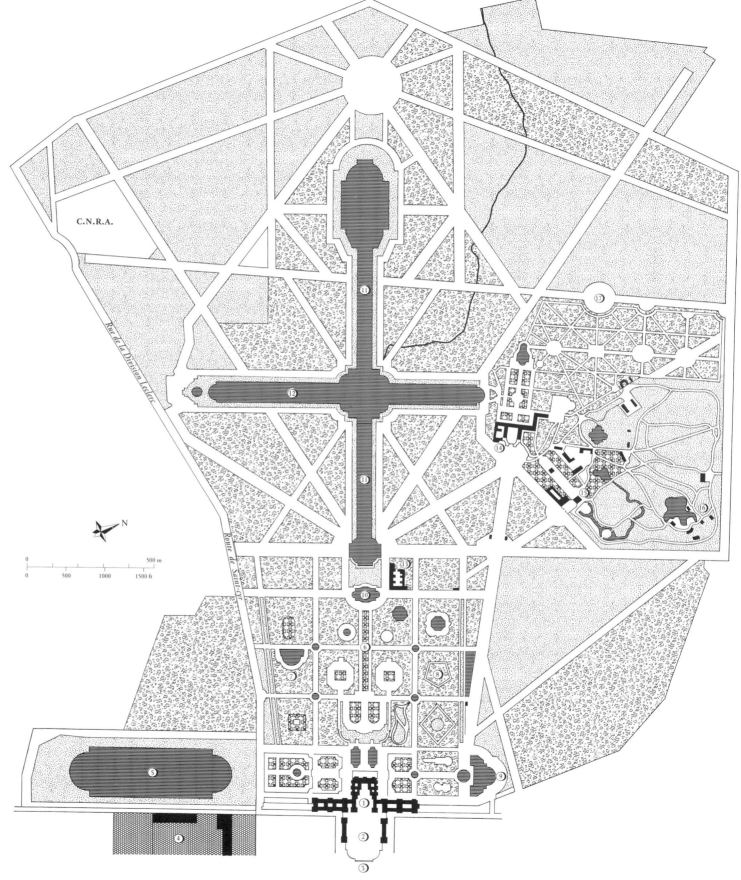

Versailles: General Plan

1 The Grand Trianon
2 The Cour d'Honneur
3 The Grille d'Honneur
4 The Petit Trianon
5 Marie-Antoinette's 'hameau'
6 The Salle des Antiques
7 The Bassin du Plat Fond
8 The Bassin du Fer à Cheval
9 Le Bassin du Rond d'Eau
10 The Jardin Bas
11 The Jardin Haut
12 The Bassin du Réservoir
   du Trèfle
13 Marie-Antoinette's theatre
14 The Pavillon Français
15 The cour d'honneur of
   the Petit Trianon
16 The greenhouses
17 The farm
18 The Grand Lac
19 Châteauneuf
20 The belvedere
21 The Petit Lac

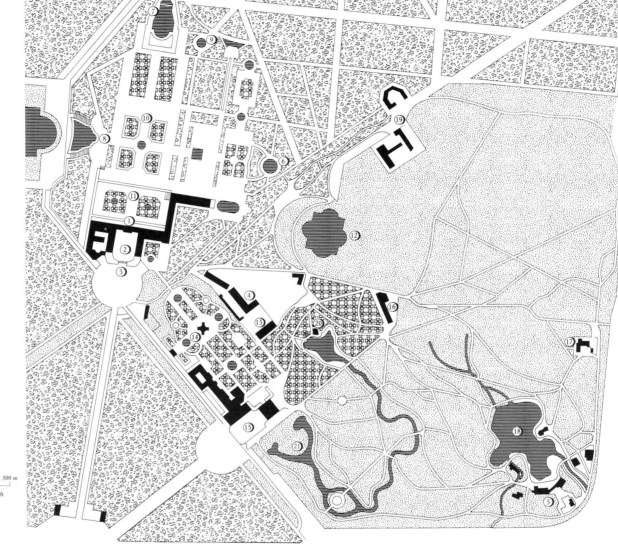

Versailles: the Trianons

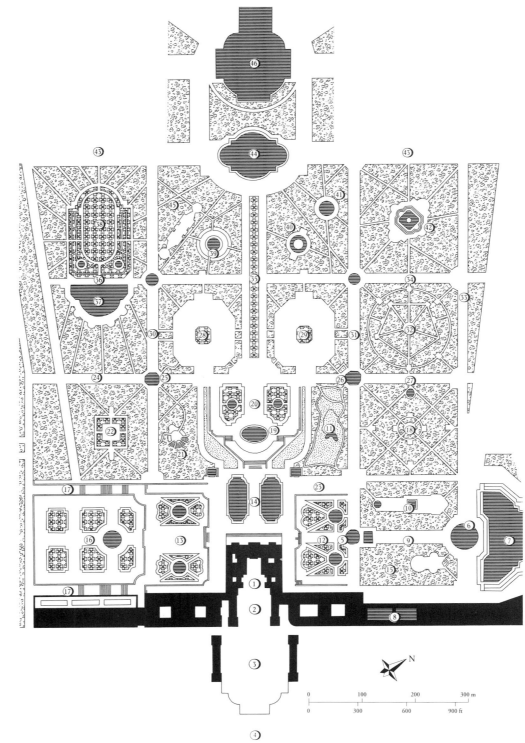

Versailles: the Gardens

N

0   100   200   300 m

0   300   600   900 ft

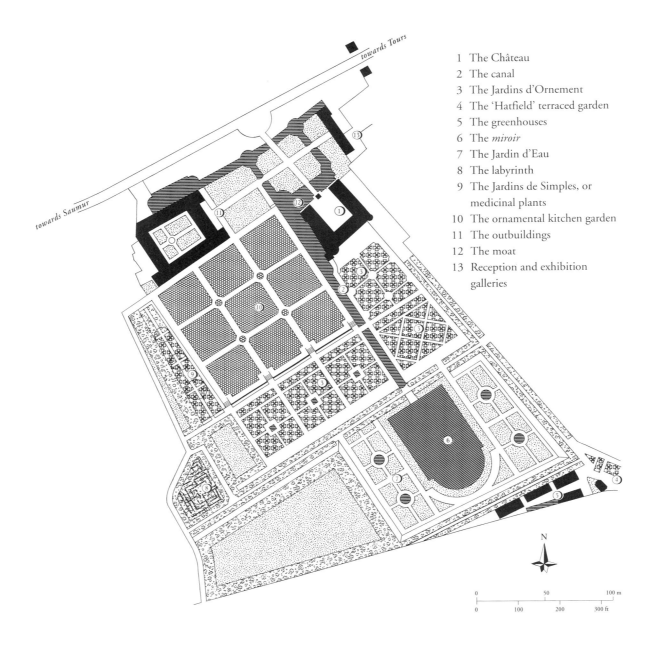

1 The Château
2 The canal
3 The Jardins d'Ornement
4 The 'Hatfield' terraced garden
5 The greenhouses
6 The *miroir*
7 The Jardin d'Eau
8 The labyrinth
9 The Jardins de Simples, or
    medicinal plants
10 The ornamental kitchen garden
11 The outbuildings
12 The moat
13 Reception and exhibition
    galleries

Villandry
Indre-et-Loire (p. 178)

How to get there: Château de Villandry, Villandry, Indre-et-Loire (37); 9 miles (15 km) west of Tours. Privately owned by M. and Mme Carvallo.

Gardens: open all the year round, from 9am to sunset; from 8.30am to 8pm in July and August.

Château: open from mid-February to the weekend of 11 November, 9.30am to 5.30pm; in July and August, 9am to 6.30pm.

Twinned with the gardens at Hatfield House in England.

'Musique et Jardins' summer festival, special Heritage days, and Kitchen Garden days (talks on the techniques and skills of the Villandry gardeners, in September).
Also illuminations, exhibitions, audio-visual displays, and shop.

Further information: Tel. 00 33 2 47 50 02 09. Fax 00 33 2 47 50 12 85.

1 The Château
2 The old wine press
3 The Tour Saint-Nicolas
4 The caretaker's lodge and
   entrance
5 The Fontaine de Jeunesse
6 The Terrasse des
   Marronniers
7 The Maison de Ninon
8 The Italian gardens
9 The Bain de Ninon
10 The windmill

11 The lake
12 The Château du Haut
13 The entrance drive
14 The orangerie
15 The *cour d'honneur*
16 The *boulingrin*

N

| 0 | 100 | 200 m |
| 0 | 200 | 400 | 600 ft |

Villarceaux
Val-d'Oise (p. 204)

How to get there: Domaine de Villarceaux, Chaussy (95); 42 miles (70 km) west of Paris.

Château and gardens: open Saturday and Sunday and public holidays, from the last weekend in April to the last weekend in October, 2pm to 6pm. Guided tours: last one begins at 5pm.

Further information: Tel. 00 33 1 34 67 74 33. Fax 00 33 1 34 67 74 79.

Festival d'Ile-de-France, Tel. 00 33 1 44 94 28 50.

Musical performance days, Tel. 00 33 1 44 94 28 78.

Managed by the Conseil régional d'Ile-de-France. Restoration of gardens by Agence des espaces verts.

Villette
Val-d'Oise (p. 208)

How to get there: Château de Villette, Condécourt, Val-d'Oise (95); 2½ miles (4 km) from Meulan. Privately owned by Mme Robert Gérard.

Château: open on Heritage Days and visits can be arranged by applying in writing.

Further information: Château, Tel. 00 33 1 34 66 34 30; in Paris, Tel. 00 33 1 43 59 79 29.

1 The Château
2 The *cour d'honneur*
3 The lodges
4 The outbuildings
5 The old wine press
6 The *miroirs*
7 The Rivière or *escalier d'eau*
8 The obelisk
9 The orangerie

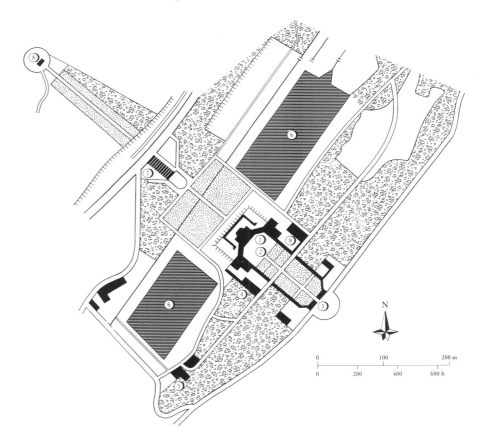

N

| 0 | 100 | 200 m |
| 0 | 200 | 400 | 600 ft |

Classic publications

BOYCEAU DE LA BARAUDERIE, Jacques, *Traité du jardinage selon les raisons de la nature et de l'art*, Paris, 1638

COLONNA, Francesco, *Hypnerotomachia Poliphili*, or *The Dream of Poliphilus*, first French translation 1554, reprinted with notes by Gilles Polizzi, Paris, 1994

DEZALLIER D'ARGENVILLE, Antoine Joseph, *La Théorie et la pratique du jardinage*, Paris, 1709, reprinted 1723, 1732, 1747

DEZALLIER D'ARGENVILLE, Antoine Nicolas, *Voyage pittoresque des environs de Paris ou description des maisons royales, châteaux*, Paris, 1762

ESTIENNE, Charles, *L'Agriculture et la maison rustique*, Paris, 1564 (French translation by J. Liébault from the original Latin publication of 1554)

LA FONTAINE, Jean de, *Elégie pour M. F[ouquet]. Aux nymphes de Vaux*, Paris, 1661

————, *Les Amours de Psyché et de Cupidon*, Paris, 1669

————, *Le Songe de Vaux*, Paris, 1671

————, *Fables*, Paris

LA QUINTINYE, Jean de, *Instruction pour les jardins fruitiers et potagers*, Paris, 1690

LIGNE, Prince de, *Coup d'oeil sur Beloeil*, 1781, reprinted 1922

LOUIS XIV, *Manière de montrer les jardins de Versailles*, S. Hoog (ed.), reprinted Paris, 1992

MOLLET, André, *Le Jardin de plaisir*, Stockholm, 1651

MOLLET, Claude, *Théâtre des plans et jardinages*, Paris, 1652

SAINT-SIMON, duc de, *Mémoires*, Paris, 1983

SAUVAL, Henri, *Histoire et recherches des antiquités de la ville de Paris*, 1724, reprinted 1974

SERRES, Olivier de, *Le Théâtre d'agriculture et mesnages des champs*, Paris, 1600, enlarged 3rd edn 1605, reprinted 1997

VOLTAIRE, François Marie Arouet de, *Oeuvres complètes*, Paris, vol. 34, 1861, p. 98 (Letter to the English architect William Chambers, 1 August 1772)

————, *Mémoires*, Paris, 1993

Modern publications

ADAMS, William Howard, *The French Garden, 1500–1800*, London, 1979

Architecture, jardin, paysage, symposium at the Centre d'Etudes supérieures de la Renaissance de Tours, Picard (*De Architectura*), 1999

BABELON, Jean-Pierre, ed., *Le Château en France*, Paris, 1986

———, *Châteaux de France au siècle de la Renaissance*, Paris, 1989

———, *Chantilly*, London, 1999

BARIDON, Michel, *Les Jardins, paysagistes, jardiniers, poètes*, Paris, 1998

BRUNON, Hervé, ed., *Le Jardin, notre double. Sagesse et déraison*, Paris, 1999 (Mutations no. 184)

CARVALLO, Robert and Henri, and LEROUX, Jean-Baptiste, *Les Jardins de Villandry*, Paris, 1999

Cent jardins à Paris et en Ile-de-France, Délégation à l'Action Artistique de la Ville de Paris, 1992

CHAMBLAS-PLOTON, Mic, and LEROUX, Jean-Baptiste, *Les Plus beaux parcs et jardins de France*, Reader's Digest selection, 1996

———, *Le Potager fleuri de Saint-Jean-de-Beauregard*, Paris, 1996

———, *Lumières de jardins*, Paris, 1998

CHARAGEAT, Marguerite, *L'Art des jardins*, Paris, 1962

CONAN, Michel, *Dictionnaire historique de l'Art des Jardins*, Paris, 1997

CONSTANS, Claire, and BABELON, Jean-Pierre, *Versailles*, Paris, 1998

CORPECHOT, Lucien, *Parcs et jardins de France: les jardins de l'Intelligence*, Paris, 1912, new edn 1937

DAUCHEZ, Chantal, *Les Jardins de Le Nôtre*, Paris, 1994

DEVILLERS, Pierre, *Les Leçons du jardin français*, 1959

DIXON HUNT, John, *L'Art du jardin et son histoire*, Paris, 1996

DUCHÊNE, Achille, *Les Jardins de l'avenir*, Paris, 1935

DUPOUEY, Catherine, and GIVRY, Jacques de, *Le Parc de Sceaux*, 1996

GANAY, Ernest de, *Les Jardins de France et leur décor*, Paris, 1949

———, *André Le Nôtre*, Paris, 1962

GANAY, Ernest de, *Coup d'oeil sur les jardins de France*, Paris, 1993

GRIMAL, Pierre, *Les Jardins romains*, Paris, 1943, reprinted 1969 and 1984

GUILLAUME, Jean, 'Château, jardin, paysage en France du XVe au XVIIe siècle', *Revue de l'art*, no. 124, 1999, pp. 13–30

HARCOURT, duc d', MOSSER, Monique, and BARIDON, Michel, *Le Style Duchêne*, 1998

HAUTECOEUR, Louis, *Les Jardins des dieux et des hommes ou la grande épopée des jardins*, Paris, 1959

HAZLEHURST, Franklin Hamilton, *Jacques Boyceau and the French Formal Garden*, Athens, USA, 1966

————, *Gardens of Illusion: the Genius of André le Nostre*, Nashville, Tennessee, 1980

HOBHOUSE, Penelope, and TAYLOR, Patrick, *The Gardens of Europe*, London, 1990

Les Jardins du Carrousel et des Tuileries, Paris, 1996

LABLAUDE, Pierre-André, *The Gardens of Versailles*, London, 1995

LAIRD, Mark, *The Formal Garden, Tradition of Art and Nature*, London, 1992

MARIAGE, Thierry, *L'Univers de Le Nostre*, Brussels, 1990

MARIE, Alfred, *Les Jardins français classiques des XVIIe et XVIIIe siècles*, Paris, 1949

MORAND, Paul, *Fouquet ou le Soleil offusqué*, 1961

MOSSER, Monique, and TEYSSOT, Georges, eds, *The History of Garden Design: The Western Tradition from the Renaissance to the Present Day*, London, 1990

NIDERST, Alain, *Le Siècle de Louis XIV*, Paris, 1997

RACINE, Michel, *Jardins en France*, Arles, 1999

SAULE, Béatrix, *Versailles Triumphant, une journée du roi Louis XIV*, Paris, 1997

TAPIE, Victor-L., *Le Baroque*, Paris, 1961

THACKER, Christopher, *The History of Gardens*, London, 1979 and 1985

TORSTEN, Olaf Enge, and SCHROER, Carl Friedrich, *L'Architecture des jardins en Europe, 1450–1800*, Cologne, 1994

WEISS, Allen S., *Miroirs de l'infini. Le jardin à la française et la métaphysique au XVIIe siècle*, Paris, 1992

WOODBRIDGE, Kenneth, *Princely Gardens. The Origins and Development of the French Formal Style*, London, 1986

ZUYLEN, Gabrielle Van, *Tous les jardins du monde*, Paris, 1994

————, *The Garden, Visions of Paradise*, London, 1995

ACKNOWLEDGMENTS

MIC CHAMBLAS-PLOTON *and* JEAN-BAPTISTE LEROUX *would like to thank all the private owners of the gardens included in this book, and the curators and administrators of the State properties and royal palaces, who helped them in their work.*

For JEAN-BAPTISTE LEROUX *this book marks the completion of a project inspired by the estate of Courances, and he would particularly like to thank the owners, Monsieur and Madame de Ganay.*

JEAN-BAPTISTE LEROUX*'s photographs are distributed by the Hoa-Qui agency, and were taken using Fuji film.*

The engraving reproduced in 'Pathways of the Sun' shows a gardener's costume by Valck, from the Musée Carnavalet, Paris. © Photothèque des musées de la ville de Paris.

The photographs of Blenheim Palace were reproduced by kind permission of his Grace the Duke of Marlborough.

STARFINDER

THE COMPLETE BEGINNER'S GUIDE TO THE NIGHT SKY

Carole Stott and Giles Sparrow

LONDON, NEW YORK, MELBOURNE,
MUNICH, AND DELHI

DORLING KINDERSLEY
Senior Editor Peter Frances
Senior Art Editor Maxine Pedliham
Project Editors Ben Hoare, Rob Houston
Project Art Editors Helen McTeer, Duncan Turner
Editor Miezan van Zyl
Jacket Design Mark Cavanagh
Jacket Editor Manisha Majithia
Jacket Design Development Manager Sophia MTT
Creative Technical Support Adam Brackenbury, John Goldsmid
Production Controllers Rita Sinha, Elizabeth Warman, Erika Pepe
Producer Mary Slater
Production Editor Phil Sergeant
Pre-Production Producer Rachel Ng
Picture Research Louise Thomas
Managing Editor Angeles Gavira Guerrero
Managing Art Editor Michelle Baxter
Publisher Sarah Larter
Art Director Philip Ormerod
Associate Publishing Director Liz Wheeler
Publishing Director Jonathan Metcalf

DK DELHI
Editors Suchismita Banerjee,
Kingshuk Ghoshal, Rupa Rao, Rohan Sinha
Designer Rajnish Kashyap
DTP Designer Pushpak Tyagi, Dheeraj Arora
DTP Coordinator Sunil Sharma
Art Director Shefali Upadhyay

**PRODUCED FOR DORLING KINDERSLEY BY
SANDS PUBLISHING SOLUTIONS**
Project Editors David & Sylvia Tombesi-Walton
Project Art Editor Simon Murrell

Important notice
Observing the Sun through any kind of optical device can
cause blindness. The author and publishers cannot accept
any responsibility for readers who ignore this advice.

This edition published in 2013
First published in Great Britain in 2007 by
Dorling Kindersley Limited
80 Strand, London WC2R 0RL
A Penguin Company

195571 – 001– Oct/2013
2 4 6 8 10 9 7 5 3 1

A CIP catalogue record for this book
is available from the British Library.

ISBN: 978-1-4093-3506-1

Colour reproduction by GRB, London
Printed and bound in China by Leo Paper Products

See our complete catalogue at
www.dk.com

Contents

Star trails
As the Earth rotates, the position of bright stars can be traced in the sky using a long exposure on a camera. In the foreground is the dome of the Canada–France–Hawaii Telescope on the summit of Mauna Kea, Hawaii.-

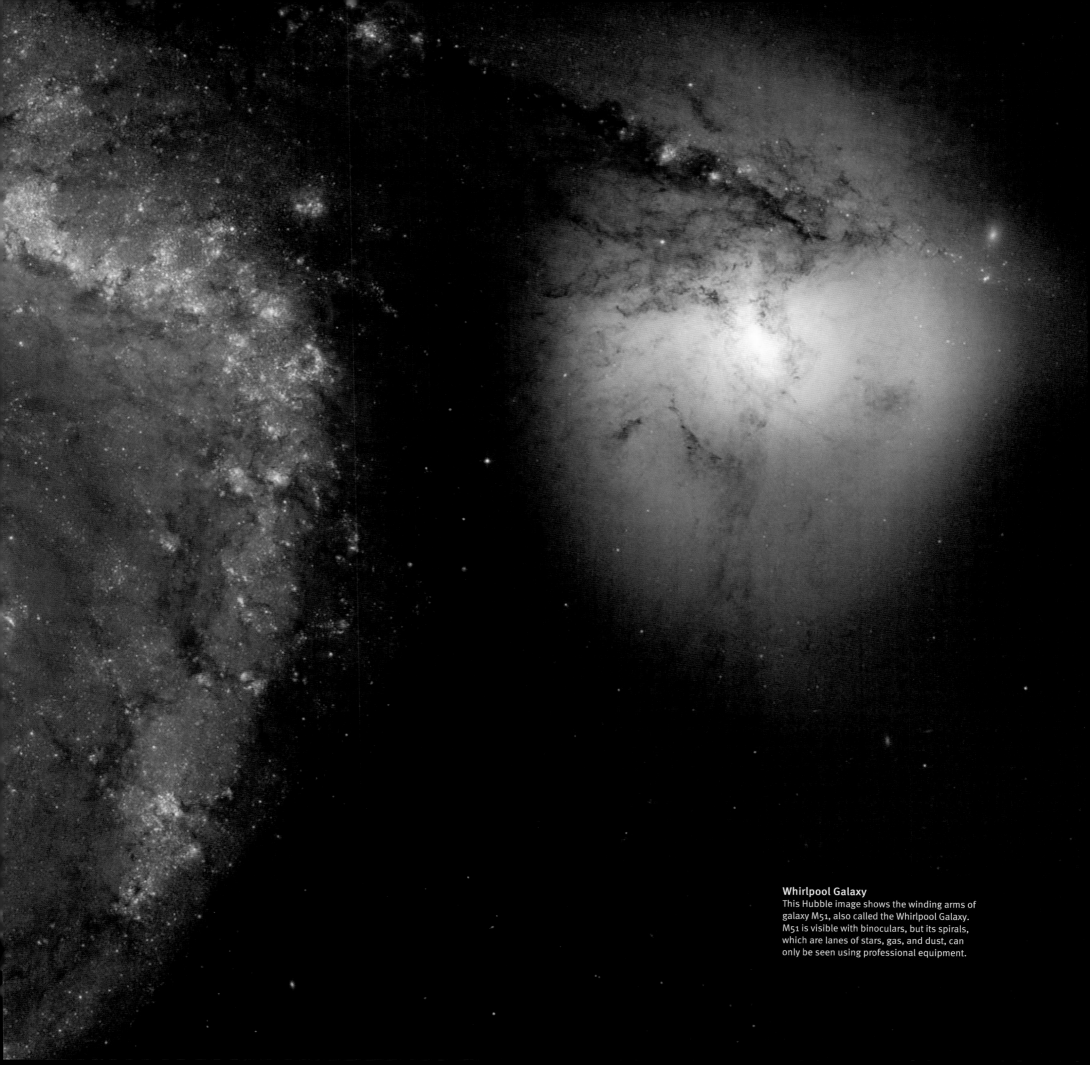

Whirlpool Galaxy
This Hubble image shows the winding arms of galaxy M51, also called the Whirlpool Galaxy. M51 is visible with binoculars, but its spirals, which are lanes of stars, gas, and dust, can only be seen using professional equipment.

Northern lights
The Aurora Borealis, also known as the northern lights, is the result of solar particles colliding with gases in the Earth's atmosphere. The levels of oxygen and nitrogen in the air determine the colour of this spectacular light show.

Southern lights
This image, taken from the space shuttle
Discovery, shows the Aurora Australis like
a crown of light encircling the South Pole.
The Aurora Australis is not as easily viewed
as the Aurora Borealis, as it is only visible
in some of the remotest parts of the world.

Amateur astrophotography
An amateur astrophotographer, working from his garden in Queensland, Australia, took this image of the Horsehead Nebula. The dark cloud that appears to be shaped like a horse's head is mostly dust.

Meteor shower
Streaks of light created by meteors, also called shooting stars, can be seen during the annual Leonid meteor showers. Leonids are associated with the constellation Leo, from where the meteors appear to originate.

Comet tails
The two tails of comet Hale-Bopp can clearly be seen in this image. The whitish tail is dust, while the blue is the ion tail. Due to its large size, Hale–Bopp was one of the brightest comets of the 20th century.

Lunar eclipse
This composite photo shows multiple
exposures taken during a lunar eclipse.
A lunar eclipse only occurs during a full
Moon and is the result of the Moon passing
through the Earth's shadow.

Finding your way

Each fresh pair of eyes looking at the night sky sees a confusion of stars. The myriad pinpoints of light all seem the same and together appear to form a starry sphere around Earth. This imaginary sphere is a key to finding your way about the sky. Soon, you'll discover that brighter stars make patterns, and these act as signposts. They guide us as our view of the Universe changes, and they form a starry backdrop to the planets as they make their stately progress across the sky. Once recognized in this way, the Universe will unfold before your eyes.

New stars
A cluster of newborn stars shines brightly in the centre of one of the most dynamic star-forming regions known. The whole area, known as N66, is in the Small Magellanic Cloud, a companion galaxy to our own Milky Way.

Eye in the sky
The planets, stars, and galaxies have been revealed to us by telescopes and space probes. The Hubble Space Telescope has been a constant eye on the Universe since 1990.

To the edge of the visible Universe
The Universe is here separated into five steps, moving farther away from our home planet. From Earth, we move to the Moon, then the Solar System, the Milky Way, and the Local Group of galaxies. Beyond this, however deep we look into space we find more galaxies.

Looking into space

The Universe is a fascinating place brimming over with countless worlds to explore, but the quantity and diversity of the worlds make exploration seem an impossible goal. Nevertheless, there is order within the Universe. Objects are grouped into types, and a grasp of the scale of the Universe adds structure and form. With this basic understanding, it is possible to begin an enthralling journey of discovery.

◼ WINDOW ON THE UNIVERSE

The sky of our home planet, Earth, is our window on the Universe. As we look away out into space, we see some of its objects. In the daytime, there is just one large object, the Sun. It is our local star, and its brilliance fills the sky.

On a cloud-free night, the dark sky is full of starry pinpoints of light. With the naked eye we can see more than 2,000 of these objects, and with binoculars the number rises to over 40,000. Looking carefully, we can discern that some are not bright points of light but disc-shaped planets, while the fuzzy patches we see can be galaxies full of stars.

The objects in the Universe are so remote that it is difficult to compare their sizes and distances. They all appear to be an equal distance from Earth. In reality, though, they are not only at varying distances from us, they are also vastly different distances from each other.

Our "neighbourhood" includes the Sun, Moon, and planets. Beyond is the realm of the stars, the Milky Way Galaxy. And outside of this are more galaxies overflowing with stars.

Earth: our home planet
A blue ball of rock 12,756km (7,926 miles) across, Earth is the only place in the Universe known to have life; and uniquely, much of it is covered by liquid water. As Earth spins and moves in space, we are able to look out to different parts of the Universe.

The Moon
Closest to Earth, and a familiar feature of its sky, is the Moon. At its brightest, it is the next brightest object in our sky after the Sun. This ball of rock accompanies Earth in space, travelling around us every 27.3 days. It is a dry, dead world covered in impact craters formed billions of years ago. The Moon is the only place that man has walked apart from Earth.

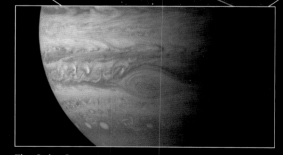

The Solar System
Earth and the Moon are part of the Solar System (above top), which is a volume of space that includes billions of objects. The central, most massive object is the Sun, and all other members of the system travel around it. Next biggest are the eight planets, and the giant of these is Jupiter (above). Comets and asteroids are more numerous but smaller.

MEASURING DISTANCE

The Universe is so vast that the units of measurement used on Earth, such as the kilometre, quickly become inadequate. They are used to describe the size of the planets within the Solar System, as well as distances between them, but beyond the Solar System, the unit commonly used is the light year (ly). One light year is 9.46 trillion (million million) km (5.88 trillion miles) and is the distance that light travels in a year. Light moves at 299,792km per second (186,282 miles per second), and nothing in the Universe travels faster. The Andromeda Galaxy is said to be 2.5 million light years away, because it takes that length of time for its light to reach us; this means we are seeing the galaxy as it was 2.5 million years ago. By contrast, the Sun's light takes just eight and a half minutes to reach Earth. In the chart below, the first division represents 10,000km (6,200 miles). Each further division marks a 10x increase in scale on the previous one.

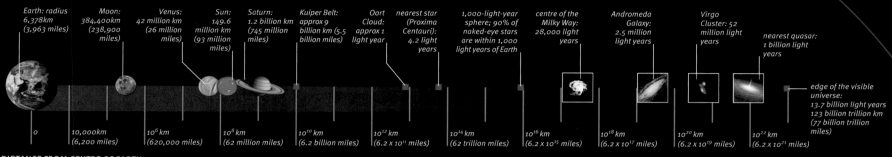

Earth: radius 6,378km (3,963 miles)

Moon: 384,400km (238,900 miles)

Venus: 42 million km (26 million miles)

Sun: 149.6 million km (93 million miles)

Saturn: 1.2 billion km (745 million miles)

Kuiper Belt: approx 9 billion km (5.5 billion miles)

Oort Cloud: approx 1 light year

nearest star (Proxima Centauri): 4.2 light years

1,000-light-year sphere; 90% of naked-eye stars are within 1,000 light years of Earth

centre of the Milky Way: 28,000 light years

Andromeda Galaxy: 2.5 million light years

Virgo Cluster: 52 million light years

nearest quasar: 1 billion light years

edge of the visible universe: 13.7 billion light years 123 billion trillion km (77 billion trillion miles)

0 | 10,000km (6,200 miles) | 10^6 km (620,000 miles) | 10^8 km (62 million miles) | 10^{10} km (6.2 billion miles) | 10^{12} km (6.2 x 10^{11} miles) | 10^{14} km (62 trillion miles) | 10^{16} km (6.2 x 10^{15} miles) | 10^{18} km (6.2 x 10^{17} miles) | 10^{20} km (6.2 x 10^{19} miles) | 10^{22} km (6.2 x 10^{21} miles)

DISTANCE FROM CENTRE OF EARTH

Solar System is in one of Milky Way's arms of stars

most Local Group galaxies are small and elliptical in shape

about 10,000 galaxies appear in this image by the Hubble Space Telescope

The Milky Way Galaxy
The Sun is just one of billions of stars in the Milky Way Galaxy (above top). The stars are in a disc shape, with a concentration of stars in the centre, and "arms" of stars spiralling out from it. All the stars we see in the night sky are in the Milky Way, along with clusters of stars (above) and giant clouds of gas and dust where new stars form.

The Local Group of galaxies
The Milky Way is one of a group of more than 40 galaxies that exist together in space. They are collectively called the Local Group (above top). The Milky Way and the Andromeda Galaxy (above) dominate the group. The Andromeda is about 2.5 times as wide as the Milky Way and is the most distant object normally visible to the naked eye.

Universe of galaxies
In whatever direction we look and however deep we peer into space, there are galaxies (above top) – an estimated 100–125 billion of them. They exist in clusters (above) that are strung together into superclusters, which are the biggest structures in the Universe. Prominent among these are the Hercules and Centaurus superclusters.

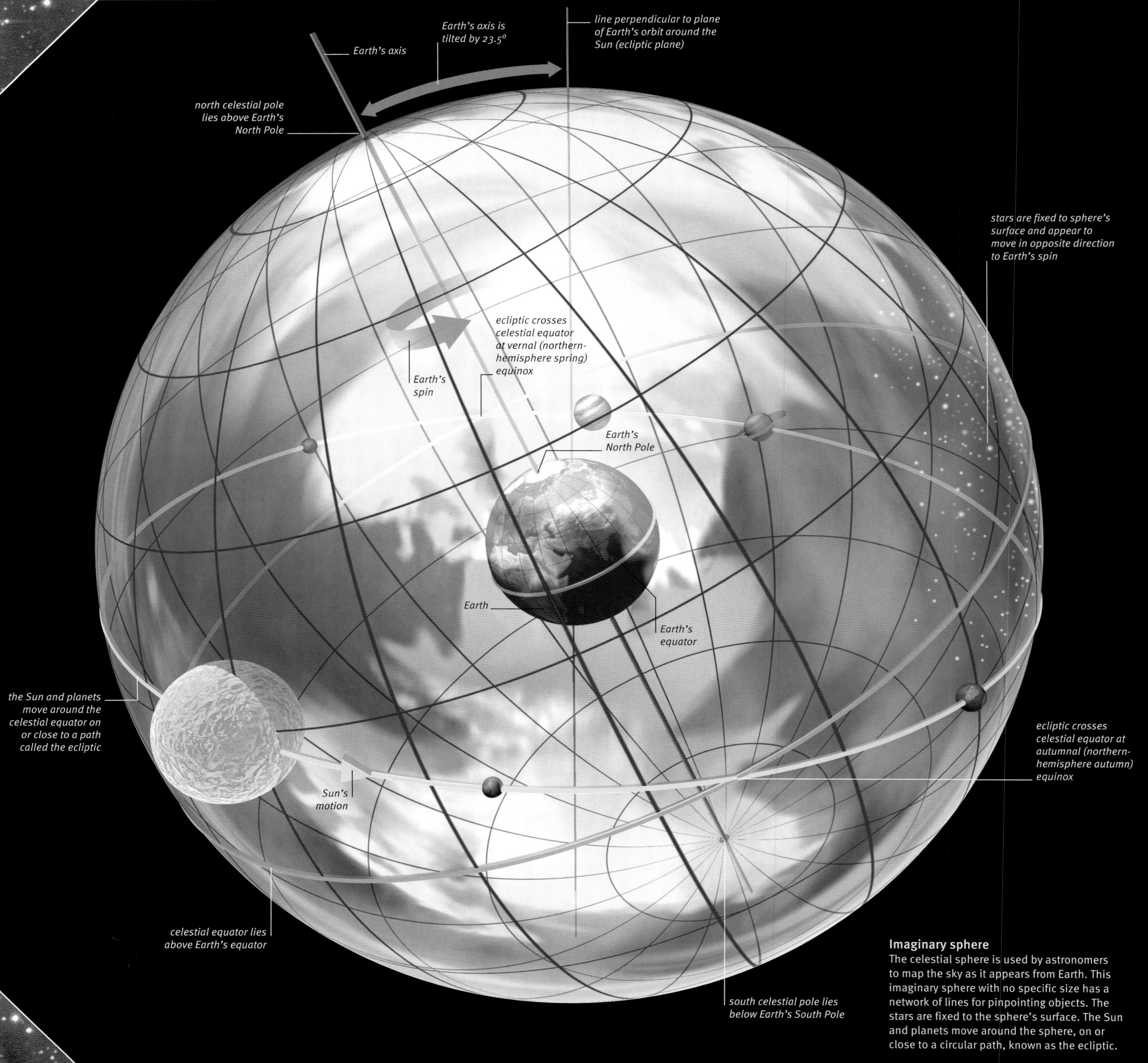

Earth's axis

Earth's axis is tilted by 23.5°

line perpendicular to plane of Earth's orbit around the Sun (ecliptic plane)

north celestial pole lies above Earth's North Pole

stars are fixed to sphere's surface and appear to move in opposite direction to Earth's spin

ecliptic crosses celestial equator at vernal (northern-hemisphere spring) equinox

Earth's spin

Earth's North Pole

Earth

Earth's equator

the Sun and planets move around the celestial equator on or close to a path called the ecliptic

ecliptic crosses celestial equator at autumnal (northern-hemisphere autumn) equinox

Sun's motion

celestial equator lies above Earth's equator

south celestial pole lies below Earth's South Pole

Imaginary sphere
The celestial sphere is used by astronomers to map the sky as it appears from Earth. This imaginary sphere with no specific size has a network of lines for pinpointing objects. The stars are fixed to the sphere's surface. The Sun and planets move around the sphere, on or close to a circular path, known as the ecliptic.

The starry sphere

Looking out from Earth we see a Universe full of stars. The stars are so far away that they all appear to be the same distance from us. As they move across the sky, they do so together, keeping their relative positions. The stars appear to be fixed to the inside of a giant globe enveloping Earth. Although it is a distortion of reality, this imaginary globe, called the celestial sphere, is a useful astronomical tool.

THE CELESTIAL SPHERE

The celestial sphere is important for anyone who wants to become familiar with the night sky. It is used by all observers, from beginners to experienced astronomers. It helps in understanding how location and time and date of observation determine what is in the sky. The sphere's network of lines pinpoints the positions of stars, and helps when navigating around the sky. The celestial equator, concentric with Earth's equator, divides the sphere into the northern- and southern-hemisphere sky. North and south celestial poles are above Earth's poles.

The distant stars are fixed on the sphere, and as Earth spins they appear to revolve around the poles. The much closer Sun and planets move against the backdrop of fixed stars. The Sun's path, the ecliptic, crosses the celestial equator at two points, known as the equinoxes. The Moon and planets follow paths close to the ecliptic.

YOUR VIEW OF THE CELESTIAL SPHERE

An observer's latitude determines which portion of the celestial sphere they see. Most people see all of one celestial hemisphere and part of the other, but not all of this is visible at once. As Earth makes its daily spin and yearly orbit around the Sun, new regions of the sphere come into view.

KEY TO SPHERES

— Horizon
● Observer

▨ Stars always visible
▨ Stars visible at some time
▨ Stars never visible

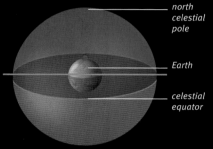

north celestial pole
Earth
celestial equator

View from the North Pole
To an observer based at Earth's North Pole, only the stars in the northern half of the celestial sphere are visible.

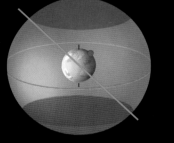

View from mid-latitudes
Stars close to the observer's celestial pole are always visible. Those further from the pole are seen as Earth spins and orbits.

View from the equator
All parts of the celestial sphere are visible. The celestial equator is overhead, and the celestial poles are on opposite horizons.

CHANGING VIEW

From any one location on Earth it is possible to see only part of the celestial sphere at a particular time. This view changes during the evening as the Earth spins. Earth turns from west to east, and so the stars move across the sky from east to west. The view also changes over the course of a year (see pp.22–23). For instance, stars that are in the winter daytime sky can be seen in the evening sky later in the year when the Sun has moved along the ecliptic and its starry backdrop has changed.

An observer's location determines not only which part of the celestial sphere is visible, but also how the stars move across the sky. Except at the equator, observers will always have part of the sky around the celestial pole above the horizon. Stars circle around the pole; the farther you are from the pole, the more circumpolar stars you will see. The position of the celestial pole in your sky corresponds to your latitude on Earth. For instance, for observers at 40°N, the north celestial pole is located 40° above their northern horizon.

ORION FROM USA

ORION FROM JAPAN

The same sky
Observers at the same latitude but on opposite sides of the world (on different longitudes) see the same sky. The constellation of Orion is clearly visible to observers in Arizona, USA, at 11pm (left). Several hours later, once Earth has turned, the same view of Orion is seen at 11pm in Tokyo, Japan (right).

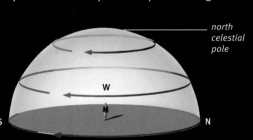

north celestial pole

Motion at the poles
At the North Pole, the stars circle overhead, around the north celestial pole. They circle anticlockwise. At the South Pole, the stars circle in the opposite direction, clockwise

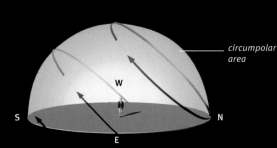

circumpolar area

Motion at mid-latitudes
At mid-latitudes, the stars rise above the eastern horizon, cross the sky obliquely, and set below the opposite, western horizon. Also, some circumpolar stars are always in the sky

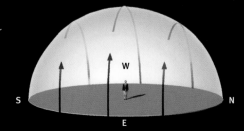

Motion at the equator
From the equator, stars are seen to rise vertically from the eastern horizon, then move across the sky over the observer's head, before setting in the west

The changing sky

Our view into the Universe is constantly changing. As Earth makes its daily spin, the Sun leaves the sky, darkness falls, and the distant stars come into view. Also, through the course of a year, the starry sky seen from a fixed point on Earth will change. The Sun, Moon, and planets follow their paths against the background of these stars. Particular star patterns – the zodiac constellations – help us locate them and track their progress.

■ YOUR CHANGING VIEW

One side of Earth is always facing the Sun, which lights up the daytime sky, while the other is facing the night-time stars. Earth spins around on its axis, and as it makes its daily spin, an observer at a fixed location is facing towards both the Sun and the stars in any 24-hour period.

WHY THE VIEW ALTERS

If Earth did not move along its path around the Sun, it would alternately face the Sun and the same piece of starry sky. But because Earth travels around the Sun, it faces progressively different stars at the same time on successive nights during the course of a year. Although this change is hardly noticeable from night to night, as the weeks stretch

into months, the difference in the sky becomes more apparent. Observers in the northern hemisphere looking south and those in the southern hemisphere looking north will each see new constellations (see pp.24–25) with the changing seasons. By contrast, the northern sky for the northern-hemisphere observers and the southern sky for the southern-hemisphere observers undergo less change. These views contain the appropriate celestial pole, and the circumpolar stars that move around it are always in view.

As Earth makes its orbit, the starry backdrop to the Sun also changes. Like the Moon and planets, the Sun is seen against the zodiac band of sky (see facing page). Northern-hemisphere observers will see this stretching across the sky to their south, and southern observers see it in the sky to their north.

1 APRIL, 8PM

8 APRIL, 8PM

15 APRIL, 8PM

Night-time sky change
With the exception of those at the North and South Poles, observers see different stars in their sky during the course of a year. An observer at 50°N sees the constellation of Orion lower and lower in the sky as April progresses. By the end of the month, it has almost disappeared below the horizon.

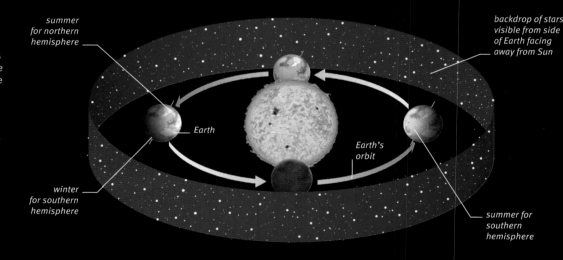

Seasonal sky change
One side of Earth faces the Sun, while the other side faces the stars. If Earth was fixed in space, it would face the Sun and the same piece of starry sky alternately as it makes its daily spin. But Earth is not fixed: it orbits the Sun. As a result, the stars we see in the summer months are different from those we see in winter.

summer for northern hemisphere

winter for southern hemisphere

Earth

Earth's orbit

backdrop of stars visible from side of Earth facing away from Sun

summer for southern hemisphere

6 AUGUST

7 AUGUST

11 AUGUST

Daytime sky change
As Earth makes its yearly orbit around the Sun, the position at which the Sun rises above the eastern horizon and sets below the western horizon changes. The three images above record sunset at a location 50°N on different days in August. The Sun sets farther and farther towards the south as the summer progresses.

DIVIDING THE SKY

At first glance, stars seem like indistinguishable pinpoints of light randomly scattered across the sky. Quite quickly, however, it is noticeable that some stars are brighter than others, and when these are linked together, recognizable patterns emerge. Astronomers have been using such patterns, the constellations (see pp.24-25), for about 4,000 years to navigate around the night sky. Today, the sky surrounding Earth is divided into 88 internationally recognized constellations, just over half of which depict mythological people and creatures. The constellation Orion depicts the eponymous Greek hunter; the constellation Scorpius is the scorpion that killed him. They range in size and complexity. Hydra, the water snake is the largest, and Crux, the southern cross, the smallest.

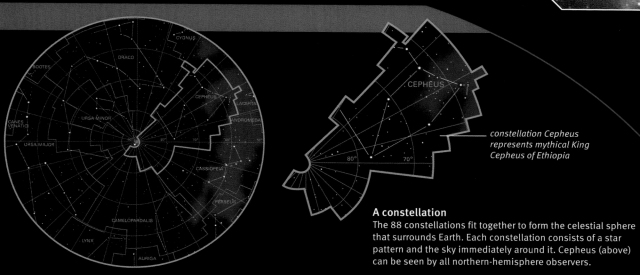

constellation Cepheus represents mythical King Cepheus of Ethiopia

A constellation
The 88 constellations fit together to form the celestial sphere that surrounds Earth. Each constellation consists of a star pattern and the sky immediately around it. Cepheus (above) can be seen by all northern-hemisphere observers.

STARRY BACKDROP

Some of the first stars to be grouped into recognizable patterns were those that form the background to the Sun as it moves across the sky. The Sun's path against the backdrop of stars is called the ecliptic. And the band of sky centred on the ecliptic is known as the zodiac.

CIRCLE OF ANIMALS

The name zodiac comes from the Greek for animal, and it refers to the patterns made by the stars within this band of sky. With the exception of Libra, which is a set of scales, the traditional zodiac is a group of creatures. The zodiac constellations are, in order around the sky: Aries, Taurus, Gemini, Cancer, Leo, Virgo, Libra, Scorpius, Sagittarius, Capricornus, Aquarius, and Pisces.

The Sun completes one circuit of its ecliptic each year. It takes approximately one month to move through each of the zodiac constellations. However, this is not the full picture. Traditionally, the zodiac is described as consisting of 12 constellations. There is, though, a 13th, Ophiuchus, and the Sun spends more time crossing this constellation than it does traversing its neighbour Scorpius.

The zodiac band of sky also forms the starry backdrop to the planets and the Moon. Their paths take them close to the ecliptic – sometimes to its north, and sometimes to its south.

The zodiac
The band of the celestial sphere that forms the backdrop to the movement of the Sun, Moon, and planets is called the zodiac. It is centred on the ecliptic, the path that the Sun traces out month by month as the Earth orbits around it. There are 13 constellations in the zodiac: the 12 traditional zodiacal constellations and Ophiuchus.

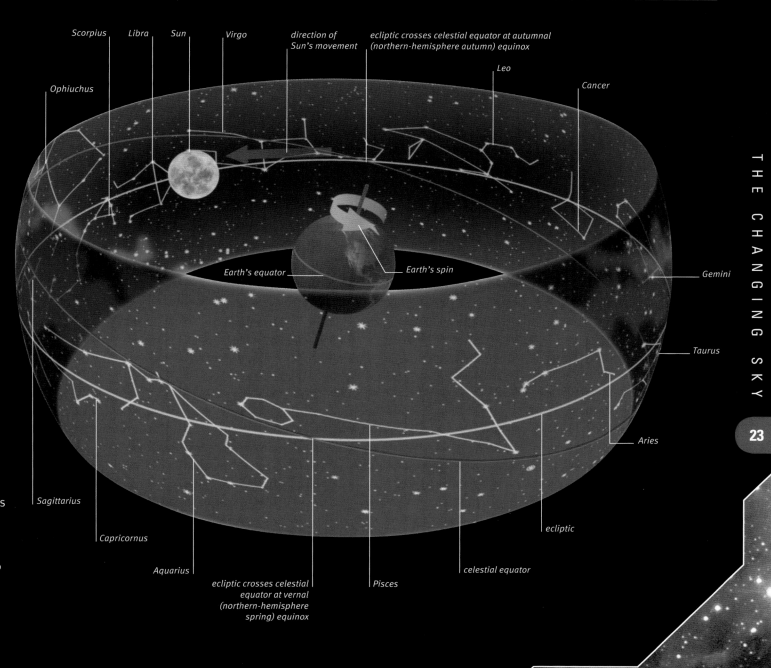

Scorpius Libra Sun Virgo direction of Sun's movement ecliptic crosses celestial equator at autumnal (northern-hemisphere autumn) equinox

Ophiuchus

Leo

Cancer

Earth's equator Earth's spin

Gemini

Taurus

Aries

ecliptic

Sagittarius

Capricornus

celestial equator

Aquarius ecliptic crosses celestial equator at vernal (northern-hemisphere spring) equinox Pisces

A piece of sky

The celestial sphere is divided into areas called constellations, each of which contains a figure produced by joining the brightest stars in dot-to-dot fashion. These figures are purely products of the human imagination – the stars have no real relationship to one another in space. The stars, as well as other objects within a constellation, are identified by name or number according to an agreed system of rules.

Sirius
The brightest night-time star of all is Sirius (below centre), in the constellation Canis Major. Its magnitude is –1.44. At 8.6 light years away, it is also one of the closest stars to us. It gives out about 20 times more light than the Sun.

■ BRIGHTNESS

It is easy to observe that the stars in the sky vary in brightness. The first star-watchers soon realized this, and so they classed the stars according to their brightness level. Their system was later formalized to produce what is known as the apparent-magnitude scale used today.

Apparent magnitude is an indication of how bright a star appears when viewed from Earth. This is not the same as the star's real brightness, its luminosity. Each star is given a number, known as its magnitude to indicate its brightness: the smaller the number, the brighter the star. The brightest stars have negative magnitude values.

The apparent-magnitude scale is also used for other objects – the full Moon is magnitude –12.5, for example. The brightness of a planet varies depending on its distance from the Sun and Earth; at its brightest, Venus measures –4.7.

TEN BRIGHTEST NIGHT-SKY STARS

The stars listed below are in order of brightness. Only the four brightest have negative values, and as the magnitude number increases, the star becomes fainter. All stars of magnitude 6 and brighter are visible with the naked eye, so each of these stars is easily seen.

1. **Sirius**
   Canis Major, –1.44
2. **Canopus**
   Carina, –0.62
3. **Rigil Kentaurus**
   Centaurus, –0.28
4. **Arcturus**
   Boötes, –0.05
5. **Vega**
   Lyra, 0.03
6. **Capella**
   Auriga, 0.08
7. **Rigel**
   Orion, 0.18
8. **Procyon**
   Canis Minor, 0.40
9. **Achernar**
   Eridanus, 0.45
10. **Betelgeuse**
    Orion, 0.45

■ RELATIVE DISTANCE

The stars on the celestial sphere all appear to be at the same distance from Earth, but the reality is quite different. The stars are scattered through space with vast expanses between them. Each star is typically 7 light years away from its nearest neighbour. And they are all so far from us that they appear to be pinpoints of light rather than huge globes.

The distance of the naked-eye stars we see, for instance, varies hugely. As we look at them, we see stars that are just a few light years from us and others that are thousands of light years away. This means that the star patterns of the constellations are illusions. They are a two-dimensional view of stars within a three-dimensional volume of space. The stars are not related at all, but far apart. Very often they are farther from each other than they are from Earth.

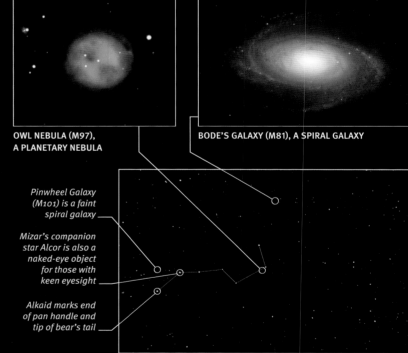

OWL NEBULA (M97), A PLANETARY NEBULA

BODE'S GALAXY (M81), A SPIRAL GALAXY

Pinwheel Galaxy (M101) is a faint spiral galaxy

Mizar's companion star Alcor is also a naked-eye object for those with keen eyesight

Alkaid marks end of pan handle and tip of bear's tail

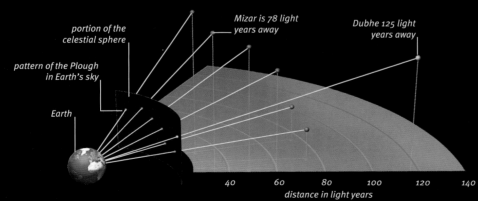

portion of the celestial sphere

pattern of the Plough in Earth's sky

Earth

Mizar is 78 light years away

Dubhe 125 light years away

40   60   80   100   120   140
distance in light years

Line-of-sight effect
The stars in the constellation Ursa Major trace out the shape of a bear in Earth's sky. The stars that form the tail and rump of the bear are known as the Plough, or Big Dipper. The stars are at vastly different distances from Earth, and seen from elsewhere in space, they would make a totally different pattern.

The Plough
Also known as the Big Dipper, the Plough (left of centre) consists of seven bright stars. Three stars form the handle, and four more the basin of a saucepan in profile. Once found, the shape can be used as a guide to other objects. The two brightest stars are known as the pointers, because they point the way to the Pole Star, Polaris.

PATTERNS IN THE SKY

Astronomers worldwide use not only the same set of 88 constellations, but also the same ways of locating and identifying objects within them.

Naming and numbering

Individual stars may be identified by names, numbers, or letters. The brightest stars in a constellation have a Greek letter: alpha (α) is usually the brightest; the next brightest, beta (β); and so on. Once the Greek alphabet is used up, small Roman letters (a,b,c, etc.) are allocated.

Many of the bright stars have names, a large number of which are Arabic in origin. The vast majority, however, are unnamed. Fainter stars, although often within naked-eye visibility, have a number allocated according to their position within the constellation. Stellar objects such as star clusters, nebulae, and galaxies have a catalogue number from one of the many volumes that list such objects. NGC numbers, for example, come from the New General Catalogue.

Asterisms

Some stars make a distinctive pattern in the sky but are not a constellation; they are a separate pattern within a constellation, or are made up of stars from more than one constellation. Such a pattern is known as an asterism. The Plough, or Big Dipper, possibly the best-known pattern in the northern-hemisphere sky, is a prime example. Four stars that form the lower torso of Hercules are known as the Keystone; and the head, neck, and shoulders of Leo is known as the Sickle.

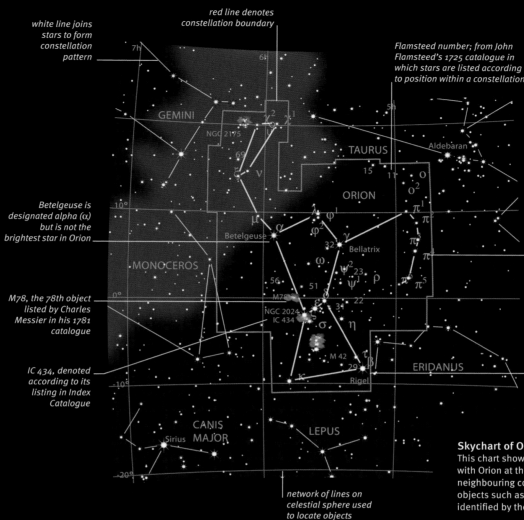

white line joins stars to form constellation pattern

red line denotes constellation boundary

Flamsteed number; from John Flamsteed's 1725 catalogue in which stars are listed according to position within a constellation

Betelgeuse is designated alpha (α) but is not the brightest star in Orion

M78, the 78th object listed by Charles Messier in his 1781 catalogue

IC 434, denoted according to its listing in Index Catalogue

Greek letter used in Bayer system; superscript numbers are used to distinguish stars assigned the same letter

Rigel is the brightest star in Orion but is designated beta (β). Its name derives from Arabic for foot, which this star represents

network of lines on celestial sphere used to locate objects

Skychart of Orion
This chart shows a portion of the celestial sphere with Orion at the centre, surrounded by its neighbouring constellations. Stars and stellar objects such as clusters, nebulae, and galaxies are identified by their own name, letter, or number.

Orion in the night sky
One of the most easily seen constellations in the night sky, Orion is an excellent target for novice star-watchers. Its simple, distinctive shape traces the figure of the mythical hunter. It is seen in both the northern- and southern-hemisphere skies.

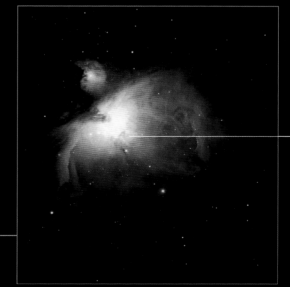

at the centre of the Orion Nebula is a small cluster of stars called the Trapezium; a small telescope shows it as four stars, while a large one reveals six

Orion's belt and sword
One of Orion's shoulders is marked by the red supergiant Betelgeuse (top left), while blue supergiant Rigel (lower right) is the constellation's brightest star. Three stars form the belt, from which hangs a sword of stars and glowing gas and dust.

Orion Nebula
The Orion Nebula, or M42, is the brightest nebula in the night sky. It is an enormous star-forming cloud of gas and dust some 30 light years across and 1,500 light years away. It is illuminated by newly born stars deep within.

Your view of the Solar System

The nearest celestial objects to Earth are members of the Solar System – a group of eight planets and smaller objects that orbit the Sun. The planets and our Moon emit no light of their own but shine by reflecting sunlight. From Earth we can see five of these planets with relative ease. As the planets, Moon, and Earth travel around the Sun, our view changes, at times creating spectacular sights for us on Earth.

Moon and Venus
The planets and the Moon all move within the zodiac band of constellations and so can often be viewed together. Here, the Moon and Venus are seen in the early evening sky.

■ VIEWING THE PLANETS

Of the eight planets, Earth is the third in distance from the Sun. Mercury and Venus are closer and, for this reason, are called the inferior planets. The five other planets – Mars, Jupiter, Saturn, Uranus, and Neptune – are all farther away than Earth and are called the superior planets. The five visible to the naked eye are Mercury, Venus, Mars, Jupiter, and Saturn, and their existence has been known of since humans first looked into space. Uranus's brightness suggests that it

is just within the range of naked-eye visibility, but it is difficult to see. Uranus was only discovered in 1781, and then through a telescope. Neptune, farthest from the Sun, is too faint to see with the naked eye.

All eight planets follow paths around the Sun, and one complete circuit of the Sun is called an orbit. As each planet orbits, and time passes, the positions of the planets relative to Earth change. The view that we have from Earth of a particular planet depends on these relative positions. For instance, when a planet is on the opposite side of the Sun to Earth, it is lost from view. The planet is still present in the daytime sky, but it is invisible because it is drowned out by the glare of the Sun. For this reason, Mercury and Venus are also invisible when situated between the Sun and Earth. Specific juxtapositions of the Earth, the Sun, and the planets have names. These act as a quick indicator of whether or not a planet is visible. They can also signify the phase, brightness, size, and time of visibility of a planet.

The close orbits of Mercury and Venus to the Sun mean that these two planets are never far from the Sun in the sky. They are best seen when at locations that are known as greatest elongation. At this point, they are at their maximum angle to the east or west of the Sun. The superior planets are best seen at opposition, when they are on the opposite side of the Earth from the Sun. In this position, a planet is close to Earth and appears particularly large and bright. At opposition, a planet is visible all night long. It is found to the south at midnight by observers in the northern hemisphere, and to the north at midnight by observers in the southern hemisphere.

RETROGRADE MOTION

The planets make their stately progress against the starry backdrop from west to east. However, planets are occasionally seen to move in the opposite direction, from east to west, with their paths seeming to loop or zigzag across the sky. This backwards movement, known as retrograde motion, is nothing more than an illusion created by our viewpoint on Earth. It is achieved when the faster-moving planet Earth overtakes a

slower-moving superior planet, such as Mars. As Earth moves along its orbit, the superior planet is seen from a different perspective. Superior planets go into retrograde motion around the time of opposition.

Planetary positions
As Earth and the seven other planets orbit the Sun, their relative positions change. The best time to see Mercury and Venus is when they are at maximum elongation; Mars, Jupiter, and Saturn are best seen at opposition. None of the planets is visible at inferior and superior conjunction.

superior conjunction of superior planet

superior conjunction of inferior planet; planet is in full phase and is not visible from Earth

greatest western elongation: planet appears as crescent in morning sky

greatest eastern elongation: planet appears as crescent in evening sky

inferior planet's orbit

inferior conjunction; inferior planet is between Earth and Sun in its new phase and is not visible from Earth

Earth

superior planet's orbit

opposition of superior planet

Mars looping the loop
The retrograde, or backwards, movement of a planet across Earth's sky is an illusion caused by our viewpoint from Earth. It is achieved when the faster-moving planet Earth overtakes a superior planet – in this case, Mars, as each moves from west to east (right to left in this diagram). As Earth overtakes on the inside, Mars seems to perform a zigzag across the sky.

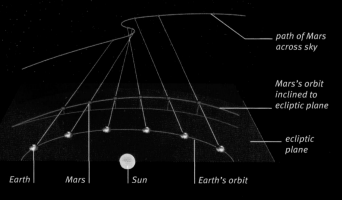

path of Mars across sky

Mars's orbit inclined to ecliptic plane

ecliptic plane

Earth   Mars   Sun   Earth's orbit

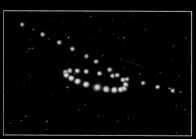

MARS SEEN OVER SEVERAL MONTHS

ALIGNMENTS

The planets and the Moon are always seen within the same band of sky. So it is not surprising that two or more are often seen close together at the same time. Such an alignment is called a conjunction. Should one object obstruct the view of another, more distant object, it is known as an occultation. The Moon regularly occults background stars. When the Moon or a planet passes in front of a star it is temporarily lost from view. In the case of the Moon, which has no atmosphere, the disappearance and later reappearance of the star happens instantly. A grazing occultation is when the star skims the upper or lower limb of the Moon. In this case, the occulted body is lost from view only as it disappears behind lunar mountain peaks along the limb. An occultation of a bright planet by the Moon occurs 10 or 11 times a year. Occultations of one planet by another – for example, an occultation of Jupiter by Venus – occur only a few times a century.

OTHER CELESTIAL PHENOMENA

When the Moon obstructs our view of the Sun it is also, technically, an occultation, but this phenomenon is better known as an eclipse. During a solar eclipse, the Moon stops the Sun's light reaching Earth. When the Moon moves into Earth's shadow, we witness a lunar eclipse.

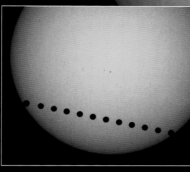

Path across the Sun
This composite image of the 2004 transit of Venus charts the progress of the planet across the Sun's disc. It took more than six hours for the planet to cross the Sun. Transits of Venus occur in pairs, and the partner to this one is due in 2012. The next pair is due in 2117 and 2125.

When a smaller body crosses the disc of a larger one, it is known as a transit. The inferior planets Mercury and Venus cross the Sun's disc when directly between Earth and the Sun. But transits do not occur every time Mercury and Venus pass between Earth and the Sun, because the planets usually pass above or below the Sun's disc. Transits of Venus occur in pairs, separated by more than 100 years, while transits of Mercury are more frequent, occurring about 12 times each century.

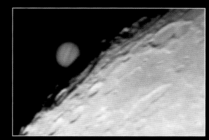

Occultation of Jupiter
This picture shows the January 2002 occultation of Jupiter, which is about to disappear from view behind the Moon. The two objects are along the same line of sight from Earth. Such an alignment often lasts long enough for an occultation to occur each lunar month until the two move out of alignment.

Planetary alignment
In April 2002, soon after the Sun had set, a line of five planets could be seen with the naked eye. Nearest to the horizon was Mercury (bottom right), above and to its left was brighter Venus, and up and to the left again were Mars and Saturn. Bright Jupiter (top left) completed the view.

MECHANICS OF ECLIPSES

The Moon is 400 times smaller than the Sun and 400 times closer to Earth, so when the three bodies are directly aligned, the Moon's disc blocks the Sun from view. This is a solar eclipse. The shadow cast by the Moon falls on Earth, and within the shadow, day turns to night as darkness falls. A total solar eclipse typically lasts for 3–4 minutes. In a lunar eclipse, when the Moon is in Earth's shadow, totality can last up to 1 hour 47 mins. There are on average four eclipses each year – two solar and two lunar.

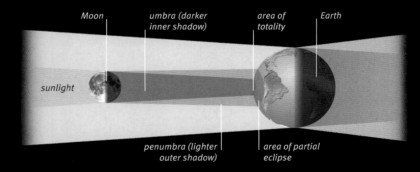

Eclipse of the Sun
When the Moon is directly between the Sun and Earth, it blots out the Sun and casts a shadow on Earth. Anyone within the umbra, the darker inner shadow, sees a total eclipse. Outside of this is a wider area of lighter shadow, the penumbra, from within which a partial eclipse is seen. An annular eclipse occurs when the Moon is farther from Earth than average, and its disc is too small to cover the Sun's disc totally.

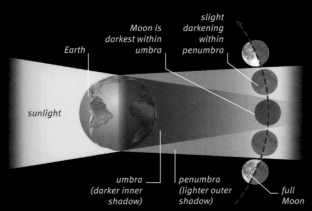

Eclipse of the Moon
The Sun, Earth, and Moon are aligned, and Earth stops sunlight reaching the Moon. When the whole of the Moon is in the umbra, it receives no light and is totally eclipsed. When only a portion of the Moon passes through the umbra, a partial eclipse can be seen.

The Milky Way and beyond

The stars that surround Earth all belong to the Milky Way Galaxy, which is an enormous disc-shaped collection of stars, as well as gas and dust. The Sun and Earth are in a spiral arm of stars about two-thirds out from the centre of the disc. It is an ideal position to observe the galaxy's stellar objects – its stars, clusters, and nebulae. We can also look beyond the Milky Way into a Universe full of galaxies.

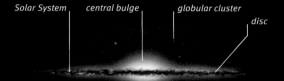

Fornax Cluster
Galaxies are not randomly spread though space; they exist in clusters huge distances apart that form superclusters. The Milky Way belongs to the Local Group, which, along with clusters such as the Fornax Cluster, forms the Local Supercluster.

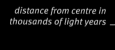

Solar System   central bulge   globular cluster

disc

Edge-on view
The Milky Way measures 100,000 light years from side to side, and its disc is roughly 4,000 light years thick. Young stars within the arms give the disc a blue-white tinge, while the bulge has a yellow tinge because it contains older stars. The disc is surrounded by a sparsely populated spherical halo of individual old stars and about 200 globular clusters.

■ LOOKING AT THE MILKY WAY

The Milky Way is disc-shaped with a bulging centre. Within the disc are spiral arms of stars. Stars also exist between the arms, but because the arm stars are young and bright, these are the ones that shine out. The centre is packed with young and old stars. In total, there are about 500 billion stars.

From our position on Earth we can look into the disc and along its plane, either towards the centre or away from it and out of the galaxy. The many stars in the disc appear as a river of milky light, hence the name Milky Way. The view to the centre is seen in Sagittarius. A view through the plane and out of the galaxy is seen, for example, in the path above Orion's head. We see the other stars in our night sky (those not in the milky path) by looking perpendicular to the disc plane, up or down into the disc.

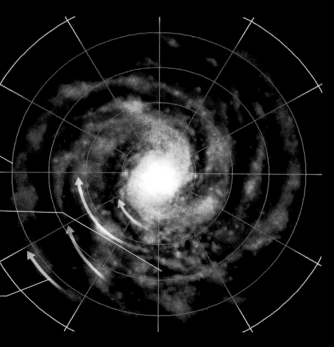

distance from centre in
thousands of light years

Solar System

direction of rotation

Bird's-eye view
This artist's impression shows what we think the Milky Way looks like from outside and above the disc. Gravity keeps the stellar objects in the Milky Way together. They do not travel as a solid disc but follow individual paths around the galaxy's centre. They move at about the same speed; the closer to the centre, the shorter the orbit time. The Sun's orbit lasts 220 million years.

Milky path of light
When we look into the plane of the Milky Way's disc, we see its stars as a path of light. This path is broadest and brightest within the constellation of Sagittarius, but the view is dappled with dark c of dust that hide more distant stars. One dust patch is known as the Dark Horse (above right of c The horse's legs point to the right edge of the image, and its head towards the top edge.

OBJECTS IN THE MILKY WAY

Most of the galaxy's visible material consists of stars at various stages in their life cycles: young, newly formed ones; middle-aged ones like the Sun; and older red giants and planetary nebulae. The rest is vast clouds of interstellar gas and dust.

STARS, CLUSTERS, AND NEBULAE

A star is a huge ball of hot, glowing gas that is held together by gravity. Like humans, each star is unique, differing from each other in size, brightness, colour, age, and mass – that is, the amount of gas making the star.

A star's size, temperature, and colour change with time. An individual star is described by the stage it has reached in its life cycle. Betelgeuse, for instance, is a red supergiant; and a planetary nebula is an old star that has pushed off its outer layer of gas.

Some stars seen from Earth are double stars. Such stars may not be related, but they look close because of our line of sight from Earth. Other doubles, such as Algol, exist together in space; stars such as this are known as binaries. Stars whose brightness varies are variable stars.

Stars form in clusters from gas and dust, and often they will drift apart. Open clusters consist of young, newly switched-on stars; globular clusters consist of older stars. A cloud of interstellar gas and dust is called a nebula. Nebulae either shine brightly or appear as a dark patch against a brighter background.

BETELGEUSE (RED SUPERGIANT)

ALGOL (BINARY)

ALDEBARAN
(RED GIANT, VARIABLE)

BUTTERFLY CLUSTER (OPEN CLUSTER)

OMEGA CENTAURI (GLOBULAR CLUSTER)

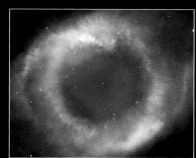
HELIX NEBULA (PLANETARY NEBULA)

LAGOON NEBULA (BRIGHT NEBULA)

HORSEHEAD NEBULA (DARK NEBULA)

BEYOND THE MILKY WAY

When we look out from Earth and beyond the stars of the Milky Way, we see galaxies. They exist in every direction we look. It is estimated that there are 100–125 billion of them. Each is a vast group of stars held together by its own gravity. A single one contains billions or trillions of stars, as well as interstellar gas and dust. Galaxies vary in width from a few thousand light years to more than a million light years. They are so remote that even the nearest look like faint blurs of light to the naked eye.

Galaxies are classified according to shape. Spirals are disc-shaped with a central bulge and spiralling arms. A spiral galaxy with a bar-shaped centre and arms winding out from those bar ends is known as a barred spiral. Ellipticals are ball-shaped, along the lines of a football, a rugby ball, a flattened ball, or something in between. Irregular galaxies have no obvious defined shape or form.

Andromeda Galaxy
The closest major galaxy to the Milky Way, Andromeda is the largest member of the Local Group. To the naked eye, this vast spiral galaxy looks like an elongated smudge of light.

LARGE MAGELLANIC CLOUD (IRREGULAR)

NGC 1300 (BARRED SPIRAL)

M87 (ELLIPTICAL)

Getting started

Anyone can observe the night sky. Simply wait until it is dark, then go outside and look up at the sky. I[t] is thrilling to see the distant stars, but even more so if you can identify them. Simple preparations, su[ch] as choosing where to observe from and knowing what you might see, make all the difference. And the successful identification of a few stars each evening will soon grow into a broad knowledge of the sky

FINDING YOUR WAY

Getting your bearings
A compass will help you get your bearings if you are away from familiar surroundings. Use it in conjunction with the planisphere to locate objects in the night sky.

CHECKLIST

- Take warm clothing, even on summer nights.
- Wear a hat in winter; fingerless gloves are useful.
- Carry binoculars around your neck for ease of use.
- Keep your torch handy: its soft light keeps your eyes adapted to the dark.
- Use a reclining chair, if possible, for extra comfort.
- Take food and drink if observing for a long time.
- Make sure your horizon is clear of obstructions.
- Set up your planisphere before going into the dark.

■ PLANNING AHEAD

The choice of an observation site dictates the quality of the sky. Stars, planets, nebulae, and galaxies are best seen in a dark sky away from houses and street lights. If the sky is clear and moonless, about 300 stars are visible from cities. Only the brightest shine out, which to the absolute beginner can be an advantage: it is the brightest stars that make the constellation patterns. A darker, village sky will yield about 1,000 stars; and the darkest country location, about 3,000. Here the constellation patterns are not so clear, and dim objects are easier to see.

Once you have chosen a location, think about what you need; the checklist (left) will help. Collect everything together before going out. A lucky few may not even need to leave the house. At the right location, bright stars, the Moon, and planets can all be observed from a window. Simply turn off the lights and look out and up.

Sirius

Sirius

Viewing location
The sky above a well-lit town or city (right) is never truly dark. But the brightest stars can, and do, shine through. The darkest skies are in country locations (above), well away from towns and cities. There may still be a bright glow on the horizon from a distant town, but the sky above is dark. The brightest stars are now joined by fainter ones.

■ READY TO GO

Any cloud-free night is an observing night, but some are better than others. Use the Monthly Sky Guide (pp.96–121) to find out the phase of the Moon. If the Moon is full, the sky will be flooded with light and stars will be lost from view. Use the Sky Guide and planisphere to plan your viewing.

IDENTIFYING THE STARS
Initially you should aim to identify two or three of the more prominent constellations and the brightest stars. You can build on this base in the nights ahead. Familiarize yourself with the constellation shapes before going outside.

Remember: as Earth spins, our view of a constellation changes as it moves across the sky. And southern-hemisphere observers should know that maps of the Moon and constellations are usually orientated for northern-hemisphere observers.

Once outside, give your eyes time to adjust to the dark. Within ten minutes or so, more stars will appear. Before 30 minutes have passed, your eyes will be fully dark-adapted, and a range of stars of different brightness will be discernible. Use the technique of averted vision to observe fainter objects. Look slightly away rather than directly at the object. It will then appear as an image, formed by the sensitive edge of the eye's retina.

Looking skywards
The darkest part of the sky is the highest part, farthest away from the horizon. If possible, lean against a wall when looking up, since this will keep your body steady.

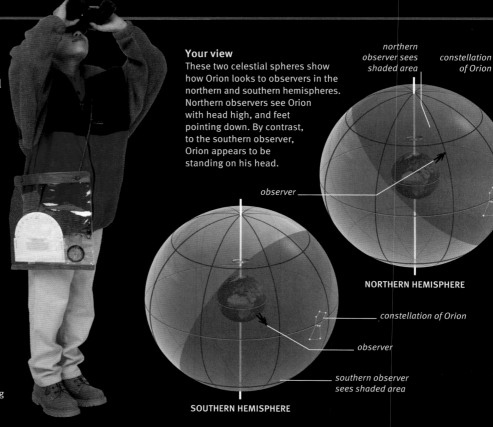

Your view
These two celestial spheres show how Orion looks to observers in the northern and southern hemispheres. Northern observers see Orion with head high, and feet pointing down. By contrast, to the southern observer, Orion appears to be standing on his head.

northern observer sees shaded area

constellation of Orion

observer

NORTHERN HEMISPHERE

constellation of Orion

observer

southern observer sees shaded area

SOUTHERN HEMISPHERE

NHANCING YOUR VIEW

ked eye alone can be used to identify
stellations, view planets and meteors,
ate dark and light features on the Moon.
r, equipment such as binoculars will
e your view by collecting more light than
han eye can. They add clarity to your view
loon's surface and of stellar objects such
clusters and the Orion Nebula, as well as
g objects not visible to the naked eye.

USING BINOCULARS

1 Try the binoculars
Everyone's eyesight is
different, so you must focus
binoculars before use.

2 Locate eyepiece focus
Find which eyepiece can be
focused independently. Look
through with that eye closed.

3 Focus left eyepiece
Rotate the binoculars'
main, central focusing ring
until the left image is in
sharp focus.

4 Switch eyes, and focus
Open only the other eye. Use
the eyepiece focusing ring to
bring the image into focus.

5 Use the binoculars
Both eyepieces should now
be in focus. Open both eyes
and start observing.

BINOCULARS

The most useful optical aid for a newcomer to
astronomy is a pair of binoculars. They are easy
to use and portable, and they show the image
the right way up (unlike telescopes). They are a
combination of two low-powered telescopes,
using both eyes for viewing.

Binoculars come in a range of sizes. The two
numbers that describe a pair of binoculars are
important. The first is magnification; the
second, the diameter of the objective lens.

Binoculars described as
7 x 50, magnify an object
seven times and collect the
starlight with a lens 50mm wide.
Larger binoculars, which have a lens of
70mm or more and magnifications of 15–20,
are used by dedicated astronomers. Binoculars
are difficult to keep steady, whatever the size.
For a stable image with handheld binoculars,
sit down, or lean against a low wall, resting the
binoculars on top.

hold steady sitting
and supporting
arms on knees

MOON THROUGH
STANDARD
BINOCULARS

ANDROMEDA
GALAXY (M31)

objective lens

eyepiece

handle for
adjusting
orientation

tripod

MOON THROUGH LARGE
BINOCULARS

ANDROMEDA GALAXY
(M31) THROUGH LARGE
BINOCULARS

Standard binoculars
Binoculars described as 7 x 50 are ideal for general use.
They are light enough to carry around and will reveal about
200 times more stars than can be seen by the naked eye.

Large binoculars
Too heavy to handhold, large binoculars should be
supported on a tripod. The larger lens and higher
magnification reveal more than standard binoculars.

ETTING EVEN CLOSER

pes bring astronomical objects even
an binoculars. They gather more light and
int objects seem brighter and larger.

OPES

e two types of telescope: refractors, which
ses; and reflectors, which use mirrors.
oduce upside-down images, but this is
iceable when looking at familiar objects.
ope is further described by the diameter
ain lens or mirror – 75mm (3 inch), for
e. The diameter, known as the aperture,
rtant. Double this, and the light gathered
elescope quadruples. This light forms an
nat is magnified by the eyepiece.
eur telescopes are now often controlled
mputer, simplifying the work of locating
cking particularly faint objects.

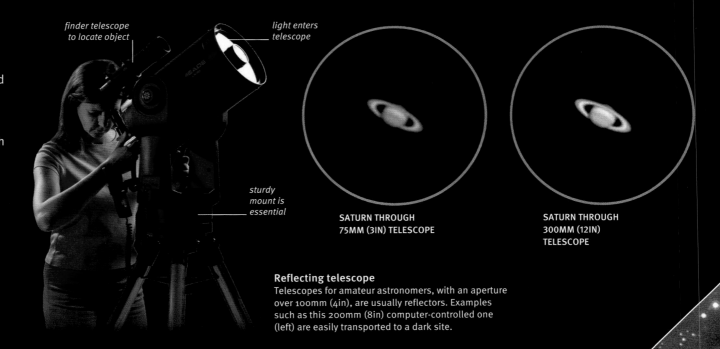

finder telescope
to locate object

light enters
telescope

sturdy
mount is
essential

SATURN THROUGH
75MM (3IN) TELESCOPE

SATURN THROUGH
300MM (12IN)
TELESCOPE

Reflecting telescope
Telescopes for amateur astronomers, with an aperture
over 100mm (4in), are usually reflectors. Examples
such as this 200mm (8in) computer-controlled one
(left) are easily transported to a dark site.

Star hopping

Bright stars and distinctive constellations stand out in the night sky. Patte[...]
the Plough are easily found and, along with stars such as Sirius, can be us[...]
navigating the sky, hopping from one star to the next. Some well-practise[...]
shown here. These, and techniques you'll develop with practice, will help

Ursa Major, the great bear
The third-largest constellation, Ursa Major can be seen from anywhere in Earth's northern hemisphere. Seven of its stars make a saucepan shape called the Plough, or Big Dipper; it is one of the most familiar patterns in the northern sky.

■ NORTHERN LATITUDES

Ursa Major and Cassiopeia are in the sky all year round. They are on opposite sides of the north celestial pole and make ideal starting points for finding your way around the northern sky.

URSA MAJOR
These routes all start at the Plough, the simple and clear pan-shaped pattern in the tail and rump of the bear.

1 A line from Merak and Dubhe, at the right side of the pan, leads to Polaris. Also known as the Pole Star, Polaris marks the north celestial pole, around which the circumpolar stars revolve. Extend the line for the same distance again to the "W" of stars that is Cassiopeia.

2 Hop from Merak to the bear's front paw; make a second hop of a similar distance to reach Castor, the brightest star in Gemini, the twins.

3 Leo, the unambiguous shape of a crouching lion, is found by extending the line at the left side of the pan. Hop between the back legs of the bear and on to Regulus.

4 Two stars at the end of the bear's tail are the starting point to find Boötes and Virgo. Extend the line away rom the bear to the brilliant

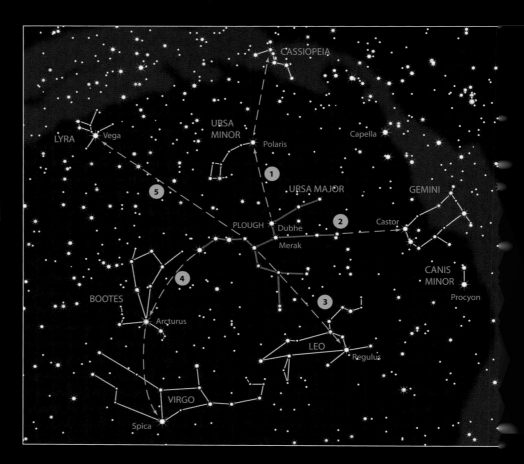

star Arcturus. Make a second hop, the same distance again, to find Spica, the brightest star in Virgo.

5 The left end of the pan can also be used to find Lyra. Its bright star, Vega, is about the same distance away but in the opposite direction from the Plough to Leo.

CASSIOPEIA
The "W" shape of Cassiopeia lies within the Milky Way and is a starting point for locating three constellations and one asterism.

1 Hop twice the length of Cassiopeia along the path of the Milky Way. The bright star you find is Deneb, representing the tail of Cygnus, the swan.

2 From Deneb, locate two brighter stars, one at either side of the Milky Way's path. These are Vega (in Lyra) and Altair (in Aquila). The three together make the Summer Triangle

MID-LATITUDES

The figure of Orion is a prominent presence. Three stars in the hunter's belt are the starting point for exploring a rewarding area of sky.

1 Extend a line from the belt, through Betelgeuse and beyond Orion's raised arm, to reach Gemini, the twins.

2 Hop from the belt of Orion to his head, go the same distance again to the star at the end of Taurus the bull's horn, and carry on to Capella.

3 Hop from the belt to Orion's left hand; hop the same distance again to reach the Pleiades star cluster, passing through Taurus's face on the way.

4 A line from Betelgeuse to Rigel and extended on through a relatively barren area of sky reaches the bright star Achernar.

5 Follow the line of Orion's belt past his lower body and on to the unmistakably brilliant Sirius.

6 Hop from Betelgeuse to Sirius and the same distance again to Procyon to make an equilateral triangle of stars called the Winter Triangle.

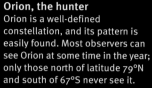

Orion, the hunter
Orion is a well-defined constellation, and its pattern is easily found. Most observers can see Orion at some time in the year; only those north of latitude 79°N and south of 67°S never see it.

SOUTHERN LATITUDES

The four bright stars in Crux and the two brightest in Centaurus are embedded in the Milky Way's path. Just a hop away are other brilliant stars.

1 Extend the long axis of Crux, the cross, and another line from between the stars Hadar and Rigil Kentaurus, the third-brightest star of all. The two lines meet at the unmarked position of the south celestial pole, which is about halfway to the bright star Achernar.

2 A triangle of lines links the south celestial pole, around which the circumpolar stars revolve, to Achernar, the ninth-brightest star of all, and to Canopus, the second brightest.

3 Find brilliant Sirius, the brightest star in all of the sky, by lengthening and curving the line from Canopus. Hop about the same distance again to Procyon, the eighth-brightest star. Sirius and Procyon are two of the three stars that form the Winter Triangle, shown in the mid-latitude sky map above.

Crux, the southern cross
Crux is the smallest constellation of all, but its four prominent stars and location in the Milky Way make it a favourite of southern observers. It can be seen from anywhere in Earth's southern hemisphere.

The Solar System

The closest celestial objects to Earth are the Moon and the planets. Along with Earth, they are part of the Solar System. The Sun is at the centre of our local space neighbourhood, and the planets, their moons, asteroids, and comets all orbit around it. As all these objects move along their orbits, we are able to observe these fascinating worlds. There are rock spheres covered by craters, volcanoes, and freezing desert; giant planets surrounded by swirling gas; and, once in a while, a dirty-snowball comet makes a spectacular appearance.

Saturn and its rings
Saturn's rings consist of pieces of dirty ice. Here, they have been coloured according to the sizes of their particles, ranging from blue for the smallest, through to green, and then purple for the largest.

What's in the Solar System?

The Solar System consists of the Sun, eight planets, five dwarf planets, more than 170 moons, and billions of asteroids and comets. The Sun is by far the most massive member of the system, lying at its centre; the other objects all orbit around it. They have existed together since they were formed from a cloud of gas and dust about 4.6 billion years ago.

■ STRUCTURE AND EXTENT

The Sun's immense gravity holds the Solar System together. It pulls on all of the other objects in the system and keeps them on their set paths around the Sun. One complete circuit of a path is called an orbit. Each object in the system – from the smallest asteroid, to Jupiter, the largest planet – orbits the Sun.

The orbits taken by the planets, which are the most significant objects after the Sun, are made close to the plane of the Sun's equator. The asteroids that form the Main Belt, between Mars and Jupiter, also tend to stay close to this plane. Consequently, the planetary part of

the Solar System is disc-shaped. The average distance from the Sun to the farthest planet, Neptune, is 4.5 billion km (2.8 billion miles).

Beyond Neptune is the Kuiper Belt – a flattened belt of icy, comet-like bodies. And outside of this are the comets themselves. The comets follow randomly inclined orbits that might be close to the planetary plane, above or below the Sun, or anywhere in between. The comets form the Oort Cloud, which is a huge spherical cloud surrounding the Kuiper Belt and the planetary region. The outer edge of the Oort Cloud, which is some 1.6 light years away and nearly halfway to the closest stars, marks the extent of the Sun's influence. Beyond this lies interstellar space.

comet orbit to edge of cloud

Sun

comet close to plane of planets

Oort Cloud

Kuiper Belt

typical comet path

Oort Cloud
The Oort Cloud, which consists of more than a trillion comets, surrounds the planetary region and the Kuiper Belt. Three comet orbits are shown here in green: one extends to the edge of the cloud; a second is close to the plane of the planets; the third is a typical elongated orbit.

Neptune's orbit

Sun

Pluto's orbit

Uranus's orbit

planetary region

Kuiper Belt
Encircling the planetary region, the Kuiper Belt extends from about 6 billion km (3.7 billion miles) from the Sun. It is thought that its outer edge is about 12 billion km (7.4 billion miles) away. The belt is believed to consist of many thousands of objects, more than a thousand of which have been identified.

twice as far from the Sun as Saturn is, Uranus is tilted on its side

Planetary orbits
The planets and asteroids orbit the Sun in an anticlockwise direction when seen from above Earth's North Pole. As they orbit, each one also spins. Orbit size and the time taken to complete an orbit increase with distance from the Sun. Orbits are elliptical, which means that a planet's distance from the Sun varies by many millions of kilometres during its orbit. The planets and their orbits in this image are not shown to scale.

the largest and most massive planet, Jupiter is the one with the fastest spin

liquid water covers more than 70 per cent of Earth, which is the only planet known to have life

Mars is the most distant rocky planet from the Sun; it is also the coldest

the hottest and slowest-spinning planet, Venus is similar in size to Earth

Mercury is the smallest and fastest-moving planet; it is also the closest to the Sun

THE PLANETS

The eight Solar System planets all fall into one of two categories: the rocky planets and the gas giants. The rocky planets are the four closest to the Sun – Mercury, Venus, Earth, and Mars. They were formed from rocky and metallic material near the newly born Sun. Each consists of a rocky mantle and crust, surrounding a metal core, yet their surfaces differ widely. Mercury and Venus are hot, lifeless, dry worlds, but while the former is covered in craters, the latter is shrouded in a thick atmosphere that hides a volcanic landscape. By further contrast, Earth is wet and teems with life, and the more distant, colder Mars is a red world of frozen desert.

The gas giants Jupiter, Saturn, Uranus, and Neptune are the four largest planets. They formed from rock, metal, gas, and ice in the cooler outer regions of the disc of material surrounding the young Sun. Each has a rock-rich core surrounded by an unfathomably deep and thick atmosphere. All four have a ring system encircling them and a large number of orbiting moons.

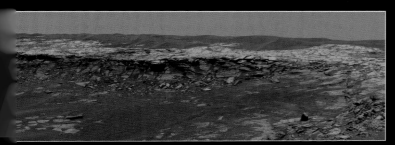

Rocky landscape
This panoramic view of Mars was produced from 28 images taken in February 2006 by the rover Opportunity during its exploration of the planet. The view is of the western edge of Erebus Crater. Layered rocks can be seen in the 1m- (3ft-) thick crater wall.

PLANET TYPES

ROCK	GAS
Mercury	Jupiter
Venus	Saturn
Earth	Uranus
Mars	Neptune

Gaseous atmosphere
The gas giants do not have solid surfaces; what we see is the cloud-top layer of their atmospheres. Jupiter's visible surface shows bands of swirling gas – and spots, which are giant storms.

more than 90 per cent of asteroids orbit in the Main Belt between Mars and Jupiter

Saturn is the second-largest planet and is nearly ten times as far from the Sun as Earth is

the smallest gas giant and most distant planet, Neptune is 30 times farther from the Sun than Earth is

MOONS AND RINGS

At present, more than 170 planetary moons are known to exist, but more are likely to be found as observing techniques improve. The majority belong to the gas giants; only Mercury and Venus are moonless. The moons are made of either rock or a mix of rock and ice, and they orbit around their planets like mini solar systems. The largest is Jupiter's moon Ganymede, which is bigger than Mercury. The smallest are hill-sized irregular lumps. All four giant planets also have ring systems comprising pieces of dirty ice. The most extensive of these is the one around Saturn.

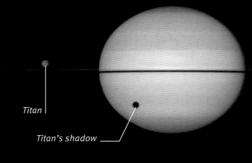
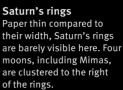

Mimas

Titan

Titan's shadow

Saturn's rings
Paper thin compared to their width, Saturn's rings are barely visible here. Four moons, including Mimas, are clustered to the right of the rings.

Contrasting moons
Titan is the second-largest moon in the Solar System, and the only one with a substantial atmosphere. A nitrogen-rich smoggy haze envelops the moon, but here it has been removed to show the moon's surface. Phoebe, another of Saturn's moons, is more typical: it is 230km (143 miles) long, potato-shaped, and covered in craters.

TITAN   **PHOEBE**

MINOR MEMBERS

There are more than a trillion smaller bodies in the Solar System. The majority are comets and asteroids, followed by thousands of Kuiper Belt objects, and finally the dwarf planets: icy rock bodies Eris, Pluto, Haumea, and Makemake, and rocky Ceres in the Main Belt of asteroids. Over a billion asteroids are thought to exist. More than 200,000 are in the Main Belt between Mars and Jupiter; these are the remnants of a failed process of planet formation. Most of the asteroids are irregular-shaped lumps of rock. Comets are huge, dirty snowballs within the Oort Cloud. When one leaves the cloud and travels in towards the Sun, it becomes large enough and bright enough to be seen.

Comet Hale–Bopp
Hale–Bopp was seen in 1997 as it travelled close to the Sun. Its large head and its tails of gas (blue) and dust (white) made it one of the brightest 20th-century comets.

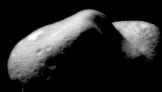

Asteroid Eros
Orbiting outside the Main Belt between Mars and Earth, the potato-shaped Eros is 31km (19 miles) long. Its surface is covered in craters where other bodies have struck it.

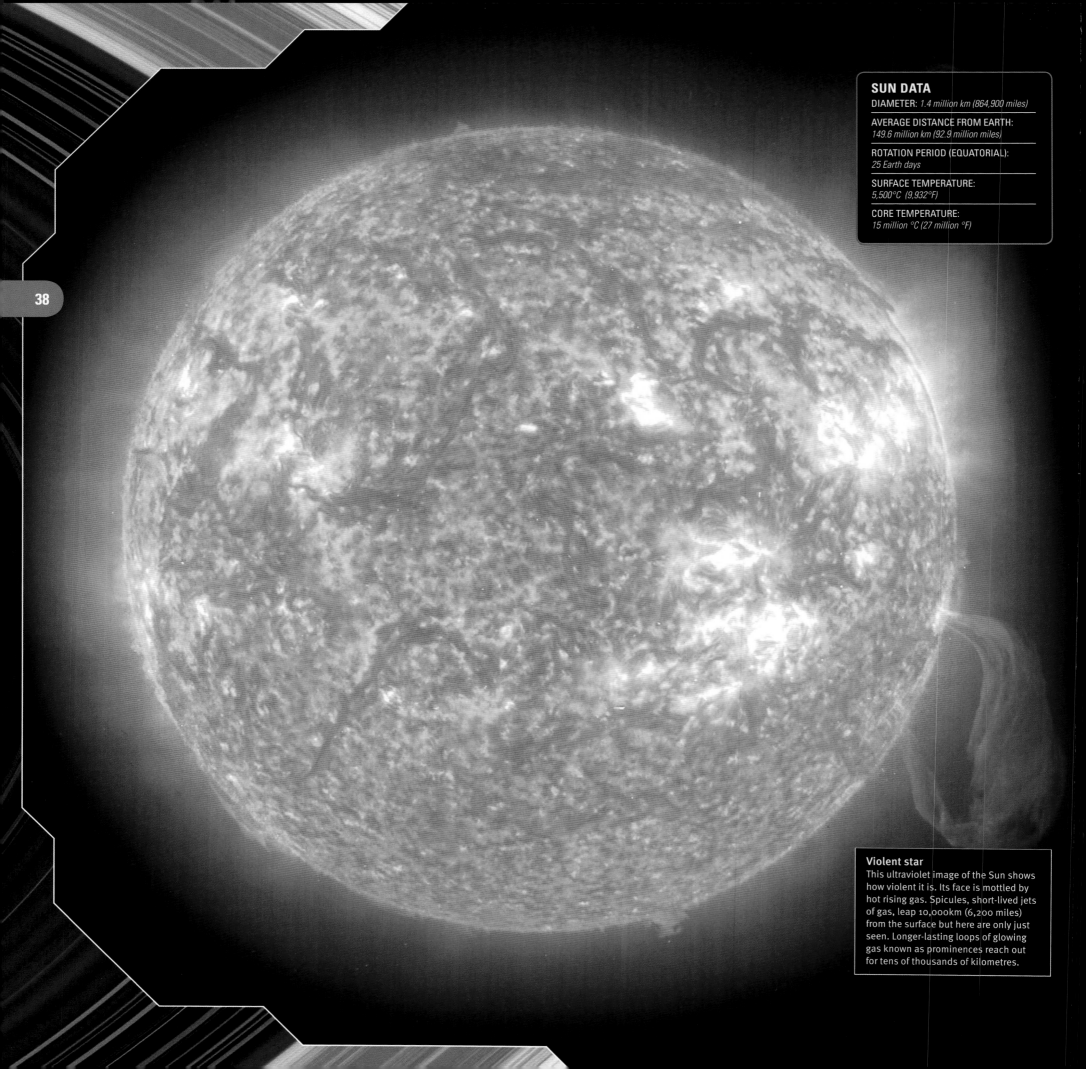

SUN DATA

DIAMETER: *1.4 million km (864,900 miles)*

AVERAGE DISTANCE FROM EARTH:
149.6 million km (92.9 million miles)

ROTATION PERIOD (EQUATORIAL):
25 Earth days

SURFACE TEMPERATURE:
5,500°C (9,932°F)

CORE TEMPERATURE:
15 million °C (27 million °F)

Violent star
This ultraviolet image of the Sun shows how violent it is. Its face is mottled by hot rising gas. Spicules, short-lived jets of gas, leap 10,000km (6,200 miles) from the surface but here are only just seen. Longer-lasting loops of glowing gas known as prominences reach out for tens of thousands of kilometres.

The Sun

The Sun is the closest star to Earth. Like all other stars, it is a vast ball of incredibly hot, brilliant gas. Gravity keeps the Sun together by pulling the gas in towards the centre, where it converts hydrogen to helium and in the process produces heat and light. The Sun has been shining for about 4.6 billion years and will do so for about another 5 billion.

■ FEATURES

The Sun is about three-quarters hydrogen and a quarter helium, with small amounts of 90 or so other elements. About 60 per cent of all this is in the core, where the temperature and pressure are extremely high and nuclear reactions occur.

The Sun is not solid but has a visible surface, the photosphere. The temperature of the photosphere gives the Sun its colour. It consists of constantly renewing granules of rising gas, each of which is about 1,000km (620 miles) across. Beyond the photosphere is the Sun's atmosphere, which is not normally visible. Nearest the Sun is the chromosphere, which extends out about 5,000km (3,100 miles), and outside of this is the corona, which extends for millions of kilometres into space.

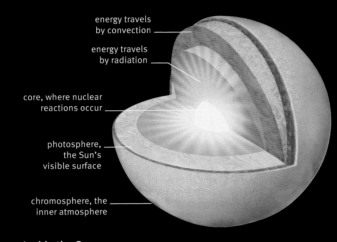

energy travels by convection

energy travels by radiation

core, where nuclear reactions occur

photosphere, the Sun's visible surface

chromosphere, the inner atmosphere

Inside the Sun
The Sun converts hydrogen to helium at about 600 million tons a second. Energy produced moves through the Sun by radiation, then nearer the surface by convection, and is released via the photosphere.

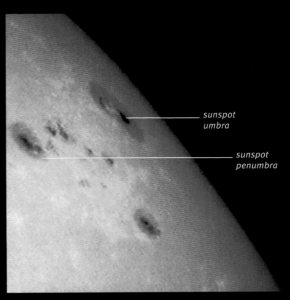

sunspot umbra

sunspot penumbra

Sunspots
Dark patches on the Sun's surface are called sunspots. These are relatively cool regions of the photosphere – about 1,500°C (2,700°F) cooler than the surrounding surface. Sunspots appear periodically, usually in pairs or groups, between 40 degrees north and 40 degrees south of the Sun's equator. They are hundreds of thousands of kilometres wide and last for a few weeks.

■ OBSERVING THE SUN

The Sun cannot be observed directly, but it is possible to view its disc safely. One way to do this is by projecting the Sun's image onto a white card using binoculars or a telescope.

A total eclipse of the Sun is a dramatic event that offers the opportunity to see the Sun's outer atmosphere and prominences flaring from the surface. Spectacular light displays called aurorae (singularly aurora) can be seen

WARNING

Never look at the Sun directly with the naked eye or with any instrument. The light will burn your retina, causing permanent blindness.

by observers in the most northerly and southerly latitudes. These are produced by the interaction between particles from the Sun and Earth's upper atmosphere.

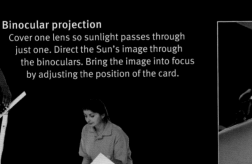

Binocular projection
Cover one lens so sunlight passes through just one. Direct the Sun's image through the binoculars. Bring the image into focus by adjusting the position of the card.

image of Sun is seen on card

image of Sun on card

finder is capped for safety

telescope is pointed at Sun

Telescope projection
Position the card about 50cm (20in) from the telescope's eyepiece, and aim the telescope at the Sun. To sharpen the Sun's image, adjust the eyepiece. Any sunspots will be seen as blackened dots on the Sun's disc.

Aurora Borealis
Also known as the Northern Lights, the Aurora Borealis can be seen from locations north of about latitude 50°N. The colourful display of glowing gas shown above was captured just after dusk from the Yukon Territory, Canada. The Aurora Australis (Southern Lights) can be seen south of about 50°S.

Total eclipse
The Sun and Moon appear the same size in the sky, so when the Moon passes directly in front of the Sun, the latter's disc is completely hidden. The Sun's outermost layer, its corona, is then visible. In this photo, red prominences are also seen.

PLANET DATA

DIAMETER *3,476km (2,160 miles)*

AVERAGE DISTANCE FROM EARTH
384,400km (238,900 miles)

ROTATION PERIOD *27.3 Earth days*

SURFACE TEMPERATURE *−150 to +120°C
(−240 to +250°F)*

Unseen Moon
This view of the Moon cannot be seen from
Earth; the Earth-facing side is at lower left.
The impacts that produced the Moon's
large craters cracked the crust so badly
that lava flooded the crater floors. It then
solidified, producing the darker areas.

The Moon

The Moon dominates the night sky. It is our only natural satellite and closest space neighbour. Many think this cold, dry, lifeless ball of rock was formed when a Mars-sized asteroid collided with Earth about 4.5 billion years ago. Molten material from Earth and the asteroid formed the Moon, before cooling and solidifying.

FEATURES

The lunar crust is solid and rigid. It is about 48km (30 miles) thick on the Earth-facing side, and 74km (46 miles) thick on the far side. Below is a rocky mantle, and because the interior gets hotter with depth, this is partly molten. A small iron core may be at the Moon's centre. Bombardments by asteroids and meteorites have pulverized the surface, producing a lunar soil, the regolith, some 5–10m (16–33ft) thick. Boulders that have been blasted out of both near and distant craters litter the landscape. The craters, formed by impacting asteroids, range from bowl-shaped ones, less than 10km (6 miles) across, to features more than 150km (90 miles) wide. These larger ones have been flooded by lava that seeped from inside the Moon.

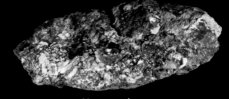

Moon rock
Between 1969 and 1972, 12 astronauts walked on the Moon. They returned with more than 2,000 samples of rock, pebbles and dust, and core material. They are very old and mainly consist of silicate rocks and lava from volcanoes.

Lunar landscape
The Moon's mountains are simply the walls of its huge craters and can be up to 5km (3 miles) high. Below, astronaut Harrison Schmitt stands on the rim of the 110m- (356ft-) wide Shorty Crater. Left, an astronaut is dwarfed by a boulder from an impact crater.

THE VIEW FROM EARTH

The Moon appears to be the largest object in the night sky. It produces no light of its own but shines by reflecting light from the Sun. From Earth we only ever see one side of the Moon because the Moon spins around in the same amount of time as it takes to complete one orbit around Earth. The Moon seems to be a different shape from day to day. But these shapes, known as phases, are simply the different amounts of the Moon's sunlit side visible from Earth. A complete cycle of phases lasts 29.5 days.

NORTHERN HEMISPHERE

SOUTHERN HEMISPHERE

Changing views
The European astronomers who first mapped the Moon called the top "north" and the bottom "south". But southern-hemisphere observers see the Moon's south pole at the top.

Phases of the Moon
The Moon's phase changes throughout the month. Two days after the new Moon, a thin crescent appears in the evening sky. A week after the new Moon, half the disc is visible. A week later, the Moon is full, as the whole bright Earth-facing hemisphere is lit by the Sun.

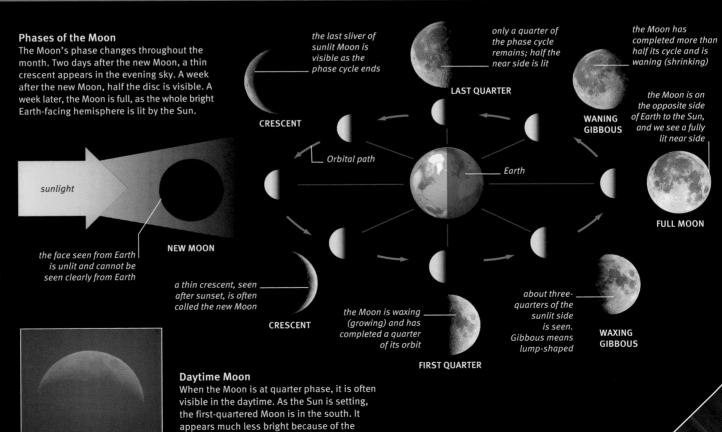

sunlight

the face seen from Earth is unlit and cannot be seen clearly from Earth

NEW MOON

a thin crescent, seen after sunset, is often called the new Moon

CRESCENT

the Moon is waxing (growing) and has completed a quarter of its orbit

FIRST QUARTER

about three-quarters of the sunlit side is seen. Gibbous means lump-shaped

WAXING GIBBOUS

Orbital path

Earth

the last sliver of sunlit Moon is visible as the phase cycle ends

CRESCENT

only a quarter of the phase cycle remains; half the near side is lit

LAST QUARTER

the Moon has completed more than half its cycle and is waning (shrinking)

WANING GIBBOUS

the Moon is on the opposite side of Earth to the Sun, and we see a fully lit near side

FULL MOON

Daytime Moon
When the Moon is at quarter phase, it is often visible in the daytime. As the Sun is setting, the first-quartered Moon is in the south. It appears much less bright because of the daylight, but surface features can still be seen.

Observing the Moon

The Moon's surface is dry, dusty, dark, and dead. The lunar landscape has remained virtually unchanged for millions of years. A "new" crater, wider than 1km (0.6 miles) across, is formed on the Earth-facing side on average every 40,000 years. A glance at the Moon will reveal that it has two types of terrain: large dark plains, called maria (mare in the singular); and brighter, heavily cratered highland regions.

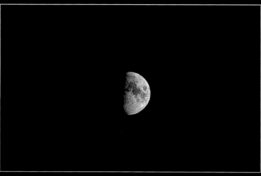

Naked-eye view
Dark and light features are visible. The full Moon looks like a face, with Mare Imbrium and Mare Serenitatis as eyes, and Mare Nubium and Mare Cognitum as the mouth.

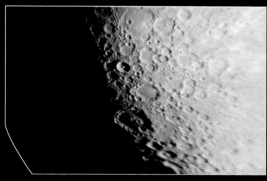

Binocular view
The Moon is still seen as a whole but a well-supported pair of binoculars reveal surface features, such as large craters. The uneven nature of the terminator (see opposite) is also visible.

Telescope view
Now only a part of the Moon is visible. Thousands of smaller craters and details of shadows, mountains, and valleys become distinct. The usable magnification depends on the turbulence of Earth's atmosphere.

■ THE NEAR SIDE

Very early in the Moon's life, when it was much closer to Earth and the interior was hotter, it became locked such that one face – the near side – always pointed towards Earth. This affected the crust, and not only is the near side, on average, 5km (3 miles) lower than the far side, the near-side crust is about 25km (15 miles) thinner. Deep craters on the near side were filled with volcanic lava in their early history; this did not happen on the far side. Dark lava plains now cover about half the near side. When the Moon was first mapped, astronomers thought these dark regions were water and referred to each as a mare (sea) or an oceanus (ocean). It is useful to learn their names and positions. More recently formed craters can be seen within the dark flat maria. The higher mountainous regions, which are older and have more craters, are twice as bright as the maria.

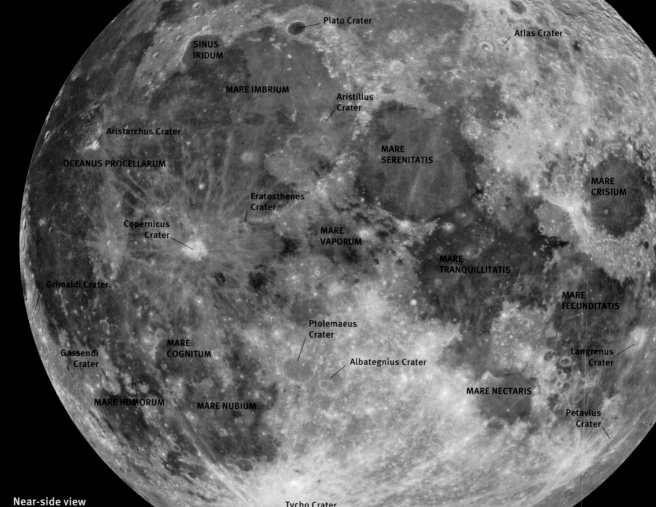

Pythagoras Crater
MARE FRIGORIS
Endymion Crater
Plato Crater
Atlas Crater
SINUS IRIDUM
MARE IMBRIUM
Aristillus Crater
Aristarchus Crater
MARE SERENITATIS
OCEANUS PROCELLARUM
MARE CRISIUM
Eratosthenes Crater
Copernicus Crater
MARE VAPORUM
MARE TRANQUILLITATIS
Grimaldi Crater
MARE FECUNDITATIS
Ptolemaeus Crater
Gassendi Crater
MARE COGNITUM
Langrenus Crater
Albategnius Crater
MARE HUMORUM
MARE NUBIUM
MARE NECTARIS
Petavius Crater
Tycho Crater

Near-side view
The near side is dominated by the large dark Oceanus Procellarum on the western side. Bright spots in the region are more recently formed craters. Copernicus is particularly prominent.

SURFACE FEATURES

You can train your eye to observe detail by concentrating on small parts of the lunar surface and sketching the craters. You will soon realize that there are far more small craters than large ones. The biggest visible crater is Mare Imbrium, some 1,100km (680 miles) across, the formation of which almost broke the Moon apart. About 4 per cent of the craters are not circular. These were produced by impactors arriving at very low angles. Some craters are "ghosts" – only the peaks of the walls protrude above the mare lava. The lunar surface also has some interesting valleys. These were not caused by flowing water but are mainly the remnants of lava tubes that have emptied and then caved in. Smaller valleys are called rills. Craters such as Gassendi and Hevelius have many rills crisscrossing their lava-filled basins. These were formed when the lava cooled and contracted.

Terminator
The terminator is the boundary between the sunlit part of the Moon and the dark part. It moves around the Moon during the month. Shadows at the terminator are very long, and features such as mountains are thrown into relief.

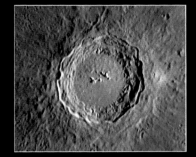

NOON: THE SUN IS OVERHEAD

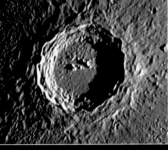

SUNRISE: THE SUN IS LOW

Sunrise over Copernicus
This crater is 800 million years old, and is 91km (57 miles) wide and 3.7km (2.3 miles) deep. It looks "washed out" when the Sun is overhead (top), but at sunrise (above), the long shadows highlight the dramatic nature of the crater's collapsed inner walls and the central mountain. The surrounding hills are also more visible.

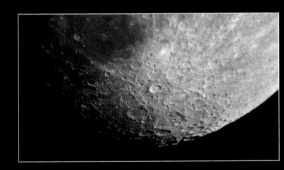

Sinus Iridum
The beautiful Sinus Iridum (Bay of Rainbows) is the western half of a 260km- (160-mile-) diameter impact crater that tilted over when the central regions of Mare Imbrium subsided. The eastern side of the crater was then lost from view as lava from beneath the lunar crust completely flooded the gigantic mare.

OBSERVING CRATERS

Craters appear at their most dramatic when they are near the terminator, which sweeps across the lunar surface as the lunar month progresses. The craters listed here have been divided into four groups according to when they are close to the terminator – that is, whether they are best observed when the Moon is a new waxing crescent, at first quarter, at last quarter, or an old waning crescent. The craters can all be viewed with binoculars. When the Moon is full, concentrate on the cratered regions around its rim.

BEST OBSERVATION TIME

◗	*Waxing crescent*	◑	*Last quarter*
◐	*First quarter*	◔	*Waning crescent*
◗	*Endymion*	◑	*Plato*
◗	*Langrenus*	◑	*Tycho*
◐	*Petavius*	◐	*Eratosthenes*
◗	*Atlas*	◔	*Aristarchus*
◐	*Albategnius*	◔	*Gassendi*
◑	*Ptolemaeus*	◔	*Grimaldi*
◐	*Aristillus*	◑	*Pythagoras*

Tycho Crater
Visible in the centre of this image, the Tycho Crater is an impressive sight through binoculars. This "young", 85km- (52-mile-) wide crater was formed 100 million years ago. In its centre is a 3km- (1.8-mile-) high mountain peak, formed when the underlying rock relaxed after being depressed by the pressure of the impact. Bright rays of material that were ejected from the crater can be seen splashed over the nearby lunar surface.

LUNAR ECLIPSES

Total lunar eclipses occur only when the Moon is full and the Sun, Earth, and Moon are lined up (see p.27). Such eclipses can be seen from anywhere on the night-time hemisphere of Earth, and no special equipment is needed to observe one. During the eclipse, the Moon is in the Earth's shadow, and the Earth is preventing sunlight from reaching its surface. At totality, a small amount of indirect sunlight still manages to reach the Moon. This travels close to the Earth and through its atmosphere. As a result, the light is a deep red-orange colour.

Onset of eclipse
The lower edge is totally eclipsed. Light from part of the Sun continues to shine on the rest of the Moon.

Halfway stage
About half of the Moon is now totally eclipsed, while the other half is still illuminated by sunlight.

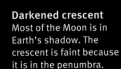

Darkened crescent
Most of the Moon is in Earth's shadow. The crescent is faint because it is in the penumbra.

Totality
The Moon is completely inside Earth's shadow and is a dusky reddish colour.

Mercury

Rocky, crater-covered Mercury is the smallest planet and the closest to the Sun. It has the barest of atmospheres, and conditions on its surface are extremely harsh. Although visible to the naked eye, Mercury is never far from the Sun and so is often difficult to find.

PLANET DATA

DIAMETER *4,875km (3,029 miles)*

AVERAGE DISTANCE FROM SUN
57.9 million km (36 million miles)

ORBITAL PERIOD *88 Earth days*

ROTATION PERIOD *59 Earth days*

SURFACE TEMPERATURE
−180°C to +430°C (−292°F to +806°F)

NUMBER OF MOONS *none*

■ FEATURES

Mercury is very dense compared to the other rocky planets, and beneath its rocky crust and mantle is a large iron core. It is not certain whether this is because the region of the Solar System where Mercury was formed was rich in iron, or whether the early cratering of Mercury has eroded its rocky mantle. The core formed when the heavy iron sank within the young planet.

The planet's surface is pockmarked by thousands of craters – from small, bowl-shaped ones to the vast Caloris Basin (right). Meteorite bombardment churned up the surface and produced a powdery soil that reflects little light and is very dark, just like lunar soil.

Mercury is too small and too hot to have anything more than a very thin atmosphere. This is either captured from the solar wind of gas constantly escaping the Sun or produced by the roasting of surface rocks. Much escapes in the daytime, and it is constantly replenished.

Mercury has the most elongated planetary orbit: its distance from the Sun varies between 46 million km (28.6 million miles) and 69.8 million km (43.4 million miles), and it spins round exactly three times during every two orbits. This makes a "day" on Mercury last 176 Earth days.

Cratered world
Mercury is a dry, rocky world reminiscent of Earth's Moon. It has a very old surface, much of which is very heavily cratered rather like the lunar highland. The remaining area is younger; it consists of more lightly cratered plains of solidified volcanic lava, rather similar to the lunar maria.

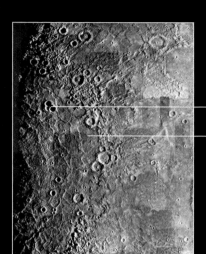

more recent impact craters

lava-filled basin floor

Caloris Basin
The huge, multiringed Caloris Basin impact crater is about 1,350km (840 miles) across (its centre lies to the left of this image). The asteroid that caused it was about 100km (60 miles) wide. The resulting seismic waves traversed Mercury, shattering the surface on the other side, before travelling back to cause fracturing and landslides.

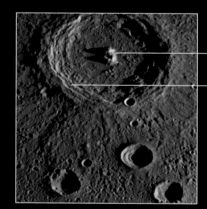

mountainous peak 3km (1.8 miles) high

walls have slipped, forming terraces

Brahms Crater
This bowl-shaped crater is 97km (60 miles) across and was formed when an asteroid hit Mercury about 3.5 billion years ago. It has a prominent central mountainous peak and inner walls that have slipped inwards due to structural weakness and the influence of gravity.

■ OBSERVING THE TWO PLANETS

Mercury and Venus are both inside Earth's orbit, so they never appear far from the Sun. Mercury is seen closer to the Sun than Venus, which orbits at a greater distance. As a result, the two are only seen in the early morning eastern sky before the Sun rises, and in the western evening sky after the Sun has set. Mercury is only visible for around a fortnight when the planet is at elongation. Venus can be very prominent at elongation and is then often by far the brightest body in the sky. Dates of elongation are included in the Special Events listings of the Monthly Sky Guide (pp.96–121).

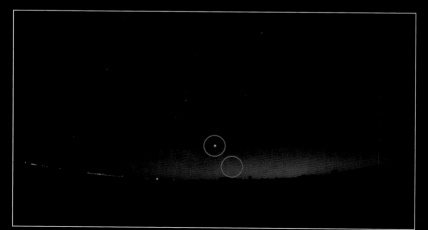

Naked-eye view
Here, the Sun is below the horizon and is illuminating the sky near the horizon. The brighter of the circled planets is Venus. Mercury is fainter because it is both smaller and has a rocky surface that reflects less sunlight. Few stars are seen in the vicinity because their light has been absorbed by Earth's atmosphere. Both planets go through a phase cycle similar to the Moon's, but these are only seen with optical aid.

Venus

Venus is the second rocky planet from the Sun and the brightest in Earth's sky. It is Earth's inner neighbour and twin, with a similar size and mass. However, Venus has lost all of its water, and its carbon dioxide has escaped to form a very dense atmosphere that acts like a greenhouse, trapping in heat.

FEATURES

The similarity between Venus and Earth means that, like Earth, Venus has a hot rocky mantle beneath its solid surface crust. This is the source of Venus's spasmodic volcanic activity. Below this is an iron-nickel core, which has a central solid region surrounded by a liquid-metal outer region. Due to the baking-hot temperature at Venus's surface, the vast majority of the water that was released from the mantle rocks in the past has escaped into space. As a result, the dry mantle rocks are very viscous, and Venus has no moving plates and no mountain ranges.

Radar systems on board orbiting spacecraft have penetrated Venus's clouds and mapped its surface. It is dominated by volcanic features: 85 per cent of it is covered with low-lying plains of lava produced about 500 million years ago, and hundreds of volcanoes are visible. Large impact craters also dot the surface.

Venus is the slowest-spinning planet, taking longer to spin than to complete an orbit of the Sun. Uniquely, it spins from east to west.

Cloudy world
Venus has a dense carbon-dioxide atmosphere and is completely shrouded by thick, highly reflective clouds made of dilute sulphuric acid droplets. These start about 45km (28 miles) above the surface and extend up to a height of 70km (43 miles). Below the clouds is an overcast, orange-coloured world.

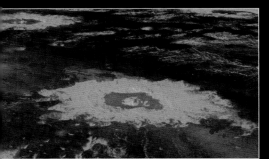

Saskia Crater
Impact craters on Venus vary from 270km (168 miles) down to 7km (4 miles) across. Saskia is middle-sized, at 37km (23 miles), and has a central mountain. This view made by radar has been coloured based on images taken on the surface.

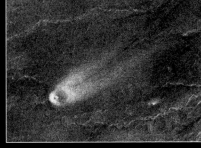

Wind streaks
The surface of Venus is windy, and since the winds generally blow in only one direction, wind streaks form. The streaks of dust and soil shown here are 35km (22 miles) long.

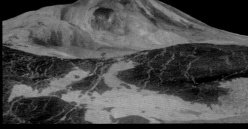

Maat Mons
This large shield volcano rises about 5km (3 miles) above the surrounding plains. Lava has poured out of the volcano, spread out in all directions for hundreds of kilometres, and then solidified.

PLANET DATA
DIAMETER *12,104km (7,521 miles)*

AVERAGE DISTANCE FROM SUN
108.2 million km (67.2 million miles)

ORBITAL PERIOD *224.7 Earth days*

ROTATION PERIOD *243 Earth days*

SURFACE TEMPERATURE
464°C (867°F)

NUMBER OF MOONS *none*

Transit of Mercury
Mercury's orbit usually takes it above or below the Sun's disc in the sky. Infrequently, it is seen to transit the Sun's face. It can take up to 9 hours for Mercury to cross the face of the Sun. The black planetary dots on this image are Mercury's transit on 7 May 2003. The transit shows just how small Mercury is in comparison to the Sun. The next transit will take place on 9 May 2016.

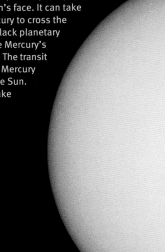

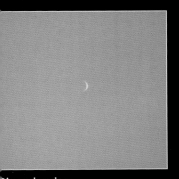

Binocular view
Venus is extremely bright when viewed through binoculars – its crescent phase is apparent – but all that is seen are the tops of the thick, cloudy blanket.

Phases of Venus
Because its distance from Earth changes with its various phases, Venus appears three times bigger when in crescent phase than it does when full.

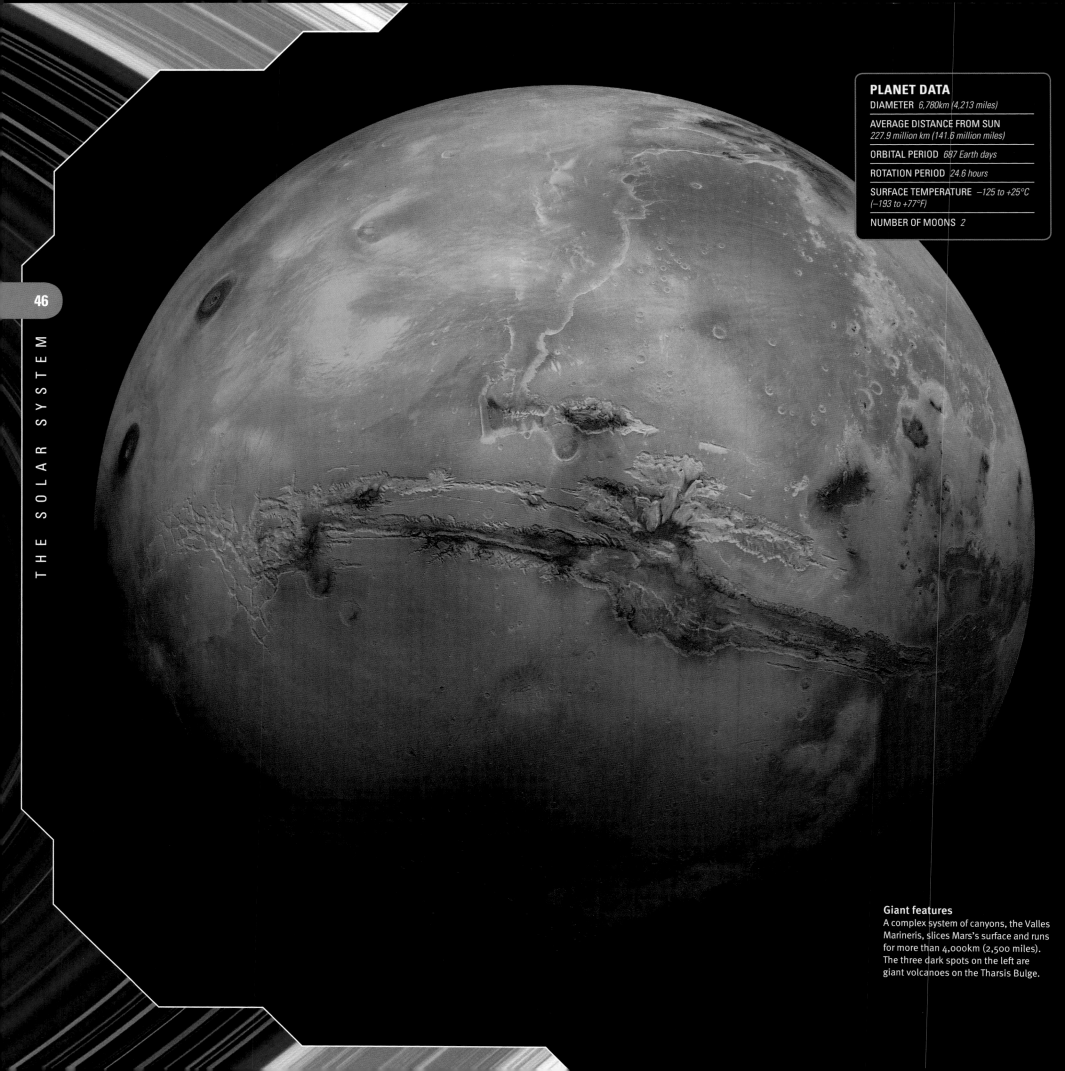

PLANET DATA

DIAMETER *6,780km (4,213 miles)*

AVERAGE DISTANCE FROM SUN
227.9 million km (141.6 million miles)

ORBITAL PERIOD *687 Earth days*

ROTATION PERIOD *24.6 hours*

SURFACE TEMPERATURE *–125 to +25°C
(–193 to +77°F)*

NUMBER OF MOONS *2*

Giant features
A complex system of canyons, the Valles
Marineris, slices Mars's surface and runs
for more than 4,000km (2,500 miles).
The three dark spots on the left are
giant volcanoes on the Tharsis Bulge.

Mars

Mars is the next planet out from the Sun after Earth, and the outermost of the four rocky planets. It is a dry, cold world with a landscape marked by deep canyons and towering volcanoes. Mars is about half the size of Earth, and like Earth it has polar ice caps and seasons, and it spins around in a little over 24 hours.

▪ FEATURES

Mars is made mainly of rock with a small, probably solid iron core. Its rocky surface has been moulded by faulting, volcanism, meteorites, water, and wind. Large-scale features such as the Valles Marineris were formed billions of years ago when internal forces split the surface. Elsewhere, huge regions such as the Tharsis Bulge were raised up above the surrounding terrain. The Tharsis Bulge is Mars's main volcanic centre and home to giant volcanoes, including Olympus Mons.

Low-lying lava plains cover much of the northern hemisphere. The highland south is older and heavily cratered from meteorite bombardment some 3.9 billion years ago. Dry riverbeds, outflow channels, and floodplains indicate that Mars once had flowing water.

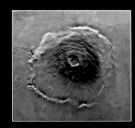
Olympus Mons
This is an overhead view of the summit of Olympus Mons. At 24km (15 miles) high, it is the biggest volcano in the Solar System.

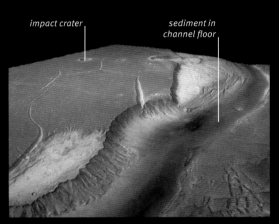
impact crater *sediment in channel floor*

Kasei Vallis
Features such as Kasei Vallis bear witness to the presence of large amounts of fast-flowing water 3–4 billion years ago. This outflow channel a few hundred kilometres wide was probably formed by catastrophic flooding and glacial activity.

Red planet
Much of Mars is rocky, sandy, and dusty, and large areas of its terrain resemble a rock-strewn desert. It is often referred to as the red planet, with its colouring coming from iron oxide (rust) in the rocks and soil.

▪ OBSERVATION

Mars is in Earth's sky for much of each year and is one of the easiest planets to see. It is prominent and red and can be spotted with the naked eye by anyone with good eyesight.

LOCATING AND LOOKING

The best time to see Mars is when the planet is close to Earth and on the opposite side of Earth to the Sun (termed "opposition"; see p.26). This is when it is at its brightest and largest; it is also above the horizon all night long. Oppositions occur roughly every other year, since they are about 26 months apart. Dates of oppositions are included in the Special Events listings in the Monthly Sky Guide (pp.96–121). All oppositions are good for observing Mars, but some are better than others. This is because Mars follows an elliptical orbit around the Sun, and so its distance from us varies. Mars's brightness at opposition is in the range −1.0 to −2.8.

Mars keeps close to the path of the ecliptic and is found within the zodiac band of sky. It is only some 78 million km (48.5 million miles) away from Earth at opposition and makes rapid progress against the background stars.

It travels west to east but goes into retrograde motion (see p.26) about every 22 months. At such a time, Mars appears to move backwards for a few weeks as Earth passes between it and the Sun before once again resuming its forward progression. Mars starts its backward motion about five weeks before opposition.

Mars is the only rocky planet with surface features visible from Earth. Its polar caps can be seen as, in turn, they are tilted towards Earth. Light and dark areas can be seen on the disc; these do not relate to real surface features but result from differences in reflectivity (dark areas reflect the least).

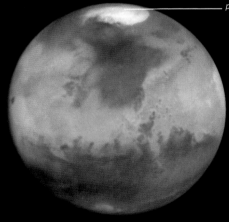
polar ice cap
Large-telescope view
The polar ice caps are the easiest features to pick out on the surface of Mars. Just one is visible at a time due to the planet's tilt. The caps change in size with the seasons, shrinking in summer and extending in winter. Light and dark marks (the result of differences in the amount of reflected sunlight) can be seen.

Naked-eye view
Mars is identified by its disc shape and red colouring. Here, it is the brighter of the two dots. Jupiter is to its right.

Binocular view
The planet's disc shape becomes obvious through binoculars, but its surface features are still not visible.

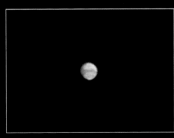
Small-telescope view
Here, Mars is visibly red. Some surface features – polar ice caps and dark regions – may be seen.

PLANET DATA

DIAMETER *142,984km (88,846 miles)*

AVERAGE DISTANCE FROM SUN
778.3 million km (483.6 million miles)

ORBITAL PERIOD *11.8 Earth years*

ROTATION PERIOD *9.9 hours*

CLOUD-TOP TEMPERATURE
–110°C (–166°F)

NUMBER OF MOONS *64*

Storm world
Jupiter's cloudy atmosphere is dominat
by storms. The smallest are like Earth'
largest hurricanes. The biggest, the Gre
Red Spot, is bigger than Earth itself. On t
left is the shadow of the moon Europa.

Jupiter

Jupiter is a giant among the planets. It is the second-largest body in the Solar System after the Sun and the most massive of all the planets. Its visible surface is not solid but the colourful top layer of a deep, thick atmosphere. An extensive family of moons orbits around Jupiter, and a thin faint ring of dust particles encircles it.

■ FEATURES

Jupiter is made of hydrogen and, to a lesser extent, helium. Its outer layer is a 1,000km- (600-mile-) deep hydrogen-rich atmosphere. Underneath this, the planet becomes increasingly dense and hot, and the hydrogen acts like a liquid; deeper still, it acts like a molten metal. At Jupiter's heart is a core of rock, metal, and hydrogen compounds.

The "surface" we see consists of colourful bands of swirling gas. Heat from inside Jupiter combined with its fast spin create the bands and the violent weather within them. The light bands of rising gas and the red-brown ones of falling gas produce winds that give rise to storms and hurricanes. The Great Red Spot is a giant storm that has raged for more than 300 years.

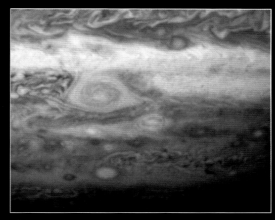

Little Red Spot
In late 2005, astronomers witnessed the birth of Jupiter's second red spot, and second-largest storm – about 70 per cent of the size of Earth. It formed between 1998 and 2000 when three white, oval-shaped storms merged.

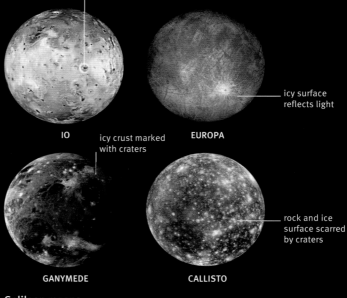

surface constantly renewed by volcanic eruptions

IO

icy crust marked with craters

EUROPA

icy surface reflects light

GANYMEDE

CALLISTO

rock and ice surface scarred by craters

Galilean moons
Jupiter's four largest moons are collectively known as the Galilean moons. These spherical bodies made of a mix of rock and ice are worlds in their own right. By contrast, most of the other moons are small and irregular in shape.

■ OBSERVATION

Jupiter shines like a bright silver star in the night sky for about ten months of each year. Its brilliance allows it to stand out from the star background and be recognized. Although its brightness varies, it is never dimmer than Sirius, the brightest star in the night sky.

LOCATING AND LOOKING

Jupiter is best seen when it is close to Earth and on the opposite side of Earth to the Sun (a position known as "opposition"; see p.26). It is then particularly bright because the sunlight that shines fully on it is reflected back by its atmosphere. Its brightness at opposition is at least −2.3 and goes up to a maximum of −2.9. Jupiter is also in the sky all night long, rising at sunset, being highest in the middle of the night, and setting at sunrise. Opposition occurs every 13 months; dates of oppositions are included in the Special Events listings in the Monthly Sky Guide (pp.96–121).

Jupiter is found within the zodiac band of sky. It takes about 12 months to cross one zodiac constellation before moving into the next. It travels from west to east against the background

of stars, but when at opposition it also goes through a period of retrograde motion (see p.26) and temporarily moves backwards in the sky.

For most of the time, Jupiter is the planet with the largest disc size. Surface detail on the planet can be seen through either powerful binoculars

or a telescope. The banded structure, the Great Red Spot, and other cloud features then come into view. A large telescope will reveal further spots and structure in the clouds. The slightly squashed appearance of Jupiter's disc, due to its fast spin, is also apparent through a telescope.

Changing view
Our view of Jupiter's surface is constantly changing due to the planet's rapid rotation. Jupiter makes one spin in just under ten hours. This means that features can be seen to move within about ten minutes. These five images show Jupiter over the course of about five hours. The planet spins from left to right, and the Great Red Spot is seen to move as the planet turns. The black dot is the shadow of a Galilean moon.

Naked-eye view
Jupiter's disc shape is clearly visible even to the naked eye. Its shape and brilliance make it easy to identify.

Binocular view
The Galilean moons are visible through binoculars either side of the planet's equator, changing position each night.

Telescope view
Here, it is possible to discern details: the bands and the Great Red Spot can be seen.

Saturn

Pale-yellow Saturn is the most distinctive planet due to its impressive ring system. It is second in size to Jupiter. Like Jupiter, its visible surface is its outer atmosphere, and it has a large family of moons. Saturn is also the most distant planet that is normally visible to the naked eye.

■ FEATURES

Saturn is made mainly of hydrogen and helium. They form the planet's gaseous outer layer, but inside, as the temperature and pressure increase with depth, the hydrogen and helium change state. Below the atmosphere they act like a liquid and, deeper still, like a liquid metal. A core of rock and ice is at the planet's centre.

Saturn and its moons
Saturn dwarfs two of its largest moons, Tethys (top) and Dione (below). Shadows cast by Tethys and the main rings are seen on the planet's globe. The limb of the planet is also visible through the Cassini Division separating the A and B rings.

Ringed world
Saturn's rings reflect sunlight well, making them and the planet easy to see. But those rings we readily see (shown here) are only part of the system; much fainter rings extend to about four times as far from the planet. Saturn is tilted relative to its orbit, so as it travels, first one hemisphere then the other is tilted sunwards. This gives Saturn seasons and offers a changing view from Earth.

PLANET DATA

DIAMETER *120,536km (74,897 miles)*

AVERAGE DISTANCE FROM SUN
1.43 billion km (886.56 million miles)

ORBITAL PERIOD *29.5 Earth years*

ROTATION PERIOD *10.7 hours*

CLOUD-TOP TEMPERATURE
−180°C (−292°F)

NUMBER OF MOONS *62*

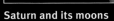

The top of the cloud layer forms the planet's visible surface. Muted dark belts and bright zones in various shades of yellow girdle Saturn. The muted appearance is due to a thin layer of smoggy haze covering the entire planet. Saturn may appear serene, but things are far from calm. Giant storms in the upper atmosphere are created by winds generated by heat from within the planet and the planet's rotation. Stormy weather leads to the regular appearances of spots and ribbon-like features.

MOONS AND RINGS

Most of Saturn's moons are small and irregularly shaped. Only Titan is larger than our Moon. Most were discovered in the past 25 years, and more are expected. The moons are mixes of rock and water-ice in varying proportions. Some moons orbit within the ring system, which is not solid but is made of billions of pieces of dirty water-ice. These range in size from dust grains to objects several metres across, and they move around Saturn on their own orbits. The system extends for hundreds of thousands of kilometres into space, but it is only a few kilometres deep.

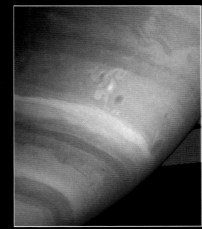

Dragon storm
In September 2004, an area in the southern hemisphere known for its storms and dubbed "storm alley" was the setting for a giant thunderstorm. Dragon Storm – the reddish feature above the centre in this false-colour image – seems to be a long-lived storm that periodically flares up.

C ring   B ring   Cassini Division   A ring

Main rings
Saturn's readily seen ring system comprises three distinct rings: A, B, and C. These are made of ringlets, which in turn are made of pieces of dirty water-ice. The Cassini Division, seen from Earth as an empty gap, is in fact full of ringlets.

OBSERVATION

Saturn is twice as remote from Earth as Jupiter but is still bright enough to be seen at some time during the night about ten months of the year. It looks like a star but can be distinguished from its stellar backdrop with the help of a star chart.

LOCATING AND LOOKING

Due to Saturn's distance from Earth, it moves more slowly across the sky than closer planets such as Jupiter. Its 29.5-year orbit means it takes about two and a half years to pass through one zodiac constellation. It travels from west to east, but every 12 months it goes into retrograde motion (see p.26), when, for about four months, it appears to move backwards.

Like other superior planets, Saturn is best seen when it is on the opposite side of Earth to the Sun termed "opposition"; see p.26). Its brightness at opposition ranges from 0.8 to a maximum of –0.3. This wide range is largely due to the varying amount of ring facing Earth. Oppositions happen annually – about two weeks later each year. Dates of oppositions are included in the Special Events listings in the Monthly Sky Guide (pp.96–121).

A small telescope or powerful binoculars will reveal the nature of the rings and give a first look at the disc's banded appearance. A larger telescope reveals more disc detail, the three main rings, the Cassini Division, and a handful of dots, which are moons. The bulging equatorial region and flattened poles are also apparent. Our view of the rings changes as Saturn orbits the Sun. Their orientation changes from edge-on (when they are virtually invisible), to open (fully visible), and then edge-on again. The rings were open last in 2002. They will be fully open and seen from above in 2017.

Cassini Division is visible

2000: rings almost fully open and seen from below

Changing view
Our view of the rings changes as Saturn and Earth move along their orbits. A full cycle is completed every 29.5 years. We see the rings edge-on first; from above as Saturn's north pole tilts towards the Sun; edge-on once again; and from below when the south pole is sunwards.

1996: rings almost edge-on

Naked-eye view
Saturn looks like a star to the naked eye, but its warm colouring and disc shape distinguish it from the stars.

Binocular view
Saturn's disc shape is more apparent here. High-powered binoculars will show the rings as bumps on its sides.

Small telescope view
The ring system can be clearly seen, and the planet's bands are just visible.

Uranus and Neptune

The two planets farthest from Earth, Uranus and Neptune are also the smallest of the gas giants. They are cold, featureless worlds, so remote that they are difficult to see from Earth. Both have sparse rings and large numbers of moons orbiting around them. And both are coloured blue by the presence of methane-ice clouds in their atmospheres.

■ URANUS

The visible surface of Uranus is its hydrogen-rich atmosphere. Below is a deep layer of water, methane, and ammonia ices, and in the centre a core of rock and possibly ice. Uranus appears calm and featureless because of upper-atmosphere haze, but the planet does undergo change. The atmosphere has some banding, and bright clouds are carried around the planet; in 2006, a dark spot was observed. Uranus's unique feature is its tilt: the planet appears to orbit the Sun on its side. The combination of the tilt and its 84-year orbit mean that its hemispheres face the Sun for 42 years at a time.

PLANET DATA

DIAMETER 51,118km (31,763 miles)

AVERAGE DISTANCE FROM SUN
2.87 billion km (1.78 billion miles)

ORBITAL PERIOD 84 Earth years

ROTATION PERIOD 17.2 hours

CLOUD-TOP TEMPERATURE
−214°C (−353°F)

NUMBER OF MOONS 27

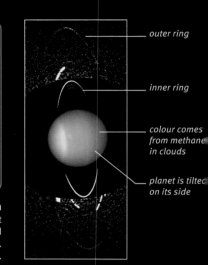

outer ring

inner ring

colour comes
from methane
in clouds

planet is tilted
on its side

Ring system
Uranus has two distinct sets of rings. Closest to the planet is a set of 11 rings; narrow and widely separated, these are more gap than ring. Outside these is a pair of faint, dusty rings.

■ NEPTUNE

Neptune is similar in structure to Uranus. It has a core of rock and possibly ice, surrounded by a mix of water, methane, and ammonia ices, and topped off with a hydrogen-rich atmosphere. The planet undergoes seasonal change, and its atmosphere is unexpectedly dynamic. It experiences ferocious equatorial winds, fast-moving bright clouds, and short-lived gigantic storms.

The planet is surrounded by a sparse system of five complete rings and one partial ring. Only one of its 13 moons, Triton, is of notable size, and four are within the planet's ring system.

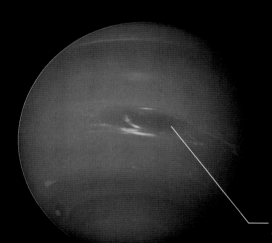

the Great Dark Spot – a huge
storm in the atmosphere

PLANET DATA

DIAMETER 49,532km (30,760 miles)

AVERAGE DISTANCE FROM SUN
4.5 billion km (2.8 billion miles)

ORBITAL PERIOD 164.9 Earth years

ROTATION PERIOD 16.1 hours

CLOUD-TOP TEMPERATURE
−200°C (−320°F)

NUMBER OF MOONS 13

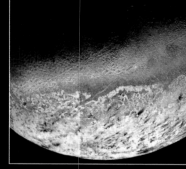

Triton
Triton is about three-quarters the size of Earth's Moon. It is a rocky world with an icy surface of linear grooves, ridges, and circular depressions.

■ OBSERVING THE TWO PLANETS

Both Uranus and Neptune are too distant to be seen easily. The sharp-sighted can see Uranus with the naked eye, but it is difficult to locate. Following its progress against the stars will confirm its identity. This will take time and patience, because Uranus's orbit is long, and the planet spends about seven years in the same zodiac constellation. Neptune moves even more slowly through the zodiac constellations, spending nearly 14 years in each. It is too faint to be seen by the naked eye, but a medium-sized telescope will reveal a blue-green disc.

Uranus and Neptune
Distant Uranus (left) is magnitude 5.5 and brighter than Neptune (right), which, at magnitude 7.8, is beyond naked-eye vision. Both appear as faint stars in this enhanced view.

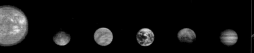

The dwarf planets

he distant, icy worlds of Eris and Pluto orbit beyond Neptune. Along with neighbours
Haumea and Makemake, they are four of the five known dwarf planets; a category of object
created in 2006. The fifth dwarf planet, Ceres is much closer to the Sun in the Main Belt of
asteroids. Only these five are known but the number is set to rise.

WARF WORLDS

ris is believed to be a mix of rock and ice with
n icy surface. It is also possibly the largest dwarf
lanet. Measuring 2,326 km (1,445 miles) across
is only just larger than Pluto. Eris was
iscovered in 2005 when images taken in 2003
ere reanalyzed. At the time, it was almost 16
illion km (10 billion miles) away and the most
istant Solar System object seen. It completes
ne circuit of its elongated and highly inclined
rbit every 557 years.

Pluto is a cold world. A thin, icy crust covers a
ody made of probably 70 per cent rock and 30
er cent water-ice. At an average distance from
he Sun of 5.9 billion km (3.7 billion miles), it is
nsurprising that its surface temperature is
bout −230°C (−382°F). This 2,304km- (1,432-
ile-) wide body has five moons. The largest,
haron, is about half the size of Pluto itself.
ach of the pair spins every 6.38 days, and
ecause Charon orbits Pluto in the same time,
he two bodies keep the same face towards each
ther. From its discovery in 1930 until August
006, Pluto had the status of a planet. It was
hen the smallest and most distant planet.

Ceres has been known since 1801. It was the
rst asteroid discovered and remains the largest
nown; it measures 960km (596 miles) across.
eres is a rocky body with water-ice near the
urface. It orbits the Sun every 4.6 years.

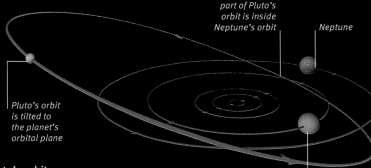

part of Pluto's
orbit is inside
Neptune's orbit

Neptune

Pluto's orbit
is tilted to
the planet's
orbital plane

Uranus

Pluto's orbit
The orbit of Pluto is elongated and tilted with respect to the orbits
of the eight planets. Pluto completes one circuit in about 248
years, and for about 20 years of each orbit its path takes it closer to
the Sun than Neptune. This last happened between 1979 and 1999.

PLANETS OR DWARF PLANETS?

After the first Kuiper Belt object was found, in 1992,
Pluto's status as a planet was questioned. The 2005
identification of an object seemingly larger than Pluto
led to the creation of the "dwarf planet" class. This
was established in August 2006 by the International
Astronomical Union, the largest professional body for
astronomers. Like planets, dwarf planets are almost
round, but unlike planets, they have not cleared their
neighbourhoods: Ceres is in the Main Belt; and Eris,
Pluto, Haumea, and Makemake are in the Kuiper Belt.
So far, only these five examples are known but about
100 likely candidates exist in the Kuiper Belt.

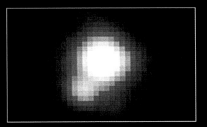

Ground view
This is how Pluto appears through the best
ground-based telescopes. The bump to the
lower left is its major moon, Charon.

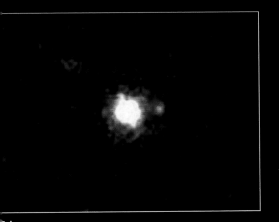

Eris
This image from the 10m (3ft) Keck telescope in Hawaii has Eris
at its centre as a large bright object. The smaller, duller object
o its right is Dysnomia. Keck astronomers realized the small
dot was a moon when it moved with Eris against the stars.

Ceres
The Hubble Space Telescope studied Ceres for
nine hours, the time it takes to complete one
rotation. It was found to be almost round: the
diameter at its equator is wider than at its poles.

Pluto and its moons
On average, Pluto is a
little under 40 times as far
from the Sun as Earth. This
image from the Hubble Space
Telescope shows Pluto with
Charon at its lower right and,
further right, the moons Nix
(top) and Hydra (bottom).

Comet McNaught
On 7 August 2006, Robert McNaught discovered a comet that within months became the brightest in Earth's sky for more than 30 years. In January 2007, when at its closest to the Sun, it had a large head and spectacular tail and was impossible to miss in the southern sky.

Comet Tempel 1
This image was taken in 2005 by the *Deep Impact* spacecraft 67 seconds after the craft released a missile to impact the nucleus. Light from the collision shows a pitted, ridged surface.

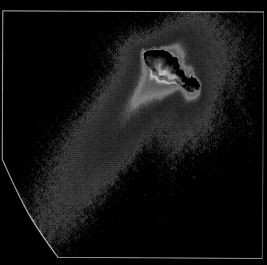

Comet Borrelly
The bowling-pin-shaped nucleus of Comet Borrelly was imaged by the *Deep Space 1* spacecraft in 2001. It is 8km (5 miles) long and orbits the Sun every 6.9 years. Colour has been added to highlight dust and gas jetting out of the nucleus.

Comets, meteors, and asteroids

Billions of comets and asteroids are invisible to us on Earth because they are too distant or too small to be seen. Yet some comets appear to grow and then make a spectacular show in the night sky. On any given night, meteors produced by cometary dust flash into view, and asteroids can crash-land on Earth's surface.

▪ COMETS

Comets are often referred to as dirty snowballs. But these cosmic snowballs are not ball-shaped, and they are on a giant scale. Comets are irregular-shaped, city-sized lumps of snow and rocky dust that follow orbits around the Sun. More than a trillion of them together make the vast Oort Cloud, where they have been since the birth of the Solar System 4.6 billion years ago.

Comets only become visible when they leave the Oort Cloud and travel in towards the Sun. Then, the snowball, called a nucleus, is warmed by the Sun's heat. The snow is converted into gas, and this and loosened dust jet away from the nucleus. When closer to the Sun than Mars, the nucleus is surrounded by a cloud of gas and dust, known as a coma, and it develops two tails.

The comet is now large enough and bright enough to be seen from Earth. Typically, two or three a year are seen as a fuzzy patch of light through binoculars. Three or four a century, such as Comet McNaught, are truly impressive and easily visible to the naked eye.

More than 2,000 comets have been recorded within the vicinity of the Sun, and about 200 are periodic. Most are named after their discoverers.

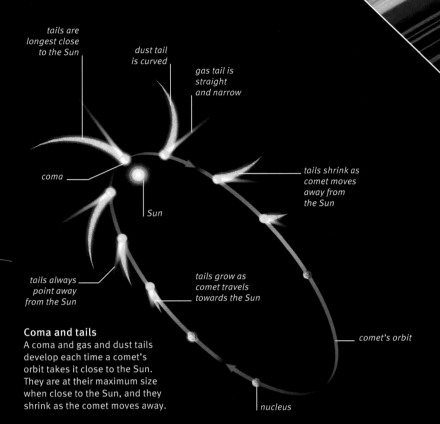

tails are longest close to the Sun

dust tail is curved

gas tail is straight and narrow

coma

Sun

tails shrink as comet moves away from the Sun

tails always point away from the Sun

tails grow as comet travels towards the Sun

comet's orbit

nucleus

Coma and tails
A coma and gas and dust tails develop each time a comet's orbit takes it close to the Sun. They are at their maximum size when close to the Sun, and they shrink as the comet moves away.

▪ METEORS

On any night of the year it is possible to see a meteor – a short-lived trail of light in the sky. These transient flashes, popularly called shooting stars, are produced by small fragments of a comet or, sometimes, an asteroid. As the fragment, or meteoroid, moves through Earth's atmosphere, it produces a trail of excited atoms, which in turn produce light. This streak of light is the meteor. It lasts for less than a second and has an average brightness of magnitude 2.5.

The best time to see a meteor is during the hours before dawn, when you'll be on the side of Earth facing the incoming meteoroids. Although meteors appear every night, they are not predictable. To maximize your chances of seeing one, it is best to observe when a meteor shower is expected. These happen on the same dates every year and are produced as Earth ploughs into a stream of comet particles. Shower details are in the Monthly Sky Guide (see pp.96–121).

Leonid shower
The Leonid meteor shower occurs in mid-November. As Earth orbits, it passes through a stream of particles lost by Comet Tempel–Tuttle. The dust particles produce meteors that appear to radiate from a point in the constellation of Leo.

▪ ASTEROIDS

Asteroids are dry, dusty lumps of rock that failed to make a rocky planet. Most are irregular in shape, and just the handful or so over about 320km (200 miles) across are round. They range in size from Ceres at 960km (596 miles), through boulders and pebbles to dust-sized particles. There are 100,000 larger than about 20km (12.5 miles) across. As size diminishes, the quantity increases. Most orbit the Sun between Mars and Jupiter.

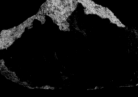

Meteorites
When an asteroid makes it through Earth's atmosphere and lands on the surface, it is called a meteorite. More than 22,500 have been catalogued. This one has a dark crust that formed as it fell through the atmosphere.

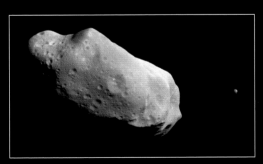

Ida and Dactyl
The asteroid Ida is 60km (37 miles) long and shows signs of past collisions. It journeys around the Sun every 4.8 years. Its tiny moon, Dactyl, just 1.6km (1 mile) long, orbits Ida every 27 hours.

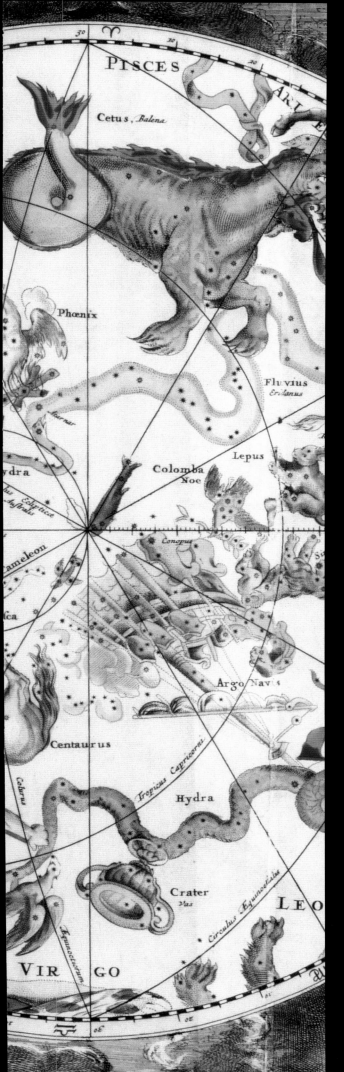

Mapping the sky

Astronomers divide the sky into 88 areas called constellations, which are interlocked like pieces of an immense jigsaw puzzle. Each of the 88 constellations are covered in this section, with a chart and a text profile that includes a list of stars and other features that can be found within its borders. Guidance on when to view them is given in the Monthly Sky Guide chapter (see pp.96–121).

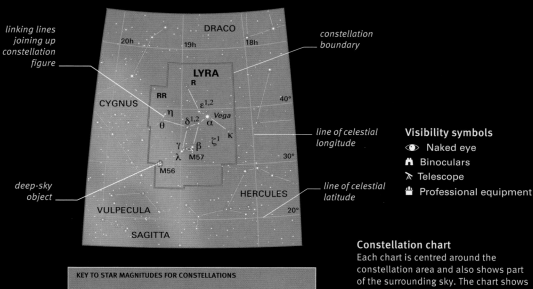

linking lines joining up constellation figure

constellation boundary

line of celestial longitude

deep-sky object

line of celestial latitude

KEY TO STAR MAGNITUDES FOR CONSTELLATIONS

-1.5–0 0–0.9 1.0–1.9 2.0–2.9 3.0–3.9 4.0–4.9 5.0–5.9 6.0–6.9

Visibility symbols

👁 Naked eye
🔭 Binoculars
➴ Telescope
🔭 Professional equipment

Constellation chart
Each chart is centred around the constellation area and also shows part of the surrounding sky. The chart shows all stars visible to the naked eye, under ideal viewing conditions, and selected deep-sky objects.

Fully Visible

Partially visible

Not visible

80°N
60°N
40°N
20°N
0°
20°S
40°S
60°S

Visibility map
The chart for each constellation is accompanied by a map that shows the parts of the world from which it can be seen. The entire constellation can be seen from the area shaded in green, and part of it can be seen from the area shaded in yellow, but it cannot be seen at all from the area shaded in red.

A view of the heavens
Since ancient times, the stars in the sky were associated with gods, legends, heroes, and mythical beasts. This 15th-century chart shows the way these figures were represented in the northern and southern halves of the night sky.

Ursa Minor The Little Bear

Fully visible 90°N–0°

The constellation of Ursa Minor is a constant feature of northern skies – as the location of the north celestial pole, it never rises or sets, but instead spins around the pole once every 24 hours. Its shape mimics that of the Plough (or Big Dipper) in Ursa Major.

FEATURES OF INTEREST

Alpha (α) Ursae Minoris (Polaris) 👁 The northern pole star, Polaris is an almost fixed point in the sky, since it lies barely half a degree from the north celestial pole. A yellow supergiant star of magnitude 2.0, Polaris lies about 430 light years away. Until quite recently, it was classed as a Cepheid variable – a type of pulsating star named after its prototype, Delta Cephei in neighbouring Cepheus. But in the past few decades its variations have died away – a sign that occasionally changes in stellar evolution can happen within a human lifetime. Polaris's 8th-magnitude companion star can be picked up with a small telescope.

Beta (β) Ursae Minoris (Kochab) 👁 Ursa Minor's second brightest star is an orange giant about 100 light years away.

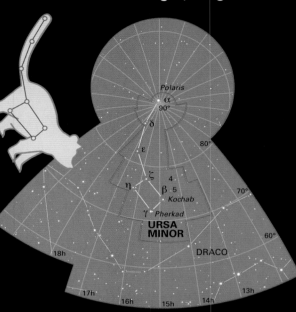

Long-tailed bear
The tail of the Little Bear curves away from the north Pole Star, Polaris (top left). Unlike real bears, the celestial bears Ursa Minor and Ursa Major both have long tails.

Draco The Dragon

Fully visible 90°N–4°S

The large constellation of Draco wraps itself around Ursa Minor and the north celestial pole. It represents a dragon from Greek mythology, slain by Hercules. Despite its size, it has no stars brighter than second magnitude.

FEATURES OF INTEREST

Alpha (α) Draconis (Thuban) 👁 Thuban is a blue-white giant star, about 300 light years from Earth. Precession, the slow wobble of Earth's axis of rotation, meant that 5,000 years ago, this star was the pole star.

16 and 17 Draconis ⚲ This pair of stars, magnitudes 5.1 and 5.5, are easily divided with binoculars, but a small telescope shows that the brighter star is itself a double.

NGC 6543 ⚲ This is one of the sky's brightest planetary nebulae.

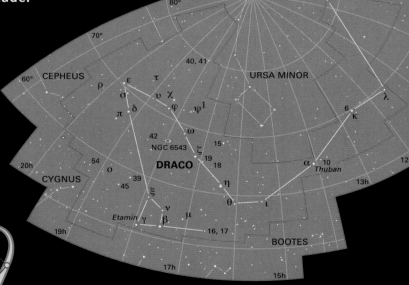

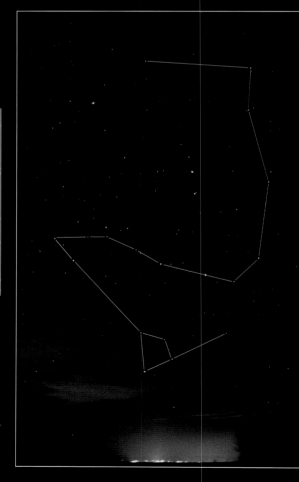

Dragon star
The lozenge-shaped head of the dragon is easily identified in the constellation Draco. This shape is formed by four stars, including Gamma (γ) Draconis, the brightest star.

Cepheus Cepheus

Fully visible 90°N–1°S

Lying in the far northern sky between Draco and Cassiopeia, this constellation represents the husband of Queen Cassiopeia in Greek myth. Although its pattern is obscure, it contains several interesting variable stars.

FEATURES OF INTEREST

Beta (β) Cephei 👁 The constellation's second brightest star is a blue giant with a faint companion. Its brightness varies in a 4.6-hour cycle, but only by 0.1 magnitudes.

Delta (δ) Cephei 👁 The prototype star for a class of variables called Cepheids, this ageing yellow supergiant is passing through a phase of its life where it expands and contracts repeatedly. It changes brightness between magnitudes 3.5 and 4.4 in a little under five days and nine hours.

Mu (μ) Cephei 👁 Called the Garnet Star due to its blood-red colour, Mu is a red supergiant. Like Delta, it is a variable star, but it is less predictable, varying between magnitudes 3.4 and 5.1 with a period of about two years.

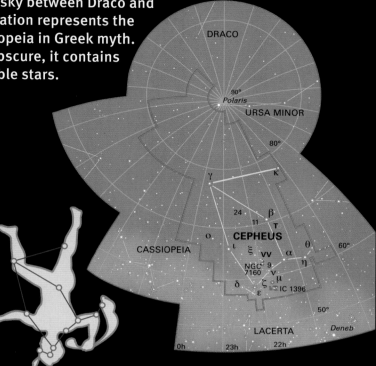

The king
Shaped like a bishop's mitre, Cepheus is not easy to pick out in the sky. He is flanked by his prominent wife, Cassiopeia, and Draco, the dragon.

Cassiopeia Cassiopeia

Fully visible 90°N–12°S

This distinctive W-shaped group of stars sits on the opposite side of the pole star from the Plough or Big Dipper, and is usually easy to locate. One of the original Greek constellations, it depicts Cassiopeia, the mother of Andromeda in Greek myth, sitting in a chair and fussing with her hair.

FEATURES OF INTEREST

Alpha (α) Cassiopeiae (Shedir) 👁 The brightest star is a yellow giant of magnitude 2.2, 120 light years away.
Gamma (γ) Cassiopeiae 👁 Gamma is one of the youngest stars obvious to the naked eye. It lies about 800 light years away, and usually shines at magnitude 2.5. However, it is still expelling material from the nebula in which it formed, and the obscuring gas can cause its brightness to vary unpredictably between magnitudes 3.0 and 1.6.
NGC 457 🔭 Cassiopeia's position in the heart of the northern Milky Way means that it is rich in star clusters, the best of which is NGC 457. This ball of 80 recently formed stars, 9,000 light years from Earth, is visible to the naked eye and rewarding in binoculars.

Polar pointer
The centre of the W shape of Cassiopeia points towards the north celestial pole. The constellation is located between Perseus and Cepheus in the Milky Way.

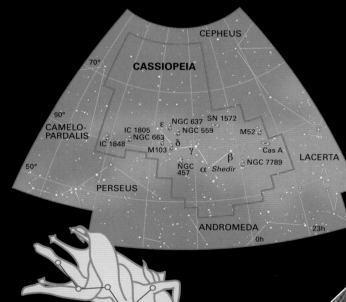

Camelopardalis The Giraffe

Fully visible 90°N–3°S

This faint constellation of far northern skies was invented in 1613 by Dutch theologian Petrus Plancius. It represents an animal from the Bible.

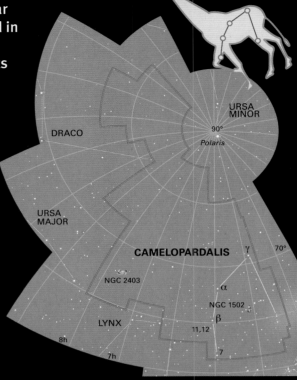

FEATURES OF INTEREST

Alpha (α) Camelopardalis 👁 Despite its designation, alpha is the constellation's second brightest star. It is a blue supergiant, but because it lies about 3,000 light years away, it shines at only magnitude 4.3.

Beta (β) Camelopardalis 🔭 Outshining alpha with a magnitude of 4.0, beta is a yellow supergiant about 1,000 light years away, with a faint, magnitude-8.6 companion star.

NGC 1502 🔭 This small star cluster, with about 45 members, is visible through binoculars and is some 3,100 light years from Earth.

NGC 2403 🔭 This spiral galaxy is relatively nearby, at 12 million light years away. A small telescope should show it as an eighth-magnitude, elliptical smudge.

Celestial giraffe
It can be difficult to relate the figure of a giraffe to the stars of Camelopardalis. Only the stars representing the giraffe's legs are visible in this picture.

Auriga The Charioteer

Fully visible 90°N–34°S

This constellation, a highlight of northern winter skies, is usually said to represent Erichthonius, an ancient king of Athens and skilled charioteer. Its southernmost star is shared with Taurus, and the Milky Way passes diagonally across it, making it rich in interesting stars and clusters.

Shared star
Auriga, the charioteer, lies in the Milky Way between Gemini and Perseus. Neighbouring Beta (β) Tauri completes the charioteer figure.

FEATURES OF INTEREST

Alpha (α) Aurigae (Capella) 👁 The sixth-brightest star in the sky, Capella shines at magnitude 0.1 and is just 42 light years from Earth. It is actually a binary system, composed of twin yellow giants that orbit each other in 104 days, far too close together for a telescope to separate them.

Zeta (ζ) Aurigae 👁 A triangle of stars close to Capella is known as "The Kids". Zeta (ζ), on the southwest point, is an eclipsing binary – a system where two stars passing in front of one another cause regular dips in brightness.

Epsilon (ε) Aurigae 👁 The northernmost "kid" is another eclipsing binary, but a very curious one whose eclipses last for about one year out of every 27. This intensely luminous supergiant is orbited by a dark eclipsing partner that seems to be huge and semi-opaque and may be a star with a young, dusty solar system.

Lynx The Lynx

This faint northern group is a relatively late addition to the classical constellations, invented by Johannes Hevelius in the 1680s. A chain of faint stars between Ursa Major and Auriga, it bears no resemblance to the European wildcat of the same name – Hevelius apparently came up with the name because it was so faint that only those with a cat's eyes would be able to spot it.

Fully visible 90°N–28°S

FEATURES OF INTEREST

Alpha (α) Lyncis 👁 This is a magnitude-3.2 red giant, 150 light years from Earth.

12 Lyncis ⚹ To the naked eye, this white star is a faint magnitude 4.9, but a small telescope will reveal a blue-white companion of magnitude 7.3, and a larger instrument will show that the brighter element is itself a binary, making this a triple system, 140 light years from Earth. The components of the brighter star have an orbital period of about 700 years.

NGC 2419 ⚹ This faint globular cluster, only visible through telescopes of moderate aperture, is 210,000 light years away from Earth, much more distant than the Milky Way's other globular clusters.

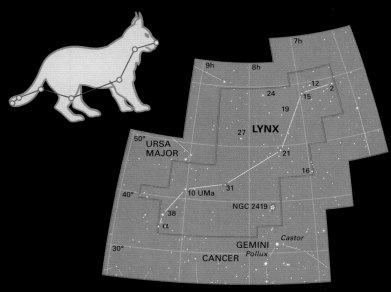

Elusive feline
Lynx consists of nothing more than a few faint stars zigzagging between Ursa Major and Auriga. The constellation has many interesting double and multiple stars.

Ursa Major The Great Bear

One of the best-known constellations of the northern sky, the seven brightest stars in Ursa Major form the familiar pattern of the Plough or Big Dipper – a useful signpost to other stars. But the constellation's fainter stars extend much farther.

Fully visible 90°N–16°S

FEATURES OF INTEREST

Alpha (α) Ursae Majoris (Dubhe) 👁 This yellow giant is just over 100 light years away, shining at magnitude 1.8. A line from beta (Merak), through Dubhe points towards the pole star in Ursa Minor.

Zeta (ζ) Ursae Majoris (Mizar) ⚹ This is a famous double star. Its neighbour Alcor just happens to lie in the same direction, but a small telescope shows that Mizar is also a true binary, with a much closer companion.

M81 ⚹ This spiral galaxy is bright and just 10 million light years away but can still be seen only through a small telescope.

A familiar sight
The saucepan shape of the Plough's stars is one of the most easily recognized sights in the night sky.

Canes Venatici The Hunting Dogs

Fully visible 90°N–37°S

This constellation depicts a pair of dogs used by the Boötes (whose constellation is adjacent) to chase the Little Bears (Ursa Major and Minor) around the north formed by Johannes Hevelius at the end of the 17th century.

FEATURES OF INTEREST

Alpha (α) Canum Venaticorum (Cor Caroli) 🔭 This star's name means "Charles's Heart" – it was named in memory of the executed British King, Charles I. Binoculars will show that it is a wide binary system, composed of white stars with magnitudes 2.9 and 5.6. It lies 82 light years from Earth.

M3 🔭 One of the northern sky's best globular clusters, M3 appears as a fuzzy "star" in binoculars and a hazy ball of light through small telescopes.

Whirlpool Galaxy (M51) 🔭 This spectacular spiral galaxy is bright and relatively close, some 15 million light years away. It happens to lie "face on" to Earth, so binoculars or, ideally, a small telescope will show the bright core, while medium-sized instruments will reveal traces of the spiral arms that give the galaxy its name.

Two bright stars
Canes Venatici represents a pair of hounds, but the unaided eye can see little more than the constellation's brightest stars, Cor Caroli and Beta Canum Venaticorum.

Boötes The Herdsman

Fully visible 90°N–35°S

The figure of Boötes is often shown driving the Great Bear (see p.61) and Little Bear (see p.58) around the north pole of the sky. Its kite-shaped pattern is quite distinctive. The brightest star in this constellation is Arcturus, which means "bear guard" or "bear-keeper" in Greek.

FEATURES OF INTEREST

Alpa (α) Boötis (Arcturus) 👁 Arcturus is one of the closest and brightest stars to us. It is an orange giant nearing the end of its life, and just 36 light years away. At magnitude -0.04, it is the fourth-brightest star in the sky.

Epsilon (ε) Boötis (Izar) 🔭 Also called Pulcherrima, this is one of the sky's most beautiful double stars. A small telescope will split it to reveal an orange giant of magnitude 2.7 accompanied by a blue star of magnitude 5.1. The pair lie around 150 light years away.

Tau (τ) Boötis 👁 This apparently uninspiring star of magnitude 4.5 is notable as host to one of the first planets discovered beyond our solar system. Tau is a yellow star quite similar to the Sun and 51 light years from Earth. A giant planet three times the size of Jupiter orbits it every 3.3 days.

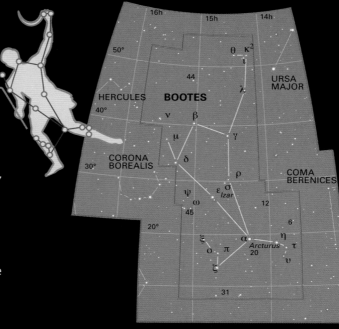

Kite-shaped constellation
Boötes, containing the bright star Arcturus, skies in the Northern Hemisphere. This larg constellation extends from Draco to Virgo.

Hercules Hercules

A large but not particularly prominent constellation depicting the mythical hero and demigod, Hercules can be hard to identify. It is best spotted by working out from the square Keystone at its centre.

Fully visible 90°N–38°S

FEATURES OF INTEREST

Alpha (α) Herculis (Rasalgethi) ☌ With a name that means "the kneeler's head" in Arabic, this is a double star system containing two stars that orbit one another 380 light years away. One is a huge red giant so large that it has become unstable, and varies in brightness between magnitudes 2.8 and 4.0. The other is a smaller giant shining steadily at magnitude 5.3.

M13 ♒ This globular cluster is the best in the northern sky, a knot of 300,000 closely packed stars about 25,000 light years from Earth. Binoculars will show it as a fuzzy ball, and a small telescope should reveal some of the more loosely packed stars around its edges.

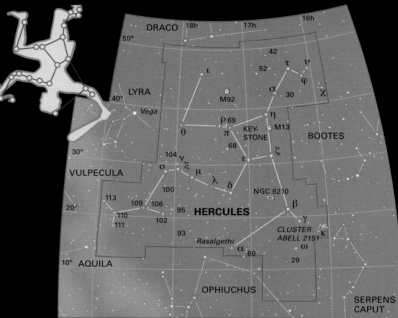

Upside down
In the night sky, Hercules is positioned with his feet pointing toward the pole (top left) and his head pointing south. He kneels with one foot on the head of the celestial dragon Draco.

Lyra The Lyre

Although it is one of the smaller constellations, Lyra is easily spotted in northern skies, thanks to the presence of the fifth-brightest star in the sky, brilliant white Vega. It represents the ancient musical instrument played by Orpheus on his journey to the underworld.

Fully visible 90°N–42°S

FEATURES OF INTEREST

Alpha (α) Lyrae (Vega) 👁 This is a white star just 25 light years from Earth. It shines at magnitude 0.0, indicating that it is some 50 times as luminous as the Sun, and it is surrounded by an intriguing disc of dusty debris that may be left over from the formation of a planetary system.

Epsilon (ε) Lyrae ☌ This famous multiple star splits into a double when viewed through binoculars, but a small telescope will show that each of these components is itself also double, making epsilon a "double double" system.

The Ring Nebula (M57) ☌ Lyra's other showpiece is the Ring Nebula, the most famous planetary nebula in the sky. Lying midway between beta and gamma, M57 is a delicate shell of gas cast off by a dying star 1,100 light years away. It shines at magnitude 9.5, and is best seen through a small telescope.

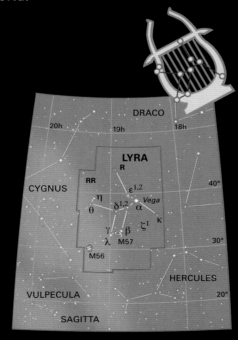

Stringed instrument
Lyra, dominated by dazzling Vega, represents the harp played by Orpheus, the musician of Greek myth. Arab astronomers visualized the constellation as an eagle or vulture. It lies on the edge of the Milky Way, next to Cygnus.

Poised in flight
One of the most prominent constellations of the northern sky, Cygnus depicts a swan flying with its wings outstretched. The beak of the swan is marked by a double star, Beta (β) Cygni.

Cygnus The Swan

Sometimes known as the Northern Cross because of its distinctive shape, Cygnus represents a swan flying down the Milky Way. As well as rich starfields, it contains many deep sky objects of interest.

Fully visible 90°N–28°S

FEATURES OF INTEREST

Alpha (α) Cygni (Deneb) 👁 Although at magnitude 1.3 it is outshone by nearby Vega, Deneb is one of the sky's most luminous stars – it lies 2,600 light years from Earth, and must be some 160,000 times brighter than the Sun.
Beta (β) Cygni (Albireo) 🔭 This is a beautiful double star of contrasting colours – binoculars will split it into yellow and blue stars of magnitudes 3.1 and 4.7.
Cygnus Rift 👁 Cygnus contains several interesting nebulae, but the most obvious is this dark cloud of gas and dust that runs alongside the swan's neck and obscures our view of the Milky Way behind it.
Cygnus X-1 🔭 Although undetectable to amateurs, this strong X-ray source is thought to mark the site where a black hole is pulling material from a companion star.

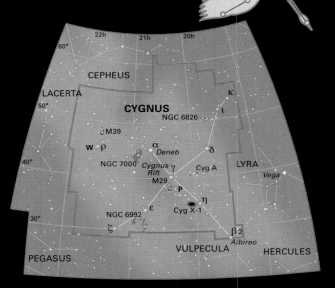

Andromeda Andromeda

Easy to find because of its link to the Square of Pegasus, Andromeda – daughter of Cassiopeia (see p.59) – represents a princess chained to a rock as a sacrifice to the sea monster Cetus, but ultimately rescued by the hero Perseus.

Fully visible 90°N–37°S

FEATURES OF INTEREST

Alpha (α) Andromedae (Alpheratz) 👁
Sometimes also referred to as Delta Pegasi, Alpheratz is a blue-white star 97 light years from Earth.
Gamma (γ) Andromedae (Almach) 🔭 Through small telescopes, Almach appears as a contrasting double, with yellow and blue stars of magnitudes 2.3 and 4.8. Larger telescopes will also show the blue star's fainter, sixth-magnitude companion.
The Andromeda Galaxy (M31) 🔭 The most distant object visible to the naked eye, this looks at first like a fuzzy, fourth-magnitude star. Binoculars or a small telescope reveal an elliptical disc – the bright central area of a huge spiral galaxy larger than the Milky Way, 2.5 million light years away. Two companion galaxies are visible through small telescopes.

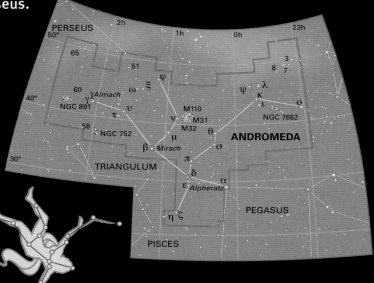

Head to toe
Andromeda is one of the original Greek constellations. Its brightest stars represent the princess's head (α), her pelvis (β), and her left foot (γ).

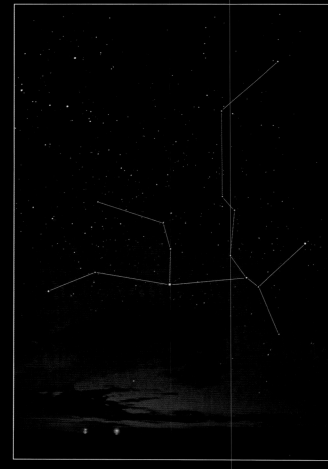

Straddling the northern Milky Way between Cassiopeia and Cygnus, Lacerta is a small and obscure constellation introduced by the Polish astronomer Johannes Hevelius in 1687. Its size means that it contains few significant deep-sky objects, but it is the site of occasional nova explosions (produced when a star brightens suddenly). It also contains the prototype of a very strange class of galaxy.

Fully visible 90°N–33°S

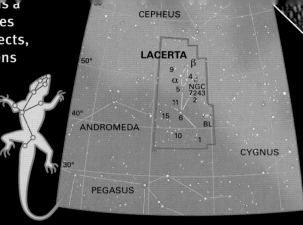

FEATURES OF INTEREST

Alpha (α) Lacertae 👁 This blue-white star shines at magnitude 3.8 and lies 102 light years from Earth. This means that it is roughly 27 times as luminous as the Sun.

NGC 7243 ✵ This loose group of blue-white stars, thought to lie about 2,800 light years from Earth, is so scattered that some astronomers suspect it is not a true open cluster at all.

BL Lacertae ⚏ This strange and rapidly varying starlike object is in fact a "blazar" – a distant galaxy with a massive black hole at its centre, that is gulping down material from its surroundings and spitting it out in a jet that points directly at Earth. Because we see these jets head-on from Earth, they tend to look starlike.

Triangulum The Triangle

This small northern constellation fills the gap between Perseus, Andromeda, and Aries. Despite its lack of bright stars, it has an ancient origin – Greek astronomers originally saw it as a version of their letter "delta". Its compact size makes it relatively easy to spot nevertheless.

Fully visible 90°N–52°S

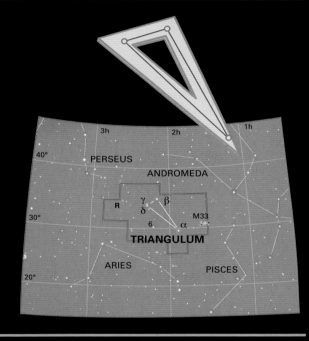

FEATURES OF INTEREST

Alpha (α) Trianguli 👁 With a magnitude of 3.4, this is a white star some 65 light years away. Although designated alpha, it is not in fact Triangulum's brightest star.

Beta (β) Trianguli 👁 Alpha's brighter neighbour shines at magnitude 3.0 and lies about 135 light years from Earth. Despite the stars' apparent similarity, beta must be considerably more luminous in order to outshine alpha – it is classed as a "giant". Apart from these two stars and M33, there is little else of note in this constellation.

M33 ⚏ Triangulum's finest sight is this spiral galaxy, one of the closest in the sky at 2.7 million light years away. In spite of its size and proximity, it is hard to spot in binoculars or a small telescope because it presents its "face" to Earth, and so its light is thinly spread. M33, also known as the Triangulum Galaxy, is the third major member of our Local Group of galaxies, after the Andromeda Galaxy (M31) and the Milky Way itself. In long-exposure photographs, it looks like a starfish. It may actually be in orbit around Andromeda.

Perseus Perseus

This constellation represents a hero of Greek myth, coming to the rescue of nearby Andromeda. He carries the head of Medusa, a creature whose gaze could turn anyone to stone. It is one of the original Greek constellations.

Fully visible 90°N–31°S

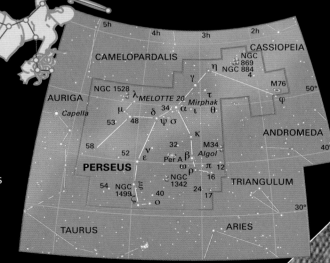

FEATURES OF INTEREST

Alpha (α) Persei (Mirphak) ⚏ Binoculars will reveal that this magnitude-1.8 yellow supergiant lies at the heart of a cluster of fainter blue stars, 590 light years from Earth.

Beta (β) Persei (Algol) 👁 This famous variable star is also known as the "winking demon". It was the first eclipsing binary to be identified – a double star with two components that pass in front of each other every 2.87 days, causing the

star's apparent brightness to dip from magnitude 2.1 to 3.4 for about 10 hours.

Double Cluster (NGC 869, NGC 884) ⚏ This famous cluster is a spectacular sight in binoculars and can be seen with the naked eye as a bright knot in the Milky Way. The clusters are both about 7,000 light years from Earth, and genuine neighbours in space.

Aries The Ram

Fully visible 90°N–58°S

The zodiac constellation of Aries represents the ram with the golden fleece in the legend of Jason and the Argonauts. Although it has astronomical and astrological significance as the original site of the "First Point of Aries" (the point where the ecliptic crosses the celestial equator, defining zero hours right ascension), this point now lies in the neighbouring constellation Pisces. Aries's pattern is relatively faint and hard to identify.

Legendary ram
From a crooked line formed by three faint stars, ancient astronomers visualized the figure of a crouching ram, with its head turned back over its shoulder.

FEATURES OF INTEREST

Alpha (α) Arietis (Hamal) 👁 This yellow giant star, about 66 light years from Earth, shines at magnitude 2.0. Its popular name is derived from the Arabic for "lamb".

Gamma (γ) Arietis (Mesartim) ⤢ This is an attractive double star – one of the first discovered to be double. It was found by English scientist Robert Hooke in 1664. Small telescopes will easily separate it to reveal twin white components of magnitude 4.8. The stars are orbiting each other some 200 light years from Earth.

Lambda (λ) Arietis 🔭 This is another double star – binoculars will reveal that the white, magnitude-4.8 primary star has a yellow companion of magnitude 7.3.

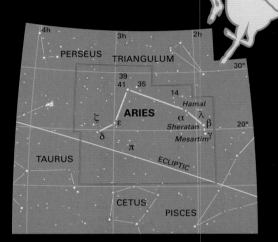

Taurus The Bull

Fully visible 88°N–58°S

This rich constellation represents a bull charging the hunter Orion. One of the oldest constellations, it has been recognized since Babylonian times – perhaps because of the distinctive "face" formed by Aldebaran and the Hyades.

FEATURES OF INTEREST

Alpha (α) Tauri (Aldebaran) 👁 This red giant star lies some 65 light years from Earth. It shines at around magnitude 1.0, but its brightness varies because this elderly star has become unstable.

The Hyades 👁 This V-shaped star cluster lies well beyond Aldebaran, some 160 light years away. Binoculars will reveal stunning starscapes.

The Pleiades (M45) 👁 Named after a group of mythical Greek nymphs, this famous open cluster marks the bull's shoulders. Naked-eye observers usually see six of the so-called "seven sisters", but binoculars or a telescope show many more hot blue stars. The cluster is just 50 million years old and lies 400 light years away.

Crab Nebula (M1) ⤢ This nebula is the shredded remnant of a star that exploded as a supernova in 1054.

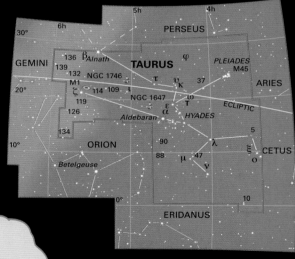

Raging bull
Taurus, the celestial bull, thrusts his star-tipped horns into the night air. The bull is said to represent a disguise adopted by Zeus in a Greek myth.

Gemini The Twins

This zodiac constellation represents the twins Castor and Pollux, who were the brothers of Helen of Troy and were among the crew of the Argo that went in search of the golden fleece. Gemini is easy to find due to its proximity to Orion.

Fully visible 90°N–55°S

FEATURES OF INTEREST

Alpha (α) Geminorum (Castor) ⚹ Castor is a fascinating multiple star system with overall magnitude 1.6. A small telescope will divide it into two white stars, while a larger one reveals a faint red companion. Each of these stars is itself a double (though none can be separated visually), giving Castor a total of six stars.

Beta (β) Geminorum (Pollux) 👁 In contrast to Castor, Pollux is a single yellow star, about 34 light years from Earth. It is also brighter than Castor, at magnitude 1.1.

M35 ♏ This open cluster can be spotted with the naked eye and is a rich target for binoculars, through which it appears as an elongated, elliptical patch of starlight spanning the same apparent width as a full moon.

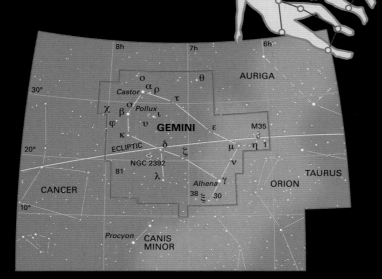

Celestial twins
Castor and Pollux, the twins of the Greek myth, stand side by side in the sky between Taurus and Cancer. The bright "star" in the middle of Gemini is actually the planet Saturn.

Cancer The Crab

Although Cancer's star pattern is faint and indistinct, it is still easy to find. This is because it lies between the brighter stars of Leo and Gemini. Cancer represents a crab that attacked the hero Hercules, but was crushed beneath his foot.

Fully visible 90°N–57°S

FEATURES OF INTEREST

Alpha (α) Cancri (Acubens) 👁 This star, whose name means "the claw", is actually fainter than nearby beta. It is a white star of magnitude 4.2, some 175 light years from Earth.

Beta (β) Cancri (Altarf) 👁 Cancer's brightest star is an orange giant, 290 light years from Earth and obviously brighter than Acubens at magnitude 3.5.

Praesepe (M44) ♏ This is a group of 50 young stars spread across an area of sky three times the size of the full Moon. Although their combined light makes them easily visible to the naked eye, binoculars are needed to resolve the individual stars. This cluster is also known as the Beehive. Its traditional name, Praesepe, means "manger".

Hidden crab
Cancer is the faintest constellation in the zodiac, but it contains a major star cluster, M44, which is just visible near the centre of the constellation.

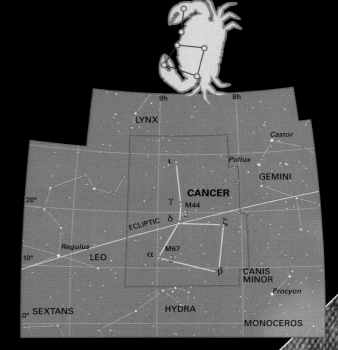

Leo Minor The Lesser Lion

This constellation was invented by Polish astronomer Johannes Hevelius around 1680. He claimed that its stars resembled nearby Leo, but the resemblance is far from obvious, and it seems as though Hevelius was simply keen to fill a gap in the sky for his great star atlas, *Uranographia*.

Fully visible 90°N–48°S

FEATURES OF INTEREST

46 Leonis Minoris 👁 The constellation's brightest star is an orange giant of magnitude 3.8. It lies about 80 light years from Earth and is nearing the end of its life. It has missed out on a Greek letter designation due to obscurity and historical accident. The 19th-century English astronomer Francis Baily overlooked recording this star as alpha (α).
Beta (β) Leonis Minoris 👁 The second brightest star in the constellation, meanwhile, does merit a Greek letter. This

yellow giant shines at magnitude 4.2 and is 190 light years away, so in reality it is considerably more luminous than 46.
R Leonis Minoris 🔭 Lying just to the west of 21 Leonis Minoris, this is an interesting star to track with binoculars. It is a pulsating red giant with a period of 372 days, similar to the famous Mira in Cetus. At its peak, of magnitude 6.3, it is easily spotted in binoculars, but at its dimmest it fades beyond the reach of small telescopes.

Coma Berenices Berenice's Hair

This constellation (whose name is often shortened to simply Coma) represents the hair of a mythical queen of Egypt. Despite a lack of bright stars, it is easily located since it lies between the brighter stars of Leo and Boötes. It contains significant clusters of both stars and galaxies.

Fully visible 90°N–56°S

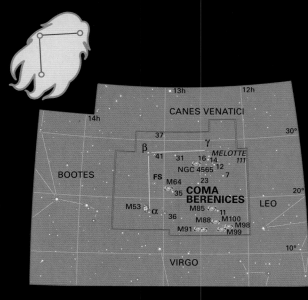

FEATURES OF INTEREST

Melotte 111 👁 The constellation gets its name from the faint strands of stars in this open cluster. Melotte 111 is one of the closest open star clusters to Earth, and more than 20 of its stars are visible to the naked eye.
M53 🔭 The brighter of two globular clusters in Coma, M53 is some 56,000 light years away, visible through binoculars but best seen in a small telescope.

Coma Cluster 🔭 Many galaxies are scattered across this part of the sky. Some are overspill from the Virgo Cluster, around 50 million light years away, while others are members of the more distant Coma Cluster, centred around a point close to beta.
M64 🔭 Coma's brightest galaxy is nicknamed the "Black Eye". It is a spiral tilted at an angle to the Earth, and is crossed by a prominent lane of dust.

Leo The Lion

This zodiac constellation, which represents the Nemean lion fought by Hercules, does bear some resemblance to a resting lion. The Leonid meteors radiate from the region around the head and neck, which is called the Sickle, every November.

Fully visible 82°N–57°S

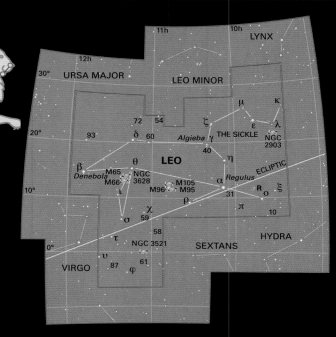

FEATURES OF INTEREST

Alpha (α) Leonis (Regulus) 👁 This bright blue-white star shines at magnitude 1.4 and is located almost 80 light years away. It lies at the foot of the pattern of six stars marking the lion's head and chest. It has a companion star of magnitude 7.8 that can be seen through binoculars.
Gamma (γ) Leonis (Algieba) 🔭 This attractive double star consists of two yellow giants some

170 light years form Earth. Easily split in small telescopes, the brighter star is magnitude 2.0 and the fainter 3.2. Both stars orbit each other every 600 years or so.
R Leonis 🔭 This red giant is 3,000 light years away. It varies in brightness over 312 days, usually staying below naked-eye visibility but peaking at fourth magnitude.

Often associated with the harvest goddess Demeter, Virgo lies to the southeast of the more identifiable Leo. Demeter is usually depicted holding an ear of wheat, which is represented by Spica, the constellation's brightest star. Virgo is also identified as Dike, the Greek goddess of justice. It is host to Earth's nearest major galaxy cluster.

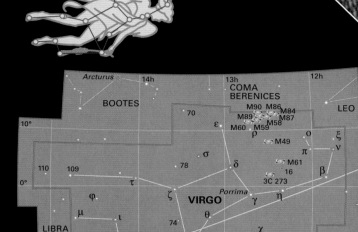

FEATURES OF INTEREST

Alpha (α) Virginis (Spica) 👁 This bright star has an average magnitude of 1.0. About 260 light years from Earth, it is actually a binary star – its elements cannot be split visually, but the companion distorts the primary's shape, causing its brightness to vary as different amounts of the surface are presented to Earth.

M87 ⚏ This huge "giant elliptical" galaxy is at the heart of the Virgo Cluster of galaxies. It shines at magnitude 8.1 and lies 50 million light years away.

Sombrero Galaxy (M104) ↗ This bright galaxy is 35 million light years away, and is considerably closer than the Virgo Cluster. It is an edge-on spiral that appears Saturn-like, and a dark lane of dust in the galaxy's plane crosses its central bulge. Only its nucleus is visible through small telescopes. The dust lane is only revealed when seen through a large-aperture telescope or on long-exposure photographs.

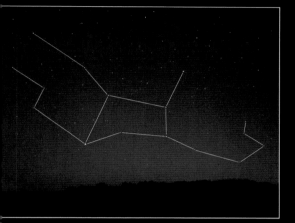

The virgin goddess constellation
Virgo straddles the celestial equator, between Leo and Libra. It is the largest constellation of the zodiac, and the second-largest overall.

Libra The Scales

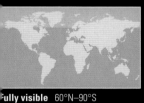

The only sign of the zodiac depicting an object rather than a living creature, Libra was once seen by the ancient Greeks as Chelae Scorpionis, the claws of neighbouring Scorpius. Since Roman times, Libra has been interpreted as the scales of justice, held by nearby Virgo.

FEATURES OF INTEREST

Alpha (α) Librae (Zubenelgenubi) ⚏ With a name meaning "the southern claw" in Arabic, alpha is a bright double easily split with binoculars or even with sharp unaided eyesight. Its two stars, a blue-white giant of magnitude 2.8 and a white star of magnitude 5.2, lie 70 light years from Earth. To the north of this pair is the constellation's brightest star, Zubeneschamali, meaning "the northern claw", or beta (β) Librae.

Mu (μ) Librae ↗ This double star, with components of magnitudes 5.6 and 6.7, is a close pairing 235 light years from Earth, but can be split by all but the smallest telescopes.

48 Librae 👁 Lying 510 light years from Earth, this young star is at an early stage of its development, and is still throwing off excess material that forms shells around the star, causing it to vary unpredictably by around 0.1 magnitudes.

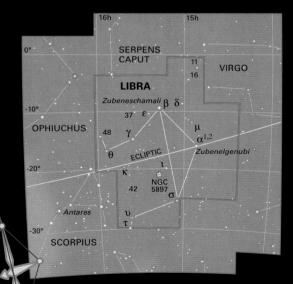

Libra's stars
Originally, the ancient Greeks visualized Libra as the claws of Scorpius, which is why the constellation's brightest stars have names meaning "northern claw" and "southern claw".

Corona Borealis The Northern Crown

The distinctive arc of Corona Borealis lies just to the east of Boötes, and is easily spotted despite the relative faintness of its stars. It contains a number of interesting variable stars. The constellation depicts a crown worn in Greek myth by Princess Ariadne at her wedding to the god Dionysus.

Fully visible 90°N–50°S

FEATURES OF INTEREST

Alpha (α) Coronae Borealis (Alphekka) ◉ This is an eclipsing binary star, similar to Algol in Perseus, although far less obvious, since it varies by only 0.1 magnitude either side of its average of 2.2 in a 17.4-day cycle.

R Coronae Borealis ◉ This intriguing variable is normally just visible to the naked eye, enclosed by the curve of the crown, shining at magnitude 5.8. But every few years it unpredictably plunges in brightness, disappearing beyond the range of most amateur telescopes. R is a yellow supergiant some 6,000 light years from Earth and seems to throw off shells of material that obscure its own light.

T Coronae Borealis ✴ Every few decades this nova system, known as the Blaze Star, does the opposite of R, brightening rapidly from magnitude 11 to around 2.

Starry crown
Like a celestial tiara, the seven main stars of Corona Borealis form an arc between Bootes and Hercules. According to the myth, Dionysus threw Ariadne's jewelled crown into the sky, where it transformed into stars.

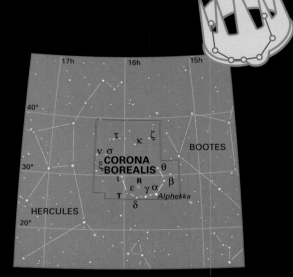

Serpens The Serpent

This is one of the 48 original Greek constellations, representing a snake coiled around Ophiuchus. Uniquely, it is split into two parts, on either side of Ophiuchus – Serpens Caput represents the snake's head, and Serpens Cauda its tail. Both parts straddle the celestial equator.

Fully visible 74°N–64°S

FEATURES OF INTEREST

Alpha (α) Serpentis (Unukalhai) ◉ Situated in Serpens Caput, this is an orange giant of magnitude 2.7, 70 light years away.

M5 ◉ An attractive globular cluster, M5 is just visible to the naked eye on dark nights, hovering around magnitude 5.6. Binoculars or a small telescope reveal a hazy ball of light, but at 24,500 light years away, larger telescopes are needed to see the curving chain of individual stars.

M16 ♁ This open cluster of about 60 stars lies 8,000 light years away at the heart of the large, faint Eagle Nebula, a huge cloud of gas and dust from which the stars have recently been born. It appears as a hazy patch covering an area of sky similar in size to a full moon.

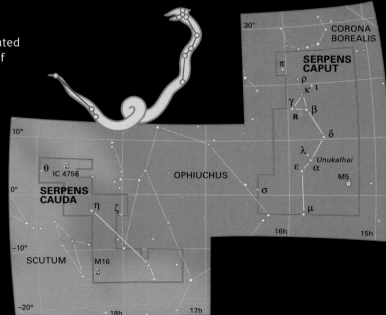

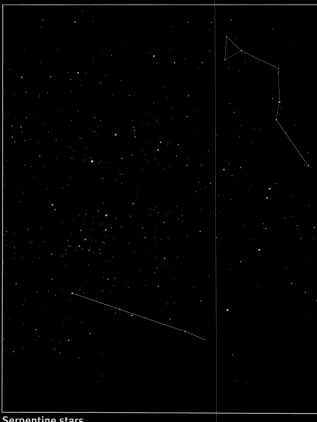

Serpentine stars
The upper part of the snake contains Unukalhai (α), which derives its name from the Arabic for "the serpent's neck". In Greek mythology, snakes were a symbol of rebirth, because of their ability to shed their skin.

Ophiuchus The Serpent Holder

This large, indistinct constellation is either represented as Hercules wrestling the snake Serpens or alternatively as Asclepius, the Greek god of healing, who carried a staff with a serpent entwined around it. The serpent is represented by adjoining Serpens.

Fully visible 59°N–75°S

FEATURES OF INTEREST

Alpha (α) Ophiuchi (Rasalhague) 👁 Ophiuchus's brightest star is this magnitude-2.1 white giant, about 50 light years away.

Rho (ρ) Ophiuchi 🔭 This fine multiple star is still embedded in the faint gas from which it formed. Binoculars will show two wide companions close to the magnitude-5.0 primary star, while a small telescope will show that the primary has a closer neighbour of magnitude 5.9.

Barnard's Star 🔭 Though too faint for binoculars, this star (found near beta) is interesting as it is the fastest-moving in the sky. It is just six light years from Earth, and moving so fast that it crosses a Moon's width of the sky every 200 years. This celebrated star is the second-closest star to the Sun.

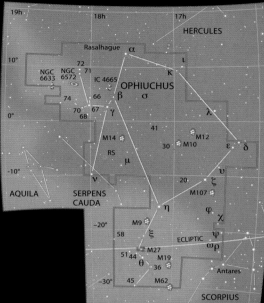

Snake man
Ophiuchus represents a man wrapped in the coils of a huge snake, the constellation Serpens. The ecliptic runs through Ophiuchus, and planets can be seen within its borders.

Scutum The Shield

This small, kite-shaped constellation was invented in the 17th century by the Polish astronomer Johannes Hevelius and was originally named Scutum Sobieski (meaning "Sobieski's shield") in honour of Hevelius's patron, the King of Poland. Lying in the Milky Way, it is best located by searching between Altair (in the neighbouring constellation Aquila) and the bright stars of Sagittarius.

Fully visible 74°N–90°S

FEATURES OF INTEREST

Delta (δ) Scuti 👁 This magnitude-4.7 star, 260 light years from Earth, is the prototype for a class of rapidly changing variable stars, though it only varies by about 0.1 magnitude over each 4.6-hour cycle.

R Scuti 🔭 This is a variable star with a slower period than Delta Scuti, and its changes are much easier to follow. It is a yellow supergiant that varies from an easy magnitude 4.5 at its peak, down to magnitude 8.8, the limit of binocular visibility, in a cycle lasting 144 days.

Wild Duck Cluster (M11) 👁 A rich open cluster, this is easy to see with the naked eye and is rewarding for binoculars. When seen through a telescope, the stars form a fan shape, like a flock of ducks in flight, hence the popular name.

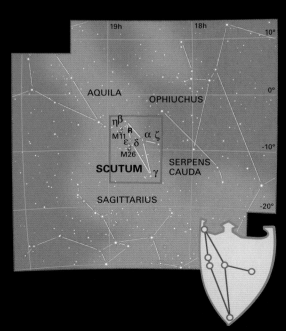

Sobieski's shield
Scutum is a minor constellation with no bright stars of its own, but it lies in an area of the Milky Way, between Aquila and Sagittarius, that is particularly rich with stars. One of the brightest parts of the Milky Way lies in Scutum and is known as the Scutum Star Cloud.

Sagitta The Arrow

Fully visible 90°N–69°S

Although this small constellation represents an arrow, and was recognized in ancient times, it has nothing to do with the larger constellation of Sagittarius, the archer. Sagitta lies in the Milky Way and represents an arrow fired by Hercules towards Aquila and Cygnus.

FEATURES OF INTEREST

Alpha (α) (Sham) and Beta (β) Sagittae 👁 Alpha and beta are twin yellow stars, both of magnitude 4.4. They are genuine neighbours in space, both lying about 470 light years away. Alpha's Arabic name, Sham, means "arrow".
Gamma (γ) Sagittae 👁 The brightest star in Sagitta, gamma is an orange giant of magnitude 3.5. It lies at a distance of 175 light years from Earth, at the tip of the arrow that points northeastward.

S Sagittae 🔭 This yellow supergiant, 4,300 light years from Earth, is a pulsating variable, ranging in brightness between magnitudes 5.5 and 6.2 every 8.38 days.
M71 🔭 This star cluster is usually classed as a globular, but its relatively loose structure means that some astronomers suspect it is really a large open cluster, as it lacks the central condensation typical of globulars. It lies about 13,000 light years away, and is visible only through binoculars.

Aquila The Eagle

This constellation is found easily by its central bright star Altair, flanked by twins. Aquila depicts the god Zeus, who took the form of an eagle to carry away the youth Ganymede (himself depicted by Aquarius).

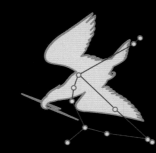

FEATURES OF INTEREST

Alpha (α) Aquilae (Altair) 👁 Altair is one of the closest bright stars to Earth, lying just 17 light years away and shining at magnitude 0.8. Along with Deneb (in Cygnus) and Vega (in Lyra), it forms the "summer triangle" of northern skies.
Beta (β) Aquilae (Alshain) 👁 Beta and gamma (Tarazed) are the near-twin stars that flank Altair. Alshain is actually

the fainter of the two. It shines at magnitude 3.7 compared to Tarazed's 2.7. It is just 49 light years away, while the giant Tarazed, which has a distinctly orange colour, is more than five times this distance.
NGC 6709 🔭 Aquila is crossed by a rich area of the Milky Way. NGC 6709 is an open cluster 3,000 light years away that appears through binoculars as a bright knot in the star clouds.

Vulpecula The Fox

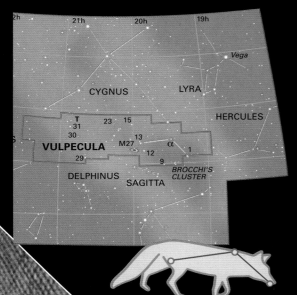

Fully visible 90°N–61°S

This constellation is another of the additions made by Polish astronomer Johannes Hevelius in the late 17th century. It consists of a handful of faint stars with no obvious pattern, and is best located by looking to the west of the brighter constellation Pegasus.

FEATURES OF INTEREST

Alpha (α) Vulpeculae 👁 The constellation's brightest star has a modest magnitude of 4.4. It is a red giant about 250 light years away from Earth.
Brocchi's Cluster 👁 This small group of stars lies on Vulpecula's southern border. Its members hover at the limit of naked-eye visibility, and the cluster is an attractive sight in binoculars.

Dumbbell Nebula (M27) 🔭 Vulpecula's most famous object, this is the brightest planetary nebula in the sky and among the easiest to spot. Appearing as a rounded patch, the nebula is one-quarter of the diameter of a full Moon, and about 1,000 light years from Earth. It is a rewarding target for small telescopes, which will reveal the twin lobes or hourglass shape for which it gets its popular name. The nebula usually appears grey-green.

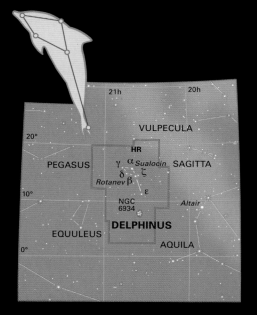

Delphinus The Dolphin

Small and faint, but still distinctive, Delphinus lies just to the west of Pegasus. It represents either one of two dolphins from Greek myth – one sent by the sea god Poseidon to rescue the drowning lyre player Arion, or another sent to persuade the mermaid Amphitrite to be Poseidon's bride.

Fully visible 90°N–69°S

FEATURES OF INTEREST

Alpha (α) Delphini (Sualocin) 👁 This hot blue-white star is located 190 light years from Earth and shines at magnitude 3.8.
Beta (β) Delphini (Rotanev) 👁 Slightly brighter than alpha, Rotanev is a pure white star of magnitude 3.6 that lies 72 light years away from Earth. The names Sualocin (see above) and Rotanev are a reversed spelling of Nicolaus Venator, the Latinized name of an Italian astronomer called Niccolò Cacciatore working at Palermo Observatory in Sicily in

around 1800, who ignored convention and mischievously named the stars after himself.
Gamma (γ) Delphini 🔭 This attractive double star, about 125 light years away from Earth, consists of two yellow-white stars of magnitudes 4.3 and 5.1. They are easily separated with a small telescope. With Sualocin (α), Rotanev (β), and delta (δ), gamma forms the asterism known as "Job's Coffin", the name possibly being a reference to its boxlike or diamond shape.

Equuleus The Foal

Equuleus is the second smallest constellation in the sky, and its stars are relatively faint. It represents the head of a young horse and since ancient times has been seen as a companion to the nearby, larger horse-shaped constellation Pegasus, although there are no myths or legends associated with Equuleus. It is located by looking in the wedge of sky between Epsilon Pegasi, in the southwest corner of Pegasus, and the diamond-shaped constellation Delphinus.

Fully visible 90°N–77°S

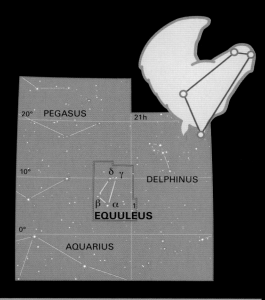

FEATURES OF INTEREST

Alpha (α) Equulei (Kitalpha) 👁 This yellow giant of magnitude 3.9 lies 190 light years from the Sun, and is 75 times more luminous than it.
Epsilon (ε) Equulei 🔭 This triple star combines a chance alignment with a genuine binary system. A small telescope

will reveal that the primary star, magnitude 5.4, has a magnitude-7.4 companion that just happens to lie in the same direction. The fainter star is actually the closer of the two, 125 light years away compared to 200 for the primary. Larger telescopes reveal that the primary is itself a double star.

Pegasus The Winged Horse

One of the largest constellations, Pegasus covers a rather empty area of sky. This constellation is very easy to find, because its four bright stars (one of which is shared with Andromeda) form the Great Square of Pegasus. It is one of the original 48 Greek constellations.

Fully visible 90°N–53°S

FEATURES OF INTEREST

Alpha (α) Pegasi (Markab) 👁 This is normally the brightest star in the constellation, blue-white and shining at magnitude 2.5. It is 140 light years away.
Beta (β) Pegasi (Scheat) 👁 This red giant shows an obvious colour difference from the other stars in the Great Square of Pegasus. It is 200 light years from Earth, and varies unpredictably – usually around magnitude 2.7,

but sometimes outshining Markab, reaching magnitude 2.3, and occasionally becoming fainter than gamma at around magnitude 2.9.
M15 🌐 This bright globular cluster of magnitude 6.2 is easily spotted through binoculars. More than 30,000 light years away, it is one of the densest star clusters in the galaxy. It contains nine pulsars, the remains of ancient supernova explosions.

Aquarius The Water Carrier

Fully visible 65°N–86°S

One of the oldest constellations, and a member of the zodiac, Aquarius has been seen as a youth (or, sometimes, an older man) pouring water from a jug since the second millennium BCE. The pattern is indistinct, but its brightest star and the Y-shaped pattern of the water jug are useful aids for locating it.

FEATURES OF INTEREST

Helix Nebula (NGC 7293) ♒ This is our nearest planetary nebula, at 300 light years away. One of the largest nebulae in apparent size, it appears the size of the full Moon. Its light, however, is diffused over a large area, so the nebula can be identified only in clear and dark skies. It is best seen through binoculars, which have a wide field of view.

Saturn Nebula (NGC 7009) ⚹ Another planetary nebula, this is 3,000 light years away and shines at magnitude 8.0. It appears to be of a size similar to the disc of Saturn, when viewed with a small telescope.

M2 ♒ This is the brighter of Aquarius's two globular clusters, at magnitude 6.5. It is 37,000 light years away.

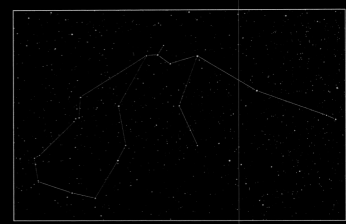

Pouring water
Aquarius is found between Capricornus and Pisces, near the celestial equator. The cascade of stars that represent the flow of water from Aquarius's jar is to the left of this image. The distinctive Water Jar is centre-top.

Pisces The Fish

Fully visible 83°N–56°S

This zodiac constellation represents two mythical fish. It is best spotted by looking to one side of the Great Square of Pegasus. According to ancient Greek myths, the goddess Aphrodite and her son, Eros, transformed into fish and plunged into the River Euphrates to escape a fearsome monster called Typhon. In another version of the same story, two fish swam up and carried Aphrodite and Eros to safety on their backs.

FEATURES OF INTEREST

Alpha (α) Piscium (Alrescha) 👁 Marking the point where the tails of Pisces's two fish join, Alrescha is a double star, though one whose components are too close in the sky to separate with small telescopes. Its white stars are 140 light years away, and have individual magnitudes of 4.2 and 5.2, giving them a combined brightness of magnitude 3.8.

Eta (η) Piscium 👁 The second brightest star in Pisces, eta is a yellow supergiant of magnitude 3.6 – brighter than either of alpha's components alone, and more than twice their distance at 300 light years.

M74 ⚹ This spiral galaxy, 25 million light years away, is face-on to Earth. Its light is so spread out that it is quite a challenging target for small telescopes.

The Circlet
The most distinctive feature of Pisces is the ring of seven stars, seen on the top right. Known as the Circlet, it lies to the south of the Great Square of Pegasus and marks the body of one of the fish.

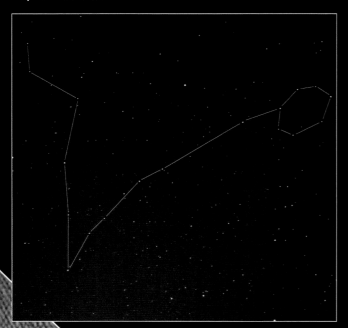

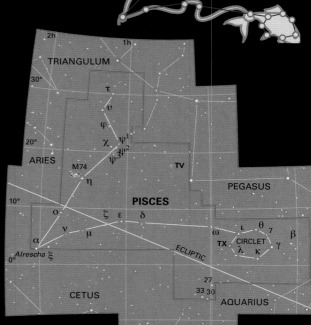

Cetus The Sea Monster or Whale

Usually seen as the figure of a whale, Cetus doubles as a sea monster for one of the sky's great legends – the story of Perseus and Andromeda. Cetus is large but relatively faint, best found by looking next to Taurus. Identification is not helped by the fact that it can vary in appearance depending on the brightness of its most famous star, Mira.

Fully visible 65°N–79°S

Lurching monster
Cetus is one of the original 48 Greek constellations listed by Ptolemy in his *Almagest*. It can be seen in the equatorial region of the sky, lying south of the constellations Pisces and Aries.

FEATURES OF INTEREST

Omicron (ο) Ceti (Mira) 👁 With a name derived from the Latin for "wonderful", Mira is among most prominent variable stars in the sky, and was recognized in 1596. It is distinctively red and varies between magnitude 10 and 2 over a cycle of 332 days. Mira is an unstable red giant, and it varies in brightness as it fluctuates in size. Depending on how much it has swollen or contracted within its cycle, Mira can be either a naked-eye star or one that is visible only with a telescope.

Tau (τ) Ceti 👁 One of the closest Sun-like stars to Earth, tau is just 11.9 light years away. Technically, it is a "yellow sub-dwarf", and if it has planets in orbit around it, they would be prime candidates for extraterrestrial life.

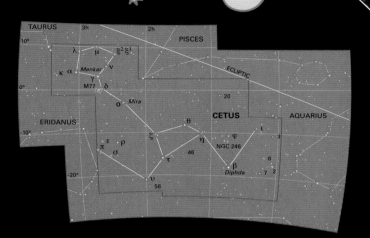

Orion Orion

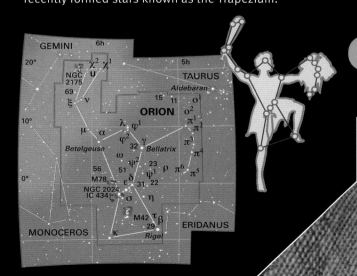

This prominent constellation, containing two of the brightest stars and the clearest emission nebula in the sky, represents a hunter from Greek myth. Orion stands in a celestial tableau, facing the charging bull Taurus, and followed by his faithful hounds, Canis Major and Canis Minor.

Fully visible 90°N–57°S

FEATURES OF INTEREST

Alpha (α) Orionis (Betelgeuse) 👁 Some 430 light years from Earth, this is one of the brightest red giants in the sky. But its magnitude varies unpredictably, between magnitude 0.0 and 1.3. It usually shines around 0.1, and is so large that astronomers have been able to map its surface.

Beta (β) Orionis (Rigel) 👁 Apart from the rare times when Betelgeuse is at its maximum magnitude, Rigel is Orion's brightest star. It is a brilliant blue-white supergiant of magnitude 0.1, and marks one of Orion's feet. Rigel lies about 770 light years away.

Great Orion Nebula (M42) 👁 Forming a "sword" below the three stars of Orion's belt, M42 is a huge star-forming region about 1,500 light years away. The nebula and its surrounding stars are visible to the naked eye, and a beautiful sight through binoculars or a small telescope. At its heart lies a small cluster of four recently formed stars known as the Trapezium.

Bright hunter
Orion is one of the most magnificent and easily recognizable constellations. A line of three stars makes up the hunter's belt, while an area of star clusters and nebulae forms his sword.

Canis Major The Greater Dog

Fully visible 56°N–90°S

Following obediently behind Orion the hunter on his journey across the sky, Canis Major is host to Sirius, the Dog Star, the brightest star in the sky. But since it lies across the Milky Way, it also contains several star clusters and other features of the deep sky.

FEATURES OF INTEREST

Alpha (α) Canis Majoris (Sirius) 👁 With a magnitude of -1.4, the famous "Dog Star" is so bright that only some planets ever outshine it. At 23 times more luminous than the Sun, Sirius is fairly average for a white star of its type, but it also happens to lie in our stellar neighbourhood, just 8.6 light years away. It is a binary system: the primary star is orbited by Sirius B – a faint white dwarf that would be more easily seen were it not for Sirius's own brilliance.

Beta (β) Canis Majoris (Mirzam) 👁 Although at magnitude 2.0, Mirzam is far outshone by Sirius, it is a much more luminous star in reality – a blue giant 500 light years from Earth.

M41 👁 This open cluster of stars is visible to the naked eye as a hazy patch the size of the full Moon, although it is 2,300 light years away. Binoculars distinguish its brightest stars, while telescopes show chains of stars radiating from its centre.

Canis Minor The Lesser Dog

Fully visible 89°N–77°S

This small constellation is easy to spot because of its bright star Procyon. It is a Greek constellation and represents the smaller of Orion's two dogs. It forms an obvious triangle in the sky, with Sirius in Canis Major and Betelgeuse in Orion. Its border lies almost on the celestial equator.

FEATURES OF INTEREST

Alpha (α) Canis Minoris (Procyon) The name of this star means "before the dog" in Greek, because from Mediterranean latitudes, it always rises shortly before the more brilliant Sirius. Shining at magnitude 0.34, it is still one of the most prominent stars in the sky, and offers a useful comparison with its brighter cousin, since both stars lie around the same distance from Earth. In reality, Procyon

is seven times more luminous than the Sun, compared to Sirius's 23 times. Like Sirius, it forms a binary system with a white dwarf companion, named Procyon B.

Beta (β) Canis Minoris (Gomeisa) This magnitude-2.9 blue-white star is far more distant than Procyon, at about 150 light years away, and is much more radiant. Its name derives from the Arabic for "the little bleary-eyed one" which referred to the weeping sister of Sirius, whom he left behind to flee for his life.

Monoceros The Unicorn

Fully visible 78°N–78°S

The W-shape of Monoceros is hard to pick out, but it can be located with reference to Orion and Canis Major. The constellation sits on the celestial equator in the middle of a triangle formed by Betelgeuse (in Orion), Procyon (in Canis Minor), and Sirius (in Canis Major). Added to the list of constellations by Dutch theologian Petrus Plancius in 1613, it depicts a unicorn.

FEATURES OF INTEREST

Alpha (α) Monocerotis 👁 This is the brightest of the constellation's stars. It is an orange giant, about 175 light years from Earth and shining at magnitude 3.9.

Beta (β) Monocerotis ☌ The constellation's stellar highlight, beta is a beautiful triple star, separated in a small telescope to reveal a chain of three fifth-magnitude, blue-white stars.

M50 ♦ This is one of several open star clusters populating a rich band of the Milky Way as it passes through Monoceros. Small telescopes should reveal its individual stars.

NGC 2244 ♦ This star cluster lies at the heart of a glowing gas cloud called the Rosette Nebula – an outlying part of a huge star-forming complex centred on Orion. The Rosette itself (NGC 2237) is diffuse, but can be seen with good binoculars on a dark night.

Hydra The Water Snake

The largest constellation in the sky is a hard-to-trace chain of mostly average-brightness stars. The head of this lengthy snake is a roughly triangular group of stars south of Cancer. The brightest star, Alphard ("solitary one"), marks its heart.

Fully visible 54°N–83°S

FEATURES OF INTEREST

M48 👁 This open cluster of stars lies close to Hydra's border with the richer starfields of Monoceros. It contains about 80 stars, and is just visible to the naked eye in dark skies.

M83 🔭 This face-on spiral galaxy, 15 million light years away, has a bright central nucleus that can be spotted with ease through a small telescope.

Long serpent
The Hydra's head, at the right in this photograph, lies south of Cancer (and, in this view, the disc of Jupiter), while the tip of its tail lies far to the left.

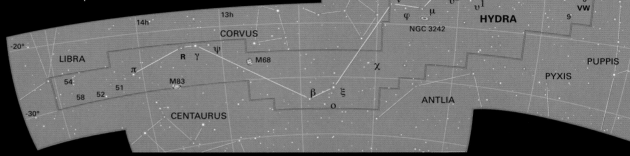

Antlia The Air Pump

French astronomer Nicolas de Lacaille introduced this constellation for his 1756 map of the southern skies. It honours the vacuum pump invented by French scientist Denis Papin and British physicist Robert Boyle. It is best found by looking to the northeast of the Milky Way as it passes through Puppis.

Fully visible 49°N–90°S

FEATURES OF INTEREST

Alpha (α) Antliae 👁 This orange giant is 500 times more luminous than the Sun, but at a distance of 365 light years, it shines at a weak magnitude of 4.3.

Theta (θ) Antliae 👁 At magnitude 4.8, theta is the constellation's second brightest star, though it is actually a double, consisting of white and yellow stars of magnitudes 5.6 and 5.7 respectively, 385 light years away. Unfortunately, small telescopes are not powerful enough to separate them.

Eight-burst Nebula (NGC 3132) 🔭 Sometimes also referred to as the Southern Ring Nebula, this nebula straddles the boundary of Antlia and Vela, at a distance of about 2,000 light years from Earth. It is a planetary nebula, which often forms when a Sun-like star becomes a red giant and throws off its outer layers. NGC 3132 shines at magnitude 8 and so is a good target for small telescopes.

North of Vela
Antlia is an inconspicuous grouping in the southern hemisphere and consists of a handful of stars to be found between Vela and Hydra.

Sextans The Sextant

Fully visible 78°N–83°S

This constellation is named after a navigational and scientific instrument used for taking star positions in the days before telescopes. The pattern is easy to find, since it lies to the south of Leo's bright star, Regulus. It was added to the sky by Polish astronomer Johannes Hevelius in 1687.

FEATURES OF INTEREST

Alpha (α) Sextantis 👁 This blue-white giant star is some 340 light years from Earth. Due to this distance, alpha shines in Earth's skies at a relatively weak magnitude 4.5.

Beta (β) Sextantis 👁 Another blue-white giant, beta is more luminous than alpha, but only reaches magnitude 5.1 in our skies because it lies 520 light years away.

Spindle Galaxy (NGC 3115) 🔭 One of the closest large galaxies, NGC 3115 lies some 14 million light years away (many dwarf elliptical galaxies lie closer but are generally too faint for amateur observers). Usually classified as lenticular (lens-shaped) galaxy, NGC 3115's huge, bulging disc of stars can appear elliptical, because it is viewed edge-on from Earth. The combined light of its stars reaches magnitude 8.5, making it just visible in binoculars, though a telescope of small to moderate aperture is needed for a proper view. It is popularly named the Spindle Galaxy because of its highly elongated shape.

Crater The Cup

Fully visible 65°N–90°S

This constellation is faint, but still relatively easy to locate due to its distinctive "bow-tie" shape. It represents the drinking cup of the Greek god Apollo, and is linked in mythology with its adjacent constellations. Supposedly Apollo sent Corvus, the crow, to fill his cup from a well, but the bird was distracted by a fig tree, and returned with an empty cup, saying that Hydra, the water-snake, had blocked the well. An angry Apollo saw through the crow's deception, and threw snake, cup, and crow into the sky, to be preserved among the stars.

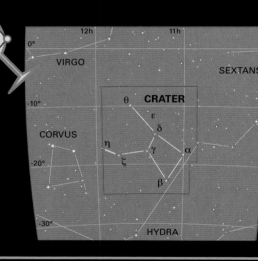

FEATURES OF INTEREST

Delta (δ) Crateris 👁 Crater's brightest star has ended up with the designation delta through historical accident. It is a magnitude-3.6 orange giant, 62 light years from Earth.

Alpha (α) Crateris 👁 Significantly fainter than gamma at magnitude 4.1, alpha is a yellow giant star, about 175 light years away.

Gamma (γ) Crateris 🔭 This white star, 75 light years away and of magnitude 4.1, has a faint binary companion that can be seen in small telescopes.

Corvus The Crow

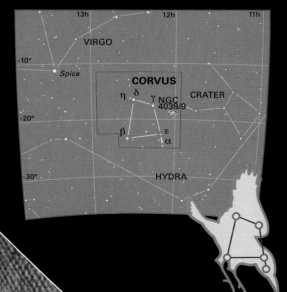

Fully visible 65°N–90°S

The roughly rectangular shape of Corvus is defined by its four brightest stars and represents a crow, the servant of the god Apollo in a story linking it with Crater and Hydra. Its pattern is indistinct, and it is best found by looking to the southwest of the bright star Spica in Virgo.

FEATURES OF INTEREST

Gamma (γ) Corvi (Gienah) 👁 Corvus's brightest star, gamma is a blue-white star of magnitude 2.6, lying at a distance of 220 light years. It shares a common name with Epsilon (ε) Cygni.

Delta (δ) Corvi 🔭 This double star, 115 light years distant, is a good target for small telescopes. The bright blue-white primary is orbited by a deeper blue or even purple star of magnitude 9.2.

Alpha (α) Corvi (Alchiba) 👁 Despite its Bayer letter designation, usually given to the brightest star, alpha is outshone by Gamma (γ), Beta (β), and Delta (δ) Corvi. It is a white star 52 light years away, shining at magnitude 4.0.

Antennae (NGC 4038 and 4039) 🔭 These faint galaxies, bare visible through small telescopes, are a pair of colliding spiral galaxies. Their name describes the long tendrils of stars, gas, and dust ripped from the galaxies during their encounter.

Centaurus The Centaur

Fully visible 25°N–90°S

Centaurus extends into the Milky Way and contains several deep-sky objects as well as the closest star to Earth. This constellation represents a mythical centaur called Chiron.

FEATURES OF INTEREST

Alpha (α) Centauri (Rigil Kentaurus) The sky's third-brightest star at magnitude -0.3, this system is our next-door neighbour, 4.3 light years away. This brilliant star is in fact a yellow star with a red companion of magnitudes 0 and 1.3 respectively. Another companion, the 11th-magnitude red dwarf Proxima Centauri, can be spotted only through a good telescope.

Omega (Ω) Centauri (NGC 5139) Despite its stellar name, omega is the sky's brightest globular cluster – a tight ball of several million stars, 17,000 light years from Earth and shining at magnitude 3.7. To the naked eye, it is a large, hazy star, and a small telescope is required to resolve the brightest individual members of this globular cluster.

NGC 5128 This bright galaxy is an active elliptical, about 15 million light years away, that gives out strong radio signals.

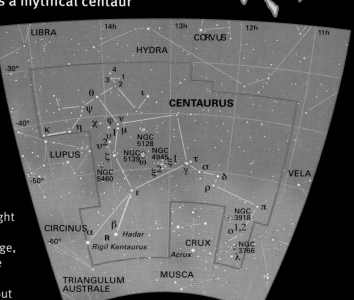

Celestial centaur
The brilliant stellar pairing of Alpha (α) and Beta (β) Centauri guides the eye to Centaurus, the celestial centaur. The familiar pattern of Crux, the Southern Cross, lies beneath the centaur's body.

Lupus The Wolf

Fully visible 34°N–90°S

Lying in the southern Milky Way and cursed with a complex jumble of stars, Lupus can be hard to spot, despite being relatively bright. However, it lies between the more recognizable Scorpius and Centaurus and contains many interesting objects.

FEATURES OF INTEREST

Alpha (α) and Beta (β) Lupi Lupus's two brightest stars are almost identical and close neighbours in space. Both are blue giants about 650 light years away, but alpha is slightly closer, giving it a magnitude of 2.3 compared to beta's 2.7.

Mu (μ) Lupi Many of Lupus's stars are double, but mu is one of the easiest to split. Small telescopes will easily show that the primary, a blue-white star of magnitude 4.3, has a magnitude-7 companion. Larger telescopes will reveal that the primary is itself a double, composed of twin stars of magnitude 5.1.

NGC 5822 This large open cluster of stars, about 2,600 light years away, has an overall magnitude of 7.0.

NGC 5986 This globular cluster also shines at magnitude 7 – its stars are much more distant than those of NGC 5822, at around 45,000 light years, but they are also far more numerous.

Bestial offering
Here, Lupus is partly surrounded by the stars of Centaurus. In Greek and Roman myths, Lupus represented a wild animal that had been speared on a long pole by Centaurus. The identification of Lupus as a wolf seems to have become common during Renaissance.

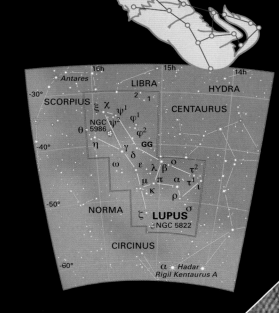

Sagittarius The Archer

Usually represented as a centaur (half man, half horse) armed with a bow, Sagittarius lies in the richest area of the Milky Way. Its central stars are best spotted by looking for a teapot-shaped pattern in the sky.

Fully visible 44°N–90°S

FEATURES OF INTEREST

Sigma (σ) Sagitarii (Nunki) 👁 This blue-white star is the constellation's brightest, with a magnitude of 2.0.
Beta (β) Sagittarii (Arkab) 👁 This apparent double star, consisting of two stars at about magnitude 4.0, can be split with the naked eye – but its stars are a chance alignment – in reality they are 140 and 380 light years away.
Lagoon Nebula (M8) 👁 Sagittarius is rich in deep-sky objects, as it lies in the direction of the galactic centre. Highlights are a chain of star-forming nebulae, including the Omega Nebula (M17). Largest and brightest of all is M8, visible to the naked eye as a lighter patch of sky and easily identified in binoculars.
M22 👁 Visible to the naked eye and a fine sight in binoculars, this is the brightest of several globular clusters on the northern edge of the constellation.

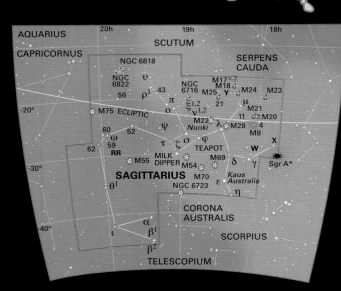

Mounted bowman
The prominent constellation of Sagittarius is found between Scorpius and Capricornus, in the southern celestial hemisphere. In Greek mythology, Sagittarius was also identified with the satyr Crotus, son of Pan.

Scorpius The Scorpion

This ancient zodiac constellation contains many dense Milky Way star clouds. Scorpius represents a scorpion that killed the hunter Orion in Greek myth – hence its location on the opposite side of the sky.

Fully visible 44°N–90°S

FEATURES OF INTEREST

Alpha (α) Scorpii (Antares) 👁 With a name that means "rival to Mars", this brilliant star varies in brightness between magnitudes 0.9 and 1.8 over a six-year period. Near-identical flanking stars Sigma and Tau Scorpii make it even easier to identify. Antares is a red supergiant, hundreds of times larger than the Sun and lying 600 light years from Earth.
M6 👁 This fine open star cluster is visible to the naked eye as a "knot" in the Milky Way, just above the scorpion's tail. Binoculars or a small telescope will reveal dozens of individual stars. M6 lies 2,000 light years away, while its chance neighbour M7 is just 800 light years from Earth, and so is rather brighter.
M4 🔭 This globular cluster, 7,000 light years away and in orbit around the Milky Way, shines at magnitude 7.4, making it a good target for binoculars or a telescope.

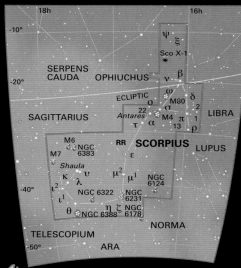

Sting in the tail
This view of Scorpius shows the scorpion raising its curving tail as though to strike. Its heart is marked by the red star Antares.

Capricornus The Sea Goat

Fully visible 62°N–90°S

Less recognizable than its southeastern neighbour Sagittarius, this constellation represents one of the stranger creatures in the sky, half fish and half goat. In ancient Greek legend, Capricornus was supposed to be the goat-headed god Pan, depicted in the sky escaping danger by transmuting into a fish.

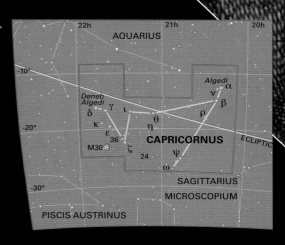

FEATURES OF INTEREST

Alpha (α) Capricorni (Algedi) ☆ This is an impressive multiple star, though not all its elements are truly related. The brightest stars, easily separated with binoculars or good eyesight, are a yellow supergiant (α^1) and an orange giant (α^2), 690 and 109 light years away and with magnitudes of 4.2 and 3.6. Small telescopes show that the yellow supergiant is a double star in its own right; larger ones will reveal that the orange giant is in fact a triple star.

Beta (β) Capricorni (Dabih) ♏ This magnitude-3.3 yellow giant reveals a faint companion through binoculars. Beta is in fact a complex multiple containing at least five, and perhaps eight, stars in orbit around each other, 330 light years away.

M30 ♏ This globular cluster, of magnitude 7.5, is 27,000 light years away and visible through binoculars. Chains of stars extend like fingers from the northern side of the cluster.

Microscopium The Microscope

Fully visible 45°N–90°S

This constellation is one of several small, faint groups added to the sky by French astronomer Nicolas Louis de Lacaille during the 1750s, most of them named after scientific instruments. Microscopium is best found by looking between the brighter stars of Sagittarius and Fomalhaut (in Piscis Austrinus).

FEATURES OF INTEREST

Alpha (α) Microscopii ☆ This double star lies 250 light years from Earth. The primary is a yellow giant of magnitude 5.0, while its companion is far fainter at magnitude 10, and visible only through telescopes of moderate aperture.

Gamma (γ) Microscopii 👁 Slightly brighter than alpha at magnitude 4.7, gamma is a yellow giant 245 light years away. To its southeast is the star epsilon (ε) Microscopii, while alpha (α) Microscopii lies at its northwest.

Theta (θ) Microscopii 👁 This is the brightest of several variable stars in the constellation, but its variations are hard to see, since it varies by only about 0.1 magnitudes from its average of 4.8 in a cycle lasting 2 days.

U Microscopii ♏ This distant red giant is a more obvious variable – it pulsates in the same way as the famous Mira in Cetus, varying between magnitudes 7.0 and 14.4 in 334 days. S Microscopii is similar but has a shorter 209-day cycle.

Piscis Austrinus The Southern Fish

Fully visible 53°N–90°S

This small ring of generally faint stars is made more obvious by the presence of Fomalhaut, one of the brightest stars in the sky. Piscis Austrinus was invented in ancient times and is one of the most southerly members of a list of 48 constellations drawn up the Greek astronomer Ptolemy.

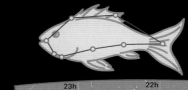

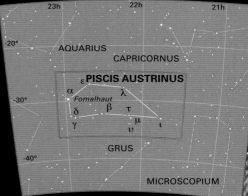

FEATURES OF INTEREST

Alpha (α) Piscis Austrini (Fomalhaut) 👁 At magnitude 1.2, Fomalhaut is the 18th brightest star in the sky. It is also relatively nearby, just 22 light years away, which means that in reality it is some 16 times more luminous than the Sun. Fomalhaut was the first star found to have a disc around it – in this case, a ring of cold, icy material, extending over about twice the diameter of our own solar system. It seems that

Fomalhaut, which is relatively young, is still in the process of forming its own planets.

Beta (β) Piscis Austrini ☆ This double star, 135 light years away, consists of a magnitude-4.3 primary with a widely spaced magnitude-7.7 star easily seen through a small telescope.

Gamma (γ) Piscis Austrini ☆ A more challenging double star, gamma's primary, of magnitude 4.5, has a closer companion of magnitude 8.0. The system lies 325 light years from Earth.

Sculptor The Sculptor's Studio

Representing a sculptor's workshop, this is one of the more bizarre constellations added to the sky by French astronomer Nicolas Louis de Lacaille.Its stars are faint and their pattern uninspiring, but the constellation is redeemed by the presence of several interesting nearby galaxies.

FEATURES OF INTEREST

Alpha (α) Sculptoris 👁 The brightest star in the constellation is a blue-white giant, 590 light years away and shining at magnitude 4.3.

NGC 55 The 8th-magnitude galaxy is only 6 million light years away, in the galaxy cluster just beyond the edge of our own Local Group. A spiral galaxy, it is mottled with dust clouds and areas of star formation. Though just visible through binoculars, it an easier target for small telescopes.

NGC 253 The largest and brightest member of the so-called Sculptor Group, this spiral galaxy is about 9 million light years away, at the heart of its galaxy cluster. It shines at around magnitude 7.5 and appears through binoculars as a fuzzy oval of light with the same diameter as the full Moon. The central region of the galaxy appears as a bright, starlike point – an indication that its heart is unusually active. Like NGC 55, it appears edge-on but it is brighter and easier to view with binoculars.

Fornax The Furnace

Another of the constellations introduced by Nicolas Louis de Lacaille during his observations from the Cape of Good Hope in the early 1750s, Fornax was originally Fornax Chemica, the Chemist's Furnace. It is mostly enclosed between the larger constellations of Eridanus and Cetus.

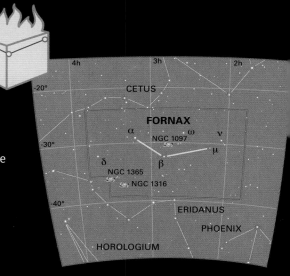

FEATURES OF INTEREST

Alpha (α) Fornacis ⟁ The constellation's brightest star is double, easily split in small telescopes to reveal a magnitude-3.9 yellow star with an orange companion that has a magnitude of 6.9.

NGC 1097 ⟁ Sixty million light years away, and shining at magnitude 10.3, this is one of the sky's brightest barred spiral galaxies. A small telescope will show its bright central nucleus,

but a larger instrument is needed to show the barred structure and a dark bar of dust through the centre. Astronomers now believe that our own Milky Way galaxy is also a barred spiral.

NGC 1316 ⟁ This unusual galaxy is associated with a strong radio source called Fornax A. It appears to be an elliptical galaxy that has recently absorbed another one. Dust and gas falling into the larger galaxy have awakened its central black hole, giving it an unusually bright and active core.

Caelum Caelum

Caelum is another of French astronomer Nicolas Louis de Lacaille's additions to the southern sky and has an unenviable reputation as one of the least impressive constellations in the heavens. Its pattern of two faint stars is supposed to represent an 18th-century engraver's chisel.

FEATURES OF INTEREST

Alpha (α) Caeli 👁 The brightest star in Caelum is a paltry magnitude 4.5. It is a white star 62 light years from Earth.

Beta (β) Caeli 👁 Like alpha, this is a white star of average luminosity. It shines at magnitude 5.1, and is a close neighbour in space of alpha, lying some 65 light years away.

Gamma (γ) Caeli ⟁ Sitting on the constellation's western boundary, gamma is a magnitude-4.6 orange giant, some

280 light years away. A small telescope will reveal that it is a binary star, with a faint companion of magnitude 8.1.

R Caeli Lying just to the south of Beta Caeli, R is a variable star. Similar in type to Mira in Cetus, it is a slowly pulsating red giant with a long period of around 400 days. At its peak, it is of magnitude 6.7 and easily spotted in binoculars, but at its dimmest, around 13.7, it sinks beyond the range of small telescopes.

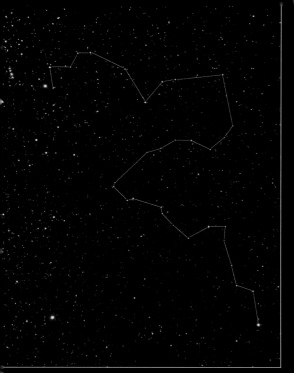

Celestial river
Eridanus has its source next to Rigel (in Orion) and flows south to Achernar. It is fully visible to almost all of the southern hemisphere and half of the Northern.

Eridanus The River

The elongated form of Eridanus, the celestial river, leads from the foot of Orion deep into southern skies.

Fully visible 32°N–90°S

FEATURES OF INTEREST

Alpha (α) Eridani (Achernar) 👁 With a name meaning "river's end" in Arabic, the constellation's one truly bright star marks its southern tip. Achernar is a blue-white giant of magnitude 0.5, some 95 light years from Earth.

Epsilon (ε) Eridani 👁 On the constellation's northern stretch, epsilon is one of the closest Sun-like stars to Earth. It lies 10.5 light years away and shines at magnitude 3.7. It is a little fainter and cooler than our Sun, and a planet-forming disc of gas and dust surrounds it.

Omicron 2 (o2) Eridani 🔭 This triple-star system is 16 light years from Earth and hosts the most easily seen white dwarf star in the sky. The primary is a magnitude-4.4 red dwarf, but its companion is a white dwarf of magnitude 9.5, which itself has a fainter red dwarf partner.

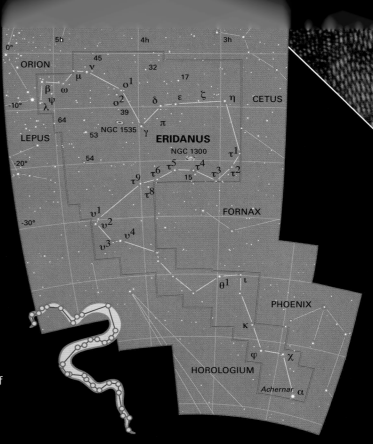

Lepus The Hare

Lying just to the south of Orion, Lepus represents a hare at the feet of the celestial hunter, hotly pursued by the dog Canis Major. It was known to the ancient Greeks and is relatively easy to spot among its sparkling neighbours, since its brighter stars form a distinctive bow-tie shape.

Fully visible 62°N–90°S

FEATURES OF INTEREST

Alpha (α) Leporis 👁 At magnitude 2.6, this star seems to be of average brightness, but it lies a distant 1,300 light years away and is actually one of the most luminous stars visible from Earth.

Gamma (γ) Leporis 🔭 Gamma is a double star, with a yellow primary of magnitude 3.9 and a magnitude-6.2 orange companion. Both stars are at a similar distance from Earth, about 30 light years away.

R Leporis (Hind's Crimson Star) 🔭 This object is a pulsating red giant variable, noted for its deep red colour. It ranges in magnitude between 5.5 and 12.0 over a 430-day cycle.

NGC 2017 🔭 This beautiful multiple star consists of eight colourful stars in all, five of which lie between magnitudes 6 and 10, and so are visible in binoculars.

M79 🔭 This globular cluster, 42,000 light years away and shining at magnitude 7.7, may have originated in a small dwarf galaxy that has recently been absorbed by the Milky Way.

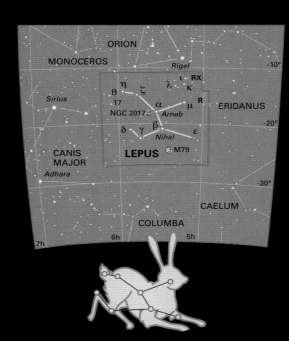

Safe Haven
Lepus. the celestial hare, crouches under the feet of Orion, like an animal trying to hide from its hunter. Orion's dogs, Canis Major and Canis Minor, lie nearby.

Columba The Dove

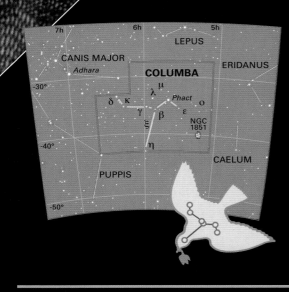

Fully visible 46°N–90°S

The faint constellation of Columba was invented by Dutch astronomer Petrus Plancius in 1592. Since Plancius was a biblical scholar, he probably intended the dove to represent the bird that Noah sent out from the Ark in search of dry land. However, others have linked it to a different dove, from classical myth, which Jason sent ahead of his ship the Argo to find a safe passage into the Black Sea. This may have been partly in Plancius's mind when he placed his dove so close to the constellation of Puppis, part of Argo.

FEATURES OF INTEREST

Alpha (α) Columbae (Phact) 👁 This star's name derives from the Arabic word for a collared dove. It is 170 light years from Earth and shines blue-white at magnitude 2.6.

Beta (β) Columbae (Wazn) 👁 The constellation's second brightest star is a yellow giant, 130 light years away,

and shining at magnitude 3.1. Its Arabic name, Wazn, means "weight".

NGC 1851 ♏ This globular cluster is Columba's most prominent deep-sky object. It lies about 39,000 light years away and, at magnitude 7.1, is visible as a faint patch through binoculars or a small telescope.

Pyxis The Compass

Fully visible 52°N–90°S

Representing a magnetic compass (as opposed to Circinus, the draftsman's compasses), Pyxis is one of Nicolas Louis de Lacaille's technological constellations, added to the sky in the 1750s. In ancient times, its stars were probably incorporated into the great ship, Argo Navis.

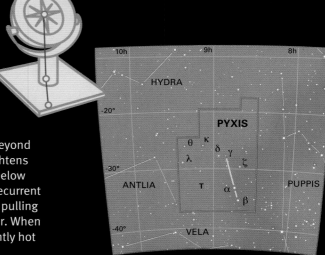

FEATURES OF INTEREST

Alpha (α) Pyxidis 👁 The brightest star, in the middle of the row of three linked stars, is a blue-white supergiant. It is 18,000 times more luminous than the Sun, yet it shines at a magnitude of only 3.7 because it is more than 1,000 light years distant.

Beta (β) Pyxidis 👁 In contrast to alpha, beta is a magnitude-4.0 yellow giant, 320 light years away.

T Pyxidis ♏ Most of the time, this variable star lies beyond the range of small telescopes, but occasionally it brightens dramatically to well within binocular range, and just below naked-eye visibility. The system is an unpredictable recurrent nova – a double star system in which a white dwarf is pulling material onto its surface from a larger neigbouring star. When the gases in the dwarf's atmosphere become sufficiently hot and dense, the star erupts in an enormous explosion.

Puppis The Stern

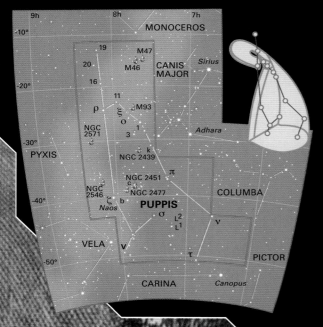

Fully visible 39°N–90°S

Puppis is one of three constellations that were once parts of the largest constellation in the sky, the huge ship Argo Navis. Puppis, representing the ship's stern, is the largest part. The stars of each section retained their original Greek letters, and in the case of Puppis the lettering now starts at Zeta (ζ) Puppis, a star that is also known as Naos.

FEATURES OF INTEREST

Zeta (ζ) Puppis (Naos) 👁 The splitting of Argo has left this blue giant as the brightest star in Puppis. It is also one of the hottest stars known, with a surface temperature six times that of the Sun. At some 14,000 light years away, it is only its vast distance that reduces Naos's brightness to magnitude 2.2.

L Puppis ♏ This line-of-sight double star consists of a blue-white star (L¹) 150 light years from Earth, and a red giant

(L²), 40 light years beyond it. L¹ shines at a steady magnitud 4.9, but L² is a pulsating variable, ranging in brightness between magnitude 2.6 and 6.2 over a 140-day cycle. Binoculars allow an easy comparison between the stars.

M47 👁 This naked-eye object is a rich sight in binoculars. Slightly brighter than the neighbouring M46, it is 1,600 light years distant and the most impressive of several open star clusters in Puppis.

Vela The Sails

Fully visible 32°N–90°S

This large constellation represents the sail of the ship Argo Navis, and once formed a single huge constellation with Puppis and Carina. It outlines a dense region of the Milky Way that contains many interesting objects.

FEATURES OF INTEREST

Gamma (γ) Velorum (Suhail) 🔭 Vela's brightest star is a multiple that contains the brightest known Wolf–Rayet star – a type of massive, superhot star that is blowing away its own outer layers with fierce stellar winds, thereby exposing its ultra-hot interior. The system shines at an overall magnitude of 1.8.

IC 2391 👁 This beautiful star cluster is also called the Southern Pleiades. Just 400 light years away, its 30 or so naked-eye stars are a spectacular sight in binoculars.

Vela Supernova Remnant 🔭 At the end of a massive star's life, it explodes as a supernova, shredding and dispersing its outer layers. The Vela Supernova Remnant (SNR), between Gamma and Lambda (λ) Velorum, results from one such explosion, 11,000 years ago. Its gas strands are diffuse and faint and are best seen through large telescopes or in long-exposure photographs.

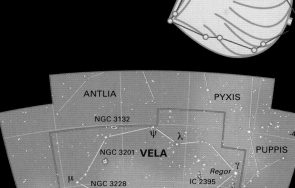

Under sail
Vela represents the mainsail of the *Argo*, the ship of Jason and the Argonauts, sailing through the southern sky in the quest for the golden fleece.

Carina The Keel

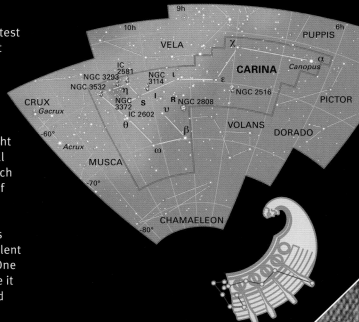

Fully visible 14°N–90°S

Marking the keel of the great ship Argo Navis, Carina lies right across the southern Milky Way, and contains many bright stars and interesting objects. As the most southerly of Argo's segments, the constellation is circumpolar (never setting) for much of the southern hemisphere.

FEATURES OF INTEREST

Theta (θ) Carinae (Canopus) 👁 The second brightest star in the entire sky, Canopus shines at a brilliant magnitude -0.7. Unlike Sirius, which outshines it purely because of its proximity to Earth, Canopus is a truly luminous star – a yellow-white supergiant some 310 light years away.

Carina Nebula (NGC 3372) 👁 This expansive emission nebula is a star-forming region 8,000 light years away. Four times the apparent size of the full Moon, it is visible to the naked eye as a bright patch in the Milky Way. The densest and brightest part of the nebula is around Eta (η) Carinae.

Eta (η) Carinae 🔭 Normally shining at magnitude 6.7 in the heart of NGC 3372, this red supergiant is rapidly nearing the end of its life, and prone to violent outbursts that brighten it to naked-eye visibility. One such flare-up in the 19th century temporarily made it the second-brightest star in the sky. The star could destroy itself in a supernova at any time.

Even keel
Carina represents the keel and hull of the Argonaut's ship, the *Argo*. The blade of the steering oar is marked by Canopus, Carina's brightest star.

Crux The Southern Cross

The sky's smallest constellation is also one of its most distinctive thanks to its four bright stars. It was first mapped as a separate pattern by explorers in the early 1500s. Crux offers a useful pointer to the south celestial pole – following the line between alpha and gamma for just under five times its length reveals its location.

Fully visible 25°N–90°S

FEATURES OF INTEREST

Alpha (α) Crucis (Acrux) 👁 Marking the southern end of the cross, magnitude-0.8 Acrux is a blue-white double star, divisible in a telescope into two stars of roughly equal magnitude.

Beta (β) Crucis (Becrux) 👁 This rapidly varying blue-white star changes its brightness by less than 0.05 magnitude, either side of an average of 1.2, every 6 hours. It lies 350 light years from Earth.

NGC 475 5 👁 This glorious star cluster, also known as the Jewel Box, appears to the naked eye as a single fuzzy star of magnitude 4.0. In fact, it is a cluster of stars 7,600 light years away. Binoculars reveal that it contains several dozen blue-white stars, with a contrasting red supergiant near the centre.

The Coal Sack 👁 This dark nebula, just 400 light years from Earth, is very noticeable because of the way it blocks out light from the dense Milky Way star fields behind it.

Musca The Fly

This is the most distinctive of several constellations invented by Dutch navigators Pieter Dirkszoon Keyser and Frederick de Houtman in the late 16th century. Its stars are relatively bright, and it is easily found by following the long axis of Crux, the Southern Cross, towards the south celestial pole.

Fully visible 14°N–90°S

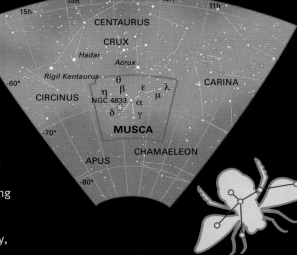

FEATURES OF INTEREST

Alpha (α) Muscae 👁 This magnitude-2.7 star is a blue-white giant, 305 light years away.

Beta (β) Muscae ⚲ To the naked eye, beta is an almost identical twin of alpha. However, a small telescope will show that it is actually a double, containing two blue stars, of magnitudes 3.0 and 3.7, that orbit each other in 383 years. The system lies some 310 light years from Earth.

Theta (θ) Muscae ⚲ This double star consists of a blue supergiant of magnitude 5.7 orbited by a star of magnitude 7.3. The faint companion, visible in binoculars, is a rare Wolf–Rayet star, a fierce white star – so hot that it is blasting its own outer layers away into space and ageing at an accelerated rate.

NGC 4833 ⚲ This globular cluster, 18,000 light years away, shines at magnitude 6.5 and is easily seen in binoculars.

Circinus The Compasses

Supposedly resembling a pair of surveyor's compasses (as opposed to Pyxis, the magnetic compass), this faint triangle of stars is another of French astonomer Nicolas de Lacaille's 18th-century additions to the sky. It is easy to locate, however, as it lies beside Centaurus's brightest stars.

Fully visible 19°N–90°S

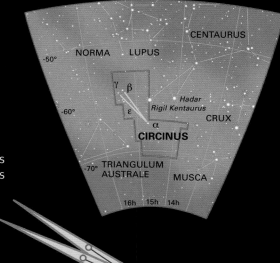

FEATURES OF INTEREST

Alpha (α) Circini ⚲ This white star of magnitude 3.2 has a faint companion of magnitude 8.6 that can be seen through a small telescope. The system is 65 light years away.

Gamma (γ) Circini ⚲ This double can be separated only with a medium-sized telescope. It consists of blue and yellow stars with magnitudes 5.1 and 5.5 respectively, orbiting each other 500 light years from Earth.

Theta (θ) Circini 👁 This is a variable, double star: its parts are too close to separate visually, but we know the system is young, since one of the stars still fluctuates unpredictably, causing theta's brightness to vary between magnitudes 5.0 and 5.4.

The Circinus Galaxy ⚱ Despite lying at a distance of only 13 million light years, this active galaxy was recently discovered, below Hadar, concealed by the Milky Way.

Norma The Level

Sandwiched between the brighter stars of Scorpius and Lupus lies this faint triangle of stars. French astronomer Nicolas Louis de Lacaille decided in the 1750s that it resembled a surveyor's level or set-square. He originally called it Norma et Regula, or the "square and ruler".

Fully visible 29°N–90°S

FEATURES OF INTEREST

Gamma (γ) Normae 🔭 Of the two components of this double star, γ² is a giant of magnitude 4.0, some 125 light years away, while γ¹ is a much more distant supergiant, 1,500 light years away but still shining at magnitude 5.0. Both are yellow, and they show how much the true brightness of apparently similar stars can vary.

Iota (ι) Muscae 🔭 This star is 220 light years from Earth and appears double through a small telescope, with a magnitude-4.6 primary orbited by a fainter star of magnitude 8.1. Much larger telescopes can split the primary again into twin stars that orbit one another in 27 years. This makes the system a triple star.

NGC 6087 👁 This open cluster of about 40 stars lies 3,000 light years away, and can be spotted with the naked eye. Its stars are mostly hot, young, and blue-white, but at its heart lies a yellow supergiant, S Normae.

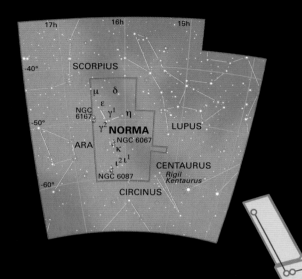

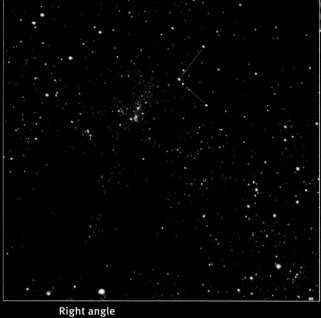

Right angle
Norma is a rather unremarkable southern constellation. Its most distinctive feature is a right-angled trio of three faint stars, which is somewhat difficult to identify among the rich Milky Way star fields.

Triangulum Australe The Southern Triangle

This distinctive pattern is easy to spot, but there are several claims to its invention. It was first recorded in *Uranometria*, the great star atlas compiled by Johann Bayer in 1603, but it may have been invented by the Dutch sailors Dirkszoon Keyser and de Houtman in the 1590s, or by a Dutch astronomer, Petrus Theodorus Embdanus, some decades earlier. Arab astronomers may also have named it independently.

Fully visible 19°N–90°S

FEATURES OF INTEREST

Alpha (α) Trianguli Australis 👁 The brightest star marks the triangle's southeast corner and is an orange giant of magnitude 1.9, lying 100 light years away.

Beta (β) Trianguli Australis 👁 This white star is about 42 light years from Earth and shines at magnitude 2.9.

Gamma (γ) Trianguli Australis 👁 Although it has the same magnitude (2.9) as beta, gamma lies over 70 light years away, so it is significantly more luminous. In keeping with its higher luminosity, its surface is hotter, and blue-white.

NGC 6025 🔭 Though visible to the naked eye at magnitude 5.4, this open cluster is best seen through binoculars.

Southern triplet
Triangulum Australe is an easily recognized triangle of stars, lying in the Milky Way near brilliant alpha (α) and beta (β) Centauri.

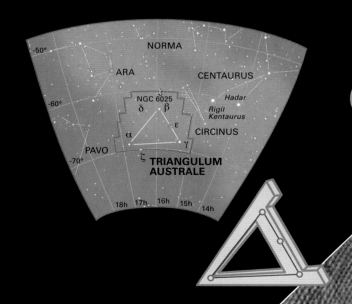

Ara The Altar

Although it lies in the far south of the sky, Ara originated with the ancient Greeks, who saw it as the altar on which the gods swore their oaths. Its pattern is obscure, but nevertheless is easy to locate to the south of Scorpius, and it is crossed by a rich band of the Milky Way's star fields.

FEATURES OF INTEREST

Alpha (α) Arae 👁 This blue-white star of magnitude 3.0 lies some 460 light years from Earth.

Gamma (γ) Arae 👁 This is one of the most luminous stars in our region of the galaxy, shining with the brilliance of 32,000 Suns. However, at a distance of 1,100 light years, it only reaches magnitude 3.3 in Earth's skies.

NGC 6193 👁 This is a bright open cluster of stars, easily spotted with the naked eye, being over half the apparent width of the full Moon. It features a central blue-white giant that just reaches naked-eye visibility (magnitude 5.7) in its own right. The cluster is 4,000 light years from Earth, and still embedded in remnants of the gas from which it was born.

NGC 6397 ♙ A relatively nearby globular cluster, at a distance of just 7,200 light years, NGC 6397 is easily seen with binoculars.

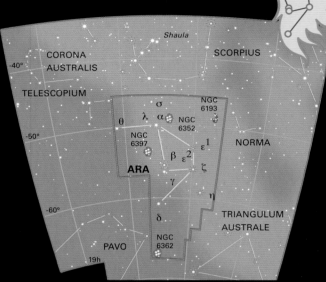

Incense burner
Ara, the celestial altar, is oriented with its top facing south. Incense burning on the altar might give off the "smoke" of the Milky Way above it.

Corona Australis The Southern Crown

Although the pattern of this celestial coronet is not as well-spaced as its northern equivalent, Corona Borealis, the southern crown is easy to recognize, just below the central "teapot" pattern of stars in Sagittarius. The constellation borders on the rich star clouds of the Milky Way.

FEATURES OF INTEREST

Alpha (α) Coronae Australis 👁 This magnitude-4.1 star is white in colour and 140 light years from Earth.

Beta (β) Coronae Australis 👁 This yellow giant shines at magnitude 4.1, with the same brightness in Earth's skies as alpha. However, in reality it is considerably further away, at a distance of 510 light years. This means it is actually 13 times more luminous than alpha. With a radius half the size of Mercury's orbit, it is 730 times more luminous than the Sun.

Gamma (γ) Coronae Australis ⚲ Both the stars in this binary system are bright enough to be seen with the naked eye (magnitudes 4.8 and 5.1). However, a small telescope is still needed to separate them.

NGC 6541 ♙ Hovering just below naked-eye visibility, this globular cluster is 22,000 light years from Earth.

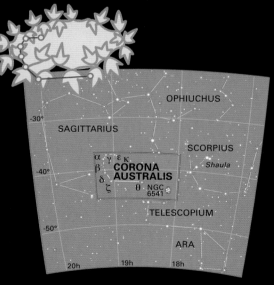

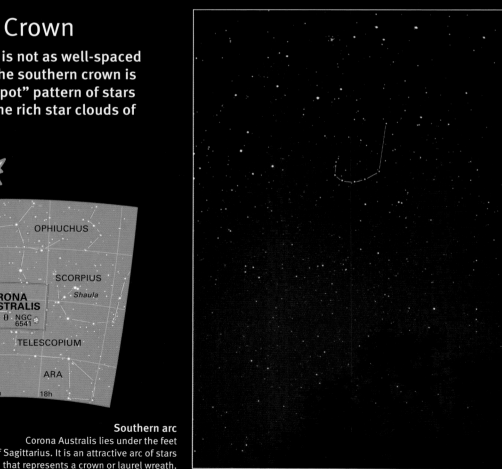

Southern arc
Corona Australis lies under the feet of Sagittarius. It is an attractive arc of stars that represents a crown or laurel wreath.

Telescopium The Telescope

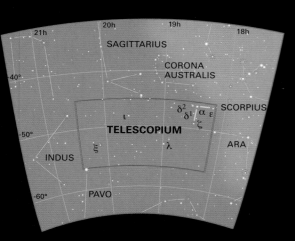

Fully visible 33°N–90°S

One of the least recognizable constellations, Telescopium seems to have been made simply by drawing a line around an arbitrary area of sky. An invention of French astronomer Nicolas Louis de Lacaille during his South African observing tour of the 1750s, the constellation does at least have an interesting history – when Lacaille compiled the pattern, he "stole" stars from several nearby constellations, including Sagittarius, Scorpius, Ophiuchus, and Corona Australis. When the constellations were standardized in 1929, these stars were returned to their rightful owners, and Telescopium was left in its current state.

FEATURES OF INTEREST

Alpha (α) Telescopii 👁 This blue-white star is around 450 light years from Earth and shines at magnitude 3.5.
Delta (δ) Telescopii 🔭 Binoculars will reveal that this star is a line-of-sight double, consisting of two unrelated blue-white stars. These stars are 650 and 1,300 light years away. They are of roughly equal brightness at around magnitude 5.0. They can even be divided with good eyesight.

Indus The Indian

Fully visible 15°N–90°S

This constellation, representing a Native American, is an invention of Dutch navigators Frederick de Houtman and Pieter Dirkszoon Keyser, who made long voyages in the southern hemisphere during the 1590s. They made the first record of the far southern stars at the request of Dutch astronomer Petrus Plancius, who had already added several new constellations to northern skies.

FEATURES OF INTEREST

Alpha (α) Indi 👁 This orange giant star, 125 light years from Earth, shines at magnitude 3.1.
Beta (β) Indi 👁 A slightly less luminous orange giant, this star is 15 light years closer than alpha, but still dimmer in Earth's skies, at magnitude 3.7.

Epsilon (ε) Indi 👁 This yellow star of magnitude 4.7 is a close stellar neighbour of the Sun, 11.2 light years away. It is orbited by a "brown dwarf" 45 times the mass of Jupiter. Though beyond the range of amateur telescopes, the brown dwarf is is a prime target for future telescopes that will search for Earth-like planets around other stars.

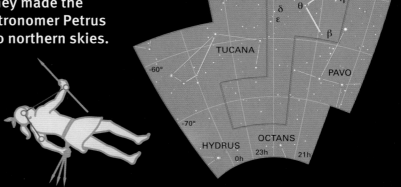

Grus The Crane

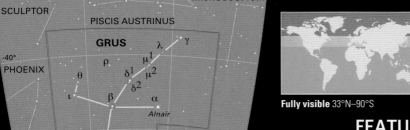

Fully visible 33°N–90°S

Grus is one of several bird-shaped constellations added to the southern sky in the 1590s by the Dutch explorers Pieter Dirkszoon Keyser and Frederick de Houtman and was later immortalized by Johann Bayer in his Uranometria star atlas of 1603. The stars of the crane's neck form a chain between the Small Magellanic Cloud in Tucana and Fomalhaut in Piscis Austrinus.

FEATURES OF INTEREST

Alpha (α) Gruis (Alnair) 👁 This blue-white star, whose name means "the bright one" in Arabic, is 65 light years away and shines at magnitude 1.7.
Beta (β) Gruis 👁 Beta is a red giant, 170 light years from Earth. It is variable, oscillating unpredictably between magnitudes 2.0 and 2.3 as it swells and shrinks.

Delta (δ) Gruis 👁 Naked-eye observers can usually tell that this star is a double, but this is in fact just a line-of-sight effect. The two components are yellow and red giants of magnitudes 4.0 and 4.1, 150 and 420 light years away respectively. Together with Mu (μ) Gruis, this star appears along the extended neck of Grus.

Phoenix The Phoenix

Fully visible 32°N–90°S

Representing the mythical firebird that regenerates from its own ashes, Phoenix is an indistinct group, although easily located because it lies beside the brilliant Achernar. Arabian astronomers named the pattern after a boat moored on the river Eridanus.

FEATURES OF INTEREST

Alpha (α) Phoenicis (Ankaa) ♙ Located 88 light years from Earth,this yellow giant shines at magnitude 2.4.

Beta (β) Phoenicis ⤳ Although to the naked eye this appears to be a yellow star of magnitude 3.3, a medium-sized telescope will show that it is actually double, consisting of twin yellow stars of magnitude 4.0, 130 light years away.

Zeta (ζ) Phoenicis ⤳ This interesting quadruple star lies 280 light years away. Its brightest component shines for most of the time at magnitude 3.9, but dips briefly to 4.4 every 40 hours. This is because it is an eclipsing binary – a close pair of stars that pass in front of each other once in every orbit. A small telescope will reveal a third star, of magnitude 6.9, while a larger instrument will show the fourth member of the system, fainter and much closer to the primary.

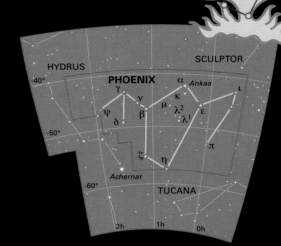

Phoenix falling
The stars of Phoenix sink toward the western horizon in the morning sky, with Grus below it. North is to the right in the photograph.

Tucana The Toucan

Fully visible 14°N–90°S

Invented, like most of the bird constellations, by Dutch navigators Pieter Dirkszoon Keyser and Frederick de Houtman, Tucana is an indistinct group of stars to the west of brilliant Achernar in Eridanus. However, it contains two outstanding objects of interest to any amateur astronomer.

FEATURES OF INTEREST

Small Magellanic Cloud 👁 The SMC is the smaller of the Milky Way's two major satellite galaxies, first recorded by Portuguese explorer Ferdinand Magellan in around 1520. It lies 210,000 light years from Earth and orbits our galaxy every 1.5 billion years. The SMC is easily visible to the naked eye, looking like a detached region of the Milky Way itself, but binoculars will reveal rich fields of stars, dust, and star-forming nebulae.

47 Tucanae 👁 Next to the SMC in the sky, but actually a foreground object within the Milky Way, this beautiful globular cluster is classified as a star but in fact contains hundreds of thousands of stars in a ball about 120 light years across. It is 13,500 light years away but is easily visible as a fuzzy star with the naked eye. Small telescopes can pick up single stars around this cluster's edge.

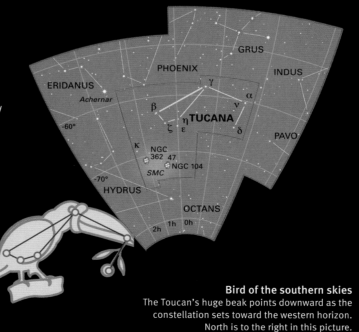

Bird of the southern skies
The Toucan's huge beak points downward as the constellation sets toward the western horizon. North is to the right in this picture.

Hydrus The Little Water Snake

While the similarly named Hydra is the longest constellation, Hydrus is compact and nestles farther to the south. Its stars are of middling magnitude and their pattern indistinct, but the constellation is easy to locate because alpha – the snake's "head" – lies near to the brilliant Achernar.

Fully visible 8°N–90°S

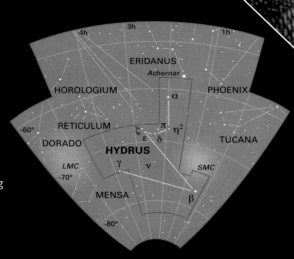

FEATURES OF INTEREST

Alpha (α) Hydri ◉ At magnitude 2.9, this white star, 78 light years from Earth, is the constellation's brightest member.

Beta (β) Hydri ◉ This Sun-like yellow star in the snake's "tail" is just 21 light years away and shines at magnitude 2.8.

Pi (π) Hydri ♏ This wide double of unrelated red giants can be split readily with binoculars. Pi-1 (π¹) is 740 light years away, while Pi-2 (π²) lies closer, at a distance of 470 light years.

VW Hydri ✶ **Lying near Gamma (γ) Hydri,** VW is an interesting star whose variations are easy to follow in a small or medium-sized telescope. The star is actually a recurrent nova system – a binary containing a white dwarf that pulls material off its companion, which occasionally ignites in a fire storm on its surface. VW erupts roughly once a month, brightening from magnitude 13 to 8 in just a few hours, then fading away over several days.

Horologium The Pendulum Clock

This faint constellation is one of Nicolas Louis de Lacaille's inventions, and, like many of them, it is a fairly arbitrary group of faint, scattered stars. Lacaille intended it to represent a clock, and it is often drawn with its pendulum suspended at alpha, and swinging back and forth between lambda and beta.

Fully visible 23°N–90°S

FEATURES OF INTEREST

Alpha (α) Horologii ◉ The constellation's brightest star is a magnitude-3.9 yellow giant, 180 light years from Earth.

NGC 1261 ♏ This globular cluster is one of the more distant of its type, 44,000 light years away from Earth. The combined light of this huge ball of stars reaches Earth at magnitude 8.0, making it a good target for binoculars.

NGC 1512 ✶ This barred spiral galaxy is about 30 million light years away and is nearly 70,000 light years across, as large as the Milky Way galaxy. Its bright centre has a magnitude of 10, and is visible through a small telescope, while detailed observations have shown that the centre is surrounded by a huge ring of infant star clusters. This region of star formation is about 2,400 light years across.

Reticulum The Net

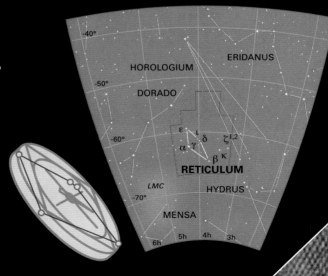

This faint but distinct diamond-shape of stars, invented by the French astronomer Nicolas Louis de Lacaille, lies a little way to the south of the brilliant star Canopus. The literal meaning of its Latin name is the "net", but it is actually supposed to represent a reticle – the set of crosshairs in the eyepiece of a telescope and some other scientific instruments.

Fully visible 23°N–90°S

FEATURES OF INTEREST

Alpha (α) Reticuli ◉ The constellation's brightest star at magnitude 3.4, alpha is a yellow giant located 135 light years away from Earth.

Beta (β) Reticuli ◉ Beta is an orange giant some 78 light years away, and shines at magnitude 3.9.

Zeta (ζ) Reticuli ♏ This double star, easily resolved through binoculars, consists of twin yellow stars – Zeta-1 (ζ¹) and Zeta-2 (ζ²). These have magnitudes 5.2 and 5.9 respectively and lie 39 light years away. The chemical composition of this system suggests that the stars in this very wide binary may be up to 8 billion years old – far more ancient than the Sun – and astronomers are eager to search for possible planets in orbit around them.

Pictor The Painter's Easel

Fully visible 26°N–90°S

Located just to the west of Canopus, the second brightest star in the sky, Pictor is one of Lacaille's 18th-century constellations. Typically for one of his inventions, it is a group of faint stars with no obvious resemblance to the object – in this case, an artist's easel – that they supposedly represent. However, Pictor is redeemed by the presence of two very interesting stars.

FEATURES OF INTEREST

Beta (β) Pictoris 👁 Uninspiring at first glance, this white star of magnitude 3.9, situated 63 light years away, nevertheless has an interesting secret that it reveals in infrared (heat) radiation. The star is surrounded by a broad disc of planet-forming gas and dust, and recent studies have shown that something close to the star (most likely a newborn planet) is warping the disc out of shape. The planets of our Solar System are believed to have developed from a similar disc that existed shortly after its formation.

Delta (δ) Pictoris 👁 This is an eclipsing binary star – a pair of stars too close to separate with even the most powerful telescope. They give themselves away by periodic dips in their brightness (from magnitude 4.7 to 4.9) as one passes in front of the other every 40 hours. They are 2,400 light years from Earth.

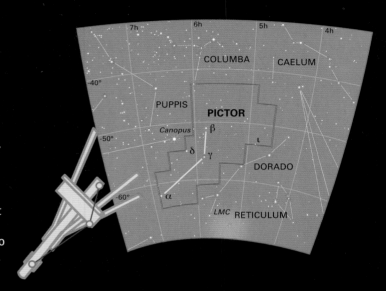

Dividing line
Pictor consists of little more than a crooked line of stars between brilliant Canopus (in Carina), seen here on the left, and the Large Magellanic Cloud.

Dorado The Goldfish

Fully visible 20°N–90°S

Invented by Dutch navigators Dirkszoon Keyser and de Houtman in the 1590s, Dorado is also called the Swordfish. Its stars form a faint chain near to Canopus. The brightest is magnitude 3.3, but Dorado contains an object far more impressive than its stars.

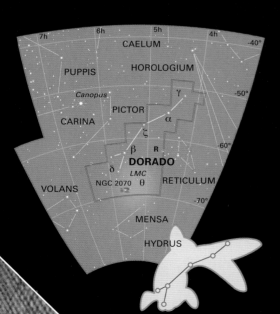

FEATURES OF INTEREST

Large Magellanic Cloud (LMC) 👁 The LMC is named after Portuguese explorer Ferdinand Magellan, who recorded it in the early 1520s, but it has been known to cultures of the southern hemisphere since prehistory. Arab astronomers in the 10th century named it Al Bakr, the "white ox". It is an irregular satellite galaxy of our own Milky Way, some 150,000 light years away, and is easily visible to the naked eye, although a small telescope gives the best views of its numerous star fields and nebulae.

Tarantula Nebula (NGC 2070) 👁 The spectacular Tarantula Nebula in the Large Magellanic Cloud is visible as a fuzzy star to the naked eye, and it also bears the stellar name 30 Doradus. But at 800 light years across, it is one of the largest star-forming regions known. A cluster of hot blue-white supergiant stars, known as R136, illuminates it from the inside.

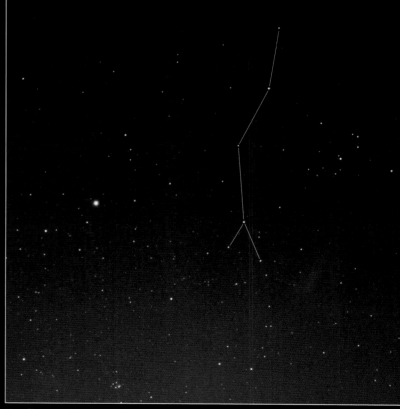

Heading south
Dorado swims through the southern skies, apparently on its way to the south celestial pole. Although known as the goldfish, the constellation in fact represents the dolphinfish found in tropical waters, not common aquarium and pond fish.

Volans The Flying Fish

Fully visible 14°N–90°S

The 16th-century Dutch explorers Peter Dirkszoon Keyser and Frederick de Houtman named many of their discoveries after birds, but Volans is an exception, because it takes its inspiration from the bizarre flying fish of the Indian Ocean. The constellation is fairly faint and indistinct, but it is easily found because it lies between the bright stars of Carina and the south celestial pole.

FEATURES OF INTEREST

Gamma (γ) Volantis ☌ The constellation's brightest star has the wrong Bayer letter due to historical accident. It is a double that can easily be split through a small telescope to reveal a golden star of magnitude 3.8 and a yellow-white companion of magnitude 5.7. Both are 200 light years away from Earth.

Epsilon (ε) Volantis ☌ This is another interesting double star, although it is not as colourful as Gamma. The blue-white primary is 550 light years away and shines at a magnitude of 4.4. It has a magnitude-8.1 companion visible only through a small telescope.

NGC 2442 ♘ A larger telescope is needed to view this face-on barred spiral galaxy, 50 million light years away from Earth. Nevertheless, it is a beautiful sight, with spiral arms extending out to an elegant "S" shape from a pronounced central bar.

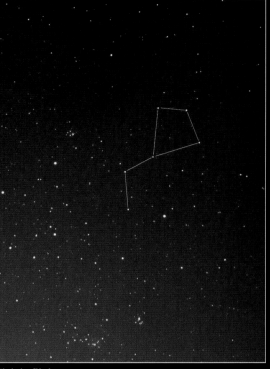

Fish in flight
The flying fish leaps into the evening sky above the eastern horizon. Beneath it are the Milky Way and the stars of Carina and Vela, with the False Cross at the left of the image.

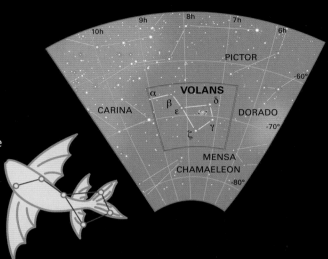

Mensa The Table Mountain

Fully visible 5°N–90°S

French astronomer Nicolas Louis de Lacaille, observing the southern skies from Cape Town in the early 1750s, named this constellation in honour of the distinctive Table Mountain that overlooks the city. Mensa is one of the faintest constellations in the sky, with no stars brighter than magnitude 5.0. However, it is fairly straightforward to locate, as it lies between the south celestial pole and the Large Magellanic Cloud (LMC) in Dorado. In fact, the southern reaches of the LMC cross over the border into Mensa itself.

FEATURES OF INTEREST

Alpha (α) Mensae 👁 The constellation's brightest star reaches a magnitude of only 5.1. It is an average yellow, Sun-like star, relatively close to Earth at a distance of 30 light years.

Beta (β) Mensae 👁 While beta is also yellow, and just slightly fainter than alpha at magnitude 5.3, it is a very different type of star. Astronomers have measured its distance at 300 light years, meaning that it must be a yellow supergiant, 100 times more luminous than alpha.

Table top
The far-southern constellation Mensa appears in this photograph above pink-tinged clouds in the dawn sky. Its main point of interest is a part of the Large Magellanic Cloud that overlaps into it from nearby Dorado.

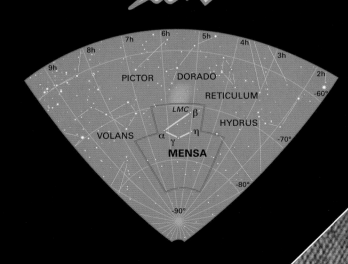

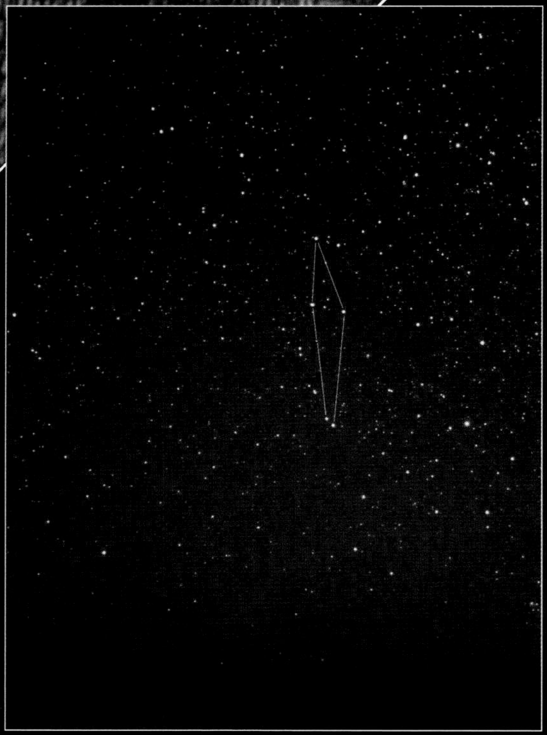

Camouflage artist
Chamaeleon lies close to the south celestial pole, which is to the left of it in this picture. To the north of this constellation are found the rich Milky Way star fields of Carina.

Chamaeleon The Chameleon

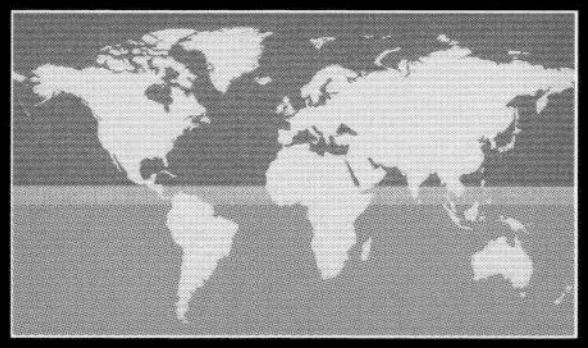

Fully visible 7°N–90°S

This skewed diamond of stars is supposed to represent a chameleon, but bears little resemblance to the lizard. It first appeared in Johann Bayer's Uranometria star atlas of 1603, and is probably another invention of the Dutch explorers Dirkszoon Keyser and de Houtman. It remains above the horizon at all times for every inhabited part of the southern hemisphere, but has few interesting objects.

FEATURES OF INTEREST

Alpha (α) Chamaeleontis This blue-white star shines at magnitude 4.1, and lies at a distance of 65 light years from Earth.

Delta (δ) Chamaeleontis Delta is a line-of-sight double star, easily separated in binoculars. Delta-1, the closer of the two stars, is an orange giant of magnitude 5.5, 360 light years away from Earth. Delta-2 is brighter but more distant, located 780 light years away and shining at magnitude 4.4.

NGC 3195 This ring-like planetary nebula, formed as a dying Sun-like star puffs its outer layers into space, shines at magnitude 10. Of similar apparent size to Jupiter, it is relatively faint and requires a medium-sized telescope to be seen. It is the most southern of all the planetary nebula in the sky, and remains completely invisible to all northern observers.

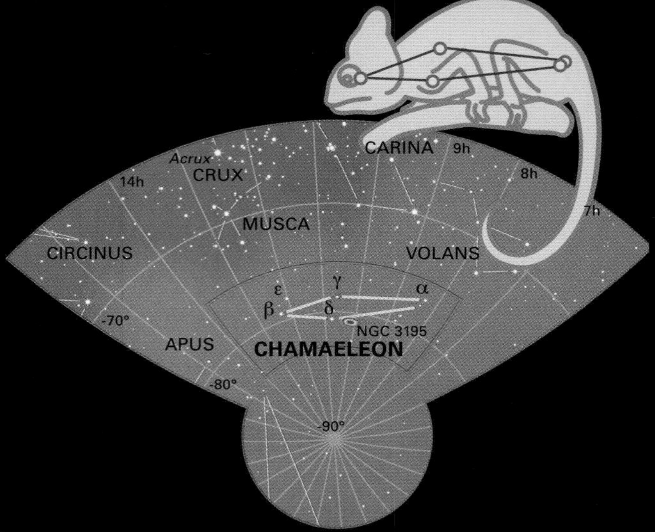

Apus The Bird of Paradise

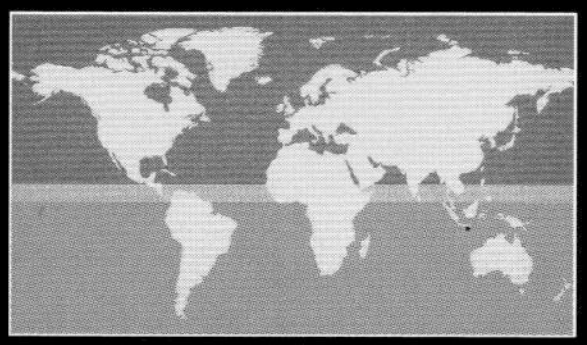

Fully visible 7°N–90°S

Pieter Dirkszoon Keyser and Frederick de Houtman named this constellation after the dazzling birds of paradise they saw during their explorations of New Guinea in the 1590s. Close to the south celestial pole, it is permanently visible in nearly all of the southern hemisphere. Despite its exotic name, the constellation is disappointingly obscure, with only a faint pattern of stars.

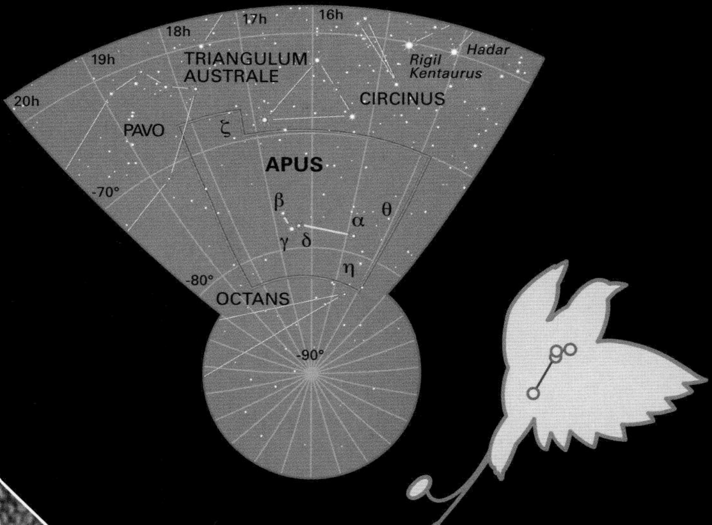

FEATURES OF INTEREST

Alpha (α) Apodis The constellation's luminary (brightest star) at a magnitude of 3.8, this orange giant is located about 230 light years from Earth.

Delta (δ) Apodis The most interesting star in Apus is this double, consisting of orange giants with magnitudes 4.7 and 5.3. The two stars orbit each other some 310 light years from Earth, and can easily be separated with binoculars – and sometimes by a sharp pair of eyes.

Theta (θ) Apodis Theta is a variable star, with fluctuations in brightness that are easily followed through binoculars. It ranges between magnitudes 6.4 and 8.0 in a 100-day cycle.

Exotic bird
Apus, which is south of the distinctive Triangulum Australe, represents a bird of paradise but is a disappointing tribute to such an exotic bird.

Pavo The Peacock

Another of the bird constellations added to the sky in the 1590s by Dutch navigators Frederick de Houtman and Pieter Dirkszoon Keyser, Pavo lies in a fairly featureless area of the sky, but is easily spotted because of its brightest star – Alpha Pavonis, the Peacock itself.

Fully visible 15°N–90°S

FEATURES OF INTEREST

Alpha (α) Pavonis (The Peacock) 👁 Alpha Pavonis is a blue-white giant star in the northeast corner of Pavo. It has a magnitude of 1.9 and is brilliant enough that, even at a distance of 360 light years from Earth, it is unmistakable.
Kappa (κ) Pavonis 👁 A yellow supergiant, 550 light years away, this is one of the brightest Cepheid variables in the sky. It expands and contracts in a 9.1-day cycle, varying in brightness between magnitudes 3.9 and 4.8 as it does so. These fluctuations can be followed with the naked eye.
NGC 6752 👁 This globular cluster of stars, 14,000 light years away, is visible to the naked eye at magnitude 5.
NGC 6744 🔭 This barred spiral galaxy has its "face" open towards Earth and is located 30 million light years away.

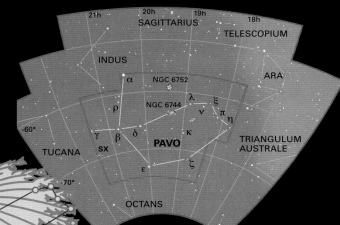

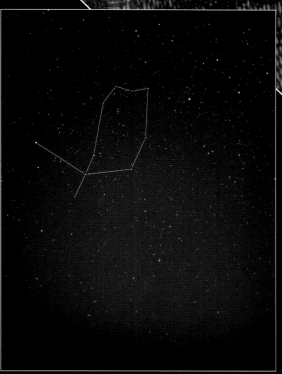

Celestial display
The constellation Pavo, the Peacock, is depicted fanning its tail across the southern skies, in imitation of a real-life peacock when attracting a male.

Octans The Octant

While the north celestial pole is marked by the bright stars of Ursa Minor, the south polar constellation is faint and indistinct. It was invented by Nicolas Louis de Lacaille during his 18th-century observations from South Africa, and represents an octant – later supplanted by the sextant.

Fully visible 0°–90°S

FEATURES OF INTEREST

Beta (β) Octantis 👁 A bright star in a dim constellation, beta is a white star that lies 110 light years from Earth. It shines at magnitude 4.1 and is outshone only by nu (n) at magnitude 3.8.
Gamma (γ) Octantis 👁 This is a chain of three stars, usually separable with the naked eye, whose members lie at different distances from Earth. Gamma-1 and Gamma-3 are both yellow giants, 270 and 240 light years away respectively, and shining at magnitudes 5.1 and 5.3. Between them lies Gamma-2, an orange giant of magnitude 5.7 at a distance of 310 light years.
Sigma (σ) Octantis 👁 The southern "pole star" is dim, white, and around 300 light years away. Its only noteworthy feature is its location within one degree of the south celestial pole, which makes it the nearest thing to a fixed reference point in the southern sky.

At the pole
Octans comprises only a scattering of faint stars. There is no bright star to mark the southern pole, which lies to the centre left in this picture.

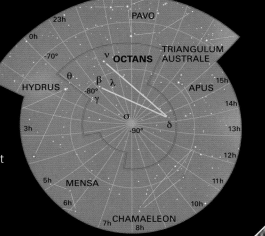

Monthly sky guide

Some constellations are always in our sky, while others appear and disappear during the course of the year. Your view of the night sky and the highlights that each month brings are described in this section. For each month, a Special Events table lists events that vary from year to year, while the positions of the naked-eye planets are shown on a locator chart.

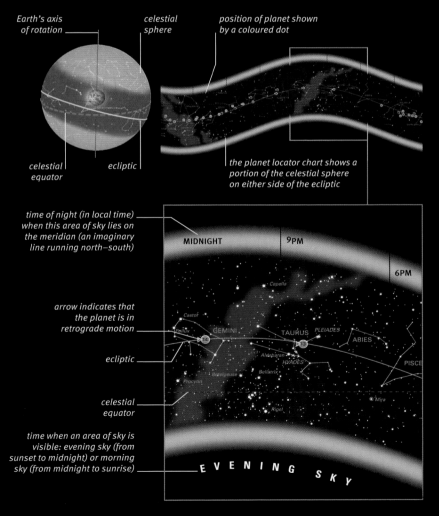

Earth's axis of rotation

celestial sphere

position of planet shown by a coloured dot

celestial equator

ecliptic

the planet locator chart shows a portion of the celestial sphere on either side of the ecliptic

time of night (in local time) when this area of sky lies on the meridian (an imaginary line running north–south)

arrow indicates that the planet is in retrograde motion

ecliptic

celestial equator

time when an area of sky is visible: evening sky (from sunset to midnight) or morning sky (from midnight to sunrise)

MIDNIGHT 9PM 6PM

Capella

Castor
Pollux
GEMINI TAURUS PLEIADES ARIES
Aldebaran
HYADES PISCE
Bellatrix
Procyon Betelgeuse
Mira
Rigel

EVENING SKY

Planet locator charts
These charts show the positions of Mercury, Venus, Mars, Jupiter, and Saturn. They give the planets' positions in relation to the constellations along the ecliptic – the part of the sky in which they are always found. The view portrayed here and described in the accompanying text is for 10pm mid-month (11pm at the start of the month, and 9pm at the end). When daylight saving time is observed, add one hour to these times.

Using the charts
Each planet is represented by a differently coloured dot (the key is repeated in the guide for each month), and the number inside the dot refers to a particular year. Once you have identified the constellation in which the planet you are looking for can be found, use the planisphere to locate it in the night sky and the constellation charts (see pp.58–95) to get a more detailed view.

An ever-changing scene
There is always something new to see in the night sky. As Earth spins, the stars that are centre stage at the start of the evening are replaced by fresh ones from the east, which in turn sink to the west before the night is over.

January

The impressive constellation of Orion dominates the scene this month. The hunter's recognizable figure, with raised club and lion pelt, is easy to spot; and in his sword is the celebrated Orion Nebula. His two hunting dogs, Canis Major and Canis Minor, are close by. Canis Major includes Sirius, the brightest star of all in Earth's night sky.

SPECIAL EVENTS

PHASES OF THE MOON

	Full Moon	New Moon
2013	27 January	11 January
2014	16 January	1, 30 January
2015	5 January	20 January
2016	24 January	10 January
2017	12 January	28 January
2018	2, 31 January	17 January
2019	21 January	6 January

ECLIPSES

2018: 31 January A total eclipse of the Moon is visible from Asia, Australia, Pacific, and western North America.

2019: 6 January A partial eclipse of the Sun is visible from northeast Asia and north Pacific.

2019: 21 January A total eclipse of the Moon is visible from central Pacific, North and South America, Europe, and Africa.

THE PLANETS

2014: 6 January Jupiter is at opposition, magnitude –2.7. At midnight it is visible to the south from northern latitudes and to the north from southern latitudes.

2014: 31 January Mercury is at greatest evening elongation, magnitude –0.5.

2015: 14 January Mercury is at greatest evening elongation, magnitude –0.6.

2015: 5 January Mercury and Venus appear three Moon widths apart in the southwestern evening sky.

2016: 9 January Venus and Saturn appear one-sixth of a Moon's width apart in the southeastern morning sky.

2017: 12 January Venus is at greatest evening elongation, magnitude –4.4.

2017: 19 January Mercury is at greatest morning elongation, magnitude –0.2.

2018: 1 January Mercury is at greatest morning elongation, magnitude –0.3.

2018: 7 January Mars and Jupiter appear a half Moon width apart, high in the pre-dawn southern sky.

2019: 6 January Venus is at greatest morning elongation, magnitude –4.5.

2019: 22 January Venus and Jupiter appear five Moon widths apart in the pre-dawn southeastern sky.

Opposition and **elongation** are explained on *page 26*

■ NORTHERN LATITUDES

Orion stands proud above the southern horizon with his dogs to the left of his feet. The dogs are located by their bright stars, brilliant Sirius in Canis Major, and Procyon, the eighth-brightest star of all, in Canis Minor. At either side of Orion's head are the constellations Gemini and Taurus. Gemini is identified by the two bright stars Castor and Pollux.

The head of Taurus, the bull, is close to the lion pelt in Orion's hand. The Hyades star cluster, easily visible to the naked eye, locates the bull's face, and the bright star Aldebaran marks its eye. Aldebaran is a red giant, and its colouring is apparent to the naked eye.

Directly overhead and within the path of the Milky Way is the constellation of Auriga, found by its bright star, Capella. The Milky Way flows into Cassiopeia, whose stars make a recognizable "W" or "M" shape in the sky, depending on whether they are above or below the north celestial pole.

Cassiopeia and the other circumpolar constellations are above the northern horizon. Cassiopeia is to the left of Polaris, the Pole Star, and the two bears, Ursa Minor and Ursa Major, are to its right.

The Quadrantid meteor shower occurs during the first week of January and is best seen after midnight. The meteors are usually faint and radiate from a point within the constellation Boötes, close to where Boötes borders the tail of Ursa Major. The short-lived peak of about 100 meteors an hour occurs on 3–4 January.

Capella and Auriga
Bright Capella (top centre) identifies the location of the constellation Auriga, the charioteer. It actually consists of two giant stars and has a yellow tint. It contains two star clusters, M36 and M38, just visible to the naked eye. Binoculars reveal them as fuzzy patches and confirm their presence.

patch, and binoculars will confirm its position. Close to M42 but nearer the belt is NGC 1981 – a scattered open star cluster that must be viewed through binoculars.

Auriga and its bright star Capella lie between Orion and the northern horizon. Procyon, the bright star of Canis Minor, is to the east of Betelgeuse, the star that marks one of the hunter's shoulders. To the east of Orion's feet is Sirius, the bright star that marks the head of the second of Orion's dogs. To the northwest and below Orion is Taurus; and to the lower right of Orion, beyond his club-holding hand, are the feet of Gemini, the twins. Closer still to the horizon, are the bright stars Castor and Pollux that mark the twins' heads.

The view looking south is one of contrasts. The eastern – that is, left – part of the sky is full of things to see, but just one bright star shines out in the western portion. This is Achernar, the ninth-brightest star. It marks one end of the meandering constellation Eridanus, which represents the mythological river of that name.

At the left, the Milky Way flows from the southeastern horizon and up into the sky towards Sirius. En route it crosses the rich starfields of Centaurus, Crux, and Carina. Centaurus, the centaur, is lying with its back almost against the horizon. Between its upward-pointing legs is Crux, the smallest constellation of all.

SOUTHERN LATITUDES

Orion is high in the sky, and his head points down to the northern horizon while his feet are tipped towards the southern horizon. The three stars that form his belt are overhead. The sword hanging from the belt is identified by stars and a bright nebula, the Orion Nebula (M42), which is the brightest and best-known nebula. Sharp-eyed observers will see it as a milky

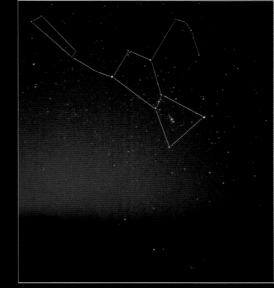

Orion the hunter
One of the most easily recognized constellations in the sky is Orion. Its stars effortlessly draw out the figure of the hunter. Single bright stars mark his shoulders, a small group of stars his head, and a line of three stars his belt. His sword is represented by stars and the star-forming region M42.

EVENING SKY

MIDNIGHT   9PM   6PM   3PM   NOON

Capella
GEMINI   TAURUS   Pleiades   ARIES
Castor
Aldebaran
Hyades   PISCES
Betelgeuse
Bellatrix   Mira
Procyon   AQUARIUS
Rigel
10°
0°
−10°
Fomalhaut   CAPRICORNUS   −20°
−30°
−40°
−50°

POSITIONS OF THE PLANETS

This chart shows the positions of Mercury, Venus, Mars, Jupiter, and Saturn in January from 2013 to 2019. The planets are represented by coloured dots, while the number inside the dot indicates the year. For all planets apart from Mercury, the dot indicates the planet's position on 15 January. Mercury is shown only when it is at greatest elongation (see p.26) – for the specific date of elongation, refer to the table on the facing page.

 Mercury   Venus   Mars   Jupiter   Saturn

EXAMPLES   16 Jupiter's position on 15 January 2016   ▶13 Jupiter's position on 15 January 2013. The arrow indicates that the planet is in retrograde motion (see p.26).

February

A triangle of bright stars and a pair of twins shine high in February's sky. The equilateral triangle is made by linking three stars in different constellations. They are Betelgeuse in Orion's shoulder, and Sirius and Procyon, the bright stars in each of Orion's two dogs, Canis Major and Canis Minor. The twins Castor and Pollux are represented by the bright stars of the same name.

ECLIPSES

2017: 26 February An annular eclipse of the Sun is visible from Pacific Ocean, Chile, Argentina, Atlantic Ocean, and Africa. A partial solar eclipse is visible from southern South America, Atlantic Ocean, and Antarctica.

2018: 15 February A partial eclipse of the Sun is visible from southern South America and Antarctica.

THE PLANETS

2013: 8 February Mercury and Mars appear half a Moon's width apart in the western evening sky.

2013: 16 February Mercury is at greatest evening elongation, magnitude −0.5.

2015: 7 February Jupiter is at opposition, magnitude −2.6. At midnight it is visible to the south from northern latitudes and to the north from southern latitudes.

2015: 21 February Venus and Mars appear a Moon width apart in the southwestern evening sky.

2015: 24 February Mercury is at greatest morning elongation, magnitude 0.1.

2016: 7 February Mercury is at greatest morning elongation, magnitude 0.0.

2019: 18 February Venus and Saturn appear two Moon widths apart in the low, southeastern pre-dawn sky.

2019: 27 February Mercury is at greatest evening elongation, magnitude −0.4.

Opposition and **elongation** are explained on *page 26*

Beehive Cluster
Also known as Praesepe, or M44, the Beehive Cluster is in Cancer, seen high to the south this month. The brightest stars in this open cluster of 350 or so stars are magnitude 6, making it visible to the naked eye as a cloudy patch. Binoculars show it as a star field of more than three apparent Moon widths.

■ NORTHERN LATITUDES

The triangle of stars formed by Betelgeuse, Sirius, and Procyon is known as the Winter Triangle (see pp.32–33). Sirius and Procyon are easy to spot to the south, since they are the first- and eighth-brightest stars. Brilliant Sirius is closest to the southern horizon; Procyon is above, to Sirius's left. Betelgeuse is in the constellation of Orion, above and to the right of Sirius.

Beyond Orion, and in the southwestern sky, is Taurus, the bull. The distinctive shape of Leo, the lion, is now in view in the southeast, and Gemini is almost overhead. The twins are nearly parallel to the horizon, with their heads pointing to Leo and their feet towards Taurus.

Capella, the bright star in Auriga, is high in the western sky. Below is Perseus, the mythological hero who rescued Andromeda from a sea monster. The chained figure of Andromeda is between Perseus and the horizon. Her mother, Cassiopeia, is to her right in the northwestern sky. The two other circumpolar constellations, Ursa Major and Ursa Minor, are to the northeast.

MIDNIGHT

3AM

6AM

9AM

NOON

20°—

10°—

0°—

−10°—

−20°—

−30°—

−40°—

LEO

Regulus

Arcturus

VIRGO

Spica

OPHIUCHUS

Altair

LIBRA

CAPRICORNUS

Antares

SAGITTARIUS

Shaula

SCORPIUS

MORNING SKY

SOUTHERN LATITUDES

The path of the Milky Way extends across the sky, stretching from the southeastern horizon to the northwest. Along its path, starting closest to the southern horizon, are the constellations Centaurus, Crux, Carina, Vela, and Puppis, and then Canis Major, which is overhead. Its bright star, Sirius, and brilliant Canopus of Carina, are the two brightest stars of all. They are seen high in the sky throughout this month.

The equilateral triangle known to northern-hemisphere observers as the Winter Triangle is made by linking orange-red Betelgeuse and the white stars Sirius and Procyon. It is seen high above the northwestern horizon. Sirius is the highest star; below it are Betelgeuse and Procyon, to the left and right respectively. Within the triangle is the constellation Monoceros, the unicorn, which also lies in the path of the Milky Way. Close to its border with Orion is the open star cluster NGC 2244, which is visible through binoculars.

The stars Castor and Pollux, which mark the heads of the Gemini twins, are seen by looking north. At magnitude 1.2, Pollux is the brighter of the two, but Castor (magnitude 1.6) is possibly the more interesting. A small telescope will show it as a pair of stars. At right, to the east, is Cancer, the crab, and the upside-down figure of Leo, the lion. His head points toward the twins, his tail to the eastern horizon.

Rosette Nebula and NGC 2244
This spectacular telescope view of the Rosette Nebula in the constellation of Monoceros, the unicorn, reveals an open cluster of stars, NGC 2244, in the heart of the nebula. The surrounding nebula shows up well in photographs but not to the eye.

The Winter Triangle
Despite urban light pollution from the horizon, the Winter Triangle is visible here. Brilliant Sirius in Canis Major is just below the centre of the image. Above and to the left is Procyon in Canis Minor. At right centre is Orion; its star Betelgeuse forms the third point of the triangle.

EVENING SKY

MIDNIGHT · 9PM · 6PM · 3PM · NOON

Castor · Pollux · GEMINI · Capella · Pleiades · ARIES · Aldebaran · TAURUS · Hyades · CANCER · Procyon · Betelgeuse · Bellatrix · PISCES · AQUARIUS · Mira · Rigel · Fomalhaut

—20° —10° 0° —10° —20° —30° —40° —50°

POSITIONS OF THE PLANETS

This chart shows the positions of Mercury, Venus, Mars, Jupiter, and Saturn in February from 2013 to 2019. The planets are represented by coloured dots, while the number inside the dot indicates the year. For all planets apart from Mercury, the dot indicates the planet's position on 15 February. Mercury is shown only when it is at greatest elongation (see p.26) – for the specific date of elongation, refer to the table on the facing page.

 Mercury   Venus   Mars   Jupiter   Saturn

EXAMPLES   **13** Jupiter's position on 15 February 2013   **14** Jupiter's position on 15 February 2014. The arrow indicates that the planet is in retrograde motion (see p.26).

March

Leo and Virgo take the place of Orion and Gemini as we herald the start of northern spring and southern autumn. On the 20th, or occasionally the 21st, of the month, the Sun crosses the celestial equator as it moves from the southern to the northern celestial sky. Briefly, day and night are of equal length before the northern-hemisphere nights grow shorter and the southern ones longer.

SPECIAL EVENTS

PHASES OF THE MOON

	Full Moon	New Moon
2013	27 March	11 March
2014	16 March	1 March
2015	5 March	20 March
2016	23 March	9 March
2017	12 March	28 March
2018	2, 31 March	17 March
2019	21 March	6 March

THE PLANETS

2013: 31 March
Mercury is at greatest morning elongation, magnitude 0.3.

2014: 14 March
Mercury is at greatest morning elongation, magnitude 0.2.

2016: March 8
Jupiter is at opposition, magnitude −2.5. At midnight it is visible to the south from northern latitudes and to the north from southern latitudes.

2018: 4 March
Mercury and Venus appear two Moon widths apart in the low, western sky at sunset. Day by day, they appear further apart; by 19 March they are six Moon widths apart.

2018: 15 March
Mercury is at its greatest evening elongation, magnitude −0.3.

Opposition and elongation are explained on *page 26*

■ NORTHERN LATITUDES

Due south and high in the sky is the distinctive constellation Leo. Its linked stars really do resemble a crouching lion. The curve of his head and the shape of his body are easy to pick out in the sky. Leo looks towards the west, past the faint constellation of Cancer, and on to the winter constellation of Orion as it disappears from view. To the left of Leo are Virgo and its bright star Spica, rising over the eastern horizon. Leo's brightest star, Regulus, marks the start of an outstretched front leg. It is a blue-white star of magnitude 1.4. Through binoculars, a dimmer, wide companion can be seen. Just below the lion's body are five galaxies, all visible with binoculars in good observing conditions.

Ursa Major is situated high in the sky above the northern horizon. The bowl of the saucepan-shaped Plough, formed from seven bright stars in the hindquarters and tail of Ursa Major, is open downwards towards Polaris, the Pole Star. Among the stars near the bear's head is M81, one of the easiest galaxies to find with binoculars. It is a spiral galaxy also known as Bode's Galaxy. About one apparent Moon width away is a second, smaller and fainter galaxy, M82. Cassiopeia, on the opposite side of Polaris, is now almost between Polaris and the horizon, forming a "W" shape.

Galaxies in Ursa Major
Galaxies M81 and M82 are in Ursa Major, above the great bear's shoulder. With binoculars, the spiral galaxy M81 (right) appears as an elongated patch of light. Cigar-shaped M82 (left) is only visible through a telescope.

■ SOUTHERN LATITUDES

The view south is packed with stars. Due south are the constellations Carina and Vela. The white supergiant Canopus marks the western end of Carina. At magnitude –0.62, Canopus is second only to Sirius, the brightest star of all. Sirius is above and west of Canopus. Eta (η) Carinae is a variable star that brightens considerably when it erupts. In 1841, it rivalled Sirius after a giant outburst of material.

The southeastern sky is dominated by the two bright stars Alpha (α) and Beta (β) Centauri, which point to the nearby tiny constellation of Crux. Further east, the first of the winter constellations are rising above the eastern horizon. Virgo is leading the way, followed by Scorpius.

Due north is Leo. Its stars draw out a crouching lion, which southern-hemisphere observers see upside-down. The lion is apparently lying on its back with its head facing west; its bright star Regulus, marking the start of an outstretched front paw, is above. Almost equidistant and at either side of Regulus are two equally bright stars: to the west, Procyon in Canis Minor; and to the east, Spica in Virgo. Closer to the eastern horizon is the red giant Arcturus and the constellation Boötes, a forerunner of the winter sky to come. On the opposite side of the sky, the summer constellation of Orion can be seen disappearing over the western horizon.

Eta Carinae Nebula
The fuzzy red object at right is the Eta Carinae Nebula (NGC 3372). Embedded within is the variable star, Eta Carinae. To its left is Crux and the dark nebula the Coalsack, which is blocking the light of more distant stars.

Leo, the lion
The recognizable figure Leo is seen in this northern-sky view. The bright star at lower right is Regulus. The curve of stars that make up his shoulders and head extend up from Regulus. Denebola, the bright star at lower left, marks the start of the lion's tail. Turn the book upside-down to see how Leo appears in the southern sky.

EVENING SKY

MARCH

103

POSITIONS OF THE PLANETS

This chart shows the positions of Mercury, Venus, Mars, Jupiter, and Saturn in March from 2013 to 2019. The planets are represented by coloured dots, while the number inside the dot indicates the year. For all planets apart from Mercury, the dot indicates the planet's position on 15 March. Mercury is shown only when it is at greatest elongation (see p.26) – for the specific date of elongation, refer to the table on the facing page.

- ● Mercury
- ● Venus
- ● Mars
- ● Jupiter
- ● Saturn

EXAMPLES ⑬ Jupiter's position on 15 March 2013 ▶⑭ Jupiter's position on 15 March 2014. The arrow indicates that the planet is in retrograde motion (see p.26).

April

Leo remains high in the sky but now starts to make room for another zodiac constellation, Virgo. And a further mythical figure is making his presence felt. Boötes, the herdsman, is well placed for all observers. The third-largest constellation, Ursa Major, the great bear, is almost overhead for those in the northern hemisphere, while those observing from Earth's south find Crux prominently placed.

Opposition and elongation are explained on page 26

SPECIAL EVENTS

PHASES OF THE MOON

	Full Moon	New Moon
2013	25 April	10 April
2014	15 April	29 April
2015	4 April	18 April
2016	22 April	7 April
2017	11 April	26 April
2018	30 April	16 April
2019	19 April	5 April

THE PLANETS

2013: 28 April
Saturn is at opposition, magnitude 0.13. At midnight it is visible to the south from northern latitudes and to the north from southern latitudes.

2014: 8 April
Mars is at opposition, magnitude −1.5. At midnight it is visible to the south from northern latitudes and to the north from southern latitudes.

2016: 18 April
Mercury is at greatest evening elongation, magnitude 0.2.

2017: 1 April
Mercury is at evening elongation, magnitude −0.1.

2017: 7 April
Jupiter is at opposition, magnitude −2.5. At midnight it is visible to the south from northern latitudes and to the north from southern latitudes.

2018: 2 April
Mars and Saturn appear 2.5 Moon widths apart, due-south, in the low, pre-dawn sky.

2018: 29 April
Mercury is at morning elongation, magnitude 0.5.

2019: 11 April
Mercury is at morning elongation, magnitude 0.4.

■ NORTHERN LATITUDES

Leo is high in the southwest sky, its distinctive shape easily picked out. The lion is looking towards the heads of the twins, Gemini, marked by the bright stars Castor and Pollux. The sky above and below is relatively barren. The long figure of Hydra, the water snake, straggles between Leo and the southern horizon. This is the largest constellation, but it is far from prominent. To the right, Virgo follows Leo across the sky. Its star Spica shines bright in the southeast. Above and to the east is Arcturus, the brightest star north of the celestial equator. At magnitude −0.05, this red giant is the fourth-brightest star.

Looking north, Ursa Major is directly above Polaris, the Pole Star, and almost overhead. Seven stars that form the tail and rump of the bear make a saucepan shape in profile. Known as the Plough, or Big Dipper, this is one of the most recognized star patterns in the northern hemisphere.

Cassiopeia is below, close to the horizon. To the northwest is the yellow-coloured Capella, which, at magnitude 0.08, is the sixth-brightest star. It is the brightest and by far the most conspicuous star in Auriga, the charioteer. To the east, Vega in Lyra heralds the arrival of the first of the summer constellations. Lyra is host to the Lyrids meteor shower, which peaks around 21–22 April. A dozen or so meteors can be seen every hour radiating from a point near Vega.

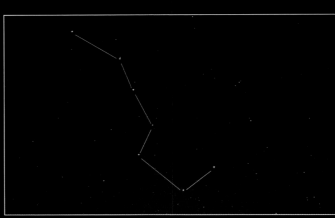

Ursa Major and the Plough
The seven stars in the great bear's tail and rump (top and centre) form the Plough. The second star in the tail is Mizar, which has a companion, Alcor. Both can be seen with binoculars or by anyone with good eyesight.

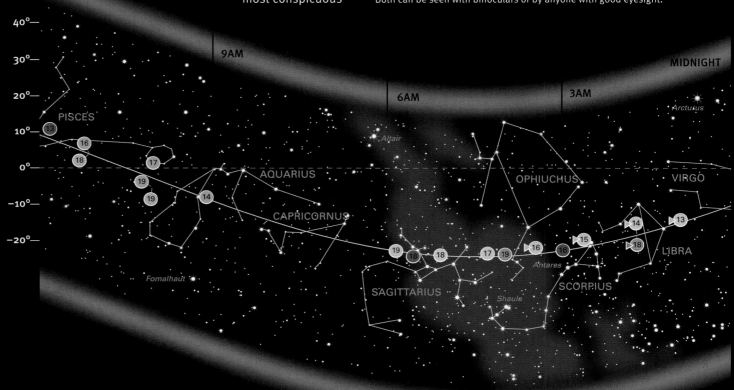

MORNING SKY

Crux and Carina

The Milky Way flows from top to bottom in this view of the southern-hemisphere sky. The four stars that form the southern cross, Crux, can be seen at the top left of the image. Below are the stars of Carina, which represent the keel of a ship.

Acux, the brightest star in the constellation Crux, marks the base of the cross. To the naked eye it is a single star of magnitude 0.8, but through a small telescope it is seen as a pair of stars. Beta (β) Crucis marks the left of the cross; it is a blue-white giant of magnitude 1.3. Between this star and the prominent dark nebula known as the Coalsack is the sparkling Jewel Box cluster. Also known as NGC 4755, this is an open star cluster visible to the naked eye. Binoculars or a small telescope will show its individual stars.

Looking north, Leo is still well placed but is heading for the western horizon. To the right of its bright star Regulus are five galaxies visible with binoculars. The bright stars Spica in Virgo and Arcturus in Boötes shine bright in the northeastern sky. Procyon is still visible in the northwest, but Gemini is now moving below the horizon.

■ SOUTHERN LATITUDES

The star-rich path of the Milky Way makes a glorious sight in the southern sky. It extends from the western horizon and climbs high in the sky to the south, before descending to the east. En route it passes Sirius and incorporates Carina, Crux and Centaurus, and the tail of Scorpius, the scorpion. Crux is almost due south and well placed for observation. The sky overhead, above Crux, is barren by comparison. It contains the long meandering body of Hydra, the water snake.

The Sombrero Galaxy

Also known as M104 or NGC 4594, the Sombrero Galaxy is a spiral galaxy in Virgo. Its dark dust lane and bulbous core resemble the traditional Mexican hat after which it is named. It is seen almost edge-on and appears elongated in a small telescope. The dark lane is visible through a larger instrument.

A P R I L

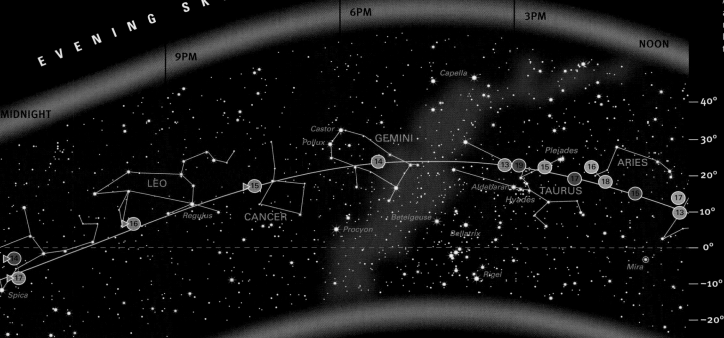

POSITIONS OF THE PLANETS

This chart shows the positions of Mercury, Venus, Mars, Jupiter, and Saturn in April from 2013 to 2019. The planets are represented by coloured dots, while the number inside the dot indicates the year. For all planets apart from Mercury, the dot indicates the planet's position on 15 April. Mercury is shown only when it is at greatest elongation (see p.26) – for the specific date of elongation, refer to the table on the facing page.

● Mercury	● Venus	● Mars	● Jupiter	● Saturn

EXAMPLES ⑬ Jupiter's position on 15 April 2013   ▶⑭ Mars' position on 15 April 2014. The arrow indicates that the planet is in retrograde motion (see p.26).

Opposition and elongation are explained on *page 26*

SPECIAL EVENTS

PHASES OF THE MOON

	Full Moon	New Moon
2013	25 May	10 May
2014	14 May	28 May
2015	4 May	18 May
2016	21 May	6 May
2017	10 May	25 May
2018	29 May	15 May
2019	18 May	4 May

THE PLANETS

2013: 25–28 May
Mercury, Venus, and Jupiter appear within five Moon widths of each other in the western evening sky.

2014: 10 May
Saturn is at opposition, magnitude 0.06. At midnight it is visible to the south from northern latitudes and to the north from southern latitudes.

2014: 25 May
Mercury is at greatest evening elongation, magnitude 0.6.

2015: 7 May
Mercury is at greatest evening elongation, magnitude 0.5.

2015: 23 May
Saturn is at opposition, magnitude 0.02. At midnight it is visible to the south from northern latitudes and to the north from southern latitudes.

2016: 22 May
Mars is at opposition, magnitude –2.1. At midnight it is visible to the south from northern latitudes and to the north from southern latitudes.

2017: 17 May
Mercury is at greatest morning elongation, magnitude 0.6.

2018: 9 May
Jupiter is at opposition, magnitude –2.5.

Boötes and Virgo are prominent for May observers in both the northern and southern hemispheres. Those to the south of the equator also see the constellations Crux and Centaurus, which are now at their highest above the horizon. In the northern hemisphere, the days are lengthening as summer approaches. Once the sky has darkened, Ursa Major stands high and proud in the northern sky.

■ NORTHERN LATITUDES

The bright star Spica and its constellation, Virgo, are due south. Higher in the sky, and almost overhead is Arcturus in Boötes. The 13th "zodiac" constellation, Ophiuchus, is seen to the southeast. The head and body of Leo are still visible in the southwest, before sinking below the horizon. Antares, the red star that marks the heart of Scorpius, the scorpion, makes a rare appearance in the northern sky for those observers south of 50°N. It can be seen close to the horizon for the summer months.

Ursa Major is high in the sky to the north. The easily recognized saucepan shape of the Plough is positioned so that the end of the handle is north and the pan tips down to the west. Dubhe and Merak, the two brightest stars in Ursa Major, form the side of the pan away from the handle. These are known as the pointers, since they point the way

Mizar and Alcor
This image shows the stars Mizar (left) and Alcor (right). They are usually seen as one star in the handle of the Plough. When seen through a telescope (above), Mizar is found to have another companion.

to Polaris. Also known as the Pole Star, Polaris marks the position of the north celestial pole.

The summer stars Vega (in Lyra) and Deneb (in Cygnus) move higher into the northeastern sky as the last of the winter stars Castor and Pollux (in Gemini), set in the northwest. Lyra is small but prominent due to its bright star Vega. It is also home to the planetary nebula, the Ring Nebula (M57), seen as a misty disc through a small telescope. The Eta Aquarid meteor shower (see opposite) is visible to observers in the lower latitudes.

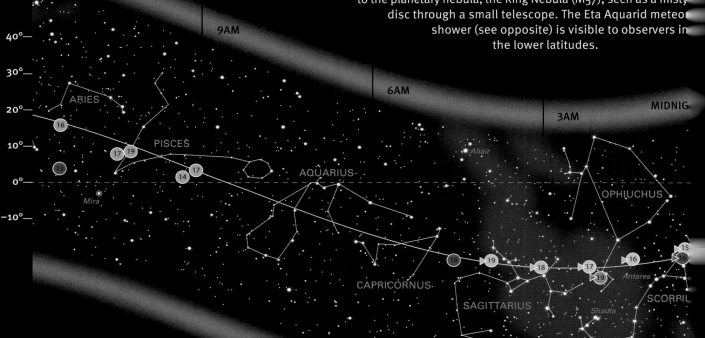

M O R N I N G   S K Y

■ SOUTHERN LATITUDES

Two bright stars, Spica (in Virgo) and Arcturus (Boötes), are centrally placed to the south. Arcturus is the lower and brighter of the two and the fourth-brightest star of all. Spica is almost overhead. To the northwest is Leo, which will soon be making way for the winter constellations. Ophiuchus, the serpent holder, is in the eastern sky. The serpent, which forms the constellation Serpens, is coiled around Ophiuchus – it is in two halves, one at either side of Ophiuchus. The head, Serpens Caput, is between Ophiuchus and Boötes; the tail, Serpens Cauda, is close to the eastern horizon.

Centaurus and Crux are high in the sky to the south. The two bright stars of Centaurus shine out, even against the starry path of the Milky Way. Alpha (α) Centauri is the brighter of the two and third brightest of all. Within the centaur's body is Omega (ω) Centauri, the brightest globular cluster in all of Earth's sky. This month also offers the first good opportunity to look at Scorpius, a winter constellation that is now rising in the southeastern sky.

The Eta Aquarid meteor shower starts in late April but peaks in the first week of May, when about 35 meteors an hour can be seen. The meteors radiate from a point in Aquarius. They are visible in the hours before dawn as Earth ploughs into a stream of dust lost by Halley's Comet.

Alpha Centauri
By the horizon in this dawn sky, Alpha Centauri, just 4.3 light years away, is often said to be our closest star after the Sun. An unseen companion, Proxima Centauri, is in fact slightly closer and truly the closest night-time star.

Omega Centauri
The largest globular cluster in the Milky Way is Omega Centauri (NGC 5139). Just some of its 10 million or so stars are visible in this 4m (13ft) telescope image. To the naked eye or through binoculars, it appears as a fuzzy star.

Boötes
The large figure of Boötes, the herdsman, raises his arm high in the sky. The top star of the kite shape marks his head. At the tail end of the kite is the red giant Arcturus, the brightest star north of the celestial equator.

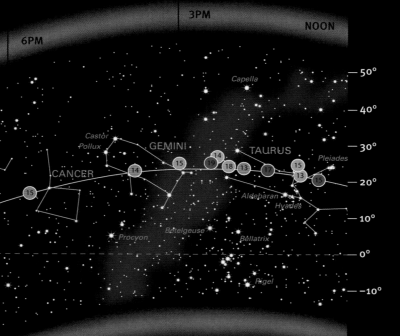

M A Y

POSITIONS OF THE PLANETS

This chart shows the positions of Mercury, Venus, Mars, Jupiter, and Saturn in May from 2013 to 2019. The planets are represented by coloured dots, while the number inside the dot indicates the year. For all planets apart from Mercury, the dot indicates the planet's position on 15 May. Mercury is shown only when it is at greatest elongation (see p.26) – for the specific date of elongation, refer to the table on the facing page.

● Mercury   ● Venus   ● Mars   ● Jupiter   ○ Saturn

EXAMPLES   Jupiter's position on 15 May 2013   Mars' position on 15 May 2016. The arrow indicates that the planet is in retrograde motion (see p.26).

EVENING SKY

June

The mythical hero Hercules moves into the June sky to join Boötes, the herdsman, and Ophiuchus, the serpent holder. Towards the end of the month, the nights are at their shortest for northern observers and at their longest for those in the southern hemisphere. This is because on 21 June, the Sun is at its farthest point north of the celestial equator.

SPECIAL EVENTS

PHASES OF THE MOON

	Full Moon	New Moon
2013	23 June	8 June
2014	13 June	27 June
2015	2 June	16 June
2016	20 June	5 June
2017	9 June	24 June
2018	28 June	13 June
2019	17 June	3 June

THE PLANETS

2013: 12 June
Mercury is at greatest evening elongation, magnitude 0.6.

2015: 24 June
Mercury is at greatest morning elongation, magnitude 0.6.

2016: 3 June
Saturn is at opposition, magnitude 0.0. At midnight it is visible to the south from northern latitudes and to the north from southern latitudes.

2016: 5 June
Mercury is at greatest morning elongation, magnitude 0.6.

2016: 3 June
Venus is at greatest morning elongation, magnitude −4.3.

2017: 15 June
Saturn is at opposition, magnitude 0.0. At midnight it is visible to the south from northern latitudes and to the north from southern latitudes.

2018: 27 June
Saturn is at opposition, magnitude 0.0. At midnight it is visible to the south from northern latitudes and to the north from southern latitudes.

2019: 10 June
Jupiter is at opposition, magnitude −2.6. At midnight it is visible to the south from northern latitudes and to the north from southern latitudes.

2019: 18 June
Mercury and Mars appear half a Moon width apart in the low, northwestern sky at sunset.

2019: 23 June
Mercury is at greatest evening elongation, magnitude 0.6.

Opposition and elongation are explained on *page 26*

■ NORTHERN LATITUDES

When looking south, Hercules and Boötes are high in the sky. The bright star Arcturus makes Boötes easy to find. Hercules, although large, is not prominent. It is best found by locating Vega in the east. Vega is in the constellation Lyra and is the fifth-brightest star of all. It is outshone in the June sky only by Arcturus. To the right of Vega is the body of Hercules. Four linked stars that form a distorted square, called the Keystone, represent his lower torso.

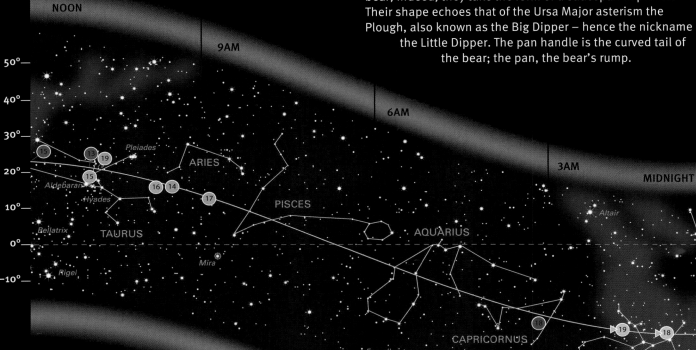

Albireo
The second brightest star in Cygnus, Albireo marks the swan's beak. It appears like a single star with the naked eye, but when viewed with powerful binoculars or a telescope, it is seen as a double star.

His legs point upwards, and his head points towards the horizon. The star cluster M13 can be spotted by the naked eye and lies on a line linking two of the stars. The head of Scorpius is just above the horizon, located by spotting red supergiant Antares.

In the east are three stars that form the asterism known as the Summer Triangle. The brightest and highest is Vega, and nearer to the horizon, Deneb (Cygnus) and Altair (Aquila) can be seen. Due north, Ursa Minor extends above Polaris, the Pole Star, which marks the tip of the bear's tail. The stars in Ursa Minor have no direct resemblance to a bear; indeed, they take the form of a saucepan in profile. Their shape echoes that of the Ursa Major asterism the Plough, also known as the Big Dipper — hence the nickname the Little Dipper. The pan handle is the curved tail of the bear; the pan, the bear's rump.

SOUTHERN LATITUDES

Boötes and Hercules are either side of due north. The figures of the huntsman and hero are found by locating the bright stars Arcturus and Vega, which is just peeking above the northeastern horizon. On the left, Boötes is head down and feet high; at right, Hercules is head high and feet down, with an arm outstretched above Vega. His lower body is represented by four linked stars known as the Keystone. The star cluster M13 lies on a line linking two of the stars. Aquila and its bright star Altair are now in the northeast.

Overhead, the distinctive shape of Scorpius with its curving tail is clearly seen. Its heart is marked by Antares, a red supergiant whose brightness varies between magnitudes 0.9 and 1.2 over a four-to-five-year period. Two open-star clusters, M6 and M7, are found near the sting in the scorpion's tail. Both are visible to the naked eye.

Scorpius and its neighbour Sagittarius lie in the Milky Way and in the direction of the centre of our galaxy. From Sagittarius and Scorpius, the milky path of light flows to the southwest, taking in the constellations Centaurus and Crux along the way. The globular cluster Omega (ω) Centauri is well placed, as are the dark Coalsack nebula and the Jewel Box (NGC 4755) open cluster, both in Crux.

Butterfly Cluster
The Butterfly Cluster (M6) is an open cluster in Scorpius. It is about 2,000 light years away and about 12 light years across. Its brightest star is an orange giant whose light varies over time. The star cluster is found near the sting of the scorpion's tail.

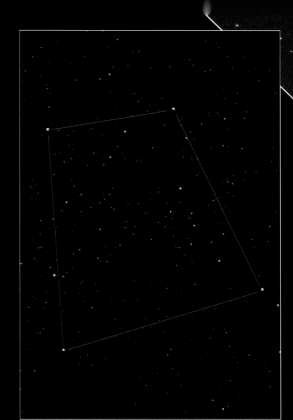

The Keystone in Hercules
The four stars that form the lower body of Hercules are known as the Keystone. The globular cluster M13 is bisected by a line joining two of the stars (seen here at left). The cluster can be seen from both northern and southern latitudes.

EVENING SKY

NOON
3PM
6PM
9PM
MIDNIGHT

50°
40°
30°
20°
10°
0°
−10°

Castor
Pollux
GEMINI
LEO
CANCER
Arcturus
Regulus
Procyon
Betelgeuse
Spica
VIRGO
OPHIUCHUS
LIBRA
Antares
SCORPIUS

J U N E

POSITIONS OF THE PLANETS

This chart shows the positions of Mercury, Venus, Mars, Jupiter, and Saturn in June from 2013 to 2019. The planets are represented by coloured dots, while the number inside the dot indicates the year. For all planets apart from Mercury, the dot indicates the planet's position on 15 June. Mercury is shown only when it is at greatest elongation (see p.26) – for the specific date of elongation, refer to the table on the facing page.

Mercury   Venus   Mars   Jupiter   Saturn

EXAMPLES   13 Jupiter's position on 15 June 2013   ▶16 Mars' position on 15 June 2016. The arrow indicates that the planet is in retrograde motion (see p.26).

July

Hercules and Ophiuchus remain centre stage, and Aquila, the eagle, has flown into view. Southern observers are treated to the rich star fields of the Milky Way. These include Sagittarius, within which, almost directly overhead, lies the centre of our galaxy. The outstretched wings of Cygnus, the swan, are now high in the sky for northern observers. Vega, in the small constellation, Lyra, shines brightly overhead.

SPECIAL EVENTS

PHASES OF THE MOON

	Full Moon	New Moon
2013	22 July	8 July
2014	12 July	26 July
2015	2, 31 July	16 July
2016	20 July	4 July
2017	9 July	23 July
2018	27 July	13 July
2019	16 July	2 July

ECLIPSES

2018: 13 July A partial eclipse of the Sun is visible from the most southerly regions of Australia.

2018: 27 July A total eclipse of the Moon is visible from South America, Europe, Africa, Asia, and Australia.

2019: 2 July A total eclipse of the Sun is visible from south Pacific, Chile, and Argentina. A partial solar eclipse is visible from south Pacific and South America.

2019: 16 July A partial eclipse of the Moon is visible from South America, Europe, Africa, Asia, and Australia.

THE PLANETS

2013: 22 July
Mars and Jupiter appear two Moon widths apart in the morning eastern sky.

2013: 30 July
Mercury is at greatest morning elongation, magnitude 0.3.

2014: 12 July
Mercury is at greatest morning elongation, magnitude 0.3.

2015: 1 July
Venus and Jupiter appear one Moon width apart in the western evening sky.

2017: 30 July
Mercury is at greatest evening elongation, magnitude 0.4.

2018: 12 July
Mercury is at greatest evening elongation, magnitude 0.5.

2018: 27 July
Mars is at opposition, magnitude −2.8. At midnight it is visible to the south from northern latitudes and to the north from southern latitudes.

2019: 5 July
Mercury and Mars appear seven Moon widths apart in the low, western sky at sunset.

2019: 9 July
Saturn is at opposition, magnitude 0.1. At midnight it is visible to the south from northern latitudes and to the north from southern latitudes.

Opposition and **elongation** are explained on *page 26*

◼ NORTHERN LATITUDES

Looking north, Ursa Minor reaches up from Polaris. Coiling around it is the long, winding figure of Draco, the dragon. Ursa Major is to the left of Polaris, in the northwest; to the right, in the northeast, are the mythical king Cepheus and his queen, Cassiopeia. Arcturus (Boötes), in the west, and Vega (Lyra), almost overhead, are the brightest stars in the July sky.

Next in brightness is Altair in the southeast, marking the neck of Aquila, the eagle, and flanked by two dimmer stars. The Milky Way flows through Aquila and on to Cygnus, high in the east. A line of stars forms the swan's body and an intersecting line its wings; this cross shape led to its other name, the northern cross. Cygnus's brightest star, the blue-white supergiant Deneb, marks its tail. One of the smallest constellations, Corona Borealis is high in the southwest; it is flanked by Hercules and Boötes. Its arc of seven stars depicts the crown of the mythical Princess Ariadne, hence its alternative name, the northern crown. Ophiuchus is well placed due south, with Hercules above. Observers south of about 45°N will see star-rich Sagittarius and Scorpius on their horizons. This is the best chance for northern observers to see the two most southerly constellations of the zodiac in the evening sky.

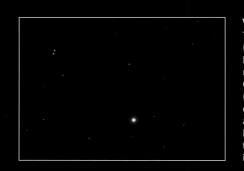

Vega
The blue-white star Vega (below centre) is the brightest star in the northern summer sky. Close by is the star Epsilon (ε) Lyrae. Sharp eyesight or binoculars will show it as a double star (upper left). A telescope reveals that each of its two stars is also a double.

POSITIONS OF THE PLANETS

This chart shows the positions of Mercury, Venus, Mars, Jupiter, and Saturn in July from 2013 to 2019. The planets are represented by coloured dots, while the number inside the dot indicates the year. For all planets apart from Mercury, the dot indicates the planet's position on 15 July. Mercury is shown only when it is at greatest elongation (see p.26) – for the specific date of elongation, refer to the table to the left.

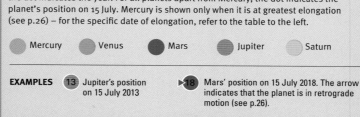

● Mercury ● Venus ● Mars ● Jupiter ● Saturn

EXAMPLES ⑬ Jupiter's position on 15 July 2013 ▶⑱ Mars' position on 15 July 2018. The arrow indicates that the planet is in retrograde motion (see p.26).

■ SOUTHERN LATITUDES

Scorpius and Sagittarius are almost overhead. The scorpion's tail is due south, and so the open clusters M6 and M7 are ideally placed for observation. The red supergiant Antares shines out. It is the brightest star in Scorpius and one of the largest stars visible to the naked eye. Estimates of its size range from 280 to 700 times that of the Sun.

The Lagoon Nebula

The bright, star-forming Lagoon Nebula (M8, NGC6523) is some 5,200 light years away, within the archer's bow of the constellation of Sagittarius. It is visible to the naked eye in a rural sky and is a good binocular object. Binoculars will reveal the cluster of stars, NGC 6530, within the nebula.

The view towards Sagittarius is towards the centre of our galaxy. A large and bright field of stars, M24 in Sagittarius, is visible to the naked eye; so, too, is the Lagoon Nebula (M8). M22, the third-brightest globular cluster, is also in Sagittarius. Easy to find with binoculars, it can also be seen by keen-eyed observers in a rural sky. A group of eight stars within Sagittarius forms the Teapot asterism, but it is difficult to pick out in this star-studded part of the sky. The arc of stars at the forefeet of Sagittarius is easier to see. It is Corona Australis, the southern crown, and one of the smallest constellations of all.

Looking north, Ophiuchus is high in the sky; below it is the figure of Hercules. Vega in Lyra is close to the horizon. Adjoining Vega is the northern-hemisphere constellation Cygnus. Observers to the north of about 30°S are able to see the complete figure of the flying swan. Above it in the northeastern sky is Aquila, the eagle.

The Delta Aquarid meteor shower reaches its peak around the 29th of this month. Up to 20 rather faint meteors an hour radiate from the southern half of Aquarius.

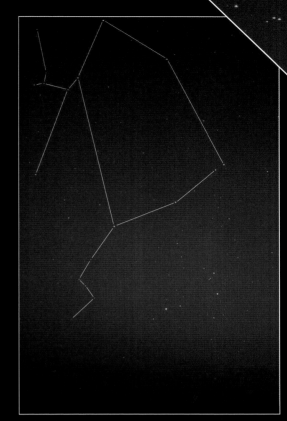

Ophiuchus

The serpent holder Ophiuchus is the 11th-largest constellation, lying on the edge of the Milky Way's starry path. The figure is seen here, head-high. Within his body are two globular clusters, M10 and M12 – both are visible through binoculars.

NOON
3PM
50°
40°
EVENING SKY
6PM
30°
Pollux
17
MIDNIGHT
9PM
Arcturus
16 14
20°
19
LEO
15 13 18
Regulus
18
15
CANCER
10°
17
16
Procyon
OPHIUCHUS
VIRGO
0°
17
−10°
13
Spica
14 18
15
16
LIBRA
19
18
17 19
16
Antares
SCORPIUS
Shaula

August

The Summer Triangle, a triangle of three brilliant stars from three different constellations, is seen from all but the most southerly latitudes. Northern observers have a glimpse towards the galaxy's centre and are treated to the Perseids, the best meteor shower of the year. Sagittarius remains well-placed for southern observers, and August also offers them the best chance of observing two celebrated planetary nebulae.

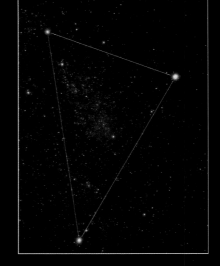

The Summer Triangle
Three bright stars make up the Summer Triangle. Deneb in Cygnus, at top left, is the dimmest of the three; the brightest, Vega in Lyra, is to the right; and Altair in Aquila is seen at lower left.

■ NORTHERN LATITUDES

The stars of the Summer Triangle, a familiar feature in northern summer and autumn skies, are overhead. As the sky darkens, blue-white Vega in Lyra is the first triangle star to appear. To its east is Cygnus, the swan, which contains the second star, blue-white supergiant Deneb. The third, Altair in Aquila, the eagle, is below, to the south.

Sagittarius, the archer, is a centaur, a mythical beast. His human head and upper body are just above the southern horizon; his horse's legs are only visible to observers south of about 40°N. Sagittarius marks the centre of the galaxy. Here the Milky Way is at its densest and brightest, but a dark horizon is needed to reveal the star-studded path. It flows up from the horizon and although the path becomes dimmer, it may be easier to see. The path moves through Aquila, overhead into Cygnus, and on to Cassiopeia in the northeastern sky.

The best meteor shower of the year, the Perseids, peaks around 12 August, with up to 80 meteors an hour, radiating from a point in Perseus. Although Perseus is not clear of the eastern horizon before midnight, some pre-midnight meteors may be seen.

Elongation is explained on *page 26*

SPECIAL EVENTS

PHASES OF THE MOON

	Full Moon	New Moon
2013	21 August	6 August
2014	10 August	25 August
2015	29 August	14 August
2016	18 August	2 August
2017	7 August	21 August
2018	26 August	11 August
2019	15 August	1, 30 August

ECLIPSES

2017: 7 August A partial eclipse of the Moon is visible from Europe, Africa, Asia, and Australia.

2017: 21 August A total eclipse of the Sun is visible from north Pacific, USA, and south Atlantic. A partial solar eclipse is visible from North America and northern South America.

2018: 11 August A partial eclipse of the Sun is visible from northern Europe and northeast Asia.

THE PLANETS

2014: 18 August
Venus and Jupiter appear half a Moon width apart in the eastern morning sky.

2014: 27 August
Mars and Saturn appear seven Moon widths apart in the southwestern evening sky.

2016: 16 August
Mercury is at greatest evening elongation, magnitude 0.3.

2016: 25 August
Mars and Saturn appear nine Moon widths apart in the southern sky at sunset.

2016: 27 August
Venus and Jupiter appear one-sixth of a Moon width apart in the western evening sky with Mercury 10 Moon widths away.

2018: 17 August
Venus is at greatest evening elongation, magnitude –4.4.

2018: 26 August
Mercury is at greatest morning elongation, magnitude –0.1.

2019: 9 August
Mercury is at greatest morning elongation, magnitude 0.3.

POSITIONS OF THE PLANETS

This chart shows the positions of Mercury, Venus, Mars, Jupiter, and Saturn in August from 2013 to 2019. The planets are represented by coloured dots, while the number inside the dot indicates the year. For all planets apart from Mercury, the dot indicates the planet's position on 15 August. Mercury is shown only when it is at greatest elongation (see p.26) – for the specific date of elongation, refer to the table to the left.

● Mercury ● Venus ● Mars ● Jupiter ● Saturn

EXAMPLES ⑬ Jupiter's position on 15 August 2013 ▶⑱ Mars' position on 15 August 2018. The arrow indicates that the planet is in retrograde motion (see p.26).

Three bright stars dominate the scene to the north, the highest of which is Altair in Aquila. Below it are Vega in Lyra, and Deneb in Cygnus. The three form a triangle known as the Summer Triangle due to its prominence in the northern-hemisphere summer sky. The constellation of Vulpecula, the fox, which is between Aquila and Cygnus, contains a relatively easy-to-spot planetary nebula, the Dumbbell Nebula (M27). It is seen through binoculars as a rounded patch of light.

A second well-known planetary nebula, the Ring Nebula (M57), is in Lyra and can be seen through a small telescope as a disc of light. The constellation Tucana, the toucan, is to the southeast. It contains the globular cluster 47 Tucanae and the irregular galaxy called the Small Magellanic Cloud.

Sagittarius and the rich star fields in the centre of the galaxy are still high overhead. The galaxy's milky path flows through Scorpius to the southwest, then through Lupus and on to Crux and the southern horizon. Alpha (α) and Beta (β) Centauri are low on the southwestern horizon and mark the front legs of Centaurus, the centaur (half man, half horse). Alpha Centauri, also known as Rigil Kentaurus, is the third-brightest star in the sky; Beta Centauri, or Hadar, is 11th brightest. The two appear to be the same distance from us, but in reality they are vastly separated. Beta is about 525 light years away, and Alpha only 4.3 light years away. A small telescope will show that Alpha Centauri is a binary star consisting of two yellow and orange stars that orbit each other every 80 years. Alpha Centauri is sometimes described as the closest star after the Sun, but Proxima Centauri, a much fainter red dwarf star possibly associated with Alpha, is a little closer. Centaurus is one of two centaurs in the sky; the second is Sagittarius.

47 Tucanae
The globular cluster 47 Tucanae is the second brightest in the sky. At 13,400 light years away, it is also one of the closest to Earth. It contains several million stars and appears as a hazy star to the naked eye.

Cygnus Rift
The path of the Milky Way flows from Cepheus (top) to Scorpius (near the horizon), where it is noticeably brighter as we look towards the galaxy's centre. The dark band of dust along its centre line is the Cygnus Rift.

EVENING SKY

September

The stars of northern autumn and southern spring are now in place as Capricornus and Aquarius move centre stage. On the 23rd, or occasionally the 22nd, of the month, the Sun moves from the northern to the southern celestial sky. When it crosses the celestial equator, day and night are of equal length. In the weeks ahead, the northern hemisphere nights lengthen and the southern ones shorten.

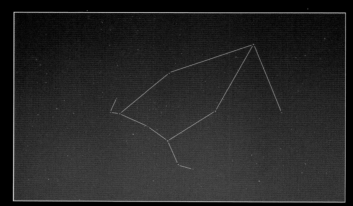

Cepheus
The head of Cepheus, the mythical king of Ethiopia, is at lower left. The constellation is not prominent but is worth seeking out for Delta Cephei, in the king's head. Its brightness changes between magnitudes 3.5 and 4.4.

■ NORTHERN LATITUDES

Capricornus and Aquarius are at either side of due south. For those at high northern latitudes, September is the best time to see Capricornus, the smallest zodiac constellation. Cygnus remains high overhead and is joined by the flying horse, Pegasus. The Summer Triangle stars, Deneb (Cygnus), Vega (Lyra), and Altair (Aquila), remain in view to the west, but Pegasus's presence in the east announces the arrival of autumn.

To the north, Ursa Major is below Polaris, while Cepheus is above. Its star Delta (δ) Cephei is the prototype of the Cepheid variables. As the star pulsates, its brightness shifts over a five-day cycle. Only two bright stars are seen to the north: Capella (Auriga), the sixth brightest of all, is close to the northeast horizon. Just brighter is Vega, high in the sky to the west.

POSITIONS OF THE PLANETS

This chart shows the positions of Mercury, Venus, Mars, Jupiter, and Saturn in September from 2013 to 2019. The planets are represented by coloured dots, while the number inside the dot indicates the year. For all planets apart from Mercury, the dot indicates the planet's position on 15 September. Mercury is shown only when it is at greatest elongation (see p.26) – for the specific date of elongation, refer to the table to the left.

● Mercury   ● Venus   ● Mars   ● Jupiter   ○ Saturn

EXAMPLES ⑬ Jupiter's position on 15 September 2013   ⑱ Saturn's position on 15 September 2018. The arrow indicates the planet is in retrograde motion (see p.26).

Small Magellanic Cloud
The Small Magellanic Cloud (left) and the globular cluster 47 Tucanae (right) seem the same distance from us. In reality, the galaxy, which is 10,000 light years across, is 210,000 light years away. 47 Tucanae is just 13,400 light years away.

the closest planetary nebula to Earth. It appears large in the sky and covers a third of the apparent width of the Moon. As a result its light is spread out, so it is difficult to spot. Binoculars will locate its pale-grey light. Close by is the bright star Fomalhaut in Piscis Austrinus.

Altair (Aquila), Vega (Lyra), and Deneb (Cygnus) form the Summer Triangle and are still visible to the northwest. September offers the last chance of seeing the triangle before Vega and, later, Deneb move below the horizon. Take a last look at Albireo, in the beak of the swan. It is a celebrated double that is clearly separated through a telescope.

The path of the Milky Way is seen in the western sky. Sagittarius remains high; below is Scorpius. Lowest of all are Centaurus and Crux, which are disappearing below the southwestern horizon. The blue-white star Achernar is well placed to the southeast. At magnitude 0.45, it is the ninth brightest of all. Achernar marks one end of the mythical river Eridanus. Its name, Arabic in origin, means "river's end".

To the right of Achernar is Tucana, representing the tropical bird, the toucan. It is home to the globular cluster 47 Tucanae (NGC 104). Close by is an elongated patch of light seven times wider than the apparent width of the full Moon. This is the Small Magellanic Cloud – a small irregular galaxy that is a companion to the Milky Way. When viewed with binoculars, this naked-eye object reveals some of its star clusters and nebulae.

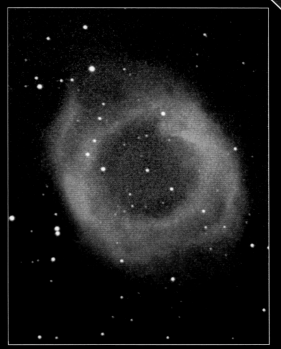

Helix Nebula
The colour and complexity of the Helix Nebula in Aquarius is seen only in images such as this one. The shells of gas, which are about 15 light years across, are material expelled by a central dying star. The nebula is about 300 light years away.

■ SOUTHERN LATITUDES

Capricornus and Aquarius are overhead. Neither has especially bright stars, but Aquarius in particular has objects of note. The brightest star in Capricornus, Alpha (α), called Algedi, is a double star. Sharp eyesight or binoculars show a giant of magnitude 3.6 and, six times more distant, a supergiant of magnitude 4.3. Aquarius, the water carrier, includes M2, a globular cluster that is easily seen as a fuzzy star through binoculars, and a notable planetary nebula. The Helix Nebula (NGC 7293) is believed to be

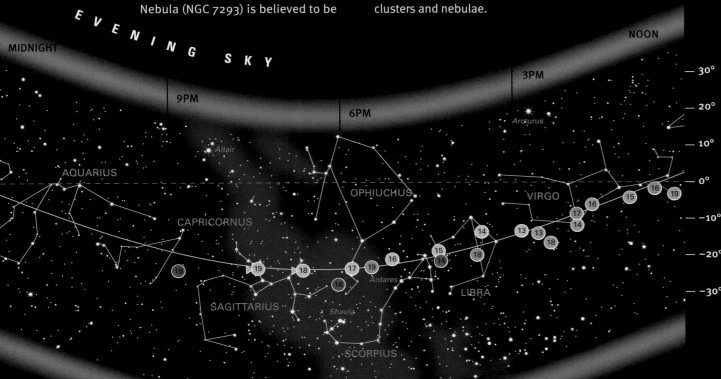

SPECIAL EVENTS

PHASES OF THE MOON

	Full Moon	New Moon
2013	18 October	5 October
2014	8 October	23 October
2015	27 October	13 October
2016	16 October	1, 30 October
2017	5 October	19 October
2018	24 October	9 October
2019	13 October	28 October

THE PLANETS

2013: 9 October
Mercury is at greatest evening elongation, magnitude 0.0.

2013: 10 October
Mercury and Saturn appear 11 Moon widths apart in the southwestern evening sky.

2015: 16 October
Mercury is at greatest morning elongation, magnitude –0.5.

2015: 17–30 October
Venus, Jupiter, and Mars appear within two Moon widths in the eastern morning sky.

2016: 30 October
Venus and Saturn appear six Moon widths apart in the southwestern evening sky.

2017: 5 October
Venus and Mars appear one-third of a Moon width apart in the pre-dawn eastern sky.

2019: 20 October
Mercury is at greatest evening elongation, magnitude –0.1.

Elongation is explained on *page 26*

The Andromeda Galaxy, the most distant object visible to the naked eye, is on view to all observers as is the Great Square of Pegasus, an asterism formed by linking stars in neighbouring Pegasus an Andromeda. Southern observers can see both of the Milky Way's companion galaxies in the sky, and Cassiopeia is well positioned for observers in northern latitudes.

■ NORTHERN LATITUDES

Pegasus and Andromeda are either side of due south. The winged horse and the princess are linked by the Great Square of Pegasus. This is formed of three stars in Pegasus and one in Andromeda, and it defines the upper body of the mythological winged horse. Close to the horse's nose is M15, a globular cluster visible to the naked eye under clear rural skies.

Andromeda is home to the Andromeda Galaxy (M31), the largest member of the Local Group cluster. It is a spiral but is tipped to our line of sight, so it looks like an elongated oval. Its central part can be seen with the naked eye and binoculars. A large telescope is needed for its spiral arms.

The Orionid meteor shower peaks around 20 October, with about 25 fast meteors an hour. It is best seen after midnight when Orion has risen in the east.

Looking northwards, Vega (in Lyra), Polaris (which marks the position of

Cassiopeia
Here, the "M" shape
bright stars in Cassio
is at upper centre. Po
is the bright star at b
right, and two bright
of Cepheus are to its
The Milky Way flows
through Cassiopeia
top right to bottom le

the north celestial pole), and Capella (in Auriga) make across the sky. The path of the Milky Way arches overh Cepheus and Cassiopeia are above Polaris and are in t optimum positions for viewing.

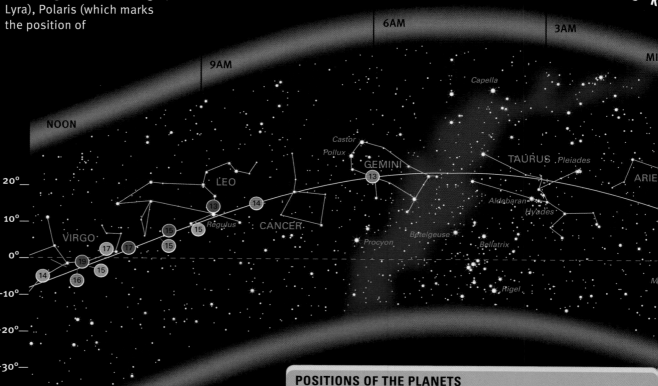

MORNING SK

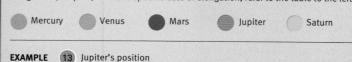

POSITIONS OF THE PLANETS

This chart shows the positions of Mercury, Venus, Mars, Jupiter, and Saturn in October from 2013 to 2019. The planets are represented by coloured dots, while the number inside the dot indicates the year. For all planets apart from Mercury, the dot indicates the planet's position on 15 October. Mercury is shown only when it is at greatest elongation (see p.26) – for the specific date of elongation, refer to the table to the left.

○ Mercury   ○ Venus   ● Mars   ◐ Jupiter   ○ Saturn

EXAMPLE   ⑬ Jupiter's position on 15 October 2013

Looking north, the Great Square of Pegasus is centrally placed. It is formed by three stars in the winged horse Pegasus, to the left, and one star in the mythological princess, Andromeda, to the right. The horse flies towards the west. His head is defined by a line of stars, below, two more lines map out his forelegs. The square makes the shape of his upper body.

Andromeda is lower in the sky and to the right of Pegasus. Alpheratz, its brightest star, marks the princess's head and is the fourth star in the Great Square. The Andromeda Galaxy (M31) is in her left knee. This spiral – similar to but larger than the Milky Way and 2.5 million light years away – appears as an elongated oval to the naked eye. Its spiral arms and two companion galaxies, M32 and M110, are seen through a larger telescope. A small telescope will reveal NGC 7662, the Blue Snowball planetary nebula near Andromeda's right hand.

The bright star Fomalhaut, in Piscis Austrinus, is almost overhead. The winter trio of stars Altair, Vega, and Deneb is setting in the northwest. The summer constellations Taurus and Orion are beginning to appear in the east. Only one bright star, Achernar (Eridanus), is high above the horizon to the south. Four relatively dim constellations depicting birds – Phoenix, Grus, Tucana, and Pavo – are centre stage. Tucana is well placed for observing the Small Magellanic Cloud and 47 Tucanae. Close to the southeastern horizon is Dorado, significant because it contains the Large Magellanic Cloud, the larger and closer of our two companion galaxies.

Large Magellanic Cloud
Binoculars and a small telescope reveal star clusters and nebulous gas and dust patches in the Large Magellanic Cloud. On its upper-left edge is the Tarantula Nebula, including a cluster of new-born stars. The Large Magellanic Cloud appears to the naked eye as a long hazy patch of light.

Pegasus, the winged horse
The Great Square of Pegasus forms the upper body of the horse. His head is here below the square, and his forelegs stretch off the image at the right. The star at left in the square belongs to Andromeda. The Moon is seen close to the horizon, and above it is the planet Venus.

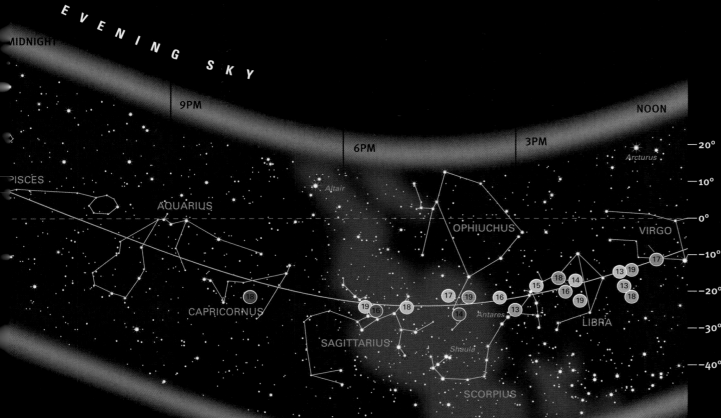

EVENING SKY

MIDNIGHT 9PM 6PM 3PM NOON

PISCES
AQUARIUS
CAPRICORNUS
SAGITTARIUS
OPHIUCHUS
SCORPIUS
LIBRA
VIRGO

Arcturus
Altair
Antares
Shaula

—20°
—10°
0°
—10°
—20°
—30°
—40°

November

Two celebrated stars – Mira in Cetus, the sea monster, and Algol in Perseus – are in the sky for both northern and southern observers. Cetus and Perseus are joined by the constellation of Andromeda, the princess rescued from Cetus by Perseus. Northern-latitude sky watchers see the Milky Way arching overhead, and southern-latitude observers see four birds as they await the arrival of the summer stars.

■ NORTHERN LATITUDES

Perseus and Andromeda are high overhead. Andromeda's parents, Cepheus and Cassiopeia, are to the north. Andromeda is well placed for observing the Andromeda Galaxy. Algol in Perseus is an eclipsing binary – two stars that exist together and orbit each other. As the dimmer of the pair passes in front of the brighter, the combined brightness drops. Algol's magnitude changes from 2.1 to 3.4 and back again.

Cetus is due south. Its red giant Mira is a variable star whose brightness varies in a cycle lasting 11 months. It changes from a naked-eye star of magnitude 3, to a star of magnitude 10 visible only through a telescope. Pisces is above Cetus; to its right is the Great Square of Pegasus.

The Summer Triangle stars of Altair (Aquila), Vega (Lyra), and Deneb (Cygnus) are low in the northwest. The winter constellations Taurus, Gemini, and Orion are to the southeast. There are two meteor showers this month: the Taurids peak in the first week and the Leonids around the 17th. About ten meteors an hour are seen in each.

Leonid meteor shower
Thirty images are combined in this view of a Leonid meteor shower. Meteors are best seen about 50 degrees above the horizon and 30–40 degrees to one side of the point from which they appear to radiate – in this case, in Leo.

POSITIONS OF THE PLANETS

This chart shows the positions of Mercury, Venus, Mars, Jupiter, and Saturn in November from 2013 to 2019. The planets are represented by coloured dots, while the number inside the dot indicates the year. For all planets apart from Mercury, the dot indicates the planet's position on 15 November. Mercury is shown only when it is at greatest elongation (see p.26) – for the specific date of elongation, refer to the table to the left.

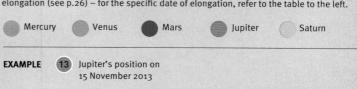

● Mercury　● Venus　● Mars　● Jupiter　● Saturn

EXAMPLE ⑬ Jupiter's position on 15 November 2013

Mira
The variable star Mira is circled in the centre of this image. It is here at its brightest and visible to the naked eye. The two brightest "stars" in this view are, in fact, planets: Jupiter is at right, with Saturn above and to its left.

■ SOUTHERN LATITUDES

The constellation Cetus is overhead. Mira, one of its stars, is a well-known variable. It is a red giant whose brightness changes over about 11 months. It is about magnitude 3 at brightest and within naked-eye visibility. At its dimmest, about magnitude 10, it is visible only through a telescope. Mira is the prototype for long-period variables known as Mira variables.

Pisces and Aries are either side of north. Pisces, depicting two fish joined with a cord, is a faint constellation. Its brightest star, alpha (α), marks the knot that ties the fish together; a telescope reveals it as two stars. Below Pisces and to the northeast are Pegasus and Andromeda, which are linked by the Great Square of Pegasus. The Andromeda Galaxy remains high enough to be seen.

November offers the chance to see Andromeda and Perseus together. Perseus, who killed the sea monster Cetus

and prevented it from devouring Andromeda, is near the horizon in the northeast. The star Beta (β) Persei, called Algol, is a well-known eclipsing binary. It consists of two stars orbiting around each other. Together they are magnitude 2.1, but when the fainter passes in front of its brighter companion, the brightness drops to magnitude 3.4. This change can be detected by the naked eye. The dip and return to full brightness takes about 10 hours every 69 hours.

Achernar in Eridanus is centre stage to the south. To its west is Fomalhaut in Piscis Austrinus, the southern fish. The fish is the parent of the two in Pisces and is the recipient of water pouring from Aquarius's jug at right. Four birds – Phoenix, Grus (the crane), Tucana (the toucan), and Pavo (the peacock) – are in the southwest. The Small Magellanic Cloud is seen in Tucana, and to its left is the Large Magellanic Cloud in Dorado. Both irregular galaxies are visible to the naked eye. Individual clusters and nebulae are seen with binoculars or a telescope. Canopus, the white supergiant and second-brightest star of all, is in the southeast. Beyond, in the east, is Sirius (Canis Major), the brightest of all. The presence of Taurus, Orion, and Canis Major above the horizon is a sign that summer is approaching.

Pisces
The distinguishing feature of Pisces is the ring of seven stars that marks the body of one of the two fish. Alpha (α) Piscium (lower left) marks the knot where the cords from the fish are tied together.

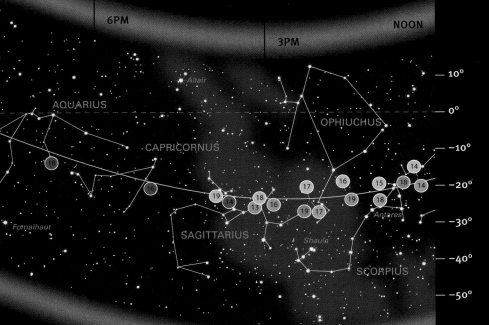

119

December

Elongation is explained on *page 26*

SPECIAL EVENTS

PHASES OF THE MOON

	Full Moon	New Moon
2013	17 December	3 December
2014	6 December	22 December
2015	25 December	11 December
2016	14 December	29 December
2017	3 December	18 December
2018	22 December	7 December
2019	12 December	26 December

ECLIPSES

2019: 26 December An annular eclipse of the Sun is visible from Saudi Arabia, India, Sumatra, and Borneo. A partial solar eclipse is visible from Asia and Australia.

THE PLANETS

2014: 30 December
Mercury and Venus appear seven Moon widths apart in the southwestern evening sky.

2015: 29 December
Mercury is at greatest evening elongation, magnitude −0.5.

2016: 11 December
Mercury is at greatest evening elongation, magnitude −0.4.

2017: 7 December
Mercury and Saturn appear a little over two Moon widths apart in the very low, early-evening southwestern sky.

2018: 15 December
Mercury is at greatest morning elongation, magnitude −1.4.

2018: 21 December
Mercury and Jupiter appear two Moon widths apart in the low, pre-dawn southeastern sky.

2019: 11 December
Saturn appears 3.5 Moon widths higher than Venus in the low, southwestern sky at sunset.

Taurus is ideally placed for everyone to observe its fine star clusters. This month also offers the first opportunity for a good look at Orion as it moves higher in the sky. The Sun is at its farthest point south of the celestial equator on 21–22 December. Northern-latitude nights are the longest of the year, while southern ones are the shortest.

◼ NORTHERN LATITUDES

Winter stars occupy half the view to the south: Taurus leads the way and is high and almost due south; Orion is in the southeast; and Gemini in the eastern sky. Two water constellations, Pisces, the fish, and Cetus, the sea monster, move towards the western horizon. Two bright stars shine out above and below the figure of Orion: yellow Capella, in Auriga and sixth brightest, shines overhead; brilliant-white Sirius, the brightest of all, is near the southeast horizon.

Taurus is easy to see due to its distinctive shape. Its stars depict a bull's head and shoulders; the bright red giant Aldebaran is its eye. Aldebaran appears to be part of the Hyades open cluster in the bull's face but is only half its distance away. The Hyades are easily visible to the naked eye; binoculars reveal many more stars. A second cluster, the Pleiades (M45), marks the start of the bull's back. About six stars are seen by eye; dozens through binoculars. A telescope shows the Crab Nebula (M1) next to the tip of a horn. It is the remains of a star that exploded in 1054.

To the north, both Ursa Major and Ursa Minor are below Polaris; Andromeda and Perseus remain overhead. A naked-eye knot of light in Perseus's hand is the Double Cluster. The Geminids, the second-best meteor shower, reaches its peak on the 13th, when up to 100 meteors an hour are seen.

Double Cluster
The Double Cluster is a pair of open star clusters within Perseus. NGC 884 is to the left, and NGC 869 to the right. Each contains hundreds of stars. The naked eye sees them as a brighter patch in the path of the Milky Way.

■ SOUTHERN LATITUDES

Looking north, the spring constellations Aquarius, Pisces, and Pegasus are moving towards the western horizon as the summer stars rise in the east. The upside-down figure of Orion, the hunter, announces that summer is almost here. It is flanked by Taurus to its lower left and Canis Major to the right. Below is the constellation Gemini, the twins. The two bright stars that mark their heads, Castor and Pollux, are near the northeastern horizon. Their legs point upwards to Orion.

Taurus is the front portion of a bull, which, from southern latitudes, is seen facing east, the direction it has come from. Its shoulders and head are close to the horizon, and its forelegs point up to the sky overhead. The Pleiades (M45), one of the finest open clusters in the sky, marks the bull's shoulder. Six of its stars are discernible with the naked eye; the keen-sighted may see seven, which gives rise to the cluster's alternative name, the Seven Sisters. Many more are visible with optical aid. The bull's face is formed of a second, V-shaped cluster, the Hyades. More than a dozen of its stars are visible to the naked eye. The unrelated red star Aldebaran represents one eye.

Eridanus, the river, is overhead. Its meandering path is traced from Orion's bright star, Rigel, a blue supergiant of magnitude 0.18. It flows overhead, then towards the southern horizon, stopping at Achernar at right of due south. Brilliant-white Canopus (in Carina) is to the left of Achernar. Between them, but closer to the horizon, are two galaxies: the Large and Small Magellanic Clouds.

The brightest star of all, Sirius in Canis Major, shines high in the east. Sirius is one corner of a triangle of stars in the east; the other two are Betelgeuse in Orion and Procyon in Canis Minor.

Canopus
The second-brightest star in the entire sky, Canopus is a white supergiant, 310 light years away. At magnitude −0.62, it is easily visible to the naked eye. It is a truly brilliant star – placed next to the Sun, it would outshine it 14,000 times.

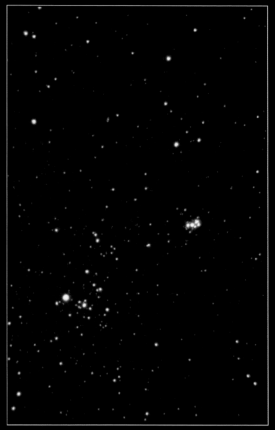

Hyades and Pleiades
The V-shaped group of stars below and left of centre is the Hyades star cluster representing the face of Taurus. The brightest star in the face is Aldebaran, which is not part of the cluster. The knot of stars at centre right is the Pleiades cluster.

EVENING SKY

MIDNIGHT
9PM
6PM
3PM
NOON

Capella
TAURUS Pleiades
ARIES
Aldebaran
Hyades
PISCES
AQUARIUS
Mira
Altair
CAPRICORNUS
Rigel
SAGITTARIUS
Shaula

10°
0°
−10°
−20°
−30°
−40°
−50°

POSITIONS OF THE PLANETS

This chart shows the positions of Mercury, Venus, Mars, Jupiter, and Saturn in December from 2013 to 2019. The planets are represented by coloured dots, while the number inside the dot indicates the year. For all planets apart from Mercury, the dot indicates the planet's position on 15 December. Mercury is shown only when it is at greatest elongation (see p.26) – for the specific date of elongation, refer to the table on the facing page.

● Mercury   ● Venus   ● Mars   ● Jupiter   ● Saturn

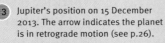

EXAMPLES (14) Jupiter's position on 15 December 2014   ▶(13) Jupiter's position on 15 December 2013. The arrow indicates the planet is in retrograde motion (see p.26).

Glossary

Words in *italics* are defined elsewhere in the glossary.

ABSOLUTE MAGNITUDE A measure of the actual brightness of an object, defined as the *apparent magnitude* it would have at a distance of 32.6 *light years*.

APERTURE The diameter of the main mirror or lens in a telescope or binoculars. A large aperture telescope can see more detail and detect fainter objects than a small aperture telescope.

APPARENT MAGNITUDE The brightness of a celestial object as seen from the Earth. This depends on the object's real brightness and its distance from the Earth.

ASTERISM A pattern of *stars* where the *stars* are either a part of a *constellation*, or are members of several *constellations*. An example is the Plough in Ursa Major.

ASTEROID A rocky body orbiting the Sun with a diameter less than 1,000 km.

ASTRONOMICAL UNIT (AU) A measure of distance convenient for use within the Solar System, defined as the mean distance between the Earth and the Sun (149,597,970 km).

ASTROPHOTOGRAPHY Photography of celestial objects in the night sky; also includes photography of the Sun and *eclipses*.

BINARY STAR Two *stars* in mutual *orbit* around a common centre of mass, and bound together gravitationally.

CELESTIAL EQUATOR The celestial equivalent of the Earth's equator. The celestial equator marks a line where the plane of the Earth's equator meets the *celestial sphere*.

CELESTIAL POLE The celestial equivalent of the Earth's poles. The night sky appears to rotate on an axis through the celestial poles.

CELESTIAL SPHERE The imaginary sphere that surrounds the Earth, and upon which all celestial objects appear to lie.

CEPHEID VARIABLE A type of *variable star* with a regular pattern of brightness changes linked to the *star*'s actual *luminosity*. Such *stars* are used as distance indicators.

CHARGE-COUPLED DEVICE (CCD) A light-sensitive silicon chip used as an alternative to photographic film.

COMET An icy body orbiting the Sun that may develop a glowing tail as it passes through the inner Solar System.

CONJUNCTION An alignment of objects in the night sky, with one passing in front of the other, particularly when a planet lines up with the Sun as viewed from the Earth.

CONSTELLATION An area of the night sky with boundaries that are determined by the International Astronomical Union; constellations are 88 in number.

DECLINATION The celestial equivalent of latitude on the Earth. It is the angle between a celestial object and the *celestial equator*, measured in degrees. The *celestial equator* has a declination of 0 degrees, and the *celestial poles* are at 90 degrees.

DEEP-SKY OBJECT Any celestial object external to the Solar System, but excluding *stars*.

DIFFUSE NEBULA A cloud of gas and dust illuminated by *stars* embedded within it.

DOUBLE STAR Two *stars* that are not physically associated with each other but appear close together through line-of-sight from the Earth.

DWARF PLANET A celestial body that is large enough to be nearly round, but that has not cleared its neighbourhood of other objects.

DWARF STAR A *star* that has lost most of its mass towards the end of its evolutionary development.

ECCENTRICITY A measure of the circularity of a body's *orbit*. An eccentricity of 0 means a circular orbit, with larger values indicating more elongated ellipses up to a theoretical maximum of 1.

ECLIPSE An alignment of a planet or moon with the Sun, which casts a shadow on another body. During a lunar eclipse, the Earth's shadow is cast on the Moon. During a solar eclipse, the Moon's shadow is cast on the Earth.

ECLIPTIC The plane of the Earth's *orbit* around the Sun, or the projection of that plane onto the *celestial sphere*.

ELONGATION The angular separation between the Sun and a planet as viewed from the Earth. Also used as the time of maximum angular separation (greatest elongation) between the inner planets, Mercury or Venus, and the Sun.

GALAXY A huge mass of *stars*, gas, and dust, containing from millions to billions of *stars*. Galaxies vary in size and shape, with diameters that range from thousands to hundreds of thousands of *light years*.

GIANT STAR A *star* that has expanded dramatically as it nears the end of its life-cycle.

GLOBULAR CLUSTER A sphere of *stars*, bound together gravitationally, and containing from tens of thousands to hundreds of thousands of *stars*.

LIBRATION A monthly variation in the parts of the Moon's surface visible from the Earth, due to the slight *eccentricity* and tilt of the Moon's *orbit*.

LIGHT YEAR The distance light can travel during the course of one year, that is, 9,460,700,000,000 km (5,878,600,000,000 miles).

LIMB The outer edge of a moon's or a planet's observed disc.

LOCAL GROUP A small cluster of over 30 galaxies which includes our own *galaxy*, the *Milky Way*.

LONG-EXPOSURE PHOTOGRAPHY Photography of the night sky where the camera shutter remains open, often for hours, in order to record very faint objects.

LUMINOSITY A measure of the amount of light that is produced by a celestial object.

MAGNITUDE The brightness of a celestial object, measured on a numerical scale, where brighter objects are given small or negative magnitude numbers, and fainter objects are given larger magnitude numbers.

MARE (plural: maria) Dark, low-lying areas of the Moon, flooded with lava, derived from the Latin word for "sea".

METEOR A small rock that burns due to friction as it enters the Earth's atmosphere.

METEORITE A *meteor* that reaches the Earth's (or another planet's) surface.

MILKY WAY A faint band of light visible on clear dark nights, consisting of millions of *stars*; the common name for our *galaxy*.

MULTIPLE STAR A system of *stars* that are bound together gravitationally and are in mutual *orbits*. Multiple *stars* consist of at least three *stars* and up to about a dozen *stars*.

NEBULA A cloud of gas and dust, visible by either being

illuminated by embedded *stars* or nearby *stars*, or by obscuring starlight.

OPEN CLUSTER A group of up to a few hundred *stars* bound by gravity; found in the arms of a *galaxy*.

OPPOSITION The time when an outer planet lies on the exact opposite side of the Earth from the Sun. The planet is at its closest to the Earth and therefore appears brightest at this time.

ORBIT The path followed by a planet, *asteroid,* or *comet* around the Sun, or a moon around its parent planet.

PARALLAX The apparent shift in an object's position as it is viewed from two different locations. The amount of shift depends on the distance of the object, and the distance between the two locations.

PHASE Illumination of the Moon or an inner planet, as seen from the Earth. At full phase, the side of the object facing the Earth is fully illuminated; at new phase, the object is fully in shadow; crescent, half phase, and gibbous phase are in between.

PLANETARY NEBULA A shell of gas thrown off by a *star* towards the end of its evolutionary development. In a small telescope, the shell resembles a planet's disc.

PRECESSION A gradual shift in the direction of the Earth's axis of rotation. It currently points towards the *star* Polaris, but it wanders over a 25,800-year cycle.

RADIO SOURCE A celestial object that appears bright when viewed with instruments that detect radio waves.

REFLECTING TELESCOPE (reflector) A type of telescope that collects and focuses light by using a mirror.

REFRACTING TELESCOPE (refractor) A type of telescope that collects and focuses light by using a lens.

REGOLITH The loose material or "soil" on the surface of a moon or planet.

RESOLVE The ability to detect detail within celestial objects, for example, craters on the Moon, or splitting *double stars*. The greater the *aperture* of a telescope, the greater its resolving power.

RETROGRADE MOTION A reversal of the usual eastward motion of a planet relative to background *stars*; occurs as it reaches *opposition*.

RETROGRADE ROTATION The rotation of a planet or moon in the opposite direction to its *orbit*. All of the planets *orbit* the Sun in the direction of the Sun's rotation: anti-clockwise when viewed from above the Sun's north pole. Most planets also rotate (spin) anti-clockwise. Venus and Uranus have retrograde rotation: clockwise compared with their anti-clockwise *orbits*.

RIGHT ASCENSION The celestial equivalent of longitude on the Earth. It is measured in hours (one hour is 15 degrees) from the point where the Sun crosses the *celestial equator* in March.

SOLAR WIND A continuous flow of charged particles (electrons and protons) outward from the sun.

SPECTRAL TYPE A code assigned to a *star* based on the characteristics of its *spectrum*. Hot young *stars* are types O, B and A, older cooler *stars* are types F, G, K, and M.

SPECTRUM The range of wavelengths of light emitted by a celestial object, as well as any emission and absorption lines. The spectrum identifies the chemical and physical properties of the celestial object.

STAR A large sphere of gas that emits heat and light as a result of thermonuclear reactions within its core.

SUPERGIANT STAR A *star* at least ten times more massive

than the Sun. Supergiants are at the end of their evolutionary development, and can be hundreds of times larger than the Sun, and thousands of times brighter.

SUPERNOVA An exceptionally violent explosion of a *star* during which it sheds its outer atmosphere; it outshines its host *galaxy*

SUPERNOVA REMNANT The outer layers of a *star* that have been ejected during a *supernova* explosion, travelling at high speed through space.

TERMINATOR The edge of the sunlit area of a moon or planet's surface, where the surface falls into shadow.

TRANSIT A planet's motion in front of the Sun, or a moon in front of its parent planet, as viewed from the Earth.

VARIABLE STAR A *star* that appears to change its brightness. This can be caused by physical changes within the *star*, or by the *star* being eclipsed by a companion.

WOLF-RAYET STAR A hot, massive *star* that produces a strong stellar wind.

ZODIAC The area of the sky, 9 degrees either side of the *ecliptic plane*, through which the Sun, the Moon, and the planets move.

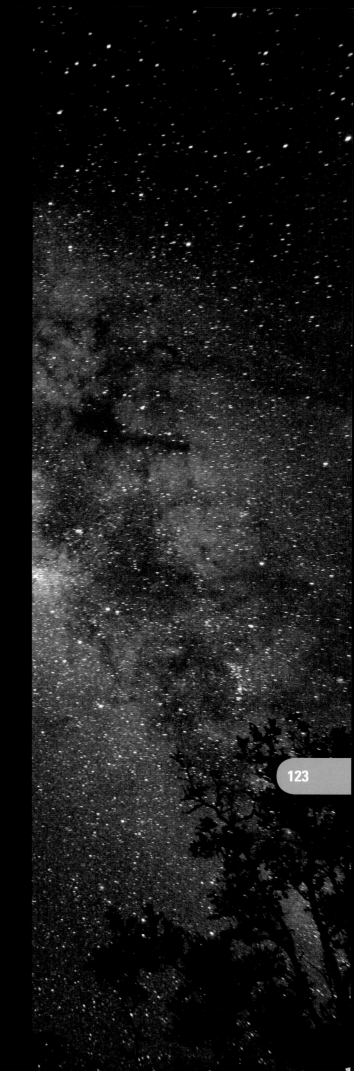

Index

127

Acknowledgements

Dorling Kindersley would like to thank Heather McCarry for design consultancy and David Hughes for his contribution to the sections on Mercury, Venus, and the Moon. The planisphere artwork and the star charts on pp.32–33 were produced by Giles Sparrow and Tim Brown.

Sands Publishing Solutions would like to thank Hilary Bird for compiling the index and Robin Scagell for his assistance with images.

Photography credits

The publisher would like to thank the following for their kind permission to reproduce their photographs:

Key: a=above; b=below/bottom; c=centre; l=left; r=right; t=top
1 Science Photo Library: Fred Espenak (c).
2–3 Ali Jarekji/Reuters/Corbis: (l, r).
4–5 Corbis: Roger Ressmeyer.
6–7 HubbleSite: NASA, ESA, S. Beckwith (STScI), and the Hubble Heritage Team (STScI/AURA).
8 Corbis: Daniel J. Cox.
9 Corbis: Terra.
10–11 Martin Pugh.
12 Corbis: Tony Hallas/Science Faction.
13 Jerry Lodriguss/Astropix LLC.
14–15 Corbis: Tom Fox/Dallas Morning News.
16–17 NASA, ESA, and A Nota (STScI/ESA): (c).
18 Detlav Van Ravensway/Science Photo Library: (cr). NASA: (tl, bc, cl, c, br).
19 NASA: (bl, bc). Science Photo Library: Mark Garlick (c); Tony and Daphne Hallas (br); David A Hardy, Futures: 50 years in space (cl). Robert Williams and the Deep Field Team (STScI) and NASA: (cr).
22 Galaxy Picture Library: Robin Scagell (bl,bc,br).
24 Galaxy Picture Library: David Cortner (tr); Robin Scagell (br). NASA, ESA, and the Hubble Heritage Team (STScI/AURA) (cr).
25 Till Credner (www.allthesky.com): (bl). NOAO (br). Science Photo Library: John Chumack (bc).
26 Galaxy Picture Library: Robin Scagell (tl).
27 Galaxy Picture Library: Jon Harper (bl). Science Photo Library: Eckhard Slawik (c, tr).
28 Science Photo Library: Chris Butler (cl); Celestial Image Co (tl); Stephen and Donna O'Meara (r).
29 HST/NOAO, ESA, and the Hubble Helix Nebula Team, M Meixner (STScI), and TA Rector (NRAO): (cr). Sven Kohle (www.allthesky.com): (br). NASA, ESA, and the Hubble Heritage Team (STScI/AURA): (brr).NOAO/AURA/NSF: (brB). NOAO: (c, crr). MPIA-HD/Birkle/Slawik: (b). Science Photo Library: Celestial Image Co (car); John Chumack (tc); Eckhard Slawik. Loke Tan (www.starryscapes.com): (ca).
30 Dorling Kindersley: Gary Ombler (tl); Andy Crawford (bc).
31 Galaxy Picture Library: Robin Scagell (c, ca, r, rb).
34–35 NASA/JPL.
37 Alamy: Yendis (br). NASA/JPL-Caltech: (brr). NASA/JPL-Caltech/USGS/Cornell: (cla). NASA/JPL/Space Science Institute: (cr, crr). NASA/JPL/University of Arizona: (c).
38 SOHO (ESA and NASA): (c).
39 Alamy: John E. Marriott (br). Dorling Kindersley: Andy Crawford (b, bl). Science Photo Library: John Chumack (tr); Jerry Lodriguss (brr).
40 NASA/JPL-Caltech: (c).
41 NASA: (t, tc, tr). Galaxy Picture Library: Robin Scagell (br, brr). Science Photo Library: John Foster (bc).
42 Alamy: Matthew Catterall (tl). Galaxy Picture Library: Robin Scagell (cl, bcl). NASA/JPL/USGS: (c).
43 Galaxy Picture Library:ESO (tr).Thierry Legault (tcr, tcrb).Robin Scagell (tcl,b).
44 Galaxy Picture Library: Martin Ratcliffe (b). NSDCC/GSFC/NASA: (tl, tc, c).
45 Galaxy Picture Library: Damian Peach (bc); Robin Scagell (bl). NASA: (c, cl, cr, tr). SOHO (ESA and NASA): (br).
46 USGS: (c).
47 ESA/DLR/FU Berlin (G.Neukum): (tc). Galaxy Picture Library: Robin Scagell (bl, bc). NASA: (tr, cr). NASA/JPL/Cornell: (cra).
48 NASA/JPL/University of Arizona: (c).
49 Galaxy Picture Library: Robin Scagell (b). NASA: (tc, tr, c).
50 NASA/JPL/Space Science Institute: (c, tl).
51 Galaxy Picture Library: Robin Scagell (b). NASA/JPL/Space Science Institute: (tr, c). NASA and the Hubble Heritage Team (STScI/AURA): (crb).
52 Galaxy Picture Library: Robin Scagell (br). NASA/JPL: (cl, cr, tl, tr).
53 NASA/ESA: (bc, br). WM Keck Observatory: (bl).
54 Galaxy Picture Library: Robert McNaught (c). NASA/JPL: (bl). NASA/JPL-Caltech/UMD: (tl).
55 Dorling Kindersley: Colin Keates, Courtesy of the Natural History Museum, London (cr). NASA/JPL: (br). Science Photo Library: David McLean.
56–57 Getty Images: Hulton Archive.
58 Galaxy Picture Library: Robin Scagell (tl).
58–95 Getty Images: Hulton Archive (borders).
58–95 Till Credner (www.allthesky.com).
77 Galaxy Picture Library: Y. Hirose (clb).
79 Galaxy Picture Library: Chris Picking (tr).
96–97 Science Photo Library: David Nunuk.
98 Till Credner (www.allthesky.com): (cl).
99 Till Credner (www.allthesky.com): (cr). Galaxy Picture Library: Yoji Hirose (tl).
100 Galaxy Picture Library: Robin Scagell (c).
101 Galaxy Picture Library: Robin Scagell (cr). NOAO/AURA/NSF: NA Sharp (tl).
102 Galaxy Picture Library: NOAO/AURA/NSF/Adam Block (c).
103 Galaxy Picture Library: Yoji Hirose (tc); Robin Scagell (cr).
104 Till Credner (www.allthesky.com): (cr).
105 Till Credner (www.allthesky.com): (tl). Galaxy Picture Library: NOAO/AURA/NSF/Todd Boroson (cr).
106 Galaxy Picture Library: Damian Peach (cra).
107 Till Credner (www.allthesky.com): (cra). Galaxy Picture Library: NOAO/AURA/NSF (cl); Robin Scagell (tl).
108 Till Credner (www.allthesky.com): (tr). Galaxy Picture Library: Damian Peach (tr/insert).
109 Galaxy Picture Library: Robin Scagell (tr). NOAO/AURA/NSF: NA Sharp, Mark Hanna, REU Program (cla).
110 Galaxy Picture Library: Robin Scagell (cra).
111 Till Credner (www.allthesky.com): (tr). NOAO/AURA/NSF: (tl).
112 Galaxy Picture Library: Robin Scagell (tr).
113 Galaxy Picture Library: Yoji Hirose (tr). NOAO/AURA/NSF: (cl).
114 Till Credner (www.allthesky.com): (ca).
115 Galaxy Picture Library: Chris Livingstone (tl); Michael Stecker (cra).
116 Galaxy Picture Library: Yoji Hirose (cra).
117 Till Credner (www.allthesky.com): (cr). Galaxy Picture Library: Chris Livingstone (cla).
118 Galaxy Picture Library: Juan Carlos Casado (cra).
119 Till Credner (www.allthesky.com): (cr). Galaxy Picture Library: Robin Scagell (tl).
120 NOAO/AURA/NSF: NA Sharp (c).
121 Galaxy Picture Library: Gordon Garradd (tl); Robin Scagell (cr).
124–128 Science Photo Library: Stephen and Donna O'Meara (r).

Endpapers: NASA: ESA, M Robberto (Space Telescope Science Institute/ESA) and the Hubble Space Telescope Orion Treasury Project Team.

Jacket front and inside: Science Photo Library: Russell Croman

All other images © Dorling Kindersley
For further information, see: www.dkimages.com